Object-Oriented Programming in Python

Object-Oriented Programming in Python

Michael H. Goldwasser

Saint Louis University

David Letscher

Saint Louis University

PEARSON

Prentice
Hall

Upper Saddle River, New Jersey 07458

Library of Congress Cataloging-in-Publication Data on File.

Editorial Director, Computer Science, Engineering, and Advanced Mathematics: *Marcia J. Horton*
Executive Editor: *Tracy Dunkelberger*
Editorial Assistant: *Melinda Haggerty*
Senior Managing Editor: *Scott Disanno*
Production Editor: *Irwin Zucker*
Cover Designer: *Jonathan Boylan*
Cover Art: © *Louie Psihovos / Science Faction / Getty Images, Inc*
Art Editor: *Gregory Dulles*
Manufacturing Manager: *Alexis Heydt-Long*
Manufacturing Buyer: *Lisa McDowell*
Senior Marketing Manager: *Tim Galligan*

© 2008 Pearson Education, Inc.
Pearson Prentice Hall
Pearson Education, Inc.
Upper Saddle River, New Jersey 07458

Printed in the United States of America
10 9 8 7 6 5 4 3 2 1

ISBN 0-13-615031-4
      978-0-13-615031-2

Pearson Education LTD., *London*
Pearson Education Australia PTY, Limited, *Sydney*
Pearson Education Singapore, Pte. Ltd
Pearson Education North Asia Ltd, *Hong Kong*
Pearson Education Canada, Ltd., *Toronto*
Pearson Educacion de Mexico, S.A. de C.V.
Pearson Education –Japan, *Tokyo*
Pearson Education Malaysia, Pte. Ltd
Pearson Education, Inc., *Upper Saddle River, New Jersey*

To Susan, who is both my wife and best friend,
and to our wonderful daughters Calista and Maya.
— Michael H. Goldwasser

To my wife Beth. Your love and support
makes everything possible.
— David Letscher

Preface

We are excited to be sharing this book with you after years of developing material for our own course at Saint Louis University. We have had a great time writing the book, and we hope that our enthusiasm is contagious as you learn to program a computer.

Software development is both a skill and an art. At times is can be challenging, yet when things work out it is very rewarding. As we guide you through the process, please read the chapters carefully. However, we also encourage you to be an *active* learner. Our lessons frequently contain examples of Python programs and a demonstration of the behavior that might be observed when running those programs. Don't take our word for it; experiment on your own computer and see if you get the same results. Feel free to change things, and see if those changes affect the outcome. While we do our best to organize the discovery with our lessons, hands-on practice is a key component to success.

Why Object-Oriented Programming?

There are many different programming styles. Our book uses a particular paradigm known as object-oriented programming. The characteristic of this style is the modeling of components in a software system as *objects* that each have independent state information represented internally, as well as a set of supported behaviors that allow for interactions with other components.

The primary advantage of object-oriented programming is that it provides a framework for modeling a large complex software system as a collection of separate components. This can aid in the initial design and implementation of software, in the subsequent maintenance of that software, and in the reuse of individual components in other contexts. For these reasons, object-oriented programming has become the dominant style in industry for large-scale software development.

Why Python?

Python is an object-oriented programming language developed by Guido van Rossum in the early 1990s. It is an open-source language that is licensed and freely distributed by the Python Software Foundation, a non-profit organization backed by several prominent companies such as Google and Microsoft.

Python is designed with an extremely simple syntax, together with a powerful built-in core. This combination facilitates the rapid development of software, making Python an attractive choice for experienced software developers.

More recently, Python had emerged as a language for teaching computer science. The very same properties that make Python popular for experienced programmers, such as simplicity and robustness, make it attractive as an instructional language for beginners. Our own switch to Python was based on the desire to spend far greater time teaching core principles and far less effort distracted by artificial hurdles of a programming language. As an object-oriented language, Python provides a simpler, more consistent model than other traditional object-oriented languages such as Java and C++. While those other languages remain prominent in industry, their complexity can easily overwhelm a beginning student. (We provide a direct comparison between Python and Java or C++ in Appendix B).

Elements of the Book

We use a variety of elements when presenting material. The most notable are as follows.

A Word of Warning

Sometimes, we raise an issue in the flow of a lesson that is too important to be accidentally overlooked. In such a case, we prominently echo the lesson in a separate displayed box, such as the following:

 A WORD OF WARNING

Everyone should read such a warning, as it draws attention to a common pitfall.

For the Guru

Other times, we find ourselves in the middle of a discussion with a perfect opportunity to present an advanced lesson, albeit one that is not immediately necessary. In these cases, we present this extra lesson in a separate displayed box, such as the following:

 FOR THE GURU

This should be considered as optional reading, providing advanced lessons for the motivated reader that are inspired by the surrounding discussion.

Case Studies

Sixteen designated case studies are incorporated into various chapters of the book. These case studies can be treated as *optional* material, as we do not use them to introduce primary lessons. Instead, they allow us to reinforce techniques that were introduced in earlier portions of a chapter. Furthermore, the case studies are often more comprehensive and demonstrate the use of computers in a variety of real-world application areas (e.g., biology, physics, mathematics, text analysis, graphics and animation, games and puzzles).

Chapter Reviews and Practice Problems

Each chapter ends in a consistent manner, with a summary of key points introduced in the chapter, followed by a glossary of relevant terminology, and finally a collection of exercises for the reader. Furthermore, some of the exercises are clearly labeled as **Practice**. For your convenience, solutions to all practice problems are given in Appendix C.

Graphics Library

The use of computer graphics can be both motivating and rewarding. Graphics can be used to provide visual feedback during the execution of a program, and to produce software that is more engaging. Although the core Python language does not include support for graph–ics, there are several standard packages used in industry. Unfortunately, those packages tend to be complex and more appropriate for experienced programmers.

    For this reason, we have developed an easy–to–use custom graphics library for this book. Our software is named `cs1graphics` and is freely distributed through the website `http://www.cs1graphics.org`, and through the publisher's companion website.

    To strike a balance between graphical and nongraphical programming, we tend to avoid the use of graphics when introducing fundamental concepts. We then use graphics prominently in selected sections to reinforce the core material. The package itself is intro–duced in Chapter 3. Those who do not intend to use graphical examples, may completely bypass this chapter. Conversely, those who love graphics (as we do) can jump quickly to this chapter for a vibrant introduction to Python programming.

Transition Guide: from Python to Java and C++

Python is a wonderful language for beginners, and one that can continue to be used as a professional software developer. However, experienced programmers must be familiar with many programming languages.

    As an aid for readers of this book who may soon transition from Python to Java or C++, Appendix B serves as a transition guide, highlighting the major distinctions between the languages, and providing side–by–side comparisons of Python source code from this book together with corresponding implementations in Java and C++. An expanded version of this guide is available through the publisher's companion website.

Companion Website: Student and Instructor Resources

Prentice Hall maintains a companion website with resources for this book at:

`http://www.prenhall.com/goldwasser`

The site includes the `cs1graphics` package, all source code for examples used in this book, and an expanded version of the Transition Guide from Appendix B. This site also includes a link to password protected instructor resources.

Comprehensive Coverage with Flexible Organization

The text is organized within two parts. Part I comprises nine chapters that represent the most fundamental topics often found in a CS1 course. These include an understanding of data types, the use of objects, control structures and functions, user–defined classes, good software development practices, input and output, and the use of inheritance in object–oriented design. Though not every instructor will wish to cover each of those topics, we expect that most instructors will cover much of the core material.

Yet we hope that instructors will find opportunity to explore a handful of more advanced topics to pique the interest of the students. Part II of the book includes coverage of the underlying memory model, recursion as a programming technique, the use of Python's many container classes, and even a glimpse at how data structures and algorithms can be implemented from scratch. Our final chapters introduce event–driven programming and network programming, two topics which are less commonly included in CS1 yet readily approachable with Python. These topics are extremely popular with students and at the heart of their view of modern computer software.

Chapter dependencies (shown on the facing page) are designed to provide flexibility in customizing the flow of a course. This organization supports a wide range of teaching styles and philosophies. Following the chapters in their natural order leads to a balanced introduction of object–oriented principles alongside the traditional programming constructs. However the flow can easily be adjusted to provide lesser or greater emphasis on the object–oriented principles. Following the leftmost boundary of that figure leads to a "Back to Basics" approach which is predominantly nongraphical and imperative. Those interested in a more "Objects First" approach may follow a more right–leaning path through the material, relying more prominently on graphics, inheritance, and coverage of event–driven programming.

As a final alternative, there is enough material in the book to support a two–course sequence in Python, including a transition to Java or C++ in the second course if desired.

Balanced approach

Ch. 1: Cornerstones of Computing
Ch. 2: Getting Started in Python
Ch. 3: Getting Started with Graphics
Ch. 4: Elementary Control Structures
Ch. 5: Additional Control Structures
Ch. 6: Defining Our Own Classes
Ch. 7: Good Software Practices
Ch. 8: Input, Output, and Files
Ch. 9: Inheritance
Ch. 10: Object Management

"Back to Basics" approach

Ch. 1: Cornerstones of Computing
Ch. 2: Getting Started in Python
Ch. 4: Elementary Control Structures
Ch. 5: Additional Control Structures
Ch. 8: Input, Output, and Files
Ch. 6: Defining Our Own Classes
Ch. 10: Object Management
Ch. 11: Recursion
Ch. 12: More Python Containers
Ch. 14: Sorting Algorithms

"Objects First" approach

Ch. 1: Cornerstones of Computing
Ch. 3: Getting Started with Graphics
Ch. 2: Getting Started in Python
Ch. 4: Elementary Control Structures
Ch. 6: Defining Our Own Classes
Ch. 7: Good Software Practices
Ch. 9: Inheritance
Ch. 15: Event–Driven Programming
Ch. 8: Input, Output, and Files
Ch. 16: Network Programming

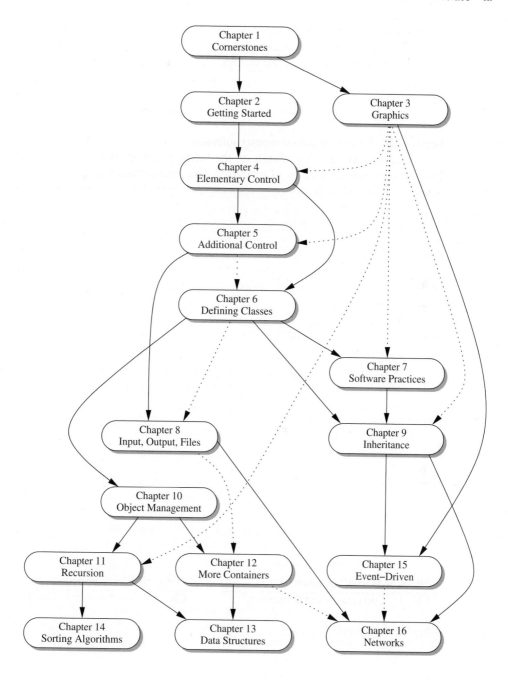

Chapter Dependencies. Solid lines denote strong prerequisite requirements that should be respected, while dashed lines denote dependencies that are relatively minor or limited to coverage of particular case studies.

Acknowledgments

This endeavor would not have been completed without the support and guidance of many individuals. We begin by thanking our colleagues in the Department of Mathematics and Computer Science at Saint Louis University, for the encouragement they offered us through all stages of this project, and for the freedom we were given in redesigning our introductory course. Of particular note, we are grateful to Kimberly Druschel for teaching a section of the class based on our first draft of the material (where first draft meant that pages were often being sent to the printer five minutes before a topic was covered in class). In similar spirit, we thank Ann McNamara for teaching a subsequent section of the course from our materials (fortunately, a second draft by that time). We are indebted to our own students, whose efforts have greatly influenced the development of these materials.

We sincerely value the feedback given by colleagues at other institutions, namely Claude W. Anderson and Curtis C. Clifton of the Rose-Hulman Institute of Technology, Andrew N. Harrington of Loyola University, Chris Haynes of Indiana University, John H. E. F. Lasseter of Willamette University, Holly Patterson-McNeill of Lewis-Clark State College, Terry Scott of the University of Northern Colorado, Michael S. Tashbook of the University of Virginia, and Michael C. Vanier of the California Institute of Technology. Of particular note, we thank Terry and his students for experimenting with an early version of cs1graphics, Claude for his remarkable eye for detail as he reported hundreds of mistakes that remained in recent months, and Andy for many extra discussion along the way and for his feedback regarding the Java and C++ Transition Guide.

We greatly appreciate the guidance of the professional staff at Pearson Education and Prentice Hall for supporting this project from its inception all the way to the product that you are reading. Following the timeline, we begin with Michael Hirsch whose early advice helped us shape (and reshape) the organization of the book. We owe our most sincere thanks to our Executive Editor, Tracy Dunkelberger, whose belief in the project led to our partnership with Prentice Hall. Tracy, we thank you for your enthusiasm and your continued patience in seeing the project through. We also acknowledge several more people who played vital roles in the publication process. We thank Jake Warde for organizing several rounds of peer review, and our copy editor at WriteWith Inc. for providing detailed comments that have greatly affected our writing. The overall presentation of this book has been greatly improved with the help of Irwin Zucker, who kept everything moving forward down the homestretch, and Scott Disanno, whose valuable suggestions and careful proofreading provided the finishing touches.

On a personal note, Michael wishes to thank his family for their utmost patience over the past two years. I owe each of you some extra time with my undivided attention; Calista and Maya, I also owe you a turn with the computer to play Webkinz. Finally, I thank my parents for their constant support, and for being the first to preorder a copy of the book (eight months in advance, it turns out).

David would like to thank his wife for her endless patience through the length of this project. Now that the book is done, I'll get started on that "Honey Do" list. I would also like to thank my family for their years of support.

Michael H. Goldwasser
David Letscher
Saint Louis University

Brief Contents

Contents

Object-Oriented Programming in Python

PART ONE

Fundamental Topics

CHAPTER 1

Cornerstones of Computing

1.1 **Data and Types**
1.2 **Operations, Functions, and Algorithms**
1.3 **High-Level Programming Languages**
1.4 **The Object-Oriented Paradigm**
1.5 **Design and Modeling**
1.6 **Chapter Review**

Throughout our study, we focus on two aspects of computing at the heart of the dis-cipline since its early history. These two are *data* and *operations*. Though we soon suggest that they be viewed in tandem, we start by exploring each of these concepts individually.

1.1 Data and Types

The Oxford English Dictionary offers a definition of data in the context of computing as

> The quantities, characters, or symbols on which operations are performed by computers and other automatic equipment, and which may be stored or trans-mitted in the form of electrical signals, records on magnetic tape or punched cards, etc.

Computing devices have become ubiquitous in society as vast information is represented and stored digitally. A piece of data may represent something as simple as a number, a character of text, or a favorite color. Yet data can represent more complex information such as a photograph, an address book, a web page, a company's sales records, or the human genome. The significance of data cannot possibly be overstated: computing devices cannot do anything useful without some form of underlying data on which to operate.

Within modern computers, all information is represented as a collection of binary digits, also known as *bits*. Each bit can be set to one of two possible states, commonly denoted 0 and 1. By combining many bits, a wider variety of patterns can be stored to represent pieces of information. For example, a set of 8 bits (known as a *byte*) can be used to distinguish between 256 different values. With thousands or even millions of bits, more interesting data can be represented; a typical four-minute song on a compact disc is represented with approximately 340 million bits (perhaps only 30 million if using a compressed format). Much of the data being used by a computer processor is stored in the computer's *main memory*, often referred to as RAM (random access memory). For example, a computer system with 128 megabytes (MB) of RAM provides just over 1 billion bits of storage; a system with 1 gigabyte (GB) of RAM provides approximately 8 billion bits of storage.

Information versus data

We have intentionally differentiated our use of the term *information* from *data*. We consider information to be a high-level abstraction, while data a low-level ***representation*** of such information, capable of being stored and manipulated by a computer. Consider the following philosophical questions. Is a picture stored in JPG format the same *data* as that picture when stored in GIF format? Is it the same *information*? If we have the text of Hamlet with characters stored in ASCII format versus Unicode format, is that the same data? Is it the same information? What if we have the text of Hamlet translated to Danish; is that the same data? Is it the same information? Our point is not to claim that there is a clear and correct answer to such philosophical questions, but to highlight the important distinction. There may be many possible representations of a piece of information. We call each such choice of representation an ***encoding***, noting that certain encodings offer advantages and disadvantages when compared to others.

Data types

It is helpful to consider information as a high-level concept, even when programming. Though all data is truly stored as a sequence of bits, it would be quite cumbersome to precisely specify the exact encoding each time we want to read, write, or otherwise manipulate a piece of data. Higher-level abstractions are supported though the definition of ***data types***. A data type is a definition that associates a particular form of information with an underlying encoding scheme for data of this type. For example, we may wish to view a particular number as an "integer" without actually worrying about how integers are represented in memory. Or we may wish to view a person's name as a string of characters from an alphabet, without worrying precisely about how those alphabet symbols are represented in memory. Some forms of data (e.g., numbers, characters, dates, lists) are so commonly needed that they exist as predefined data types. These are often called the ***primitive*** or ***built-in*** data types. Other times, a programmer may want data abstractions that are specific to her own implementation, and thus not built in. For example, an online vendor may wish to treat a "shopping cart" as a high-level concept that is implemented to meet its needs. Most programming languages support such abstractions by allowing a programmer to define custom data types that can subsequently be used. These are typically called ***user-defined types***. It is up to the programmer to choose an appropriate encoding for the underlying representation of a user-defined type.

1.2 Operations, Functions, and Algorithms

As intrinsic as data is for computing, it would be nothing more than storage if there were no way to process it. What makes computing devices so useful is the remarkable combination of operations that they can perform. The hardware component that controls the entire computer is known as its ***central processing unit (CPU)***. Interestingly, most computing architectures support a rather limited repertoire of instructions. Commonly supported instructions are as simple as loading data from main memory into the CPU, storing data from the CPU into main memory, performing basic arithmetic operations such as addition or multiplication, or checking whether a value is less than, equal to, or greater than zero. Yet with a well-crafted sequence of such instructions, it is possible to manage a large database, generate three-dimensional animations, choose optimal driving directions, or control a rover on the surface of Mars.

Of course, achieving such grand results requires complex software, perhaps with hundreds of millions of instructions. It is next to impossible to design such software by thinking of each of these instructions individually. Instead, a series of low-level operations are grouped and considered as a single higher-level operation. These larger abstractions allow us to develop a large project by composing it from smaller manageable pieces. Those pieces can be easier to understand, implement, and test, making the overall software development more efficient and less prone to error.

Control structures and functions

We noted that some data types are so commonly used that they have built-in support while others are custom-defined by a programmer as needed. The same basic principle holds true with operations. Tasks such as incrementing a counter, computing the length of a name, and sorting a list of values are commonly supported. There also exist built-in commands, known as ***control structures***, that determine when other instructions are executed or repeated. For example, we may wish our software to follow one set of instructions when a particular condition is met, and a different set of instructions otherwise. We may wish to specify that a series of operations is to be repeated a certain number of times, or even repeated continuously so long as a given condition is met.

Yet there will often be cases in which a programmer wants to describe a high-level behavior that is not among the built-in operations, for example computing the sales tax for a purchase. Such behaviors are often described as user-defined ***functions***. This programming technique provides a way to abstract a more complicated series of instructions by giving it a simple name, such as computeTax. Once the instructions for the behavior are defined, the programmer can use the high-level name throughout the rest of the software, just as if it had been a built-in operation. In fact, once written, these functions can be stored in a library and reused in future software.

Algorithms

In the end, it is important to keep in mind that the computer does not think for itself. It blindly follows the instructions it has been given. No matter how complex a high-level task it solves, there must be unambiguous instructions behind the scene. Such a set of instructions is typically called an ***algorithm***, defined by Merriam-Webster as

> A step-by-step procedure for solving a problem or accomplishing some end especially by a computer.

Everyday life is filled with algorithms: baking a cake, changing a flat tire, assembling a piece of furniture. Common algorithms in the context of computing include calculating the sum of a list of numbers, saving a file to disk, and authenticating a user's password. Sometimes it is quite challenging to describe a technique precisely, even one that may be second nature to us. For example, although you can (presumably) perform a long division, could you clearly explain the process to a child who does not know how? Worse yet, there are times we perform actions without clear recognition of our own problem-solving techniques. For example, how do you compose an original short story?

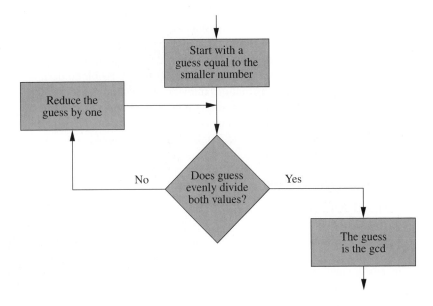

FIGURE 1.1: Flowchart for an algorithm that computes the gcd of two integers.

To fully explore an algorithmic concept, we devote the rest of this section to a common mathematical problem that many students learn to solve in grade school: reducing a fraction to its lowest terms. For instance, the fraction $54/42$ is equivalent to $9/7$ when in lowest terms. When reducing a fraction to lowest terms, we implicitly need the largest possible integer that divides both the numerator and the denominator, the so-called ***greatest common divisor (gcd)*** of the two. For instance, we reduce fraction $54/42$ by recognizing that 6 is the largest factor that we can remove, as $54/42 = \frac{54/6}{42/6} = 9/7$. Just as there are different representations for the same high-level information, there can exist different algorithms for accomplishing the same high-level task. We describe two distinct algorithms for computing the gcd of a pair of positive integers.

A straightforward approach is to try all numbers less than or equal to the smaller of the original values. For each candidate, we check if it divides both original numbers (notice that performing this step implicitly presumes our ability to perform divisions). By testing from bigger to smaller values, we are assured that the first solution we find is the greatest possible. This process eventually succeeds, as 1 is guaranteed to be a divisor of both numbers if no other common divisor is found. We describe this approach graphically using a diagram that is termed a ***flowchart***, as shown in Figure 1.1. This helps portray the conditional branching and repetition that occurs during the algorithm.

Although our first algorithm succeeds, it is not the most efficient. For example, when computing the gcd of 54 and 42 it starts by checking if 42 is a common divisor. Since 42 does not go evenly into 54, this guess is incorrect. So it next tries (unsuccessfully) the guess of 41, then 40, then 39, then 38, and so on, until finally discovering that 6 is a legitimate common divisor. This approach is very time consuming when working with extremely large numbers.

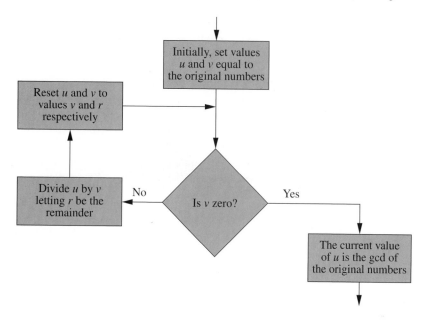

FIGURE 1.2: Euclid's algorithm for computing the gcd of integers u and v.

A much more efficient algorithm was first described by the Greek mathematician Euclid around 300 B.C. As such, it is one of the earliest examples of an explicitly expressed algorithm.[1] The idea is clever, but before discussing why it works, let us simply explain the rules to follow. We maintain two values u and v which are initially set equal to the original numbers. When we reach a point at which v is zero, we report the current value of u as the answer. When v is greater than zero, we reduce both u and v in the following way. We compute the remainder r that results when dividing u by v. We then replace the values u and v respectively by v and r and repeat the process. A flowchart describing this algorithm is shown in Figure 1.2. As a demonstration, the sequence of computations when applying Euclid's algorithm to 54 and 42 are shown as follows, concluding with gcd 6.

u	v	r
54	42	12
42	12	6
12	6	0
6	**0**	

Why this algorithm produces the correct answer requires a bit of number theory (for those interested, see *For the Guru* on the following page). Yet if the steps are programmed as a user-defined function, it can subsequently be treated as a single high-level operation. The significance of the algorithm is its amazing efficiency, especially when compared to the first algorithm we described. Even if the original numbers are each near a billion, Euclid's algorithm is guaranteed to find the answer in fewer than 50 rounds.

---

1.   Informal algorithmic techniques existed for other mathematical problems some 1000 years earlier.

FOR THE GURU

Why Euclid's Algorithm Works. If r is the remainder of u divided by v, then we we have that $u = k \cdot v + r$ for some integer k. Therefore $r = u - k \cdot v$ and so anything that evenly divides both u and v must be a divisor of r. By similar algebra, any divisor of v and r must be a divisor of u as well. Therefore the gcd of v and r is the same as the gcd of u and v.

Furthermore, the process is guaranteed to terminate. Notice that remainder $r < v$, and so the subsequent value of v is strictly smaller than before yet nonnegative. So eventually v must reach 0.

1.3   High-Level Programming Languages

Every piece of software that runs on a computer is executed by that computer's *central processing unit*. The CPU design varies between different computing systems, but in general each CPU provides the core support for the most primitive data types (e.g., integers) and instructions (e.g., addition). Each CPU technically has its own programming language called its *machine language*. This is the only language that is genuinely understood by the processor. Because a machine language supports only the most basic data types and operations, it is often described as a *low-level programming language*. It is possible to develop software directly for a particular CPU but doing so is quite cumbersome with such limited built-in support.

More often, software is developed with what are termed *high-level programming languages*. These languages ease the development process by offering a richer set of data types and operations beyond those directly supported by a low-level language. For example, incrementing a value in a low-level language may require a sequence of three separate instructions: reading the value from memory, adding one to that value, and storing the result back into memory. Yet this is often expressed as a single operation in a high-level language.

It is important to remember that the computer's hardware only understands the low-level language. A person programming in a high-level language typically creates one or more text files that are called *source code*. In order to be executed, that high-level source code must in some way be translated into equivalent low-level instructions. Fortunately, this translation process can be automated. There are special pieces of software designed to translate code from a high-level language to a low-level language. The most common two forms of such translators are known as *compilers* and *interpreters*. A compiler typically takes the entire original code and translates it into a low-level program known as an *executable*. This executable can then be run directly by the computer. In contrast, an interpreter proceeds piecewise, translating an instruction, executing it, then translating the next instruction, and so on.

Hundreds of different high-level programming languages have been developed, each designed to make software development easier. Some of the most commonly used languages are (in alphabetical order): Ada, C, C++, C#, Cobol, Fortran, Java, JavaScript, Lisp, Perl, PHP, Prolog, Python, Ruby, Smalltalk, and Visual Basic. No one language is "the best" for all occasions. They have relative advantages and disadvantages in terms of expressiveness, flexibility, and efficiency.

Each language has its own ***syntax*** and ***semantics***. The syntax of a language is the precise set of rules regarding how characters, words, and punctuation should be used in a program. English has a syntax defining how words are spelled, the grammar for combining words into sentences, and proper use of capitalization and punctuation. Dutch has its own syntax, as does each natural language. In similar spirit, each programming language has its own well-defined syntax. The syntax for a programming language is generally far more rigid that that of a natural language. When communicating with a person, that person may still understand you even if you do not use perfect syntax. With computer languages, there is no room for ambiguity. A compiler or interpreter insists that you use perfect syntax in expressing your desires and reports what is known as a ***syntax error*** if the characters that you type are not properly formatted according to the rules of the language.

While the syntax of a language determines which statements are well formed, the **_semantics_** capture the underlying meaning of those statements. As an example, the syntax of a language may dictate that the statement `print 'hello'` is legitimate, while the semantics dictates that the characters `hello` are to be displayed to the user as a result of this command. When a programmer gives a computer legal instructions, but ones that do not lead to the correct behavior, this is known as a **_semantic error_** (or logical error). So long as the syntax is correct, the computer blindly does as it is told. If the overall behavior is flawed, that is the programmer's responsibility.

 # FOR THE GURU

The astute reader will note that there is not such a clear demarcation between data and operations. The instructions themselves can be viewed as a form of information and encoded as data. When we buy software, those instructions are stored as data either on external media such as a CD or DVD, or downloaded via a network. When installed, those instructions are stored on the computer's hard drive, and when executed those instructions are loaded into the computer's main memory and eventually the CPU. This recognition of an instruction as yet another form of data is a hallmark of the modern computer architecture that has remained since early work in the 1940s. This design is generally referred to as a **_von Neumann architecture_**, crediting John von Neumann who was an early pioneer in this work, although admittedly only one of many researchers in that era who were developing similar approaches.

1.4   The Object-Oriented Paradigm

High-level programming languages have been developed to support various ways of con–ceptualizing and expressing software. The ***paradigm*** used in this book, known as ***object-oriented programming (OOP)***, is based upon modeling data and operations as intimately paired, rather than as separate elements.

As a first example, we consider a digital picture. Some may choose to think of this purely as a type of data. Yet in an object-oriented framework we view it as a higher-level piece of information that supports a set of relevant operations. Thus a picture is an object that can be rotated, scaled, cropped, color-enhanced, cataloged, indexed, displayed, and so on. By considering the set of desired operations in the early design, one may better choose a suitable encoding of the information when designing the data representation. Our goal in this section is to introduce the major themes of object-oriented programming and the associated terminology.

1.4.1   Objects and Classes

We call the various entities that interact during the execution of a program ***objects***, and organize these into ***classes*** based upon their commonalities. More formally, objects of the same class share a common encoding of their underlying data representation and support a common set of operations. For example, in the previous discussion, DigitalPhoto may be the name of a class. A single object from a given class is termed an ***instance*** of that class, for example meAtTheArch and honeymoonInEurope. Internally, each instance is repre–sented by one or more pieces of data which we call ***attributes*** (although we occasionally use synonyms such as ***data members***, ***fields***, or ***instance variables***). The fact that objects are drawn from the same class means that they are represented using the same group of attributes, yet the *values* of those attributes may or may not be the same. For example, each photo has a width and height, but the dimensions of each photo are not necessarily the same. Taken together, the attribute values of a particular instance comprise what we term the ***state information***, representing the precise condition of the object at a given time. Notice that over time some attributes of an object (and thus the overall state) may change.

The operations supported by instances of a class are known as ***methods*** (although we occasionally use synonyms such as ***actions***, ***behaviors***, or ***member functions***). The methods supported by an object provide the mechanism for interacting with that object. Collectively, the attributes and methods of an instance are called its ***members***.

Example: the obedient dog

In general, we think of an object as a passive thing that does not do anything unless explic–itly told to do so. As an analogy, we compare it to the stereotypical well-trained dog. If we were to define a class Dog, we might take time to consider what attributes and meth–ods should be included. Perhaps we would include attributes such as birthdate, hairColor, eyeColor, weight, location, posture, and temperament, and methods such as sit, lieDown, rollOver, and fetch. If an instance of the Dog class, named spot, is created, it would pas–sively await commands from others. To interact with spot, an entity ***calls*** one of its sup–ported methods (this is synonymously termed ***invoking*** a method). The entity that invokes the method is termed the ***caller*** and will often be some other object in the larger system;

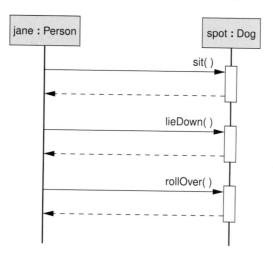

FIGURE 1.3: A sequence diagram demonstrating interactions between jane, an instance of a presumed Person class, and spot, an instance of Dog.

the entity upon which the method is invoked is termed the ***callee***. The typical syntax used for such a method call in an object-oriented programming language is spot.sit( ). Behind the scene, a message reaches the callee when one of its methods has been called, and in this case spot would perform whatever behavior is associated with the method sit. If a sequence of method calls are made, they are performed one at a time in the order in which they are invoked.

Figure 1.3 contains a graphical representation of a simple sequence of interactions. We call such a figure a ***sequence diagram***. At the top is a label for each object, identifying a unique name (e.g., jane) as well the class from which it is drawn (e.g., Person). The vertical line drawn down from the label represents the chronological lifespan of that object. Each solid arrow represents the invocation of a method, oriented from caller to callee (e.g., jane invoking the sit method upon spot). When a method is called, we say that the flow of control is passed from the caller to the callee. At that time, the caller waits until the callee completes the action. In our diagram, a white rectangle on the callee's side denotes the duration of time when that action is being performed. At its conclusion, the flow of control is passed back to the caller, as diagrammed with a dashed line in our figure. So in this example, after spot finishes sitting, we see that jane invokes the lieDown method, waits for that to complete, and then finally calls the rollOver method.

Each method has its own semantics based upon an underlying algorithm. Instances of the same class rely upon an identical implementation that is specified as part of the class definition. Yet that is not to say that each invocation of a given method causes the identical behavior. The instructions may take into account the current state of an object. For example, the precise mechanics of how a dog with short legs sits may be different from that of a dog with long legs. Even a single object can exhibit different behaviors for a method at different times, depending on the current state. If we call spot.sit( ) at a time when spot is in a lying posture, the execution of that command would presumably be

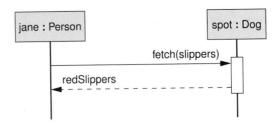

FIGURE 1.4: Sequence diagram in which jane invokes spot.fetch(slippers)

different than if called when spot is in a standing posture. However, it is worth noting that the behavior of the callee does not depend overtly upon the identity of the caller. In this way, our analogy of an object as a well-trained dog is fallacious; a well-trained dog might behave differently when its master tells it to sit as opposed to a stranger.

The methods serve as the primary avenue of communication with an object. Even in its simplest form, as in spot.sit( ), there is an aspect of communication captured purely in the decision to invoke this method (as opposed to calling spot.lieDown( ) or calling no method whatsoever). Yet in some cases, additional information must be passed from the caller to the callee. We call such a piece of information a *parameter*. Consider the fetch method of class Dog. There could be several possible things that one might ask a dog to fetch. A parameter can be used to designate this information, as in spot.fetch(slippers) as opposed to spot.fetch(newspaper). Of course, there must be an a priori agreement for each method as to how many parameters are expected, what types of information are to be sent, and in what order. We note that in the case of spot.sit( ), we intentionally use parentheses to clearly denote this as an invocation of a method with zero parameters.

Often, we wish to have a way for the *callee* to communicate information back to the caller after performing some action. For example, at the conclusion of spot.fetch(slippers), spot may have an object to return to the caller (ideally, the slippers). This kind of information passing is supported by allowing a callee to send a ***return value*** back to the caller at the conclusion of a method call. Figure 1.4 shows a sequence diagram for the call to fetch, with both the parameter and return value displayed. As with parameters, there should be a clear agreement as to what information will be returned, if any. The overall agreement regarding the expected parameters and return value for a method is called its ***signature***, and is documented as part of the class definition.

Methods serve various purposes. Some do not cause any change in the object's current state, but rather are used by the caller to request information about that state. Such methods are commonly termed ***accessors*** or ***inspectors*** and necessitate the use of a return value. For example, our Dog class might support the syntax getPosture( ) to let a caller know whether a dog is currently sitting, standing or lying. Other methods, such as sit( ), may affect the state of the callee; such a method is termed a ***mutator***. Although sit( ) does does not use any parameter or return value, other mutators may. Finally we note that some methods are neither accessors or mutators. For example if we presume that a dog returns precisely to the original position after fetching an object, the fetch method has no lasting effect on the state of the dog nor does it inform the caller about that state. Instead, it is used to initiate a broad action, in this case one that affects a third object, the slippers.

1.4.2   The Design of a Television Class

To further demonstrate these concepts, we consider the design of a Television class. A single television would be an *instance* of this class. In identifying what constitutes the *state* of a television, consider the following hypothetical scenario. Can you determine if your roommate uses your television while you are away? The state of a television should capture information that may help you determine the answer to such a question. For example, if you are sure that you left the television tuned to channel 5 yet when you come back it is set to channel 2, its state has certainly changed. The volume level of the television is another aspect of its state, as is whether or not the television is currently turned on.

Behind the scene, when an object is created the system sets aside a particular chunk of memory for storing the attributes values that represent the state of the new instance. The designer of the class specifies how those attribute values should be initially set. Some attributes, such as the brand and model of a television, are likely to be determined at the time the object is created and never again changed. Other aspects of state, such as the channel number and volume, might be initialized to certain settings at the time the object is created, but readily changeable after that. Although an object may be in different states at different times, the history of state changes are not automatically recorded. So when you return to find the television tuned to a different channel, you cannot necessarily determine what brought about that change. Perhaps your roommate is to blame; but maybe the cat changed it, or the power went out, or a neighbor's remote control triggered the change. Likewise, if you come back to find the state of your television precisely as you left it, this does not necessarily mean that the television was unused in the interim. Taking our hypo—thetical a step further, if your roommate accidentally broke your television and replaced it without telling you, would you know? It is possible to have two distinct objects in identi—cal states. Of course in this example, the roommate had better select the same brand and model, as well as ensure that the channel, volume, and other aspects of the state are set to match the previous state of the original.

Thus far, we have considered high-level aspects of a television's state, but not the pre—cise set of attributes used in representing that state. Before deciding upon those attributes, we should consider the desired behaviors for our televisions and the likely interactions between a user and a television instance. Consider the volume. A natural internal repre—sentation for this aspect of state might be a single numeric attribute, aptly named volume. But we must consider the user interactions associated with the volume of the television. A typical television does not allow the user to specify an arbitrary volume in a single oper—ation, but instead provides two buttons to respectively increase or decrease the volume. We model this interface by including two behaviors volumeUp and volumeDown. The user does not specify the actual increment for a single invocation of volumeUp; rather it is a fixed increment. To significantly increase the volume, a user must repeatedly invoke volumeUp. Therefore, we design the signature of the volumeUp method without any need for parameters. We can return the current setting of the volume to the caller as a way to model a typical television's behavior in displaying the updated volume setting immediately after the user invokes the volumeUp behavior.

Suppose we also wish to support functionality allowing the user to mute the televi—sion. Since the interface for muting and unmuting is typically a single button, we model this as a single method named toggleMute. The signature for this method would be simple,

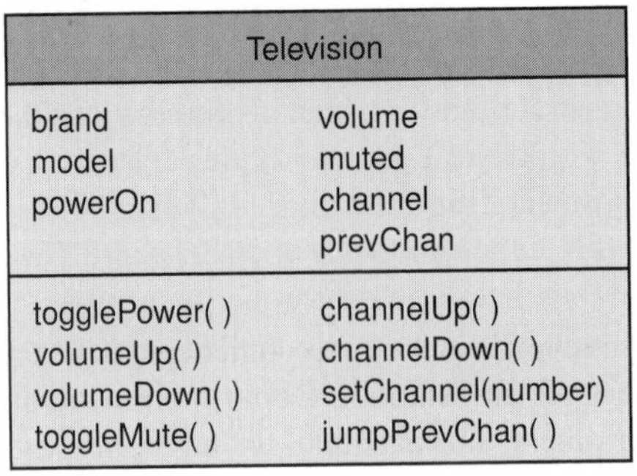

Television	
brand	volume
model	muted
powerOn	channel
	prevChan
togglePower( )	channelUp( )
volumeUp( )	channelDown( )
volumeDown( )	setChannel(number)
toggleMute( )	jumpPrevChan( )

FIGURE 1.5: A Television class diagram.

as there are no necessary parameters nor any relevant return value. For the implementation of the toggleMute behavior, a naive approach is to set the value of the volume attribute to zero. While this may seem an appropriate design at first glance, a problem arises when the mute button is pressed a second time. The volume should then be restored to the level that existed before it was muted. Yet if we had changed our internal representation to volume zero, we no longer have such a previous level stored as part of the object's state. A more robust design is to represent this aspect of the state with two separate attributes: a numeric volume and an attribute, named muted, set to either **True** or **False** to reflect whether or not the television is currently muted. With this representation, the toggleMute method reverses the setting for the muted attribute yet leaves the volume attribute unchanged. In this way, a second application of toggleMute has the effect of restoring the volume level. Of course, the speaker system of the television must take both attributes into account when controlling the physical audio output.

Next, we consider interactions involving the television channel. As was the case with volume, the television should support incremental control through methods such as channelUp( ) and channelDown( ). Yet unlike volume, televisions allow the user to set the channel directly to a specified value. We define an additional method with signature setChannel(number) for this purpose. The parameter number represents the desired channel as specified by the user. Suppose we wish to support another common feature of televisions, namely the ability to jump back to the most recently viewed channel. To do so, we must carefully consider our state representation. It is not sufficient to simply have an attribute channel that represents the current selection; we must also maintain an attribute such as prevChan as part of the internal state.

Although our television model is not yet complete, this discussion should give the flavor of the design process. A sketch of the basic design for our class is shown in Figure 1.5. We call such a figure a *class diagram*. The top portion of the diagram identifies the class name, the middle portion the attributes, and the bottom portion the supported methods. Our class diagram explicitly indicates the expected parameters sent to each method. We do not explicitly display the use of a return value in our diagram, although this could be included if desired. We will come back to this example in Chapter 6, providing a complete implementation of a Television class.

1.4.3 The Design of a Student Registration System

In the preceding section, the design of the Television class was self contained. For larger software systems, many different objects of various classes must be defined in modeling a complete application. The challenge in designing larger systems is in identifying a reason–able set of classes and envisioning the interactions between objects of those classes.

Although we do not undertake a complete design of such a large system, we briefly examine the high-level design of a hypothetical student registration system. Some obvious candidates for classes are Student, Department, Course, Professor, and Major, yet there may be need for others. For example, we might propose a Schedule class to represent an individual student's current schedule. In similar fashion, a Transcript class might be defined to represent a student's complete history of courses. Attributes of an object can reference other objects. For example the Course object might maintain a list of enrolled students or the responsible teacher; a Schedule or Transcript instance would reference associated courses. These relationships are often described as ***has-a relationships***. A Course has a teacher; a Schedule has courses. One instance may even reference another instance from the same class, for example if keeping track of a roommate attribute for each Student.

When modeling the set of behaviors supported by each class, it is important not to view each class in isolation but to consider the likely interactions. In performing a particular behavior, an object may rely on intermediate calls to behaviors of that same object or of other associated objects. These method calls serve as a way to pass messages back and forth between objects as well as to initiate change in the state of the objects. Sequence diagrams are often used as modeling tools. Consider, for example, what may take place behind the scene when an advisor wishes to enroll a student bob in the course cs102. Presumably that action begins with the invocation of bob.enroll(cs102). Figure 1.6 shows a straightforward model for this action. Notice that the Professor communicates with the Student object and awaits completion of the method call. It is the Student instance that manages the underlying Schedule instance when adding the new course. Take note of the timing portrayed by this diagram. When the call to bob.enroll(cs102) is made, this triggers a call to bobSch.addCourse(cs102). The first action does not terminate until *after* the second method completes. Only then does bob return control back to the original caller.

Yet the model portrayed in Figure 1.6 is overly simplistic. In Figures 1.7–1.9 we present a series of refinements, adding additional underlying detail to each version. First we model the fact that a student cannot automatically add a course. A request must be made, presumably to the object that represents the course, asking whether this student can

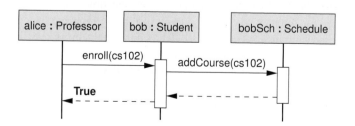

FIGURE 1.6: Simple sequence diagram for invocation of bob.enroll(cs102).

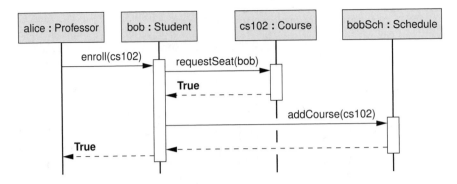

FIGURE 1.7: A refined sequence diagram for invocation of bob.enroll(cs102), which includes explicit approval for a seat in the course.

have a seat. So in Figure 1.7 we have bob make an explicit request for a seat in cs102, waiting until that is confirmed before reflecting the new course in his schedule. Notice that this particular diagram shows only one possible sequence; presumably there would be a different consequence if that seat had been denied. Even in this new model, there is no explanation for the process used in deciding whether a seat in the course is granted to the given student. So in Figure 1.8 we add an additional layer of complexity showing this step. The difference between this version and the previous is the call bob.hasTaken(cs101) to check whether the student has taken the prerequisite course. Note carefully the direction of the arrow. Although most of our calls have been made from left to right, that was somewhat arbitrary. With respect to the hasTaken call, the cs102 object is the *caller* and bob is the *callee*. In a sense, this interaction is like a small conversation between those two entities, animated perhaps as follows:

bob: "I would like a seat in your course (cs102)."

cs102:   "Have you taken the prerequisite cs101?"

bob: "Yes, I have."

cs101:   "Then yes, you may have a seat."

Another new feature of this diagram is the activation of the hasTaken method overlaid on top of the (ongoing) activation of bob.enroll(cs102). As method calls lead to intermediate calls, it is not uncommon for a particular object to perform behaviors in this sequence.

In Figure 1.9 we provide our most detailed model of the interactions. Here we see a process in which the student makes sure that he can fit the number of hours into his current schedule. Also, when a seat is requested in a course, the course "asks itself" whether there is room for the new student, in addition to the prerequisite check for the student. Also, the course instance records the student's enrollment in its own internal state (while the student object continues to record the enrollment in its associated schedule). Again we wish to emphasize that this is a diagram of one particular sequence. A very different set of actions might take place, for example, had the course been full or the student's schedule overloaded. Given time, we would develop sequence diagrams for other cases in a fully functional registration system, such as how a professor assigns grades for students in a class or how the university checks whether a student has met the requirements for graduation. But this is enough for now to give the flavor of the design process.

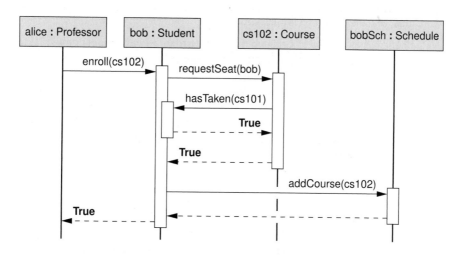

FIGURE 1.8: A sequence diagram in which bob is required to have taken the prerequisite cs101.

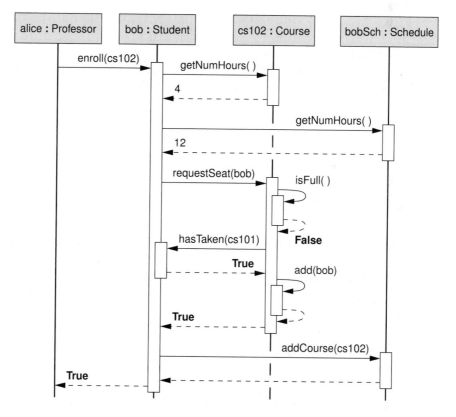

FIGURE 1.9: Our most detailed model of an invocation of bob.enroll(cs102).

1.4.4   Class Hierarchies and Inheritance

The key to good object-oriented design is to identify and model commonalities and differences among entities. As we start to consider the modeling of different classes, we should consider how those classes compare to one another. By identifying commonalities, we can organize a *class hierarchy*. Such classification of objects based upon commonality is not unique to computer science. The standard biology taxonomy is organized in similar fashion (e.g., kingdom, phylum, class[2]). Organisms in the Mammalia class share common structural properties (e.g., three middle ear bones, body hair) and behaviors (e.g., the production of milk for offspring). There are certainly differences among mammals as well, hence a further breakdown into subclasses and orders based upon further commonalities.

To demonstrate a simple hierarchy, we revisit the student registration system introduced in the preceding section. We suggested the need for several classes, such as Student and Professor, yet did not flesh out the details at that time. For the sake of demonstration, presume that we had settled on the Student model and Professor model portrayed in Figure 1.10. Although these two classes could be designed and implemented independently, there is a better way. Some of the attributes and methods we suggest for the Professor class (e.g., those involving the name, birthdate, phone number) are identical in purpose to those of the Student class. Yet there are also clear differences between the two classes, as a student has a GPA and a major while a professor has an office and holds office hours.

Student
name
phoneNumber
birthdate
curSchedule
advisor
transcript
declaredMajor
getName( )
getPhone( )
setPhone(number)
getAge( )
getMajor( )
declareMajor(major)
enroll(course)
drop(course)
getGrade(course)
assignGrade(course, grade)
hasTaken(course)
checkGraduation( )
getGpa( )

Professor
name
phoneNumber
birthdate
curSchedule
department
office
officeHours
getName( )
getPhone( )
setPhone(number)
getAge( )
getOffice( )
setOffice(room)
getDepartment( )
getOfficeHours( )
addHours(time)
removeHours(time)
assignGrade(course, student, grade)

FIGURE 1.10: Class diagrams for independent Student and Professor classes.

---

2.   Hey, they even use the term *class*!

We prefer to model the Student and Professor classes using a technique known as *inheritance*. We first define a more generic Person class based precisely upon the identified commonalities. Every Person instance has a name, phoneNumber, birthdate, and curSchedule, and related methods such as getName( ) and setPhone(number). Then we define both the Student class and the Professor class relative to the Person class. A revised diagram demonstrating the class hierarchy is shown in Figure 1.11 (thereby replacing the original designs of Figure 1.10). When modeling the Student class relative to the Person class, a Student instance *inherits* all of the attributes and methods of the Person class. We must only identify changes or additions to the set of attributes and methods that are specifically appropriate for a Student. For example, a student has a declared major and an advisor, and supports methods such as declareMajor(major) or getGpa( ). In similar fashion, the Professor class inherit from Person and then specify additional members, for example those involving the office hours.

When discussing inheritance relationships, we refer to Person as the *parent class* or *base class* of Student, and likewise Student as a *child class* or *subclass* of Person (as children inherit from their parent). The relationship between a parent and child class is often termed an *is-a relationship*, in that every Student is a Person, although a Person is not necessarily a Student. Note the distinction from the *has-a* relationship described in Section 1.4.3, which applies when a class has attributes that are instances of another class.

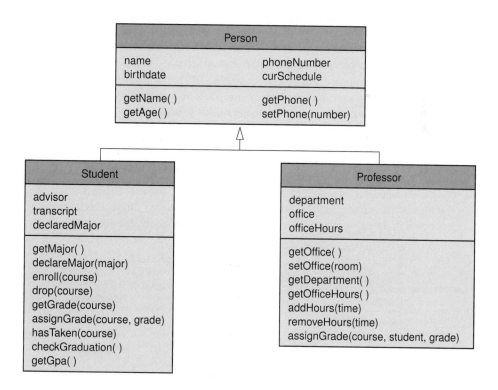

FIGURE 1.11: A hierarchy showing Student and Professor classes derived from Person.

A drawing package

As a larger example we consider the design of a system for creating and displaying a variety of graphical objects. Our system will include support for objects such as circles, squares, line segments, polygons, and text, and will provide the ability to vary positions, sizes, and colors of these objects. Rather than develop each type of object in isolation, we design a hierarchy to take maximal advantage of the inherent commonality.

We start our design with a generic Drawable class that is meant to capture aspects that are common to all such objects. We do not expect a user to create an instance of the Drawable class directly. It is designed to serve as a parent class in our inheritance hierarchy, unifying the common traits and behaviors. For this reason it is known as an **abstract class**. For example, there is a notion of position relative to the canvas which transcends all of our graphical objects. That is, a circle will not just be defined by its radius but also its position on the canvas; the same concept applies to a rectangle, a piece of text, and a line segment. We therefore include a referencePoint as an attribute of all drawable objects in our model. The reference point may be interpreted differently for different shapes, such as the center of a circle, the top-left corner of a piece of text, or one end of a line segment. Then we can provide support for all drawable objects by providing an accessor, such as getReferencePoint( ), and mutators for altering the position of an object. In fact, we will offer two such mutators for convenience. The method move(dx, dy) allows a caller to specify the change in coordinates *relative* to the current position. The second mutator moveTo(x, y) takes parameters x and y, which designate the desired position in *absolute* coordinates. In similar fashion, the concept of rotating, scaling, or flipping an object transcends all shapes, so we provide methods for those operations and an internal transformation that keeps track of the current setting.

The complete design of our Drawable class is outlined in Figure 1.12. The depth attribute is used to control the appearance when the position of two or more objects overlap. One with lesser depth obscures another with greater depth, with those values observed or modified using the getDepth( ) and setDetph(depth) methods respectively. We also offer a clone method that can be used to create a new instance that is an exact copy of an existing object. Our model for this class includes an abstract method *draw( )* that cannot be implemented generically. For this reason, we italicize its name (in fact, we also italicize the name of the Drawable class since that class as a whole is abstract). Our presumption is that any concrete class that inherits from Drawable (e.g., Circle, Rectangle) will provide a true definition for draw( ), controlling how that particular shape is drawn.

Drawable		
depth	transformation	referencePoint
move(dx, dy) moveTo(x, y) getDepth( ) setDepth( )	rotate(angle) scale(factor) flip(angle) clone( )	getReferencePoint( ) adjustReference(dx, dy) *draw( )*

FIGURE 1.12: Our design for the top-level class Drawable.

At this point, we might be tempted to complete our design by defining a separate child class of Drawable for each of the graphical primitives we want, such as Text, Circle, Rectangle, Square, Polygon, Segment, and so on. Yet such a design would not properly leverage the object–oriented paradigm. Although we cannot identify any other properties that are common to all of these objects, they are not entirely unrelated. For example, many of the drawing primitives have borders with a specified thickness or color. To capture this generality, we define a Shape class. Not all Drawable objects belong to this specialized subclass. For example, we treat a text object as Drawable, yet not supporting the concept of a configurable border. In similar fashion, we further specialize a FillableShape class for those elements that have an interior that might be colored, such as a circle, square, or rectangle (yet not a line segment).

At the lower levels of the hierarchy we finally define individual classes such as Circle, Rectangle, and Segment that specify the structure and behaviors that make those objects unique. For example, a Circle has a radius attribute with an associated accessor and mutator for that value. A Rectangle has a height and width. Each of these classes is responsible for providing a concrete implementation of the draw( ) method to capture the semantics of its instances. Putting all of this together, we offer the hierarchy of Drawable objects shown in Figure 1.13. While this is just a design, we will introduce in Chapter 3 a package which implements these classes, allowing us to create pictures and animations.

1.5 Design and Modeling

Creating a good object–oriented design is not a straightforward task, even for the most experienced software designers. There is no one "best" design and no standard formula for identifying the various classes, attributes, and behaviors. Design decisions must carefully weigh the overall functionality needed for the end product, as well as internal factors that affect the ease of development and efficiency of the software.

Looking back at our own designs, we find some decisions that warrant more thought. For example in our Television design, what should happen if setChannel is called with a parameter value that is not a legitimate channel number? For our Student class, we suggested the inclusion of a declaredMajor attribute. How might we represent students who have more than one major or students who are currently undeclared? In our graph–ics design, we intentionally defined the Rectangle class without making it a child of the Polygon class, even though geometrically a rectangle is an instance of a polygon. Why might we prefer this model?

As you gain programming experience, you will start to recognize good and bad design decisions that you have made. For now, we wish to emphasize that design is a very important part of the programming process. As a beginner, there will be a temptation to sit at a computer and start typing; in fact, this is a great way to learn. But for experienced programmers, it becomes far more important to think about the overall design of a project long before the first line of code is written. It is a terrible waste of resources to move ahead with the implementation of a seriously flawed design. Although designs can evolve and be refined to remedy shortcomings, a major change to the core design can be very difficult to implement. In an extreme case, all of the source code might have to be thrown away and redeveloped from scratch.

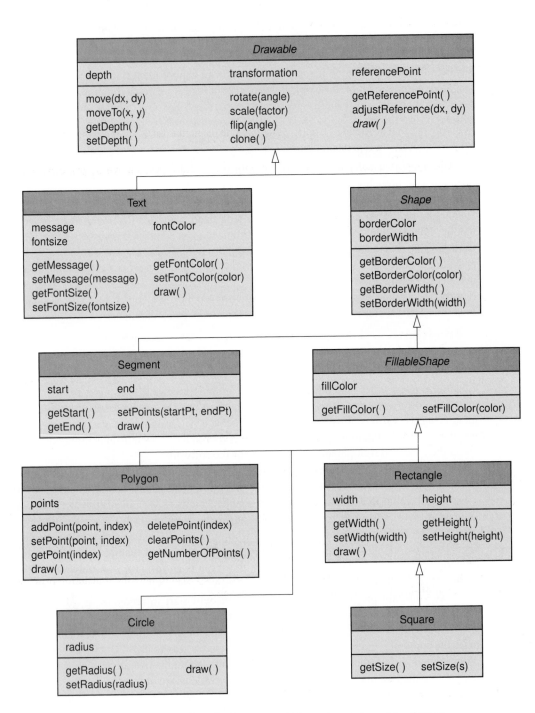

FIGURE 1.13: A proposed hierarchy of drawable objects.

1.6 Chapter Review

1.6.1 Key Points

Data and Types

- All data is stored in memory as a collection of *bits*.
- There may be several possible data *representations* for a high-level piece of information.
- A *data type* is an abstraction used to associate one particular form of high-level information with an underlying representation.
- Built-in support usually exists for commonly used data types, known as *primitive data types*.
- A programmer can design and implement *user-defined data types*.

Operations, Functions, and Algorithms

- Built-in support exists for many commonly used operations.
- *Control structures* are operations that are used to control when other operations are executed or repeated.
- A programmer can provide an abstraction for a higher-level task by designing and implementing a *function*.
- An *algorithm* is a well-defined series of operations used to perform a task.
- We use a *flowchart* to portray the general sequence of steps in an algorithm.
- There often exist different algorithms for accomplishing the same high-level task, each with its own advantages and disadvantages.

High-Level Programming Languages

- The instructions supported by a CPU comprise its *machine language*. These are the only instructions that can be executed by that computer's hardware.
- A CPU supports a rather limited repertoire of primitive data types and instructions. For this reason, a machine language is viewed as a *low-level programming language*.
- A *high-level programming language* supports greater abstraction by providing a richer set of data types and operations, beyond those supplied by the CPU.
- Software written in a high-level programming language must be translated back to the low-level language to be executed on the computer.
- *Compilers* and *interpreters* are software tools designed to automate the translation process from a high-level language to a low-level language.
- The *syntax* of a programming language defines the precise format of characters, words, and punctuation used when programming.
- The *semantics* of a language describe the underlying meaning associated with each statement.

The Object-Oriented Paradigm

- We design *classes* to take advantage of similarities in the way we represent and interact with objects.
- One object from a class is called an *instance* of that class.

- Instances of a given class have their *state information* represented using a common set of *attributes*. Each instance has its own attribute values stored independently in memory.
- The values of an object's attributes may change over the lifespan of the object.
- Objects drawn from the same class support a common set of *methods* and rely upon the same algorithm when performing those behaviors.
- *Parameters* provide a way for the caller to send information to the callee when invoking a method.
- *Return values* provide a way for the callee to send information back to the caller upon completion of a method.
- The *signature* of a method is a summary of the number and order of parameters and the use of return values.
- The precise behavior of a method invocation may depend upon the parameters sent from the caller as well as the current state of the object itself.
- A method that never changes the state of the callee is called an *accessor*; a method that might change the state of the callee is called a *mutator*.
- A class can be defined relative to an existing class, *inheriting* the members of that *parent class*. The *child class* can also establish additional attributes or methods.

1.6.2 Glossary

abstraction A high-level model for a piece of information or an algorithmic process, independent of low-level implementation details.

accessor A method whose invocation cannot affect the state of the callee.

algorithm A step-by-step procedure for accomplishing a task.

attribute One of the pieces of data used in representing the state of an object. Equivalently termed a data member, field, or instance variable.

base class *See* parent class.

behavior *See* method.

bit A binary digit; the smallest unit of memory. It can be set to one of two distinct states.

callee The object whose method is being executed.

caller The object that initiates the execution of a method.

central processing unit (CPU) The hardware component that controls the computer.

child class A class that is defined to inherit from another class, known as the parent class.

class A group of objects that share commonality in their underlying encoding and supported behaviors.

class diagram A figure used to model the design of a class by identifying its name, its attributes, and its methods.

class hierarchy A taxonomy of related classes.

control structure A command that describes the order in which some other instructions are executed.

CPU *See* central processing unit.

data The low-level representation of information, as stored and manipulated by a computer.

data member *See* attribute.

data type A definition that associates a particular form of high-level information with an underlying representation scheme.

encoding *See* representation.

executable A low-level program that can be run directly by a computer's hardware.

field *See* attribute.

flowchart A diagram demonstrating the sequence of steps associated with a particular algorithm.

function A programming construct for encapsulating a (user-defined) behavior.

has-a relationship An instance of one class having an instance of another class as an attribute (e.g., a Course has a Teacher).

high-level programming language A language designed to ease the task of specifying a complex set of instructions to be followed by a computer. High-level languages support more general abstractions than low-level programming languages.

inheritance A technique by which one class is defined based upon another.

inspector *See* accessor.

instance A single object drawn from a given class.

instance variable *See* attribute.

is-a relationship A description of the relation between child and parent classes (e.g., a Student is a Person).

low-level programming language A programming language with very basic support for primitive data types and operations, for example, a CPU's machine language.

machine language The particular low-level programming language supported by a CPU.

main memory The portion of the computer system's storage in which the program and its data are stored while the program is executing.

member Any of the attributes or methods associated with a class or an instance of that class.

member function *See* method.

method A formal operation supported by all objects of a given class.

mutator A method whose invocation may affect the state of the callee.

object An entity of an executing program, which typically represents some real-world item or concept.

object-oriented programming A paradigm in which data and operations are modeled as intimately paired, rather than as separate elements.

operation A basic instruction that may be performed by a computer.

paradigm   A general approach to conceptualizing and expressing computer software (e.g., the object–oriented paradigm).

parameter   A piece of information sent from the caller to the callee upon invocation of a function.

parent class   A class used as the basis for another (child) class through inheritance.

primitive data type   A data type that is so commonly used it is already defined as part of a programming language.

representation   A low–level way of storing some high–level information.

return value   A piece of information sent back from the callee to the caller at the conclusion of a function call.

semantics   The underlying meaning associated with a particular syntax.

sequence diagram   A figure used to model the chronological flow of control between interacting objects.

signature   The interface of a function; specifically its name, parameters, and return value.

source code   The characters that comprise commands for a program in a high–level language. Source code is typically stored in one or more text files and translated with an interpreter or compiler.

state   The current condition of an object, as represented by its set of attribute values.

subclass   *See* child class.

syntax   The precise rules for the use of characters, words, and punctuation when writing in a particular programming language.

user-defined type   A custom data type that is defined by a programmer (as opposed to a primitive type of the language).

1.6.3   Exercises

Data

Practice 1.1: We mentioned ASCII and Unicode as two different encodings for text. If you are not already familiar with these, do some research and describe the difference between the two.

Exercise 1.2: We mentioned JPG and GIF as two different encodings for pictures. If you are not already familiar with these, do some research and describe the difference between the two.

Exercise 1.3: We list several natural types of information that are commonly stored and manipulated by computers (e.g., text, photographs, sales records). Suggest some other examples.

Exercise 1.4: What data might be stored when representing the concept of an online shop–ping cart?

Operations

Practice 1.5: Write down the steps of the algorithm taught in elementary school for adding two numbers.

Exercise 1.6: Simulate Euclid's algorithm for computing the gcd of 180 and 75, listing all pairs of numbers that were considered along the way.

Exercise 1.7: Write down the steps of the algorithm taught in elementary school for sub-tracting one number from another.

Exercise 1.8: Write down the steps of an algorithm for tying your shoes.

Exercise 1.9: Write down the steps of an algorithm for a common everyday task.

Exercise 1.10: Give a flowchart portraying the algorithm you use to find a name in a phonebook.

Class Design

Practice 1.11: The volumeDown behavior of a television generally decrements the vol-ume, and the channelDown behavior generally decrements the channel. However, the precise semantics of these two behaviors is not quite the same. Explain any differences.

Exercise 1.12: When you turn your television off and then on again, does this sequence of actions have any lasting effect? Explain.

Exercise 1.13: In Section 1.5, we discussed a possible flaw in the design of our Student class regarding the representation of a declared major. Identify other potential flaws in that design and suggest ways you might remedy the design.

Exercise 1.14: Imagine that you have been hired to design a computer system to support a video store. Describe several classes that you envision in your design. You do not need to provide details of the exact attributes and behaviors for each class; the focus should be on identifying the general purpose of each class.

For Practice 1.15 through Exercise 1.19, you are asked to describe a class design. In each case, clearly specify the following aspects of your design:

- Give a list of attributes, describing the purpose of each.
- Give a list of supported behaviors, clearly indicating the action that takes place and whether or not this behavior has any effect on the state information. Also indicate the purpose of any parameters and the purpose of a return value, if applicable.

Practice 1.15: We suggest that the university registration system include a Course class, although we never provide details of its design. Please develop an initial design.

Exercise 1.16: Describe an initial design for a basic Calculator class.

Exercise 1.17: Describe an initial design for an AnsweringMachine class.

Exercise 1.18: Describe an initial design for a SodaMachine class.

Exercise 1.19: Describe an initial design for a ShoppingCart class, as used by a typical online merchant.

Interactions Among Objects

For Practice 1.20 through Exercise 1.24, you are asked to give a sequence diagram in the style of Figure 1.9. Such a diagram should clearly identify the following aspects:

- Which object initiates each interaction (i.e., the caller)?
- Upon which object is the interaction invoked (i.e., the callee)?
- What information, if any, is passed from the caller to the callee?
- What information, if any, is returned from the callee back to the caller?

Practice 1.20: Draw a sequence diagram for an invocation of bob.enroll(cs102) in which Bob is denied enrollment due to an unfulfilled prerequisite course.

Exercise 1.21: Draw a sequence diagram modeling the action of a professor assigning a grade, as in alice.assignGrade(cs102, bob, 'A'). Make sure that the grade is reported on Bob's transcript.

Exercise 1.22: Give a sequence diagram modeling the purchase of a sandwich at a typical sandwich shop. Use three objects: Cashier, Customer, and SandwichMaker.

Exercise 1.23: Give a sequence diagram modeling the purchase of a 75-cent soda using a dollar bill.

Exercise 1.24: Give a sequence diagram modeling some other example of a real-world interaction between two or more objects.

Inheritance

Practice 1.25: Design a Staff class that inherits from the Person class of Section 1.4.4.

Exercise 1.26: The Square class modeled in Figure 1.13 does not include any attributes. Why is that?

Exercise 1.27: Consider the high-level design of two classes: BasicClock representing a basic digital clock, and AlarmClock representing a clock with an alarm. Describe a high-level design using inheritance to model an AlarmClock class as a child of BasicClock. List the attributes and behaviors that you would include in each class.

For Practice 1.28 through Exercise 1.32, please diagram a class hierarchy for the given domain. You do not need to detail the precise members of each class, only the relationships among classes. Your hierarchy should have at least 4 levels and include 10 or more overall classes.

Practice 1.28: Diagram a hierarchy of foods.

Exercise 1.29: Diagram a hierarchy of animals.

Exercise 1.30: Diagram a hierarchy of gifts.

Exercise 1.31: Diagram a hierarchy of motor vehicles.

Exercise 1.32: Pick some other general class of objects from everyday life and diagram a natural hierarchy for that domain.

CHAPTER 2

Getting Started in Python

Throughout this text, we use the Python programming language. This is a high-level language that was originally developed in the early 1990s. Python includes many existing data types and functions to support the manipulation of text, numbers, logical expressions, files, and larger collections of objects. In this chapter, we start with an early exploration of the language, interacting with objects from many of the built-in types. This allows us to reinforce the principles of object-oriented programming while also being exposed to many important tools of the language. By the end of the chapter we will be ready to write complete programs.

2.1   The Python Interpreter

Python is an example of an interpreted language. There is a piece of software known as the **Python interpreter** that executes commands in the Python programming language. If not already installed on your computer, it is freely available at `http://www.python.org`.

The procedure for starting the Python interpreter depends upon your computer system. It may be as simple as typing `python` at a command prompt. The standard Python distribution also includes a graphical development environment, known as IDLE, that is used by many programmers (and is described in Appendix A). When the Python interpreter starts, it displays some introductory lines including the software version number, and then the following line.

```
>>>
```

31

We call this the ***Python prompt*** and will see it often. Whenever this appears as the last line on the screen, the interpreter is waiting for us to enter further commands. Each time a command is entered, the computer executes it and presents another prompt.

From the Python prompt, we can create an instance of a class and view and manip-ulate its state. For most of this chapter, we explore Python through interactive sessions with the interpreter. By the end of the chapter, we discuss how to save our commands in pre-written files that can be executed by the Python interpreter. This means we do not have to start over every time we sit down at the computer.

2.2   Using Objects: the list Class

We begin our exploration by examining one of the most interesting of Python's built-in types, the **list** class. This class is used to maintain an ordered list of items, be it phone numbers, people you are inviting to a party, or groceries. A list serves as an excellent first example of an interesting object that supports a variety of behaviors. This lets us reinforce many of the object-oriented principles that were first discussed in Section 1.4. A list is also an extremely valuable tool used regularly by experienced Python programmers. This section serves to introduce many features of the class.

2.2.1   Constructing and Naming Instances

We create a list of groceries as our first example, typing the following at the Python prompt.

```
>>> groceries = list()
>>>
```

The command groceries = **list**( ) demonstrates several key principles. The syntax **list**( ) creates a new instance of the **list** class by invoking what is termed the ***constructor*** of the **list** class. A constructor is responsible for configuring the initial state of a new object in memory. In this case, the newly created list is initially empty. It truly is an instance of the **list** class, simply one that represents a list of zero items. The construction of a new object from a given class is called ***instantiation***. The parentheses that follow the class name designate this syntax as an action (as opposed to **list**, without parentheses, which is the name of the class).

The word groceries is a name we have chosen that serves as an ***identifier***. We can essentially pick whatever we want to use as an identifier, although good programming style dictates a meaningful choice. There are a few limitations. An identifier must consist of letters, digits, or underscore characters (_) yet cannot use a digit as the first character. The identifiers are case sensitive; thus groceries and Groceries are not the same. Furthermore, Python reserves a few keywords, such as **class**, to have special meaning in the syntax of the language. Those keywords cannot be used as identifiers.

The overall command groceries = **list**( ) is an ***assignment*** statement. The seman-tics are to associate the identifier on the left-hand side of the = operator with the object expressed on the right-hand side. Identifiers are like labels that can be stuck onto an under-lying object. In this regard, the assignment statement is used to assign a label to an object. Figure 2.1 shows the result of our first complete statement. Looking back at the interpreter session, the display of a new Python prompt >>> lets us know that the interpreter awaits further instruction.

FIGURE 2.1: The steps in the execution of the groceries = **list**( ) statement: (a) creation of an empty **list** instance, and (b) the assignment of identifier groceries to the newly created object.

2.2.2   Calling Methods

Having associated the identifier groceries with an initially empty list, we wish to add some items. We do so by calling theappend method using the following syntax:

```
>>> groceries.append('bread')
>>>
```

We will see this general format often as we invoke methods upon our objects. This is similar to the notation introduced in Chapter 1, as in spot.sit( ) or spot.fetch(slippers). Let's take a closer look at the precise syntax of one of these statements. The information conveyed by this syntax includes several key components:

$$\underbrace{\text{groceries}}_{\text{object}}.\underbrace{\text{append}}_{\text{method}}(\underbrace{\text{'bread'}}_{\text{parameters}})$$

Starting at the left we must identify the particular object with which we want to interact. In this example we use the identifier groceries, which had been established earlier. Next comes a period (often pronounced "dot"). The dot indicates that we wish to access a member of the given object. Next is the name of a method, in this case append. Finally, we find a set of parentheses with any expected parameters included between them. Each piece of this syntax is significant.

The leftmost identifier is critical in starting such an interaction. Keep in mind that we may have many objects in our environment. For example if planning a party, we might use a list groceries when shopping for our supplies, and another list guests of those people who are invited to the party. We could begin as

```
>>> groceries = list()
>>> guests = list()
```

In this case, two distinct instances of the **list** class are constructed, one labeled with the identifier groceries and the other labeled with the identifier guests. If we want to add 'Chip' to our guest list, we must use the syntax guests.append('Chip') as opposed to groceries.append('Chip').

The method name must be clearly identified because objects support many different behaviors. For example, we will soon see that lists support other methods such as remove and sort. In this example, we are specifically invoking the append method.

Finally, the parentheses are used to formally invoke the method and to delimit parameters that are being sent. In our example, the parameter 'bread' is intentionally enclosed in quotation marks although this is not always the case. The quotation marks denote this as a string of characters (more about strings is coming in Section 2.3). Had we not included quotes, the term bread in the context groceries.append(bread) is presumed to be the name of another identifier. The interpreter reports an error if no such identifier exists.

```
>>> groceries.append(bread)
Traceback (most recent call last):
  File "<stdin>", line 1, in -toplevel-
NameError: name 'bread' is not defined
>>>
```

Don't be too alarmed by the gibberish of the error message. As a beginning programmer you will see many of them. Even experienced programmers make errors quite often when developing software. In fact, many of the details shown in Python's error messages are meant to provide important diagnostic information to the programmer as to the cause of the error. The final line of the error message is usually the most informative, describing the type of error that occurred, in this case a NameError. Notice that the error does not cause the interpreter to quit. It simply ignores the troublesome command and presents us with a new prompt so that we can continue.

Another common error occurs when a method is called without the proper parameters. It is important that the number and type of parameters agree with the signature of the given method. In the case of append, the caller must send a single parameter, namely the object that is to be added to the list. It makes no sense to invoke append without such a value and doing so results in an error message from the interpreter.

```
>>> groceries.append()
Traceback (most recent call last):
  File "<stdin>", line 1, in -toplevel-
TypeError: append() takes exactly one argument (0 given)
>>>
```

Going back to our lesson, the append method is an example of a ***mutator***. It changes the internal state of the list, adding the specified item to the *end* of the list. Of course, we do not typically see that internal state. However, we can take a peek by typing the identifier itself into the interpreter. This causes it to display a textual representation of our object.

```
>>> groceries
['bread']
```

In the case of lists, that representation uses square brackets with the contents of the list between those brackets. To see an example of a longer list, let's add some more groceries.

```
>>> groceries.append('milk')
>>> groceries.append('cheese')
>>> groceries
['bread', 'milk', 'cheese']
```

We see the individual elements separated by commas when displayed. Notice that each element was appended to the end of the list. Thus 'milk' was placed after 'bread', and then 'cheese' after that. The same item can be added to the list in more than one position, as shown here.

```
>>> groceries.append('bread')
>>> groceries
['bread', 'milk', 'cheese', 'bread']
```

The insert method

The order of items on a grocery list may or may not be significant in real life. As our next example, we focus on a list where order is very significant: a restaurant's waiting list. Here, the append method has natural semantics, adding a new person to the end of the list.

```
>>> waitlist = list()
>>> waitlist.append('Kim')
>>> waitlist.append('Eric')
>>> waitlist.append('Andrew')
>>> waitlist
['Kim', 'Eric', 'Andrew']
```

Perhaps by slipping some money to the maître d', a new customer can improve his or her position on the list. The more money, the higher up the list! In Python, we simulate such a possibility by calling a method named insert, which allows us to add an item at a desired position. The signature of the method uses two parameters; the first specifies the position and the second the new item. We describe the desired position using a value known as an *index*. The index of the newly inserted item is the number of existing items that should remain in front of it. By this convention, inserting an item with index 0 places it at the very beginning of the list, with index 1 it is placed after the first item, and so on. As an example,

```
>>> waitlist.insert(1, 'Donald')
>>> waitlist
['Kim', 'Donald', 'Eric', 'Andrew']
>>> waitlist.insert(3, 'Grace')
>>> waitlist
['Kim', 'Donald', 'Eric', 'Grace', 'Andrew']
```

Notice that a new element does not replace any existing item; the trailing items are implic–itly pushed back one position in the list.

A WORD OF WARNING

The index of an element equals the number of elements that precede it. Therefore, the first element of a list has index 0, the second has index 1, and so forth. For this reason, we say that lists are *zero-indexed*.

The remove method

What if somebody gets tired of waiting in line and decides to leave our restaurant? We can adjust our list accordingly by calling the remove method, specifying the item to be removed as a parameter.

```
>>> waitlist.remove('Eric')
>>> waitlist
['Kim', 'Donald', 'Grace', 'Andrew']
```

Earlier, we mentioned that a list may have several occurrences of the same value. So what happens if we use the syntax waitlist.remove('Alan') when our list has two or more people named 'Alan'? In this case, the semantics of the method are defined to remove the *first* such entry that it finds, searching from beginning to end. As an example, consider the following longer list:

```
>>> waitlist
['Rich', 'Elliot', 'Alan', 'Karl', 'Alan', 'William']
>>> waitlist.remove('Alan')
>>> waitlist
['Rich', 'Elliot', 'Karl', 'Alan', 'William']
```

Notice that the first person named 'Alan' was removed while the subsequent individual remains. Finally, we point out that if you try to remove an item that is not actually on the list, an error occurs.

```
>>> waitlist.remove('Stuart')
Traceback (most recent call last):
  File "<stdin>", line 1, in -toplevel-
ValueError: list.remove(x): x not in list
```

This particular error is known as a ValueError; we sent a parameter, as expected by the signature, but the *value* of that parameter was not legitimate for the intended action.

2.2.3   Return Values

In our original discussion of Section 1.4 we describe parameters as a means for the caller to send information to the callee. A ***return value*** is a mechanism used by the callee to send information back to the caller. None of the methods that we have examined thus far provide a return value. Each one executes, presumably performing its job, and then returns control to the interpreter, which awaits our next command. Here is an example of one of our earlier interactions.

```
>>> groceries.append('bread')
>>>
```

In contrast, let's look at a method that provides a return value. Our first example is the count method. This takes one parameter and returns the number of times this item occurs on the list. To demonstrate its use, let's go back to an earlier example with a list of groceries having the contents ['bread', 'milk', 'cheese', 'bread']. In this case, we could observe the following result.

```
>>> groceries.count('bread')
2
>>> groceries.count('milk')
1
>>> groceries.count('apple')
0
>>>
```

After each command, we see the interpreter display the value that was returned. Notice that it is perfectly legal to call count using a parameter that is not actually contained in the list (e.g., 'apple'). It returns 0 as the natural result (remember that calling remove using a nonexistent element causes an error).

When working interactively, it may suffice to have the interpreter display the return value visually, as we see above. But more often, we want to save the returned information for continued use in the larger context of our program. This is done by using an assignment statement with the method call on the right-hand side of the = symbol. As an example, we might execute

```
>>> numLoaves = groceries.count('bread')
>>>
```

This assignment statement associates the numLoaves identifier from the left-hand side with the object expressed on the right-hand side. In this case, the method is evaluated and then the identifier is assigned to the return value. Notice that the interpreter no longer explicitly displays the return value. But we can use the numLoaves identifier in subsequent commands to manipulate that underlying value.

2.2.4 Constructing Lists

Python's lists support many other behaviors; we will introduce several more in the coming section. But before we go further, we would like to describe several convenient ways to construct a list. We have already demonstrated one approach, which is to create an initially empty list with the syntax **list( )** and subsequently populate the list using the append and insert methods. But this style is cumbersome for initializing longer lists. When the initial contents of a list are known in advance, a more convenient approach is to use a *literal* form to instantiate a list, as shown here.

```
>>> favoriteColors = ['red', 'green', 'purple', 'blue']
```

This form should seem familiar; it is precisely that which Python used when displaying a list to us. Square brackets delimit the list, with individual elements of the list separated by commas. The literal form can even be used when creating an empty list.

```
>>> groceries = []
```

Although the syntax groceries = **list( )** more clearly designates the new object as a list, the literal form is the one used more commonly by Python programmers (primarily because it involves less typing).

Copying an existing list

By default the syntax **list( )** is used to construct an initially empty list. However, a new list can be created that is a copy of an existing list. This is done by sending the existing list as a parameter to the constructor. For example, based on the favoriteColors list we created a moment earlier, we can do the following:

```
>>> primaryColors = list(favoriteColors)
>>> primaryColors.remove('purple')
>>> favoriteColors
['red', 'green', 'purple', 'blue']
>>> primaryColors
['red', 'green', 'blue']
```

The expression **list**(favoriteColors) creates a brand new **list** instance, yet one that has the same contents. After the new list is constructed, those two lists are independent objects rep–resented in memory and can be manipulated separately. Notice that removing 'purple' from the copy did not have any effect on the original list.

The range function

Lists are often used to represent a range of integers. Python supports a built–in function range to help construct such lists. There are three different forms for its use. The simplest form range(stop) takes a single parameter and constructs a list of numbers starting at zero and going up to *but not including* stop.

```
>>> range(5)
[0, 1, 2, 3, 4]
```

This convention is intentionally designed to be consistent with the zero-indexing of lists in Python. We will see the advantage of this choice in later uses of range. There is also a two parameter form range(start, stop) that constructs a list of integers starting at start and going up to but not including stop.

```
>>> range(23, 28)
[23, 24, 25, 26, 27]
```

A third form range(start, stop, step) results in a list starting at start, advancing by the given step size so long as it does not reach or pass the given stopping value. The step size can be positive or negative, as shown below.

```
>>> range(100, 130, 4)
[100, 104, 108, 112, 116, 120, 124, 128]
>>> range(8, 3, -1)
[8, 7, 6, 5, 4]
```

 A WORD OF WARNING

The list produced by range goes up to, but does not include, the specified stopping value. Thus range(5, 8) produces the list [5, 6, 7].

2.2.5 Operators

Thus far, we have suggested that all of an object's behaviors are invoked by means of a method call. Technically this is true, but some behaviors are so commonly used that Python supports a more convenient syntax that we call an *operator*.

For the sake of example, suppose that we have a list of people from a race, which is sorted from fastest to slowest finishers, and that contestants is our identifier. We have seen how to display the entire list in the interpreter. But that list may be very long. What if we wanted to access one particular entry of the list? We can use an index as the natural way to describe the position of interest. For example the bronze medalist is the third-fastest finisher, and thus at index 2 of the list. We can access that particular element of the list using the syntax contestants[2] as shown in the following session:

```
>>> contestants = ['Gomes', 'Kiogora', 'Tergat', 'Yego']
>>> contestants[2]
'Tergat'
```

This use of square brackets is typically called *indexing* the list. The square brackets serve an entirely different purpose than the parentheses that are used to enclose parameters when invoking a method. In the above example, we did not specify a method name, just the identifier for the list itself. The developers of Python could have supported such queries using a method-calling syntax, perhaps as contestants.getItem(2). Yet because accessing an element of a list is such a common task, their goal was to provide a simpler syntax.[1] List indexing can also be used to *replace* an existing element of a list with another. This is done by using the square bracket notation on the *left-hand side* of an assignment statement, as shown here.

```
>>> groceries = ['cereal', 'milk', 'apple']
>>> groceries[1] = 'soy'
>>> groceries
['cereal', 'soy', 'apple']
```

The second line has the effect of replacing the element originally at index 1 of the list, namely replacing 'milk' with 'soy'. For convenience, Python also allows the use of negative indices, which are interpreted relative to the *end* of the list. The index −1 denotes the last position of the list, −2 the second-to-last and so forth.

```
>>> contestants = ['Gomes', 'Kiogora', 'Tergat', 'Yego']
>>> contestants[-1]
'Yego'
>>> contestants[-4]
'Gomes'
>>> contestants[-2]
'Tergat'
```

Based upon the conventions, positive indices can range from zero up to one less than the length of the list, whereas negative indices range from −1 down to the negative length of the list. Python also supports access to a larger portion of a list using a syntax known as *slicing*, which we discuss in more detail in Section 2.3.

Behind the scene, syntactic shorthands such as these are translated back to standard method calls. For example, the shorthand contestants[2] is technically translated to a call of the form contestants.__getitem__(2). The shorthand groceries[1] = 'soy' is translated to a method call of the form groceries.__setitem__(1, 'soy'). At this time, there is little need to focus on these underlying method calls, but we mention this in passing because you may see names such as __getitem__ when viewing Python documentation. We will investigate such special methods far more thoroughly when it comes time to implement our own classes in Chapter 6.

---

1. Not coincidentally, the use of square brackets for indexing stems from the same convention used in many earlier programming languages.

2.2.6 Additional Behaviors

We have been exploring a list as a representative example of an object that can be manip–ulated, and to demonstrate a typical syntax for such interactions. We have seen how to construct instances, to call methods and communicate with parameters and return values, and to invoke common behaviors using operator shorthands. These lessons carry over to many other classes that we will see.

Of course lists are a valuable tool for Python programmers and there are many more behaviors we have yet to discuss. In the remainder of this section we provide an overview of the most commonly used behaviors supported by lists. If you are interested in digging deeper into the use of lists right now, continue reading this section. Otherwise, feel free to skip ahead to Section 2.3 on page 49, but please keep these pages in mind as a reference when the time comes to write more significant programs using lists.

Getting documentation

Although we have promised an introduction to other behaviors, and will provide this shortly, here is probably a good place to point out that it is difficult to memorize the proper use of each and every method. More important is to have a general idea of what can be accomplished and then to seek documentation when it comes time to use a feature. This is not just true of the **list** class, but of any class that you use.

Documentation can be found at http://www.python.org/ or in many other resources. More conveniently, the Python interpreter provides its own direct documenta–tion using a command called help. Let's say you want to use the insert method of the **list** class and you know it takes two parameters (the new item and the desired index), but can–not remember in which order they are sent. The standard documentation can be accessed as follows:

```
>>> help(list.insert)
Help on method_descriptor:

insert(...)
    L.insert(index, object) -- insert object before index
```

Given a prototypical **list** instance L, this describes the syntax L.insert(index, object) used when invoking the method. Based on the description, the first parameter is the desired index and the second is the object to insert. More generally, we can get documentation on the complete **list** class by typing help(**list**) rather than help(**list**.insert).

That said, it is nice to have written documentation as a reference. For this reason, Figure 2.2 contains our own brief description of the most commonly used methods of the **list** class.

We organize these behaviors into three major categories: (1) those that mutate the list, (2) those that return information about the current state of the list, and (3) those that generate a new list that is in some way modeled upon the contents of one or more existing lists. For each entry, we demonstrate a prototypical syntax and provide a brief description of the semantics.

Behaviors that modify an existing list (i.e., mutators)	
data.append(val)	Appends val to the end of the list.
data.insert(i, val)	Inserts val following the first i elements of the list.
data.extend(otherlist)	Adds the contents of otherlist to the end of this list.
data.remove(val)	Removes the earliest occurrence of val found in the list.
data.pop( )	Removes and returns the last element of the list.
data.pop(i)	Removes and returns the element with index i.
data[i] = val	Replaces the element at index i with given val.
data.reverse( )	Reverses the order of the list's elements.
data.sort( )	Sorts the list into increasing order.

Behaviors that return information about an existing list (i.e., accessors)	
len(data)	Returns the current length of the list.
data[i]	Returns the element at index i.
val **in** data	Returns **True** if the list contains val, **False** otherwise.
data.count(val)	Counts the number of occurrences of val in the list.
data.index(val)	Returns the index of the earliest occurrence of val.
data.index(val, start)	Returns the index of the earliest occurrence of val that can be found starting at index start.
data.index(val, start, stop)	Returns the index of the earliest occurrence of val that can be found starting at index start, yet prior to stop.
dataA == dataB	Returns **True** if contents are pairwise identical, **False** otherwise.
dataA != dataB	Returns **True** if contents *not* pairwise identical, **False** otherwise.
dataA < dataB	Returns **True** if dataA is lexicographically less than dataB, **False** otherwise.

Behaviors that generate a new list as a result	
data[start : stop]	Returns a new list that is a "slice" of the original, including elements from index start, up to but not including index stop.
data[start : stop : step]	Returns a new list that is a "slice" of the original, including elements from index start, taking steps of the indicated size, stopping *before* reaching or passing index stop.
dataA + dataB	Generates a third list that includes all elements of dataA followed by all elements of dataB.
data * k	Generates a new list equivalent to k consecutive copies of data (i.e., data + data + ... + data).

FIGURE 2.2: Selected **list** behaviors, for prototypical instances data, dataA, and dataB.

The pop method

Often we find that accessors, such as count, return information to the caller but leave the list unchanged. Mutators, such as append, insert, and remove, typically change the under-lying state of the list yet do not provide a return value. The pop method is an interesting example that mutates the list and returns relevant information to the caller. By default, pop is used to remove the very last object from the list and to return that item to the caller. We can see the effect in the following interpreter session:

```
>>> groceries = ['salsa', 'pretzels', 'pizza', 'soda']
>>> groceries.pop()
'soda'
>>> groceries
['salsa', 'pretzels', 'pizza']
```

Notice that the immediate response upon completion of the pop call is the display of the return value 'soda'. Behind the scene that value has also been removed from the list, so when we redisplay the list afterward we see the updated state. It is also possible to label the return value using an assignment statement nextToBuy = groceries.pop( ), as in Section 2.2.3.

There is another form of pop that takes a specific index as a parameter and removes and returns the element at that given index (rather than the last item of the list). For exam-ple, in the context of a restaurant waiting list, when a table opens up the person at the *front* of the list should be served and removed from the list, as

```
>>> waitlist = ['Kim', 'Donald', 'Grace', 'Andrew']
>>> toBeSeated = waitlist.pop(0)
>>> waitlist
['Donald', 'Grace', 'Andrew']
>>> toBeSeated
'Kim'
```

This form of pop can be used with any valid index (positive or negative). The two forms of pop are not separate methods, but one and the same. This is our first example of what is called an ***optional parameter***. The formal signature of the method is pop(i); if the caller does not explicitly send an index, the value -1 is assumed, thereby popping the last ele-ment of the list.

We wish to emphasize that pop is most appropriately used when there is a desire to remove an element from a list based upon a known index. When you have knowledge of the value and the index, it is much better to rely on pop than remove. A call to remove requires extra time to search for the given value; worse yet, it may find one that occurs earlier than the one you intended to delete. Also, pop is not the proper choice when trying to *replace* one element with another. The ideal syntax in that case is

```
>>> data[i] = newValue
```

Although it is possible to simulate the same effect using a combination of pop and insert, as

```
>>> data.pop(i)
>>> data.insert(i, newValue)
```

this is unnecessarily inefficient. The assignment syntax data[i] = newValue caters to just this kind of replacement. The disadvantage of the latter approach is that for a very long list, a lot of time is wasted shifting the elements of the list after the old item is removed, and once again shifting elements to make room for inserting the new value.

Other mutators

Lists support three other mutators, each of which is valuable when used properly. The first of these is named extend. It is a close relative of append but with different semantics. append is used to add a single element to the end of an existing list. Yet sometimes we may have a sequence of elements that we wish to add to a list. We could append them one at a time, but it is easier to add then en masse using the extend method.

```
>>> groceries = ['cereal', 'milk']
>>> produce = ['apple', 'oranges', 'grapes']
>>> groceries.extend(produce)
>>> groceries
['cereal', 'milk', 'apple', 'oranges', 'grapes']
>>> produce
['apple', 'oranges', 'grapes']
```

The extend method takes a single parameter that is another sequence of items. This causes each element contained in the parameter sequence to be added onto the end of the indicated list, while leaving the state of the parameter itself unaffected. In our example, notice that 'apples', 'oranges' and 'grapes' have been added to the end of the groceries list (yet still remain on the produce list).

FOR THE GURU

In describing extend, we used the syntax groceries.extend(produce). This command can easily be confused with groceries.append(produce), which is syntactically legal but with a very different effect. Since a list is an object, it can be added to another list as a single element. So in our earlier configuration, the command groceries.append(produce) causes groceries to become a list with three elements, the string 'cereal', the string 'milk' and the list ['apple', 'oranges', 'grapes']. Python would display this new list as ['cereal', 'milk', ['apple', 'oranges', 'grapes']].

The other two mutators are used to rearrange the overall order of a list. The reverse method rearranges the list to be in the opposite order and the sort method alphabetizes the list. This is demonstrated with our previous grocery list.

```
>>> groceries.reverse()
>>> groceries
['grapes', 'oranges', 'apple', 'milk', 'cereal']
>>> groceries.sort()
>>> groceries
['apple', 'cereal', 'grapes', 'milk', 'oranges']
```

Notice that neither of these methods accepts any parameters; there is no additional information to pass other than the clear desire for the list to be rearranged with the given method. It is very important, however, that the empty parentheses be included. The parentheses let the interpreter know that it should call the method. Without the parentheses, the expression groceries.sort is valid syntax; it serves to identify the name of the method itself. But if the intended goal is to sort the list, this will not work.

Another common mistake is to use a command like groceries = groceries.sort( ). Unfortunately, the effect of this statement is disastrous. Calling the sort method is not a problem in and of itself. The problem is the assignment statement. This reassigns the groceries identifier to the value returned by the sort method. However, *nothing is returned*. We see evidence of the problem in the following simple session:

```
>>> groceries = ['milk', 'bread', 'cereal']
>>> groceries = groceries.sort()
>>> groceries
>>>
```

A diagram of the semantics in this case is given in Figure 2.3. Although the original list was indeed sorted as part of the process, by the end of the session we no longer have a way to reference the list. The groceries identifier has been reassigned to a special Python value **None**, signifying a nonexistent object.

 A WORD OF WARNING

When calling a method that does not require any parameters, it is still necessary to include a set of parentheses, as in groceries.sort( ). The expression groceries.sort is the name of the method, not an invocation of the method.

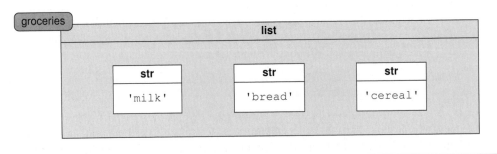

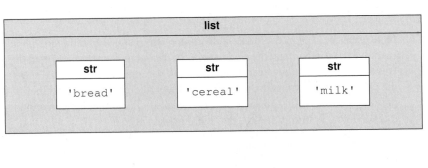

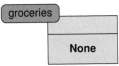

FIGURE 2.3: A before-and-after view of the command groceries = groceries.sort( ).

Additional accessors

There are several other ways to access pertinent information about a list. Let's return to the restaurant waiting list example. If someone walks into the restaurant and wants to know how many people are already on the waiting list, this can be determined using the syntax len(waitlist).

```
>>> waitlist = ['Kim', 'Donald', 'Grace', 'Andrew']
>>> len(waitlist)
4
```

Another common task is to find out whether someone is already on the waiting list. One way to do this is to count the number of occurrences of the name and see whether it is greater than zero. But there is a more direct way. The syntax `'Michael'` **in** waitlist, evaluates accordingly to **True** or **False**.

```
>>> waitlist = ['Kim', 'Donald', 'Grace', 'Andrew']
>>> 'Michael' in waitlist
False
>>> 'Grace' in waitlist
True
```

Another common question when waiting in a restaurant is "where am I on the list?" Presuming that someone is actually on the list, we can determine how far he is from the front by using a method named index. In its simplest form, this method takes one parameter, which is a value that is assumed to be on the list. It returns an integer that denotes the index of that element within the list using the standard zero-indexed convention.

```
>>> waitlist = ['Kim', 'Donald', 'Grace', 'Andrew']
>>> waitlist.index('Donald')
1
```

In this case we find that 'Donald' has one person ahead of him. When using index it is imperative that you ensure the parameter exists on the list (presumably because you previously checked with **in** or count). An error occurs otherwise, demonstrated as follows:

```
>>> waitlist.index('Michael')
Traceback (most recent call last):
  File "<stdin>", line 1, in -toplevel-
ValueError: list.index(x): x not in list
```

When multiple occurrences of an item are on a list, the index method returns the *earliest* such position.

```
>>> waitlist = ['Rich', 'Elliot', 'Alan', 'Karl', 'Alan']
>>> waitlist.index('Alan')
2
```

If we want to find other positions, there exists an alternative syntax. The index method accepts an optional second parameter, which is treated as a starting index for the search. As an example, consider the following:

```
>>> waitlist.index('Alan', 3)
4
```

This call asks the list to find the first occurrence of 'Alan' starting the search from index 3 rather than from the beginning of the list. Most often, this starting parameter is based upon a previous return value, as shown here.

```
>>> firstIndex = waitlist.index('Alan')
>>> secondIndex = waitlist.index('Alan', firstIndex + 1)
```

After locating the index of the first occurrence, we intentionally start the second search *one spot further* in the list. As was the case with pop, this alternative form is really based on an optional parameter. index('Alan') is treated similarly to index('Alan', 0), finding the first occurrence starting from index 0. In fact, there exists an optional third parameter stop. A call to index(val, start, stop) returns the index of the first occurrence of val that can be found starting from index start, yet prior to index stop (or causes an error if none is found).

Finally, we introduce operators used to compare the contents of one list to another. For example with two popular restaurants on the same street, there may be many people who impatiently put themselves on both waiting lists. Perhaps both lists end up looking the same. We can compare them to each other using a syntax waitlistA == waitlistB. This returns **True** if the elements match each other *in the respective order*, and **False** otherwise. This is typically called an equivalence test. Being equivalent does not mean that the two restaurants are maintaining a single list; it means that the same values appear and in the same order. We use the == operator (pronounced "double equal") for testing equivalence as opposed to the single equal sign =, which is used when assigning an identifier to a value. There is also the != (pronounced "not equal") operator that has the opposite semantics of ==. The expression waitlistA != waitlistB will be **True** when the lists do *not* match, and **False** when they do match.

Generating new lists

Some operators exist to create new lists based upon the contents of existing lists. For exam–ple, the + operator is used to "add" two lists, creating a third list that has the contents of the first followed by the contents of the second list.

```
>>> produce = ['apple', 'orange', 'broccoli']
>>> drygoods = ['cereal', 'bread']
>>> groceries = produce + drygoods
>>> groceries
['apple', 'orange', 'broccoli', 'cereal', 'bread']
```

It is worth noting that the third list is created based upon the *current* contents of the other two lists at that time the addition was performed. Once created, it is an independent list. Subsequent changes to the original list do not affect the third list, as seen in the following example:

 A WORD OF WARNING

Be careful not to confuse the = and == operators. The single equal sign (=) is the assignment operator. The syntax a = b is used to assign identifier a to whatever object is referenced by identifier b. The double equal sign (==) is the equivalence operator. The syntax a == b is used to test the equivalence of the two objects.

```
>>> produce.append('grapes')
>>> groceries
['apple', 'orange', 'broccoli', 'cereal', 'bread']
```

You can also create a list that consists of multiple consecutive copies of an existing list. The syntax is based on use of the * operator, which is traditionally used to denote multiplication. Thus myList * 3 produces the same result as myList + myList + myList. A convenient use of this syntax is to initialize a list of identical items. For example, we might wish to track spending for each month of a year by maintaining a list of 12 values, each of which is initially zero. We can accomplish this succinctly as

```
>>> monthlySpending = [ 0 ] * 12
>>> monthlySpending
[0, 0, 0, 0, 0, 0, 0, 0, 0, 0, 0, 0]
```

We included square brackets in the expression [0] to denote this part as a list, whereas 12 is an integer. We could equivalently write 12 * [0]. However, it would be quite a different thing to write 0 * 12, which denotes standard multiplication of numbers and it is illegal to write [0] * [12], as a list cannot be multiplied by another list.

Finally we can create a new list that is a sublist of another by using a notation known as *slicing*. The syntax groceries[start : stop] produces a new list containing all elements of the original list that were stored starting at index start up to but *not* including index stop. We will discuss this notion more fully on page 51, in the context of strings.

2.3 Other Sequence Classes: str and tuple

We chose Python's **list** as the first class to explore because of its very rich support for a variety of behaviors. A **list** is a *mutable* object. Even after it is created, we can interact in ways that change its state, such as adding, removing, or reordering its elements. Indeed, most classes are composed of mutable objects, as these allow for the most significant inter-action. Yet there do exist classes of *immutable* objects. Once constructed, those instances can no longer be modified. At first, one might question the purpose of designing a class of immutable objects. What sort of interactions can we have with an object that never changes? In this section we examine two important immutable classes that are used to represent ordered sequences in Python.

The first of these is the **str** class (commonly called "string") that is specially designed for a sequence of characters. We also introduce the **tuple** class, which is essentially an immutable version of the **list** class. A tuple represents a sequence of arbitrary objects, yet a sequence that cannot be altered. Although **list**, **str**, and **tuple** are three distinct classes, we will see that they were designed to support many of the same operations. For example, the syntax data[i] can be used to retrieve the element at index i whether data is a list, a string, or a tuple. This type of a generic syntax is called *polymorphic* (Greek for "of many forms"). The advantage of this design is that many of Python's functions are able to accept any of the sequence types interchangeably.

2.3.1 Character Strings

Because the majority of computer applications are used by humans, software requires the ability to store and manipulate textual information. Since text can be modeled as a sequence of individual characters, it is possible to use the **list** class to represent a portion of text, as with ['s', 'e', 'q', 'u', 'e', 'n', 'c', 'e']. However, Python supports a dedicated **str** class to represent a sequence of characters. The advantage of this string class are twofold. First, it supports many methods (e.g., capitalize) that are designed for behaviors that only make sense when dealing with characters. Secondly, the class is intentionally immutable, allowing Python to optimize internal implementation details (since existing strings will never be changed). As an immutable class, the style of the behaviors are somewhat different. For example we mentioned that there is a capitalize method, but this method does not alter the existing string. Instead, it returns a *new* string that is a capitalized version of the original.

If you need a behavior for processing strings that seems generally useful, there is a good chance it is already supported. In the remainder of this section, we demonstrate the most commonly used behaviors of the **str** class. At the very end of the section, Figure 2.5 provides our own summary of these selected behaviors. Keep in mind that you can get a complete overview of strings by typing help(**str**) in the interpreter or by seeking online documentation.

Literals

The constructor for the string class can technically be invoked as **str**( ), but by default this creates the empty string ' '. Given that the instance is immutable, this is not very helpful. The most common way to create a string object is by using a literal form. We have already been using such a form, namely specifying a character string between quotes, as with 'bread'. An alternative form "bread" uses double-quote symbols rather than single quotes. This choice is especially convenient if you wish to use a single quote character as part of the actual string, as in "Who's there?".

Typically, string literals cannot span multiple lines. However, a newline character can be embedded directly within a literal by using the special symbol \n. For example, the string literal "Knock Knock\nWho's there?" could be displayed to a user as

```
Knock Knock
Who's there?
```

The backslash (\) in such context is used as an escape character, allowing us to specify a character that cannot otherwise be expressed naturally. This same technique is used to specify many other special characters that may be part of an extended alphabet but not otherwise naturally expressible. In fact, this can also be used as a way to place a single quotation mark as a character within a literal delimited by single quotation marks, as in 'Who\'s there?'. A third literal form uses either the delimiter ''' or """, to begin and end the string. The advantage of these literals is that they can span multiple lines without the need for escape characters. We will not typically use them from within the interpreter, but they will become more significant when writing source code in a file.

Behaviors common to lists and strings

Strings use the same zero-indexing conventions as lists and also many of the same acces-sors. For example, the length of a string is computed using a syntax such as len(greeting) and individual characters can be accessed by indexing.

```
>>> greeting = 'Hello'
>>> len(greeting)
5
>>> greeting[1]
'e'
```

However, because strings are immutable, using the indexing syntax on the left-hand side of an assignment statement is illegal, as shown in the following example.

```
>>> greeting = 'Hello'
>>> greeting[0] = 'J'
Traceback (most recent call last):
  File "<stdin>", line 1, in -toplevel-
TypeError: object does not support item assignment
```

Often we wish to retrieve a contiguous portion of a sequence. We call such a portion a *slice*. The syntax for slicing is demonstrated as follows:

```
>>> alphabet = 'abcdefghijklmnopqrstuvwxyz'
>>> alphabet[4:10]
'efghij'
```

Rather than a single index, a slice is described by a pair of indices separated by a colon. The slice starts at the first of the two indices and continues *up to but not including* the second index. In the above example, the character j has index 9. By this convention, the number of items in the slice is the difference between the indices, and consecutive slices are defined so that alphabet[4:10] + alphabet[10:15] is equivalent to alphabet[4:15]. When specifying a slice, both arguments are optional; if the first is omitted the slice starts at the beginning of the string and if the last is omitted the slice continues to the end.

```
>>> alphabet[:6]
'abcdef'
>>> alphabet[23:]
'xyz'
```

An optional step size can be specified as a third argument in the slice syntax. For example with a step size of k, the slice begins at the first index, takes each k-th character, continuing so long as the index does not reach or pass the end point. If you want to step backwards, the step size can be negative. Both forms are demonstrated in our next example.

```
>>> alphabet[9:20:3]
'jmps'
>>> alphabet[17:5:-3]
'roli'
```

There are other similarities between lists and strings. In Section 2.2, we encountered several behaviors used to check whether a particular value is contained in a list, and if so, where and how often. In the case of strings, those same operations can be used not just to check if a single character is within a string, but whether a larger pattern appears as a substring. A demonstration of those behaviors is shown here.

```
>>> musing = 'The swallow may fly south with the sun'
>>> 'w' in musing
True
>>> 'ow ma' in musing
True
>>> 'South' in musing
False
>>> musing.count('th')
3
>>> musing.index('th')
23
>>> musing.index('ow ma')
9
```

We see the operator **in** used to check whether a pattern is contained in the string. We note that the pattern need not be a single word, as seen with 'ow ma'. Strings are case sensitive, and so 'South' is not in the musing (although 'south' is). This is also why count only finds three occurrences of 'th'. The first two characters 'Th' of the musing are not a match; the three occurrences are in sou<u>th</u>, wi<u>th</u>, and <u>th</u>e. The location of the leftmost occurrence of a pattern is reported by the index method.

Strings can also be compared to each other using a syntax similar to lists. Keep in mind that strings are case sensitive, and thus 'Hello' == 'hello' evaluates to **False**. Operators for common inequalities (e.g., <, >, <=, >=) are supported, based on what is known as *lexicographical order* (similar to the standard dictionary order when alphabetizing words). The two words are compared letter by letter, until a difference is found. For example, 'Goodbye' < 'Hello' because G proceeds H alphabetically; 'Good' < 'Goodbye' as the first is a prefix of the second. However, the rule for comparing characters depends on the precise encoding of the underlying alphabet. With the standard encoding (typically ASCII or Unicode), all uppercase letters come before any lowercase letters, thus 'Z' < 'a'.

Finally, strings can be concatenated or repeated using the + and operators respectively. Thus 'over' + 'load' evaluates to 'overload' (notice that there is no space inserted unless one was present in one of the originals). Multiplication can be used to easily create simple patterns; thus 'HO' * 3 evaluates to 'HOHOHO'.

Additional methods

Strings support a variety of additional behaviors that can be very convenient for text pro‑cessing. Many of these generate new strings as variants of existing ones. A typical such example is the lower method, which is used to form a lowercase version of a string. The semantics of lower is very different in style from behaviors often seen with mutable objects. For example, we saw that the sort method of the **list** class alters the state of the given list, rather than returning a new list. Calling lower does not change the state of the given string; instead it returns a new string that is a lowercase version of the original. In similar fashion, upper returns a version of the string using all uppercase letters. Their use is demonstrated as follows:

```
>>> formal = 'Hello.  How are you?'
>>> informal = formal.lower()
>>> screaming = formal.upper()
>>> formal
'Hello. How are you?'
>>> informal
'hello. how are you?'
>>> screaming
'HELLO. HOW ARE YOU?'
```

Punctuation, spacing, and other nonalphabetic characters remain unchanged when lower‑case or uppercase. Also notice that upper causes *all* letters to be uppercase, not just the leading character (the capitalize method can be used for that purpose).

We emphasize that strings are immutable, and thus there is no way to alter the con‑tents of an existing string. However, it is possible to reassign an existing *identifier* to a dif‑ferent string. A typical example of this technique is the command person = person.lower( ). The invocation of person.lower( ) on the right‑hand side of the assignment does not alter the original underlying string; it creates a new string. Yet the assignment statement causes the name person to subsequently be reassigned to this resulting string. Figure 2.4 portrays this situation.

Strings also support a few additional accessors that are not available for general sequences. For example if country is a string, the syntax country.startswith('Aus') returns **True** or **False** accordingly. Other specialized accessors include isalpha, isdigit, islower, and isupper. These four methods also return **True** or **False** according to whether a given string consists entirely of alphabetic characters, digits, lowercase characters, or uppercase characters respectively It is important to understand the difference between methods such

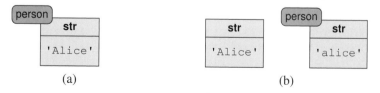

FIGURE 2.4: A before-and-after look at the command person = person.lower( ).

as lower and islower. The former produces a new string that is a lowercase version of the original; the latter evaluates whether a string is itself made of lowercase letters.

Finally, there are two extremely important methods of the **str** class used to convert from strings to lists and vice versa. These methods can be very helpful for processing formatted text. The first of these is the split method, which creates a list of pieces formed when using a chosen separator to divide a string. It can be used in two ways. If used in a form without any parameter, the original string is divided by all blocks of whitespace (i.e., spaces, tabs, or newline characters). In the following example, the result is a list of five substrings that were originally separated by whitespace:

```
>>> request = 'eggs and milk and apples'
>>> request.split()
['eggs', 'and', 'milk', 'and', 'apples']
```

Notice that the whitespace itself is not included in any of the pieces. This form is sometimes a good way to determine the words in a sentence, although punctuation may complicate the task. The second form of split takes a single parameter, which is a pattern that should be used as the separator when dividing the original. Revisiting the previous example with 'and' as the separator results in the following:

```
>>> request = 'eggs and milk and apples'
>>> request.split('and')
['eggs ', ' milk ', ' apples']
```

Note carefully that in this case, the spaces around the word 'and' are not explicitly part of the separator pattern, and therefore we see that they remain within the results. If we knew that there would be spaces around the word 'and' in the original text, we could instead use a separator of ' and ', as follows:

```
>>> request = 'eggs and milk and apples'
>>> request.split(' and ')
['eggs', 'milk', 'apples']
```

As a dual to the split method, the **str** class supports join. This takes a sequence of strings as a parameter and joins them together placing a copy of the original instance between each pair. What is important to note is that the desired separator string is the actual object upon which the join method is invoked. Typically, the parameter is a list of strings. For example, if guests is currently set to ['John', 'Mary', 'Amy', 'Frank'], we can perform the following:

```
>>> conjunction = ' and '
>>> conjunction.join(guests)
'John and Mary and Amy and Frank'
```

In the above example, it is important that we explicitly include a leading and trailing space as part of our conjunction.We should also note that since a string literal is a legiti–

mate object, join can be invoked directly upon such a literal, as in `' and '`.join(guests). When an empty string is used as the separator, all strings in the sequence are concatenated together. As a final example, we note that a string is itself a sequence of characters and can serve as the *parameter* to join. Thus `'-'`.join(`'respect'`) evaluates to `'r-e-s-p-e-c-t'`.

Summary of the str class

Figure 2.5 provides our own summary of many behaviors of the **str** class. We organize these behaviors into three major categories: (1) those that return information about given strings, (2) those that generate a new string that is modeled upon an existing string, and (3) those that translate from a string to a list and vice versa.

FOR THE GURU

Strings do not technically support a reverse method, even though such a behavior would clearly be useful. The reason for the lack of a method is likely that such a reversal is already possible by slicing the entire string with a step size of negative one. Thus an experienced Python programmer would use the syntax greeting[: : −1] to produce a reversed version of string greeting.

2.3.2 The tuple Class

Python's **list** represents a *mutable* sequence of arbitrary elements. In contrast, a **tuple** is used to represent an *immutable* sequence of objects. Because tuples are immutable, Python can implement them more efficiently than the corresponding lists and need only support a subset of the behaviors afforded to lists. The primary purpose of a tuple is to encapsulate multiple pieces of information into a single composite object that can be stored or transmitted. For example, a common representation for digital colors is based upon three separate values to denote the intensity of the red, green, and blue components. But using three separate identifiers to store the components of a color lacks intuitive coherency. So a more typical approach is to use a tuple, as shown here.

```
>>> skyBlue = (136, 207, 236)
```

As you can see, the literal form for tuples uses enclosing parentheses, with commas separating individual elements. As for behaviors, tuples support all of the *nonmutating* behaviors of lists that were summarized in Figure 2.2 on page 42, with the exception of count and index.

Behaviors that return information about the existing string s	
len(s)	Returns the current length of the string.
s[i]	Returns the character at index i.
pattern **in** s	Returns **True** if the given pattern occurs as substring of s, **False** otherwise.
s.count(pattern)	Returns the number of distinct occurrences of pattern within s.
s.find(pattern)	Returns the index starting the leftmost occurrence of pattern within s; if pattern is not found, returns -1.
s.find(pattern, start)	Returns the index starting the leftmost occurrence of pattern found at or after index start within s; if no such pattern is found, returns -1.
s.rfind(pattern)	Returns the index starting the rightmost occurrence of pattern within s; if pattern is not found, returns -1.
s.rfind(pattern, start)	Returns the index starting the rightmost occurrence of pattern found at or after index start within s; if no such pattern is found, returns -1.
s.index(pattern)	Same as s.find(pattern) except causes ValueError if not found.
s.index(pattern, start)	Same as s.find(pattern, start) except causes ValueError if not found.
s.rindex(pattern)	Same as s.rfind(pattern) except causes ValueError if not found.
s.rindex(pattern, start)	Same as s.rfind(pattern, start) except causes ValueError if not found.
s.startswith(pattern)	Returns **True** if s starts with the pattern, **False** otherwise.
s.endswith(pattern)	Returns **True** if s ends with the pattern, **False** otherwise.
s.isalpha( )	Returns **True** if all characters are alphabetic, **False** otherwise.
s.isdigit( )	Returns **True** if all characters are digits, **False** otherwise.
s.isspace( )	Returns **True** if all characters are whitespace, **False** otherwise.
s.islower( )	Returns **True** if all alphabetic characters are lowercase, **False** otherwise.
s.isupper( )	Returns **True** if all alphabetic characters are uppercase, **False** otherwise.
s == t	Returns **True** if strings are identical, **False** otherwise.
s != t	Returns **True** if strings are *not* identical, **False** otherwise.
s < t	Returns **True** if string s is alphabetized before t, **False** otherwise.

FIGURE 2.5: Selected behaviors supported by Python's **str** class (continued on next page).

Behaviors that generate a new string as a result	
s.capitalize( )	Returns a capitalized version of the original string.
s.lower( )	Returns an entirely lowercase version of original.
s.upper( )	Returns an entirely uppercase version of original.
s.center(width)	Returns a new string of the specified width containing characters of the original centered within it.
s.ljust(width)	Returns a new string of the specified width containing characters of the original left justified within it.
s.rjust(width)	Returns a new string of the specified width containing characters of the original right justified within it.
s.replace(old, new)	Returns a copy of s, with every occurrence of the substring old replaced with new.
s.strip( )	Returns a copy of s with leading and trailing whitespace removed.
s.strip(chars)	Returns a copy of s with as many leading and trailing characters from the string chars removed.
s[start:stop]	Returns a new string that is a "slice" of the original, including characters of original from index start, up to but not including index stop.
s[start:stop:step]	Returns a new string that is a "slice" of the original, including characters of original from index start, taking steps of of the indicated size, continuing up to but not including index stop.
s + t	Generates a third string that is the concatenation of the characters of s followed by the characters of t.
s * k	Generates a new string equivalent to k consecutive copies of s (equivalent to s + s + ... + s).

Behaviors that convert between strings and lists of strings	
s.split( )	Returns a **list** of strings obtained by splitting s into pieces that were separated by whitespace.
s.split(sep)	Returns a **list** of strings obtained by splitting s into pieces that were separated by sep.
s.join(stringSeq)	Returns a string that is a concatenation of all elements of stringSeq with a copy of s inserted between each pair.

FIGURE 2.5 (continuation): Selected behaviors supported by Python's **str** class.

2.4 Numeric Types: int, long, and float

Numbers are very significant in computing. In fact, they have already appeared in earlier examples of this chapter, such as when indexing a sequence, or as the return value of the count method. Python supports three[2] different primitive types for storing numbers: **int**, **long**, and **float**. Each differs in purpose according to the range of numbers that can be represented and the internal encoding of the values. The most common of the numeric types is the **int** class, which is used to represent a number that is integral. Example literals for this class are: 5, −273, and 299792458. There is a maximum magnitude for a value stored as an **int**, although this limit depends upon the underlying computer architecture. For integer values that have magnitude beyond that limit, Python supports a **long** class that can perfectly represent integers with arbitrarily large magnitudes (although with a more complicated internal encoding). We will probably not see much use of longs in this book, but they arise in various scientific computing applications. Fortunately, Python does a nice job of automatically converting from the use of **int** to **long** when necessary.

When manipulating numbers that are not necessarily integral, there is a slight problem. Some mathematical values cannot typically be stored with perfect precision in digital form. For example, the value $\sqrt{2}$ has a conceptual meaning but the traditional decimal value of the square root cannot be perfectly represented in a finite number of bits. In computing systems, values such as these are stored in an approximate form using a standard encoding known as *floating-point* representation. In Python, these are stored using a class named **float**. Example literals for this class include: 3.14159, 0.125, and −0.618. Floating-point numbers may coincidentally be integral. That is, the literal 3.0 belongs to the **float** class even though it happens to correspond to a number that has no fractional part. In fact Python even treats the literal 3. as a floating-point value because of the decimal point.

Numeric operators

All three numeric classes support a common set of operations (another example of *polymorphism*, as observed with the three sequence types in Section 2.3). Figure 2.6 summarizes the most commonly used operations. There are two major categories: arithmetic operations and comparison operations. The semantics for most arithmetic operators are quite natural. The symbols + and − are used for addition and subtraction, and ∗ for multiplication. When adding two integers, the result is an **int**; when adding two floating-point numbers, the result is a **float**. Thus 5.25 + 2.75 evaluates to the **float** 8.0, even though the value happens to be a whole number. If addition is performed using one integer and one floating-point number, the result is expressed as a floating-point number. The same is true when using subtraction or multiplication.

The conventions involving division are more subtle. With the other three arithmetic operators, a calculation involving two integers naturally results in an integer. With division, there is potential ambiguity; for example, how should the calculation of 14 divided by 3 be viewed? Should this evaluate to a floating-point form, as 4.66666667? Should it be viewed as an integer, and if so, rounded up or down? To resolve such questions we describe two

---

2.   Actually, Python supports a fourth numeric type complex for representing the mathematical notion of a complex number.

Syntax	Semantics
x + y	Returns the sum of the two numbers.
x − y	Returns the difference between the two numbers.
x * y	Returns the product of the two numbers.
x / y	Returns the result of a true division[a] of x divided by y.
x // y	Returns the integral quotient of x divided by y.
x % y	Returns the remainder of an integer division of x divided by y.
x ** y	Returns x^y; also available as pow(x,y).
−x	Returns the negated number.
abs(x)	Returns the absolute value of the number.
x == y	Returns **True** if x and y are equal, **False** otherwise.
x != y	Returns **True** if x is not equal to y, **False** otherwise.
x < y	Returns **True** if x is less than y, **False** otherwise.
x <= y	Returns **True** if x is less than or equal to y, **False** otherwise.
x > y	Returns **True** if x is greater than y, **False** otherwise.
x >= y	Returns **True** if x is greater than or equal to y, **False** otherwise.
cmp(x, y)	Returns −1 if x < y, 0 if x = y, and 1 if x > y.

FIGURE 2.6: Selected operators supported by Python's numeric types.

[a]Technically, this performs integer division when both operands are **int** or **long**. However, starting with Python version 3.0, the semantics will be changed to true division in such a case.

distinct forms of division. *True division* results in a floating-point number, providing the maximum level of accuracy, such as 4.66666667. In contrast, *integer division* is more akin to the long division method that we learned as children. An integer division results in a *quotient* and a *remainder*. For example, if we perform 14 divided by 3 using long division, we will get a quotient of 4 with a remainder of 2, as $\frac{14}{3} = 4\frac{2}{3}$.

Given this distinction between true division and integer division, Python supports three related operators: /, //, and %. True division is accomplished using the / operator, so long as at least one of the two operands is of type **float**. To perform a true division of two **int** objects, it is necessary to first convert at least one of the two to the corresponding **float**, as in **float**(14) / 3 which evaluates to approximately 4.66666667. The operators // and % are used to perform integer division, returning the quotient and remainder of that calculation respectively. Thus 14 // 3 evaluates to 4, and 14 % 3 evaluates to 2. The % operator is sometimes called the *modulo* operator (pronounced "mod" for short).

The basic comparison operators (e.g., x < y) return **True** or **False** based upon natural mathematical meanings. When comparing a floating-point value to an integral value, the necessary internal conversion will be performed before the evaluating the comparison.

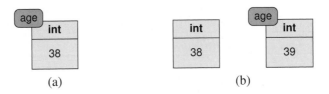

(a)   (b)

FIGURE 2.7: A before-and-after look at the command age = age + 1.

Immutability of numeric types

Just as with strings, all of Python's numeric types are *immutable*. Once an instance is created, that particular object cannot be changed. An expressions such as x + y does not have any effect on the underlying values x and y, rather it creates a third number with value equal to the sum of the other two. However, it is quite common to reassign an existing *identifier* to a new value using the arithmetic operators. A typical example is the command age = age + 1, as portrayed in Figure 2.7. Behind the scene, the expression age + 1 does not alter the value of the original object representing value 38; it causes the creation of a new object with value 39, that is subsequently associated with the identifier age.

2.5   Type Conversions

The encoding scheme used to store an object depends upon the object's data type. Thus the integer value 35 is stored differently from the string representation '35', or the floating–point value 35.0. It is often necessary to convert information from one data type to another. In general, this process is called ***casting***. In Python, casting is typically done by construct–ing a new instance of the desired class, using the original data as a model.

For example, the syntax **int**(x) is used to create an integer with a value that depends upon the parameter x. When the parameter is a floating–point value, such as **int**(3.8), a question arises as to which of the neighboring integers results. In Python a conversion from a floating–point value to an integer is performed by *truncating* any fractional part. Thus **int**(3.8) evaluates to 3, and **int**(−3.8) evaluates to −3. To convert a **float** to the *near-est* integer, there exists a function named round. Technically, round returns the nearest integer value, although still represented as a floating–point number (although that **float** can then be converted to the corresponding **int**).

```
>>> int(3.8)
3
>>> round(3.8)
4.0
>>> int(round(3.8))
4
```

More generally, the round function accepts an optional second parameter specifying the desired number of digits after the decimal point. Thus round(3.14159, 3) returns 3.142.

There are two different notions used when converting back and forth between strings and numbers. Typically, we are interested in converting between a string representation of a number and the true number. For example, when asked to enter a number, a user tech-nically entered a sequence of characters (that we hope symbolizes a number). Converting that string of characters to an **int** or **float** is done using a similar syntax as above. Thus **int**('1776') results in the value 1776, while **int**('hello') causes an error. In reverse, we can take an underlying numeric value x and create the string representation of that value using the syntax **str**(x). For example, **str**(1776) results in the string '1776'. More generally, **str**(x) is defined to create a string representation of any type of parameter x.

A second notion of conversion between text and numbers involves the low-level encoding of text characters. Each individual character of a string is stored in memory as an integer, using a particular convention known as a code; most common is *ASCII*, though *Unicode* provides greater support for internationalization. For most software, there is no need to worry about the low-level encoding (after all, this is the beauty of a high-level abstraction). However, it is possible to examine this encoding if necessary. The ord function takes a one character string and returns its integer code. For example, ord('a') returns 97, and ord('b') returns 98. The chr function does the opposite; it converts a code value into the corresponding character. Thus chr(97) returns 'a'. These underlying numeric codes determine how letters are ordered; 'Z' < 'a' because ord('Z') is 90 and ord('a') is 97.

It is also possible to convert from one sequence type to another. In Section 2.2.4, we noted that the syntax **list**(produce) constructs a new list that is a copy of the existing list. As it happens, the parameter to the **list** constructor can be any type of sequence. So we can easily create a list based upon a tuple, or even a list based upon the sequence of characters in a string. Thus **list**('hello') produces the list ['h', 'e', 'l', 'l', 'o']. In similar fashion, the **tuple** constructor can be used to create a tuple based on the contents of an existing list or string.

2.6   Calling Functions

On page 33, we characterize the general object-oriented syntax for calling a method as *object.method(parameters)*. Yet we have also seen functions that are called outside the context of a particular object or class. For example, the previous section introduced the round function. We use the syntax round(val) rather than the syntax val.round( ) because this behavior is not formally a method of the numeric classes. We refer to these as *pure functions* to distinguish them from member functions defined as part of a class. We have already seen several other examples, such as ord and chr from the previous section and len and range from earlier sections. There are many other built-in functions defined for both beginning and advanced tasks. Figure 2.8 highlights a handful of commonly used ones.

For example, if transactions is a list of numbers, the sum can be computed as sum(transactions). The minimum or maximum of a list of values can be computed as min(transactions) or max(transactions) respectively. In fact, these two functions are more general. The minimum or maximum can be computed for any data type, based upon the underlying definition of comparisons. For example, the "minimum" of a list of strings is the one that comes earliest alphabetically. The min and max functions can be used in another way. Rather than sending a single parameter that is a sequence, those functions can be sent an arbitrary number of individual parameters. Thus the syntax max(a, b, c) returns the largest of three given values.

Sample Syntax	Semantics
range(stop)	Returns list of integers from 0 up to but not including stop.
range(start, stop)	Returns list of integers from start up to but not including stop.
range(start, stop, step)	Returns list of integers from start up to but not including stop.
len(sequence)	Returns the number of elements of the sequence.
abs(number)	Returns the absolute value of the number.
pow(x, y)	Returns x^y.
round(number)	Returns a **float** with integral value closest to the number.
ord(char)	Returns the integer alphabet code for the given character.
chr(code)	Returns the character having the given integer alphabet code.
min(a, b, c, ...)	Returns the "smallest" of the given parameters.
min(sequence)	Returns the "smallest" item in the sequence.
max(a, b, c, ...)	Returns the "largest" of the given parameters.
max(sequence)	Returns the "largest" item in the sequence.
sum(sequence)	Returns the sum of the given sequence of numbers.
sorted(sequence)	Returns a copy of the given sequence that is sorted.[a]

FIGURE 2.8: Several commonly used built-in functions.

[a]Introduced in version 2.4 of Python.

2.7 Python Modules

All of the classes and functions that we have seen thus far are built in. These are automat‐
ically available as soon as the Python interpreter begins. Yet there are hundreds of other
useful tools that have been written by developers of Python. These are deemed to be not
quite as commonly needed as the built‐in ones, so they have been placed into libraries,
called *modules*, that can be individually loaded as needed.

For example, there exists a sqrt function to calculate the square root of a number.
Although it is possible to implement our own algorithm to compute a square root (in fact
we will do so in Section 5.4), it is far more convenient to use the existing one. However, that
function is not officially included among the built‐ins. It is part of a larger library of math‐
ematical functions and constants defined in the mathmodule!math module. That library
includes not only functions, but definitions for several important mathematical constants
such as pi. In order to use these tools, we must first *import* it. There are three distinct ways
this can be done. The first is to import the module as a whole with the following command:

```
>>> import math
```

Name	Overview
math	Various mathematical constants and functions (e.g., pi, sqrt, sin, cos, tan, log).
random	Classes and functions used to support randomization of data according to various distributions (e.g., randint, sample, shuffle, uniform).
time	Various functions to manipulate time (e.g., sleep, time).
datetime	Classes and function to manipulate dates and times (e.g., time, date, datetime classes).
re	Support for string matching with *regular expressions*.
os	Support for interactions with the operating system.
sys	Values and functions involving the Python interpreter itself.

FIGURE 2.9: Several commonly used modules.

After importing the module in this form, we must give a *qualified name*. The simpler syntax sqrt(2) is still not directly available; the caller must clearly designate this function as math.sqrt(2) as shown in the following session:

```
>>> import math
>>> math.pi
3.1415926535897931
>>> math.sqrt(2)
1.41421356237
```

Because the use of qualified names requires more typing throughout the rest of a program, there is an alternative approach when importing, which we use in this book. We may handpick precisely the things we need from the module and make them *directly* available, as demonstrated below.

```
>>> from math import sqrt, pi
>>> pi
3.1415926535897931
>>> sqrt(2)
1.41421356237
```

A similar form can be used to import *everything* from the module in one fell swoop, using a syntax **from** math **import** * with an asterisk (*) as a wild card.

Having demonstrated the syntax for importing, we note that many modules are available, providing useful support in a variety of settings. Some of our own favorite modules are described briefly in Figure 2.9. We will introduce details as needed later in the book. A more complete list of modules exists at python.org. Furthermore, documentation on an individual module becomes available within the interpreter once it is imported. For example, after executing **import** math we can type help(math) for more information.

2.8 Expressions

At this point, we have discussed the use of many operations in isolation (e.g., 18 + 5). However, it is quite common to perform several operations as part of a single compound *expression*. For example, the arithmetic expression

```
18 + 5 + 2
```

evaluates to 25. This expression involves two occurrences of the + operator. Behind the scene, the larger expression must be evaluated as two distinct steps. In this case, 18 + 5 is evaluated first, resulting in the value 23. That intermediate result is then used as an operand for the second addition 23 + 2 leading to 25.

Of course the precise order of evaluation in this first example is immaterial, as the end result is 25 no matter which addition is performed first. But in general, the order of evaluation can be very significant. For example the expression 18 − 5 + 2 evaluates to 15 if viewed as (18 − 5) + 2, yet to 11 if viewed as 18 − (5 + 2). Because there is no room for ambiguity when executing a program, Python uses strict rules when evaluating expressions that involve more than one operation. In this section we detail many of the rules that determine how expressions are evaluated. Along the way, we will also introduce some new operations and one more primitive data type.

2.8.1 Precedence

When there are two or more operations as part of an expression, some determination must be made as to which action is performed first. In general, we say that the operation performed first is given *precedence* over the others. Python defines a strict set of rules for how precedence is determined when several operations are expressed in a single statement.

The precedence rules are based on two principles. The most significant issue in determining precedence is the type of operation being used. Every available operator has a precedence relative to others. For example, multiplication and division are given priority over addition and subtraction, to follow the standard algebraic conventions. So with the expression 1 + 2 * 3, the multiplication is performed first, and then the addition. We portray the evaluation order graphically using a hierarchical *evaluation tree*, as shown in Figure 2.10.

The use of explicit parentheses allows a programmer to specify some evaluation order other than the default. For example if our intent is to perform the addition before the multiplication, we can do so by parenthesizing as (1 + 2) * 3, which evaluates to 9. Python resolves any subexpression enclosed within parentheses before that result is used within a larger expression. Even when desiring the default precedence, it is permissible to use explicit parentheses for clarity, as in 1 + (2 * 3).

The above example described how expressions are evaluated when using operators that have different precedence (as with multiplication over addition). Some operators are given equal precedence, such as addition and subtraction. Looking back at the earlier example 18 − 5 + 2, the default evaluation proceeds from left to right, thus as (18 − 5) + 2. Formally this is because addition and subtraction have equal precedence yet are *left-associative* operators, just as with traditional algebraic rules for numbers.

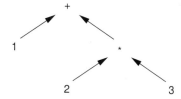

FIGURE 2.10: An evaluation tree demonstrating the order of operations for the expression 1 + 2 * 3.

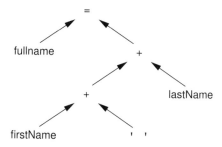

FIGURE 2.11: An evaluation tree demonstrating the order of operations for the expression fullName = firstName + ' ' + lastName.

The great majority of operators are left–associative but there are a few exceptions that are right–associative. For example exponentiation is right–associative, so 4 ** 3 ** 2 evaluates by default as 4 ** (3 ** 2). Again, this is to mimic standard mathematical conventions which consider $4^{3^2} = 4^{(3^2)} = 4^9 = 262144$.

Although the precedence rules are intuitively based on algebraic traditions, they are consistently enforced for operations on any data types. Consider the following statement:

```
>>> fullName = firstName + ' ' + lastName
```

This statement actually involves *three* different operators. There are two additions and also an assignment. Technically, the assignment operator (=) has the *lowest* precedence so that it is performed last, therefore allowing the entire right–hand side to be evaluated before the left–hand side identifier is assigned to the value. Within the right–hand side subexpression, the addition operators are performed from left to right. Figure 2.11 shows the evaluation tree for this expression. If we were to fully parenthesize the expression, it would appear as

```
>>> fullName = ((firstName + ' ') + lastName)
```

Of course, if we understand what is happening, it is nicer to avoid so many parentheses. But in case of doubt when writing a complicated expression, it is better to be explicit.

2.8.2 Boolean Expressions and the bool Class

Earlier in the chapter, we gave several examples of expressions that produce a result that is **True** or **False**. For example we could compare two values, as in `'Goodbye' < 'Hello'`. Also we saw several methods of the string class that return such a **True/False** value, as with country.startswith(`'Aus'`).

Formally, the literals **True** and **False** are instances of the simplest of all classes. The class is named **bool**, which is an abbreviated form of the term boolean, a tribute to the name of mathematician George Boole who pioneered the study of many logical properties. These values are a mainstay of digital computing and closely related to the concept of a bit. They are typically used to represent some logical condition that is assumed to be either true or false. For example if we model the weather as a boolean value, we might be forced to characterize it either as "sunny" or "not sunny," without any room for variations such as "mostly sunny" or "partly sunny." We will see significantly more use of this class in Chapter 4, when we begin using control structures to determine under what condition an instruction should be performed, skipped, or repeated. Our goal for now is to summarize the most important aspect of this class, the basic logical operators that can be used to express more complex conditions.

One example of a logical operator is **not**. You can get the opposite value by placing this keyword in front of any other boolean expression. For example, we could evaluate the expression **not** country.startswith(`'Aus'`).

An operator that takes two operands is **and**. We use this word in English to express two conditions that must both be satisfied. For example, the Bill of Rights guarantees "the right to a speedy and public trial." The meaning is that a trial must be speedy as well as public. It does not suffice for the government to hold a trial that is speedy yet private. Nor does it suffice to hold a trial that is public yet greatly delayed. It most certainly does not suffice to hold long-delayed, secretive trials. If we assume that the condition speedy is a boolean property (that is, we overlook the fuzziness in defining what time frame qualifies as speedy) and similarly for private, then there are only four possible scenarios. We generally describe the semantics of a logical operator by enumerating all possible results in what is called a truth table. Figure 2.12 provides such a truth table showing the semantics of **and** as well as other common boolean operators.

x	y	**not** x	x **and** y	x **or** y	x == y	x != y
False	False	True	False	False	True	False
False	True	True	False	True	False	True
True	False	False	False	True	False	True
True	True	False	True	True	True	False

FIGURE 2.12: Truth table for the common boolean operators. Given the values of x and y shown in the left two columns, the remaining columns show the resulting value of subsequent expressions.

Another logical operator is **or**. We might rely again upon our intuition as to its meaning, but there is some ambiguity in our use of the word in English. For example, the President of the United States can be impeached if convicted of treason or bribery. In this context, the term *or* means at least one of the conditions. That is, if a president were convicted of both offenses, impeachment is warranted. This notion is commonly called *inclusive or*. In other contexts, the use of the word *or* means precisely one of the two, as in Patrick Henry's famous quote, "give me liberty or give me death" — but presumably not both. This is an *exclusive or*. Because there is no room for ambiguity in a programming language, there are two distinct syntaxes for these meanings. The standard **or** operator provides the *inclusive* meaning, which is the most common usage. The easiest way to get the *exclusive* behavior is to rely on the != operator to compare one boolean value to another; the expression x != y is **True** precisely when one of the original two operands is **True** and the other is **False**.

We can also test the equality of two boolean values using ==. However, we note that this is only necessary when comparing two expressions whose truth values are not known at the time the programmer writes the code. Using a boolean literal as one of the operands is redundant. For example, assume that the identifier sunny denotes a boolean value. Although it is valid syntax to have an expression such as sunny == **True**, it is far bet-ter style to use the simpler expression sunny by itself; notice that expression sunny == **True** is itself true when sunny is true, and false when sunny is false. In similar fashion, the con-dition sunny == **False** is more simply expressed by the equivalent syntax **not** sunny.

Finally, consider a typical example of a compound boolean expression.

```
3 < x and x < 8
```

This checks whether the value of x is both strictly greater than 3 and strictly less than 8. When the same value, such as x, appears as an operand of two sub-expressions, those oper-ators can be *chained* as follows.

```
3 < x < 8
```

Chaining provides convenience as a programmer, and often a more legible form intuitively.

2.8.3 Calling Functions from Within Expressions

Calling a function is another operation that can be interleaved as part of a larger expression. Consider the use of len in the following example.

```
len(groceries) > 15 and 'milk' in groceries
```

The invocation of function len(groceries) is just another operation that must be considered when evaluating the overall expression. Function calls have very high precedence so that their return values can be used within the larger context. In this example, the length of the list is evaluated, and only then is that value compared to 15. The complete evaluation tree in this case appears in Figure 2.13. As another example of a function call as part of an expression, consider the following.

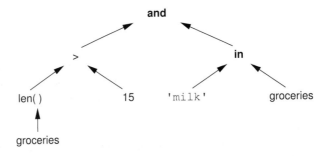

FIGURE 2.13: An evaluation tree demonstrating the order of operations for the expression len(groceries) > 15 **and** 'milk' **in** groceries.

```
>>> fullName = 'George Washington'
>>> fullName.split()[1]
'Washington'
```

This statement has the effect of first splitting the string to produce the intermediate list ['George', 'Washington'], and then indexing that list.

When multiple function calls are used in the same expression, they are typically evaluated from left to right, as in the following example:

```
>>> person = 'George Washington'
>>> person.lower().count('g')
3
```

The subexpression person.lower() is first evaluated, producing as an intermediate result the string 'george washington'. That intermediary is then used as the object when invoking the count method. A rather different evaluation order is demonstrated by the second command in the following session:

```
>>> groceries = ['cereal', 'milk', 'apple']
>>> groceries.insert(groceries.index('milk') + 1, 'eggs')
>>> groceries
['cereal', 'milk', 'eggs', 'apple']
```

That statement includes two method calls as well as an addition. In this case, the first step in the evaluation is the call to index. The reason that insert is not yet evaluated is that we need to resolve its parameters; things within parentheses are evaluated before using them in the greater context. Therefore, the call to groceries.index('milk') returns the value 1 in this case. That result is then used as the first operand of the addition, and only after that is the effective call to groceries.insert(2, 'eggs') performed.

2.9   Using a File for Source Code

Until now, we have directly interacted with the Python interpreter to execute statements. Although this sufficed for tinkering, it is limited as well. Every time we restart the interpreter, we have a clean slate and have lost all of the work we might have done in a past session. Furthermore, as a software developer our eventual goal is to write programs that can be executed by users who are not likely to be software developers. Those users should not need to know much about the Python interpreter.

As we begin to write larger programs, we will place our commands into separate text files that can be saved and later executed. Python programs are conventionally stored in files named with the .py extension, as in sample.py. Because the commands in a file are fed to the interpreter, they are typically known as *source code*. Fortunately, the format used for authoring source code is almost identical to that used when working in the interpreter, except that the source code only contains characters typed by the programmer (not the Python prompt or other interpreter displays). For example, when working in the interpreter, we may have started a program as follows:

```
>>> groceries = list()
>>> groceries.append('bread')
>>> groceries.append('milk')
>>> groceries.append('cheese')
>>>
```

For clarity, we have underlined those parts of the sessions that were literally typed by the programmer, to distinguish them from the characters that are generated by the system. This same sequence of commands, if authored as source code, would appear as follows:

```
groceries = list( )
groceries.append('bread')
groceries.append('milk')
groceries.append('cheese')
```

As another classic example, the following is a one-line program that displays the text Hello World to a user (we will discuss the purpose of the **print** command momentarily):

```
print 'Hello World'
```

Let's assume that we save this code in a separate text file, perhaps named hello.py. A user could then execute the program in one of several ways, depending on the computing environment. In a console environment, the user may execute the program by issuing the command python hello.py to the operating system. It may also be that the operating system recognizes the file as Python source code because of the .py extension and allows a user to simply click on the file icon to execute the program. Some Python programming environments (e.g., IDLE, which is discussed in Appendix A) provide additional means for executing source code.

As we make the transition from interactive Python sessions to executing source code from a file, there are a few important considerations to observe. Most notably, we must carefully distinguish between the role of the programmer and the role of the software's user. The remainder of the section is organized around the following four issues:

- Section 2.9.1 — Commands for getting output displayed to the user.
- Section 2.9.2 — Commands for receiving input from the user.
- Section 2.9.3 — Further details about executing software from a file.
- Section 2.9.4 — How a programmer can leave comments for other programmers.

2.9.1 Producing Output

An interactive session in the Python interpreter is very much like a conversation between a software developer and the interpreter. The developer issues commands to the interpreter and the interpreter at times displays information to be seen by the developer. For example, here is a simple session indicative of those from earlier in the chapter.

```
>>> waitlist = ['Kim', 'Eric', 'Andrew', 'Nell']
>>> waitlist.pop(0)
'Kim'
>>> waitlist
['Eric', 'Andrew', 'Nell']
```

Notice that when we issue a call to a function that provides a return value, the return value is displayed by the interpreter. When we type the identifier waitlist by itself, the interpreter responds by displaying a representation of that list. If, however, we were to type the very same commands into a separate file, as follows,

```
waitlist = ['Kim', 'Eric', 'Andrew', 'Nell']
waitlist.pop(0)
waitlist
```

and execute the source code, *no output is generated*. Although these responses are shown by the interpreter during an interactive session, they are not automatically displayed to the user. The **print** command allows the programmer to control what information is displayed to the user. For example, when issuing the pop command, had we wanted the return value to be displayed to the user, we must write

```
print waitlist.pop(0)
```

In this case, the following output is explicitly displayed to the user:

```
Kim
```

Notice that when a string is displayed with **print**, the quotation marks are not actually printed; those were only shown within the interpreter to clearly designate that information as a **str** instance.

Of course, displaying such a name without any further explanation is not very help‑
ful; remember that the user does not know that this output was generated as a result of
being popped from a waiting list. We should probably compose more informative output,
perhaps with the command

```
print waitlist.pop(0), 'your table is ready.'
```

In this case, the user would see the output

```
Kim your table is ready.
```

Here, the syntax we use for the **print** statement has two arguments, separated by commas.
The first argument is the value returned from the pop and the second is the string literal
`'your table is ready.'`. When multiple arguments are outputted with a single
print command, they appear on the same line with a single space automatically inserted
between each pair. That is why a space appears between `'Kim'` and `'your'` in this
example. Notice that the comma is not displayed as part of the output; that syntax is used
in the source code to separate the arguments. If we want the comma to appear within the
output it must be included as a character within the string. We might try the following,
with the comma and space within the second argument:

```
print waitlist.pop(0), ', your table is ready.'
```

Unfortunately this does not quote produce the desired format. It literally outputs the
following:

```
Kim , your table is ready.
```

Python still inserts a space between the two arguments, in this case lying between the name
and the displayed comma. An alternative approach to get the desired output is to use string
concatenation to compose a *single* argument, as follows:

```
print waitlist.pop(0) + ', your table is ready.'
```

By using the + operator, the two strings are concatenated into a single string *without* any
additional space. Then that composite string is printed.

If two separate **print** statements are used, then by default, the user sees two separate
lines of output. For example, if the above had been programmed as

```
print waitlist.pop(0) + ', your table is ready.'
print 'Please come this way.'
```

the user would see

```
Kim, your table is ready.
Please come this way.
```

The default newline can be suppressed and replaced with a single space by putting a final comma at the end of the first **print** statement. Thus the code

```
print waitlist.pop(0) + ', your table is ready.',
print 'Please come this way.'
```

produces the output

```
Kim, your table is ready. Please come this way.
```

Printing nonstring data types

In these first examples, the arguments to the **print** statement happen to be string instances. However, we can also use **print** with arguments from other types. In this case, those arguments are automatically converted to a string representation by Python. For example, it is perfectly acceptable to issue a command, as follows

```
print 'There are', waitlist.index('Nell'), 'people ahead of Nell.'
```

If this command were executed at the end of our program, the output would appear as

```
There are 2 people ahead of Nell.
```

We specified three arguments to the **print** command, the second of which is formally the **int** instance returned by the call to index. When faced with a nonstring object, the **print** command automatically casts it to a string, using the implicit syntax **str**(x) for argument x. Mixing different arguments of different types is okay; each is independently cast to a string.

Finally we note that a single **print** command may cause multiple lines of output if newline characters are contained within any of the arguments. For example, we could print the entirely waiting list in a more user-friendly manner with the single command

```
print 'Current list\n-----------\n' + '\n'.join(waitlist)
```

 A WORD OF WARNING

Although strings can be concatenated with the + operator, they cannot be directly concatenated to other data types. For example, the expression `'The number of guests is ' + `len(guests) is illegal because the first operand is a string and the second is an integer. Instead, the integer must be cast to a string, as in `'The number of guests is ' + `**str**(len(guests)).

This results in the following output, given our sample waiting list:

```
Current list
------------
Eric
Andrew
Nell
```

2.9.2 Receiving Input

When working in an interactive session, there is no distinction between programmer and user. Since we can enter whatever data we needed directly into the interpreter, there is no need for special commands that request input. For example, we can set the value of an identifier as

```
>>> favoriteFruit = 'apple'
```

When executing a saved program, we often need to gather input from the user. The primary command we use to this end is the **raw_input** function. It takes a single optional parameter, which is a string displayed as a prompt. The function outputs the given prompt, waits for the user to enter a line of text, and then returns the string that was entered. So we might gather information from the user using a command such as

```
favoriteFruit = raw_input('What is your favorite fruit? ')
```

When executed, this code may produce the following interaction:

```
What is your favorite fruit? apple
```

The underlined portion indicates characters entered by the user. Notice that the user is not expected to enter quotation marks around the response (unless those quotation marks are actually meant to be included as characters of the string).

Formally, the return value of the **raw_input** function is a **str** instance that contains precisely those characters typed by the user prior to hitting the enter key (yet not a newline character). If intending to read a number from the user, it is the programmer's responsibility to cast the result, as discussed in Section 2.5. Consider, for example, the following code fragment:

```
age = int(raw_input('What is your age? '))
print 'Soon you will be', age + 1
```

When executed by the user, it might produce the following interaction:

```
What is your age? 38
Soon you will be 39
```

2.9.3 Executing the Program

At the beginning of the section, we indicated that source code in a file named `sample.py` might be executed by starting the interpreter using the command `python sample.py`, rather than simply `python`. The interpreter executes the commands in the given file until one of two things happens. If all goes well the program executes, displaying output as instructed, continuing until there are no further commands to execute. At that point the program is complete and the interpreter automatically exits. If, on the other hand, an error occurs while a program is running, the execution halts at that point and the relevant error message is displayed on the screen. Suppose the example from the end of the previous section had incorrectly attempted to concatenate a string and a number, written as

```
1   age = int(raw_input('What is your age? '))
2   print 'Soon you will be' + age + 1
```

Here is a possible execution, as observed by the user.

```
What is your age? 38
Traceback (most recent call last):
  File "sample.py", line 2, in -toplevel-
    print 'Soon you will be' + age + 1
TypeError: cannot concatenate 'str' and 'int' objects
```

Along with the usual description, notice that the error message clearly indicates the file name and the line number at which the error occurred. This can be extremely helpful information in diagnosing the problem.

Above, we described the typical way that a user would run a Python program. But as a developer, there is an extremely convenient alternative to run a program. Rather than starting the program with the syntax `python sample.py`, we can execute the program with the syntax `python -i sample.py`. The `-i` designation indicates that we would like to enter an inspection mode as soon as the execution stops. Whether it reaches the end of the commands or an error occurs, the interpreter will not exit but will instead present us with a standard Python prompt. All of the objects from the original program still exist in memory and we can interact with them by typing further commands at the Python prompt. If we had started the above program in this way, we could continue with a session such as

```
What is your age? 38
Traceback (most recent call last):
  File "sample.py", line 2, in -toplevel-
    print 'Soon you will be' + age + 1
TypeError: cannot concatenate 'str' and 'int' objects
>>> age
38
>>> nextYear = age + 1
```

Although we would never expect a typical (non–Python–speaking) user to be interested in interactive mode, it is quite a valuable tool when developing our own programs.

2.9.4   Leaving Comments in Source Code

When writing source code, it is very helpful to be able to leave messages that can be visible to another programmer yet unseen by the user who executes the program. Python supports a syntax for embedding such **comments** directly in the code. When the symbol # is used in a line of code, the rest of the line is considered a comment and ignored by the Python interpreter. There are two common styles, the first of which is to have a comment on a line by itself to explain what is about to come, as in

```
# start with an empty shopping list
groceries = list( )
```

Another style is to inline a comment on the right-hand side of an existing command, as in

```
groceries = list( )          # start with an empty shopping list
```

It is a matter of taste to decide when to include comments and which visual style to use. Comments can serve to landmark major components of a program, or to highlight a subtlety in technique that might otherwise be overlooked. They can be quite useful if another programmer ever needs to read or modify your code. In fact, it can even be quite helpful if *you* ever need to read or modify your code after some time has passed. We will demonstrate the use of comments quite often in our own examples.

2.10   Case Study: Strings and Lists

To demonstrate the techniques we have already learned, we present a code fragment that converts a date from one string format to another. Specifically, we would like to take a date originally formatted as the string 07-19-1997 and to output the date in the form July 19, 1997.

The task can be broken into several stages: getting the original input, breaking apart this format, reassembling the desired result, and outputting the result to the user. To get the data, we choose to prompt the user as follows:

```
original = raw_input('Please enter a date (MM-DD-YYYY): ')
```

The identifier original is used to denote the complete string entered by the user. Next we wish to break apart the components of the date, as delimited by dashes. The split command is perfectly suited for such a manipulation, as in

```
pieces   = original.split('-')
```

After this command, pieces is a list which presumably contains the three relevant portions of the original date. We can use indices to retrieve each piece, but to avoid confusion, we associate more meaningful identifiers with those pieces. Also, it is important to remember that each piece is still technically a string, even though we might think of each component as a number in the context of dates.

```
month  = pieces[0]              # this is a string of numerals (e.g., '10')
day    = pieces[1]
year   = pieces[2]
```

The biggest challenge in reassembling the desired format is in converting the numeral form of the month into the corresponding name. Our strategy for converting the integer into a name is to take advantage of the consecutive numbering of months. We begin by defining a tuple containing the names of the twelve months, in the standard order.

```
monthNames = ('January', 'February', 'March', 'April',
              'May', 'June', 'July', 'August', 'September',
              'October', 'November', 'December')
```

This is a very natural case for using a tuple rather than a list, as the contents never need change. To convert a month number (e.g., 10) into a name (e.g., 'October'), we carefully index the tuple, remembering that the proper index is one less than the conventional numbering of months. This discrepancy occurs because we index starting at 0, yet months are traditionally numbered starting at 1; that is, 'January' is stored at index 0, 'February' at index 1, and so forth.

At this point, we are ready to reassemble the alternate format for our original date. Remembering that the identifier month still represents a string (e.g., '10'), we must first convert this to an **int**, then subtract one, and then use it as an index into the tuple of month names, as monthNames[**int**(month)−1]. Finally, we need to put all of the final pieces together, with proper spacing and punctuation. Although we could do each of these intermediate manipulations as a separate command, we choose to rely upon a single compound statement that does the job.

```
alternate = monthNames[int(month)−1] + ' ' + day + ', ' + year
```

Notice that we did not have to convert day or year into strings when concatenating our result, because they were already represented as strings from the original split. Our complete source code is given in Figure 2.14. This code works properly, so long as the user enters the original date in the expected format. A more professional piece of software should gracefully handle unexpected scenarios if the user strays from that format, but we will leave this topic for another chapter after we have more experience.

2.11 Chapter Review

2.11.1 Key Points

General Use of Objects

- When a new instance of a class is created, we say it is *instantiated*. Typically this is done using a constructor, which is invoked with the class name followed by parentheses, for example **list**( ).
- An identifier is a name, chosen by a programmer, that is used to keep track of an object.
- An identifier is *assigned* to an underlying object using the = symbol, as in groceries = **list**( ).

```
1   monthNames = ('January', 'February', 'March', 'April',
2               'May', 'June', 'July', 'August', 'September',
3               'October', 'November', 'December')
4
5   # get input from user
6   original = raw_input('Please enter a date (MM-DD-YYYY): ')
7
8   pieces  = original.split('-')
9   month   = pieces[0]                    # this is a string of numerals (e.g., '10')
10  day     = pieces[1]
11  year    = pieces[2]
12
13  alternate = monthNames[int(month)-1] + ' ' + day + ', ' + year
14  print alternate
```

FIGURE 2.14: Our complete program for formatting a date.

- A method is invoked using the form *object.method(parameters)*, as in groceries.append('bread').

- When programming in interactive mode, the return value of a function call is displayed within the interpreter.

- An identifier can be assigned to the return value of a function for later use, as in nextToBuy = groceries.pop( ).

- Some methods accept one or more optional parameters. If those parameters are not explic-itly sent, default values are used instead.

- A mutable class is one that contains objects whose state may be changed over time. The **list** class is the only example of a mutable class from this chapter.

- An immutable class is one that contains objects whose state cannot be changed, once con-structed. Most of Python's primitive types are implemented as immutable classes, includ-ing **str, tuple, int, float, long,** and **bool**.

- The semantics of an operator depends upon the type of operands that are used. For example with integers, 13 > 5 is true because it compares values. With strings the comparison is evaluated according to alphabetical order, and so '13' > '5' is false.

Sequence types (list, str, tuple)

- Instances of the **list, str,** and **tuple** classes are designed to represent an ordered sequence of elements. A **list** is a mutable sequence of general objects. A **tuple** is an immutable sequence of general objects. A **str** is specifically an immutable sequence of characters.

- A position in an ordered sequence is described using an integer *index*, equal to the number of items that precede the position. By definition, the first element has index 0, so we say that sequences are *zero-indexed*.

- An individual element of a sequence can be accessed by index, as in waitlist[0].

- A slice of a sequence, denoted as data[start:stop:step], is a new sequence that begins at the specified start index, advances by the indicated step size, and continues up to but not including or passing the specified stop index. If not explicitly provided, the start is 0, the stop is the end of the list, and the step size is 1.

- All sequences support containment queries using the syntax value **in** seq and all report their length using len(seq).

- The literal form of a **list** uses square brackets, as in ['cereal', 'milk', 'apple'].

- The range function can be used to create a list of integers over a certain range. The syntax range(start, stop, step) is used to create a list, starting at start (0 by default), advancing by the given step size (1 by default), going up to but not including or passing the specified stopping value. For example, range(4) returns [0, 1, 2, 3], range(3,6) returns [3, 4, 5], range(18,6,−5) returns [18, 13, 8].

- Mutator methods supported by the **list** class include: append, insert, pop, remove, reverse, and sort.

- Accessor methods supported by the **list** class include: count and index, as well as the special methods associated with operators.

- The literal form of a **str** uses either a single quote to begin and end it (e.g., 'bread'), or a double quote to begin and end it (e.g., "bread"), or triple quotes to begin and end it (e.g., """bread""").

- The **str** class supports many convenient methods that generate a new string that is a variant of an existing string. These include: lower, upper, capitalize, center, ljust, rjust, strip, and replace.

- The **str** class supports many convenient methods that return information about a given string. These include: startswith, isalpha, isdigit, islower, and isupper.

- The **str** class supports two important methods involving lists. The split method takes one long string and breaks it up according to a given delimiter, producing a list of pieces. The join method takes a list of strings and reassembles them separated by a delimiter, producing one long string.

- The literal form of a **tuple** uses parentheses, as in ('cereal', 'milk', 'apple').

Numeric types (int, long, float)

- The **int** class is used to represent integral values.

- The **long** class is used to represent integral values too large to be directly supported by the computer architecture.

- The **float** class is used to represent floating-point numbers, which are similar to the mathematical notion of a *real number*, yet with limited precision.

- All numeric types support basic operators for performing arithmetic and for comparing one value to another.

- Division is a bit tricky with numeric types because there are several possible semantics. For example if dividing 14 by 3, a *true division* results in a floating-point number 4.6666667. The / operator is typically used to perform true division. In contrast, an *integer division* results in a quotient of 4 and a separate remainder of 2. The // operator is used to report the quotient, while the % operator is used to report the modulus (i.e., remainder).

Casting among types

- The process of converting data from one type to another is known as *casting*. In Python, casting is performed by reconstructing a new instance of the desired type, using the existing value as a parameter to the constructor.

- For example **str**(1776) produces a string representation `'1776'` of the original integer value.

- **list**(`'hello'`) produces the list [`'h'`, `'e'`, `'l'`, `'l'`, `'o'`] of characters occurring in the given string.

- The syntax **int**(x) casts an object to an integer, if possible. For example, **int**(`'1776'`) results in value 1776.

- When converting from a floating-point number to an integer, the fractional part is always truncated. Thus **int**(3.8) evaluates to 3.

- The built-in function round can be used to compute the nearest integral value to a given floating-point value (although the result is still a **float**). Thus round(3.8) evaluates to 4.0. That result can subsequently be cast to an **int** if desired.

- The underlying integer encoding of a character is reported by the syntax ord(character), where character is a one-character string. Conversely, an integer code can be converted to the corresponding one-character string using the syntax chr(code).

Functions and Modules

- Some functions (e.g., round) are defined outside the context of any particular class. We call these *pure functions*.

- Other common built-in functions include len, sum, min, and max.

- An enormous library of additional values, functions, and classes have been implemented by Python developers but not automatically included as built-ins. These additional tools are organized into *modules* that can be imported if desired.

- Importing and using a tool such as the sqrt function from the math module can be accomplished in three styles.

```
>>> import math
>>> math.sqrt(2)
1.41421356237

>>> from math import sqrt
>>> sqrt(2)
1.41421356237

>>> from math import *
>>> sqrt(2)
1.41421356237
```

Expressions

- When multiple operations are expressed in a single statement, the Python interpreter evaluates them one at a time.

- By default, Python dictates a set of *precedence rules* that are used to determine the order in which operations of a compound expression are performed.
- Certain operators are always given precedence over others, such as multiplication over addition.
- Operations of equal precedence are usually evaluated from left to right, although there are a few operators that are evaluated from right to left.
- A programmer can use parentheses to explicitly specify the order of evaluation.
- An *evaluation tree* can be used to diagram the order in which pieces of an expression are computed.
- The **bool** class is the simplest of all. It has only two instances, **True** and **False**. The class supports the expression of logical statements using operators such as **not, and,** and **or**.
- Python syntax allows for compound expressions, including function calls, such as len(groceries) > 15 **and** `'milk'` **in** groceries.

Python Interpreter

- The Python interpreter can be started in one of three ways from a command line:
  - `python`
    starts a purely interactive session of the interpreter
  - `python sample.py`
    executes the code from a file, such as `sample.py`, ending the interpreter either when the program completes or when an error occurs.
  - `python -i sample.py`
    similar to previous, except rather than quitting the interpreter, it switches to interactive mode so that we can inspect the existing objects.
- Documentation for a class, function or other object can be accessed directly from the interpreter by using the syntax help(*topic*).

Using a file for source code

- Although we can experiment interactively in the interpreter, source code is usually written in a separate file, which can later be executed.
- The **print** command is used to generate output that will be visible to a user when executing a program.
- If multiple arguments are designated in a **print** command, separated by commas, they are printed on the same line of output with a space between each pair.
- By default, a newline character is printed at the conclusion of each **print** statement. However, this newline is suppressed if a comma appears at the end of a print statement.
- The **raw_input** function can be used to get input from the user. A prompt for the user can be specified as an optional parameter. The return value is a string object containing the characters typed by the user in response.
- Comments can be added to a Python program following a # symbol. Those comments are ignored by the interpreter, and unseen by the user, but visible to programmers who review the source code.

2.11.2 Glossary

ASCII A standard ordering for an alphabet of 128 common characters, used for representing text digitally.

assignment A statement that associates an identifier on the left-hand side of the = operator with the object expressed on the right-hand side.

casting A conversion of data from one type to another.

comment An explanatory note in the source code that is ignored by the Python interpreter yet visible to a programmer.

constructor A special method that is implicitly called whenever an object is instantiated. It is responsible for establishing the initial state of the object.

default parameter value *See* optional parameter.

exclusive or Meeting one of two conditions but not both.

expression A single statement consisting of one or more operations.

identifier A name associated with some underlying object.

immutable The characteristic of an object whose state cannot be modified once constructed.

inclusive or Meeting at least one of two conditions.

index An integer value used to identify a position in a sequential structure, such as a string or list. Indices are measured by the offset from the beginning, and thus the first position has index 0.

instantiation The construction of a new object in a given class.

left-associative Operators that are evaluated from left to right as part of an expression, as in $18 - 5 + 2$ which is equivalent to $(18 - 5) + 2$.

list A built-in class used to manage a mutable sequence of elements.

literal An explicit value of an object drawn from one of the built-in classes.

module A library defining a combination of identifiers, functions and classes. Modules must be imported when needed.

mutable The characteristic of an object whose state can be changed by one or more of its methods.

operator A symbol (e.g., +) that triggers a special behavior in Python.

optional parameter A parameter that can be sent to a function, yet which is assigned a default value if not sent.

parameter A piece of information sent from the caller to the callee upon invocation of a function.

polymorphism A technique in which objects of different types support a common syntax or when a single function supports multiple behaviors depending upon the type of parameter it receives.

precedence When one operation is performed before another in evaluating an expression. Python defines strict rules for how precedence is determined.

pure function A function that is defined outside the context of any class.

Python interpreter The software that accepts and executes Python commands.

qualified name A syntax using "dot" notation (e.g., math.pi) for accessing a name defined in another context (such as a module).

slice A selected portion of a sequence, such as a **list**, **str**, or **tuple**, using a syntax such as data[start:stop].

source code The characters that comprise commands for a program in a high-level language. Source code is typically stored in one or more text files and translated with an interpreter or compiler.

special method A method that provides implicit support for an alternative syntax in Python. For example, the __add__ method supports the + operator.

2.11.3 Exercises

Lists

Practice 2.1: Suppose the list astronauts has the value

```
['Yuri Gagarin','John Glenn','Neal Armstrong']
```

Give a single statement that adds 'Alan Shepard' between 'Yuri Gagarin' and 'John Glenn'.

Practice 2.2: Write a program that takes a list of strings named people and rearranges that list into reverse alphabetical order.

Practice 2.3: Write a statement that takes a list named houses and creates a new list someHouses containing every other house starting with the second (i.e., the second, fourth, sixth and so on).

Practice 2.4: Explain how to use range to create a list with contents [2, 4, 6, 8].

Exercise 2.5: Assume that we have a list initialized as

```
fruits = ['orange', 'banana', 'grape', 'lime', 'strawberry']
```

Give a single command that replaces the occurrence of 'lime' with the string 'kiwi'.

Exercise 2.6: Give a series of statements that determine and print the string that comes second, in alphabetical order, from an initially unordered list friends.

Exercise 2.7: Repeat Exercise 2.6, ensuring that the original list remains unchanged.

Exercise 2.8: The command groceries.append('milk') adds the element to the end of the list. Explain how to implement this action using the insert method rather than the append method.

Exercise 2.9: What is the result of the command range(13, 40, 5)?

Exercise 2.10: Explain how to use the range command to create a list with contents [8, 5, 2].

Exercise 2.11: Suppose that numbers is a list of values. Give a command or sequence of commands that outputs the median value from that list.

Exercise 2.12: Assume that groceries is a list and that you have been told that 'milk' occurs five times on the list. Give a command or sequence of commands that removes the *second* occurrence of 'milk' while leaving the rest of the list intact.

Exercise 2.13: Assume that the identifier stuff references a list. Give an expression that represents the number of times the first item of this list occurs elsewhere on the list.

Strings

Practice 2.14: Consider the string defined as

```
example = 'This is a test. This is only a test.'
```

(a) Give the *type* and *value* of the expression example[12].

(b) Give the *type* and *value* of the expression example[6:12].

(c) Give the *type* and *value* of the expression example.count('is').

(d) Give the *type* and *value* of the expression example.index('a').

(e) Give the *type* and *value* of the expression example.index('is', 6).

(f) Give the *type* and *value* of the expression example.split('a').

Practice 2.15: Write an expression that is **True** if stringA and stringB are equivalent to each other in a case-insensitive manner.

Practice 2.16: Give an expression that is equal to the number of times the letter b occurs in the string song, including both uppercase and lowercase occurrences.

Practice 2.17: Assume that person is a string of the form 'firstName lastName'. Give a command or series of commands that results in the corresponding string 'lastName, firstName'.

Practice 2.18: Consider the following code fragment:

```
message = 'Hello, my name is Frank'
start = message[ :18]
name = message[18: ]

letters = list(name)
letters.remove('F')
letters.sort( )
letters[1] = 'N'

name = ' '.join(letters)
name = name.replace('r', '.')

print start + name.capitalize( )
```

What is the output of the print statement?

Exercise 2.19: Write an expression that is **True** precisely when stringA is a capitalized version of stringB.

Exercise 2.20: Assign identifier numVowels to the number of vowels in the given string poem.

Exercise 2.21: Assume that fruits is a list containing strings representing the names of various fruits. Give a command or sequence of commands that produces a single string diet containing all of the fruits from the list, alphabetized and with spaces and a plus sign between each fruit. As an example, if the list of fruits happened to be

```
fruit = ['lime', 'apple', 'grape', 'cherry', 'orange', 'banana']
```

the resulting diet should have value

```
'apple + banana + cherry + grape + lime + orange'
```

Exercise 2.22: Assume that person is a string of the general form
`'firstName middleName lastName'`.
Give a command or series of commands that results in the creation of the corresponding string `'firstName middleInitial. lastname'`. For example, if person = `'Elmer Joseph Fudd'`, the result should be `'Elmer J. Fudd'`.

Exercise 2.23: Give a code fragment that converts a general date string from the format `'07/13/2007'` into the associated format `'13 July 2007'`.

Expressions

Practice 2.24: Give the *type* and *value* of each expression.

(a)	23 + 8	(j)	`'Python'`.islower( )
(b)	3.5 − 1.1	(k)	`'hocuspocus'`.split(`'o'`)
(c)	2 * 3.1	(l)	`'A' == 'a'`
(d)	17 / 5.0	(m)	range(10,20)[3]
(e)	17 // 5	(n)	len(range(10))
(f)	2 + 6.4 / 2	(o)	`'expression'`[2:7]
(g)	4 >= 6	(p)	len(`'hello'`[1:4])
(h)	3 * `'12'`	(q)	3 + 4 == 7 **and** 1 + 1 != 4
(i)	`'a' + 'b'` * 3	(r)	**True or (True and False)**

Practice 2.25: Assume that r represents the radius of a circle. Give an expression for the area of that circle.

Practice 2.26: An error occurs when evaluating each of the following expressions. Give the official type of error, as reported by the interpreter, and explain in your own words the precise reason for the error.

(a) `'hello' * 'goodbye'`

(b) `' + '`.join(range(10))

(c) range(10).split(`', '`)

(d) range(10).reverse( )[3]

(e) len(range(10).pop( ))

Exercise 2.27: Give the *type* and *value* of each expression.

(a)	3 − 8	(j)	`'Python'`.lower( )
(b)	8 − 1.5	(k)	`'computer' < 'science'`
(c)	17 % 5	(l)	3 > 7 **or** 2 < 1
(d)	15.5 // 4.1	(m)	**False and (False or True)**
(e)	3 * 2 + 4 * 5	(n)	range(10,20).pop( )
(f)	4 − 2 + 5 // 3 − 2	(o)	len(range(10,20,4))
(g)	4 > 4	(p)	[5][0]
(h)	**str**(12 + 34)	(q)	`'sample'`[1:4]
(i)	(`'a'` + `'b'`) * 3	(r)	`'sample'`[1:4:2]

Exercise 2.28: An error occurs when evaluating each of the following expressions. Give the official type of error, as reported by the interpreter, and explain in your own words the precise reason for the error.

(a) [`'Do'`, `'Re'`, `'Mi'`].join(`'-'`)

(b) `'High'` + 5

(c) [`'Do'`, `'Re'`, `'Mi'`].insert(`'Fa'`)

(d) `'hello'`.remove(`'a'`)

(e) **list**(`'hello'`).remove(`'a'`)

Exercise 2.29: Draw an evaluation tree for the following statement:

alternate = monthNames[**int**(month)−1] + ' ' + day + ', ' + year

User input/output

Practice 2.30: Write a short program that asks the user to enter his or her name, and says hello. For example,

```
What is your name?   Frank
Hello Frank!
```

Practice 2.31: Write a program that asks the user to enter two integers (separated by a space) and outputs the sum. For example,

```
Enter two integers:   5 16
Their sum is 21.
```

Exercise 2.32: Write a code fragment that prompts the user to enter an arbitrary number of values separated by commas and prints out the average of the numbers. The output should be a floating-point number. For example,

```
Enter some numbers separated by commas: 5, 18, 14
The average is 12.33
```

Projects

Exercise 2.33: Write a program that asks the user to enter a temperature in Fahrenheit and reports the equivalent temperature in Celsius. You may use the formula $c = \frac{5}{9}(f - 32)$ for doing the conversion. A sample session might appear as follows:

```
Enter a temperature in Fahrenheit:  85
85 Fahrenheit is equivalent to 29.4444 Celsius.
```

Exercise 2.34: The Body Mass Index is a screening measure meant to approximate a person's body fat based upon his or her height and weight. Let W represent a weight (measured in pounds), and let H represent a height (measured in inches). Then the index is calculated according to the formula $\text{BMI} = 703 \cdot W/H^2$.

Write a program that asks the user for their height and weight and reports the BMI. The user should enter the height in a format such as 5'8" to signify 5 feet 8 inches. A sample session might appear as follows:

```
What is your height (e.g., 5'8"):  5'10"
What is your weight (in pounds):  140
Your BMI is 20.0857.
```

(The normal range is listed as 18.5 to 24.9, according to the Department of Health and Human Services.)

Exercise 2.35: Write a program that asks the user to enter the name of a month and prints out the birthstone for that month. A sample session might appear as

```
Enter a month:  April
April's birthstone is Diamond.
```

As part of your program, you may make use of the following two lists:

```
monthNames = ['January', 'February', 'March', 'April',
    'May', 'June', 'July', 'August',
    'September', 'October', 'November', 'December']
birthstones = ['Garnet', 'Amethyst', 'Aquamarine', 'Diamond',
    'Emerald', 'Pearl', 'Ruby', 'Peridot',
    'Sapphire', 'Opal', 'Topaz', 'Turquoise']
```

Exercise 2.36: Write a program that inputs a date and outputs how many days into the year it is. For example, May 5 is the 125th day of the year. (Do not worry about leap year.)

Exercise 2.37: DNA can be modeled as a string of characters using the alphabet: A, C, G, and T. One form of DNA mutation occurs when a substring of the DNA is reversed during the replication process. Usually, such a reversal occurs between what are termed *inverted pairs*. For example, if the pattern TGAA is later followed by the inverted pattern AAGT, it is possible that the slice of DNA delimited by those patterns could be inverted and reattached, since the bonds at each end will be locally the same. An example is shown here.

Design a program that works as follows. It should ask the user for an original DNA string as well as the particular pattern that is inverted. It should then locate the leftmost occurrence of that pattern, and the next subsequent occurrence of the inverted pattern. The output should be the mutated DNA, with the segment between the inverted pair reversed. An example session might appear as follows:

```
Enter a DNA sequence: CGATTGAACATTAAGTCCAATT
Enter the pattern:     TGAA
Mutated DNA sequence: CGATTGAATTACAAGTCCAATT
```

Note: the challenge of reversing a string is discussed in *For the Guru* on page 55.

C H A P T E R   3

Getting Started with Graphics

In Section 1.4.4 we designed a hierarchy for a hypothetical set of drawable objects. Those classes are not actually built into Python, but we have implemented precisely such a package for use with this book. Our software is available as a module named cs1graphics, which can be downloaded and installed on your computer system. This chapter provides an introductory tour of the package. Since these graphics classes are not a standard part of Python, they must first be loaded with the command

```
>>> from cs1graphics import *
```

The package can be used in one of two ways. To begin, we suggest experimenting in an interactive Python session. In this way, you will see the immediate effect of each command as you type it. The problem with working interactively is that you start from scratch each time. As you progress, you will want to save the series of commands in a separate file and then use that source code as a script for controlling the interpreter (as introduced in Section 2.9).

Our tour begins with the Canvas class, which provides the basic windows for displaying graphics. Next we introduce the various Drawable objects that can be added to a canvas. We continue by discussing techniques to control the relative depths of objects that appear on a canvas and to perform rotations, scaling, and cloning of those objects. Near the end of the chapter we discuss more advanced topics, including the use of a Layer class that provides a convenient way to group shapes into a composite object, techniques to create dynamic animations rather than still images, and preliminary support for monitoring a user's interactions with the mouse and keyboard.

FIGURE 3.1: A new Canvas on the desktop; the exact appearance depends upon the computing environment.

3.1 The Canvas

We begin by introducing the Canvas class. A canvas represents a window upon which we draw. We can create a canvas by calling the constructor as follows:

```
>>> Canvas()
>>>
```

After entering this command, a new window should appear on the screen, such as the one shown in Figure 3.1. However, we have an immediate problem; we have no further way to interact with the canvas because we did not assign an identifier to the newly created object. A more useful beginning is the following:

```
>>> paper = Canvas()
>>>
```

This creates an instance of the Canvas class that appears on the screen, and it also assigns the identifier paper to that object. This is similar to the syntax groceries = **list**( ) which we used when instantiating a **list** in Section 2.2.1.

By default, a newly created canvas is 200 pixels wide and 200 pixels tall, has a white background color, and is titled "Graphics Canvas." But a canvas is mutable, so we can change several aspects of its state by calling appropriate methods. For example, the fol-lowing commands modify the canvas that was earlier identified as paper:

```
>>> paper.setBackgroundColor('skyBlue')
>>> paper.setWidth(300)
>>> paper.setTitle('My World')
```

As each individual command is entered into the interpreter, the change to the Canvas is immediately visible. When the desired characteristics of a canvas are known in advance, they can be specified as *optional parameters* to the constructor (see page 43 for further

Canvas	
Canvas(w, h, bgColor, title, autoRefresh)	add(drawable)
getWidth( )	remove(drawable)
setWidth(w)	clear( )
getHeight( )	open( )
setHeight(h)	close( )
getBackgroundColor( )	saveToFile(filename)
setBackgroundColor(color)	setAutoRefresh(trueOrFalse)
getTitle( )	refresh( )
setTitle(title)	wait( )

FIGURE 3.2: Overview of the Canvas class.

discussion of optional parameters). In the case of the Canvas class, the constructor accepts optional parameters respectively specifying the initial width, height, background color, and title. So we could have created and configured the previous Canvas succinctly as follows:

```
>>> paper = Canvas(300, 200, 'skyBlue', 'My World')
>>>
```

The caller may elect to fill in only some of the parameter values, although only when starting from the leftmost. So the syntax Canvas(500, 270) creates a new canvas with the specified width and height, yet using the default color of white and the default window title. The simple syntax Canvas( ) relies upon all of the default values. On the other hand, the syntax Canvas('black') fails because the first parameter sent must be the width. The interpreter reports the problem with an error message similar to the following:

```
Traceback (most recent call last):
  File "<stdin>", line 1, in -toplevel-
  File "cs1graphics.py", line 862, in __init__
    raise TypeError('numeric value expected for width')
TypeError: numeric value expected for width
```

As we continue, we will explore many other important behaviors of the Canvas class. A more complete reference is given in the form of a class diagram in Figure 3.2. There are methods that allow a user to query and to alter aspects such as the width, height, background color, and title. In the next section, we discuss how drawable objects can be added to or removed from a canvas. The canvas can be explicitly closed (i.e., iconified) and reopened, and the canvas's image can even be saved to a file. Finally, there are methods that involve what we term the "refresh" mode of the canvas; we delay discussion of this issue until page 113.

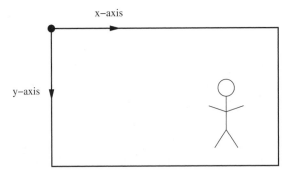

FIGURE 3.3: The canvas coordinate system, with the origin at the top left corner.

The coordinate system

Before introducing the individual shapes, we discuss the coordinate system used to describe the positions of those objects relative to a canvas. We have already seen that each canvas has a width and a height, measured in pixels. To describe the locations of shapes, we consider a coordinate system with the x-axis running horizontally and the y-axis vertically. The standard coordinate system for computer graphics uses the *top left* corner of a canvas as the origin, as shown in Figure 3.3. A typical position in the canvas is then specified as a pair of coordinates, with the x-coordinate measuring the number of pixels to the *right* of that corner, and the y-coordinate measuring the number of pixels *below* that corner.

When we want to place one of our graphical objects upon a canvas, we specify the coordinates for a key *reference point* of that shape, for example, the center of a rectangle. As a physical analogy, assume that our canvas is a bulletin board and that our shapes are made of paper. Each shape is attached to the canvas by an imaginary thumbtack that pokes through the shape at its reference point. We specify the location of the overall shape relative to the canvas by designating the placement of that thumbtack in the canvas's coordinate system. Later we will discuss how we can even rotate or scale an object about its reference point.

 A WORD OF WARNING

Do not confuse the coordinate system used for computer graphics with the traditional mathematical convention. The computer graphics system uses the top left corner as the origin, with the positive y-axis oriented *downward* from the origin; the usual mathematics convention uses the bottom left corner as the origin, with the positive y-axis oriented *upward* from the origin.

3.2   Drawable Objects

The cs1graphics module supports a variety of objects that can be drawn onto a canvas. These objects are organized in a class hierarchy originally modeled in Section 1.4.4. A more detailed summary of the various classes is given in Figure 3.4. This diagram is packed with information and may seem overwhelming at first, but it provides a nice summary that can be used as a reference. The use of inheritance emphasizes the similarities, making it easier to learn how to use each class.

When examining this diagram, remember that classes in a hierarchy inherit methods from their parent class. For example, each type of FillableShape supports a setFillColor method. So not only does a Circle support the setRadius method, but also the setFillColor method due to its parent class, and the setBorderWidth method due to its grandparent Shape class. Many of the names should be self-explanatory and formal documentation for each class can be viewed directly in the Python interpreter as you work. For example, complete documentation for the Circle class can be viewed by typing help(Circle) at the Python prompt.

Once you know how to create and manipulate circles, it will not take much effort to learn to create and manipulate squares. Circles and squares are not identical; there are a few ways in which they differ. But there are significantly more ways in which they are similar. To demonstrate the basic use of the individual classes, we spend the rest of this section composing a simple picture of a house with scenery. This example does not show every single feature of the graphics library, but it should provide a good introduction.

Circle

As our first concrete example of a drawable class, we examine the Circle class. A new circle can be instantiated as

```
>>> sun = Circle()
```

However, the Circle is *not* automatically added to our Canvas. In general, a programmer may wish to have multiple canvases and shapes, choosing which shape is added to which canvas. So a drawable object is not placed onto any canvas until we explicitly add it. This is done by using the add method of the Canvas class. Assuming that we are still working with the original canvas that we created in Section 3.1, the syntax we use is

```
>>> paper.add(sun)
```

Having typed the command to add the sun to the paper, we might wonder where it is. By default, this circle has a radius of 10 pixels, a black border, transparent interior, and a center position of (0,0). So it has indeed been added; you just need to look carefully at the top left corner of the screen (shown in Figure 3.5). We see only the portion of the circle that is within the canvas view. The rest of the circle is there in spirit, but not currently visible. Since this is not exactly how we envisioned the sun, let's go ahead and change the settings by calling several methods supported by the Circle class.

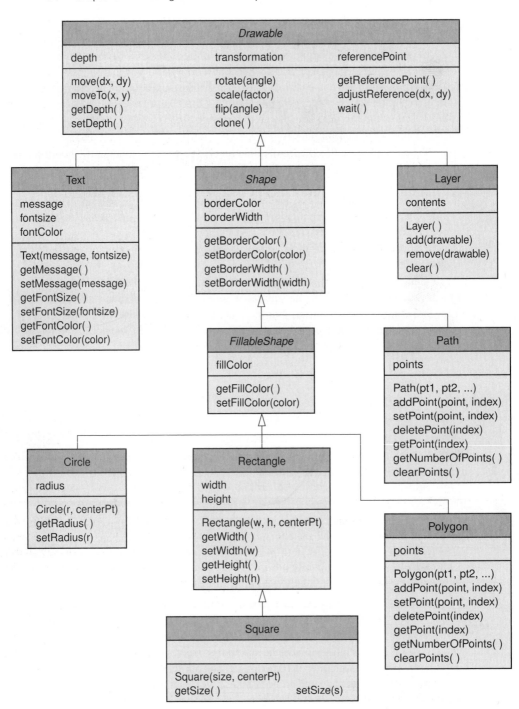

FIGURE 3.4: An overview of the Drawable objects.

FIGURE 3.5: A Canvas with a brand new Circle added (centered at the top left).

```
>>> sun.setRadius(30)
>>> sun.setFillColor('yellow')
>>> sun.move(250, 50)
```

Having made these changes to our sun, our scene now appears as shown in Figure 3.6. The first of these commands changes the radius of the circle. The second command changes the interior color of the shape to yellow (rather than the default, which is transparent). The third command repositions the shape relative to the canvas. The two parameters sent to move represent a change along the x-axis and y-axis respectively. Since our circle was originally centered at position $(0,0)$, it will be centered as a result at position $(250, 50)$. However, each move is relative to the previous position. So if we were to call sun.move(0, 20) at this point, the sun would not move to position (0, 20) but would instead move 0 pixels to the right and 20 pixels down, and therefore be positioned at $(250, 70)$.

Although it is fine to create a default circle and then to mutate it, some (but not all) of its settings can be specified as optional parameters to the constructor. The Circle constructor accepts up to two additional parameters. The first parameter specifies the initial radius. Thus a call to Circle(30) could be used to create a circle with radius 30, although still centered at the origin with a black border and transparent interior. A second optional parameter can be used to choose a different initial center position. This param-eter should be an instance of another class from our graphics package, named Point. A Point is a rather simple class that allows us to represent the two coordinates of a posi-tion as a single object, rather than as two distinct integers (in Chapter 6 we will even implement such a class). A new Point instance can be created using a syntax such as

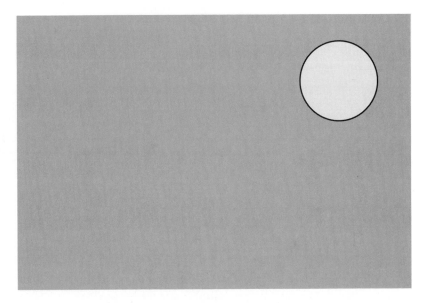

FIGURE 3.6: Our scene after reconfiguring the sun.

Point(250,50). Therefore, we could have partially configured our original sun using the syntax sun = Circle(30, Point(250,50)). That circle would still have a default border of black and a transparent interior. Alternative colors can only be selected *after* constructing the circle. (As the designers of the cs1graphics package, we could have included further optional parameters for the constructor, but we opted for the simpler design.)

Square

As the next piece of our scene, we use a white square as the front of the house. The Square class is another example of a FillableShape. In fact, it supports almost the identical behav‐iors of a circle, except that its size is described based upon the length of a side instead of the radius of the circle. The constructor for the class accepts two parameters, the first being the width (and thus height) of the square and the second being a Point that designates the initial placement of the square's center. If these parameters are not specified, a default square is 10×10 and centered at $(0,0)$. We create the front of our house and add it to our scene as follows:

```
>>> facade = Square(60, Point(140,130))
>>> facade.setFillColor('white')
>>> paper.add(facade)
```

It is also possible to change the size of a square after it has been created, using a syntax such as facade.setSize(60).

Rectangle

Another available shape is a Rectangle, which is similar to a Square except that we can set its width and height independently. By default, a rectangle has a width of 20 pixels, a height of 10 pixels, and is centered at the origin. However, the initial geometry can be specified using three optional parameters to the constructor, respectively specifying the width, the height, and the center point. Adding to our ongoing picture, we place a chimney on top of our house with the following commands:

```
>>> chimney = Rectangle(15, 28, Point(155,85))
>>> chimney.setFillColor('red')
>>> paper.add(chimney)
```

We carefully design the geometry so that the chimney appears to rest on top of the right side of the house. Recall that the facade is a 60-pixel square centered with a y-coordinate of 130. So the top edge of that facade has a y-coordinate of 100. To rest above, our chimney is centered vertically at 85 but with a height of 28. So it extends along the y-axis from 71 to 99. Alternatively, we could have waited until after the rectangle had been constructed to adjust those settings, using the setWidth and setHeight methods.

We take this opportunity to distinguish between the interior of a shape and its border. The chimney as described above has a red interior but a thin black outline. For all of the shapes we have seen thus far, we can separately control the color of the interior, via setFillColor, and the color of the border, via setBorderColor. If we want to get rid of the border for our chimney, we can accomplish this in one of three ways. The first is chimney.setBorderColor('red'). This does not really get rid of the border but colors it the same as the interior. It is also possible to set the border color to a special color 'Transparent', in which case it is not even drawn. Finally, we can adjust the *width* of the border itself. A call to chimney.setBorderWidth(0) should make the border unseen, even if it were still designated as black.

Polygon

The Polygon class provides a much more general shape, allowing for filled polygons with arbitrarily many sides. The geometry of a polygon is specified by identifying the position of each corner, as ordered along the boundary. As was the case with other shapes, the initial geometry of a polygon can be specified using optional parameters to the constructor. Because polygons may have many points, the constructor accepts an arbitrary number of points as optional parameters. For example, we might add an evergreen tree to our scene by creating a green triangle as follows:

```
>>> tree = Polygon(Point(50,80),Point(30,140),Point(70,140))
>>> tree.setFillColor('darkGreen')
>>> paper.add(tree)
```

The resulting scene is shown in Figure 3.7. When specifying the points, they must come in order as seen on the border of the polygon, but it does not matter whether that order is clockwise or counterclockwise. By default, the polygon's reference point is its first point.

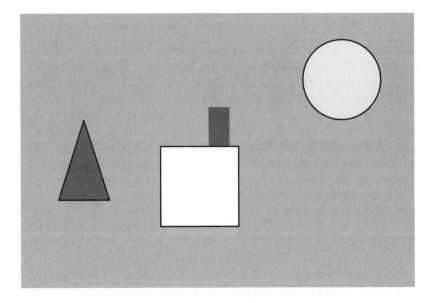

FIGURE 3.7: Further progress on our scene.

It is also possible to add additional points to a polygon after it is constructed. This is done by calling the addPoint method. By default the new point is appended to the end of the current sequence of points. For example, we could have created our tree as follows:

```
>>> tree = Polygon()
>>> tree.addPoint(Point(50,80))
>>> tree.addPoint(Point(30,140))
>>> tree.addPoint(Point(70,140))
>>> tree.setFillColor('darkGreen')
>>> paper.add(tree)
```

The addPoint method can also be used to add a new point into the middle of the existing sequence of points. In this case, an optional second parameter is used to designate the index of the new point within the sequence of points. Just as with Python's lists in Section 2.2, the first point is considered to have index 0, the next point index 1, and so on. For example, a concave angle could be added at the bottom of the tree by inserting a new point as

```
>>> tree.addPoint(Point(50,120), 2)
```

An existing point can be replaced with a new value using the setPoint method. The first parameter is the new point value and the second is an integer index. For example, we could raise the tip of our tree using the syntax tree.setPoint(Point(50,70), 0). An existing point can be removed altogether using the syntax deletePoint(i), where i is the index.

Path

A Path is a shape that connects a series of points; in this respect, it is very similar to a Polygon. However, there are two key differences: the ends of a path are not explicitly con–nected to each other, and a path does not have an interior. A Path qualifies in our hierarchy as a Shape but not as a FillableShape. We can change the color by calling setBorderColor, and the thickness by calling setBorderWidth. Its behaviors are otherwise similar to those described for the Polygon (e.g., addPoint, setPoint, deletePoint). As a simple example of a path, we add a bit of smoke coming out of the top of our chimney.

```
>>> smoke = Path(Point(155,70), Point(150,65),
                 Point(160,55), Point(155,50))
>>> paper.add(smoke)
```

A path between two points is simply a line segment (akin to the hypothetical Segment class modeled in Figure 1.13). Let's add a few rays around our sun using four simple paths. We place one ray to the left of and below the sun; we will call this object sunraySW to des–ignate this as the "southwest" of the four rays. The biggest challenge in this case is to determine the proper coordinates. We create it as follows:

```
>>> sunraySW = Path(Point(225,75), Point(210,90))
>>> sunraySW.setBorderColor('yellow')
>>> sunraySW.setBorderWidth(6)
>>> paper.add(sunraySW)
```

Sun rays emanating in other directions can be declared in similar fashion. Our updated drawing to this point is shown in Figure 3.8.

Text and Image classes

Two additional classes are not used in the current drawing of a house but are very helpful in general. The first of these is the Text class, used for rendering character strings within the drawing area of the canvas. The constructor takes two parameters: the first is a string designating the actual message to be displayed, and the second is a font size (12 by default). This class fits into our hierarchy somewhat separately; it does not even qualify as being a Shape (as it does not support a concept of a border). Instead, it has dedicated methods to support the manipulation of the message, the font size, and the font color. Once created, the text can be repositioned to a desired location. By default, the reference point for a text object is aligned with the center of the displayed message. The summary of its methods is included in Figure 3.4 on page 94; we provide an example usage in a later case study in this chapter.

Although not shown in Figure 3.4, cs1graphics includes an Image class that pro–vides support for using a raw image loaded from a file. An image object is constructed by specifying the underlying file name, as in Image('lightbulb.gif'). However, the precise set of supported file formats (e.g., gif, jpg, bmp, tiff) will depend upon your com–puter system. When controlling the placement of an image on a canvas, the reference point is aligned with the top left corner of the image.

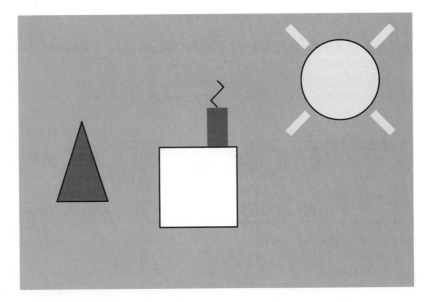

FIGURE 3.8: Sun rays and smoke have been added to our scene.

3.2.1 Colors

We have seen the use of various colors for the borders and interiors of our shapes. Thus far we have relied upon names like 'skyBlue' when specifying a desired color. A color is represented behind the scene by what is known as its **RGB value**. This is a **tuple** of three numbers that represent the intensity of red, green, and blue respectively (hence the acronym, RGB), using a scale from 0 (no intensity) to 255 (full intensity). Names like 'skyBlue' are predefined for convenience by the cs1graphics package and mapped to an appropriate RGB value, for example, (136, 206, 235).

The set of predefined color names is somewhat arbitrary; you may type help(Color) in the interpreter for more information. However, you may define new colors by directly specifying the underlying RGB tuple in place of a name. As an example, if we wanted our sky to be slightly brighter blue than the official 'skyBlue', we could use the command paper.setBackgroundColor((136, 206, 244)). Note the use of parentheses here. The caller is sending a tuple as a single parameter; see Section 2.3.2 for a discussion of tuples.

3.2.2 Depths

To further improve our scene we wish to add grass to the picture. We do so by placing one very large green rectangle to cover the bottom portion of the sky blue background. We also add a window, and roof to our house. The updated image we have in mind is shown in Figure 3.9, however, achieving this effect brings up a new issue. While the shapes for the grass, window and roof are simple, we have to consider the apparent overlap among the objects. The tree and house must appear to be in front of the grass, the window in front of the house, and the roof behind the chimney yet in front of the facade of the house.

FIGURE 3.9: Demonstrating the use of depths in placing the grass, window, and roof.

The relative ordering of conflicting shapes is controlled by an underlying numeric attribute representing the "depth" of each drawable object. By default, all objects are assigned a depth value of 50 and their relative ordering is arbitrary. However, those depths can be changed to control the image. When two or more objects overlap, the one with the smallest depth will be drawn "nearer" to the viewer. For example, by giving the grass a greater depth than the default, say grass.setDepth(75), it will be drawn behind both the tree and the house. This is not a three-dimensional rendering, so the picture will look the same no matter whether we set this depth to 75 or 100 or 1000. In similar spirit, we might give the window a depth of 30 so that it is drawn in front of the house facade. We set the depth of the roof to 30 so that it is in front of the facade, yet the chimney a depth of 20 so that it appears even nearer than the roof. Although we have given both the window and the roof a depth of 30, those shapes do not overlap so the conflict is irrelevant. The complete source code used to generate our latest image is given in Figure 3.10.

 A WORD OF WARNING

When objects have overlapping geometries, their relative appearance on a canvas is based upon specified depths. An object with greater depth will appear to be obscured by one with lesser depth. Items with equal depths are ordered arbitrarily.

```
1   from cs1graphics import *
2   paper = Canvas(300, 200, 'skyBlue', 'My World')
3
4   sun = Circle(30, Point(250,50))
5   sun.setFillColor('yellow')
6   paper.add(sun)
7
8   facade = Square(60, Point(140,130))
9   facade.setFillColor('white')
10  paper.add(facade)
11
12  chimney = Rectangle(15, 28, Point(155,85))
13  chimney.setFillColor('red')
14  chimney.setBorderColor('red')
15  paper.add(chimney)
16
17  tree = Polygon(Point(50,80), Point(30,140), Point(70,140))
18  tree.setFillColor('darkGreen')
19  paper.add(tree)
20
21  smoke = Path(Point(155,70), Point(150,65), Point(160,55), Point(155,50))
22  paper.add(smoke)
23
24  sunraySW = Path(Point(225,75), Point(210,90))
25  sunraySW.setBorderColor('yellow')
26  sunraySW.setBorderWidth(6)
27  paper.add(sunraySW)
28  sunraySE = Path(Point(275,75), Point(290,90))
29  sunraySE.setBorderColor('yellow')
30  sunraySE.setBorderWidth(6)
31  paper.add(sunraySE)
32  sunrayNE = Path(Point(275,25), Point(290,10))
33  sunrayNE.setBorderColor('yellow')
34  sunrayNE.setBorderWidth(6)
35  paper.add(sunrayNE)
36  sunrayNW = Path(Point(225,25), Point(210,10))
37  sunrayNW.setBorderColor('yellow')
38  sunrayNW.setBorderWidth(6)
39  paper.add(sunrayNW)
```

FIGURE 3.10: Complete source code for drawing our house (continued on next page).

```
40   grass = Rectangle(300, 80, Point(150,160))
41   grass.setFillColor('green')
42   grass.setBorderColor('green')
43   grass.setDepth(75)                  # must be behind house and tree
44   paper.add(grass)
45
46   window = Rectangle(15, 20, Point(130,120))
47   paper.add(window)
48   window.setFillColor('black')
49   window.setBorderColor('red')
50   window.setBorderWidth(2)
51   window.setDepth(30)
52
53   roof = Polygon(Point(105, 105), Point(175, 105), Point(170,85), Point(110,85))
54   roof.setFillColor('darkgray')
55   roof.setDepth(30)                   # in front of facade
56   chimney.setDepth(20)                # in front of roof
57   paper.add(roof)
```

FIGURE 3.10 (continuation): Complete source code for drawing our house.

3.3   Rotating, Scaling, and Flipping

By design, all of the Drawable objects can be rotated, scaled, or flipped. For these operations, the object's reference point has greater significance. It serves as a point of the shape
that stays fixed during the transformation. Earlier, we used the analogy of a shape's reference point as the place where a thumbtack attaches it to a canvas. When an object is
moved, the reference point moves relative to the canvas but stays in the same place within
the context of the shape. The thumbtack and shape move together as they are stuck elsewhere on the canvas. The effect of rotating a square that is tacked through its center is
quite different than if rotating that square when tacked near a corner.

In Section 3.2, we noted that each shape has a natural location for its initial reference point. For example, the reference point of a Square, Circle, Rectangle, or Text is
initially at its center; for a Polygon or Path, it is initially the location of the first point;
for an Image it is the top left corner. However, we can change the relative location of
that reference point if we wish. All drawable objects support a method with the signature
adjustReference(dx, dy). A call to this method behaves as follows. The shape is not moved
at all relative to the canvas. Instead, the thumbtack holding it is taken out and moved by
the specified amount in each direction, and then stuck back through the shape to hold it in
its place. This call has no immediately visible effect on the screen. But it can be used as a
precursor to a later rotation or scaling to achieve desired results.

We should note that the reference point is not actually required to lie within the
boundary of the shape; in this way, our thumbtack analogy breaks down somewhat. For
example, we could choose to move the reference point for a circle to be 100 pixels to its
left, making it easier to animate the moon orbiting around the earth.

Rotating

With the preceding discussion of the reference point, we are ready to discuss rotation. Formally, drawable objects support a rotate method that takes a parameter specifying the clockwise rotation measured in degrees. That value can be an integer or floating-point number. As an example, we can rotate a Square $20°$ about its center point as follows:

```
>>> diamond = Square(40, Point(100,100))
>>> diamond.rotate(20)
```

This rotates the square, leaving its center point fixed. If we want to rotate the square about its bottom left corner, we need to first adjust the reference point. For example,

```
>>> block = Square(40, Point(100,100))
>>> block.adjustReference(-20, 20)
>>> block.rotate(20)
```

Both of these scenarios are diagrammed in Figure 3.11, with the original and new positions superimposed and the reference point highlighted.

Scaling

For the most basic shapes, we already have specialized methods to accomplish scaling. For example, we can directly modify the radius of a circle, or the width and height of a rectangle. Yet there is a more general approach that applies to all drawable objects. Each supports a method scale that takes a single parameter specifying a (positive) multiplicative factor by which the object is to be scaled. If that factor is greater than one, it causes the size to increase; when the factor is less than one it causes the size to decrease. For intricate shapes, the use of the scale method can help simplify otherwise complicated geometry.

When performing a scale, the reference point remains fixed. All other points in the shape are scaled relative to that reference point. To demonstrate the effect, Figure 3.12 shows two examples of a pentagon being scaled. In each example, the pentagon is scaled by a factor of 0.5. Yet in the first case, it is scaled with the center as the reference point; in the second case, the rightmost corner serves as the reference point.

Flipping

Another convenient transformation is to take a mirror image of an object. For this reason, drawable objects support a flip( ) method. By default, this causes a flip to take place across a *vertical axis of symmetry* passing through the reference point. In effect, this causes a left-to-right, right-to-left flip as shown in the first part of Figure 3.13.

To allow a flip in an arbitrary direction, the method accepts an optional parameter that specifies the clockwise rotation of the axis of symmetry away from vertical. For example the call flip(10) produces the result shown on the right side of Figure 3.13, with a slightly askew axis of symmetry. As is the case with the other transformation, notice that the reference point always remains fixed by this operation.

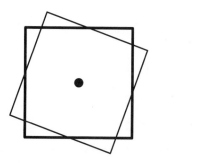
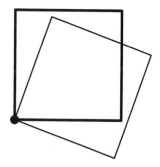

FIGURE 3.11: Rotating a square $20°$ in the clockwise direction. In both diagrams the original position is drawn with darker border and the resulting position with lighter border. In the case on the left, the square is rotated about its center point. On the right, the same square is rotated about its lower left corner.

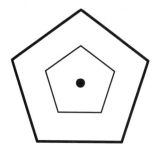
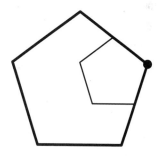

FIGURE 3.12: Scaling a pentagon about two different reference points. In both diagrams the original position is drawn with darker border and the resulting position with lighter border. On the left, the pentagon is scaled relative to its center point. On the right, the pentagon is scaled about the rightmost corner.

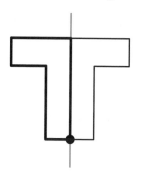
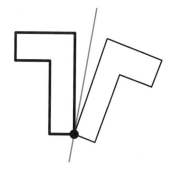

FIGURE 3.13: Flipping a flag about two different axes of symmetry. In both diagrams the original position is drawn with darker border and the resulting position with lighter border. On the left, the flag is flipped about the vertical axes by default with flip( ). The right shows the result of flip(10).

FIGURE 3.14: A scene with two trees; the right tree is drawn larger than the left.

3.4 Cloning

Although an exact copy of an existing shape could presumably be constructed and con-figured from scratch, the Drawable types support a convenient clone method that returns a brand new copy. The clone has precisely the same settings as the original element, but is not automatically added to any canvases. Once created, the clone can be manipulated independently of the original. Figure 3.14 shows an updated version of our scene with a cloned tree that has the same shape but a different location and size from the original.

```
otherTree = tree.clone( )
otherTree.move(170,30)
otherTree.scale(1.2)
paper.add(otherTree)
```

3.5 Case Study: Smiley Face

Many interesting pictures can be drawn using the techniques we have learned thus far; we encourage you to have some fun. As an example, we draw the "smiley face" shown in Figure 3.15 using the code in Figure 3.16. We start with a yellow circle with black border for the overall head. The crescent-shaped mouth is a clever illusion. There is no shape in the package for representing a crescent directly. Instead, the visual effect is created with depths. A black circle is drawn on top of the original face (see lines 9–13), then a well-placed yellow circle on top of that black circle (see lines 15–19). The remaining facial features are drawn with the default depth, and thus appear in front of the mouth.

FIGURE 3.15: A smiley face drawn using the graphics package.

```
1   from cs1graphics import *
2   paper = Canvas( )
3
4   head = Circle(75, Point(100,100))
5   head.setFillColor('yellow')
6   head.setDepth(60)
7   paper.add(head)
8
9   mouth = Circle(40, Point(100,110))
10  mouth.setFillColor('black')
11  mouth.setBorderWidth(0)
12  mouth.setDepth(52)
13  paper.add(mouth)
14
15  mouthCover = Circle(40, Point(100,100))
16  mouthCover.setFillColor('yellow')
17  mouthCover.setBorderWidth(0)
18  mouthCover.setDepth(51)
19  paper.add(mouthCover)
20
21  nose = Polygon(Point(100,90), Point(92,110), Point(108,110))
22  nose.setFillColor('black')
23  paper.add(nose)
24
25  leftEye = Circle(10, Point(70,80))
26  leftEye.setFillColor('black')
27  rightEye = Circle(10, Point(130,80))
28  rightEye.setFillColor('black')
29  paper.add(leftEye)
30  paper.add(rightEye)
```

FIGURE 3.16: Code to draw a smiley face (continued on next page).

```
31   leftEyebrow = Path(Point(60,65), Point(70,60), Point(80,65))
32   leftEyebrow.setBorderWidth(3)
33   leftEyebrow.adjustReference(10,15)      # set to center of left eyeball
34   leftEyebrow.rotate(−15)
35   paper.add(leftEyebrow)
36
37   rightEyebrow = leftEyebrow.clone( )
38   rightEyebrow.flip( )                    # still relative to eyeball center
39   rightEyebrow.move(60,0)                 # distance between eyeball centers
40   paper.add(rightEyebrow)
```

FIGURE 3.16 (continuation): Code to draw a smiley face.

The eyebrows are created using a combination of techniques. We start at lines 31 and 32, creating the left eyebrow as a thickened path which is centered directly above the left eye. To achieve a crooked appearance, we then rotate the eyebrow counterclockwise about the center of the eye itself. This requires careful use of the eyebrow's reference point. Upon construction, the path's reference point is aligned with the first declared point of that path: $(60, 65)$ in this case. Since the left eye is centered at $(70, 80)$ we adjust the eyebrow's reference point by $(10, 15)$ at line 33. Once that has been done, we rotate $15°$ in the counterclockwise direction at line 34.

Though we could create the right eyebrow using a similar technique, we instead make a clone of the left eyebrow and then flip that clone horizontally. Because the reference point for the brow was already re-aligned with the center of the eyeball, the flip at line 38 causes the new brow to be cocked to the right rather than the left. However the new brow is still located near the left eye. Line 39 translates the new brow rightward, precisely the distance separating the two eyes. This causes the right eyebrow to be aligned above the right eye rather than the left eye.

3.6 Layers

Our next class is an extremely valuable tool (and one of our favorites). It allows us to treat a collection of other elements as a single composite object that we term a Layer. For motivation, let's add a car to our earlier scene. Visually, we could achieve the image of a car perhaps by using three separate shapes: the car body and two tires that appear nearer than the body. However, if we want to move the "car" elsewhere we have to move the body and each tire. Separately moving each piece the same amount is time consuming and error prone. We might accidentally forget to move a tire, or move it by the wrong amount. Things get even more complicated when working out the correct geometry for scaling or rotating the car or when working with a more intricate design using more elements. A much better programming technique is to group those related shapes into a single composite object. In this section, we introduce a Layer class for this purpose. A Layer is sort of a hybrid of a Canvas and a Drawable. It serves as a container for other shapes while also serving as a Drawable object that can itself be added to a Canvas (or even to another Layer).

Earlier, we explained our drawing package through the analogy of physical shapes being attached to a canvas. We wish to extend this analogy to layers. We consider a layer to be a thin clear film. We can attach many shapes directly to this film rather than to the canvas. Of course the film itself can be positioned over the canvas and combined with other shapes to make a complete image. In fact, this is precisely the technology that advanced the creation of animated movies in the early 1900s. Rather than drawing the artwork on a single piece of paper, different layers of the background and characters were separated on clear sheets of celluloid. These were commonly called animation cels. The advantages were great. The individual cels could still be layered, with appropriate depths, to produce the desired result. Yet each cel could be moved and rotated independently of the others to adjust the overall image. For example, a character could be on a cel of its own and then moved across a background in successive frames.

We demonstrate the use of the Layer class by adding a car to our earlier house scene. Before concerning ourselves with the overall scene, we compose the layer itself. A layer is somewhat similar to a canvas in that it has its own relative coordinate system. Shapes can be added to the layer, in which case the shape's reference point determines the placement of that shape relative to the *layer's* coordinate system (i.e., the shape is tacked to a position on the layer). We use the origin of the layer as a landmark when placing individual elements. A sketch of our suggested geometry for the components of a car is given in Figure 3.17. We place the car so that the tires rest on the x-axis and so that the car is centered horizontally about the origin. We build this model using the code in Figure 3.18. Three individual parts are added to a new layer with coordinates based upon our sketch. When placed on a layer, a shape's depth determines how that shape appears relative to other shapes on the same layer. We set the body's depth to 60 so that it appears behind the two tires, which have default depth of 50.

At this point, we have created our layer but not yet displayed it. Yet the layer is itself a Drawable object, and so it supports all of the familiar behaviors. If we add the layer to a canvas, the reference point of the layer (its origin, by default) represents where that layer is tacked upon the canvas. A layer has its own depth attribute, used to determine whether

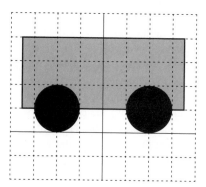

FIGURE 3.17: Geometric sketch of a car, within the coordinate system of a layer. The solid grid lines represent the x-axis and y-axis. The dashed grid lines designate a separation of 10 pixels each.

```
car = Layer( )
tire1 = Circle(10, Point(−20,−10))
tire1.setFillColor('black')
car.add(tire1)

tire2 = Circle(10, Point(20,−10))
tire2.setFillColor('black')
car.add(tire2)

body = Rectangle(70, 30, Point(0, −25))
body.setFillColor('blue')
body.setDepth(60)              # behind the tires
car.add(body)
```

FIGURE 3.18: Code to create a Layer that represents a car.

the layer is considered to be above or below other objects on the canvas. So to add the car to our house scene, we position in properly relative to the canvas's coordinate system. This is accomplished with the following:

```
car.moveTo(110,180)
car.setDepth(20)
paper.add(car)
```

The resulting image is portrayed in Figure 3.19. It is important to keep straight the distinction between the canvas's frame of reference and the layer's frame of reference. The car's placement on the canvas was made according to the coordinate (110, 180) of the canvas. More specifically it is the reference point of the layer (the hypothetical thumbtack through the layer's origin) that is tacked to the canvas at that coordinate. This example also demonstrates an important subtlety in the use of depths. Recall that when building the layer we left the tires with the default depth of 50 and gave the car body a depth of 60. That is why the body appears behind the tires. However, you will notice that the car body appears in front of the house facade, even though that facade has depth 50. The reason is that the depths of individual components are only relevant when compared to other elements in the same context. There are three objects added to the layer and their depths distinguish how those objects are interleaved. But the placement of the layer as a whole onto the canvas is based upon the depth attribute of the layer object. In this case we intentionally set the layer's depth to 30 so that the entire car appears nearer than the house.

As a Drawable object, a layer can be rotated, flipped, cloned, or scaled about its reference point. For example, if we were to scale our car, that imaginary thumbtack through the origin of the layer remains fixed, and so the bottom of the tires remain at the same y-coordinate. So if our car appears to be resting on top of a street or driveway, it will remain so when scaled. Similarly, a rotated car could be placed properly on a hill by placing its origin on the edge of the hill.

FIGURE 3.19: Adding a car in front of our house.

3.7 Animation

Most of our efforts thus far have been used to design a single static image, albeit with increasing complexity. Yet graphics can be used to generate intricate animations, involving multiple scenes and moving objects. Creating an animation can be straightforward. In this section we address several new issues that arise in the context of animation.

Controlling timing

When working within an interactive interpreter session, we see the immediate effect of each command displayed on the screen. However, if we type a long series of graphical commands into a file and execute that file, chances are that all of the intermediate stages will go by in a blink of an eye. For example, we might wish to move a car across the screen using a series of calls to the move method. Yet the computer is rather quick and may display the images too fast for the eye to see.

To better control the images seen by a viewer, we can use a sleep function that is part of Python's standard time library. We can load this module using the command **from** time **import** sleep, as originally described in Section 2.7. Once the library is loaded, a call to the sleep function causes the program to wait a given number of seconds before proceeding. For example, sleep(1.5) will wait one and a half seconds before proceeding. This command can be used not just in graphical programs, but as part of any software. Within the context of graphics, a pause can be used to give the impression of motion. Consider the following code fragment to move our car.

```
from time import sleep
timeDelay = .25                    # one-quarter second
car.move(−10, 0)
sleep(timeDelay)
car.move(−30, 0)
sleep(timeDelay)
car.move(−60, 0)
sleep(timeDelay)
car.move(−100, 0)
sleep(timeDelay)
```

The speed of the animation can be adjusted by altering the time delay or by having a longer series of motion. Another use for sleep is to produce an animation with multiple frames. We can develop an intricate scene, and then intentionally pause so that the user can take in the scene for a certain amount of time. After the pause, additional code can alter portions of the scene or even compose an entirely new scene for the viewer.

Controlling flicker

There is a drawback in trying to create multiframe animations as we have described. When there are a large number of shapes, or a significant number of separate changes that take place from one frame to the next, there is the possibility that the user may see some partially composed images that we may not intend to have viewed. For example, if one command moves a character's head and the next moves the body, the viewer might glimpse the frac-tion of a second in which the head is detached. Although the viewer may not know exactly what happened, this sort of "flicker" can be distracting.

The use of a layer was one approach to have such motion coordinated, but if several different changes in a scene are to be made, there may still be unwanted artifacts. A common technique for trying to minimize flicker in computer graphics is called **double buffering**. If we need to make ten separate changes when moving from one frame to the next, the idea is the following: don't change the displayed image at all in the interim. While the original frame is still in view, we would like to perform all ten of the hypothetical changes behind the scene. Only after the next frame is computed internally, should it be displayed on the screen for the viewer.

FOR THE GURU

In this chapter, we create motion and frames in an ad hoc way, manually repeating commands to produce the effect. This is not really a good programming style. In Chapter 4, we will introduce a technique known as a **loop** for more elegantly expressing the repetition of commands. Loops can be extremely useful when creating animations.

The cs1graphics package supports a form of double buffering as follows. Until now, we have relied upon the default behavior of a Canvas, which is to immediately display each change to the screen. We refer to this behavior as "auto-refresh" mode. Although it is the default, we can change it by using the setAutoRefresh method. This takes a single boolean parameter. If we call paper.setAutoRefresh(**False**), this turns off the automatic refresh mode and instead reverts to a manual refresh mode. When in this mode, no changes are rendered to the screen unless an explicit call to paper.refresh( ) is made. In the context of an animation, we can enact all of the changes that we want to make behind the scene and then refresh the canvas (and perhaps pause) each time we want to show a new frame to the viewer. To demonstrate this mode, try the following in an interactive session.

```
>>> paper = Canvas(200, 200, 'skyBlue')
>>> ball = Circle(25, Point(100,75))
>>> paper.add(ball)              # ball immediately appears
>>> ball.setRadius(50)          # ball immediately changes
>>> paper.setAutoRefresh(False)
>>> ball.setFillColor('red')    # no visible change
>>> ball.move(50,0)             # no visible change
>>> paper.refresh()             # image is updated
```

When there are relatively few objects in the scene, or relatively few changes being made at a time, there is really not much difference between the quality of automatic refresh mode and manual refresh. However, if you ever start to notice artifacts like flicker in complicated animations, you might try switching to manual refresh. If you want, you can always turn automatic refresh back on using a syntax such as paper.setAutoRefresh(**True**).

3.8 Graphical User Interfaces

When using purely text-based software, the only way a user can interact with a program is by entering text into the console, and only when prompted to do so. For most modern software, users interact with programs through a combination of keyboard strokes and mouse movements and clicks. Users select from menus, click on buttons, and enter text within boxes. Such an interface is known as a ***graphical user interface***, or GUI for short (pronounced "gooey"). In this section, we outline some of the basic support for building simple GUIs using the cs1graphics package.

One of the most important issues for a graphical interface is being able to detect a user ***event***, such as a mouse click or a keystroke. We will explore this concept of ***event-driven programming*** as an advanced topic in Chapter 15, but for now we wish to introduce a few simple features that you can use right away. All of our Drawable objects support a method, named wait( ), that causes the program to pause indefinitely until an event is detected upon the given object. To demonstrate the technique, we provide the following very simple example.

```
1  paper = Canvas( )
2  light = Circle(20, Point(100,100))
3  light.setFillColor('red')
4  paper.add(light)
5  light.wait( )
6  light.setFillColor('green')
```

The key to this example is line 5. When this command is executed, the flow of the program waits indefinitely. You will not immediately see the light change to green. The program is waiting for the user to trigger an event, such as a mouse click, upon the circle. After such a click, the program continues where it left off, causing the light to turn green.

Because wait( ) was specifically called upon the circle instance, the program only continues with a click upon that circle. Mouse clicks elsewhere on the canvas will be ignored. It is possible to wait upon the canvas as a whole. For example, the above program could be augmented with the final two lines.

```
7  paper.wait( )
8  paper.close( )
```

In this case, after turning the light green it waits for another event, this time anywhere on the canvas. Note that such an event does not necessarily need to be on the background; clicking on any part of the canvas (including the circle) suffices.

In the first example, we used wait to control the timing of our program, but we did not take notice of the type of event or the location of the event. However, the wait( ) method provides a return value. To see this, try the following interactively in the interpreter:

```
>>> paper = Canvas()
>>> paper.wait()
```

After typing the second command, the program is waiting for us to trigger an event (notice that we do not yet have a subsequent prompt). If we go ahead and click on the canvas, we get the following continuation:

```
<cs1graphics.Event object at 0x6d52f0>
>>>
```

That return value is an instance of the Event class. Each event stores information about the type of event that occurred (e.g., mouse, keyboard), and additional characteristics. For example, a mouse event stores the coordinates of where the click occurred and which but-ton was used. A keyboard event indicates which key was pressed. Figure 3.20 provides a brief overview of the accessors supported by the Event class. We will explore use of events more fully in Chapter 15, but for now we offer a simple example. The getMouseLocation( ) method returns a Point that represents the location of the mouse at the time the event occurred. For example, here is a program that adds a circle to the canvas centered at the indicated location.

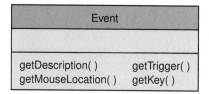

Event
getDescription( )   getTrigger( ) getMouseLocation( )   getKey( )

FIGURE 3.20: The Event class.

```
paper = Canvas( )
cue = paper.wait( )                              # wait indefinitely for user event
ball = Circle(10, cue.getMouseLocation( ))
ball.setFillColor('red')
paper.add(ball)
```

Widgets

We note in passing that the cs1graphics package includes several additional classes to support graphical user interfaces. Typically these tools are known as *widgets*. A TextBox allows a user to enter text that can later be retrieved from the program, and a Button serves as a clickable rectangle with a label. More complete documentation on their use is available online, and we will discuss their implementations in later chapters. For now, we provide the following brief demonstration.

```
paper = Canvas( )
nameInput = TextBox(150, 50, Point(100,10))
paper.add(nameInput)
submit = Button('Enter name', Point(100,80))
paper.add(submit)
submit.wait( )
welcome = Text('Hello, ' + nameInput.getMessage( ))
welcome.move(100, 150)
paper.add(welcome)
```

This interface displays a textbox and a button. When the button is pressed, it incorporates the characters previously entered into the text box into a newly displayed greeting.

 A WORD OF WARNING

If you call wait( ) on an object such as a circle that has a transparent interior, it will only respond to clicks that take place *on the border*.

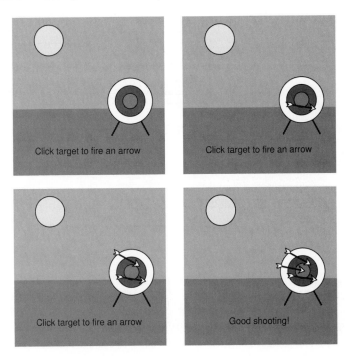

FIGURE 3.21: A few frames from the animation.

3.9 Case Study: Flying Arrows

We will combine the skills that we have learned to create an animated scene. It consists of a target and arrows flying at the target whenever the canvas is clicked on; see Figure 3.21 for a few images from the animation. The complete code for the program is given in Figure 3.22. In lines 1–13 we begin by setting up a sky blue canvas with grass and a sun. Next, in lines 15–33, we assemble the target as a separate layer. The local geometry of the target is designed so that the center of the bullseye coincides with the origin of the layer's coordinate system. Three concentric circles are added so that smaller circles appear in front of larger circles, with a path used to represent the legs holding up the target. Finally, the entire layer is added to the scene and positioned accordingly.

In our eventual animation, we will shoot three separate arrows. However, since all of the arrows have the same geometry and initial position, we create a model for the first (lines 36–48) and then clone it (lines 49 and 50). Each arrow is a layer with three components: a shaft, a tip and a fletching. The geometry is designed with the arrow facing right and with the tip of the arrow aligned with the origin of the layer. So when we rotate the arrow, the tip serves as the reference point. We note that none of the arrows are in the scene yet. We will add them one at a time, based upon the user's interactions.

To control the animation, we rely upon use of the wait method. For example, the call to target.wait( ) at line 56 causes the entire program to delay indefinitely. The program will continue only after the user clicks the mouse on the target. Since the target is a layer, the program recognizes a click on any portion of that target (including the legs). That causes

```
1    from cs1graphics import *
2    from time import sleep
3
4    scene = Canvas( )
5    scene.setBackgroundColor('skyBlue')
6    grass = Rectangle(200, 80, Point(100,160))
7    grass.setFillColor('green')
8    grass.setBorderColor('green')
9    grass.setDepth(100)
10   scene.add(grass)
11   sun = Circle(20, Point(50,30))
12   sun.setFillColor('yellow')
13   scene.add(sun)
14
15   target = Layer( )
16   outside = Circle(30)
17   outside.setFillColor('white')
18   outside.setDepth(49)
19   target.add(outside)
20   middle = Circle(20)
21   middle.setFillColor('blue')
22   middle.setDepth(48)
23   target.add(middle)
24   inside = Circle(10)
25   inside.setFillColor('red')
26   inside.setDepth(47)
27   target.add(inside)
28   legs = Path(Point(-25,45), Point(0,0), Point(25,45))
29   legs.setBorderWidth(2)
30   target.add(legs)
31   target.move(160,110)
32   target.setDepth(75)            # in front of grass; behind arrows
33   scene.add(target)
34
35   # prepare three arrows, but do not yet add to scene
36   arrow1 = Layer( )
37   tip = Polygon(Point(0,0), Point(-8,5), Point(-5,0), Point(-8,-5))
38   tip.setFillColor('white')
39   arrow1.add(tip)
40   shaft = Path(Point(-30,0), Point(-5,0))
41   shaft.setBorderWidth(2)
42   shaft.setDepth(51)
43   arrow1.add(shaft)
```

FIGURE 3.22: The code for the arrow scene (continued on next page).

```
44   fletching = Polygon(Point(-30,0), Point(-33,-3), Point(-40,-3),
45                       Point(-36,0), Point(-38,3), Point(-36,3))
46   fletching.setFillColor('white')
47   arrow1.add(fletching)
48   arrow1.move(15,120)              # initial position
49   arrow2 = arrow1.clone( )
50   arrow3 = arrow1.clone( )
51
52   dialogue = Text('Click target to fire an arrow')
53   dialogue.move(100,170)
54   scene.add(dialogue)
55
56   target.wait( )                   # wait indefinitely for user event on target
57   scene.add(arrow1)
58   arrow1.rotate(-20)
59   sleep(0.25)
60   arrow1.move(41,-15)
61   arrow1.rotate(7)
62   sleep(0.25)
63   arrow1.move(41,-5)
64   arrow1.rotate(7)
65   sleep(0.25)
66   arrow1.move(41,5)
67   arrow1.rotate(7)
68   sleep(0.25)
69   arrow1.move(41,17)
70   arrow1.rotate(7)
71
72   target.wait( )                   # wait indefinitely for user event on target
73   scene.add(arrow2)
74   arrow2.rotate(-40)
75   sleep(0.25)
76   arrow2.move(39,-22)
77   arrow2.rotate(17)
78   sleep(0.25)
79   arrow2.move(39,-12)
80   arrow2.rotate(17)
81   sleep(0.25)
82   arrow2.move(39,3)
83   arrow2.rotate(17)
84   sleep(0.25)
85   arrow2.move(39,13)
86   arrow2.rotate(17)
```

FIGURE 3.22 (continuation): The code for the arrow scene (continued on next page).

```
 87  scene.add(arrow3)
 88  arrow3.rotate(−30)
 89  sleep(0.25)
 90  arrow3.move(37,−26)
 91  arrow3.rotate(10)
 92  sleep(0.25)
 93  arrow3.move(37,−11)
 94  arrow3.rotate(10)
 95  sleep(0.25)
 96  arrow3.move(37,6)
 97  arrow3.rotate(10)
 98  sleep(0.25)
 99  arrow3.move(37,21)
100  arrow3.rotate(10)
101  dialogue.setMessage('Good shooting!')
102
103  scene.wait( )                    # wait for user event anywhere on canvas
104  scene.close( )
```

FIGURE 3.22 (continuation): The code for the arrow scene.

the first arrow to be added to the scene (line 57) and the subsequent animation (lines 58–70) as it moves toward the target. The second and third arrows are handled in similar fashion in lines 72–101, although with slightly different flights. Finally, we call scene.wait( ) at line 103, before closing the window. This has a similar effect to the earlier delays, but since wait is being invoked on the canvas as a whole, the user may click anywhere to continue.

To create a smoother animation we could have more frames with a smaller time step. Unfortunately, we would need many more lines of code if using the current programming style. In the next chapter, we will learn new techniques that could be used to better automate the animation of the arrow. Notice as well that the flight of the arrows is predetermined in our program; it has no relation to the location of the mouse click (though an interesting challenge for an exercise).

 FOR THE GURU

Python supports use of several graphics libraries. Our cs1graphics package is based upon another common library known as *Tkinter*. While cs1graphics is useful for many purposes, Tkinter is designed to support more industrial applications.

3.10   Chapter Review

3.10.1   Key Points

Graphics Primitives

- Creating a Canvas instance constructs a window. Various objects can be visualized by calling the add method of the canvas.

- The window for a canvas does not close unless the user manually closes the window through the operating system or the close method of the canvas is called.

- Coordinates are measured from the top left corner of the window. The x-coordinate speci-fies the number of pixels to the right of this point and the y-coordinate specifies the number of pixels below this point.

- Only Drawable objects can be added to a canvas.

Modifying Drawable Objects

- There are mutators to change the location, color, border color, position, and other features for each drawable object.

- A drawable object can be rotated, scaled, or flipped relative to its reference point. This reference point can be reconfigured using the adjustReference member function.

Depths

- When two or more drawable objects overlap on a canvas, the relative ordering of those objects is determined according to their specified depth attribute. Shapes with smaller depths are drawn in front of those with larger depths.

Layers

- A Layer represents a collection of objects that is treated as a single shape. They layer can be added, moved, rotated or scaled, just as with any other Drawable instance.

- Depths of objects within a layer only affects how the objects in the layer appear relative to each other. The depth of the layer controls whether all the shapes in that layer appears in front or behind objects that are not part of the layer.

Animation

- A time delay for an animation can be achieved by calling the sleep function imported from the time module.

- Flicker can be reduced in an animation by turning auto-refresh off for the canvas and calling refresh each time you want the canvas's image rendered to the screen.

Events

- Calling the wait( ) method of the Canvas class causes the program to wait indefinitely until the user triggers an event on the window, such as a mouse click or keypress.

- Calling the wait( ) method on an individual drawable object waits until the user triggers and event specifically upon that particular object.

- The wait( ) function returns an Event instance that contains information about which mouse button or key was pressed, and the cursor location at that time.

3.10.2 Glossary

canvas A graphics window on which objects can be drawn.

clone A copy of an object.

double buffering A technique for avoiding flicker in animation by computing incremental changes internally before displaying a new image to the viewer.

event An external stimulus on a program, such as a user's mouse click.

event-driven programming A style in which a program passively waits for external events to occur, responding appropriately to those events as needed.

graphical user interface (GUI) A design allowing a user to interact with software through a combination of mouse movements, clicks, and keyboard commands.

pixel The smallest displayable element in a digital picture.

reference point A particular location for a cs1graphics.Drawable instance that is used when determining the placement of the object upon a canvas's coordinate system. The reference point remains fixed when the object is scaled, rotated, or flipped.

RGB value A form for specifying a color as a triple of integers representing the intensity of the red, green, and blue components of the color. Typically, each color is measured on a scale from 0 to 255.

widget An object that serves a particular purpose in a graphical user interface.

3.10.3 Exercises

Graphics Primitives

Practice 3.1: The following code fragment has a single error in it. Fix it.

```
1  from cs1graphics import *
2  screen = Canvas( )
3  disk = Circle( )
4  disk.setFillColor('red')
5  disk.add(screen)
```

Practice 3.2: Write a program that draws a filled triangle near the middle of a canvas.

For Exercise 3.3 through Exercise 3.7, try to find the errors *without* using a computer. Then try running them on the computer to help find the errors or confirm your answers.

Exercise 3.3: After starting Python, you immediately enter

```
can = Canvas(100,100)
```

Python reports an error with the last line saying

```
NameError: name 'Canvas' is not defined
```

What did you do wrong? How do you fix it?

Exercise 3.4: Assuming that you have already created an instance of the Square class called sq, what's wrong with the statement

```
sq.setFillColor(Red)
```

Give two different ways to fix this statement.

Exercise 3.5: Assuming that you have already successfully created a Canvas instance called can, you enter the following to draw a blue circle centered in a red square:

```
sq = Square( )
sq.setSize(40)
sq.moveTo(30,30)
sq.setFillColor('Red')
can.add(sq)

cir = Circle( )
cir.moveTo(50,50)
cir.setRadius(15)
cir.setFillColor('Blue')
can.add(cir)
```

But the circle never appears. What's wrong with the above program? Edit the program so it works as desired.

Exercise 3.6: Consider the following:

```
can = Canvas(200,150)

rect = Rectangle( )
rect.setWidth(50)
rect.setHeight(75)
rect.moveTo(25,25)

rect = Rectangle( )
rect.setWidth(100)
rect.setHeight(25)

can.add(rect)
can.add(rect)
```

Only one rectangle appears? Why? How would you get two different rectangles to show up? (There are several ways to fix this.)

Layers

Exercise 3.7: The following runs but does not display anything. What is wrong?

```
can = Canvas( )
lay = Layer( )
sq = Square( )
lay.add(sq)
```

Exercise 3.8: Use the Layer class of the graphics library to create a pine tree. Make copies of the tree and use it to draw a forest of pine trees.

Exercise 3.9: Redo the smiley face described in the chapter as a layer. Test the code by rotating and scaling the layer and ensuring the face does not get distorted.

Exercise 3.10: Create an airplane as a layer and animate it flying across the screen and doing a loop. Hint: think carefully about the placement of the reference point.

Graphics Scenes

Exercise 3.11: Use the graphics library to create a picture of your favorite animal with an appropriate background scene.

Exercise 3.12: Use the graphics library to draw an analog clock face with numbers at the appropriate locations and an hour and minute hand.

Events

Exercise 3.13: Display the text "Click Me" centered in a graphics canvas. When the user clicks on the text, close the canvas.

Exercise 3.14: Create a program that draws a traditional traffic signal with three lights (green, yellow, and red). In the initial configuration, the green light should be on, but the yellow and red off (that is, black). When the user clicks the mouse on the signal, turn the green off and the yellow on; when the user clicks again, turn the yellow off and the red on.

Exercise 3.15: Write a program that displays a Text object graphically and adds characters typed on the keyboard to the message on the canvas.

Exercise 3.16: Write a program that allows the user to draw a path between five points, with each point specified by a mouse click on the canvas. As each successive click is received, display the most recent segment on the canvas.

Projects

Exercise 3.17: Use the graphics library to draw an analog clock face with hour, minute, and second hands. Use the datetime module to start the clock at the current time and animate the clock so that it advances once per second.

Exercise 3.18: Write a game of Tic-tac-toe using a graphical interface. The program should draw the initial board, and then each time the mouse is clicked, determine the appropriate square of the game board for drawing an X or an O. You may allow the game to continue for each of the nine turns. (As a bonus, read ahead to Chapter 4 and figure out how to stop the game once a player wins.)

Exercise 3.19: Think of your own cool project and have fun with it.

CHAPTER 4

Elementary Control Structures

The order in which commands are executed by a program is its *flow of control*. By default, statements are executed in the order in which they are given. However, a different execution order can be specified using what is known as a *control structure*. In this chapter we introduce two of Python's most widely used control structures. The first, known as a *for loop*, is used to repeat a series of commands upon each element of a given sequence. The second control structure introduced in this chapter is a *conditional statement* (also known as an *if statement*). This allows a programmer to specify a group of commands that are only to be executed when a certain condition is true.

We will explain the basic syntax and semantics for these two control structures and show how they can be combined with each other to accomplish a variety of tasks. One common goal is to take an original list and produce a new list that is based upon a selection of elements from the first list that meet a certain criterion. This can be accomplished using a combination of the two control structures, yet Python supports a more concise syntax termed *list comprehension*.

This chapter serves to introduce these elementary control structures. We continue in Chapter 5 by introducing several more control structures. As a collective group, these provide great flexibility in designing code that is more elegant, robust, and maintainable.

4.1 For Loops

We often need to repeat a series of steps for each item of a sequence. Such a repetition is called *iteration* and expressed using a control structure known as a *for loop*. A for loop always begins with the syntax **for** *identifier* **in** *sequence*: followed by a block of code we call the *body* of the loop. The general schema of a for loop is diagrammed in Figure 4.1. As an example, we can print the name of each person from a guest list, one per line, with the following syntax.

for *identifier* **in** *sequence* :

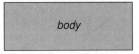

body

FIGURE 4.1: General form of a for loop.

```
for person in guests:
   print person
```

The identifier (i.e., person) is used like any other identifier in the language. Informally, we call this the *loop variable*; its name should suggest its meaning. The sequence (i.e., guests) can be any object that represents a sequence of elements, usually a list, string, or tuple. It can be specified with a literal, an identifier, or an expression that results in a sequence. At the end of that first line we use a colon (**:**) to designate the forthcoming body. The body itself (i.e., **print** person) specifies the command or commands that are to be executed for each iteration of the loop. This body is indented, although the precise amount of indentation is up to the programmer.

The semantics of a for loop is as follows. The identifier is assigned to the first item in the sequence and the body of the loop is executed. Then the identifier is reassigned to the next item of the sequence and again the loop body is executed. This iteration continues through the entire list. As a concrete example, consider the following loop, which might be used to generate name tags for a party:

```
guests = ['Carol', 'Alice', 'Bob']
for person in guests:
   print 'Hello my name is', person
```

The changing value of identifier person during this iteration is diagrammed in Figure 4.2. When Python executes this loop, the actual flow of control is equivalent to the following series of statements:

```
person = 'Carol'
print 'Hello my name is', person
person = 'Alice'
print 'Hello my name is', person
person = 'Bob'
print 'Hello my name is', person
```

Of course, the advantage of the for loop syntax is that it allows us to express this repetition succinctly and for a general sequence of elements, rather than specifically for 'Carol', 'Alice', and 'Bob'.

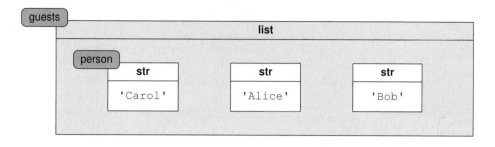

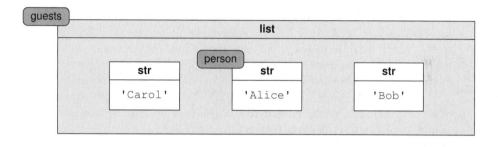

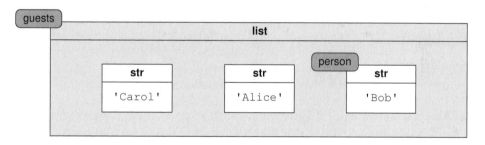

FIGURE 4.2: The assignment of person during three iterations of a for loop.

 A WORD OF WARNING

Although a for loop can technically iterate upon an empty sequence, the body of the loop is never executed; there are no elements.

As a more interesting application, suppose that a bank keeps a chronological log of all transactions for an individual's account. We model this as a list of numbers, with a positive entry representing a deposit into the account and a negative entry, a withdrawal. With this representation, the bank can perform many common tasks. For example, the overall balance for the account is simply the sum of all transactions (keeping in mind that "adding" a withdrawal decreases the balance). This sum can be computed as follows:

```
balance = 0                                    # initial balance
for entry in transactions:
    balance = balance + entry
print 'Your balance is', balance
```

Figure 4.3 shows the progression of this code on a simple example. The top drawing represents our state immediately *before* the loop is reached. Notice that balance is explicitly initialized to zero prior to the loop. The three remaining diagrams show the state at the *end* of each of the three passes of the loop. By the final configuration, we have calculated the true balance. The **print** statement is not part of the body of the loop because it is not indented. So that command is only executed once, after the loop is complete.

We use this example as a demonstration, but we can simplify our code by taking better advantage of Python. First, Python supports an operator += that adds a value to a running total. So the body of our loop could be expressed as

```
balance += entry
```

rather than as balance = balance + entry. Corresponding shorthands exist for other arithmetic operators (e.g., $-=$, $*=$, $/=$, $//=$, $\%=$). More importantly, computing the sum of a list of numbers is such a common task, there exists a built-in function sum(transactions), which returns the sum (presumably by performing just such a loop internally).

As our next example, let ['milk', 'cheese', 'bread', 'cereal'] represent the contents of list groceries. Our goal is to output a numbered shopping list, as

```
1.  milk
2.  cheese
3.  bread
4.  cereal
```

We can generate this output using the following code fragment:

```
count = 1
for item in groceries:
    print str(count) + '.  ' + item
    count += 1
```

Unlike our earlier examples, the body of this loop consists of multiple statements. Python relies upon the indentation pattern for designating the loop body. Since the command count += 1 is indented accordingly, it is part of the body.

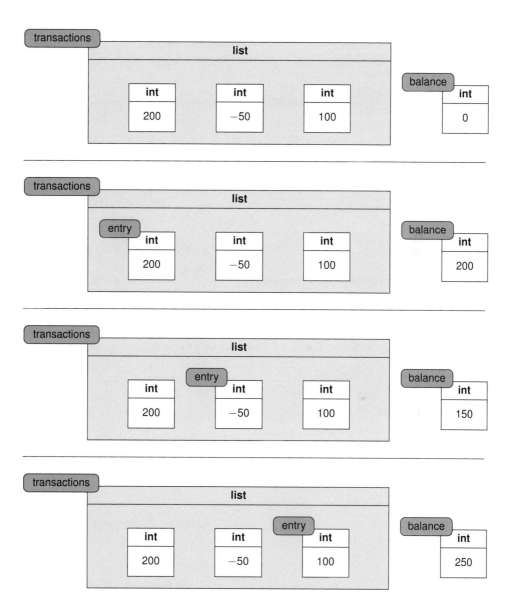

FIGURE 4.3: The changing state of variables as we compute the sum of a list. The top picture shows the state just before the loop. Subsequent pictures show the state at the *end* of each iteration.

Specifying loops from the interpreter prompt

We typically execute code that has been saved in a file. Yet it is possible to designate a loop as part of an interactive session with the Python interpreter. Try the following:

```
>>> guests = ['Carol', 'Alice', 'Bob']
>>> for person in guests:
...
```

After entering the second line, Python does not immediately present its usual >>> prompt. The interpreter recognizes the beginning of a control structure that is not yet complete. Instead, it presents the ... prompt (or if using IDLE, that next line is automatically indented to await our command). If we continue by specifying the indented command **print** person we find the following response:

```
>>> guests = ['Carol', 'Alice', 'Bob']
>>> for person in guests:
...     print person
...
```

The interpreter still does not execute the for loop. Since a loop body might have more than one statement, the interpreter cannot yet be sure whether the body is complete. For this reason, the end of a body is designated by a separate empty line when working interactively. Only then does the loop execute, as seen in the following:

```
>>> guests = ['Carol', 'Alice', 'Bob']
>>> for person in guests:
...     print person
...
Carol
Alice
Bob
>>>
```

Notice that a new >>> prompt is presented at the very end, once the loop has executed.

 A WORD OF WARNING

Although a mix of tabs and spaces may appear to be equivalent indentation to you, they are not considered identical to the Python interpreter. You must be consistent in your usage or avoid tabs altogether. Some editors will automatically convert tabs to spaces for this reason.

4.1.1 Index-Based Loops

The range function, introduced in Section 2.2.4, generates a list of designated integers. These ranges are quite convenient for iteration in the context of a for loop. For example the following code produces a countdown for a rocket launch:

```
for count in range(10, 0, −1):
  print count
print 'Blastoff!'
```

When writing source code in a file, there is no need to leave a full blank line to designate the end of the loop body. The command **print** `'Blastoff'`! is aligned with the original **for** statement, and thus no longer considered part of the body.

Ranges can often serve as a sequence of valid indices for another list. For example, let's go back and look at the goal of producing a numbered shopping list. On page 128 we accomplished this by using a traditional loop over the elements of the list and keep–ing a separate counter for numbering. Another approach is to base our loop on the list range(len(groceries)). This produces a list of integers ranging from 0 up to but not includ–ing len(groceries). So when the length of our grocery list is 4, the result is a list [0, 1, 2, 3]. By iterating over that list of numbers, we can use each index to generate the appropriate label as well as to access the corresponding list entry. Although we want our displayed labels numbered starting with one, we must recognize that indices of a list start at zero. Our code is as follows:

```
for position in range(len(groceries)):
  label = str(1 + position) + '. '        # label is one more than index itself
  print label + groceries[position]
```

To better understand this code, we examine its behavior on a grocery list with contents [`'milk'`, `'cheese'`, `'bread'`, `'cereal'`]. The loop iterates over positions in the range [0, 1, 2, 3]. The key expressions for each iteration are shown in the following table:

position	label	groceries[position]
0	`'1. '`	`'milk'`
1	`'2. '`	`'cheese'`
2	`'3. '`	`'bread'`
3	`'4. '`	`'cereal'`

This technique, called an ***index-based loop***, is especially helpful for tasks that require explicit knowledge of the position of an element within the list. As a motivating example, consider the goal of converting each name of a guest list to lowercase. A (flawed) first attempt to accomplish this might be written as

```
for person in guests:
  person = person.lower( )
```

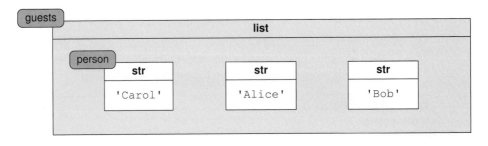

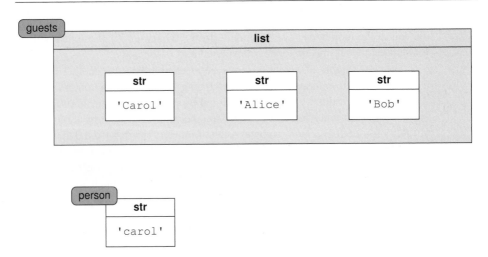

FIGURE 4.4: The effect of the command person = person.lower( ) in the context of a for loop.

Unfortunately, this code does not work as intended. Before suggesting a fix, let's make sure that we understand the shortcomings of the attempt. The issue working against us is that we have a list of strings, yet strings are immutable objects. The command person = person.lower( ) generates a new string that is a lowercase version of the origi-nal, and then reassigns identifier person to that result. This has no effect on the original element in the list. Figure 4.4 diagrams the first iteration of this loop. When the second iteration of the loop begins, the identifier person will be reassigned to the second element of the list, but the execution of the body produces another auxiliary string.

Going back to our goal, since we cannot mutate the original elements of the list we must mutate the list itself. We can replace one entry of a list with a new value using a syntax such as guests[i] = *newValue*, but this requires knowledge of the element's index within the list. We use an index-based loop as a solution.

```
for i in range(len(guests)):
    guests[i] = guests[i].lower( )
```

As before, the right-hand side of the expression guests[i] = guests[i].lower( ) evaluates to a new lowercase string. But this time, the assignment statement has the effect of altering the list composition. With practice, the choice between traditional loops and index-based loops will become more clear. The index-based form is generally used when the behavior of the loop body depends upon the location of an item within the list; otherwise, the traditional form is preferred.

4.1.2 Nested Loops

We have already seen examples where the body of the loop includes several statements. In fact, the body can even include another loop. The technique of using one control structure within the body of another is called ***nesting***. As a first example, consider the following code fragment:

```
1   for chapter in ('1', '2'):
2       print 'Chapter ' + chapter
3       for section in ('a', 'b', 'c'):
4           print '  Section ' + chapter + section
5   print 'Appendix'
```

To understand the behavior of this code, we view the nesting hierarchically. Line 1 defines a loop, which we will refer to as the *outer* loop. The body of this loop consists of lines 2–4. We recognize this because an indentation level is established at line 2, and the code remains indented at least this much until line 5. Since line 5 is back to the original level of indentation, it is not part of the outer loop body. In essence, the indentation allows us to abstract the high-level structure of the code as follows.

 A WORD OF WARNING

We gave an example of a for loop that iterates through an underlying list while mutating that list. However, the mutation was a one-for-one replacement of an element of that list and so the overall structure of the list remained intact.

The behavior of a for loop is unpredictable if the underlying list is mutated in a way that alters its overall structure. In the following example, we remove and reinsert elements as the loop is executing. Can you guess how it will behave?

```
original = ['A', 'B', 'C', 'D', 'E', 'F']
for entry in original:
    print entry
    original.remove(entry)
    original.append(entry)
```

```
1  for chapter in ('1','2'):
2      # the loop body
3      # will be repeated
4      # for each chapter
5  print 'Appendix'
```

Although we are blurring over the details of the loop body, we can already see that the body will be executed with chapter set to '1', then re-executed with chapter set to '2', and finally the word 'Appendix' printed at the conclusion of the loop. Now, let's focus narrowly on the body.

```
2    print 'Chapter ' + chapter
3    for section in ('a','b','c'):
4        print '  Section ' + chapter + section
```

In isolation, this block of code is straightforward. Assuming that the identifier chapter is well defined, line 2 prints out a single statement, and lines 3–4 comprise a loop. For example, if someone told us that chapter was set to '1', then it would be easy to see that this block of code produces the following output:

```
Chapter 1
  Section 1a
  Section 1b
  Section 1c
```

We could similarly determine the output that would be produced if chapter were set to '2'. Going back to the original version, we can put all the pieces together to predict the following output:

```
Chapter 1
  Section 1a
  Section 1b
  Section 1c
Chapter 2
  Section 2a
  Section 2b
  Section 2c
Appendix
```

The use of nested control structures can lead to many interesting behaviors. We demonstrate one such example as part of the case study in Section 4.3 in the context of drawing graphics. We will see many more examples of nested control structures as we implement more complex behaviors.

4.2 Case Study: DNA to RNA Transcription

A strand of DNA is composed of a long sequence of molecules called nucleotides or bases. Only four distinct bases are used: adenine, cytosine, guanine, and thymine, which are respectively abbreviated as A, C, G, and T. An organism uses DNA as a model when constructing a complementary structure called RNA. This process of creating RNA from DNA is known as *transcription*. The RNA is then used to create proteins.

RNA also consists of four nucleotides, three of them being A, C, and G, and a fourth one uracil, which is abbreviated as U. Transcription creates an RNA sequence by matching a complementary base to each original base in the DNA, using the following substitutions:

DNA	⟶	RNA
A	⟶	U
C	⟶	G
G	⟶	C
T	⟶	A

In this case study, we develop a program that asks the user to enter a DNA sequence and returns the transcribed RNA. An example session will look like

```
Enter a DNA sequence: AGGCTACGT
Transcribed into RNA: UCCGAUGCA
```

Our complete program is in Figure 4.5. The strings established in lines 1 and 2 encode the substitution rules for transcription. Those letters are intentionally ordered to give the proper mapping from DNA to RNA. Since the dna string entered by the user is itself a sequence, we use the for loop starting at line 6 to iterate through each individual DNA character. Line 7 finds the index of the DNA character within the dnaCodes. That index determines a corresponding RNA base from rnaCodes at line 8, which is then added to an auxiliary list rnaList at line 9. The overall RNA string is compiled at line 10, as the join of rnaList.

```
1   dnaCodes = 'ACGT'
2   rnaCodes = 'UGCA'
3
4   dna = raw_input('Enter a DNA sequence: ')
5   rnaList = [ ]
6   for base in dna:
7       whichPair = dnaCodes.index(base)        # index into dnaCodes
8       rnaLetter = rnaCodes[whichPair]         # corresponding index into rnaCodes
9       rnaList.append(rnaLetter)
10  rna = ' '.join(rnaList)                     # join on empty string
11  print 'Transcribed into RNA:', rna
```

FIGURE 4.5: Transcribing DNA to RNA.

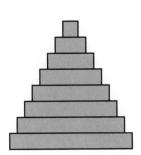

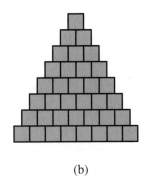

(a)   (b)

FIGURE 4.6: Two versions of a pyramid. In (a) each level is a single rectangle; in (b) each level comprises a series of squares.

4.3   Case Study: Drawing a Pyramid

In this case study, we develop two different programs for drawing a picture of a pyramid. In the first version a level is drawn as a single rectangle, while in the second a level is composed of individual squares. An example of each style is shown in Figure 4.6.

We begin by examining the first style. Our goal is not simply to draw the exact pic‒ture of Figure 4.6(a), but to develop a more general program that allows us to easily adjust the number of levels and the relative size of the drawing. To aid in the development of our code, we begin by assigning meaningful identifiers to two key measures: the number of levels and the desired height of each individual level.

```
numLevels = 8                          # number of levels
unitSize = 12                          # the height of one level
```

The unitSize serves as the height of each level and indirectly as a factor in determining the width of a level. For example, when setting the overall width and height of the canvas, we do not use numeric literals, but instead the expression unitSize * (numLevels + 1). This provides enough space for all of the levels, together with a small amount of margin around the pyramid.

```
screenSize = unitSize * (numLevels + 1)
paper = Canvas(screenSize, screenSize)
```

By writing the rest of our program to depend upon these named variables rather than the actual numbers, it becomes easy to later change the proportions of our pyramid.

Next, we must construct the levels of the pyramid. The biggest challenge is to get the details of the geometry correct. Although the levels are not identical to each other, there is clearly a repetitive pattern. We build the pyramid level by level, using a for loop that begins as follows.

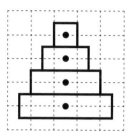

FIGURE 4.7: Geometric sketch for a 4-level pyramid. The dotted lines mark units in the coordinate system. The solid rectangles represent the levels of the pyramid, with each dot highlighting the desired center point for a level.

```
for level in range(numLevels):
```

With this convention, level will iterate over values [0, 1, 2, 3, 4, 5, 6, 7] for the case of eight levels. For convenience, we build the pyramid starting at the topmost level. Therefore level 0 is at the top, level 1 is the one under that, and so on (yes, we realize that in real life, it helps to build the bottom of the pyramid first!). In designing the rest of the code, we must determine the inherent geometric pattern. Each rectangle in our figure must be defined with a specific width, height, and center point. Sometimes it helps to sketch a small example by hand to determine the pattern. Figure 4.7 provides such a sketch for a 4-level pyramid. From this sketch, we can develop the following table of values, remembering that the origin of the screen is at the top left corner:

level	(measured in multiples of unitSize)			
	width	**height**	**centerX**	**centerY**
0	1	1	2.5	1
1	2	1	2.5	2
2	3	1	2.5	3
3	4	1	2.5	4

We see both similarities and differences among the levels. Each level has the same height, namely the unitSize, yet the width varies. Examining the table, we see that the width of a level is precisely one more than the level number (as level 0 has width 1, level 1 has width 2, and so on). So within each iteration of the loop, we compute the proper width and construct a new rectangle as follows:

```
width = (level + 1) * unitSize       # width varies by level
block = Rectangle(width, unitSize)   # height is always unitSize
```

Placing each rectangle requires an understanding of the pattern from our sample geometry. The center x-coordinate is the same for each level, in fact it is precisely half of the screenSize. Since this value is the same for all levels, we can compute it once before the loop begins, rather than recomputing within the body of the loop. On the other hand,

```
1   from cs1graphics import *
2
3   numLevels = 8                          # number of levels
4   unitSize = 12                          # the height of one level
5   screenSize = unitSize * (numLevels + 1)
6   paper = Canvas(screenSize, screenSize)
7   centerX = screenSize / 2.0             # same for all levels
8
9   # create levels from top to bottom
10  for level in range(numLevels):
11      width = (level + 1) * unitSize     # width varies by level
12      block = Rectangle(width, unitSize) # height is always unitSize
13      centerY = (level + 1) * unitSize
14      block.move(centerX, centerY)
15      block.setFillColor('gray')
16      paper.add(block)
```

FIGURE 4.8: Code for drawing a pyramid made of rectangles.

the y-coordinate varies between levels so we recompute it within the body of the loop. Fortunately, we see a familiar pattern with level 0 having a value of 1, level 1 a value of 2, and so on. Our complete code is given in Figure 4.8. Notice that the central x-coordinate is computed only once, prior to the loop at line 7. The individual y-coordinates are computed within the body of the loop at line 13, and then assigned to the rectangle at line 14. Line 16 adds each block to the canvas.

In conclusion, we wish to emphasize the advantage of relying upon the named variables numLevels and unitSize. By simply altering lines 3 and 4, we can reconfigure the pyramid's geometry. No other lines of code need to be changed. As a simple exercise, you could prompt the user for those key parameters. Another amusing modification is to make an animation of the process. By importing the time module and then inserting the command sleep(1.0) within the body of the loop, the visual construction of the pyramid will proceed level by level.

Pyramid made of squares

We next turn our attention to the second goal, a version of the pyramid made entirely from squares rather than rectangles, as shown in Figure 4.6(b). The general idea is quite similar; in fact the first ten lines of the code are identical. We create a screen of the appropriate size, and then begin a loop to create the pyramid, one level at a time. The difference in our two versions involves the body of the loop, since that determines how each level of the pyramid is built. In our first version, this body creates a single rectangle. In our next version, we use a nested loop to create and position a series of squares that comprise the level. Again, it helps to graph a small example. We find the general pattern is that level k is comprised of $(k + 1)$ unit squares. All of the squares on a given level are centered with the same y-coordinate. In fact, this is the same coordinate that we used when centering the rectangle in our first version. In this case, we compute it at line 12, prior to the inner loop. What differs among those squares is the x-coordinate. We approach the design by first considering where the leftmost square should be centered. By considering the width of the level, we determine the following equation:

leftmostX = centerX − unitSize * level / 2.0

As a check, notice that the leftmost square of level 0 will be placed precisely at the center of the diagram. The leftmost square of level 1 will be one-half a unit to the left of center, and so on. With that knowledge, we place all of the squares of the level using an inner loop that begins as follows:

```
for blockCount in range(level + 1):
    block = Square(unitSize)
    block.move(leftmostX + unitSize * blockCount, centerY)
```

Based on the selected range, we view the blocks of our level numbered from left to right, so that the leftmost is block 0, the one after that block 1, and so on. The x-coordinate of each block is set based upon an offset from the leftmost x-coordinate. So block 0 is the leftmost, block 1 is centered one full unit to the right of that, and so on. The complete second version of our code is given in Figure 4.9.

```
1   from cs1graphics import *
2
3   numLevels = 8                              # number of levels
4   unitSize = 12                              # the height of one level
5   screenSize = unitSize * (numLevels + 1)
6   paper = Canvas(screenSize, screenSize)
7   centerX = screenSize / 2.0                 # same for all levels
8
9   # create levels from top to bottom
10  for level in range(numLevels):
11      # all blocks at this level have same y-coordinate
12      centerY = (level + 1) * unitSize
13      leftmostX = centerX − unitSize * level / 2.0
14      for blockCount in range(level + 1):
15          block = Square(unitSize)
16          block.move(leftmostX + unitSize * blockCount, centerY)
17          block.setFillColor('gray')
18          paper.add(block)
```

FIGURE 4.9: Code for drawing a pyramid made of squares.

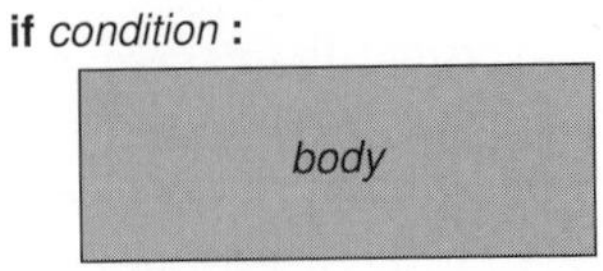

if *condition* :

body

FIGURE 4.10: Schema of a simple conditional statement.

4.4   Conditional Statements

Our next control structure is known as a ***conditional statement*** or, more commonly, an ***if statement***. It allows us to specify one or more instructions that are only to be executed when a certain condition is true. This is an extremely valuable tool as it allows execution to vary depending upon values that are not known until the program is running, such as input received from a user, data read from a file, or other forms of information that cannot be determined at the time the software is being written. A very simple example using a conditional statement is the following:

```
1  dinner = raw_input('What would you like for dinner? ')
2  if dinner == 'pizza':
3      print 'Great!'
4      print 'I love pepperoni and black olives.'
```

The first line gets input from the user. The conditional construct is on lines 2–4. It begins with the keyword **if** followed by a boolean expression which we call the ***condition***. That condition is followed by a colon and then an indented body. This format is shown in Figure 4.10. The semantics of a conditional statement is quite natural. If the condition evaluates to **True**, the body is executed; if the condition evaluates to **False**, the body is bypassed. This flow of control of an if statement is portrayed graphically in Figure 4.11.

The condition

The condition (e.g., dinner == 'pizza') can be an arbitrary boolean expression, as intro-duced in Section 2.8.2. This may be a single variable of type **bool**, or a more complex expression that evaluates to a boolean. The challenge for a programmer is crafting a con-dition that captures the desired semantics. Consider the following rule:

```
if len(groceries) > 15 or 'milk' in groceries:
    print 'Go to the grocery store'
```

With this condition, we go to the store whenever we need lots of things or whenever we need more milk (even if few other things). This is very different from the following:

```
if len(groceries) > 15 and 'milk' in groceries:
    print 'Go to the grocery store'
```

In this case, we only go to the store when we need lots of things including milk.

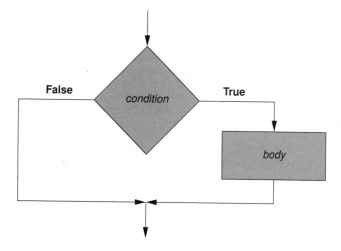

FIGURE 4.11: Flowchart for an **if** statement.

The body

Following the statement of the condition is the body of the conditional. As is the case with the for loop, the first statement of the body establishes a level of indentation for the rest of the body. The body can be as simple as one line, or more generally a larger block of code.

We can even nest one conditional within the body of another. Consider the scenario of a person approaching the site of a party, with someone guarding the door. The response of the guard may depend on whether the party has started and whether the person is on the guest list. Here is a reasonable behavior for the guard:

```
if partyStarted:
  if person in guests:
    print 'Welcome'
```

First, the guard checks to see if the party has started. If the party has started, then the guard must test the second condition to see whether this individual is invited. It is only in the case where *both* conditions succeed that the actual **print** statement is executed. Notice that when the party has not started, the guard does not even bother checking the guest list. The result of such a check is irrelevant and performing the test could be time consuming for a large party. Interestingly, this nested logic is identical to the evaluation of a single compound conditional.

```
if partyStarted and person in guests:
  print 'Welcome'
```

The outcome is clearly the same; the **print** statement executes only when both conditions are true. Yet the evaluation mechanism is similar as well. Python uses a technique known as ***short circuiting***, where a partial evaluation of a boolean expression suffices as soon as

FOR THE GURU

Although we suggested that a condition must be a boolean expression, Python actually allows many other data types to be used as a condition. For example, when a *sequence* serves as the condition, the body of the statement is executed if that sequence is nonempty. Thus we may write

   if waitlist**:**

as a compact shorthand for the actual boolean expression

   if len(waitlist) > 0**:**

The same style can be used to differentiate between empty strings and nonempty strings. For example, the following code demonstrates a common technique for prompting the user for information while providing a default value when the user presses the enter key without typing any other characters.

```
dinner = raw_input('What would you like for dinner? ')
if not dinner:              # empty string entered by user
    dinner = 'pizza'
```

Based on the condition **not** dinner, the body will be executed only when dinner is an empty string (i.e., when it does not have length greater than zero).

The use of a nonboolean object as a condition allows experienced program-mers to make code more concise. However, there are pitfalls for a beginner who accidentally uses a nonboolean object. Consider the following code, which is syntactically legal but tragically flawed:

```
response = raw_input('Shall we play a game? ')
if response == 'y' or 'yes':
    # play the game
```

The condition is treated as if it were parenthesized as follows:

   if (response == 'y') **or** ('yes')**:**

Since the right–hand operand of the **or** is a nonempty string, the overall condition will be treated as **True**, regardless of the actual response value. Of course, this can be a very nasty bug to uncover, as the condition will seem to be satisfied even when the user types 'Definitely not'.

By the way, one way to express the intended logic is with the condition response == 'y' **or** response == 'yes'. An even more concise form uses a containment check on a tuple, with the condition response **in** ('y', 'yes').

the outcome can be properly determined. When the left-hand side of the **and** operator fails (in this case partyStarted), it reports **False** as the overall result without bothering to check the second condition. A similar optimization is used when the first clause of an **or** operator is **True**.

As another illustration of nested control structures, we return to the example of a list of bank account transactions. We used a for loop to calculate the overall sum of the transactions, and thus the final balance. Yet for a series of transactions to be legitimate, the intermediate balance should remain nonnegative throughout the process. Here is a variant of our original code that uses a conditional to check for such inconsistencies.

```
balance = 0
for entry in transactions:
  balance += entry
  if balance < 0:
    print 'Overdraft warning'
```

4.4.1 if-else Syntax

In its simplest form, a conditional is used to specify instructions that are executed when a given expression is **True**. An alternate set of steps can be expressed as an **else** clause, to be performed when the condition is **False**. Consider the following:

```
dinner = raw_input('What would you like for dinner? ')
if dinner == 'pizza':
  print 'Great!'
  print 'I love pepperoni and black olives.'
else:
  print 'How about pizza?'
```

The general syntax of an **if-else** statement is given in Figure 4.12. The associated semantics are shown by the flowchart in Figure 4.13. If the condition is **True**, the first body will be executed; otherwise the second body will be executed. As a more elaborate example, the following code computes separate totals for the deposits and withdrawals of a list of transactions (rather than the overall sum).

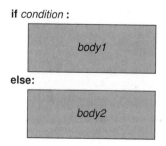

FIGURE 4.12: Schema of an **if-else** statement.

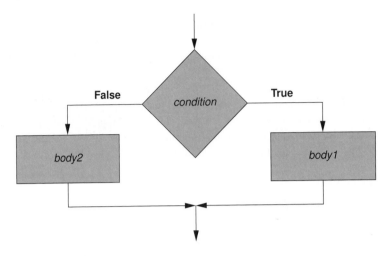

FIGURE 4.13: Flowchart for an **if-else** statement.

```
depositTotal = 0
withdrawalTotal = 0
for entry in transactions:
  if entry > 0:
    depositTotal += entry
  else:
    withdrawalTotal += entry
```

For each individual entry, we add it to one side of the ledger or the other based upon whether it is a positive value.

4.4.2   if-elif Syntax

Next, we revisit our rule for buying groceries, as originally given on page 140. By that logic, we make a trip to the grocery store whenever we need lots of things or whenever we run out of milk. With nested conditionals, we can define the following more intricate rule:

```
if len(groceries) > 15:
  print 'Go to the grocery store'
else:
  if 'milk' in groceries:
    print 'Go to the convenience store'
```

When we need lots of things we will make a trip to the grocery store, but we do not bother going to the grocery store when our list is short. Instead, we consider making a quick trip to the convenience store based upon a second condition, namely that we need milk. A flowchart for this logic is given in Figure 4.14. There are three possible paths through this chart: we might go to the grocery store, we might go to the convenience store, or we might

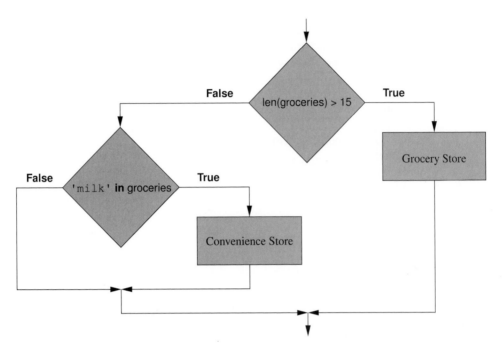

FIGURE 4.14: Flowchart for an **if**-**elif** statement.

do neither. However, we will never go to both stores. Notice that when we need lots of things, it is irrelevant whether milk is on the list; we will be going to the grocery store. The need for milk only comes into play once we have ruled out a full trip to the grocery store.

len(groceries) > 15	`'milk'` **in** groceries	Action
True	True	Grocery Store
True	False	Grocery Store
False	True	Convenience Store
False	False	(nothing)

Placing a second conditional within the body of an else clause is so common, Python supports a convenient shorthand using the keyword **elif** (short for "else if"), followed by a secondary boolean expression. Thus the above example could be rewritten as

```
if len(groceries) > 15:
    print 'Go to the grocery store'
elif 'milk' in groceries:
    print 'Go to the convenience store'
```

The distinction may seem slight in this first example, but an advantage is that we avoid increasing the level of indentation when there are additional conditions.

More generally, we can chain together multiple **elif** clauses and optionally a final **else** clause. To demonstrate this use, we consider the following biological application. Recall from the case study of Section 4.2 that DNA strands are often represented as long character strings over the bases A, C, G, and T. A simple computational task is to count the number of occurrences of each individual base within a string dna. We can accomplish this using the following implementation:

```
numA = numC = numG = numT = 0
for base in dna:
  if base == 'A':
    numA += 1
  elif base == 'C':
    numC += 1
  elif base == 'G':
    numG += 1
  else:                    # presumably a T
    numT += 1
```

The first line initializes four separate counters to zero (see page 67 for a similar use of operator chaining). The for loop is then used to consider each individual base, with the compound **if** statement used to distinguish between the possibilities. The final **else** clause executes if all of the earlier conditions have failed. In this context, if we assume that the DNA data is legitimate, then if a base is not an A, C, or G, it must be a T.

The convenience of the **elif** syntax in this example is more significant. If we had been forced to nest multiple **if-else** constructs, this code must be formatted as

```
numA = numC = numG = numT = 0
for base in dna:
  if base == 'A':
    numA += 1
  else:
    if base == 'C':
      numC += 1
    else:
      if base == 'G':
        numG += 1
      else:                 # presumably a T
        numT += 1
```

FOR THE GURU

The DNA example brings up another interesting lesson, beyond the syntactic issues. A careful reader may recall from Section 2.3.1 that the suite of methods supported by the **str** class includes a count method that calculates the number of occurrences of a specified substring. Therefore, we could accomplish our goal with the following approach.

```
numA = dna.count('A')
numC = dna.count('C')
numG = dna.count('G')
numT = dna.count('T')
```

The question is whether one approach is clearly superior to the other. The code on this page is much simpler to develop and perhaps more intuitive to read.

Efficiency becomes a significant issue when working on a large strand of DNA (for example the human genome has roughly 3 billion bases). The fact that code appears simpler syntactically does not actually mean it is more efficient. In some respect, the work is shifted behind the scene into the count method. We might suspect the approach on this page to be slower, as the four separate calls to count probably cause four separate passes through the original data, as opposed to the single loop in our earlier approach.

Interestingly, if we run our own tests on large DNA strands, we find that the approach on this page is actually significantly faster than that of page 146 (roughly 5 times faster on our system). The primary reason for this discrepancy is that the implementation of the built-in count method is optimized to take advantage of the internal representation of a string. A conclusion we can draw from this example is that there is a strong argument to be made for using existing tools rather than reinventing them, especially if the tools are well suited and presumably optimized. Of course this is only a guideline; there are many ways to destroy the efficiency of a program by relying on tools that are not well suited for a task (such as using a screwdriver to drive nails).

4.5   List Comprehension

In Section 4.1.1 we considered the goal of mutating a list of guests to convert all names to lowercase. A closely related task is that of creating a new list with lowercase versions while leaving the original unchanged. This is easily accomplished with the following code:

```
auxiliary = [ ]
for person in guests:
  auxiliary.append(person.lower( ))
```

This approach uses a general pattern in which we create a new empty list and then populate the new list by adding a corresponding entry for each item of the original list. While this implementation is straightforward, Python supports an even simpler syntax for such tasks known as *list comprehension*. This syntax resembles a list literal, but allows us to generate contents for a new list based upon entries of an existing list. As an example, the preceding code fragment can be replaced by the single command

```
auxiliary = [ person.lower( ) for person in guests ]
```

This syntax provides a compact way of designating the four key components in the above example, using the form *result* = [*expression* **for** *identifier* **in** *sequence*]. In evaluating this statement, Python iterates the for loop, appending the given expression to the new result during each pass. Notice that the expression person.lower( ) is allowed to depend upon the loop variable person.

There is a more general form of list comprehension with a condition that must be true in order for a corresponding entry to be appended to the result during each given iteration. That form is expressed using the syntax

```
result = [ expression for identifier in sequence if condition]
```

This statement is evaluated similarly to the following nested control structures:

```
result = [ ]
for identifier in sequence:
  if condition:
    result.append(expression)
```

For example, suppose we want to scan a list of transactions and produce a supplemental list of all *deposits* from that original list. This can be done using the following list comprehension:

```
deposits = [entry for entry in transactions if entry > 0]
```

4.6 Chapter Review

4.6.1 Key Points

For Loops

- A for loop is used to repeat a series of steps for each item of a sequence (e.g., a list, string, tuple).

- The general syntax of a for loop is the following:

    for *identifier* **in** *sequence***:**
      body

- For each element of an original sequence, the for loop identifier is assigned to that element and then the body is executed.

- The body of a loop can be an arbitrarily long block of code. The first line of the body establishes an indentation level. When the indentation returns to that of the word **for**, it is no longer considered to be part of the loop body.

- The body of the loop may contain an additional *nested* control structure.

- The list produced by the range function is a convenient sequence for iteration.

- An index–based loop is one that iterates over a list of indices of a list rather than over the original list, for example, **for** i **in** range(len(guests)).

Conditionals

- A conditional construct is used to specify commands that are only to be executed when a certain condition is met. The basic syntax of a conditional is the following:

    if *condition***:**
      body

  When the condition evaluates to **True** the body will be executed; otherwise the body is bypassed. The condition can be an arbitrarily complex boolean expression.

- An **if** statement can be followed by an **else** clause using the following syntax:

    if *condition***:**
      body1
    else:
      body2

  With this syntax, either the first or the second body will be executed (but not both).

- An **if** statement can be followed by one or more **elif** clauses to express subsequent conditions to be checked should the first one fail.

    if *condition1***:**
      body1
    elif *condition2***:**
      body2

- An **if–elif** construct can optionally be followed by a final **else** clause that will be performed if all earlier conditions have failed.

List Comprehension

- Python offers a convenient syntax for creating a new list that has contents based upon the entries of an original list. The general form,

    result = [*expression* **for** *identifier* **in** *sequence* **if** *condition*]

produces a result equivalent to that of

    result = [ ]
    for *identifier* **in** *sequence*:
      if *condition*:
        result.append(*expression*)

4.6.2 Glossary

body A block of (indented) code used within the context of a control structure.

conditional statement A control structure that specifies one or more blocks of code to be executed only if certain conditions are true.

control structure A command that describes the order in which some other instructions are executed.

flow of control The order in which a series of statements is executed.

for loop A control structure used to iterate a block of code for each item of a sequence.

if statement *See* conditional statement.

index-based loop A loop that iterates over a range of integers representing indices of a list, rather than iterating directly over the elements of that list.

iteration The process of repeating a step for each item in a sequence.

list comprehension A syntax for creating a new list that is populated based upon the con–tents of an existing list, as in deposits = [entry **for** entry **in** transactions **if** entry > 0].

loop variable An identifier that is assigned to each element of the sequence during the execution of a for loop.

nesting A technique in which one control structure is placed within the body of another.

short circuiting A technique used by the computer in evaluating compound boolean expressions, whereby a partial evaluation suffices as soon as the outcome can be properly determined.

4.6.3 Exercises

For loops

Practice 4.1: Consider the following program:

```
foods = ['eggs', 'broccoli', 'peas', 'salt', 'steak']
for ingredient in foods:
    print ingredient[1]
```

Predict the output that results when this code is executed.

Practice 4.2: Given the string original create a new string dramatic that has two consecu-tive copies of each letter from the original string. For example, the dramatic version of `'argh'` appears as `'aarrgghh'`.

Practice 4.3: Given an original list of integers intList create a list strList that contains the associated string representations of those integers. For example, when starting with intList = [4004, 8080, 6502, 8086, 68000, 80486], the resulting list of strings should be [`'4004'`, `'8080'`, `'6502'`, `'8086'`, `'68000'`, `'80486'`].

Practice 4.4: Write a program that draws an *n*-level staircase made of rectangles, such as the example for *n* = 4 shown here.

Exercise 4.5: Consider the following program:

```
t = 0
for k in range(5):
    t += k
    print k, t
```

Predict the output that results when this code is executed.

Exercise 4.6: Write a short program that uses a **for** loop to animate a circle moving across a canvas.

Exercise 4.7: Rewrite the program for drawing a pyramid in Figure 4.8 so that it prompts the user for the number of levels and the *overall* height of the pyramid.

Exercise 4.8: Assume that word is a string, for example `'slice'`. Write code to print out the following pattern for the given word:

```
s
sl
sli
slic
slice
```

Exercise 4.9: Write a program that prints an *n*-level staircase made of text, such as the example for *n* = 4 shown here.

```
      *
    *  *
  *  *  *
*  *  *  *
```

Exercise 4.10: Write a program that draws an *n*-level staircase made of squares, such as the example for $n = 4$ shown here.

Exercise 4.11: Write a program that draws an *n*-level staircase as a single polygon, such as the example for $n = 4$ shown here.

Exercise 4.12: Assume that people is a list of names, each represented as a string using the format `'firstName lastName'`. Print out the names one per line, yet alphabetized by *last* name.

Exercise 4.13: Given a positive integer k, write a program that calculates the factorial of k, defined as

$$k! = k \cdot (k-1) \cdot (k-2) \cdots 2 \cdot 1.$$

Exercise 4.14: The mathematical constant *e*, which serves as the base of the natural logarithm, is an irrational number with value approximately 2.718281828459. The precise value of this constant is equal to the following infinite series:

$$e = \sum_{k=0}^{\infty} \frac{1}{k!}$$

Although we cannot compute the entire infinite series, we get a good approximation of the value by computing the beginning of such a sequence. Write a program that approximates *e* by computing the sum of the first *n* terms, for some *n*.

Exercise 4.15: The syntax **int**(`'314'`) converts the string of numerals to the corresponding (base ten) number. However, Python also allows you to interpret strings in a nonstandard base, specified as an optional parameter. For example the syntax **int**(`'314'`, 5) returns the decimal value 84. If viewed as a base five number, the string `'314'` represents $(3 \times 5^2) + (1 \times 5^1) + (4 \times 5^0)$ and thus equivalent to the (base ten) value 84. Your goal is to convert such strings from scratch, without relying on the optional parameter form of Python's **int**( ) conversion. Write a program that asks the user for the original string as well as the designated base (you may assume that the base is at most ten). Your program should compute and print the associated (base ten) value.

Exercise 4.16: In *A Word of Warning* on page 133, we consider the effect of a **for** loop body that mutates the structure of the list over which it is iterating. Run that code on your computer and report the output that you see. Give a hypothesis, consistent with your observations, as to what is happening behind the scene.

Exercise 4.17: Starting on page 146 of Section 4.4.2, we use conditionals to count the number of occurrences of each base type in a DNA strand. Show how to accomplish this task using a for loop, yet without any conditionals (nor use of **str**.count). Hint: maintain a list of four counters, indexing that list using a technique similar to the Case Study of Section 4.2.

Conditionals

Practice 4.18: Lists support a method to count the number of times that a specified value appears in a list. Show that you can compute such a count without relying upon that method. Specifically, assume that you have a list collection and a target value. You are to compute the number of times that the value appears in the given collection.

Practice 4.19: Write a block of code that does the following. Assuming that words is a list of strings, generate a new list shortWords that includes all of the original strings with length 3 or less.

Practice 4.20: Carefully consider the following program:

```
for x in range(20):
  if x % 9 == 0:
    print x, 'is divisible by 9'
  elif x % 3 == 0:
    print x, 'is divisible by 3'
```

Predict the output that results when this code is executed.

Practice 4.21: Carefully consider the following program:

```
x = int(raw_input('Enter a value for x: '))
y = int(raw_input('Enter a value for y: '))
if x > 5:
  if y <= 3 and x > 8:
    print 'answer is A'
  else:
    print 'answer is B'
elif y > 6 or x < 2:
  print 'answer is C'
else:
  print 'answer is D'
```

(a) Predict the output if the user enters 4 and then 4.

(b) Predict the output if the user enters 9 and then 4.

(c) Predict the output if the user enters 1 and then 9.

(d) Predict the output if the user enters 6 and then 2.

Exercise 4.22: Carefully consider the following program:

```python
x = int(raw_input('Enter a value for x: '))
y = int(raw_input('Enter a value for y: '))
if y >= 7:
  print 'answer is A'
elif x < 4:
  if y > 4:
    print 'answer is B'
  else:
    print 'answer is C'
else:
  print 'answer is D'
```

(a) Predict the output if the user enters 4 and then 4.

(b) Predict the output if the user enters 2 and then 4.

(c) Predict the output if the user enters 1 and then 9.

(d) Predict the output if the user enters 2 and then 6.

Exercise 4.23: Consider the following program:

```python
foods = ['eggs', 'broccoli', 'peas', 'salt', 'steak']
for k in range(len(foods) - 1):
  if len(foods[k]) < len(foods[k+1]):
    print k
```

Predict the output that results when this code is executed.

Exercise 4.24: Carefully consider the following program:

```python
answer = 1
if greeting.count('a') == 1:
  if 'o' in greeting:
    if greeting.endswith('o'):
      answer = 2
    else:
      answer = 3
elif len(greeting) < 6:
  answer = 4
print answer, greeting
```

For each of the following greeting values, predict the output that would result.

(a)	`'adieu'`	(h)	`'hallo'`
(b)	`'aloha'`	(i)	`'hola'`
(c)	`'bonjour'`	(j)	`'jambo'`
(d)	`'ciao'`	(k)	`'shalom'`
(e)	`'dia duit'`	(l)	`'salaam'`
(f)	`'goeie dag'`	(m)	`'terve'`
(g)	`'guten dag'`	(n)	`'zdravo'`

Exercise 4.25: Assume that we have a list of strings named indonesian. Give a sequence of commands that alters the list so as to replace *each* occurrence of the value `'java'` with the value `'python'` in its place.

Exercise 4.26: Write a code fragment that processes a list items and prints out all values that occur more than once on the list. Take care to only print out each such value once. For example, given the list

```
items = ['apple', 'grapes', 'kiwi', 'kiwi', 'pear',
         'grapes', 'kiwi', 'strawberry']
```

your program should print

```
grape
kiwi
```

(or kiwi, grape; either order will suffice).

Exercise 4.27: On page 141 we show how the short-circuit evaluation of the boolean oper–ator **and** is equivalent to a nested conditional statement. The evaluation of the oper–ator **or** also relies upon short-circuiting semantics. When the first condition is satis–fied, there is no need to test the second condition; the compound condition is already satisfied. Give a nested conditional statement with semantics equivalent to

```
if weather == 'rainy' or day == 'Monday':
    down = True
```

Exercise 4.28: Starting on page 144, we gave code to compute separate totals for the deposits and withdrawals on a list of transaction. That code used a single **for** loop with a nested **if-else** statement. Give an alternate implementation that achieves the same end results using a single **for** loop and a single **if** statement (without use of an **else** or **elif** clause).

Exercise 4.29: The precise value of the mathematical constant π is equal to the following infinite series:

$$\pi = 4 \cdot \left(\frac{1}{1} - \frac{1}{3} + \frac{1}{5} - \frac{1}{7} + \cdots \right)$$

Although we cannot compute the entire infinite series, we get an approximation to the value by computing the beginning of such a sequence. Write a program that approximates π by computing the first n terms, for some n.

Exercise 4.30: In Exercise 4.15 we examined the conversion of a numeric string from a nonstandard base back to decimal. In that problem, we assumed that the original base was at most ten. For a base larger than ten, the issue is that we need a differ‐ ent symbol for each possible value from 0 to (base − 1). The standard convention in computer science is to begin using alphabet symbols, with A representing ten, B representing eleven, and so on. As an example, **int**('FAB4', 16) evaluates to $64180 = (15 \times 16^3) + (10 \times 16^2) + (11 \times 16^1) + (4 \times 16^0)$.

Update your earlier program to allow for the conversion for bases up to 36. When considering an alphabet character from the original string, you can determine whether it is a true digit using the **str**.isdigit method. When it is not a true digit, you can compute the appropriate value (such as 15 for 'F') by taking advantage of ASCII encoding with the following formula: value = 10 + ord(symbol) − ord('A').

List Comprehension

Practice 4.31: Redo Practice 4.2 taking advantage of list comprehension. Note that string comprehension can be used to iterate upon a string, but the result is always a list.

Practice 4.32: Redo Practice 4.3 using list comprehension.

Practice 4.33: Redo Practice 4.19 using list comprehension.

Exercise 4.34: Use list comprehension to create the list of values [1, 2, 4, 8, 16, 32, 64, 128, 256, 512].

Exercise 4.35: Use list comprehension to generate the list of floating‐point numbers [1.5, 2.5, 3.5, 4.5, 5.5, 6.5, 7.5, 8.5, 9.5]

Exercise 4.36: The range function is only able to produce a list of integers. Given floating‐ point values start, stop, and step, show how to create a list of floating‐point values, starting at start, taking steps of size step, going up to but not including or passing stop. For example with start = 3.1, stop = 4.6, and step = 0.3, the result should be the list [3.1, 3.4, 3.7, 4.0, 4.3].

Exercise 4.37: In the Case Study of Section 4.2 we used a for loop to create the rnaList base by base. Show how lines 5–9 could be replaced by a single list comprehension statement.

Exercise 4.38: Given a list orig, possibly containing duplicate values, show how to use list comprehension to produce a new list uniq that has all values from the original but with duplicates omitted. Hint: look for indices at which the leftmost occurrence of a value occurs.

Projects

Exercise 4.39: Write a program that uses loops to generate an $n \times n$ multiplication table for positive integer n. As a model, here is a 4 × 4 version of the desired format.

```
    |   1   2   3   4
 ---+----------------
  1 |   1   2   3   4
  2 |   2   4   6   8
  3 |   3   6   9  12
  4 |   4   8  12  16
```

Hint: to properly line up the columns, you may rely upon the rjust method to right justify strings. For example, the expression **str**(value).rjust(3) produces a string of three characters with necessary leading spaces. For an $n \times n$ table, the maximum number of characters needed for one entry will be len(**str**(n*n)).

Exercise 4.40: Use the graphics library to create an image of a checkerboard with pieces placed in their initial configuration, as shown here.

Exercise 4.41: Animate a ball moving across a canvas under the effect of gravity. You should maintain the position and velocity of the ball. During each iteration of the animation, the velocity should be used to update the position of the ball, and gravity should have a downward effect on the vertical component of the velocity.

CHAPTER 5

Additional Control Structures

In Chapter 4 we introduced two important control structures: a *for loop* and a *conditional statement* (a.k.a., an *if statement*). In this chapter we add several more control structures to our toolbox, giving us greater flexibility as a programmer. The first of these is known as a *while loop*. As is the case with a for loop, this construct allows us to designate a block of code to be repeated in succession. However, when using a for loop, the repetition is based upon an iteration through a *pre-existing sequence* of objects. The while loop provides us greater flexibility by performing repetition in cases where we cannot provide such a sequence in advance. This is accomplished by designating a condition in the form of a boolean expression, and continuing to repeat the body so long as the condition evaluates to **True**.

Next we introduce what is perhaps the most versatile of all control structures: the *function*. We have already seen that Python provides many built-in functions. Those functions typically support a simple syntax, such as max(score), that encapsulates the steps of what might be a complex behavior. As programmers, we have the ability to define our own functions, encapsulating our own algorithms and better organizing our code. Furthermore, since a function can be called multiple times from different places in our code, this provides greater support for expressing repetition without the explicit duplication of code. More generally, we discuss how the full range of control structures can be effectively used to avoid unwanted duplication of efforts.

Later in the chapter, we explore the role of *exceptions* (e.g., ValueError) in Python. We have seen the interpreter report such errors when we do something wrong, such as send an invalid parameter. Typically, this causes the entire program to stop. We discuss the topic of *error checking*, explaining how to gracefully recover from certain errors or to report errors from within our own code.

5.1 While Loops

We have seen that a *for loop* allows for repetition by iterating over a well-defined sequence of elements. In some situations, we need to express repetition even though we cannot determine the precise number of iterations in advance. For example, we may wish to write a game that concludes by offering the user the question, "Would you like to play again?" At the time we are writing the software, we have no way to know how a user will respond to such an offer. We can describe this form of potential repetition using a control structure known as a *while loop*. The general syntax appears as follows:

```
while condition:
    body
```

The condition can be an arbitrary boolean expression, and the body is an indented block of code. As a simple example, here is code that might be used for our hypothetical game.

```
response = raw_input('Shall we play a game? ')

while response.lower( ) in ('y', 'yes'):
    # ... code for playing a fun game ...
    response = raw_input('Would you like to play again? ')
```

The resulting flow of control is diagrammed in Figure 5.1. If the user declines the original invitation to play, the body of the while loop is never entered. In this case, the flow resembles that of an *if statement* (see Figure 4.11 on page 141 for comparison). However, when the condition is true, the body of the while loop is executed and the flow of control reverts to the top. The condition is reevaluated and if still true, the body is executed again. This process is repeated indefinitely, stopping only when a subsequent evaluation of the condition fails (in Section 5.1.1 we discuss what happens when the condition never fails).

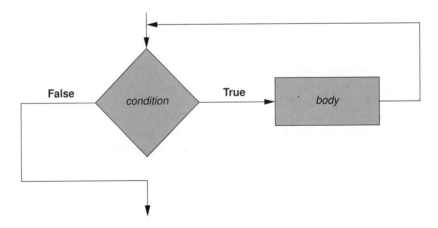

FIGURE 5.1: Semantics of a while loop.

To better demonstrate the use of while loops, we consider a series of representative examples in which we are unable to predict the number of repetitions.

Finding the greatest common divisor

In Section 1.2 we introduced two different high-level algorithms for computing the greatest common divisor of two integers. Both of these algorithms rely upon a form of repetition, but one in which the number of iterations is not immediately clear.

The first algorithm searches for possible common divisors, incrementally testing from largest to smallest so that the first success is the greatest divisor. A flowchart describing the algorithm was given in Figure 1.1 on page 8. We implement it as follows:

```
u = int(raw_input('Enter first number: '))
v = int(raw_input('Enter second number: '))

guess = min(u,v)                        # can't be bigger than this
while u % guess > 0 or v % guess > 0:   # nonzero remainder
  guess -= 1

print 'The gcd is', guess
```

If either of the remainders u % guess or v % guess is nonzero, then the current guess is not a common divisor so we decrement it and retry. Although this code works, it is inefficient on really large numbers. A better approach is Euclid's algorithm, originally diagrammed in Figure 1.2 on page 9. We implement it as follows:

```
u = int(raw_input('Enter first number: '))
v = int(raw_input('Enter second number: '))

while v != 0:
  r = u % v
  u = v
  v = r

print 'The gcd is', u
```

Although this loop is guaranteed to end eventually, the precise number of iterations is difficult to predict at the onset. A sample trace of Euclid's algorithm when finding the greatest common divisor of 1,234,567,890 and 987,654,321 is shown here.

u	v	r
1,234,567,890	987,654,321	246,913,569
987,654,321	246,913,569	45
246,913,569	45	9
45	9	0
9	0	

Checking whether an element is contained in a list

Consider the task of determining whether a given value is contained in a list. Python already supports this behavior using a syntax such as val **in** data. But for the sake of example, let's consider how to implement this ourselves (and perhaps how it was implemented for Python's **list** class). A typical approach is to use a technique known as *sequential search*, in which we scan the list from beginning to end while looking for the desired value. We might implement this using a for loop as follows:

```
found = False              # pessimism
for item in data:
    if item == val:
        found = True       # we found it
```

So long as at least one of the items matches the given value along the way, the end result of found will be **True**. However, this implementation is unnecessarily inefficient because the for loop always iterates through the entire data set.

Clearly, if we happen to find the target value along the way, there is no reason to continue scanning; the answer is **True**. We prefer this more efficient strategy. One possible implementation relies on a while loop.

```
1   i = 0                              # index—based search
2   found = False                      # pessimism
3   while i < len(data) and not found:
4       if data[i] == val:
5           found = True               # we found it
6       else:
7           i += 1                     # keep looking...
```

This is really just an index-based loop. Index i is used to track our scan through the data, starting from the beginning. The boolean value found denotes whether or not we have found the desired value. At line 2 we initialize found = **False** because our presumption is that the value is not contained in the list unless we find evidence to the contrary.

The most significant aspect of this code is the precise expression used as the loop condition on line 3. This can be paraphrased as follows. To continue our search there must still be unsearched items, hence i < len(data), and we should not yet have found the value. The body of the loop checks to see whether the currently considered element matches the target, noting any success. If the element does not match, we increment the index i in preparation for a subsequent iteration. When the loop finally completes, the boolean found correctly represents whether the value is contained in the data. If found is **True**, it must have been because it was set as such at line 5. In fact when the value is found, the resulting value of i denotes the actual index at which the value was first located. Alternatively, if found remains **False**, the loop can exit only when i has advanced beyond all valid indices of the data.

FOR THE GURU

Python provides two special commands that can be used to alter the standard flow of control of a loop. These apply to for loops as well as while loops. The **continue** command causes an immediate interruption of the current iteration of the loop body, forcing control to proceed immediately to the next iteration of the loop (if any). The **break** command, when executed within the body of a loop, causes an immediate stop to the *entire* loop. The current iteration is interrupted and control skips beyond the end of the loop, regardless of remaining items in a for loop sequence or the particular condition of a while loop.

Going back to our previous example for checking containment within a list, we could have described the efficient version of sequential search as follows:

```
found = False         # pessimism
for item in data:
    if item == val:
        found = True      # found it
        break             # quit the loop right now
```

This uses a for loop to iterate through the data, but as soon as we find a match, we set found to **True** and immediately break out of the loop.

It is a matter of programming style whether to use these commands. In some scenarios, they help simplify the immediate code. For example, the above version of a sequential search is arguably more legible than the version from page 162 which used a while loop. The criticism surrounding these commands is that their use may obscure the underlying logic of the code. Typically, the first line of a for loop or while loop gives the reader the flavor of the repetition that is taking place. For example, if a programmer sees a loop beginning with the syntax

```
while total <= 50:
```

the implication is that by the time this loop ends, the value of total will be greater than 50. However, the subtle placement of a **break** statement farther down within the body leaves open an avenue for exiting the loop without regard for the official loop condition. This can lead to a behavior that contradicts initial intuitions.

For the remainder of the text, we will avoid the direct use of **break** or **continue** statements. We recommend that you use them sparingly, if at all, and only when their use improves the legibility of your program.

Reading data from a user

There are many scenarios in which we want repetition that is based in some way upon a user's responses. Our previous example of replaying a game is one such case. Here we look at another such example, demonstrating a slightly different technique.

Assume we wish to build a guest list for a party by having the user enter names, one per line. There are two typical approaches for controlling such an interaction. One approach is to start by explicitly asking the user how many guests are to be entered. With this information, we could use a for loop to iterate the proper number of times, but ask-ing for this count in advance places an unnecessary burden on the user. A better interface allows the user to continue entering names and to signify the end of the list through a sig-nal, such as an empty line. One workable approach is the following:

```
1  guests = [ ]
2  name = raw_input('Enter a name (blank to end): ')
3  while name:                    # so long as nonempty string
4      guests.append(name)
5      name = raw_input('Enter a name (blank to end): ')
6  print 'You entered', len(guests), 'guests.'
```

We should highlight a subtlety in the statement of the loop condition at line 3. Notice that name is actually a string object, not a boolean value. Python allows a nonboolean value to be used in place of a boolean expression, with the precise interpretation dependent on the data type. This was something we discussed in *For the Guru* on page 142. In our current context, a nonempty string is evaluated as **True** versus an empty string that is treated as **False**. Therefore line 3 is really shorthand for the syntax **while** name != ' ': .

With that subtlety aside, this code can be paraphrased as follows. Starting with an empty list, we ask the user for a name. If they enter a legitimate name, we add it to the list, ask them for another name, and repeat. Though correct, the style is less than pleasing due to the duplication of the command for reading a name, seen both at line 2 and line 5. Ideally, we should not have to type such a command twice to express the desired repetition. This type of example is informally called a "loop and a half." We have a command that is executed once outside the loop body and then repeatedly within the loop body. Although we might hope for a way to remove the duplication, there is not a clear solution.

We could wait until we are within the loop body to read the initial name, but if we were to remove line 2 altogether then name is presumably undefined, causing a NameError upon the initial test of the loop condition. Instead, we offer the following work–around:

```
1  guests = [ ]
2  name = 'fake'
3  while name:
4      name = raw_input('Enter a name (blank to end): ')
5      if name:
6          guests.append(name)
7  print 'You entered', len(guests), 'guests.'
```

At line 2 of this version, we set the name to a fake value to force an initial execution of the loop body. Of course, we do not wish to append this fake name to the list. Therefore, the first step once we are within the loop body is to prompt the user for a real name. However, there will come a time when the user enters an empty string to end the list, yet that string should not appear on the guest list. The conditional at line 5 is used to avoid the unwanted append.

We have successfully avoided the duplication of the **raw_input** present in the first attempt. However, notice that we have instead duplicated the test of whether name is a nonempty string, at lines 3 and 5. A more clever approach is to blindly add each name to the list, including the final blank name, and then to remove the extra entry after the loop completes.

```
guests = [ ]
name = 'fake'
while name:
  name = raw_input('Enter a name (blank to end): ')
  guests.append(name)
guests.pop( )                                    # remove the very last (blank) entry
print 'You entered', len(guests), 'guests.'
```

Another common task involving user input is to read data with error checking. Consider the goal of reading a number from 1 to 10 from the user. If the user enters a number that is out of range, we can print an error message and reprompt for a new choice as follows:

```
number = 0                                       # not valid
while not 1 <= number <= 10:
  number = int(raw_input('Enter a number from 1 to 10: '))
  if not 1 <= number <= 10:
    print 'Your number must be from 1 to 10.'
```

5.1.1 Infinite Loops

When working with a for loop, the overall number of iterations is naturally bounded based on the length of the original sequence. When working with a while loop, the overall number of iterations is not explicitly bounded. It is determined by a combination of the particular loop condition and the changing state of the underlying values. This introduces a potential pitfall with serious consequences, namely the possibility that the while loop never ends. We commonly call such a situation an ***infinite loop***. Here is a blatant example,

```
while True:
  print 'Hello'
```

Clearly this loop condition will never fail, and so the loop continues forever. As a side note, this may be a good time to learn how to manually force the interpreter to stop its execution; this is typically done by entering the control-c keystroke.

Although we may be wise enough to avoid such a silly example, many reasonable–looking efforts may mistakenly lead to infinite loops. For example our loop to play a game multiple times as written on page 160 might technically lead to an infinite loop if the user is addicted to the game. As a programmer, we have no guarantee that the user will ever turn down the offer for another game. Of course, we do not consider such design an error in the judgment of the programmer (we might eventually raise questions as to the judgment of the player). Other infinite loops are clearly the fault of the programmer, not the user. Looking back at our index–based while loop on page 162, we see that we had to explicitly increment the value of i as part of the loop body. This was a step that was implicit in the equivalent for loop construct. If we were to forget that important step, we end up with the following infinite loop (presuming that the sequence has one or more entries and that the first entry does not match the target value):

```
i = 0                              # index–based search
found = False                      # pessimism
while i < len(data) and not found:
    if data[i] == val:
        found = True               # we found it
```

Since i is never incremented, the condition i < len(data) remains true, and since we continually compare data[0] to val we never find it.

In general, determining whether a while loop repeats infinitely requires a deeper understanding of the logic. For example, our code for Euclid's algorithm on page 161 has a loop condition **while** v != 0. It is not immediately clear that this loop will ever end, although it turns out that it always does (see *For the Guru* on page 10). But it is the responsibility of the programmer to ensure the appropriate termination.

5.2   Functions

Functions can serve as the ultimate control structure. They allow a series of complicated instructions to be encapsulated and then subsequently used as a single high–level operation. We are already familiar with the use of functions from the perspective of a *caller*. When a function is called, control is passed behind the scene to instructions that accomplish some task. Parameters might be sent by the caller to affect the behavior. The function may return some final information to the caller when the action is completed.

There exists a built–in max function, but for strings it returns the "maximum" relative to the alphabetical ordering of those strings. In many contexts, we are interested in the maximum–length string. For example, a healthy eater may scan a list of ingredients with a suspicious eye on the longest entry (e.g., monosodium glutamate). A person preparing name tags for a party may be interested in the length of the longest name from a guest list.

As a concrete example, we will design and implement a function that locates the maximum–length string from a sequence of strings. In this section, we are ready to take a look backstage, bridging the gap between the perspectives of the caller and the callee.

Usage

The key to creating a new function is to first consider how it will be used. What will the function's name be and what high-level task will it accomplish? What information will a caller need to send and what information should the function return?

For the case of determining a maximum-length string, we choose to name our function maxLength (this differentiates it from the existing max function). We expect the user to send us a sequence of strings as a parameter. Our function will locate the string that has the longest length and return that string to the caller. With these decisions in place, we can already envision code that might be used by a caller. For example in the context of analyzing foods, the following syntax can be used:

```
ingredients = ['carbonated water', 'caramel color',
    'phosphoric acid', 'sodium saccharin', 'potassium benzoate',
    'natural flavors', 'citric acid', 'caffeine',
    'potassium citrate', 'aspartame', 'dimethylpolysiloxane']

concern = maxLength(ingredients)      # calling our function
print concern
```

Notice that the calling syntax is maxLength(ingredients). Our function is not an official method of the **list** class, so it cannot be invoked using the syntax ingredients.maxLength( ). For a function to be an official method of a class, it must be defined as part of the original class definition (this will be the focus of the next chapter).

Implementation

A straightforward algorithm to find the maximum-length string is to scan the entire list, keeping track as we go of the longest entry that we have seen. In case of a tie, our function will return the first of the equally long strings it encounters. Our function definition is written as follows:

```
1  def maxLength(stringSeq):
2      longSoFar = ' '               # empty string, by default
3      for entry in stringSeq:
4          if len(entry) > len(longSoFar):   # even longer
5              longSoFar = entry
6      return longSoFar
```

A function declaration always begins with the keyword **def** (short for define). It is followed by the name of the function (in this case maxLength). Next, parentheses enclose a series of parameters that are to be sent by the caller (in this case, stringSeq). If a function does not require any parameters, there still must be opening and closing parentheses to demarcate the lack of parameters. Finally, an indented body contains the code that is executed when the function is invoked. Let's analyze the components of this example more carefully.

FIGURE 5.2: The parameter is identified as ingredients from the context of the caller, yet as stringSeq within the context of the function body.

Parameters

The name stringSeq we chose for the parameter is up to our discretion. This is known as a *formal parameter*; it serves as a placeholder for that piece of information indicated by the caller, known as the *actual parameter*. We cannot assume to know the variable name used by the caller. One caller may use the syntax maxLength(ingredients), while another maxLength(guests). To provide guidance, we choose a formal parameter name that suggests its meaning (although there is no guarantee that this is what the caller sends; more on this in Section 5.5). Each time our function is called, the system assigns the identifier we chose as a formal parameter to the actual parameter indicated by the caller, as shown in Figure 5.2. The code in the body of the function uses the formal parameter to identify the underlying piece of information (in this example, at line 3).

Body

The body of our function, shown in lines 2–6, implements our scanning algorithm. The identifier longSoFar is introduced at line 2 to track the longest string we have seen. Initially, we have not seen any strings, so we let the empty string be the longest thus far. The for loop of lines 3–5 checks each entry of the caller's sequence, looking for a string longer than any thus far. When the loop completes, longSoFar will identify the overall longest string in the original sequence.

However, the identifier longSoFar has what we term *local scope*. That identifier cannot be directly accessed by any block of code other than the body of the function; it is created solely for our use in processing the current function call. This is a good thing because it means that we do not need to worry about what variable names are used by the caller, and vice versa. If we declare a variable x and the caller also has a variable named x, these do not interfere with each other.

However, this local scope means that the caller cannot directly access the final result using the variable longSoFar. Instead, we rely on an explicit use of a **return** statement to communicate this information back to the caller.

Return value

At line 6 of our function body, we use the command **return** longSoFar. This indicates the value to be communicated back to the caller. It is not our concern what the caller plans to do with this information; we simply have a responsibility to inform the caller based upon the desired semantics of our function. Let's assume that the caller originally invoked our function with a command, such as concern = maxLength(ingredients). From the caller's perspective, the identifier concern is being assigned to the return value of the function.

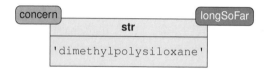

FIGURE 5.3: The mechanism for passing a return value is similar to that for a parameter. Upon return, the caller's identifier concern is associated with the object identified internally as longSoFar.

The internal mechanism for communicating an underlying object is quite similar to that of parameter passing. The caller's identifier is simply associated with the indicated return value, as shown in Figure 5.3. Although the local identifier longSoFar will cease to exist as the function ends, the underlying object will be available to the caller.

The **return** statement happened to be the last line of the body in our example, yet this is not always the case. If a **return** command is executed elsewhere within the body (for example, within a conditional), the execution of the function immediately ends with any specified value passed back to the caller. It is also possible to use a **return** statement without any subsequent value. Such a syntax is used to end the execution of the function without returning any formal value to the caller. Without an explicit object returned the special value **None** will be returned. In fact, if the execution of a function reaches the end of the body without an explicit **return** statement, **None** is automatically returned.

5.2.1 Flow of Control

We want to emphasize that calling a function is a form of a control statement. For the sake of analogy, we consider calling a function like hiring a contractor to perform a specific job. Parameters are sent to the contractor to describe the details of our particular request. Once we make the request, we do not get involved in the low-level work to be done. Moreover, we assume that we must wait for the contractor to complete the job before we continue doing any more of our own work.[1] So the moment the caller invokes the function, control is passed to the body of the function.

Ideally, the function will complete without any noticeable delay, but there is no guar-antee. Just like contract work, some function calls may take more time to complete than others. In fact it is possible that a function might never return (if stuck in an infinite loop), just as a contractor might never return (if a swindler). Of course, we should try to inter-act only with well-written functions and reputable contractors. If we consider the original caller to be "sleeping" during the execution of the function, that caller is woken the moment control is returned. The caller's code resumes precisely where it had been suspended. We typically diagram the flow of control of a single function call as shown in Figure 5.4.

More generally, we can nest function calls just as we nest other control structures. If the original caller entrusts a contractor to manage a task, it is entirely up to the contractor to handle the details. If the contractor wants to do all of the work personally, that is fine. But

---

1.   In real life, this depends upon whether our next task relies upon the completed job. If we have independent work, perhaps we can keep busy while the contractor is also working. With computer programs, there is a corresponding way to have two different processes progressing in parallel, but we leave this as an advanced topic (see *thread* in index).

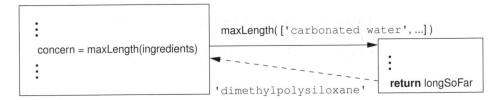

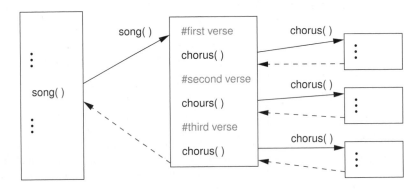

FIGURE 5.4: Flow of control for a function call.

FIGURE 5.5: Flow of control for nested function calls.

the contractor may also choose to hire one or more subcontractors to complete portions of the work. In fact, a subcontractor may hire yet another person, and so on. Notice that the original caller remains unaware of these details, while waiting for the contractor to return.

From a technical perspective, this process is accomplished by having the body of the original function make calls to one or more functions. As a simple example, suppose that we want a function song( ) that prints the lyrics to our favorite song. Since the chorus of a song is often repeated verbatim, we could have a second function chorus( ) that is solely responsible for the lyrics of the chorus. In this scenario, an original caller may invoke song( ), which itself invokes chorus( ), perhaps several times. Notice that there are two levels of suspended control each time the chorus( ) body is executing. The original caller is waiting, as is the execution of the song( ) function. When the chorus( ) returns control, it is returned to the entity that invoked it, in this case the song( ) function. We diagram the flow of control for this scenario in Figure 5.5.

5.2.2 Optional Parameters

In earlier chapters, we have encountered functions with optional parameters. A caller can choose to send a value for such a parameter, but otherwise a default value is substituted. We can provide default values for our own functions, as shown in the following simple example. A classic countdown (e.g., for a rocket launch), progresses from ten down to one. However, in creating a function for such a countdown, we may wish to allow the caller to pick an alternative starting point. Syntactically, this is done as follows.

```
def countdown(start=10):
  for count in range(start, 0, −1):
    print count
```

In this signature, start is a parameter that can be sent by the caller. However, if the caller does not send it, the value 10 will be used. So a call to countdown( ) will count down from ten, yet a call to countdown(3) will count down from three. For the record, we note that the longer syntax countdown(10) is still legal, that is, the caller may explicitly send the same value as the default.

   As a more complicated example, it is possible to declare multiple parameters with default values. The above version allows the user to choose the starting point of the count-down, but the last value printed in the countdown as defined is 1. We could write a two-parameter version of the function defined as follows:

```
def countdown(start=10, end=1):
  for count in range(start, end − 1, −1):
    print count
```

Notice that the definition specifies separate default values for each parameter. If someone uses the syntax countdown( ) the countdown will proceed from ten down to one. However, a caller can explicitly send other values, such as countdown(5, 0) to count from five down to and including zero. If the caller specifies only one parameter, such as countdown(3), that value is used for the *first* parameter, and the default is used for the second (in this case, counting down from three to one). It is also possible to define functions for which some parameters have default values and others do not. However, to avoid ambiguity, those parameters without default values must always be listed first in the signature.

FOR THE GURU

Each time a function is invoked, the system creates an internal structure, known as an ***activation record***, to keep track of important information relevant to this particular execution of the function. The activation record is maintained until the call is completed.

   The activation record tracks the values associated with all local identifiers, including the parameters. Furthermore, if the function invokes another and is therefore temporarily suspended, the activation record keeps track of where the work was interrupted. If many nested function calls are made, each call has an associated activation record. When control is returned to a function, the stored information allows it to properly resume its progress.

   We see evidence of these records when an exception halts a program, as Python displays a trace of the activations records for all currently active calls.

5.3 Avoiding Duplicate Code

The control structures we have introduced (loops, conditionals and functions) can be very valuable when programming. They provide convenient means for expressing tasks elegantly and succinctly. They help in designing code fragments that are reusable and easily maintained. Unfortunately, beginning programmers often miss opportunities to make best use of these constructs.

One common habit is to reuse a portion of code by simply copying it to another portion of a program, and modifying it if necessary. Text editors enable this style by supporting a copy-and-paste operation. Yet there are relatively few cases where copy-and-paste is the best choice of techniques. As a general rule, if you are tempted to copy and paste lines of code, there is probably a better way to design your code through the use of control structures.

We will explore several examples in this section. To frame our discussion, we begin with a blatant misuse of copy-and-paste. A classic punishment in school is to write a sentence such as "I will not chew gum in class" one hundred times on the blackboard. This is a time-consuming task by hand, although clearly straightforward. In the context of computing, generating this sort of output is easily automated. Of course, one possible program for doing so would have 100 lines of code, starting as follows:

```
print 'I will not chew gum in class'
print 'I will not chew gum in class'
print 'I will not chew gum in class'
print 'I will not chew gum in class'
print 'I will not chew gum in class'
...
```

Typing such a program seems burdensome, but with a basic text editor, the programmer could type the first line and then just repeatedly paste copies of that line to complete the rest of the program. While it's obvious that a more elegant program might be written as

```
for i in range(100):
    print 'I will not chew gum in class'
```

we want to discuss why the first version is such a bad program.

The biggest problem is that it is difficult to maintain. Suppose that we had inadvertently misspelled a word when typing the original line, but did not notice this until after copying it. To fix that mistake, we would need to edit all 100 lines (or edit the first line and then repaste 99 copies of that fixed line). With the more elegant approach, we would only have to fix the mistake in one place. In similar fashion, the first program is not easily adaptable if we were instead asked to print some other phrase one hundred times (e.g., "I will not use my cell phone in class.").

Now even a beginning programmer would probably recognize that such blatant repetition should be accomplished with a loop. But what about if the repetitions are not identical? For example, we presented the following code on page 112 of Chapter 3 (albeit, before we had formally introduced control structures).

```
 1  from time import sleep
 2  timeDelay = .25                    # one-quarter second
 3  car.move(−10, 0)
 4  sleep(timeDelay)
 5  car.move(−30, 0)
 6  sleep(timeDelay)
 7  car.move(−60, 0)
 8  sleep(timeDelay)
 9  car.move(−100, 0)
10  sleep(timeDelay)
```

This could have been entered by typing the first four lines, then pasting three additional copies of lines 3 and 4 and modifying them to adjust the x-coordinate of the move. We call this a copy–paste–and–modify approach. If we wanted even more frames of such an animation, we could continue to paste and modify those lines.

Since the repetitions are not identical, the use of a loop may not seem obvious. But there is clearly a repetitive pattern. The key to using a control structure in such a case is to isolate the particular part of the pattern that is being changed, the "modify" that takes place after the paste. In this case, the only modification is the x-coordinate of the move. So we should think of that as a variable when describing the repetition. For example, we could get the same effect with the following code:

```
from time import sleep
timeDelay = .25
for deltaX in [−10, −30, −60, −100]:
    car.move(deltaX, 0)
    sleep(timeDelay)
```

This code is significantly easier to maintain than the original. For example, we could easily divide all movements by two with a single change, using deltaX/2 rather than deltaX within the loop body. With the original code, we would have to edit each of the individual moves. We can add additional iterations to our new code by augmenting the list (it would be even more sophisticated to take advantage of the underlying pattern, namely that the car is accelerating to the left by ten units per iteration).

Functions

Designing useful functions is another classic way to avoid unnecessary duplication of code. Consider the structure of a typical song (for example as shown in Figure 5.5 from page 170). Often there is a verse, then a chorus, then a different verse, then a repeat of the same chorus, and so on. We want to avoid having duplicate code for each of the three chorus repetitions, but since the choruses are not repeated back–to–back, a loop may not be appropriate. Defining a single function that encapsulates the repeated task allows us to avoid the duplication. Once defined, the function can be called numerous times.

As a more tangible example of the wise use of functions, we revisit another example from the graphics chapter. The code for the animation case study from Section 3.9 has much unnecessary duplication. For example, constructing the target in lines 15–33 of Figure 3.22 involves the creation of three different circles representing the rings. Each of those circles has a different radius, color, and depth. We could simplify that code by defining a separate function for generating a custom circle as follows:

```
def createRing(radius, color, depth):
    c = Circle(radius)
    c.setFillColor(color)
    c.setDepth(depth)
    return c
```

With this function defined, lines 16–27 of the original code can be replaced as follows:

```
target.add(createRing(30, 'white', 49))
target.add(createRing(20, 'blue', 48))
target.add(createRing(10, 'red', 47))
```

Conditional statements

Another common temptation involves the use of copy-and-paste when working with different branches of a conditional statement. For example, consider the following code fragment which might be used in software for the checkout process for a store's website:

```
1  if destination == 'Missouri':
2      subtotal = sum(shoppingCart)
3      tax = subtotal * 0.04225
4      total = subtotal + tax
5  elif destination == 'Illinois':
6      subtotal = sum(shoppingCart)
7      tax = subtotal * 0.0625
8      total = subtotal + tax
```

We see that the program is calculating the total for a shopping cart, including sales tax based on the destination address. If the vendor operates in all 50 states, then presumably we might see versions of that four-line block repeated for each state.

Yet this program contains some unnecessary duplication, as the different branches are almost identical. The same technique is used to compute the total; the only difference between states is the tax-rate. Two of the three commands within each branch are not truly conditional. The command subtotal = sum(shoppingCart) is always executed first, no matter what state to which the order is being shipped. If that command is always executed, then it really should not be hidden within a conditional. We could move it ahead of the conditional, resulting in the following code.

```
subtotal = sum(shoppingCart)
if destination == 'Missouri':
    tax = subtotal * 0.04225
    total = subtotal + tax
elif destination == 'Illinois':
    tax = subtotal * 0.0625
    total = subtotal + tax
```

Similarly, the final command of each branch is the same, and so we could move it beyond the conditional, as follows:

```
subtotal = sum(shoppingCart)
if destination == 'Missouri':
    tax = subtotal * 0.04225
elif destination == 'Illinois':
    tax = subtotal * 0.0625
total = subtotal + tax
```

At this point, we have reduced the branching to the particular command that varies from state to state. There are only two lines of code per state in the new version versus four in the original. So with 50 states, 200 lines of code would be reduced to 100.

　　Still, the placement of the conditional within the flow of the program is somewhat distracting for a reader. We could further improve the readability of our program by defining a lookupTaxRate function for reporting the sales tax rate for a given state. We could then use the function as follows:

```
1  subtotal = sum(shoppingCart)
2  tax = subtotal * lookupTaxRate(destination)
3  total = subtotal + tax
```

The original branching is presumably displaced to within the function body. Yet this reorganization makes the primary portion of our code read more naturally.

5.4　Case Study: Computing the Square Root

Suppose that we want to compute the square root of a given value. While the math library already includes a sqrt function for this purpose, it is instructive to see that we can perform the calculation ourselves.

　　We will use an approach known as Newton's method. The technique is based on developing successive approximations to the answer. That is, we will start with a guess and repeatedly improve our guess. When computing a square root, if guess == number/guess, we have the right answer (by rearranging, we see guess*guess == number). More importantly, if the guess is wrong, the true square root lies between guess and number/guess. By taking their average, we get a new guess that is better than the previous one. By repeating this process, we get closer to the correct answer.

As a first attempt we suggest the following implementation, which we name sqrtA to distinguish it from the sqrt function of the math library:

```
def sqrtA(number):
  guess = 1.0
  while guess != number / guess:
    guess = (guess + number / guess) / 2.0    # use average
  return guess
```

Interestingly, this function works in some cases but not others. For instance, a call to sqrtA(4.0) will probably return 2.0, and a call to sqrtA(100.0) will return 10.0. Yet something goes wrong in other cases. As an experiment, try to compute a handful of other values: sqrtA(2.0), sqrtA(3.0), sqrtA(5.0), sqrtA(6.0). You will find that many of these calls never return; the culprit is an infinite loop.

In theory, Newton's method leads to better and better approximations to the true square root. But there is no guarantee that it will ever reach the *exact* square root. This fact is compounded by an inherent limit in precision when using floating-point values. Even though floating-point values can represent a wide range of numbers, they cannot perfectly represent every possible number. As a result, some of the arithmetic operations may have a small but noticeable error. Worse yet, the exact behavior may depend on your computer system, as Python typically relies upon the underlying computer hardware to perform floating-point computations. Different computers may use different floating-point implementations.

For the sqrtA implementation, the problem is that this while loop terminates only when we reach values that *precisely* satisfy the equation guess == number/guess. For some numbers, this is impossible when using floating-point values. Although we have to live with the fact that we cannot compute square roots exactly, it does not seem reasonable to live with a function that never returns. Our challenge is to determine a better way to halt the loop. We look at several possible approaches.

Fixed number of iterations

A sure way to avoid an infinite loop is to perform only a fixed number of iterations of Newton's method using a for loop. The question then becomes, how many iterations? For example, we could perform 100 iterations using the following code:

```
def sqrtB(number):
  guess = 1.0
  for trial in range(100):
    guess = (guess + number / guess) / 2.0    # use average
  return guess
```

But it is not clear why to pick 100. There is a clear trade-off. The more iterations we do, presumably the better answer we reach. We could go further and do one million iterations while still ensuring that we avoid an infinite loop. But the more iterations we do, the more time consuming the process will become. In fact in some cases, we reach our final answer

FOR THE GURU

If you want to dig deeper into the oddities that stem from the limited precision of floating-point values, try the following experiment on your machine. Different machines may have different behaviors, so don't be surprised if the experiment does not turn out the same way for you. Feel free to try similar experiments with other values.

When using one of the standard floating-point implementations, a call to sqrtA(5.0) actually returns an answer (approximately 2.2360679774997898). Yet in reality, we know that $\sqrt{5}$ is an irrational number and so there is no finite representation for the true value. We might wonder why our implementation of New-ton's method ever completes.

The explanation of such behavior is to recognize that we did not need to locate the true square root in order for our while loop to end. We simply needed to reach a value satisfying the equality guess == number/guess. This happens to be satisfied by our "solution" to sqrtA(5.0). We have a value that is not quite the true square root, but which matches the result of a (slightly inaccurate) division. The following interpreter session demonstrates the experiment:

```
>>> s = sqrtA(5.0)
>>> print s == 5.0/s
True
```

Perhaps even stranger yet, floating-point numbers can defy the basic rules of algebra. If s and 5.0/s are the same then algebraically s*s should equal 5.0. Yet in our experiment, the following test fails:

```
>>> print s*s == 5.0
False
```

The moral of this story is to be very cautious when using the precision of floating-point numbers. You should not rely on precise equality tests (i.e., ==) when using floating-point numbers, and similar oddities can be observed with many other arithmetic operations.

much earlier. For example, on our machine the computation of sqrtB(4.0) reaches the answer 2.0 after the fifth iteration. From that point on, we spend iteration after iteration revising our guess to be the average of 2.0 and 2.0. In cases where the process converges on an answer, it typically does so in 10 to 20 iterations, though this is not guaranteed. By picking a fixed number of iterations in advance, we may get a good answer but perhaps not the best result that would be achieved if we had been willing to do more iterations.

Iterate until gap is small

Intuitively, another approach is to use a while loop that dictates that we continue comput–ing successive approximations until we get "close enough." Of course, we need to define what constitutes close enough. One way to do this is to ask the user for an acceptable error bound; another way is for us to choose the error bounds. The following implementation accepts the allowable error as a parameter, yet with a default value of one millionth:

```
def sqrtC(number, allowableError=.000001):
    guess = 1.0
    while abs(guess – number / guess) > allowableError:
        guess = (guess + number / guess) / 2.0    # use average
    return guess
```

Notice that the while loop formulation is quite similar to that of sqrtA, but instead of requiring that guess precisely equal number/guess, we now continue looping so long as the difference between the two (in absolute value) is greater than the acceptable level of error. Our default error bound seems to be reasonable, and indeed it ensures that the function completes for many inputs. But it may cause the calculations to stop sooner than necessary, when more iterations could continue to improve the accuracy.

Even worse, the use of an error bound does not guarantee that the loop always ends. For example, if the user were to specify an allowable error of 0.0, we are in a situation similar to sqrtA. Even with our default error bound we can end up in an infinite loop. The precision of floating–point numbers decreases when the numbers are large, and so there may not be a solution that satisfies the error bound. Admittedly, we only seem to run into this trouble when taking the square root of a sextillion or more (that is, over 21 digits long).

Iterate until no more improvement

Our final approach uses a while loop to iterate so long as our estimate continues to improve. In this way, we can get as good a solution as possible with floating–point precision, while ensuring that we do not enter an infinite loop nor waste time doing extra iterations that do not improve the result.

Our way to measure improvement is based on the following. If we had infinite pre–cision the two key values in Newton's method, namely guess and number/guess, serve as bookends. If they are not precisely equal to each other then one will be less than the true answer and the other greater. Each successive approximation causes those bookends to move closer to each other. With the limited precision of floating–point numbers, what happens is that the numbers reach a point where no further improvement can be made or, worse yet, take a step farther apart due to error introduced into the calculation.

To implement this approach, we need to alter our code slightly from previous ver–sions. Because we want to know whether we have improved from one iteration to the next, we need to keep track of not just the current guess, but also the previous guess. Our goal will be to measure whether the lower of the two bookends continues to increase (with previous implementations, our guess oscillates between too small and too big). Our implementation is as follows.

```
def sqrtD(number):
  prevGuess = 0.0
  guess = min(1.0, number)
  while prevGuess < guess:
    prevGuess = guess
    avg = (guess + number / guess) / 2.0
    guess = min(avg, number / avg)
  return guess
```

The strict inequality in our while loop condition prevGuess < guess ensures our notion of continued improvement. As a technicality, we had to make sure to declare an initial "previous" guess of 0.0 to ensure that the loop was entered.

This final implementation is superior to any of our earlier versions. If the calculations converge to an answer after only a few iterations, our loop stops and returns the result. If it can keep making progress it does so. More importantly, calling this function will never result in an infinite loop. If we had infinite precision, Newton's method would go on forever in certain cases, such as calculating approximations to the irrational number $\sqrt{2}$. But since a floating-point number has finite granularity, we cannot continue finding better floating-point values indefinitely.[2] Eventually the guess fails to improve, ending our loop.

Taking square roots of negative numbers

None of the implementations we have suggested work properly if the user sends a negative number as the parameter. Of course there is no real number representing the square root of a negative number, so Newton's method is doomed to fail. The successive approximations fluctuate wildly with no possibility of convergence. Our various implementations fail in subtly different ways. The while loops of sqrtA and sqrtC will typically be infinite. The sqrtB function is based on a for loop, so it will return a result, although it has little relevance. Technically, the while loop of sqrtD is never entered because the original guess is less than zero, so the original negative number is always returned as the answer.

Clearly, none of these responses seems appropriate. In these cases, we must decide whether the blame lies with us as the programmer or with the caller (or both). As a programmer, we might wish to blame the caller, yet it seems unhelpful for an invalid input to lead to a misleading answer or a never-ending function call (imagine if this were the case for a handheld calculator). A better design would check for such a situation and respond in a more useful fashion. We address just this issue in the next section.

5.5 Error Checking and Exceptions

In your experiences thus far, you have undoubtedly run across situations in which the Python interpreter informs you of an error. Looking back at our earlier chapters, we have seen a NameError on page 34, TypeError's on pages 34 and 51, and ValueError's on pages 36 and 47. Each of these types of standard errors is a subclass of a general Exception class. In this section, we explore the role of exceptions in the language.

---

2. Proving such a guarantee relies upon international standards for floating-point implementations, as recommended by the IEEE organization.

Exceptions are used to report scenarios that are out of the ordinary, such as an attempt to use an identifier that is undefined, or a call to a function with the wrong number or type of parameters. Typically, the result of such an exception is to immediately stop the currently executing code. For a programmer, the exception describes the immediate cause of a significant problem. For a nonprogrammer who is the end user of software, seeing such a reported error is not helpful and reflects poorly on the quality of the software.

Consider the code from page 165, which prompts the user for a number from 1 to 10. At the time we used a while loop in an effort to ensure that a number typed by the user really is from 1 to 10. However, even that program is defective. If a user were to enter something other than an integer, for example banana, the following occurs:

```
Enter a number from 1 to 10: banana
Traceback (most recent call last):
  File "oneToTen.py", line 3, in -toplevel-
    number = int(raw_input('Enter a number from 1 to 10: '))
ValueError: invalid literal for int(): banana
```

To someone familiar with Python programming, this error message has meaning. The problem occurred when executing the following line of our program:

```
number = int(raw_input('Enter a number from 1 to 10: '))
```

The call to **raw_input** returns the actual character string entered by the user, and the separate call to **int**( ) is used to convert that string to the corresponding integer. The problem is that the string 'banana' is not a valid literal for an integer. This gets reported as a ValueError because the value of the given string is not legitimate for this purpose.

While we are able to make sense of this error, such outward behavior should never be accepted in consumer-quality software. Abruptly quitting the program is an unreasonable reaction to an errant input. A more reasonable response is to remind the user that an integer is expected, and then to reprompt.

5.5.1 Catching an Exception

To design a more robust piece of software, we need to introduce a new control structure termed a *try statement*. It is used to encase a block of code containing one or more statements that might cause an exception. Informally, we refer to this as *catching* the exception. The most straightforward syntax for the statement appears as follows:

```
try:
    body
except errorClass:
    recoveryBody
```

This code works as follows. The primary body of the try statement begins executing, and if all goes well it completes as normal. However, if the specified type of exception is raised during the execution of the body, the execution of the body is immediately interrupted and the appropriate commands from the recovery body are executed.

As an example, here is a new version of the program for reading an integer, this time taking care to respond gracefully when a noninteger string is entered by the user.

```
1  number = 0                                    # not valid
2  while not 1 <= number <= 10:
3    try:
4      number = int(raw_input('Enter a number from 1 to 10: '))
5      if not 1 <= number <= 10:
6        print 'Your number must be from 1 to 10.'
7    except ValueError:
8      print 'That is not a valid integer.'
```

Let's consider the flow of control for three possible scenarios shown in the following execution:

```
Enter a number from 1 to 10: 23
Your number must be between 1 an 10.
Enter a number from 1 to 10: banana
That is not a valid integer.
Enter a number from 1 to 10: 9
```

During the first pass of the loop, the user enters 23. At line 4, this is converted (without error) to the corresponding integer number. Because this number is not within the desired range, the conditional at line 5 triggers the output at line 6. At this point, the body of the try statement has completed without error; therefore the except clause is irrelevant to this scenario. However, we are still within the context of the while loop body, so the condition at line 2 is reevaluated and because it fails, the while loop body is executed again.

During the second pass, the user enters the string banana. This causes a ValueError to be raised by line 4 during the attempted conversion to a number. This error causes the immediate interruption of the try statement body. Thus we do not execute lines 5 and 6 in this scenario. Instead, control is taken to the body of the except clause in which we print a more appropriate error message. Still, we are within the context of the while loop body and so control proceeds back to the condition at line 2. As a technical note, when we executed line 4 in the previous scenario the error occurred *before* the assignment to number. So that variable still holds its preceding value (in this example, 23). Because that number is not in the desired range, the body of the while loop is entered again.

In the third pass, the user enters 9. This is correctly converted to a number at line 4. Then the conditional of line 5 is evaluated. Since our new number is within the desired range, the conditional body is bypassed, bringing us to the end of the try body and also to the end of the while loop iteration. Once again, control is brought back to the while condition at line 2 and in this case the loop exits.

So our new version does a much better job of handling errors gracefully. Still it is not perfect. Although we seem to be prepared for any string that the user might enter, the user can cause our software to crash by typing the control-d keystroke when prompted for a response. This causes the following response.

```
Enter a number from 1 to 10: control-d
Traceback (most recent call last):
  File "oneToTen.py", line 4, in -toplevel-
    number = int(raw_input('Enter a number from 1 to 10: '))
EOFError
```

Technically the problem is that the control-d keystroke closes the input console and so the call to **raw_input** fails with an EOFError. When the error is raised the original **try** body is interrupted, and because this particular type of error was not caught by the except statement we again have an uncaught exception, resulting in the interruption of the overall program. In cases where different types of error are possible, we can provide multiple **except** clauses. However, in the case of an EOFError we cannot simply print an error message and reprompt, because the input console has already been closed; all subsequent **raw_input** calls would similarly fail. Instead, our design is to simply pick a number on the user's behalf so that we can move on beyond the while loop. Our revised implementation is

```
number = 0                                    # not valid
while not 1 <= number <= 10:
  try:
    number = int(raw_input('Enter a number from 1 to 10: '))
    if not 1 <= number <= 10:
      print 'Your number must be from 1 to 10.'
  except ValueError:
    print 'That is not a valid integer.'
  except EOFError:
    print 'Why did you do that?'
    print 'We will choose for you.'
    number = 7
```

It is also possible to have a final **except** clause without any explicit designation for an exception type. That clause will be triggered by any exceptions that were not already handled.

5.5.2 Raising an Exception

In the preceding discussion, we saw how to gracefully catch errors that occur. We also have the ability to raise exceptions from within our own code. As a motivating example, we revisit the function for computing a square root (specifically, we use the sqrtD version from Section 5.4 as our basis).

That code works properly so long as the caller sends a nonnegative value as a parameter; however, it malfunctions in the case where a negative number is sent, such as sqrt(-5). While we might blame a caller who sends such a parameter, it still reflects poorly on us if our function returns an inaccurate result without drawing attention to the problem. This is a perfect situation for raising an exception, in particular a ValueError which is the standard error used in a case where a parameter is of the correct data type but not a legitimate value of that type. A more robust version of this function appears as follows.

```
1   def sqrtE(number):
2     if number < 0:
3       raise ValueError('sqrt(number): number is negative')
4     prevGuess = 0.0
5     guess = min(1.0, number)
6     while prevGuess < guess:
7       prevGuess = guess
8       avg = (guess + number / guess) / 2.0
9       guess = min(avg, number / avg)
10    return guess
```

The addition to the code involves lines 2 and 3. When we recognize the problem situation, we raise an exception using the syntax at line 3. When raising an exception, we technically create an instance of the appropriate error class, providing a descriptive error message as a parameter to its constructor. Lines 4–10 of this code could be expressed within an **else** clause of the conditional, but this is unnecessary. When an exception is raised, this immediately suspends execution of the function, passing control back to the caller. This is similar to the way in which a **return** statement ends the execution of a function.

The purpose of raising an exception is to draw attention to a clear problem. This gives the opportunity for the caller's side of the code to catch the potential exception and gracefully recover. Even if the caller did not foresee the error and catch it, raising an exception causes the entire program execution to stop with an appropriate error message. While we have said that this is not a good final result in consumer-quality software, it is more helpful to a developer when debugging than the alternative of quietly returning a misleading result.

5.5.3 Type Checking

Our latest implementation of a square root function is still flawed. We are conscientious enough to perform the explicit check number < 0. But we never bother to check whether the parameter is really a number. If the caller invokes sqrt('hello'), this leads to a very unpredictable error. We wish to improve our function so that it explicitly checks that the data sent matches the expected type. We call this technique *type checking*.

Our strategy is as follows. We first check that the parameter is of the expected type. If not, the traditional response is to raise a TypeError. Once we are content with the parameter type, we perform the additional check to see whether the value is nonnegative. Our preferred tool for type checking is a built-in function isinstance. This function takes two parameters, the first of which is the object in question and the second of which is typically a class. If the object is an instance of that class then it returns **True**; otherwise it returns **False**. For example, we could evaluate the expression isinstance(number, **float**) to check whether the user has sent a floating-point value as a parameter.

Of course, we want to allow the user to send either an integer or a floating-point number. Although we could accomplish this as two separate checks, there is a more convenient way. Rather than specifying a single class as the parameter to isinstance, we are allowed to send a *tuple* of classes, as shown in the following version.

```
def sqrtF(number):
  if not isinstance(number, (int,float)):
    raise TypeError('sqrt(number): number must be numeric')
  if number < 0:
    raise ValueError('sqrt(number): number is negative')
  # done error checking;  can safely perform our calculation...
```

How much type checking is enough?

We do not mean to suggest that you perform strict type checking for every parameter sent to every Python function that you ever write. In some sense, the great advantage of Python is its simplicity. A function has a presumed interface, dictating the number and type of parameters to be sent by the caller. Although Python enforces that the correct number of parameters are sent, the expected type of those parameters is only implied by default. So long as the caller uses the function properly, everything works. For example, here is a simple function that could be used to scale a sequence of numbers by a given factor.

```
def scaleData(data, factor):
  for i in range(len(data)):
    data[i] = factor * data[i]
```

Presumably the data parameter is a sequence of numbers and factor is a number; this could be documented formally if we choose (more on documentation in Chapter 7). The point is that if the caller sends the expected information, the function works.

We could write a more strictly type-checked version of this function as follows:

```
1  def scaleData(data, factor):
2    if not isinstance(data, list):
3      raise TypeError('data must be a list')
4    for item in data:
5      if not isinstance(item, (int,float)):
6        raise TypeError('data items must all be numeric')
7    if not isinstance(factor, (int,float)):
8      raise TypeError('factor must be numeric')
9    for i in range(len(data)):
10     data[i] = factor * data[i]
```

Lines 3 and 4 are used to ensure that the first parameter is indeed a **list**. However, we must also ensure that each individual entry of that list is indeed a number, as checked in lines 4 and 5. Finally, lines 7 and 8 check the second parameter. If all goes well, then we finally perform the intended operations in lines 9 and 10.

Writing a program with such type checking clearly takes additional effort. Also, as the program executes, evaluating all of those tests takes additional time. The program runs more efficiently if we just trust that the caller knows what to do. Of course, if the caller makes a mistake, the lack of type checking can cause unexpected problems. There is a

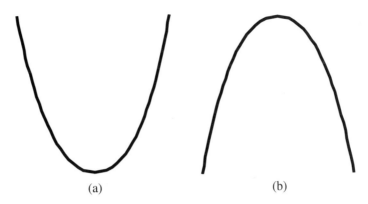

(a)   (b)

FIGURE 5.6: (a) A chain at equilibrium under the force of gravity. (b) The Gateway Arch.

trade-off involved. If you are writing functions for your own program, then you are both the caller and the callee; perhaps you can trust yourself. However, when you are writing code that you envision being imported and used by other programmers, there is more of a case for type checking. For example, you will find that almost all of the built-in functions for Python perform rather extensive checks.

5.6   Case Study: Simulating a Chain under the Force of Gravity

Our final case study is more intricate, incorporating many control structures in a single application. If you fix the two ends of a long chain and allow the rest of the chain to fall under the force of gravity, it naturally forms a shape known as a ***catenary curve***, shown in Figure 5.6(a). Although it looks somewhat like a parabola, it is not the same. This curve has some interesting properties and the inverted curve is used in architecture (e.g., the Gateway Arch in St. Louis) due to its stability. Our goal is to compute the catenary curve using a physical simulation. As was the case with square roots, our high-level approach is to compute successive approximations until reaching (near) equilibrium.

The model

We represent the shape of the chain by keeping track of the position of a number of inter-mediate points. We imagine a *link* connecting each pair of neighboring points. The more links we use, the better precision we can get at the cost of increased computational time. In our experiments, we use a total of 50 links. We model links with elasticity. Each link will have a natural resting length, yet it can be stretched beyond that length with sufficient force. The force required is proportional to the distance beyond the resting length.

The catenary curve is reached when all of the interior points of the chain are locally at equilibrium. For each interior point, there are three directional forces involved. If the left neighbor is farther away than the resting link length, then an elastic force will try to pull the point back toward the left neighbor. Similarly, there may be a force pulling the point toward its right neighbor. Finally, a fixed gravitational force pulls the point downward. A diagram of these three forces is shown in Figure 5.7. The point is at equilibrium if the sum of those three forces is precisely zero. Otherwise, we try to improve our approximation by

FIGURE 5.7: Three forces act upon each interior point of our chain.

altering the position of the point in the direction of the combined force. During one pass of our algorithm, we perform this calculation for each interior point of our chain (the two extreme points are never moved).

Another issue that remains is when to stop the process. In an ideal world, we reach a time when each interior point is perfectly at equilibrium. This is the case when the chain is at rest in nature. However, we cannot guarantee such an convergence using our technique. There are two problems involved. One is the inaccuracy of floating-point calculations, as was the problem when computing square roots in Section 5.4; but there is an additional problem here. We cannot guarantee that each new approximation is better than the previous one. When computing square roots, our approximation was a single number and Newton's method guaranteed that the average of the previous lower and upper bounds was a better approximation. In this case study, our approximation is a series of points and there is not such a clear definition for it being better as a whole. When we adjust the position of points, some estimates may improve while others degrade. The success depends subtly on the precise constants used for modeling gravity and the elasticity of links. With the proper choice, our algorithm terminates as follows. We pick a small positive value epsilon, and consider an individual point to be at approximate equilibrium if each coordinate of the combined force has magnitude at most epsilon. We consider the chain as a whole to be at approximate equilibrium if every interior point is so.

The implementation

We represent the chain as a list of points, where each point is represented as an (x, y) tuple. We also use (x, y) tuples to represent the components of the forces during our internal cal-culations. There are several key constants that control aspects of our simulation. In our own experiments, we have chosen the following values; you may experiment with other values at your own risk!

numLinks	= 50
restingLength	= 20.0
totalSeparation	= 630.0
elasticityConstant	= 0.005
gravityConstant	= 0.110
epsilon	= 0.001

The first value is the overall number of links. Keep in mind that a chain of 50 links has 51 points. The second constant defines the natural resting length of a single link, while the third defines the overall separation between the two ends of the chain. The elasticity constant will be used in calculating the force between neighbors while the gravity constant models the downward force upon all points. The final constant is used as part of the stopping criteria, as previously discussed.

Before describing the primary algorithm, we define some convenient utility functions. As a first utility function, we consider the need for adding tuples that represent (x, y) coordinates. We find the need to compute sums, for example in calculating the composite force from the left neighbor, the right neighbor, and gravity. Also, an updated point position is adjusted as the sum of the old position plus the composite force. Although we use tuples as our representation for coordinates, the semantics of addition for tuples does not match our needs. A tuple is a sequence of values and so addition is defined so that (1, 4) + (2, 5) evaluates to (1, 4, 2, 5). In the context of geometry, we prefer such a sum to be evaluated as (3, 9). For convenience, we define our own function to combine these tuples. At one point we will need to combine three tuples and at another point only two tuples. We implement a single function to handle both of these scenarios by cleverly using a default parameter. We write our function to accept three tuples, but with a default value of (0, 0) for the third. Our code appears as follows:

```
def combine(A, B, C=(0,0) ):
    return (A[0] + B[0] + C[0], A[1] + B[1] + C[1])
```

Notice that the return value of this function is a single tuple, with two entries that represent the sum of the three original tuples. Because of the default parameter, the expression combine((1, 4), (2, 5)) is legal and evaluates to the result (3, 9) as desired.

Next, we consider the computation of the force exerted due to the elasticity of a link between two neighboring points. This is a good opportunity for defining a function, as we will need to perform such a computation repeatedly. Furthermore, although the physics is relatively straightforward, the code is rather detailed. Separating that logic makes the main part of our program more clear.

So we define a calcForce function that determines the local force that one neighbor exerts upon another. As input to our function, we expect the user to send us the position of the two points in question, each expressed as an (x, y) tuple. Our goal will be to return a directional force, also as a tuple, that represents the force exerted upon point A due to neighbor B. The physical equations are performed as follows. We first compute the relative separation between the two points along the separate x-axis and y-axis. Then we compute the separating distance using the Pythagorean theorem. There will only be an elastic force if that distance is strictly greater than the prescribed resting length for a link. If it is greater, we define the "stretch" to be the amount by which the actual distance exceeds the resting length. The resulting force is aligned as a vector pointing directly from A to B, but scaled by our elasticity constant times the amount of stretch. A diagram of the mathematics is shown in Figure 5.8. Our actual implementation is as follows.

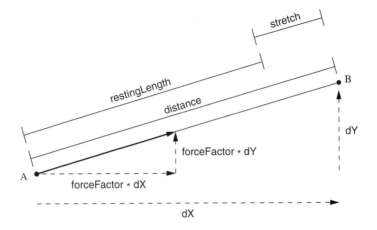

FIGURE 5.8: Computing the force exerted on point A due to neighbor B.

```
def calcForce(A, B):
  dX = (B[0] − A[0])
  dY = (B[1] − A[1])
  distance = sqrt(dX * dX + dY * dY)
  if distance > restingLength:                 # link being stretched
    stretch = distance − restingLength
    forceFactor = stretch * elasticityConstant
  else:
    forceFactor = 0
  return (forceFactor * dX, forceFactor * dY)  # returning a tuple
```

Notice that tuples A and B are sent as parameters by the caller. Technically, our function makes reference to the other special constants restingLength and elasticityConstant. We could have asked the user to send those as parameters, but for this application we want to treat them as constants so it seems unnecessary to have them sent each time. Since they will be constants, we could actually write this code to hardwire the literal 0.005 in place of elasticityConstant, for example. However, it is better for clarity to use descriptive names in place of such constants. Although we did not explicitly discuss this in Section 5.2, a function body is allowed to access identifiers that have what is termed *global scope*. Reliance on global identifiers is generally discouraged, but commonly used when those globals represent constant values. We will discuss the issue of global scope more specifically in Section 12.6.1.

At this point, we are ready to implement the primary logic of our simulation. We begin by establishing the initial state of our chain to be a straight line along the x-axis. We place the first endpoint at position (0,0), the final point at position (totalSeparation,0), and all intermediate points spaced evenly between. We accomplish this initialization using an index-based for loop to interpolate the positions.

```
chain = [ ]
for k in range(numLinks + 1):
  X = totalSeparation * k / numLinks
  chain.append( (X, 0.0) )                        # add new position
```

We compute successive approximations using a while loop that continues so long as we detect sufficient movement in at least one point. Our implementation of this logic appears as follows (the line numbers are from the complete program shown in Figure 5.9).

```
49  somethingMoved = True                          # force loop to start
50  while somethingMoved:
51    somethingMoved = False                       # default for new iteration
52    oldChain = list(chain)                        # record a copy of the data
53    for k in range(1, numLinks):                  # alter all interior points
54      gravForce = (0, gravityConstant)            # downward force
55      leftForce = calcForce(oldChain[k], oldChain[k−1])
56      rightForce = calcForce(oldChain[k], oldChain[k+1])
57      adjust = combine(gravForce, leftForce, rightForce)
58      if abs(adjust[0]) > epsilon or abs(adjust[1]) > epsilon:
59        somethingMoved = True
60      chain[k] = combine(oldChain[k], adjust)
```

For clarity, we rely upon a boolean somethingMoved to track this loop condition. We set the value to be **True** at line 49 so that we enter the loop the first time. But within each iteration of the loop, we begin optimistically by setting somethingMoved to **False** at line 51. If it remains that way throughout the current iteration, it becomes the final iteration. But if we ever find ourselves adjusting a point by strictly more than epsilon in either dimension, line 59 notes that a point has sufficiently moved thereby causing at least one more pass.

An important subtlety in our approach is seen at line 52. This line causes oldChain to be a *copy* of the chain. Note that this is quite different semantics from the command oldChain = chain, which would simply make the identifier oldChain reference the same underlying list. The need for this copy is as follows. The inner for loop is used to recompute the position of each interior point of the chain, one by one. We want to do all of those computations based upon a coherent state of the chain. If we had not made a copy, we would run into the following trouble. The adjustment to the second point in the chain depends on the positions of the first and third points. Suppose that we were to make that adjustment and then continue. The next step would be to calculate the adjustment to the third point, which depends on the positions of the second and fourth points. But now there would be a discrepancy between the preceding position of the second point and its updated position. We want to use the preceding position of the second point for consistency. For this reason, we compute all forces based upon the copy of the old chain.

The body of the inner for loop is straightforward, thanks to the use of our two functions. Lines 54–56 compute the three individual forces affecting point oldChain[k] and line 57 adds them together to have a single composite force. That force is used at line 60 to introduce a small adjustment to the position of the point to form its new position.

Visualization

The implementation from the preceding section correctly calculates the catenary curve. However, the results are stored internally as a list of positions. Although we could print out all the data, it is more satisfying to visualize the data graphically. In this section, we augment our implementation to include such a display. Our goal is not only to display the final curve, but to animate the various approximations that are used along the way.

We use the Path class of the cs1graphics package to display the chain. After we initialize the original chain representation, we perform the following initialization of the graphical components of the program:

```
paper = Canvas(totalSeparation, totalSeparation)
paper.setAutoRefresh(False)
curve = Path( )
for p in chain:
  curve.addPoint(Point(p[0], p[1]))
paper.add(curve)
```

Notice that we intentionally turned off the auto-refresh nature of the canvas, as discussed in Section 3.7. The displayed path has many points and those points will be adjusted one at a time in succession. If the canvas attempted to automatically refresh its image after each individual point of the path were moved, the user might notice artifacts. It is a much better strategy to rely on explicit refresh commands, so that we can move all points of the path before redisplaying the image. We have chosen to define one more utility function responsible for updating the points on the graphical path to match the current positions in the chain data. The function appears as follows:

```
def drawChain(chainData, chainPath, theCanvas):
  for k in range(len(chainData)):
    chainPath.setPoint(Point(chainData[k][0], chainData[k][1]), k)
  theCanvas.refresh( )
```

The first parameter is a reference to the underlying list of data points, the second a reference to the graphical Path object, and the third the canvas so that we can force a refresh. This function can be used in several ways. If we only want to display the final result, we can call the function once at the end of our program. For a more interesting animation of the progression, we place a call to drawChain within the body of the while loop itself, so that we see each successive approximation to the curve, leading to the final one. Depending upon the speed of the graphics, this animation may seem tediously slow given that there are thousands of passes through the loop. In our own implementation, we only draw every hundredth approximation. To do this, we keep track of an additional counter within the while loop that counts down from 100 to 0. Each time it reaches 0, we draw an update of the curve and reset the counter to 100. Our final implementation of the complete project is shown in Figure 5.9.

```
1   from cs1graphics import *
2   from math import sqrt                              # use the official sqrt function
3
4   # chosing constants which give nice result
5   numLinks           = 50
6   restingLength      = 20.0
7   totalSeparation    = 630.0
8   elasticityConstant = 0.005
9   gravityConstant    = 0.110
10  epsilon            = 0.001
11
12  # convenient function for adding up to three (x,y) tuples
13  def combine(A, B, C=(0,0) ):
14      return (A[0] + B[0] + C[0], A[1] + B[1] + C[1])
15
16  # function returns a tuple representing the force being
17  # exerted upon point A due to the link joining A to B.
18  def calcForce(A, B):
19      dX = (B[0] − A[0])
20      dY = (B[1] − A[1])
21      distance = sqrt(dX * dX + dY * dY)
22      if distance > restingLength:                    # link being stretched
23          stretch = distance − restingLength
24          forceFactor = stretch * elasticityConstant
25      else:
26          forceFactor = 0
27      return (forceFactor * dX, forceFactor * dY)     # returning a tuple
28
29  # function to alter the graphical path and refresh canvas
30  def drawChain(chainData, chainPath, theCanvas):
31      for k in range(len(chainData)):
32          chainPath.setPoint(Point(chainData[k][0], chainData[k][1]), k)
33      theCanvas.refresh( )
34
35  # initialize the chain; one end at (0,0) other at (totalSeparation,0)
36  chain = [ ]
37  for k in range(numLinks + 1):
38      X = totalSeparation * k / numLinks
39      chain.append( (X, 0.0) )                        # add new position
```

FIGURE 5.9: Code for simulating a chain under gravity (continued on next page).

```
40   # initialize the graphics
41   paper = Canvas(totalSeparation, totalSeparation)
42   paper.setAutoRefresh(False)
43   curve = Path( )
44   for p in chain:
45     curve.addPoint(Point(p[0], p[1]))
46   paper.add(curve)
47   graphicsCounter = 100                          # draw every 100th iteration
48
49   somethingMoved = True                          # force loop to start
50   while somethingMoved:
51     somethingMoved = False                       # default for new iteration
52     oldChain = list(chain)                       # record a copy of the data
53     for k in range(1, numLinks):                 # alter all interior points
54       gravForce = (0, gravityConstant)           # downward force
55       leftForce = calcForce(oldChain[k], oldChain[k−1])
56       rightForce = calcForce(oldChain[k], oldChain[k+1])
57       adjust = combine(gravForce, leftForce, rightForce)
58       if abs(adjust[0]) > epsilon or abs(adjust[1]) > epsilon:
59         somethingMoved = True
60       chain[k] = combine(oldChain[k], adjust)
61
62     graphicsCounter −= 1
63     if graphicsCounter == 0:
64       drawChain(chain, curve, paper)
65       graphicsCounter = 100
66
67   curve.setBorderWidth(2)                         # emphasize final result
68   drawChain(chain, curve, paper)
```

FIGURE 5.9 (continuation): Code for simulating a chain under gravity.

5.7   Chapter Review

5.7.1   Key Points

While Loops

- A while loop allows for iteration based upon a given condition, rather than upon a given sequence of values. This is most helpful for cases when the number of iterations is not apparent at the onset of a loop.

- The generic syntax of a while loop appears as follows:

    while *condition***:**
       body

- If the while loop condition is originally **False**, the body of the loop is never executed.

- If the while loop condition is **True**, the body of the loop is executed, then the condition is rechecked, continuing in this fashion until the condition fails.

- If the while loop condition remains **True**, the loop never ends; this is an *infinite loop*.

User-Defined Functions

- The generic syntax of a user-defined function appears as follows:

     def *functionName*(*parameters*)**:**
        body

- The formal parameters are specified within parentheses as a series of identifiers separated by commas. If no parameters is expected, a set of parentheses is still required.

- The formal parameters are used locally within the context of the function body.

- When the function is invoked, each formal parameter is assigned the value of the corresponding actual parameter that was provided by the caller.

- If a function definition includes a default value for a parameter, that parameter becomes optional. If the caller does not explicitly send a value, the formal parameter is assigned to the default.

- When a caller invokes a function, the flow of control is passed from the caller to the body of the function. The body of the function then executes until reaching an explicit **return** command or the bottom of the body.

- The **return** command causes the immediate end of a function call. If a value is given after the word **return**, that value is returned to the caller.

- The body of a function can invoke another function. We call these nested calls.

Avoiding Duplicate Code

- If you are tempted to copy and paste lines of code, there is probably a better way to design your code through the use of control structures.

- If a block of code is repeated more than once without modification, then a simple loop can be used to express the repetition.

- If a block of code is repeated but with modification, the key to reducing the duplication is to maintain variables for the modified portions when possible.

- If a block of code is repeated but not in immediate succession, a function can be defined to avoid duplication, with parameters to represent any varying values.

Error Checking and Exceptions

- Exceptions (e.g., ValueError, TypeError) are used by Python to report execution errors.

- By default, an exception causes an executing program to stop, with the error reported.

- An exception can be caught through the use of a **try-except** statement of the form:

     try:
        body
     except *errorClass***:**
        recoveryBody

- If no errors occur while executing the **try** body, then the **except** clause has no effect.

- If an error occurs within the body of a **try** statement, the flow of control immediately exits the body and proceeds to the matching **except** clause.
- We can raise an exception from within our own code using the command **raise**, with an instance of an appropriate exception class.
- We can test whether an object belongs to a certain class by using the boolean function isinstance. For example, we might write isinstance(age,**int**).

5.7.2 Glossary

activation record An internal record kept by the system to track each invocation of a function. It maintains the state of all parameters and local identifiers as the execution proceeds.

actual parameter The object that is sent by a caller when invoking a function; *compare to* formal parameter.

error checking The general practice of ensuring that data (for example, that sent by a caller or entered by a user) has the appropriate type and value.

exception A general class used to report unexpected errors during the execution of a program.

formal parameter An identifier used in the signature of a function declaration that serves as a placeholder for the value of an actual parameter sent by the caller.

function A programming construct for encapsulating a (user-defined) behavior.

global scope The context of an identifier that is introduced at the top level of a program.

infinite loop A while loop that executes indefinitely because the loop condition remains satisfied.

local scope The context of an identifier that is introduced within the body of a function and is only accessible for the duration of the function call.

optional parameter A parameter that can be sent to a function, yet which is assigned a default value if not sent.

parameter A piece of information sent from the caller to the callee upon invocation of a function.

return value A piece of information sent back from the callee to the caller at the conclusion of a function call.

scope The context of a program within which an identifier is defined.

sequential search An algorithm used to find a value in a sequence by scanning from beginning to end, until either finding the value or exhausting the entire sequence.

try statement A control structure used to encase a block of code that might generate an exception.

type checking A technique by which data is explicitly examined to ensure that it belongs to the expected class.

while loop A control structure used to repeat a block of code so long as a given condition remains true.

5.7.3 Exercises

While Loops

Practice 5.1: Consider the following program:

```
val = 5
while val < 10:
    val = val + 1
    print val
```

Predict the output that results when this code is executed.

Practice 5.2: Consider the following program:

```
A = 2
B = 1
while A + B < 24:
    print A, B
    if A > B:
        B = B + 6
    else:
        A = A + 2
```

Predict the output that results when this code is executed.

Practice 5.3: Write a code fragment that prompts the user to enter numbers and prints out the average of the numbers. The program should keep asking the user to enter another number until he enters the number 0, at which point the program shoud print out the average and stop. The output should be a floating-point number. For example,

```
Enter a number: 5
Enter a number: 17
Enter a number: 14
Enter a number: 0

The average is 12.0
```

Exercise 5.4: Consider the following program:

```
val = 9
while val > 4:
    print val
    val = val - 1
```

Predict the output that results when this code is executed.

Exercise 5.5: Consider the following program:

```
A = 10
B = 64
while A < B:
  print A, B
  A = A − 1
  B = B / 2
```

Predict the output that results when this code is executed.

Exercise 5.6: Consider the following program:

```
A = 19
B = 7
while A > B:
  print A, B
  if A + B < 24:
    B = B + 5
  else:
    A = A − 2
```

Predict the output that results when this code is executed.

Exercise 5.7: On page 131, we used an index-based for loop to print a numbered shopping list. Rewrite that code using a while loop instead of a for loop.

Exercise 5.8: Write a program that answers the following question. Starting with x = 1, how many times can x be doubled before reaching one million or more?

Exercise 5.9: Write a program that allows the user to enter words, continuing until the user first enters a duplicate. Your program should work as shown in the following script (the underlined parts are those parts typed by the user).

```
Start entering words:
kiwi
apple
banana
apple
You already entered apple.
You listed 3 distinct words.
```

Exercise 5.10: In Exercise 4.29, you computed an approximation of π by using finitely many terms from the beginning of the infinite series. It turns out that a very accurate approximation can be imported from Python's math module, as the identifier pi.

Recompute your own approximation from scratch, this time using a **while** loop to continue until your approximation is accurate to within one-millionth when compared to the value given in the math module. Have your program report the overall number of iterations used.

Exercise 5.11: You can check whether one string is contained as a substring of another using the built-in syntax `'era' in 'average'`. Implement such a test on your own. Do not use any behaviors of the string class other than the fact that strings are a sequence of characters.

Exercise 5.12: Give numbers x and y that are both less than 1000, yet which require five or more iterations of the while loop in our implementation of Euclid's algorithm.

Exercise 5.13: In Section 5.1 we saw two ways to calculate the gcd of two numbers. Here is another proposal.

```
u = int(raw_input('Enter first number: '))
v = int(raw_input('Enter second number: '))

smallest = min(u,v)                      # biggest possible choice
gcd = 1
for d in range(2, smallest + 1):
  if u % d == 0 and v % d == 0:          # d is a divisor
    gcd = gcd * d
    u = u / d
    v = v / d

print 'The gcd is', gcd
```

Often this program finds the correct gcd, but it does not always do so. Give an example in which the algorithm fails and then fix the implementation.

Exercise 5.14: In Exercise 4.15 the goal was to convert a string representing a number in a nonstandard base (with 1 <= base <= 9) into the equivalent (decimal) integer. In this problem we want you to do the converse. Ask the user for a (decimal) integer value as well as a base from 2 to 9. Your goal is to produce the string that represents that same value expressed in the indicated base.

One algorithm for performing this conversion determines the individual characters of the result from right to left as follows.

- Start with the original value and an initially empty string result.
- While the value is greater than zero, do the following:
    - Compute both the quotient and remainder of that value divided by the desired base.
    - The character representing the remainder should be added as the next digit to the left side of the result.
    - The computed quotient should be subsequently used as the value.

Implement this algorithm. For example if the user gives you the value 84 and indicates base 5, you should generate the string `'314'`, which is the equivalent base 5 representation.

Exercise 5.15: Redo Exercise 5.14, this time allowing for bases from 2 to 36 (see discussion in Exercise 4.30 regarding digits in higher bases). Recall that the function ord converts a character to the underlying integer code, for example ord('A') returns 65. The function chr converts the integer code to the corresponding character, for example chr(65) returns 'A'. As a test of your program, if the user gives you the value 64180 and requests base 16, the result should be the string 'FAB4'.

Exercise 5.16: An integer $k \geq 2$ is a *prime number* if it is not evenly divisible by any numbers in range(2,k). Build a list of all prime numbers less than or equal to a value n entered by a user. For each $2 \leq k \leq n$, test its primality by looping over range(2,k) looking for a factor of k.

Exercise 5.17: The approach suggested in Exercise 5.16 for finding primes less than or equal to n is not the most efficient approach. When testing the primality of a specific k, do not bother checking all possible factors in range(2,k). Just check for factors among those smaller values that have already been determined to be prime (if k is not divisible by a prime factor, it cannot be divisible by any other factors).

Functions

Practice 5.18: Consider the following definitions:

```
def silly(x):
    print 'start silly'
    print x
    funny(2 * x)
    goofy(x - 1)
    print 'end silly'

def funny(y):
    print 'start funny'
    print y
    goofy(y + 1)
    print 'end funny'

def goofy(z):
    print 'start goofy'
    print z
    print 'end goofy'
```

Predict the output that results when silly(5) is invoked.

Practice 5.19: On page 161, we give an implementation of Euclid's algorithm that receives its input from the user. Design a function gcd(u, v) that returns the greatest common denominator as the result.

Practice 5.20: Redo Practice 4.2, defining a function with signature dramatic(original) that returns the result.

Practice 5.21: Define a function sumOfSquares(n) that returns the sum of the first n positive integers, $\sum_{k=1}^{n} k^2$.

Exercise 5.22: Redo Exercise 4.13, this time defining a top-level function with signature factorial(k), that returns the result.

Exercise 5.23: Write a function sliding(word, num) that behaves as follows. It should print out each slice of the original word having length num, aligned vertically as shown below. As an example, a call to sliding('examples', 4) should produce the output

```
exam
 xamp
  ampl
   mple
    ples
```

By default, use the value 3 for the parameter num.

Exercise 5.24: Within the chapter, we gave a maxLength function, that reports the longest entry in a list of strings. Write a corresponding minLength function.

Exercise 5.25: Write a function pairSum(data, goal) that returns **True** if the data contains two *distinct* elements whose sum equals the goal, and **False** otherwise. As an example, if data = [5, 12, 3, 8, 12, 11, 2, 6], then pairSum(data, 14) would return **True** because 12 and 2 sum to 14. pairSum(data, 24) would return **True** because 12 and 12 are distinct elements that sum to 24. Yet pairSum(data, 4) returns **False** (in particular, we cannot use 2 + 2 because there is only a single instance of 2 on this list).

Exercise 5.26: Write a function with signature toDecimal(string, base) that returns the integer value that is represented by the given string when interpreted as a number in the given integer base, for 2 <= base <= 36 (see Exercise 4.30 for discussion).

Exercise 5.27: Write a function with signature fromDecimal(value, base) that returns a string representing the original integer value when converted to the given base, for 2 <= base <= 36 (see Exercise 5.15 for discussion).

Exercise 5.28: Define a function threshold(dailyGains, goal) that behaves as follows. The first parameter is a sequence of numbers that represent daily gains in a stock value. The second parameter is a single positive number that is a profit goal. The function should return the minimum number of days for which the stock must be owned in order to achieve a profit at least as much as the stated goal. In the case that the goal is unreachable, the function should return 0.

As an example, threshold([5, 3, 8, 2, 9, 1], 17) should return 4 because the goal can be reached after the first four days (e.g., 5+3+8+2).

Exercise 5.29: Assume that data is a list of sorted elements, and that our goal is to find the *index* of the first element that is strictly greater than value. Using existing machinery, we could accomplish this by temporarily inserting the value, re-sorting the data to get the new value in the correct place, then calling data.index(value) to see where it ended up, and finally removing the value to restore the original data set. However, this approach is unnecessarily inefficient.

Write a function greaterIndex(data, value) that performs a sequential search to determine the index of such a next greater element. In the case that no elements are found greater than the given value, you should return len(data) as your result.

Exercise 5.30: Write a function with signature cheerlead(word) that prints a typical cheer as follows. For example, a call to cheerlead('robot') should print

```
Gimme  an  R
Gimme  an  O
Gimme  a   B
Gimme  an  O
Gimme  a   T
What's that spell?
robot
```

Note that the individual letters appear capitalized during the cheer, even if they were not capitalized when sent as a parameter. Furthermore, note the careful use of the article a versus an as appropriate (you can accomplish this by identifying in advance those letters of the alphabet that require use of an).

Error handling

Practice 5.31: Write a function yesOrNo(prompt) that asks the user a question with the given prompt, and demands a response of 'yes' or 'no'. If any other response is received, an appropriate reminder should be printed and then the user should be reprompted until a legitimate response is received. Return **True** if the eventual response is 'yes' and **False** if 'no'.

Practice 5.32: Redo Practice 5.19 but with strict error checking, ensuring that the caller has sent two nonnegative integers.

Exercise 5.33: Write a function getInt(small, large), based on the ideas from page 182, asking the user for an integer in the range from small to large (inclusive). You may assume that the parameters are legitimate and that small < large. The eventual inte–ger result should be returned to the caller. A sample user session for a call getInt(5,8) might appear as follows:

```
Enter a number from 5 to 8: 12
Your number must be between 5 and 8.
Enter a number from 5 to 8: no
That is not a valid integer.
Enter a number from 5 to 8: 7
```

Exercise 5.34: Redo Exercise 5.23 with strict error checking. Make sure that the user sends a string and then a positive integer that is less than or equal to the length of the string. Raise appropriate exceptions otherwise.

Exercise 5.35: Redo Exercise 5.26 with strict error checking. Not only should you ensure that the base is legitimately in range, but also that the given string given is a legiti–mate literal for that base.

Projects

Exercise 5.36: Write a simple version of the classic game Hangman. As the heart of your program, implement a function playHangman(secret) that manages a single round of the game. The parameter is presumed to be a string which is the secret answer; consider it unknown to the player.

The game should begin by displaying a version of the answer with the original spacing and punctuation, but with each alphabetic character replaced by an under-score '_' character. Then start asking the player to enter a single character as a guess. If that character is hidden in the answer, inform the user of his success and redisplay the disguised message but with all occurrences of the letter displayed. If the guess was wrong, inform the user. This process should continue either until the entire message has been uncovered or until there have been seven incorrect guesses.

Exercise 5.37: Redo Exercise 5.36 using graphics to animate the game in progress.

Exercise 5.38: In Section 3.9 we developed an animation for shooting arrows at a target. At the time, we had not yet introduced control structures, so the source code was very poorly designed.

Create a new version of such a project with improved use of control struc-tures. In particular, you should make the following three improvements. Allow for six arrows to be shot rather than three (but without resorting to cut-and-paste programming). Rather than using the course coordinates for the trajectory, use a loop to produce a smoother animation of the movement. Finally, the initial program required that the user click on the target to shoot the next arrow, but the trajectory of that arrow did not depend in any way on the location of the mouse click. Redesign the program so that all arrows start at the same location, but so that the final location of each arrow is with its tip precisely at the point on which the user clicked.

Defining Our Own Classes

Until now, we have relied upon the use of objects that belong to classes written by others. In this chapter, our goal is to learn how to design and implement our own classes. We begin by defining an extremely simple Point class to support the representation and manipulation of a two-dimensional point. This first example serves to demonstrate the basic syntax of a class definition. We then go on to develop a more robust Point class, supporting more interesting behaviors and operators.

In the remainder of the chapter, we implement classes with more intricate semantics. We implement a Television class based on the model originally introduced in Chapter 1. The Point and Television classes are naturally mutable. As an example of an *immutable* class, we develop a Fraction class akin to Python's built-in numeric classes.

6.1   A Simple Point Class

We begin by implementing a simple Point class for representing a two-dimensional point. Our main goal is to introduce the syntax of a class definition. This begins with the line

```
class Point:
```

The keyword **class** declares this to be a definition of a new class. The subsequent identifier Point is our own choice for naming this particular class. The final colon marks the beginning of the block of code that serves as the body of the class definition. As is the case with other language constructs, indentation is used to set apart the body from the surrounding code. Within the body of the class definition, we must define all *methods* (a.k.a. *member functions*) that will be supported by the class. The function definitions will be nested within the class body, leading to a general structure shown in the schematic diagram of Figure 6.1. The precise order in which the methods are defined is irrelevant, so long as they are all present.

The first method we discuss is a very special one named __init__. Informally, we refer to this method as the *constructor*. Each time a caller instantiates one of our points,

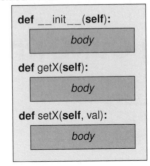

FIGURE 6.1: General indentation pattern for a class definition.

this method is automatically called by Python. Its primary purpose is to establish initial values for the ***attributes*** of the newly created object. In the context of our Point class, we offer the following constructor:

```
1  class Point:
2    def __init__(self):
3      self._x = 0
4      self._y = 0
```

As was the case with stand-alone functions in Section 5.2, the method declaration begins with the keyword **def**, followed by the ***signature*** and then the function body. A distin-guishing aspect of our member function definition is the use of the **self** parameter in the formal signature. A user instantiates a point using the syntax Point( ), without sending any explicit parameter. The *implicit* parameter **self** serves internally to identify the particular instance being constructed. In the long run there may be many different points, each of which will have its own state stored in memory.

The **self** identifier allows us to access members of this instance using the standard syntactic form *object.membername*. For example at line 3 of the constructor we assign **self**._x = 0 to establish an initial value for the _x attribute of this point. That attribute becomes part of the object's internal representation. In contrast, had line 3 appeared as

```
  _x = 0
```

it has no effect on the internal state of our point. Instead, it would establish _x as a ***local variable*** within the function body (as originally seen in Section 5.2).

The choice of each attribute name is up to us. In this implementation, x and y might be natural options yet we intentionally chose the names _x and _y. This convention is used to "hide" the attributes from users of our class and indicate that they are for internal use only. Although others are allowed to directly access our data members, we generally prefer that they leave the direct management of the state information to the designers of the class (we will motivate this point in later discussions). Instead, we provide users with some simple *accessors* and *mutators* for interacting with Point instances and accessing their state information. For example, the following two methods are used to manipulate a point's x-coordinate:

```
def getX(self):
    return self._x

def setX(self, val):
    self._x = val
```

The getX accessor returns the value of the existing attribute to the caller, while the setX reassigns that attribute to a new value (essentially forgetting the previously stored value). Notice that the signature for setX is declared with two parameters: the implicit **self** and the explicit val. Let's look more carefully at the mechanism of a method call. A typical user of this class might write code for some application as follows:

```
side = 8
bottom = 6
corner = Point( )
corner.setX(side)       # changing the x-coordinate
corner.setY(bottom)     # changing the y-coordinate
```

When the call to corner.setX(side) is made, the formal parameters of the method signature are matched up with the actual values indicated by the user.

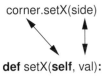

In this example, **self** is associated with the object that the caller refers to as corner, while val is associated with the object known as side in the caller's perspective. This relabeling of names is diagrammed in Figure 6.2. With this image in mind we note that the parameter val has *local* scope within the body of the method. This fact accounts for the distinction seen in the syntax **self**._x = val; the attribute _x is qualified with **self** to designate it as part of the internal state of our point, but we do *not* qualify the parameter val in such a way.

FIGURE 6.2: Two perspectives for the call corner.setX(side). The labels to the left of the objects are identifiers seen by the caller; the labels to the right of the objects are identifiers seen within the function body.

6.1.1 Testing Our Class

The complete implementation of our (simple) Point class is given in Figure 6.3. Keep in mind that this is not a built-in class for Python, so we cannot start a new interpreter session and immediately instantiate corner = Point( ). We must first make sure that our class definition has been loaded. There are several ways in which we can accomplish this.

Typically, we begin by placing the class definition in its own file. For the sake of argument, let's assume the file is named SimplePoint.py. Notice that the filename does not need to match the class name, although in many cases that would be a convenient choice. Once that file has been saved, it serves as a ***module*** that can subsequently be utilized in several ways.

The module can be preloaded into an interactive session by using the command python -i SimplePoint.py when starting Python. If using IDLE, this can be done by selecting Run Module from the Run menu for the module. Alternatively we can

```
1   class Point:
2     def __init__(self):
3       self._x = 0
4       self._y = 0
5
6     def getX(self):
7       return self._x
8
9     def setX(self, val):
10      self._x = val
11
12    def getY(self):
13      return self._y
14
15    def setY(self, val):
16      self._y = val
```

FIGURE 6.3: The complete definition of a simple Point class.

 A WORD OF WARNING

When declaring a method within a class definition, **self** should be explicitly listed as the first parameter in the signature. This parameter identifies the particular object upon which the method is invoked. The members of that object are qualified syntactically as **self**.*membername*. Variables that are not qualified within the body of the method have local scope.

import the Point class from the SimplePoint module by using the command

```
from SimplePoint import Point
```

from within a fresh interpreter session or from within another file.

It is also possible to use the class in the same file in which it is defined (unindented, so as not to be part of the class definition itself). For example, we might write the following:

```
class Point:
    def __init__(self):
        ...

    def getX(self):
        ...

corner = Point( )
corner.setX(8)
corner.setY(6)
```

This technique is appropriate for initial testing or when writing a class that is only needed in the context of that file. If, however, the class must be imported from elsewhere, these additional commands are disruptive. In Section 7.7, we will describe a more appropriate way to embed test code within the same file as the class definition.

6.2   A Robust Point Class

To demonstrate some additional techniques, we redesign the Point class to support more interesting behaviors. In fact, this more robust implementation matches the design of the cs1graphics.Point class seen in Chapter 3.

A constructor that accepts optional parameters

Our first modification involves the definition for the constructor. The original definition supports the syntax Point( ) for instantiation. In that case, a new point is configured to have an initial setting with x−and y−coordinates set to zero. While having such default values is reasonable, we want to design our constructor so that a user can choose some other initial configuration. We do this by using *optional parameters*, as introduced in Section 5.2.2. Our new constructor appears as

```
def __init__(self, initialX=0, initialY=0):
    self._x = initialX
    self._y = initialY
```

This signature has two explicit parameters used to specify the desired initial settings. This form allows a caller to instantiate a point using the syntax Point(6,2), for example. Yet the previous syntax Point( ) is still supported by this definition.

Scaling: a mutator that alters several attributes

A simple mutator like setX is designed specifically for changing an underlying attribute. But mutators can bring more far-reaching effects. Our next example is a method for scaling both coordinate values by a multiplicative factor.

```
def scale(self, factor):
    self._x *= factor
    self._y *= factor
```

Recall from page 128 that **self**._x *= factor is a shorthand for **self**._x = **self**._x * factor.

Computing the distance between two points

Another new feature we might offer is a way to compute the distance from one point to another. It is up to us to design an interface for the behavior. Our choice is to support the following syntax, as seen by a hypothetical user of our class.

```
topLeft = Point(5,20)
bottomRight = Point(45,60)
diagonal = topLeft.distance(bottomRight)
```

By this design, we will support a distance method that is formally invoked on one point, with the other point specified as a parameter. Our implementation appears as follows:

```
def distance(self, other):
    dx = self._x − other._x
    dy = self._y − other._y
    return sqrt(dx * dx + dy * dy)        # imported from math module
```

The two different points specified by the original caller are seen by us as two parameters: **self** and other. With knowledge of those two points (and a bit of geometry) we can calculate the distance.

We draw attention to three separate issues in the body of this function. The first is the use of identifiers dx and dy. We have intentionally *not* qualified them (e.g., as **self**.dx), because we do not want those calculations to be stored as additional attributes of the point instance. We only need those values temporarily, when performing the current calculation. So they are defined as *local* variables of this function, providing only short-term memory until the function call completes. Avoiding the introduction of an unnecessary attribute saves memory and also make the transient nature of those values more clear to another programmer who sees this code.

The second issue is our use of the expression other._x. Prior to this we have only seen examples where the _x attribute is retrieved from **self**. Yet the other parameter is also presumed to be an instance of the Point class. That instance has its own state information, and so other._x is used to access the x-coordinate of that other point.

Finally, we note that a distance calculation requires a square root. So we must ensure that we import the sqrt function from the math module, somewhere earlier in the file.

Normalizing an existing point

As another interesting behavior, we support a method to "normalize" a point. A point is normalized by scaling it proportionally so that its distance to the origin becomes 1. We implement it as follows:

```
def normalize(self):
    mag = self.distance( Point( ) )
    if mag > 0:
        self.scale(1/mag)
```

This function demonstrates several techniques. In the first line of the body, we deter-mine the magnitude of the original point by computing the distance from that point to the origin. Although we could have done this computation from scratch, we already have a perfectly good method for computing these distances. Much as a user can call topLeft.distance(bottomRight) where topLeft and bottomRight are references to points, we can use the syntax **self**.distance(Point( )); the parameter **self** identifies a point, and the expression Point( ) constructs a new point which represents the origin by default.

Once we have the proper magnitude, we want to scale by 1/mag, so long as that magnitude is nonzero; if the original point is the origin, we leave it unchanged. For this reason, we use a conditional statement. For the body of that conditional, we rely upon the existing scale method, rather than reimplementing the low-level computation.

How is our point printed?

Based on our initial design, a user who wants to find out the coordinates can separately print the values reported by getX and getY. However, an interesting thing occurs if the user were to try to print the point itself, perhaps as

```
>>> topLeft = Point(5,20)
>>> print topLeft
<SimplePoint.Point instance at 0x386968>
```

Although the precise format of that last line may differ on your system, it should be some-thing like we show. Python knows how to print instances of the classes that it defines, but this is an object from a user-defined class. Given the artistic license that we have when designing our own classes, Python has no way to guess an appropriate way to display an instance. So by default it prints the above representation, identifying that this is an instance of the given class and showing a number that is actually the memory address of where this particular instance is being stored.

Of course, such a representation would make little sense to a user who is not a Python programmer. As the designer of the class, we have a way to customize how our instances are printed. This is done by implementing a method named __str__. Python relies upon many specially named methods like this to perform various tasks. We have already seen that when a new instance of a class is first constructed, the interpreter looks for an __init__ method, which presumably initializes the state of an object. When an object is being printed, the interpreter looks for a method named __str__. That method is responsible for returning the appropriate string. For our Point class, we chose the following implementation:

```
def __str__(self):
    return '<' + str(self._x) + ', ' + str(self._y) + '>'
```

We display the coordinates as a string of the general form '<x, y>'. Angle brackets are used to avoid confusion with parentheses, which are used for tuples, or square brackets, which are used for lists. Notice that the method itself does *not* actually print the string; it simply returns it. The rest of the system takes the responsibility for displaying it. The method composes the appropriate string based upon our desired format and the current values of the underlying attributes. With this routine implemented, the user would see the following:

```
>>> topLeft = Point(5,20)
>>> print topLeft
<5,20>
```

Note that this only defines the form for displaying our point; the user can not legally use this form as a literal when trying to create a point. An error occurs if such an attempt is made.

```
>>> topLeft = <5,20>
  File "<stdin>", line 1
    topLeft = <5,20>
              ^
SyntaxError: invalid syntax
```

There is no way for us to introduce new literals into the syntax of the language; those decisions were reserved for the designers of Python.

Operator overloading

Just as __init__ and __str__ serve a particular purpose, there are many other specially named methods that support various shorthand syntaxes in Python. In fact all of the operators that are defined for built-in classes can be defined with custom semantics for a user-defined class.

As an example, suppose that we wanted to be able to "add" two points together, producing a third point as a sum. A very convenient syntax would be the following:

```
>>> bottomRight = Point(45,60)
>>> offset = Point(5,5)
>>> corner = bottomRight + offset
```

Unfortunately, without explicit instructions, Python does not know how two points should be added. It reports a TypeError, with a message saying something like

```
unsupported operand type(s) for +:  'Point' and 'Point'.
```

We provide semantics for the + operator by implementing a method named __add__. Since addition involves two points, we use a signature somewhat similar to the one we used for distance, with two parameters **self** and other. **self** is the point on the left-hand side of the addition sign and other is on the right. The typical semantics for addition is to leave the existing instances unchanged and to produce a third point that represent the sum of the other two. This can be implemented as shown here.

```
def __add__(self, other):
    return Point(self._x + other._x, self._y + other._y)
```

Notice that the return value is a newly instantiated point with the given initial configuration.

FOR THE GURU

Even after including the __str__ method in our Point implementation, a conscientious observer might stumble upon the following discrepancy when working in the interpreter.

```
>>> topLeft = Point(5,20)
>>> print topLeft
<5,20>
>>> topLeft
<SimplePoint.Point instance at 0x386968>
```

When an object x is printed, Python automatically calls **str**(x), which converts it to a string based principally upon the underlying __str__ method for that class. When an object x is displayed natively within the interpreter, it calls a built-in function **repr**(x), that produces an alternate string *representation* of the object based upon a call to the underlying __repr__ method. If the class has not provided a __repr__ implementation, Python reports the type and memory address as a default representation.

For many classes, expressions **str**(x) and **repr**(x) result in the same output. But sometimes a distinction is made. For example, if the preceding experiment were repeated with a string instance such as greeting = 'Hello', the quotation marks are not displayed when the string in printed as output, but they are displayed in the representation to denote it clearly as a string.

Polymorphism

A programming language's ability to perform an operation differently depending on the specific context is called ***polymorphism***. For example the implementations of 2 + 3 and bottomRight + offset are quite different. As our next example, we consider support for multiplication. Given a Point p, the syntax p * q is implemented with a special method named __mul__. However, there are several possible meanings for multiplication in the context of points.

If the second operand q is a number, we can treat a syntax like p * 3 as one that produces a new point with coordinates three times as large as the original. This is similar to our scale method, except that we defined scale to mutate the existing point rather than produce a new point. Yet this is not the only notion of multiplication. Another commonly used notion is that of a dot product of two points. Given two points $p = \langle p_x, p_y \rangle$ and $q = \langle q_x, q_y \rangle$, the dot product $p \cdot q$ is a number computed as $p_x q_x + p_y q_y$. So perhaps the syntax p * q should be defined to support the computation of a dot product.

Fortunately, we can support both notions at once! The key is to perform type check-ing (see Section 5.5.3) on the second operand to determine which behavior to use. If that operand is numeric, then we presume that the user wants us to produce a new point that is a scaled version of the original. Alternatively, if the operand is a point, then we can presume the user wants us to compute the dot product of the two points. (If the operand is neither of those types, we should probably raise an exception, but we will ignore that issue for simplicity). Our implementation of this method appears as

```
def __mul__(self, operand):
    if isinstance(operand, (int,float)):          # multiply by constant
        return Point(self._x * operand, self._y * operand)
    elif isinstance(operand, Point):              # dot product
        return self._x * operand._x + self._y * operand._y
```

In this way, our polymorphic function takes on different behaviors depending upon the type of parameters it receives.

Summary

Putting all of these pieces together, Figure 6.4 presents the full code for our robust Point class; this code forms the basis of the cs1graphics.Point class. However, there are two addi-tional methods supported in that version. First we note that the __mul__ method supports a syntax such as p * 3, in which the point is the left-hand operand. When the point is to the right of the operator, as in 3 * p, another method named __rmul__ is applied. Rather than implementing the behavior from scratch, we can have that method rely upon our existing __mul__ by remultiplying with the point as the left operand. The cs1graphics.Point class also overloads the syntax p ^ 45 to generate a new point that is a copy of the original one rotated clockwise about the origin (in this case, by 45 degrees).

```
1    from math import sqrt                                          # needed for computing distances
2
3    class Point:
4      def __init__(self, initialX=0, initialY=0):
5        self._x = initialX
6        self._y = initialY
7
8      def getX(self):
9        return self._x
10
11     def setX(self, val):
12       self._x = val
13
14     def getY(self):
15       return self._y
16
17     def setY(self, val):
18       self._y = val
19
20     def scale(self, factor):
21       self._x *= factor
22       self._y *= factor
23
24     def distance(self, other):
25       dx = self._x − other._x
26       dy = self._y − other._y
27       return sqrt(dx * dx + dy * dy)                            # imported from math module
28
29     def normalize(self):
30       mag = self.distance( Point( ) )
31       if mag > 0:
32         self.scale(1/mag)
33
34     def __str__(self):
35       return '<' + str(self._x) + ', ' + str(self._y) + '>'
36
37     def __add__(self, other):
38       return Point(self._x + other._x, self._y + other._y)
39
40     def __mul__(self, operand):
41       if isinstance(operand, (int,float)):                     # multiply by constant
42         return Point(self._x * operand, self._y * operand)
43       elif isinstance(operand, Point):                         # dot product
44         return self._x * operand._x + self._y * operand._y
```

FIGURE 6.4: A more robust implementation of a Point class.

6.3 A Television Class

Consumer electronics (e.g., televisions, phones, music players, home appliances) typically support many behaviors, chosen through a series of switches, button presses, and movements. These devices are controlled internally by embedded computing systems specially designed to support the user experience. A great deal of work goes into planning the user interface and in implementing the desired semantics.

As an example of the complexity, we revisit the design of a Television class as originally discussed in Section 1.4.2. In modeling the embedded system for a television, we associate the user's physical interactions (e.g., button presses) as method calls to our internal system. For simplicity, we will use a combination of print statements and return values to simulate forms of feedback that our system would provide to the consumer in the end (e.g., through on-screen displays or audio). In exploring this example, the challenge is to carefully model and implement more nontrivial semantics. We wish to address many of the same questions that the manufacturers face: "what should happen when the user does this followed by that?"

Having already explored some of these issues in Chapter 1, we have chosen the high-level design shown in Figure 6.5. Our implementation begins with the constructor.

```
class Television:
  def __init__(self):
    self._powerOn = False
    self._muted = False
    self._volume = 5
    self._channel = 2
    self._prevChan = 2
```

All television instances are initially created with the same "factory settings." As the designer of the class, the precise choice of initial values is up to us. In this case, a newly minted television has the power off; once turned on it will be unmuted with a volume level of 5 and tuned to channel 2. You will notice that we set the _prevChan attribute to 2 as well. Therefore, if the user's first interaction is to "return" to the previous channel, the television will appear to stay on channel 2.

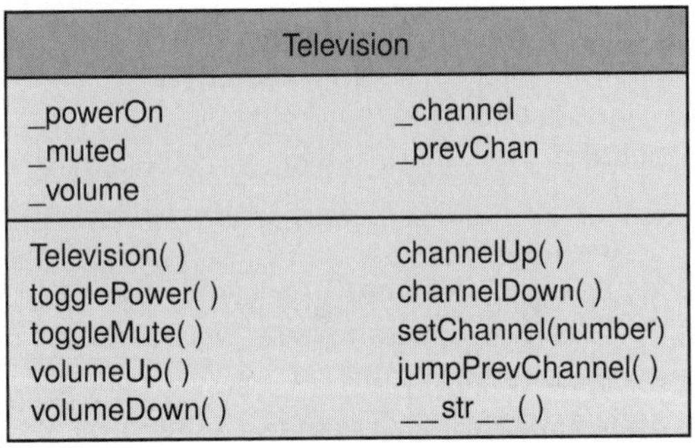

Television	
_powerOn _muted _volume	_channel _prevChan
Television( ) togglePower( ) toggleMute( ) volumeUp( ) volumeDown( )	channelUp( ) channelDown( ) setChannel(number) jumpPrevChannel( ) __str__( )

FIGURE 6.5: A Television class diagram.

togglePower method

The next method we look at is togglePower. This is quite a simple method, with its complete implementation appearing as follows:

```
def togglePower(self):
    self._powerOn = not self._powerOn
```

The body of the togglePower method effectively reverses the setting of the **self._powerOn** attribute. This is accomplished through an assignment statement with clever use of the boolean operator **not**. If the attribute value was **False** at the onset of the call, then the resulting value is **True**. Conversely, if **True** at the onset, the result will be **False**.

toggleMute method

At first glance, toggleMute is similar to togglePower in reversing the setting of a boolean attribute. Yet there is a key difference; toggleMute should only have an effect if the television's power is currently on. We use a conditional statement to ensure so.

```
def toggleMute(self):
    if self._powerOn:
        self._muted = not self._muted
```

If the power is currently on when this method is invoked, then indeed the value of the mute attribute is reversed. Yet if the power is off, there is no effect. This semantics is meant to model a real television, where pressing the mute button has no effect if the power is off. Physically, there is still a mute button which the user might press; the television is simply designed to ignore it. In fact, we use such a conditional to ensure that the power is on before performing any of our behaviors — with one exception. The togglePower method was not shielded in such a fashion; a real television is responsive to the power button even when currently off.

volumeUp and volumeDown methods

In simplest form, a call to volumeUp causes an increase in the current volume level by a fixed increment. Yet more care is necessary to accurately model the behavior of a real television. We not not want to increase the volume beyond some maximum level, such as 10. Also, many televisions have the following subtle semantics. Pressing the volume up button on a muted television automatically unmutes it. We suggest the following implementation:

```
def volumeUp(self):
    if self._powerOn:
        if self._volume < 10:
            self._volume += 1
        self._muted = False
        return self._volume
```

As was the case with toggleMute, the conditional statement on the second line shields the remainder of the body so that nothing happens unless the television is currently on. The inner conditional makes sure that we do not increase the volume past the maximum level. An interesting command is **self**._muted = **False**, which is designed to unmute the television. At first glance it may seem like we should use a conditional, as this behavior is only relevant when the television is currently muted. Yet our implementation is correct. If **self**._muted was previously **True** it is changed to **False**. If it had previously been **False** the assignment is technically performed, yet leaves the setting as **False**. The final **return** statement loosely models how a television explicitly displays the updated volume level to the user upon completion of the action. The technique for volumeDown is quite similar.

channelUp and channelDown methods

In many respects, these methods are similar to the corresponding methods used to alter the volume. However, there are key differences in the semantics. When a real-world television is at the highest allowable channel, an invocation of channelUp results in "wrapping around" to the minimum channel (as opposed to volume, which stays capped at the maximum). Likewise, invoking channelDown when at the minimum channel causes us to wrap around to the maximum channel. We also wish to support the user's option to later jump back to the most recently watched channel. For this purpose, we maintain a separate _prevChan attribute. It is important that we update the _prevChan attribute to match the current _channel value, *before* we change _channel. Keeping these issues in mind, we implement channelUp as follows:

```
def channelUp(self):
  if self._powerOn:
    self._prevChan = self._channel        # record the current value
    if self._channel == 99:
      self._channel = 2                    # wrap around to minimum
    else:
      self._channel += 1
    return self._channel
```

As before, none of this activity takes place unless the television is on. When it is on, we make sure to record the current channel setting as _prevChan before making any changes to the current channel. The subsequent **if-else** construct is used to achieve the wrap around semantics, assuming a valid channel range from 2 to 99. Finally, the return statement informs the caller of the resulting channel. The channelDown method is analogous.

setChannel method

There is another key difference between the user interface for manipulating the volume versus the channel. The volume can be altered incrementally through the volumeUp or volumeDown methods, yet there is no way to go directly to volume 7. The channel can be altered incrementally or by going straight to a desired setting, such as 7.

For this reason, we support a setChannel method. Unlike the previous methods, setChannel requires additional information to be sent from the caller, namely the desired channel value. We wish to support a syntax such as myTv.setChannel(7) for those calling this method. We define the method as follows:

```
def setChannel(self, number):
  if self._powerOn:
    if 2 <= number <= 99:
      self._prevChan = self._channel      # record the current value
      self._channel = number
    return self._channel
```

Notice that the signature includes the implicit parameter **self**, followed by the explicit parameter number. After checking that the power is on, another conditional is used to ensure that the user has sent a legitimate value for the channel. Although we might hope that the user avoids making calls such as myTv.setChannel(−28), it is better to protect our class against reaching incoherent states. The boolean expression 2 <= number <= 99 relies upon the chaining of operators, as introduced on page 67 of Section 2.8.

As was the case with channelUp, this routine is responsible for managing the value of the _prevChan attribute as well as the _channel attribute. We make sure to record the previous setting before changing the channel value. We trace a typical execution of this method in Figure 6.6. We should note that we intentionally alter the _prevChan only *after* verifying that the new number is legitimate. If someone inadvertently invokes myTv.setChannel(999), we will not be changing the channel and thus we wish to leave the previous channel setting intact as well.

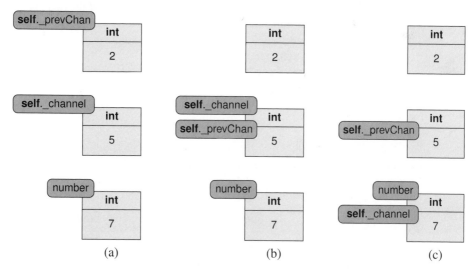

FIGURE 6.6: Trace of an execution of setChannel(7) upon a television that is currently tuned to channel 5, and had recently been on channel 2. Part (a) shows the state at the onset of the call; (b) shows the state after executing **self**._prevChan = **self**._channel; (c) after executing **self**._channel = number. The local identifier number goes out of scope as soon as the method call ends.

jumpPrevChannel method

Our other methods carefully maintain the _prevChan attribute to support the ability to later jump back. The jumpPrevChannel method is the one used to invoke such a jump. If the television is in a state where it is currently on channel 11 yet had most recently been on channel 5, an application of the jumpPrevChannel method should end up changing the channel setting to 5. But we must also consider the desired semantics if jump were invoked a second time. Since the television is now on channel 5, channel 11 should be considered as the previous channel. So it is important that the first call to jump properly maintains _prevChan before changing the current channel. In this way, jumping repeatedly toggles the channel between 5 and 11.

Given this understanding, the body of jumpPrevChannel must exchange the values of the _channel and _prevChan attributes with each other. A naive attempt might read as

```
self._channel = self._prevChan
self._prevChan = self._channel
```

but unfortunately this implementation is critically flawed. The problem can be observed by carefully tracing the changing state of the television, as shown in Figure 6.7. The first statement has the effect of altering the _channel attribute so as to reference the value 5. The problem at this point is that variables _channel and _prevChan both reference this value. We no longer have any reference to the channel value from which we came (i.e., 11), and so no way to properly record such value as _prevChan. The second statement still executes but has no meaningful effect, as the two variables are already assigned to the same object.

Perhaps the problem could be fixed by inverting the order of the two lines, so that we accurately record the incoming channel setting before losing that information.

```
self._prevChan = self._channel
self._channel = self._prevChan
```

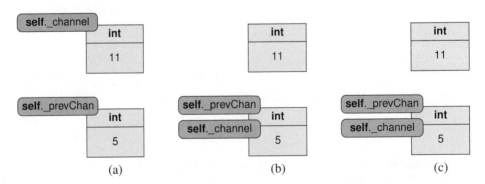

FIGURE 6.7: Trace of a flawed swap. Part (a) shows the initial state; (b) shows the state after executing **self**._channel = **self**._prevChan; (c) after executing **self**._prevChan = **self**._channel.

Yet this is not successful either. Although the first command properly records the incoming channel setting, it does so at the expense of losing track of the previous channel setting, which we need to enact the intended jump.

The following approach is a correct implementation:

```
def jumpPrevChannel(self):
    if self._powerOn:
        incoming = self._channel
        self._channel = self._prevChan
        self._prevChan = incoming
        return self._channel
```

The key is the creation of the new (local) identifier incoming that is assigned to the incom−ing channel setting. With that information recorded, we can safely alter the setting of **self.**_channel, and then **self.**_prevChan, as diagrammed in Figure 6.8.

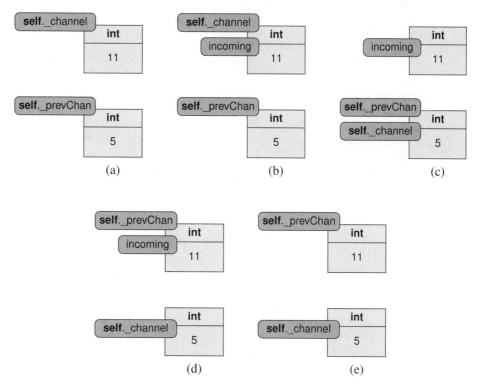

FIGURE 6.8: Trace of a successful swap.   Part (a) shows the initial state; (b) shows the state after executing incoming = **self.**_channel; (c) shows the state after executing **self.**_channel = **self.**_prevChan; (d) shows the state after executing **self.**_prevChan = incoming; (e) shows the state after the disappearance of the local vari-able incoming.

FOR THE GURU

Our careful manipulation of the _channel and _prevChan attributes demonstrates why it is better to have the designer of the class manipulate the internal representation and why we chose attributes names that attempt to hide those data members from outside users. If an outsider were to directly alter the value of data member _channel rather than call our methods, the consistency of the state might be compromised.

Complete Television implementation

Our complete Television class definition is shown in Figure 6.9. We have added a natural implementation for a __str__ method that displays the current observable settings of a television. This allows for usage such as **print** myTv, either for debugging purposes or perhaps as a simple model for displaying current settings to a user.

```
1   class Television:
2     def __init__(self):
3       self._powerOn = False
4       self._muted = False
5       self._volume = 5
6       self._channel = 2
7       self._prevChan = 2
8
9     def togglePower(self):
10      self._powerOn = not self._powerOn
11
12    def toggleMute(self):
13      if self._powerOn:
14        self._muted = not self._muted
15
16    def volumeUp(self):
17      if self._powerOn:
18        if self._volume < 10:
19          self._volume += 1
20        self._muted = False
21        return self._volume
```

FIGURE 6.9: A complete implementation of our Television class (continued on next page).

```
22   def volumeDown(self):
23     if self._powerOn:
24       if self._volume > 0:
25         self._volume -= 1
26       self._muted = False
27       return self._volume
28
29   def channelUp(self):
30     if self._powerOn:
31       self._prevChan = self._channel        # record the current value
32       if self._channel == 99:
33         self._channel = 2                    # wrap around to minimum
34       else:
35         self._channel += 1
36       return self._channel
37
38   def channelDown(self):
39     if self._powerOn:
40       self._prevChan = self._channel        # record the current value
41       if self._channel == 2:
42         self._channel = 99                   # wrap around to maximum
43       else:
44         self._channel -= 1
45       return self._channel
46
47   def setChannel(self, number):
48     if self._powerOn:
49       if 2 <= number <= 99:
50         self._prevChan = self._channel      # record the current value
51         self._channel = number
52       return self._channel
53
54   def jumpPrevChannel(self):
55     if self._powerOn:
56       incoming = self._channel
57       self._channel = self._prevChan
58       self._prevChan = incoming
59       return self._channel
60
61   def __str__(self):
62     display = 'Power setting is currently ' + str(self._powerOn) +'\n'
63     display += 'Channel setting is currently ' + str(self._channel) +'\n'
64     display += 'Volume setting is currently ' + str(self._volume) +'\n'
65     display += 'Mute is currently ' + str(self._muted)
66     return display
```

FIGURE 6.9 (continuation): A complete implementation of our Television class.

FOR THE GURU

Python offers a simpler syntax, termed *simultaneous assignment*, that can be used to effectively swap values, as seen in the following implementation:

```
def jumpPrevChannel(self):
    if self._powerOn:
        self._channel, self._prevChan = self._prevChan, self._channel
        return self._channel
```

Note the use of a comma on each side of the equality operator (=) to separate pieces of the expressions. Each identifier on the left-hand side will be assigned to the respective value being expressed on the right-hand side. This syntax is not necessarily more efficient than the earlier approach with explicit temporary variables; behind the scene, the Python interpreter makes its own temporary variables. The advantage is in simplifying the outward appearance of the code.

Simultaneous assignment can also be used as a concise form for more traditional assignments, as in the following example:

```
a, b, c = 1, 2, 3          # assigns a=1; assigns b=2; assigns c=3
```

6.4 A Fraction Class

In this section, we develop an *immutable* Fraction class. Our internal representation of a fraction consists of two numbers, a numerator and denominator. We wish to ensure that all fractions are *reduced to lowest terms* and stored with a nonnegative denominator. A fraction with denominator of zero is viewed arithmetically as an "undefined" value. Using the style of Python's built-in numeric types, our implementation will consist solely of special methods that provide support for selected operators. We consider four general flavors of such methods.

The constructor

Since our Fraction instances will be immutable, the value cannot be changed once constructed. It is therefore imperative that the caller be allowed to customize an instance when using the constructor. For greatest flexibility, we suggest the following signature:

```
def __init__(self, numerator=0, denominator=1):
```

With these defaults, legal instantiations of the fractions $\frac{16}{9}$, $\frac{3}{1}$ and $\frac{0}{1}$ appear respectively as

```
aspectRatio = Fraction(16, 9)
oddsToWin = Fraction(3)
zero = Fraction( )
```

The primary goal of the constructor is to take the original parameters and to com–pute the reduced form for our internal representation. For example, if a user instanti–ates Fraction(2,4) we want an internal representation akin to $\frac{1}{2}$; if the user instantiates Fraction(10, −6) we want an internal representation of $\frac{-5}{3}$. To accomplish this, we rely on our previous implementations of Euclid's algorithm for computing the greatest common denominator from Chapter 4. We assume that we can import such a gcd function from a file gcd.py (see solution to Practice 5.19 for the precise code). Our constructor is then implemented as follows:

```python
def __init__(self, numerator=0, denominator=1):
    if denominator == 0:                        # fraction is undefined
        self._numer = 0
        self._denom = 0
    else:
        factor = gcd( abs(numerator), abs(denominator) )
        if denominator < 0:                     # want to divide through by negated factor
            factor = -factor
        self._numer = numerator // factor
        self._denom = denominator // factor
```

In general, we want to divide both parameters by their greatest common denominator, taking a bit of care to properly handle the treatment when the original denominator was not a positive value. Our attributes are established with names _numer and _denom.

Arithmetic operators

Although each Fraction instance is immutable, we can allow users to use arithmetic to compute new values. A typical example is to use the syntax x + y to produce a new result. As we saw with the Point class in Section 6.2, the + operator is supported by implementing the special __add__ method.

To implement the proper semantics, we rely on our mathematical knowledge. For example, when calculating $\frac{3}{4} + \frac{1}{3}$, we use the product of the individual denominators as a common denominator, scaling each fraction appropriately. Thus

$$\frac{3}{4} + \frac{1}{3} \;=\; \frac{3}{4} \cdot \frac{3}{3} + \frac{1}{3} \cdot \frac{4}{4} \;=\; \frac{9}{12} + \frac{4}{12} \;=\; \frac{13}{12}.$$

More generally, addition can be calculated symbolically as $\frac{a}{b} + \frac{c}{d} = \frac{ad+bc}{bd}$. Translating this calculation back to the syntax of our operator implementation, we have

```python
def __add__(self, other):
    return Fraction(self._numer * other._denom + self._denom * other._numer,
                    self._denom * other._denom)
```

Notice that our __add__ implementation makes no explicit effort to reduce the resulting sum to lowest terms. For example, if faced with the addition $\frac{3}{4} + \frac{1}{2}$, this arithmetic has the apparent result of $\frac{10}{8}$. However, because this method returns a newly constructed fraction, in this case as Fraction(10, 8), the constructor guarantees a reduced representation, in this case $\frac{5}{4}$. This saves us the trouble of reimplementing that logic here. To support other arithmetic operators we need to implement the associated special methods, __sub__ (for −), __mul__ (for *), and __div__ (for /). The implementations of those methods are based upon similar algebraic rules and given in our final implementation at the conclusion of the section.

Comparison operators

While use of an arithmetic operator returns a new fraction, the typical comparison operator returns a boolean value. Consider the evaluation of the expression x < y. This operator is evaluated with the special method __lt__ ("less than"). Our implementation is based upon a cross-multiplication technique. Symbolically, $\frac{a}{b} < \frac{c}{d}$ if and only if $ad < bc$. This leads to the following definition:

```
def __lt__(self, other):
    return self._numer * other._denom < self._denom * other._numer
```

Another important behavior is testing equivalence, such as x == y. This operator is supported by an underlying __eq__ method. Although a similar multiplication would work, the job is even easier knowing that all fraction instances are already in lowest terms. The only way two instances can be truly equivalent is if they have the same numerator values and the same denominator values. We implement equivalence testing as

```
def __eq__(self, other):
    return self._numer == other._numer and self._denom == other._denom
```

Other comparison operators (e.g., >, >=, <=, !=) are generally supported by another batch of specially named methods. For example, we could provide a __ne__ method ("not equal") to define our notion of !=. However, Python is quite clever in this regard. If we define __eq__ but do not explicitly define __ne__, the presumption is that x != y can be automatically evaluated as **not** x == y. Similarly, x > y is presumed to be the same as y < x. So long as we provide the two methods __lt__ and __eq__, Python automatically generalizes to support the full slate of comparison operators.

Type conversions

Finally, we consider methods that take an existing fraction and produce a corresponding instance of another built-in type. For example, if $x = \frac{11}{3}$, we might want the Python expression **float**(x) to generate a corresponding instance of the **float** class with value 3.667.

The syntax **float**(x) invokes the constructor for the **float** class, which is not ours to implement. But the designers of Python have provided a way for us to affect the process. When the **float** constructor is sent a parameter that is an instance of a user-defined class, Python looks for a special method named __float__ for that class. That method is responsible for returning a floating-point value associated with the user-defined instance. In the case of fractions, we simply rely on performing a true division of the numerator by the denominator.

```
def __float__(self):
    return float(self._numer) / self._denom
```

To allow our fractions to be converted to an integer, we provide a method named
__int__. To closely mimic the semantics used by Python when converting a **float** to an
integer, we wish to truncate the remainder. In fact, we implement this by converting a
fraction to a **float** as an intermediate step in the calculation, as follows:

```
def __int__(self):
    return int(float(self))                    # convert to float, then truncate
```

Finally, we consider a design for the __str__ method, which is responsible for
creating a string representation of a fraction instance. We have complete artistic license
in designing our representation. In general, we choose a representation like '16/9' for
an underlying fraction $\frac{16}{9}$. However, we have implemented two notable exceptions to this
rule. If the denominator is zero, we use the string 'Undefined' as our representation,
to highlight this designation. If the denominator is precisely one, we display only the
numerator. Our complete Fraction implementation is given in Figure 6.10.

```
1   from gcd import gcd
2
3   class Fraction:
4
5     def __init__(self, numerator=0, denominator=1):
6       if denominator == 0:                       # fraction is undefined
7         self._numer = 0
8         self._denom = 0
9       else:
10        factor = gcd( abs(numerator), abs(denominator) )
11        if denominator < 0:                     # want to divide through by negated factor
12          factor = −factor
13        self._numer = numerator // factor
14        self._denom = denominator // factor
15
16    ######## Arithmetic Methods ########
17    def __add__(self, other):
18      return Fraction(self._numer * other._denom + self._denom * other._numer,
19                   self._denom * other._denom)
20
21    def __sub__(self, other):
22      return Fraction(self._numer * other._denom − self._denom * other._numer,
23                   self._denom * other._denom)
```

FIGURE 6.10: An implementation of our Fraction class (continued on next page).

```
24    def __mul__(self, other):
25      return Fraction(self._numer * other._numer, self._denom * other._denom)
26
27    def __div__(self, other):
28      return Fraction(self._numer * other._denom, self._denom * other._numer)
29
30    ######## Comparison Methods ########
31    def __lt__(self, other):
32      return self._numer * other._denom < self._denom * other._numer
33
34    def __eq__(self, other):
35      return self._numer == other._numer and self._denom == other._denom
36
37    ######## Type Conversion Methods ########
38    def __float__(self):
39      return float(self._numer) / self._denom
40
41    def __int__(self):
42      return int(float(self))              # convert to float, then truncate
43
44    def __str__(self):
45      if self._denom == 0:
46        return 'Undefined'
47      elif self._denom == 1:
48        return str(self._numer)
49      else:
50        return str(self._numer) + ' / ' + str(self._denom)
```

FIGURE 6.10 (continuation): An implementation of our Fraction class.

6.5 Advanced Lessons

In this final section, we revisit the Television class of Section 6.3. We wish to demonstrate two techniques that could be used to improve the overall quality and maintainability of our implementation.

6.5.1 Class-Level Attributes

One less than appealing part of our original implementation is that we used some "magic" constants in our code, such as 2 and 99, without clearly indicating the significance of those numbers as the minimum and maximum channel numbers. This approach is typically called *hardwiring* values and frowned upon as a poor programming style.

The problems are twofold. First, the significance of hardwired values may not be immediately evident to a reader of the code. This makes it far more challenging to audit the logic being expressed or to locate the cause of bugs. Worse yet, if someone wanted to redesign the television, for example to support 150 channels, great care would be needed in locating the lines to be changed. This is compounded by the fact that these hardwired values appear in multiple places (in our implementation, the value 2 is used five different times and 99 three different times). If some of those occurrences were changed but not all of them, this may lead to very inconsistent semantics that are difficult to remedy.

In these situations, the better approach is to have a well named identifier, such as _maxChannel, that captures the significance of the underlying value. But where should that identifier be declared? We could introduce _maxChannel as an attribute to each television instance, but this is somewhat wasteful. Attributes should be used for aspects of an object that may change from instance to instance (such as the current channel number). Yet in our model, all televisions use the same constants for the minimum and maximum levels. Storing a value like _maxChannel as an attribute causes extra memory to be set aside in each instance's representation.

Instead, we can introduce what is termed a ***class-level attribute*** which can be shared by all instances of the class. In Python, any identifier that is introduced within the body of the class definition, yet outside any of the methods is considered to have class-level scope. So our revised Television class could begin as follows:

```python
class Television:
    # class-level attributes will be shared by all
    _minVolume = 0
    _maxVolume = 10
    _minChannel = 2
    _maxChannel = 99

    def __init__(self):
        self._powerOn = False
        self._muted = False
        self._volume = (Television._minVolume + Television._maxVolume) // 2
        self._channel = Television._minChannel
        self._prevChan = Television._minChannel
```

Lines 3–6 introduce attributes within the context of the class. To access these from within the body of a method, we qualify the name, for example as Television._minChannel at lines 12 and 13. By coding our constructor this way, the default settings would auto-matically adjust if our television no longer supported channel 2. With these class-level attributes, the setChannel method of our implementation might be written as

```python
def setChannel(self, number):
    if self._powerOn:
        if Television._minChannel <= number <= Television._maxChannel:
            self._prevChan = self._channel        # record the current value
            self._channel = number
        return self._channel
```

In this method, we see identifiers drawn from three completely different scopes. The parameter number is used without any qualification and has scope that is local to a single call of the function. The identifier **self.**_channel references an attribute stored within the state of the particular television instance upon which the method is invoked. Finally, we see Television._maxChannel, as a class-level attribute.

6.5.2 Methods that Call Other Methods

When implementing the Point class in Section 6.2, the body of the normalize method made calls to the existing distance and scale methods. This allowed us to reuse portions of code rather than to reimplement low-level details of a computation in multiple places. The same technique can be used to greatly simplify our Television implementation. Properly managing the _channel and _prevChan attributes takes great care. Yet those details entered the implementation of each of the channelUp, channelDown, setChannel, and jumpPrevChannel methods. Although we cannot completely avoid programming the desired semantics, we do have a way to avoid programming it four times.

For the sake of argument, let's assume that we have an existing implementation of setChannel. That method changes the current channel while recording the previous channel, although only in the case where the television is turned on and the requested channel number is legitimate. It also returns the resulting channel number to the caller, presuming the power is on. Now let's consider the channelUp method. There were two distinct issues to cope with when originally implementing that method. One challenge was in implementing the "wrap around" semantics to determine the next channel. The other issue was to properly enact the change of channels. In the following revision, we focus on implementing the "wrap around" logic while deferring the remaining burden:

```
def channelUp(self):
  if self._powerOn:
    if self._channel == Television._maxChannel:
      goto = Television._minChannel
    else:
      goto = self._channel + 1
    return self.setChannel(goto)              # rely upon other method
```

The inner **if-else** statement computes the new channel number, but it does not actually enact the change. That task is accomplished by the last command. Not only does this cause the channel to change, but it properly cares for the _prevChan attribute. For example, if a television is currently on channel 4, and someone invokes channelUp, we determine that the new channel should be 5 and then we invoke setChannel(5) upon the television. The implementation of that method has the effect of changing the current channel to 5, but not before recording the value 4 as _prevChan. Furthermore, since setChannel returns the resulting channel to us, we simply return that same value to the caller of our function.

As a more extreme example of the potential savings, the following is a complete and correct implementation of jumpPrevChannel:

```
return self.setChannel(self._prevChan)
```

Compare this to the original version from page 219. That version has explicit code to check whether the power is on, to implement a careful swap of the _channel and _prevChan values, and finally to report the new channel setting as its return value. Yet if you carefully trace what happens when this new version is invoked, it behaves identically. We take advantage of the existing semantics of the setChannel method. For example, Figure 6.8 on page 219 diagrammed the effect of a television that is currently tuned to channel 11 but had previously been tuned to channel 5. With our new implementation, we in effect make a call to setChannel(5). Not only does this change the channel to 5, but it records 11 as the new value of _prevChan. In fact, setChannel even returns the value to which the television has been changed, and so we simply forward that value to the caller of jumpPrevChannel.

And what about when the power is off? A call to jumpPrevChannel should do noth-ing and return nothing. But this is precisely what is accomplished by our subsequent call to setChannel. Since the power is off, the implementation of setChannel will not alter any of the attributes nor return any explicit value. Instead, the return value is implicitly **None**, and this same response is forwarded to our caller.

6.6   Chapter Review

6.6.1   Key Points

- A class definition begins with the line,

  class *classname***:**

  and is followed by an indented body that contains definitions for all methods.
- Since methods are functions, they are defined with a syntax as described in Section 5.2.
- The constructor is a special method named __init__ that is used to establish the initial state of a newly created instance.
- When implementing an immutable class, it is important that a caller is allowed to customize its setting when calling the constructor (since its state can never again be changed).
- The signature for each method should begin with the implicit parameter **self**. When the method is called, this parameter identifies the particular instance upon which the method is invoked. For example, a method that is invoked syntactically as obj.foo( ) would be declared in the class definition starting with **def** foo(**self**):.
- Instance members are accessed using the syntax **self**.membername. As a general practice, we name our data members beginning with an underscore character (_) to emphasize that we do not wish to have those manipulated directly by users of our class.
- An identifier that is introduced in the body of a method without the **self** qualifier has local scope, existing only until the end of the current invocation.
- It is perfectly acceptable for the implementation of one method to depend upon a call to one or more of the other methods of that class.
- Support for the use of operators is provided by implementing the corresponding special method (e.g., __add__ supports the + operator, __eq__ supports ==).
- Casting from a user-defined type to an **int**, **float**, or **str** can be supported by providing special methods __int__, __float__, and __str__ respectively.

6.6.2 Glossary

accessor A method whose invocation cannot affect the state of the callee.

attribute One of the pieces of data used in representing the state of an object. Equivalently termed a data member, field, or instance variable.

caller The object that initiates the execution of a method.

class A group of objects that share commonality in their underlying encoding and supported behaviors.

class-level attribute An attribute introduced within the context of a class, as opposed to one introduced within the context of an *instance* of the class.

constructor A special method that is implicitly called whenever an object is instantiated. It is responsible for establishing the initial state of the object.

data member *See* attribute.

immutable The characteristic of an object whose state cannot be modified once constructed.

instance A single object drawn from a given class.

member Any of the attributes or methods associated with a class or an instance of that class.

member function *See* method.

method A formal operation supported by all objects of a given class.

module A library defining a combination of identifiers, functions and classes. Modules must be imported when needed.

mutable The characteristic of an object whose state can be changed by one or more of its methods.

mutator A method whose invocation may affect the state of the callee.

optional parameter A parameter that can be sent to a function, yet which is assigned a default value if not sent.

parameter A piece of information sent from the caller to the callee upon invocation of a function.

polymorphism A technique in which objects of different types support a common syntax or when a single function supports multiple behaviors depending upon the type of parameter it receives.

return value A piece of information sent back from the callee to the caller at the conclusion of a function call.

signature The interface of a function; specifically its name, parameters, and return value.

special method A method that provides implicit support for an alternative syntax in Python. For example, the __add__ method supports the + operator.

state The current condition of an object, as represented by its set of attribute values.

6.6.3 Exercises

Class Definitions: Fix the error

Practice 6.1: Consider the following definition for the Widget class:

```
 1   def Widget:
 2
 3     def Widget(self):
 4       self._msg = 'Hello, I'm a widget!'
 5
 6     def replace(self)
 7       index = self.index('w')
 8       self._msg[index] = 'g'
 9
10     def __str__(self):
11       print 'My string is: ' + self._msg
```

There are several errors in the above program (a combination of syntax and semantics). Locate and *correct* at least four of them.

Exercise 6.2: The following code defines a Radio class that implements a (very) simple model of a radio. Although we might critique the realism of the model (e.g., volume being unlimited, or the radio operating without power), there are more serious problems. Specifically, there are five critical errors with the syntax of the given class definition. Identify the five errors and explain how to correct each.

```
 1   class Radio( ):
 2     def init(self):
 3       self._powerOn = False
 4       self._volume = 5
 5       self._station = 90.7
 6       self._presets = [ 90.7, 92.3, 94.7, 98.1, 105.7, 107.7 ]
 7
 8     def togglePower(self):
 9       self._powerOn = not self._powerOn
10
11     def setPreset(self, ind):
12         self._presets[ind] = _station
13
14     def gotoPreset(self, ind):
15       self._station = self._presets[ind]
16
17    def increaseVolume(self):
18       self._volume = self._volume + 1
19
20     def decreaseVolume(self):
21       self._volume = self._volume − 1
```

```
22
23    def increaseStation(self)
24      self._station = self._station + .2
25
26    def decreaseStation(self):
27      self._station = self._station - .2
```

Class Definitions: Comprehension

Practice 6.3: Assume that we have an instance of the Television class that is currently tuned to channel 9. In this scenario, does the call setChannel(9) have any effect on the overall state of that television?

Exercise 6.4: Consider the following definition for class Thing:

```
class Thing:

    def __init__(self):
        self._a = 1
        self._b = 4

    def foo(self, param):
        self._a = self._a + param
        self._b = self._b + param
        return (self._a + self._b)

    def bar(self, param):
        a = self._a + param
        b = self._b + param
        return (a + b)

    def __str__(self):
        return 'a is '+str(self._a)+', b is '+str(self._b)
```

Predict the *precise* output that results when executing the following code.

```
it = Thing( )
print it.foo(2)
print it.bar(3)
print it
```

Class Definitions: Implementation

Practice 6.5: Consider the following partial definition for the Date class:

```
class Date:

    monthNames = ('January', 'February', 'March',
        'April', 'May', 'June', 'July', 'August',
        'September', 'October', 'November', 'December')

    def __init__(self):
        # By default: January 1, 2000
        self._month = 1
        self._day = 1
        self._year = 2000
```

(a) Define a getDay function that returns the day as an integer.

(b) Define a setYear function that takes an integer parameter specifying the year and sets the value of the year attribute.

(c) Define the __str__ function. This should return a string that represents the date in the format 'January 1, 2000'.

Practice 6.6: In Practice 4.18, we showed how we could count the number of occurrences of a value within a list. Show how such an implementation might appear if defined *within* the context of the original **list** class. That is, give a presumed body of the **list** method count(**self**, value).

Practice 6.7: On page 162, we gave logic for checking whether a given value is contained in a list. Show how such an implementation might appear if defined *within* the context of the original **list** class. That is, give a presumed body of the **list** method __contains__(**self**, value).

Exercise 6.8: Our Television design is such that the state information is maintained, even when the power is turned off. Thus when the television is subsequently turned on, the volume, channel, and mute settings remain as they had last been. However, many televisions behave as follows. Even if they were muted at the time they were last turned off, when they are turned back on the volume is no longer muted. Show how to alter our Television implementation to capture the revised semantics.

Exercise 6.9: Implement a factoryReset( ) method for our Television class that sets all dynamic attributes other than powerOn back to the original factory settings. Also, rewrite the original constructor to take advantage of this new method.

Exercise 6.10: The syntax −x for an object x is supported by that class's __neg__ method. Implement such a method for the Fraction class that returns a new fraction that is the negation of the original.

Exercise 6.11: Add an invert method to the Fraction class that returns a new fraction that is the reciprocal of the original.

Exercise 6.12: In the solution to Practice 6.7, we implement the __contains__ method in the context of the **list** class. In similar style, give an implementation of the index method of that class, with signature index(**self**, value). This method returns the index of the first occurrence of the given value on the list; however, if the value is not found, it throws a ValueError exception.

Exercise 6.13: The **str** class supports a method replace(old, new), that returns a new string that is the same as the original, except with every occurrence of the pattern old replaced by the pattern new. The **list** class does not support such an operation.

Imagine that you were originally designing the **list** class. Show how you might implement the body for such a method, declared in the context of the original **list** class definition as replace(**self**, old, new). As lists are mutable, we presume that the desired behavior is to change the original list (as opposed to the **str** class which is immutable, and thus returns a new string).

Projects

Exercise 6.14: Revise the robust Point implementation so that it can be used for represent‐ing and manipulating three‐dimensional points (<x, y, z>).

Exercise 6.15: Define a class Set that keeps track of a collection of *distinct* objects. Inter‐nally, you should use a **list** as an instance variable, but you should make sure not to allow duplicates into your set. We recommend the following design:

Set	
_contents	
Set( )	add(value)
__contains__(value)	discard(value)

The add method should insert the value into the set if not already there. The discard method should remove the value from the set if it is there (or do nothing otherwise). The __contains__ method is used to support the syntax value **in** s, returning **True** or **False** appropriately.

Exercise 6.16: Redo Exercise 6.15, this time defining a SortedSet class that ensures that the contents of the set are internally sorted. To verify the order, provide a __str__ method that displays the set (you can design your own string representation, or sim‐ply echo the underlying list).

Exercise 6.17: Redesign the Television class to add support for maintaining a list of favor‐ite channels as an attribute. Three additional methods should be supported.

- Calling addToFavorites( ) should add the *current* channel to the list of favorites (if not already present).
- Calling removeFromFavorites( ) should remove the *current* channel from the list of favorites (if it is present).
- Calling jumpToFavorite( ) should change the current channel setting to a par‐ticular channel from the favorite list. Specifically, the favorite that is the next higher in value when compared to the current channel should be chosen. If no favorites exist that are higher in value than the current channel, the lowest of

the favorite channels should be used. In the case that the favorite list is empty, the channel should not be changed.

Take care to ensure that jumpToFavorite( ) properly maintains the prevChan attribute for use with subsequent calls to jumpPrevChannel( ).

Exercise 6.18: Design an immutable class BinaryNumber, in the style of our Fraction class. Internally, your only instance variable should be a text string that represents the binary value, of the form '1110100'. Implement a constructor that takes a *string* parameter that specifies the original binary value. Provide natural implementations for the special methods __add__, __sub__, __lt__, __gt__, __eq__, __str__, and __int__. Note: with the exception of __int__, you are not to convert the internal values back to integers when implementing the operations; perform the arithmetic directly upon the internal binary representations.

Exercise 6.19: Design a class Ball, that can be used to model the physics of a ball in motion based upon the following high-level design.

Ball	
_posX	_velX
_posY	_velY
Ball(px, py, vx, vy)	advance( )
getPositionX( )	getVelocityX( )
getPositionY( )	getVelocityY( )

The advance method should update the state of the ball to simulate the effect of a single time unit. That is, the position should be altered based upon the current velocity and the velocity itself should be altered based upon the force of gravity. Assume that gravity acts upon the ball with a constant force in the y direction.

Exercise 6.20: Redo Exercise 6.19, but instead of assuming a constant downward gravity, model gravity around a star with a given position and mass. The gravitational pull should be toward the center of the star with a magnitude that is inversely proportional to the square of the distance from the ball to the star.

Exercise 6.21: Use our graphics library together with your Ball class to provide a visualization of the ball in motion.

Exercise 6.22: Rewrite the Television class using graphics to creatively animate the semantics on a Canvas that is created as part of the constructor. Perhaps each "channel" results in the display of a different image (or at least a different color). Also, the user displays can be shown visually when appropriate, with the channel number as text, and perhaps the volume represented with a form such as '=========---' for volume 3 of 10.

CHAPTER 7

Good Software Practices

In the previous chapters you have acquired skills for using Python's built-in classes and for developing your own classes. With a little planning and thought these skills can be used to construct larger, more intricate programs. However, larger programs require more time spent on design, testing, and careful documentation. In this chapter we demonstrate how fundamental skills can be combined to successfully create larger programs, highlighting good programming practices used to organize the software development process.

7.1 Overview of Mastermind

In the game Mastermind™, one player picks a secret pattern of colored pegs for another player to guess. Each guess gets scored with black and white pins. Each black pin represents a peg in the guess that is in the same position as a peg of the same color in the secret pattern. Roughly speaking, each white pin represents a peg of the guess that matches the color of a peg in a different position that has not otherwise been matched. To be more specific, the number of white pins is equal to the maximum number of additional matches that could be formed if we were allowed to rearrange the pegs. The object of the game is to determine the pattern in as few guesses as possible. In Figure 7.1, we show two stages of a sample game, one in progress and one when complete.

At first thought, developing a program as complicated as this game may seem like a daunting task; it can be difficult to know how to get started. Many beginning programmers are tempted to sit down and start writing code. This, however, is not a very good strategy. Poorly designed code is much harder to maintain and sometimes must be scrapped entirely.

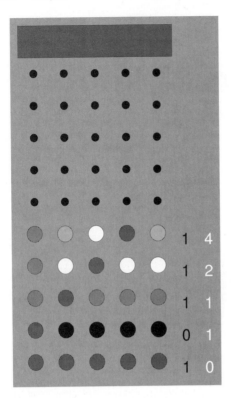 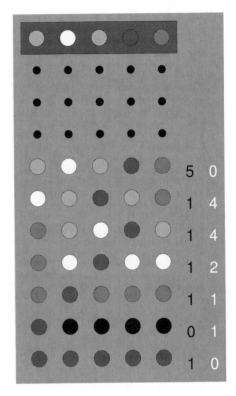

FIGURE 7.1: A mastermind board, shown during play of a game on the left, and after the player has won on the right. The numbers on the right side of a guess denote the number of black and white pins.

A well written program generally stems from a good initial design. In the remainder of this chapter, we walk through the design and implementation of software that manages a game of Mastermind in which the computer picks the secret and the player has to guess it. Our goal is to demonstrate several important techniques in software development.

7.2 Top-Down Design and Bottom-Up Implementation

Before we write any portion of a large program we should consider its overall design. One of the foremost challenges is to identify potential classes and the way in which objects from those classes will interact. This thought process was exemplified by the themes of Chapter 1. A starting point is to envision the use of our final product and design a top-level class and its interface. From there we expand our design to include classes that the top-level class will need in order to perform its tasks. We repeat this process until we have designed a collection of individual components that can be written and tested independently.

This approach is known as ***top-down design***. Once the design is fixed, implementation should start at the lowest level and work up to the top level; this technique is known as ***bottom-up implementation***. For the approach to be successful, every component must

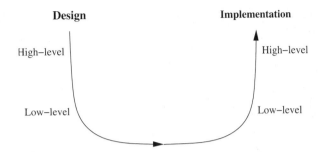

FIGURE 7.2: A development cycle with a top-down design followed by a bottom-up imple-mentation.

be tested thoroughly before moving on to the next higher level, as the higher-level code will depend upon use of the lower-level components. An overview of a typical develop-ment cycle is portrayed in Figure 7.2. The time initially spent developing a top-down plan is rewarded in the form of a better design that is easier and quicker to implement in the long run. Furthermore, because the integration of components has been planned, it is less likely that we spend time writing code that must later be thrown away due to unforeseen complications.

The existence of smaller independent pieces is called *modularity*. One advantage of this design is that the pieces can be implemented and tested in parallel by a team of software developers. Furthermore, many of the components may have more general value, allowing for *code reuse* across multiple portions of the program or in other projects.

7.3 Our Mastermind Design

Using the principles of the previous section as a framework, we begin designing our Mas-termind game. A good first step is to imagine the use of our complete software. One vision was already given in Figure 7.1, although that image is simply a sketch of a user interface. A program's interface greatly influences the user's experience, but it can often be designed relatively independently of the core program. In the case of Mastermind, for example, we need to input a guess from a user, but the logic of the game is unaffected by whether that input is typed on a keyboard, indicated with the mouse, or sent through a network. In similar spirit, the program must provide feedback to the user during the progression of the game, but we have flexibility in designing that aspect of the interface.

As an initial prototype, we design a purely text-based version of the game. This serves as a useful tool during our software development cycle, and it may be of interest for users who wish to play the game without reliance on graphics. Figure 7.3 shows a sample text-based session for a single game, corresponding to the same game shown graphically in Figure 7.1.

We will be careful in separating the primary management of the game from the user interface. We develop a Mastermind class as a high-level controller to manage the play of the game as a whole. Yet we intentionally encapsulate all aspects of the user interface into separate classes. In our initial prototype, we will develop a TextInput class for gather-

```
How many pegs are in the secret (from 1 to 10)? 5
How many colors are available (from 2 to 8)? 5
How many turns are allowed (from 1 to 20)? 10

Enter a guess (colors are RBGWY): RRRRR
On turn 1 of 10 guess RRRRR scored 1 black and 0 white.

Enter a guess (colors are RBGWY): RBBBB
On turn 2 of 10 guess RBBBB scored 0 black and 1 white.

Enter a guess (colors are RBGWY): GRGGG
On turn 3 of 10 guess GRGGG scored 1 black and 1 white.

Enter a guess (colors are RBGWY): GWRWW
On turn 4 of 10 guess GWRWW scored 1 black and 2 white.

Enter a guess (colors are RBGWY): GYWRY
On turn 5 of 10 guess GYWRY scored 1 black and 4 white.

Enter a guess (colors are RBGWY): WYRYG
On turn 6 of 10 guess WYRYG scored 3 black and 2 white.

Enter a guess (colors are RBGWY): YWYRG
On turn 7 of 10 guess YWYRG scored 5 black and 0 white.

Congratulations, you won!
The secret was YWYRG

Would you like to play again? N
```

FIGURE 7.3: An example of a text-based session for Mastermind. The underlined portions denote input entered by the user.

ing input from the keyboard and a TextOutput class for displaying results on the console. However, we later develop other user interfaces. By the end of this chapter, we will have a version that can produce graphical output, as originally shown in Figure 7.1 although still reading input from the keyboard. In Section 15.5 we will demonstrate how input can be gathered based upon mouse actions, and in Chapter 16 we will introduce techniques that could be used to develop a networked version of the game in which input is received from another computer.

Beyond the user interface, we consider aspects of the core game. For example, as a way to alter the difficulty of the game, we allow for variation in the number of pegs per pattern and the number of colors that are available for use. Continuing with our top–down design, we start to envision other components that are necessary to manage the game,

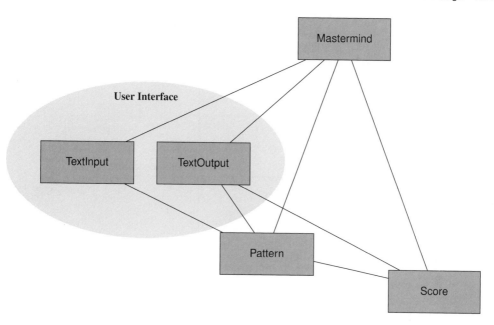

FIGURE 7.4: The major components of our Mastermind game prototype.

leading to the design of additional classes. A pattern of pegs plays a role representing both the secret and each guess; these needs can both be met with a Pattern class. The outcome of a single round may be modeled with a Score class.

The relationships between the major components of the design is shown in Fig–ure 7.4. Higher–level classes are nearer to the top and lower–level classes are nearer to the bottom. For example, the Pattern class is needed by the Mastermind class to keep track of the secret and guesses, by the TextInput class to allow a user to input a guess, and by TextOutput to display the guesses made by the player. The Pattern class generates a Score instance when determining how good each guess is.

Having identified many of the needed classes, we next consider what behaviors should be supported by each class and how a class will rely upon the behaviors of other classes. A *sequence diagram*, as introduced in Chapter 1, is a powerful modeling tool at this stage. For example, a single turn of the game involves a great deal of interaction. We may imagine this process starting with the main Mastermind object contacting a TextInput object requesting a guess from the user. That guess can be compared to the secret pat–tern, resulting in a score. That score can then be displayed to the user via a TextOutput object, which in turn needs detailed information about the particular guess and score. This hypothetical sequence of interactions is portrayed in the sequence diagram of Figure 7.5.

By envisioning other such sequences of interactions, we can begin to identify pre–cise behaviors that must be supported by individual classes to allow for needed interaction between classes. This helps us focus on the necessary flow of information between the caller and callee for each method. Soon we develop an initial sketch of the classes based upon the modeled interactions. After careful consideration, we settled upon the design

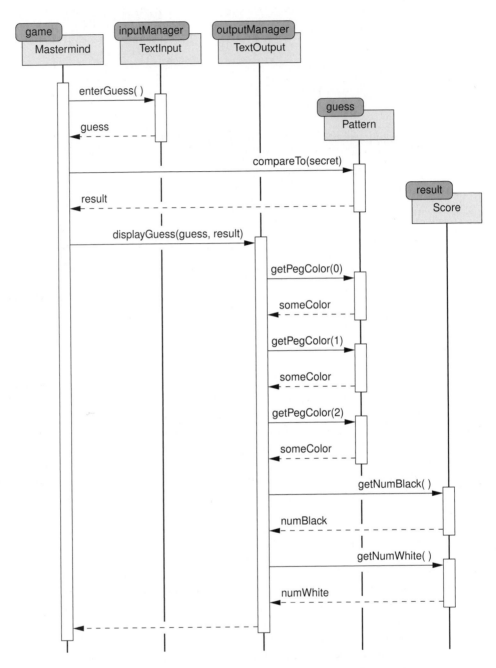

FIGURE 7.5: Sequence diagram for a single turn in Mastermind. First a guess is inputted and then the score is calculated. The rest deals with the display of the guess and the score. A series of queries is made to determine what color each peg is and to find the components of the score. All of this information is needed to display the output.

Mastermind
Mastermind(inputManager, outputManager)

Score
Score(numBlack, numWhite) getNumBlack( ) getNumWhite( )

Pattern
Pattern(numPegs) __len__( ) getPegColor(index) setPegColor(index, colorID) compareTo(otherPattern) randomize(numColors)

TextInput
TextInput(colorNames) queryLengthOfPattern( ) queryNumberOfColors( ) queryNumberOfTurns( ) queryNewGame( ) enterGuess( )

TextOutput
TextOutput(colorNames) startGame(lengthOfPattern, maxNumberOfTurns) displayTurn(guess, result) announceVictory(secret) announceDefeat(secret)

FIGURE 7.6: The publicly supported methods for each class in our design.

given in Figure 7.6 for this case study. Note that we have not yet described the implemen‑tation details for these classes, but instead have focused only on what we term the ***public members*** of each class, namely those members that are designed to provide an external means for interaction among objects. With the high‑level design complete, we should be able to move ahead and implement each of the classes independently.

In many cases, the eventual implementation closely resembles the sequence of events from our initial model. To demonstrate this relationship, we take a quick peek ahead at our final software. The following code fragment corresponds to the play of a single turn, as seen from within the Mastermind class:

```
# enact a single turn
guess = self._inputManager.enterGuess( )
result = guess.compareTo(secret)
self._outputManager.displayTurn(guess, result)
```

If you compare this code to the sequence diagram of Figure 7.5, you sould see that the three method calls initiated by the Mastermind instance in that diagram correspond precisely to the above lines of code.

In subsequent parts of this chapter, we give a detailed discussion of each of the classes, starting with the lowest‑level class and working towards the higher‑level classes. For Mastermind, the Score class is the lowest level and does not depend on any of the others. Once this class is completed the Pattern class will be implemented, as it only depends on the Score class. The TextInput and TextOutput classes can then be written before implementing the main Mastermind class.

7.4 Naming Conventions

As programmers, we have almost free rein when picking the names associated with various aspects within our software, including the functions, classes, attributes and methods of those classes, and so on. Reviewing our first mention of identifiers in Section 2.2.1, the limitations are that an identifier cannot begin with a numeral, cannot have any spaces, and cannot be among a short list of reserved keywords in the language (e.g., **class**). Furthermore, it is important to remember that identifiers are case sensitive, so Pattern and pattern are not the same.

Although the particular choice of an identifier does not generally provide syntactic meaning for the interpreter, it can provide a great deal of semantic meaning to another programmer. A name should be descriptive, clearly suggesting an underlying purpose so as to improve the overall readability of the code. In a forthcoming section, we discuss ways in which a programmer can *formally* document the precise purpose and use of classes, function, and parameters. Yet we wish to emphasize that the thoughtful choice of a name can go a long way in establishing correct intuition.

Because programmers must read, use, and modify another programmer's code, it helps to establish naming conventions that clarify the broad use of an identifier, distinguishing between class names, method names, variable names, and so on. There are a variety of existing naming conventions. The ones that we adopt are not identical to Python's built-in naming conventions, but are very typical of the conventions used by programmers developing Python code as well as those writing code in other object-oriented languages.

Classes

Class names are chosen to begin with a capital letter, as in Television, Fraction, Pattern, and Score. To enhance the readability of code, the class name should serve as a singular noun. For example, although we develop a class of patterns, we use the singular term Pattern because a single instance is created by the syntax Pattern( ). When the class name involves two or more English words, we concatenate those words while capitalizing the first letter of each word (e.g., TextOutput). The name should be descriptive, giving a general idea about its features and purposes even in the absence of further documentation. While longer names require more typing, they may greatly improve the understandability of subsequent code. For example, we could have named the TextOutput class as Output; however our name suggests additional information about the class. Furthermore it distinguishes it from other possible classes, such as GraphicsOutput.

Functions

The name of a function, whether stand-alone or a method of a class, typically begins with a lowercase letter, as in move, randomize, and run. If a name is the concatenation of multiple words, the first begins with a lowercase letter, but each additional word is capitalized, as in jumpPrevChannel, getPegColor, and announceVictory. The name should serve as a verb portraying the primary semantics of the function, as with the announceVictory method of the TextOutput class. An experienced programmer is likely to understand the general purpose of the method, even before reading any further documentation.

Data

Identifiers associated with data are named using the same capitalization style as functions, starting with a lowercase letter and capitalizing subsequently concatenated words. A name should be a noun, although it may be singular or plural depending on its usage. It is important to choose names that clearly indicate what type of data is being stored and how it will be used. For example, the names guestList and idNumber not only make the purpose of a variable clear, they also suggest that the underlying data types are lists and integers respectively. These conventions can almost make a fragment of code read like an English sentence. As an example,

for guest **in** guestList:

reads clearly and the purpose and type of each variable is clear by context.

Parameters

As a form of data, parameters are named using the same conventions discussed in the preceding section. Proper naming of parameters is particular important as these serve as a guide for a caller wishing to invoke a function. For example, the startGame method of the TextOutput class accepts two parameters (lengthOfPattern, maxNumberOfTurns). A wise user knowing something about the game may correctly predict the expectations for these three parameters even before referring to any formal documentation. Notice the greater ambiguity if those parameters had been named as (length, turns) or worse yet as (l,t).

The advantage of naming conventions

By following these conventions, it is often possible to tell exactly what a name represents, even with limited context. Consider the expressions, Game( ), calculate( ), and number. The capitalization suggests that the first is the constructor for the Game class and the second is a function call. The lack of parentheses suggests that number is a piece of data.

 A WORD OF WARNING

Using the same names for different purposes in a program can be confusing and lead to errors. We also recommend against use of differently cased versions of the same word, as in pattern = Pattern( ). Likewise, using a variable named average for an object or module that supports a function named average leads to unusual statements such as average.average( ).

Ironically, the creators of Python seem less concerned about such a naming conflict. There exists a module time that supports a function time.time( ) and similarly a random.random( ) function within the random module.

7.5   Formal Documentation: Python Docstrings

As you write more complicated code, the importance of good documentation increases. Documentation informs another programmer how to properly use your classes and functions, and serves as a formal specification of the promised behavior that must be internally implemented, whether by you or another programmer. From a planning perspective, the expected outward behavior of a class or function should be well defined and documented before the actual implementation is written.

In Section 2.9.4, we introduced use of the # symbol for directly embedding comments within source code. This style of comment is ignored by the interpreter yet visible to a programmer, making it very valuable for someone who must examine or modify a piece of source code. However, there are many circumstances where one programmer wishes to import and use a class or function written by another, without taking time to closely examine the original source code. In fact a user of a class may not even have access to its source code, such as when using one of Python's built-in classes.

To provide a more accessible form of documentation, Python supports another style of documentation using well-placed strings known as **docstrings**. These strings are not only visible within the source code, they are used to provide information seen in the Python interpreter through use of the help command, and to generate documentation on web pages using a corresponding utility pydoc. A docstring is technically a string literal that occurs as the very first element within the body of a class or function. Typically, triple quote delimiters (" " ") are used since these allow for multiline strings. A docstring should begin with a brief one line description. If further explanation is warranted, such as the purpose or type of parameters and return value, that information should be provided after a subsequent blank line within the docstring.

Score class

As a first example, we document the source code for the Score class of the Mastermind game, as shown in Figure 7.7. There are four different docstrings embedded in this code. The first occurs at lines 2–7, as the first element of the overall class body. This multiline docstring describes the broad purpose of the Score class, including a brief explanation of the notion of black and white components in the context of a Mastermind game. The next docstring occurs at line 10, describing the __init__ method. We use a single line docstring because the purpose of this method is rather clear and the parameters are well named. Similarly, we provide docstrings at lines 15 and 19 for the getNumBlack and getNumWhite methods.

The docstrings embedded with the source code can be viewed by others in one of two ways. If someone imports the Score class, its documentation can be viewed by typing help(Score) in the Python interpreter. This produces a view as shown in Figure 7.8(a).

Similar documentation can be generated in the form of a web page using a utility program named pydoc which is distributed with Python. Figure 7.8(b) shows the Score documentation in this format. In addition to a more pleasing use of color and layout, an advantage of the web page format is that documentation for a larger collection of files will contain navigational links, for example to related classes in the Mastermind project.

```
1   class Score:
2     """A score for a single turn from game of Mastermind.
3
4     A "black" component designates the number of pegs that are
5     exact matches for the answer.  A "white" component counts
6     pegs that are correctly colored but not well positioned.
7     """
8
9     def __init__(self, numBlack, numWhite):
10        """Create score with given black and white components."""
11        self._numBlack = numBlack
12        self._numWhite = numWhite
13
14     def getNumBlack(self):
15        """Return the black component of the score."""
16        return self._numBlack
17
18     def getNumWhite(self):
19        """Return the white component of the score."""
20        return self._numWhite
```

FIGURE 7.7: Implementation of the Score class.

Pattern class

A user can often discern the purpose and use of a class or function based on the naming conventions. However, sometimes more documentation is needed to provide additional details. As an example, the Pattern class includes a function named compareTo with a single parameter otherPattern. While an experienced user can probably infer that the parameter is a second parameter that is compared to the first, it is not evident what this function returns. We prefer to provide further guidance as part of the following docstring:

```
    def compareTo(self, otherPattern):
      """Compare the current pattern to otherPattern and calculate the score.

      otherPattern    the pattern to be compared to the current one

      Return a Score instance representing the result.
      See the Score class for details on the components of the score.
      """
```

This makes clear that the function returns a resulting Score instance (it also makes clear that the parameter is expected to be another pattern, just in case the naming convention is not already sufficient). This extra information allows the programmer to confidently use this method.

(a)

```
class Score
 |  A score for a single turn from game of Mastermind.
 |
 |  A "black" component designates the number of pegs that are
 |  exact matches for the answer.  A "white" component counts
 |  pegs that are correctly colored but not well positioned.
 |
 |  Methods defined here:
 |
 |  __init__(self, numBlack, numWhite)
 |      Create score with given black and white components.
 |
 |  getNumBlack(self)
 |      Return the black component of the score.
 |
 |  getNumWhite(self)
 |      Return the white component of the score.
 |
```

(b)

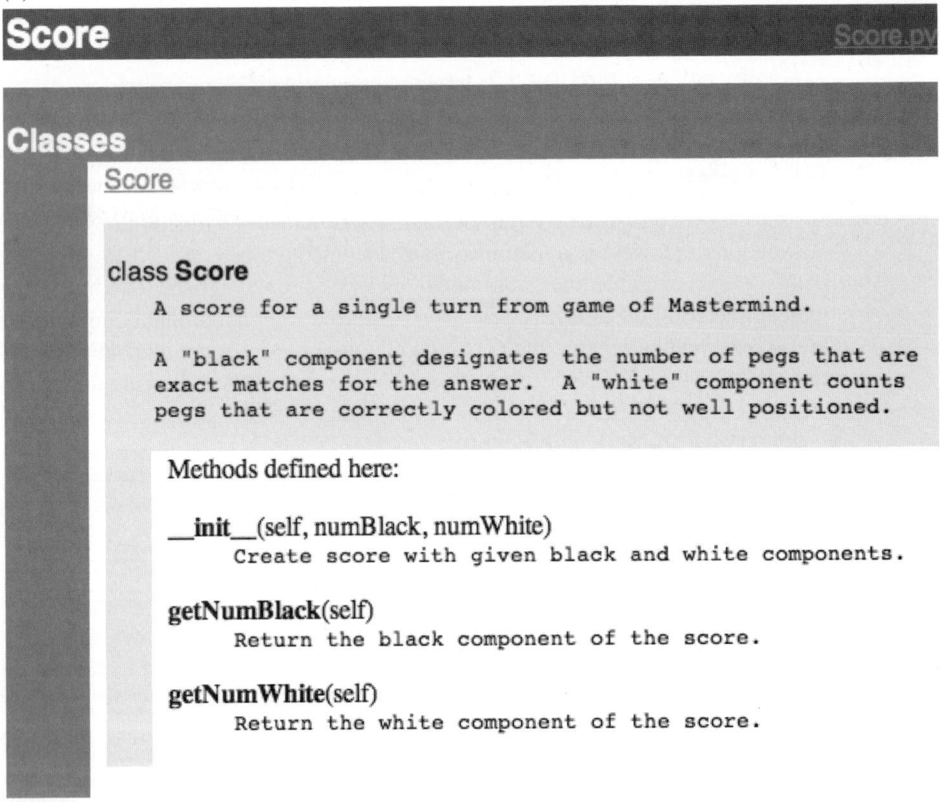

Score

Score.py

Classes

Score

class **Score**

A score for a single turn from game of Mastermind.

A "black" component designates the number of pegs that are
exact matches for the answer. A "white" component counts
pegs that are correctly colored but not well positioned.

Methods defined here:

__init__(self, numBlack, numWhite)
    Create score with given black and white components.

getNumBlack(self)
    Return the black component of the score.

getNumWhite(self)
    Return the white component of the score.

FIGURE 7.8: Documentation for the Score class. View (a) is obtained by typing help(Score) in the interpreter, and (b) from a web page created by pydoc.

Television class

As a further example, we revisit the Television class from Section 6.3. Its constructor had the following simple signature:

```
def __init__(self):
```

Based on just this information, it is clear that Television( ) is the correct calling syntax for creating a new instance. However, a user would probably want to understand the initial state for a television. That information is not evident without viewing the body of the constructor. For this reason, we provide the information as part of a docstring.

```
def __init__(self):
    """Create a new Television instance.

    The power is initially off. The first time the TV is turned on, it will be set to channel 2
    with a volume level of 5 (unmuted).
    """
    self._powerOn = False
    self._muted = False
    self._volume = 5
    self._channel = 2
    self._prevChan = 2
```

The channelUp method is another one that deserves more detailed explanation. Its name provides good intuition as to the effect of the function, but there are two particular circumstances worth noting. The method only has an effect when the television's power is on. Also, if invoked when at the maximum channel, this method causes the value to wrap around to the lowest channel. Both of these properties are documented accordingly.

```
def channelUp(self):
    """Increment the channel and return the resulting setting.

    If power is off, there is no effect.

    If channel had been set to the maximum of the valid range of channels, the effect
    is to wrap around to the minimum channel.
    """
```

Without precise details of what the function does, a user of our Television class may not expect such behavior, and as a result may develop errant code.

As a general rule, every class and function that we expect others to be using should be given an informative docstring. The appropriate level of detail may depend on the complexity of the behavior and the level of intuition that is already provided by the naming conventions. While it is true that it takes time to provide good documentation, that effort can save time in the long run for both the writer and user of a class.

7.6 Encapsulation of Implementation Details

A programmer who wishes to use a software component must have a solid understanding on the component's public interface. For this reason, all aspects of a software component that are intended for public use must be well documented, as discussed in the preceding section. However, we take a very different approach in respect to *internal* aspects of a component. Another programmer's utilization of our software component depends only on the public interface; so long as our code supports the promised interface, the details of how we accomplish that task should be irrelevant to others. This principle of treating internal implementation details of a software component as private is known as ***encapsulation***.

The primary advantage of encapsulation is that it limits the interdependence between software components. Consider the two roles, one being the author of a software component and the other being a client who is writing further software that depends on this component. Having a clear designation of the public and private aspects of the component benefits both programmers. For the client, the identification of the public portion draws focus to only that which must be understood to properly use the component; the private details are an unnecessary distraction in this regard. For the author, the encapsulation of private details provides greater flexibility in the development and maintenance of the soft-ware. Since other programmers may depend on the public interface, that interface cannot be altered without far-reaching consequences. Yet by assuming that other programmers are *not* depending upon any of the private details, the author is free to implement the compo-nent as she sees fit. The author can subsequently reorganize the internal implementation, whether to fix a bug or improve performance. In the remainder of this section, we explore ways in which the principle of encapsulation manifests itself in our Mastermind project.

7.6.1 High-Level Design

The use of encapsulation begins with the creation of the high-level design for a software project. The design of the various public interfaces depends upon the degree of information sharing that is necessary.

As an example, we consider the role of colors in our Mastermind game. For the user, colors are at the forefront of the play of the game. Yet internally, the logic of the game depends only on the fact that there exists a certain number of distinguishable color choices; the actual palette of colors is insignificant. Our core design simply represents the "colors" as integer IDs, numbered from zero. Looking back at the public interface for Pattern from Figure 7.6, we see that setPegColor relies on such a colorID as a parameter. In similar respects, the return value of getPegColor is such an integer. Internally, the state of a Pattern consists solely of a list of integers. The representation does not include any concept of color names like "red" or "blue," but there is a presumption that color #2 in one pattern denotes the same underlying color as color #2 in another. This suffices for comparing patterns to each other when computing a score.

The only portion of the code that uses the true identities of the colors is the user interface. Since colors are a central theme from a user's perspective, the identities of those colors must be used when gathering input from the user or displaying output. To coordinate the palette, the constructors for the TextInput and TextOutput classes accept a list of color names to be used. Those classes manage the mapping from those names to the corresponding indices of the list that serves as the color's ID.

7.6.2   Underscored Names in Python

Python supports the notion of encapsulation through naming conventions. If the identifier given to a class, or to a method or attribute of a class, begins with an alphabetic character (e.g., Pattern, getPegColor) that element is presumed to be of public interest. To designate something as private, we choose an identifier that begins with a single underscore character (e.g., the _channel attribute of a Television). This designation of privacy is supported by Python in several ways. When methods of a class are named with a leading underscore, they are not displayed in documentation generated by the help command or the pydoc util–ity. This keeps a reader's attention focused on the public aspects of the software. Further–more when the wildcard form of an import is performed (e.g., **from** cs1graphics **import** *), only the public elements of the module are loaded.

Although these features help shield a user from knowledge of the private details, Python does not strictly enforce the notion of privacy.[1] If another programmer some–how learned of an underscored name, it can be directly accessed using a syntax such as myTV._channel = 30. But such usage is strongly discouraged in general.

As an aside, we note that the single underscore naming convention is unrelated to the double underscore naming used for special methods such as __init__. Also, local vari–ables within a function body are not typically underscored, as they are already inherently private due to their local scope.

7.6.3   Data Members

In order to protect the integrity of an object's state, we generally encapsulate all attributes of a class as private, preferring public access through designated accessors and mutators. This convention has been followed in all of our earlier examples. Looking back at Chap–ter 6, we see that our Point class has attributes _x and _y, whose underlying values can be accessed through public methods such as getX and setX. Since we allow the user to set arbitrary values, we might have chosen a design with public data members that are directly manipulated. Yet we still prefer to use encapsulation, as the required use of method calls affords us some notion of control and monitoring.

The encapsulation within our Television class is more significant. Users may create an inconsistent state if directly manipulating our underlying attributes. For example, a programmer may set the volume or channel to an out–of–range value, or change the channel without properly tracking the previous channel. For our Fraction class, the encapsulation of attributes _numer and _denom allowed us to enforce its immutability.

7.6.4   Private Methods

Just as attributes can be designated as private by naming them with a leading underscore, we can designate certain methods as private. While the public methods are ones that we expect to be called by others, private methods are used for our own convenience when implementing a class; they should only be called from within the remainder of the class. Often these functions are used to perform some common task for the rest of the class to improve the overall organization.

---

1.   Many object–oriented languages formally enforce a notion of privacy.

As an example, we consider our implementation of the TextOutput class. One of the burdens for this class is displaying a Pattern to the user. There are three different situations in which a pattern is displayed: displayTurn is used to echo a recent guess together with its score, while both announceVictory and announceDefeat involve displaying the secret pattern. To avoid rewriting code three times for translating a Pattern to its string representation, we create a private method named _patternAsString. This represents the pattern as the sequence of leading characters from the names, relying upon the fact that the color names have distinct first letters.

Figure 7.9 shows the full implementation of the TextOutput class. Our private method is at lines 40–45. We have provided a descriptive docstring as part of that method, although this function is not normally included within the result of help(TextOutput). Even so, the documentation is available as help(TextOutput._patternAsString) for someone who knows of the function's existence and name. Syntactically, the private method is invoked just as a regularly named member of the class (see lines 25, 32, and 37).

7.7 Modules and Unit Testing

The source code for a large project is typically split into several files. This helps improve the organization, supports reuse of code, and allows for different developers to edit different components with less interference. In the case of our Mastermind game, we put each class in its own file, using the class name followed by the .py suffix as the filename, for example placing the Score definition in file Score.py.

If one class relies upon definitions from a separate file, the latter elements must be imported into the former before they can be used (as discussed in Sections 2.7 and 6.1.1). As an example, our Pattern implementation depends on several external features. It supports a compareTo method that is supposed to generate a Score as a result, therefore we must import the Score definition from the file Score.py. Our Pattern class also supports a randomize method, used eventually for the automated generated of secrets. To accomplish the randomization, we need several tools imported from Python's standard random module. Therefore, the first two lines of Pattern.py read as follows:

```
from Score import Score
from random import seed, randint
```

Another important principle of good software development is to test each individual component as it is written. If one were to wait until the entire project were written before testing any part of it, there would likely be many errors and it might be difficult to isolate the source of those errors. Testing a class individually, instead of as part of the larger program, is called *unit testing*. This practice goes hand in glove with bottom–up implementation. By developing code from lower–level to higher–level, a newly written class can be immediately tested because those classes upon which it depends will have already been implemented. More importantly, with unit testing we should have reason to believe that those earlier classes are reasonably error free. As a result, we can more easily localize and correct errors.

```
1   class TextOutput:
2     """Provide text-based output for the Mastermind game."""
3
4     def __init__(self, colorNames):
5       """Construct a new TextOutput instance.
6
7       colorNames      a sequence of strings (each color must start with a different letter)
8       """
9       self._colorOptions = ' '                              # initials for color choices
10      for color in colorNames:
11        self._colorOptions += color[0].upper( )
12      # following will be reset when startGame is called
13      self._currentTurnNum = self._lengthOfPattern = self._maxNumberOfTurns = 0
14
15    def startGame(self, lengthOfPattern, maxNumberOfTurns):
16      """Game is beginning with specified parameters."""
17      self._currentTurnNum = 0
18      self._lengthOfPattern = lengthOfPattern
19      self._maxNumberOfTurns = maxNumberOfTurns
20
21    def displayTurn(self, guess, result):
22      """Display recent guess Pattern and resulting Score to the screen."""
23      self._currentTurnNum += 1
24      print 'On turn', self._currentTurnNum, 'of', self._maxNumberOfTurns,
25      print 'guess', self._patternAsString(guess), 'scored',
26      print result.getNumBlack( ), 'black and', result.getNumWhite( ), 'white.'
27
28    def announceVictory(self, secret):
29      """Inform the player that he/she has correctly matched the secret Pattern."""
30      print
31      print 'Congratulations, you won!'
32      print 'The secret was', self._patternAsString(secret)
33
34    def announceDefeat(self, secret):
35      """Inform the player that he/she has lost and reveal the secret Pattern."""
36      print
37      print 'The secret was', self._patternAsString(secret)
38      print 'Good luck next time.'
39
40    def _patternAsString(self, thePattern):
41      """Returns string representation of given Pattern using color shorthands."""
42      display = ' '
43      for i in range(self._lengthOfPattern):
44        display += self._colorOptions[thePattern.getPegColor(i)]
45      return display
```

FIGURE 7.9: The TextOutput class.

Unit tests in Python

Python provides a convenient manner for embedding unit tests inside the same file as the class implementation. These tests are placed within a special conditional statement, following the complete class definition. The basic form of the file should appear as follows:

```
class Pattern:
  # implementation here

if __name__ == '__main__':
  # unit test here
```

The conditional serves the following purpose. We want to have a way to execute commands as part of an isolated unit test, yet to have those commands ignored when the file is being incorporated into the larger software project.

When a Python program is executed, the flow of control begins with an indicated module. For example, our complete Mastermind program may be executed from the command line as `python Mastermind.py`, or by running the Mastermind module from within IDLE. Of course, that top-level module may import other modules along the way. Within an individual module, the special variable __name__ serves to identify the context in which that module is currently being loaded. If the module is the one upon which the interpreter was initially invoked, this variable will be automatically set to the string '__main__'. Alternatively, if the module is being imported from elsewhere, then __name__ will be set to this module's own name.

Therefore, when a user runs the complete program by executing the Mastermind module, the subsequent import of the Pattern module proceeds with the special condition failing; therefore the Pattern unit test will not be executed at that time. However, a developer can intentionally run the unit test by invoking Python directly upon the Pattern module, as in `python Pattern.py`, causing the body of the conditional to be executed.

Example: the Pattern class

A unit test should be designed to ensure the correctness, as best as possible, of all of the behaviors and features of a class. The goal is to make sure that the implementation respects the semantics of the formal documentation. The tests should be comprehensive, testing every method in a variety of settings. It should not just test the easy cases, but also the exceptional cases that might have been overlooked by the developer. While unit testing never guarantees that an implementation is flawless, if used properly it can find most errors and provide some confidence that the code works as advertised. The unit test can be re-executed throughout the development cycle, ensuring that the class continues to work properly each time modifications are made to the source code.

As a demonstration, we examine our implementation and unit test for the Pattern class. The complete contents of our `Pattern.py` file is given in Figure 7.10. As originally discussed in Section 7.6, we represent a pattern as a list of integers (_pegList), denoting the sequence of colored pegs. For simplicity, the color of each peg is initialized to 0 in the constructor. The __len__, getPegColor, setPegColor, and randomize methods are straightforward. The most complicated behavior is surely compareTo, which is modeled upon the scoring rules of Mastermind. There are several possible algorithms for computing that score; hopefully our embedded comments help to explain how the score is calculated, although walking through a few examples by hand may be helpful.

Our unit testing begins at line 71. We have chosen to design our test so that it generates output only when an error is discovered. In truth, the tests we have shown are not comprehensive enough but serve to demonstrate the concept. We should have tested all of the functions, each with multiple settings. The more complicated the behavior, the more prone it is to errors.

Lines 72–82 test the most basic of behaviors. We create a pattern of length five, individually setting the peg colors as desired. Then we test the __len__ and getPegColor accessors to make sure we get the expected response. If a problem were reported, we could not immediately know whether the problem was with setting the state or retrieving the state. In either case, a further examination of the code is warranted.

Since compareTo is the most complicated of the behaviors, the remainder of our unit test is devoted to verifying its performance. We make a copy of the same pattern and check whether it is scored as all black when compared to itself. Starting at line 92 we introduce a second pattern that can be compared to the first. The expected result at line 98 is based on our own manual computation of the expected score for the two given hands. Finally, we vary the second pattern and recompute the score.

Although our test does not examine the randomize method, a good unit test should do so. A complicating factor is that a call to randomize does not lead to a predictable result. However, we could verify that it does produce colors that are all within the requested range. A more rigorous test would be to make thousands of calls while tracking statistics to ensure that the randomness appears uniform.

```
1   from Score import Score
2   from random import seed, randint
3
4   class Pattern:
5     """Class for storing a color pattern for Mastermind."""
6
7     def __init__(self, numPegs):
8       """Construct a new pattern.
9
10      Initially, the pattern consists of numPegs pegs, each set to color 0.
11      """
12      self._pegList = [0] * numPegs              # Create a list of 0's with given length
13
14    def __len__(self):
15      """Return the length of the current pattern."""
16      return len(self._pegList)
```

FIGURE 7.10: The Pattern class with unit test (continued on next page).

```
17    def getPegColor(self, index):
18        """Return the current color setting (an integer) of the specified peg.
19
20        index               the index of the peg
21        """
22        return self._pegList[index]
23
24    def setPegColor(self, index, colorID):
25        """Set the color of a peg at the given index of the pattern.
26
27        index               the index of the peg
28        colorID             the desired color identifier (an integer)
29        """
30        self._pegList[index] = colorID
31
32    def compareTo(self, otherPattern):
33        """Compare the current pattern to otherPattern and calculate the score.
34
35        otherPattern     the pattern to be compared to the current one
36
37        Return a Score instance representing the result.
38        See the Score class for details on the components of the score.
39        """
40        # First calculate the black component of the score
41        black = 0
42        for i in range(len(self._pegList)):
43            if self.getPegColor(i) == otherPattern.getPegColor(i):
44                black += 1
45
46        # The white component is a little more difficult to calculate.
47        # First find out the colors used in the current pattern
48        colorsUsed = [ ]
49        for color in self._pegList:
50            if color not in colorsUsed:
51                colorsUsed.append(color)
52
53        # For each color used find the smaller number of times
54        # it appears in each pattern and add them up.
55        white = 0
56        for color in colorsUsed:
57            white += min(self._pegList.count(color), otherPattern._pegList.count(color))
58        white -= black                                    # Don't count pegs that are paired up.
59
60        return Score(black, white)
```

FIGURE 7.10 (continuation): The Pattern class with unit test (continued on next page).

```
61      def randomize(self, numColors):
62        """Make a random pattern.
63
64        numColors    the maximum number of colors to use in the pattern
65        """
66        seed( )                                    # reset random number generator
67        for i in range(len(self._pegList)):
68          self._pegList[i] = randint(0, numColors−1)
69  ####### end of Pattern class #######
70
71  if __name__ == '__main__':
72    modelA = (1, 3, 0, 3, 2)                      # will use as sample pattern
73    patternA = Pattern(5)
74    for i in range(len(modelA)):
75      patternA.setPegColor(i, modelA[i])
76
77    if len(patternA) != 5:
78      print 'Pattern length is miscalculated'
79
80    for i in range(5):
81      if patternA.getPegColor(i) != modelA[i]:
82        print 'Color at index', i, 'not properly set/retrieved'
83
84    copy = Pattern(5)
85    for i in range(5):
86      copy.setPegColor(i, patternA.getPegColor(i))
87
88    score = patternA.compareTo(copy)
89    if score.getNumBlack( ) != 5 or score.getNumWhite( ) != 0:
90      print 'Score miscalcuated'
91
92    modelB = (3, 1, 2, 3, 1)                      # another sample pattern
93    patternB = Pattern(5)
94    for i in range(len(modelB)):
95      patternB.setPegColor(i, modelB[i])
96
97    score = patternA.compareTo(patternB)
98    if score.getNumBlack( ) != 1 or score.getNumWhite( ) != 3:   # our expected score
99      print 'Score miscalcuated'
100
101   patternB.setPegColor(1, 3)   # turns second peg to black, disqualifies a previous white
102   score = patternA.compareTo(patternB)
103   if score.getNumBlack( ) != 2 or score.getNumWhite( ) != 2:   # our expected score
104     print 'Score miscalcuated'
```

FIGURE 7.10 (continuation): The Pattern class with unit test.

7.8 Error Checking

Because we unit test each of the individual components of our software, the code for one component is written with the assumption that other components behave properly. Yet we should not make such an assumption when it comes to the user's interactions with our software. We do not want a user's mistake to cause our program to crash.

To ensure the robustness of our Mastermind software, we should check all input received from the user, responding appropriately in case of an error. Conveniently, our high-level design encapsulates all gathering of user input within the TextInput class. Our implementation of that class is given in Figure 7.11. Our text-based interface relies upon the use of a color name's initial character. For this reason, our constructor accepts a list of color names that are presumed to start with different letters. We take those names and form the string _palette that consists of the initial characters; the _palette string includes all possible colors, yet an individual game may be limited to a subset based upon the value _numColorsInUse read as a game begins.

There are five separate forms of user interaction in our program. Three of them are used to gather numeric parameters when beginning a game, namely the desired pattern length, the number of colors to be made available, and the maximum number of turns given to a player. Since each of these responses is expected to be an integer within a given range, we define a private utility function _readInt that can be used for each purpose. This function, shown at lines 16–27, uses the same techniques introduced in Section 5.5 for reading a number from 1 to 10. In this case, we parameterize the behavior to allow for a custom prompt and designated small and large limits on the allowable response. The body of the function ensures that the user's response is indeed an integer and within the allowable range. Applications of this function can be seen at lines 32, 38 and 42.

Another form of interaction occurs at the end of the game, when we ask the user if he would like to play again. Our implementation of queryNewGame is rather straightforward and shown at lines 44–48.

The remaining form of input comes as we ask the user for a guess during the game. This is supported by the enterGuess method, implemented at lines 50–75. There are several aspects of error checking in this case. Users are expected to enter a pattern as a text string using the one character codes representing color names (e.g., YWYRG). Our function ensures that the user enters a pattern of the appropriate length, and using only color options that are currently allowable. Although we suggest uppercase characters for the code, we assist the user at line 65 by intentionally filtering the entered character with a call to upper. However, if any other error is detected when examining the input, the user is given an appropriate error message and then reprompted for a pattern.

As an aside, we note that we do not perform any error checking upon the colorNames parameter sent to the constructor. For the software to function properly, this must be a sequence of strings with each string using a different initial character. We could rewrite the code to explicitly check the validity of the parameter, but these names are not being provided by the user of our software. They are presumed to be sent from within the overall body of code. So we clearly document the requirements and trust that our instructions will be followed (or that errors will be remedied during the testing phase).

```
1    from Pattern import Pattern
2
3    class TextInput:
4      """Class for dealing with text—based input for the Mastermind game."""
5
6      def __init__(self, colorNames):
7        """Create a new text input instance.
8
9        colorNames       a sequence of strings (each color must start with a different letter)
10       """
11       self._lengthOfPattern = 0                    # will later be queried from the user
12       self._palette = ' '                          # initials for color choices, e.g., R for red
13       for color in colorNames:
14         self._palette += color[0].upper( )
15
16     def _readInt(self, prompt, small, large):
17       """Robustly prompt the user for an integer from small to large."""
18       prompt = prompt + ' (from ' + str(small) + ' to ' + str(large) + ') ? '
19       answer = small − 1                           # intentionally invalid
20       while not small <= answer <= large:
21         try:
22           answer = int(raw_input(prompt))
23           if not small <= answer <= large:
24             print 'Integer must be from '+str(small)+' to '+str(large)+'.'
25         except ValueError:
26           print 'That is not a valid integer.'
27       return answer
28
29     def queryLengthOfPattern(self):
30       """Ask the user how many pegs in the secret pattern."""
31       self._lengthOfPattern = \
32                   self._readInt('How many pegs are in the secret', 1, 10)
33       return self._lengthOfPattern
34
35     def queryNumberOfColors(self):
36       """Ask the user how many colors to use for secret pattern."""
37       self._numColorsInUse = \
38         self._readInt('How many colors are available', 2, len(self._palette))
39       return self._numColorsInUse
40
41     def queryNumberOfTurns(self):
42       """Ask the user maximum number of guesses to be allowed."""
43       return self._readInt('How many turns are allowed', 1, 20)
```

FIGURE 7.11: The TextInput class (continued on next page).

```
44    def queryNewGame(self):
45      """Offer the user a new game. Return True if accepted, False otherwise."""
46      print
47      response = raw_input('Would you like to play again? ')
48      return response.lower() in ('y', 'yes')
49
50    def enterGuess(self):
51      """Get a guess from the user and return it as a Pattern instance."""
52      validPattern = False
53      while not validPattern:
54        print                                # intentional blank line
55        prompt = 'Enter a guess (colors are '
56        prompt += self._palette[:self._numColorsInUse] + ') : '
57        patternString = raw_input(prompt)
58
59        validPattern = True
60        if len(patternString) != self._lengthOfPattern:
61          print 'The pattern must have', self._lengthOfPattern, 'pegs'
62          validPattern = False
63        else:
64          for i in range(self._lengthOfPattern):
65            if patternString[i].upper() not in self._palette[:self._numColorsInUse]:
66              validPattern = False
67          if not validPattern:
68            print 'The color options are', self._palette[:self._numColorsInUse]
69
70        if validPattern:
71          pattern = Pattern(self._lengthOfPattern)
72          for i in range(self._lengthOfPattern):
73            pattern.setPegColor(i, self._palette.index(patternString[i].upper()))
74
75      return pattern
```

FIGURE 7.11 (continuation): The TextInput class.

7.9   Mastermind: Pulling It Together

With the completion of all lower-level classes, we are prepared to write the Mastermind class. Our complete implementation is given in Figure 7.12 and presumed to be saved within a file named `Mastermind.py`. This code contains two components. Lines 4–46 provide the formal definition of a Mastermind class that controls the high-level flow of a series of games. Following that class definition, is a block of code embedded within a `__name__ == '__main__'` conditional. Recall that this block of code will be executed when Python is invoked on `Mastermind.py`. In this case, the block initiates the complete Mastermind program on behalf of the user.

One of the key aspects of our high-level design is the decision to separate the user interface from the primary game logic. Looking at the main portion of the program in lines 48–57, we instantiate a TextInput and TextOutput object that manage the user interface for input and output respectively. Those objects are sent as parameters to the constructor of the Mastermind class.

When a Mastermind object is constructed, the flow of control immediately enters a while loop to repeatedly play a single game at a time, so long as the user wishes to continue. The Mastermind class does not directly interact with the user; it relies upon the given inputManager and outputManager objects for that purpose. Notice the use of command **self.**_inputManager.queryNewGame( ) at line 18; this is but one example of our reliance on the external objects for managing the user interface.

The primary game logic is encapsulated in the private _runSingleGame method. At the beginning of each game, lines 22–24 are used to request the necessary game parameters from the input manager. We make a call to **self.**_outputManager.startGame at line 25, allowing the output manager to coordinate its state based upon the settings for the newly started game.

Continuing at line 27, the secret is constructed and then individual rounds of the game are carried out until the maximum number of turns is exhausted or until the user succeeds in guessing the secret pattern. The logic for a single turn, at lines 36–41, should look familiar; this code is based primarily on the sequence diagram of Figure 7.5 and was previewed on page 243. We request a guess from the user, compare it to the secret, display the result, and take note if victory was achieved. Once the while loop completes, it is time to either congratulate or console the user by announcing victory or defeat.

```
1   from Score import Score
2   from Pattern import Pattern
3
4   class Mastermind:
5       """Main class for the Mastermind game."""
6
7       def __init__(self, inputManager, outputManager):
8           """Create a new instance of the Mastermind game.
9
10          inputManager      instance of class that gathers input from the user
11          outputManager     instance of class that displays output to the user
12          """
13          self._inputManager = inputManager
14          self._outputManager = outputManager
15          playAgain = True
16          while playAgain:
17              self._runSingleGame()
18              playAgain = self._inputManager.queryNewGame()
```

FIGURE 7.12: The Mastermind class with text-based driver (continued on next page).

```
19   def _runSingleGame(self):
20     """Play one game."""
21     # get parameters from the user
22     lengthOfPattern = self._inputManager.queryLengthOfPattern( )
23     numberOfColors = self._inputManager.queryNumberOfColors( )
24     maxNumberOfTurns = self._inputManager.queryNumberOfTurns( )
25     self._outputManager.startGame(lengthOfPattern, maxNumberOfTurns)
26
27     # pick a new secret
28     secret = Pattern(lengthOfPattern)
29     secret.randomize(numberOfColors)
30
31     # start playing
32     round = 0
33     victory = False
34     while round < maxNumberOfTurns and not victory:
35       round += 1
36       # enact a single turn
37       guess = self._inputManager.enterGuess( )
38       result = guess.compareTo(secret)
39       self._outputManager.displayTurn(guess, result)
40       if result.getNumBlack( ) == lengthOfPattern:
41         victory = True
42
43     if victory:
44       self._outputManager.announceVictory(secret)
45     else:
46       self._outputManager.announceDefeat(secret)
47
48 if __name__ == '__main__':
49   from TextInput import TextInput
50   from TextOutput import TextOutput
51
52   # text-based version
53   palette = ('Red', 'Blue', 'Green', 'White', 'Yellow', 'Orange',
54             'Purple', 'Turquoise')
55   input = TextInput(palette)
56   output = TextOutput(palette)
57   game = Mastermind(input, output)
```

FIGURE 7.12 (continuation): The Mastermind class with text-based driver.

7.10 Flexibility in Design: Graphical Output

Our original Mastermind software is entirely text based. However, the game may be more enjoyable if visualized graphically. Because the user interface is encapsulated in our high–level design, we can easily adapt our software to use cs1graphics for displaying the game as originally portrayed in Figure 7.1.

We accomplish this by creating a new GraphicsOutput class that supports the same public interface as the TextOutput class (i.e., startGame, displayTurn, announceVictory, announceDefeat). This allows us to use a GraphicsOutput instance as the outputManager when constructing a Mastermind game. We will discuss the details of our graphics class in a moment, but we first wish to describe how easy it is to incorporate such a class with the rest of our Mastermind project. We do not need to edit any of our existing source code. Instead we will create a new main program in a separate file, say `Mastermind2.py`, written simply as

```python
from Mastermind import Mastermind
from TextInput import TextInput
from GraphicsOutput import GraphicsOutput

if __name__ == '__main__':
    palette = ('Red', 'Blue', 'Green', 'White', 'Yellow', 'Orange',
               'Purple', 'Turquoise')
    input = TextInput(palette)
    output = GraphicsOutput(palette)        # choose the graphics output this time
    game = Mastermind(input, output)
```

By importing the Mastermind class and then providing our own main program, we bypass the text–based prototype. In this new version, we again use a TextInput instance to manage the input, but we create a GraphicsOutput instance to manage the output. In this way, the command `python Mastermind.py` can still be used to execute the text–based version, while `python Mastermind2.py` executes the graphical version.

Figure 7.13 provides our implementation of the GraphicsOutput class. The most intricate details involve the precise placement of the various elements. This is organized by laying out the placement of the pegs and the score designations on a grid with row 0 at the bottom representing the original guess, and row len(**self**._maxNumberOfTurns) at the top representing the placement of the secret pattern. The actual size of this grid is scaled according to the designation of the individual peg radius sent to the constructor.

For each game, a new canvas is created from within the startGame method, with the original image generated within a call to the _setupBackground utility function. Just as our TextOutput class relied upon a _patternAsString utility for the three cases in which a pattern must be displayed, our GraphicsOutput class defines a _drawPattern method for this purpose. It is subsequently called from within announceVictory, announceDefeat, and displayTurn (the call to displayTurn is responsible not just for displaying the most recent guess, but also the score for that guess). We leave the remaining details for the interested reader to study. An even more advanced interface will be introduced in Section 15.5, using the graphics system for input as well as output.

```
1   from cs1graphics import *
2
3   class GraphicsOutput:
4     """Provide graphics—based output for the Mastermind game."""
5
6     def __init__(self, colorNames, pegRadius = 10):
7       """Construct a new GraphicsOutput instance.
8
9       colorNames      a sequence of strings (each color must start with a different letter)
10      pegRadius       radius of a displayed peg (default 10)
11
12      pegRadius technically describes the radius of a single peg, yet
13      the entire display is scaled accordingly.
14      """
15      self._colorNames = colorNames
16      self._pegRadius = pegRadius
17
18      # following will be reset when game starts
19      self._currentTurnNum = self._lengthOfPattern = self._maxNumberOfTurns = 0
20      self._canvas = None
21
22    def startGame(self, lengthOfPattern, maxNumberOfTurns):
23      """Game is beginning with specified parameters."""
24      if self._canvas:      # from previous game
25        self._canvas.close( )
26      self._currentTurnNum = 0
27      self._lengthOfPattern = lengthOfPattern
28      self._maxNumberOfTurns = maxNumberOfTurns
29
30      # Set the size of board that works for the given parameters
31      width = (4*self._lengthOfPattern + 7) * self._pegRadius
32      height = (4*self._maxNumberOfTurns + 6) * self._pegRadius
33      self._canvas = Canvas(width, height, 'tan', 'Mastermind')
34      self._canvas.setAutoRefresh(False)
35      self._setupBackground( )
36
37    def _drawPattern(self, thePattern, row):
38      """Display the given Pattern at indicated row."""
39      for i in range(self._lengthOfPattern):
40        peg = Circle(self._pegRadius, self._getCenterPoint(row, i))
41        peg.setFillColor(self._colorNames[thePattern.getPegColor(i)])
42        self._canvas.add(peg)
```

FIGURE 7.13: The GraphicsOutput class (continued on next page).

```
43   def announceVictory(self, secret):
44     """Inform the player that he/she has correctly matched the secret Pattern."""
45     self._drawPattern(secret, self._maxNumberOfTurns)
46     self._canvas.refresh( )
47
48   def announceDefeat(self, secret):
49     """Inform the player that he/she has lost and reveal the secret Pattern."""
50     self._drawPattern(secret, self._maxNumberOfTurns)
51     self._canvas.refresh( )
52
53   def displayTurn(self, guess, result):
54     """Display recent guess Pattern and resulting Score to the screen."""
55     self._drawPattern(guess, self._currentTurnNum)
56
57     black = Text(str(result.getNumBlack( )), 2*self._pegRadius)
58     black.move((4*self._lengthOfPattern+2)*self._pegRadius,
59       (4*(self._maxNumberOfTurns−self._currentTurnNum−1)+7)*self._pegRadius)
60     black.setSize(2*self._pegRadius)
61     black.setColor('black')
62     self._canvas.add(black)
63
64     white = Text(str(result.getNumWhite( )), 2*self._pegRadius)
65     white.move((4*self._lengthOfPattern+5)*self._pegRadius,
66       (4*(self._maxNumberOfTurns−self._currentTurnNum−1)+7)*self._pegRadius)
67     white.setSize(2*self._pegRadius)
68     white.setColor('white')
69     self._canvas.add(white)
70
71     self._canvas.refresh( )
72     self._currentTurnNum += 1
73
74   def _getCenterPoint(self, row, col):
75     """Locate the position for a peg.
76
77     Return a Point instance positioned at the center of the peg.
78
79     row    the row that the peg is in
80     col    the column that the peg is in
81     """
82     return Point((4*col + 3) * self._pegRadius,
83       (4*(self._maxNumberOfTurns−row−1) + 7) * self._pegRadius)
```

FIGURE 7.13 (continuation): The GraphicsOutput class (continued on next page).

```
84   def _setupBackground(self):
85       """Draw the background to the graphics canvas."""
86       block = Rectangle(4*self._lengthOfPattern*self._pegRadius, 4*self._pegRadius,
87           Point((1 + 2*self._lengthOfPattern)*self._pegRadius, 3*self._pegRadius) )
88       block.setFillColor('brown')
89       block.setDepth(100)
90       self._canvas.add(block)
91
92       for row in range(self._maxNumberOfTurns):
93           for col in range(self._lengthOfPattern):
94               hole = Circle(self._pegRadius/2, self._getCenterPoint(row,col))
95               hole.setFillColor('black')
96               hole.setDepth(90)
97               self._canvas.add(hole)
98       self._canvas.refresh( )
```

FIGURE 7.13 (continuation): The GraphicsOutput class.

7.11 Chapter Review

7.11.1 Key Points

Top-Down Design and Bottom-Up Implementation

- Software development should proceed with a *top-down design*, starting at the highest-level with a vision of the software use, proceeding downward to developing necessary lower-level classes.

- The coding of a project should proceed with a *bottom-up implementation*. The lowest-level classes can be implemented and tested in isolation. Then work can proceed to implement and test higher-level classes that depend upon the completed lower-level classes.

Naming Conventions

- All names should be chosen to give a reasonable indication of its use, following consistent naming conventions.

- The name of a class should begin with a capital letter (e.g., Pattern), and when the name involves two or more English words, those should be concatenated with each word capitalized (e.g., TextOutput).

- Grammatically, the name of a class should represent a noun.

- The name of a function, whether stand-alone or a method of a class, should begin with a lowercase letter (e.g., move). If the name is the concatenation of multiple words, the first begins with a lowercase letter, but each additional word is capitalized (e.g., getPegColor).

- Grammatically, the name of a function should represent a verb.

- The name of a piece of data should represent a noun, using the same capitalization style as functions, starting with a lowercase letter and capitalizing subsequently concatenated words.

Formal Documentation

- Each public class and function should provide a formal documentation string, known in Python as a *docstring*.

- A docstring is a string literal that occurs as the very first element within the body of a class or function. Typically, triple quote delimiters " " " are used since these allow for multiline strings.

- A docstring should begin with a brief (one line) description. If further explanation is warranted, such as the purpose or type of parameters and return value, that information should be provided after a subsequent blank line within the docstring.

- The documentation for a class can be viewed through use of the help command within the Python interpreter, or as a web page generated by the `pydoc` utility.

Encapsulation of Implementation Details

- *Encapsulation* is the principle of identifying a public interface to a software component that is relied upon by other programmers, while treating the remaining internal implementation details as private.

- The primary advantage of encapsulation is that it limits the interdependence between soft– ware components. It helps the user of a component to focus upon that which must be understood to properly use the component, while it offers the author greater flexibility in choosing internal details of the implementation without far-reaching consequences.

- Typically, all attributes of a class should be private, as should any methods that are intended only for internal use.

- Private aspects of a component are conventionally named with a leading underscore in Python (e.g., _channel). Elements so named will not be automatically imported, nor described by the help command.

Unit Testing and Error Checking

- An important principle of good software development is to test each individual component as it is written. If one were to wait until the entire project were written before testing any part of it, there would likely be many errors and it may be difficult to isolate the source of those errors.

- Testing a class individually, instead of as part of the larger program, is called *unit testing*.

- In a bottom–up implementation, each class should be thoroughly tested before being used by a higher–level class.

- In Python, a unit test is placed inside the body of the conditional

      if __name__ == '__main__':

  If the current module is the one upon which the Python interpreter was initially invoked, the unit test will be executed. If the module is being imported from elsewhere, the conditional body is ignored.

- All input that is received from the user of a program should be explicitly checked to avoid unexpected behavior.

7.11.2 Glossary

bottom-up implementation Writing and testing low-level classes first and then using them in the implementation of higher-level code.

code reuse Writing portions of a program so that components can be applied in several places of the same program or as part of other projects.

docstring A Python string embedded within source code to provide formal documentation. Technically, a docstring is a string literal that is placed as the very first element within the body of a module, class, or function.

encapsulation A principle by which internal implementation details of a software component are treated as private (as opposed to the public interface to that component, which must be well documented for others).

modularity The design of a program as a series of smaller independent pieces.

private The designation of a class, or member of a class, as one that is not meant for public use from outside the component. Private aspects are typically named with a leading underscore in Python (e.g., _channel).

public The designation for a class, or member of a class, that is designed to provide an external means of interaction.

sequence diagram A figure used to model the chronological flow of control between interacting objects.

top-down design An approach for software development in which functionality is first described at a very high level and subsequently organized into smaller and smaller components suitable for coding.

unit testing Testing to ensure that a class or function works properly in isolation.

7.11.3 Exercises

Naming Conventions

Practice 7.1: Use the context to determine which of the following identifiers are classes, functions, variables, etc.

(a)	foo( )		(e)	myFoo.fooBar( )
(b)	Widget		(f)	my._stuff
(c)	bar		(g)	helpMe( )
(d)	data._analyze( )		(h)	Table( )

Documentation

Practice 7.2: A Television class was discussed and implemented in Section 6.3, but not documented. Provide appropriate docstrings for the volumeUp and jumpPrevChannel methods.

Exercise 7.3: Follow up on Practice 7.2 by documenting the remainder of the Television class. Be sure to describe the role of each parameter and return value, and clearly describe any special situations involving its behaviors.

Exercise 7.4: Provide appropriate docstrings for the Fraction class of Section 6.4 and all of its methods. Be sure to describe the role of each parameter and return value, and clearly describe any special situations involving its behaviors.

Exercise 7.5: Provide appropriate docstrings for the robust version of the Point class from Section 6.2 and all of its methods. Be sure to describe the role of each parameter and return value, and clearly describe any special situations involving its behaviors.

Unit Testing and Error Checking

Practice 7.6: Write a unit test for the __add__ member function of the Fraction class from Section 6.4.

Exercise 7.7: Write a unit test for the Television class in Section 6.3.

Exercise 7.8: Follow up on Practice 7.6 by providing a unit test which evaluates all of the methods of the Fraction class. Make sure to test its treatment of positive and negative values, and undefined values.

Exercise 7.9: In Section 6.4 we implemented the __int__ method for the Fraction class as

```
def __int__(self):
  return int(float(self))
```

An alternative implementation would be

```
def __int__(self):
  return self._numer / self._denom
```

however, this alternative does not produce the same result in all cases. Give a test case for which these two implementations produce different results.

Exercise 7.10: As described in Section 7.8, our implementation of TextInput trusts that the parameter colorNames contains a sequence of strings with unique leading characters. Give code which we could have been used to explicitly verify such a condition.

Exercise 7.11: Write a Date class with documentation and a unit test. The class should be able to deal with a date in numerical and text format and support a computeNext method that returns the next day of the year. Make sure that your unit test ensures proper treatment of leap year.

Mastermind

Practice 7.12: The implementation of the method compareTo in the Pattern class is rather complicated and can be confusing. For each of the turns in the game displayed in Figure 7.1 simulate this method by hand.

Exercise 7.13: The compareTo method of Pattern could have been written using a different algorithm. Come up with a substantially different way of calculating the score and implement it.

Exercise 7.14: Add a method isCompatible behavior to Pattern that takes as parameters a list of guesses and a list of scores, deciding whether the current pattern is compatible with the given scores for the respective guesses (i.e.,, whether this may be the secret).

Exercise 7.15: Modify the Mastermind game to have multiple players that take turns trying to guess the secret pattern; the first one to guess it wins.

Projects

Exercise 7.16: Develop a component that could be used in place of an input manager, yet with an automated strategy for making guesses. A simple but effective strategy is to pick the first pattern you can find that is consistent with all previous scores (see Exercise 7.14).

Exercise 7.17: Write a Hangman game using a collection of classes. Like Mastermind, user interaction should be separated from the game management. Also, try to write both text and graphical based output.

Exercise 7.18: Design and implement a Tic-tac-toe game where you can play against another person or the computer.

C H A P T E R 8

Input, Output, and Files

8.1   **Standard Input and Output**
8.2   **Formatted Strings**
8.3   **Working with Files**
8.4   **Handling Newline Characters**
8.5   **Case Studies**
8.6   **Chapter Review**

In the opening chapter, we emphasized data as one of the cornerstones of computing. In this chapter we focus more carefully on how data is originally gathered by a program as input and how results of a program are subsequently presented as output. We begin with a review of the most basic forms for interacting with a standard user of a program, expanding upon the options that are available to precisely control the format.

In many situations, data is so voluminous that it is not directly entered or viewed by a user, but rather read from or written to an underlying file on the computer. To support access to data in files, Python supports a built-in class named file, which we introduce in this chapter. With access to larger data sets from files, we exercise many of our programming techniques for data processing in a series of case studies.

8.1   Standard Input and Output

When we originally transitioned from interactive sessions within the interpreter to more traditional execution of programs, we needed a way to interact directly with a user. Section 2.9 contained a basic introduction to the commands **raw_input** and **print**. We review that discussion here.

Standard input

The simplest form for receiving input from a user is through the use of the **raw_input** function, as in the following example:

```
favoriteFruit = raw_input('What is your favorite fruit? ')
```

The parameter sent to this function is a string that serves as a prompt the user; if the method is called without a parameter, as in **raw_input**( ), no prompt is displayed. In either case, the system then waits while the user presumably types a string of characters. When the user presses the enter key (a.k.a., return key) on the keyboard, the **raw_input** function returns the string of entered characters, up to but not including the final newline. For example, if

the user presses the enter key without typing any previous characters, the **raw_input** function returns the empty string ' '. The following demonstrates a common style for asking a
question yet offering a default response that can be chosen by entering a blank line:

```
color = raw_input('What is your favorite color? [blue] ')
if color == '':
  color = 'blue'
```

If the user enters a response such as red, it is used, but if the user simply presses the enter
key without offering a response, we revert to blue as the default. An alternative style for
expressing this logic uses the nonboolean expression **not** color in place of the equivalent
color == ' ' (see *For the Guru* on page 142).

```
color = raw_input('What is your favorite color? [blue] ')
if not color:       # empty string received
  color = 'blue'
```

Standard output

The simplest form for generating output is based on use of the **print** command. This command accepts zero or more subsequent arguments separated by commas, as in

```
print 'I like', favoriteFruit, 'and the number', myAge
```

Note that **print** is not formally a function but instead a keyword of the language.[1] It is
important to note that its arguments are not specified within parentheses, as is done with
parameters to a regular function.

We wish to highlight several subtleties in the behavior of the command. The arguments may be literals, identifiers, or compound expressions. If an individual argument is
not already an instance of the string class, it is automatically converted to a string. For
example, even though myAge is presumably an integer, the resulting output displays the
string **str**(myAge).

When multiple arguments are given, an explicit space is automatically inserted into
the output between successive arguments. By default, the **print** command generates one
final newline character after printing all the arguments. However, this newline character
can be suppressed if a trailing comma is given following the last argument. In this case,
the arguments are printed, as well as a final space after the last argument, but the output of
a subsequent print statement will continue on the same line. So, the following two **print**
statements generate a single line of output:

```
print 'I like', favoriteFruit,            # note the trailing comma
print 'and the number', myAge             # automatic newline character
```

---

1.   Starting with version 3.0 of Python, **print** will become a regular function. At that time, the typical
      syntax will appear as print('I like', favoriteFruit, 'and the number', myAge).

8.2   Formatted Strings

Consider the goal of composing a string from individual components, such as the string `'Cardinals: ranked 5 of 30 teams'`, where values `'Cardinals'`, 5, and 30 are associated with identifiers **team**, **rank**, and **total** respectively. We can attempt to output such a string with the **print** command, as in

print team, `': ranked'`, rank, `'of'`, total, `'teams'`

Although close to the goal, there is a slight problem in that an undesired space is automatically inserted between the team and the subsequent colon. We can achieve the precise goal using string concatenation instead, as in

print team + `': ranked '` + **str**(rank) + `' of '` + **str**(total) + `' teams'`

Notice that when concatenating, it is necessary to explicitly convert any nonstring types via **str**( ). This style is quite cumbersome and masks the general structure. It may be more intuitive to view such formatting as the following fill-in-the-blank:

$$\text{'}\underline{\hspace{1.5cm}}: \text{ranked } \underline{\hspace{1.5cm}} \text{ of } \underline{\hspace{1.5cm}} \text{ teams'}$$
$$\quad\text{(team)} \qquad\qquad \text{(rank)} \quad\;\; \text{(total)}$$

When the values to be filled in are basic built-in types, such an arrangement can be achieved through a syntax that we refer to as ***string formatting***. The desired format is expressed as a string literal using the % character to denote each blank. The actual arguments used to fill in those blanks are subsequently specified in the respective order. We use our continuing example to introduce the precise syntax.

print `'%s: ranked %d of %d teams'` % (team, rank, total)

We see two distinct parts of the formatting syntax. The first part is a string, in this case `'%s: ranked %d of %d teams'`. Each % character designates a part of the eventual result to be completed. The character that follows each % designates the particular type of expected data. For example, the `%s` is a placeholder for a coming string; `%d` is a placeholder for a coming integer.[2] In our sample format, there are a total of three missing pieces to be filled in. Immediately following the string is another % character followed by the second part of the syntax, a tuple that specifies all of the missing values (see Section 2.3.2 for review of **tuple** class). In the special case where there is only one substitution, a single value can be specified rather than a tuple. The arguments are substituted into the original string in lieu of the respective placeholders. Thus in our example, string **team** replaces the `%s`, integer **rank** replaces the next `%d`, and integer **total** replaces the final `%d`.

The string formatting syntax can also be used to control the precise format of each argument. For example, the minimum width used in displaying an argument can be specified as a number between the % sign and the type designator. For example, `%4d` causes an integer to be printed with a minimum of four characters. If the number is naturally less than

---

2.   The syntax `%d` is chosen for historical reasons, based on similar use in the C programming language as a shorthand for "decimal." If you prefer the "integer" mnemonic, Python allows `%i` to be used.

Expression	Result, if printed
`'%d out of %d dentists'% (9,10)`	`9 out of 10 dentists`
`'You owe $%.2f, cash.'% 350`	`You owe $350.00, cash.`
`'%d%% of %s is water'% (70, 'Earth')`	`70% of Earth is water`
`'   %7.3f\n+ %7.3f'% (80.0/3.0, 3.0/4.0)`	`   26.667` `+   0.750`

FIGURE 8.1: String formatting examples.

four digits, it is right justified by default; thus, the expression `'%4d'% 12` is displayed as `'  12'`. Numbers are padded with leading zeros if we use the form `'%04d'% 12` which evaluates to the string `'0012'`. If we wish to use left-justification instead, we insert a negative sign in front of the numeral, as in `%-4d`, which results in the substitution `'12  '`. In either case, the specified number of characters is only treated as a minimum; if the natural representation of the value requires more characters, more will be used.

Further control of the format is possible when displaying floating-point values. Consider the following example:

```
>>> share = 100.0/7.0
>>> print share
14.2857142857
```

The reported output is not the precise numeric value stored internally, but an abbreviated version used when displayed as a string. The shown precision is based upon the implicit conversion from the float class via the **str**( ) method. If we wish to have more explicit control of the displayed precision we can use another feature of string formatting. The default type designator for a float value in a formatted string is `%f`. However, the precise number of digits following the decimal can be specified using a placeholder such as `%.3f`, which designates three digits after the decimal point. The result will then be rounded appropriately to the desired precision, 14.286 in the preceding example.

Although we have only discussed `%s`, `%d`, and `%f`, there are other available type designators and many further ways to control the precise output format. Note that since the character `%` has been given special meaning in formatted strings, it is necessary to use the combination `%%` in order to get an actual percent symbol in the result. Figure 8.1 gives several additional examples; more complete documentation can be found at `python.org`. Finally, we note that string formatting is not dependent on use of the **print** command. It is a formal behavior supported by the string class that can be used to generate a string for other purposes. Thus we could have stored the result as

```
message = '%s: ranked %d of %d teams' % (team, rank, total)
```

FOR THE GURU

String formatting has the general form template % arguments, where the template is a string and the arguments are typically a tuple. In reality, the % symbol is just a standard operator (we have seen this operator for computing the remainder of a division when both operands are integers). Yet when the first operand is a string and the second is a tuple, it performs string formatting.

In all of our examples thus far, the template has been a string literal, but we can generate a template string dynamically if we wish. As an example, assume that we wanted to print a list of numbers using three characters for each, yet we did not know how many numbers would be in the data set. If we knew there were two numbers, we might use the format template '%3d %3d'. If we knew there were three entries, we might use the format template '%3d %3d %3d'. More generally we could use the string '%3d ' * len(data) as our template and then fill in the arguments using the original data, converted to a tuple. For example, the following code

```
data = [145, 3, 98, 263, 15]
print '%3d  ' * len(data) % tuple(data)
print '---  ' * len(data)
```

generates the following output:

```
145    3  98 263  15
---  ---  ---  ---  ---
```

In this particular example, we relied upon the fact that all entries need at most three characters to be displayed. As an extra challenge, we could first compute the maximum-length string representation for all entries on the list, and then substitute that value in place of the constant 3 in our format template.

8.3 Working with Files

Because so much information is stored in the form of files on a computer system, programs must be able to read data from or write data to such files. For this reason, Python supports a built-in class named file to manipulate files on the computer. Objects from this class are not the same as the underlying computer files; they serve as an intermediary, allowing for easy and efficient access to a file.

The constructor for Python's file class requires a string parameter, identifying the underlying filename on the computer system. For example, the command

```
doorToDoor = file('directions.txt')
```

creates a new file object that is used to read the underlying file directions.txt. By default, a newly instantiated file object provides *read-only* access to an existing file. If no

Syntax	Semantics
close( )	Disconnects the file object from the associated file (saving the underlying file if necessary)
flush( )	Flushes buffer of written characters, saving to the underlying file.
read( )	Returns a string representing the (remaining) contents of the file.
read(size)	Returns a string representing the specified number of bytes next in the file.
readline( )	Returns a string representing the next line of the file.
readlines( )	Returns a list of strings representing the remaining lines of the file.
write(s)	Writes the given string to the file. No newline is added.
writelines(seq)	Writes each of the strings to the file. No newlines are added.
for line **in** f	Iterates through the file~f, one line at a time.

FIGURE 8.2: Selected behaviors of Python's file class.

file exists with the specified name or if such a file is unreadable, the call to the constructor results in an IOError. It is also possible to create a file object providing modes other than read-only access. The file constructor accepts an optional second parameter that specifies the **access mode**. The most common three modes are `'r'` to read a file (the default), `'w'` to (over)write a file, and `'a'` to append information to the end of an existing file.[3] Figure 8.2 provides a summary of the most common behaviors of Python's file class. We discuss most of these in the remainder of this section.

8.3.1   Reading from a File

To demonstrate the use of a file, we develop several implementations mimicking a standard Unix tool known as wc (a.k.a., "word count"). That program reads a text file and reports the number of characters, words, and lines that are contained in a file. Our three versions are given in Figures 8.3–8.5. All three programs begin by prompting the user for a filename and then creating a Python file object to access the underlying file. The difference is in how those programs subsequently process the contents of the file. At line 4 of Figure 8.3, the read( ) method is called. This returns a single string containing all characters of the file, including spaces and newlines. Once the file is read, our existing knowledge of string processing allows us to complete the task of counting. The overall number of characters is simply the length of the text string. We compute the number of words by using the default form of the split( ) method. Finally, we calculate the number of lines by using the newline character as the delimiter with split(`'\n'`). Although a simple approach, there is a potential disadvantage to this program. If the text file is huge, the use of read( ) may require a lot of temporary memory in the system, since it reads the entire contents at once.

---

3.   The syntax file(`'sample.txt'`) is equivalent in effect to the use of a built-in function open(`'sample.txt'`) that returns an associated file instance. We prefer the former to more clearly denote the construction of a file instance. However, for historical reasons the use of the open syntax is more commonplace in the Python community.

```
 1  filename = raw_input('What is the filename? ')
 2  source = file(filename)    # read-only access
 3
 4  text = source.read( )       # read the entire contents as one string
 5  numchars = len(text)
 6  numwords = len(text.split( ))
 7  numlines = len(text.split('\n'))
 8
 9  print numlines, numwords, numchars
10  source.close( )
```

FIGURE 8.3: A program for computing a count of lines, words, and characters.

```
 1  filename = raw_input('What is the filename? ')
 2  source = file(filename)
 3
 4  numlines = numwords = numchars = 0
 5  line = source.readline( )
 6  while line:                    # line length is nonzero
 7      numchars += len(line)
 8      numwords += len(line.split( ))
 9      numlines += 1
10
11      # done with current line; read the next
12      line = source.readline( )
13
14  print numlines, numwords, numchars
15  source.close( )
```

FIGURE 8.4: A program processing the file line by line with a **while** loop.

```
 1  filename = raw_input('What is the filename? ')
 2  source = file(filename)
 3
 4  numlines = numwords = numchars = 0
 5  for line in source:
 6      numchars += len(line)
 7      numwords += len(line.split( ))
 8      numlines += 1
 9
10  print numlines, numwords, numchars
11  source.close( )
```

FIGURE 8.5: A program processing the file line by line with a **for** loop.

Our second version of the program, in Figure 8.4, processes the file one line at a time. It relies upon another method of the file class, readline( ). Each time this method is called, it returns a subsequent line of the file in the form of a string, including a trailing newline character if present. When there are no further lines of input, a call to this method returns an empty string. So we use a **while** loop, starting at statement 6 of the code, continuing so long as a nonempty string is retrieved. The overall loop structure is a typical example of the loop–and–a–half style, as we read the first line of the file before the loop and each remaining line within the body of the loop. Notice that if we omitted statement 12, the result is an infinite loop; we would repeatedly count the same (nonempty) line.

The third variant of the program, in Figure 8.5, demonstrates that files support the **for** loop syntax for iterating line by line. This is similar in spirit to the second version, but with greater legibility due to the simplicity of the for loop syntax.

8.3.2   Writing to a File

Writing to a text file from within a program is also quite simple. The first step is to create a file object with the appropriate access mode. For example, the command

```
result = file('output.txt','w')
```

can be used to prepare for writing the results of a program to a file named output.txt. If there already exists a file with that name, this command will *overwrite* the existing file with a new file, thereby losing all of the previously stored information. As users of modern computer software, we have come to rely upon protective messages such as the following:

A file already exists with that name.
Are you sure you want to overwrite it?

No such safety net exists for the programmer. If we wish to offer such a safety net to the users of our software, we must implement the check for an existing file.[4] Alternatively, a file can be opened with append access mode ('a'), in which case a previously existing file is not overwritten; any newly written text is appended to the end of the existing file.

Once a file is successfully opened, text can be written to that file using of a method named write. That method takes a single string as a parameter, which is the text to be writ–ten to the file. Here is an example writing to the result file, opened in the previous example.

```
result.write('This is a test.')
```

We carefully distinguish between the syntax of the **print** and write commands. Although nonstring arguments to **print** are automatically converted to strings, this is not so with the write method. Thus the following code fragment would fail.

---

4.   To do this involves further interaction between the Python program and the underlying operating system. We will not cover such interactions at this time, but they can be accomplished with the help of Python's os module.

```
pi = 3.14159
result.write(pi)
```

If you wish to write nonstring data to the file, you must explicitly convert that data to a string, perhaps by casting it as in result.write(**str**(pi)), or by using a formatting string as in result.write('%5.3f'% pi).

When is the underlying file saved?

When introducing Python's support for files, we drew a distinction between a file object and the underlying file on the computer system. This distinction is quite important in the context of writing to a file. Calling the write method of a Python file does not necessarily cause any immediate change to the underlying file. The file object acts as an intermediary, and it is up to the discretion of that object when to write the data to the underlying file. It may do so immediately, but may choose to hold it in a buffer indefinitely to combine that data with a future write, for efficiency. When you call the close( ) method of the associated file object, it is obligated to write all of its stored data to the underlying file. In this regard, it is important that you remember to call close when you are finished using a file. Although some Python implementations may give you the benefit of the doubt and close those files on your behalf, there is risk involved. If the program or system were to catastrophically fail before reaching the eventual close( ), all might be lost. There exists another method, named flush( ), which forces the file object to write all of its currently buffered output to the underlying file while leaving the file object open for subsequent writes. Informally, the close( ) method is analogous to a "Save and Close" command for a typical word processor, whereas the flush( ) is analogous to a "Save" without closing the file.

8.4   Handling Newline Characters

We draw attention to several important distinctions regarding the treatment of newline characters when using standard input and output versus file input and output. The default behavior of the **print** statement generates a trailing newline character. So the code fragment

```
print 'One'
print 'Two'
```

generates output that appears as

```
One
Two
```

Yet when writing to a file, no automatic newline character is generated. The statements

```
result.write('One')
result.write('Two')
```

result in a file with the following contents.

```
OneTwo
```

A newline character will not be written to the file unless explicitly part of the string parameter, as in results.write('One\n').

There exists a similar distinction in the treatment of the newline character when gathering input. The **raw_input** command waits as the user enters a sequence of characters.
Even though the user must physically press the enter key to signify the completion of the
input, the returned string does *not* include a newline character. In contrast, the readline
method of the file class returns the next line of the file *including* any explicit newline character ending that line. For example, a blank line within a file will appear as the string '\n'.
This can be differentiated from an empty string '', which is conventionally returned if a
call to readline is made when already at the end of the file. It is also important to realize
that the very last line of the file may or may not contain an explicit newline character.

To emphasize the importance of proper treatment of newline characters, we consider
the following example. Spell checkers often rely upon a list of known words in a language,
called a *lexicon*. This is typically stored in a file with a single word or phrase per line.
At first glance, the following code appears to read such a file, building a list of strings
containing the entries:

```
wordfile = file('words.txt')
lexicon = list( )
for entry in wordfile:
   lexicon.append(entry)
```

Yet there is a problem. Assume that the word dog was included in the original file. Even
so, we would observe the following, based upon the above implementation:

```
>>> 'dog' in lexicon
False
```

The problem is that the line of the original file that contained the word dog was read as the
string 'dog\n' and that is the actual string we appended to our list. The string 'dog\n'
is not the same as the string 'dog', thus the **False** result.

One possible solution is to take a slice of each individual entry so as to intentionally
exclude the last character, which we presume to be an unwanted newline. However, if
the last line of the file ends without a newline character, we would be ignoring a desired
character. The best way to handle this situation is to rely upon the rstrip method supported
by the **str** class, which can be used to strip off a potential newline from the right side of a
string. Our revised version appears as follows:

```
wordfile = file('words.txt')
lexicon = list( )
for entry in wordfile:
   lexicon.append(entry.rstrip('\n'))   # remove trailing newline
```

FOR THE GURU

A careful observer may notice a slight difference in the behavior of the three programs given in Figures 8.3–8.5, which each purport to count the number of characters, words, and lines of a file. The discrepancy arises precisely when the last character of the input file is a newline character. For such a file, the program of Figure 8.3 reports a count of one additional line compared to the programs of Figures 8.4 and 8.5. The correct behavior is a matter of interpretation. If a newline is the last character of the file, should we consider there to exist one further line that happens to be empty? Either interpretation might be desired. Yet as a programmer, we wish to ensure that our software's behavior matches the desired intent.

The differing behaviors in our example are due to subtleties in our use of split('\n') in the first program, readline( ) in the second, and the **for** loop in the third. In particular, when Python splits a string based upon a specified delimiter, if that delimiter is found at the very end of the given string, the resulting list will include an additional empty string as the final item in the list. So in Figure 8.3, our use of lines = text.split('\n') is equivalent to the interpretation that there exists an additional line in the file, albeit an empty line. If that were not our intent, we would have to explicitly strip off any trailing newline character. If we carefully examine the behavior of Figure 8.4, we find that after reading the line with the last newline character, the next call to readline( ) returns an empty string. With our stated loop condition, the occurrence of an empty string ends our loop, and so the numlines count is not explicitly incremented as a result of that line. Similarly, the behavior of the for loop is to iterate over all of the lines of the file, yet with the interpretation that a line does not exist if there are no characters.

Note also that the issue with this last line of the file is quite different from the issue of a blank line earlier in the file. Such blank lines are represented not by an empty string, but by a string with a single newline character. All three of our variants properly account for those lines.

8.5   Case Studies

In this section we examine several case studies that combine our newfound use of files with several processing techniques from earlier chapters. We begin by developing a set of general tools for more reliably opening files and dealing robustly with errors. Then we develop a program that creates an annotated version of an existing file, with line numbers added on the left-hand side of the individual lines. Finally, we develop programs that compute and report frequency counts for numeric or alphabetic data files.

8.5.1 File Utilities

In spirit, opening a file is rather simple. In Section 8.3.1, we used the following two lines to prompt a user for a filename and then to open the selected file:

```
filename = raw_input('What is the filename? ')
source = file(filename)
```

Everything works as planned if the user enters a legitimate filename. However, if no file with the given name is found, the program crashes with the following exception trace displayed to the user:

```
What is the filename? junk
Traceback (most recent call last):
  File "wc1.py", line 2, in -toplevel-
    source = file(filename, 'r')
IOError: [Errno 2] No such file or directory: 'junk'
```

While some blame may lie with the user for giving the wrong filename, our program should do a better job in handling the scenario. The user should never be exposed to such internal debugging information.

The broader theme of error handling was the focus of Section 5.5. Here we incorporate those techniques into the current setting. Whenever we attempt to open a file, there is a risk of an IOError. So we should write our code within the confines of a **try-except** clause, although it is up to us as to how to react in the case of an error. If nothing else, we could craft a more appropriate message for the end user, as follows:

```
filename = raw_input('What is the filename? ')
try:
    source = file(filename)
except IOError:
    print 'Sorry. Unable to open file', filename
```

For clarity, we intentionally leave the original **raw_input** line outside the try statement, as that particular command is not at risk for causing an IOError. The potential for error arises when trying to construct a file object based upon the given filename.

There is a larger question as to how a program should continue upon encountering a problem with a user-provided filename. Since the file constructor never completed, the identifier source is not assigned to any result. A reasonable alternative is to embed this logic within a while loop so that we can reprompt until a file is successfully opened. Since such a tool might be useful in many programs, we define it as a function named openFileReadRobust and place it within a file FileUtilities.py so that it can be imported as a module into other programs. That function is displayed in lines 2–14 of Figure 8.6. We assign source to **None** at line 7 to denote our initial lack of an open file. The subsequent condition at line 8 causes the loop to continue until source is reassigned following a successful call to the file constructor.

```
1    """A few utility functions for opening files."""
2    def openFileReadRobust( ):
3      """Repeatedly prompt user for filename until successfully opening with read access.
4
5      Return the newly open file object.
6      """
7      source = None
8      while not source:                        # still no successfully opened file
9        filename = raw_input('What is the filename? ')
10       try:
11         source = file(filename)
12       except IOError:
13         print 'Sorry. Unable to open file', filename
14     return source
15
16   def openFileWriteRobust(defaultName):
17     """Repeatedly prompt user for filename until successfully opening with write access.
18
19     Return a newly open file object with write access.
20
21     defaultName    a suggested filename. This will be offered within the prompt and
22                    used when the return key is pressed without specifying another name.
23     """
24     writable = None
25     while not writable:                      # still no successfully opened file
26       prompt = 'What should the output be named [%s]? '% defaultName
27       filename = raw_input(prompt)
28       if not filename:                       # user gave blank response
29         filename = defaultName               # try the suggested default
30       try:
31         writable = file(filename, 'w')
32       except IOError:
33         print 'Sorry. Unable to write to file', filename
34     return writable
```

FIGURE 8.6: FileUtilities module (stored in `FileUtilities.py`).

We define a similar utility function named openFileWriteRobust (lines 16–34) for opening files with write access. This function has an additional feature, accepting a default name as a parameter which is then suggested to the user. We use a technique similar to that of page 272, prompting the user for a response but using the default in case an empty string is entered. The call to open the file (line 31) is still shielded within a try clause. Also note that the second parameter `'w'` provides write access to the newly created file.

8.5.2 Annotating a File

Our next goal is to create a program that makes a copy of an original file, providing line numbers aligned on the left-hand side. So if the original input file has contents

```
Dear Editor,

  I greatly enjoyed your article on Python.

Sincerely,
David
```

the resulting file appears as

```
   1   Dear Editor,
   2
   3      I greatly enjoyed your article on Python.
   4
   5   Sincerely,
   6   David
```

Our program will prompt the user for the name of the original input file. We will suggest that the output file be named `annotated.txt` although the user can override that choice if desired. We want to ensure that all of the line numbers are right-aligned with each other, thus with line numbers 9 and 10 formatted as

```
   9   ...
  10   ...
```

We use string formatting to right-align numbers, however the question arises as to how many characters to use for those numbers. In our code, we take a somewhat lazy approach, always using the leftmost four columns for the number. Of course, this does not work as intended if there are 10000 or more lines in the file; also it uses more space than necessary when there are only a few lines. But it is easy to write our program this way (Exercise 8.14 challenges you to find a better approach). Our complete program is given in Figure 8.7. The primary processing involves keeping a counter of the current line number, initially set to 1 in statement 10 of the code. Then the for loop iterates over each line of the original file. To annotate the line number, we make use of the formatted string shown in statement 12. Note that we do not explicitly include a newline character in that format string because there will already be one included in the line read from the original file (with the possible exception of the final line).

8.5.3 Computing Frequency Counts

As our final case study, we develop software to perform frequency analysis upon data read from a file. This is an important step in statistical analysis. Numeric data sets might represent ages, weights, test scores, and other measures. Equally important is the frequency analysis of textual data. The relative frequency of letters in a sample text is a key in

```
1   from FileUtilities import openFileReadRobust, openFileWriteRobust
2
3   print 'This program annotates a file, by adding'
4   print 'Line numbers to the left of each line.\n'
5
6   source = openFileReadRobust( )
7   annotated = openFileWriteRobust('annotated.txt')
8
9   # process the file
10  linenum = 1
11  for line in source:
12      annotated.write('%4d   %s' % (linenum, line) )
13      linenum += 1
14  source.close( )
15  annotated.close( )
16  print 'The annotation is complete.'
```

FIGURE 8.7: Annotating a file with line numbers.

basic cryptanalysis as well as in developing good compression strategies. In biology, DNA analysis includes the computation of relative frequencies among the four underlying bases.

We used the DNA problem as an example, starting on page 146 of Chapter 4, but the approach we took at the time is not very general. We relied heavily upon the fact that there were four distinct symbols. We maintained four separate identifiers (e.g., numA, numC) and used an **if-elif** construct with multiple branches to determine which counter to increment at each step. In this section, our goal is to develop a better approach that can handle the computation of frequency counts for a larger range of numbers or letters.

The key insight is that we can take advantage of a single list of counters rather than maintaining many separate variables. As a very simple example, assume that we are computing frequency counts for a set of integers that are known to lie between 0 and 99 inclusive. If using separate variables, we might choose names such as numOnes, numTwos, and so on. Of course writing such code with one hundred separate names is tiring, as would be writing a series of conditionals to determine the proper counter to increment. Instead, we maintain a single list, perhaps named tallies, containing 100 counters as elements. Although we still maintain 100 underlying counters, we have a more convenient syntax for manipulating them based on the use of list indices. The counter for the number of zeros is simply tallies[0]; the counter for ones is tallies[1]; the counter for seventies is tallies[70]. As we encounter an occurrence of value val, we want to increment tallies[val]. In this way, we avoid a complicated sequence of conditionals for locating the proper counter.

In this case, the approach works so conveniently because we assume the data are integers in the range from 0 to 99 and thus can serve directly as indices into a list. The question is how to handle the situation if scores are drawn from some other domain. Suppose we have a list of birthdates and want to calculate the distribution of years in the range from 1900 to 2000. We could create one big list with some 2000 counters, but we know that the majority of them will never be used. This allows us to use list indexing, but it seems to be an unnecessary waste of memory. A better approach, given the limited range of numbers, is to artificially shift the sequence of possible values into indices so that the minimum value is associated with the index 0. This can be done by precisely subtracting the minimum possible value from the original value. For the year-counting example, we could count the year 1900 with the entry tallies[0], the year 1901 with tallies[1], and so on, leading to tallies[100] for the year 2000. So long as we remember to adjust for the sequence shift, this allows us the convenience of list indexing while removing the unnecessary waste of keeping counters for values that never arise.

Although not immediately intuitive, this same approach can be used to maintain frequency counts for letters of the alphabet. We can use tallies[0] to count the occurrences of A, tallies[1] for B, up to tallies[25] for Z. We can perform this translation quite efficiently by taking advantage of the fact that the letters A to Z are ordered consecutively in the underlying ASCII encoding. Given a variable letter, we can determine its underlying integer code using the syntax, ord(letter). We then obtain the zero-index numbering by subtracting an offset equal to the ordinal of character A, computing ord(letter) − ord('A').

Designing a TallySheet class

As we work towards the development of complete frequency analysis software, we carefully consider the various aspects of the task. We need to read and interpret data from a file and to compute frequencies of those values. These are independent tasks; our strategy for managing a list of tallies has nothing to do with the way in which the data is gathered. However, we need to take care when converting an arbitrary range of values to list indices.

To encapsulate the low-level details of our counting strategy, we envision the creation of a class we name TallySheet. An object from this class will be used to keep a set of tallies for a consecutive range of values, which may be drawn either from an integer domain or a character domain. Before worrying about the internal implementation, we first consider the minimal public support that a class must provide to suit our top-level needs. This leads us to a public interface diagrammed in Figure 8.8. When constructing a new TallySheet, the caller will designate the precise range of values by sending the minimum and maximum values to be tracked. We use this interface no matter whether those values are integers or characters (our class will rely internally upon type checking to distinguish).

Once a TallySheet is created, a particular count is advanced by calling increment(val) for a given value, (e.g., increment('G')). All the details of managing the list of counters and of converting values to list indices is encapsulated within the TallySheet class.

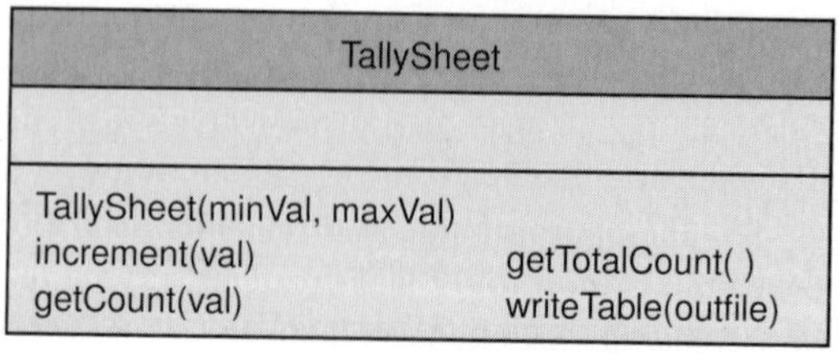

TallySheet
TallySheet(minVal, maxVal) increment(val)   getTotalCount( ) getCount(val)   writeTable(outfile)

FIGURE 8.8: Public interface to the TallySheet class.

We offer several methods for retrieving information about the tallies. An invocation of getCount(val) returns the particular count for the given value; a call to getTotalCount( ) returns the aggregate count of all tallies. Although these two suffice, we provide a third supporting method called writeTable. This method provides a formatted table of the results. Rather than printing the table directly, this method accepts a currently open file as a param– eter and writes the table directly to that file.

TallySheet usage

With our vision of such a class, we can go ahead and write the top–level code for our frequency analysis software. Although we eventually have to implement the TallySheet class, those internal details are irrelevant when writing applications that use the class.

Our first program is the one for computing frequency counts of letters of the alpha– bet. This program tracks the occurrences of A to Z within a file, folding lower and upper– case together and ignoring any nonalphabetic characters. Figure 8.9 contains the source code. The necessary tools from the FileUtilities and TallySheet modules are imported at lines 1 and 2. Since the letter range is known at the onset, at line 7 we initialize TallySheet('A', 'Z') before opening the data file. Once the file is open, we process it reading one character at a time with the call to read(1) at line 11. That function eventu– ally returns an empty string, signifying the end of the file and causing an end to our while loop. The tally sheet itself is only incremented when encountering an alphabetic character, using the uppercase form of that character at line 13. When the entire input file has been processed, the tallies are complete and we call the writeTable method to report the results.

```
1   from FileUtilities import openFileReadRobust, openFileWriteRobust
2   from TallySheet import TallySheet
3
4   print 'This program counts the frequency of letters.'
5   print 'Only alphabetic characters are considered.\n'
6
7   sheet = TallySheet('A', 'Z')
8   source = openFileReadRobust( )
9   character = 'FAKE'            # forces us inside the loop
10  while character:
11      character = source.read(1)    # read single (ascii) character
12      if character.isalpha( ):
13          sheet.increment(character.upper( ))
14  source.close( )
15
16  tallyfile = openFileWriteRobust('frequencies.txt')
17  sheet.writeTable(tallyfile)
18  tallyfile.close( )
19  print 'The tally has been written.'
```

FIGURE 8.9: Computing frequency of letter usage.

```
1   from FileUtilities import openFileReadRobust, openFileWriteRobust
2   from TallySheet import TallySheet
3
4   print 'This program tallies a set of integer scores.'
5   print 'There should be one integer per line.\n'
6
7   source = openFileReadRobust( )
8   values = [ ]
9   for line in source:
10    try:
11      val = int(line)
12      values.append(val)
13    except ValueError:
14      pass                # ignore noninteger line
15  source.close( )
16
17  small = min(values)
18  large = max(values)
19  sheet = TallySheet(small, large)
20  for v in values:
21    sheet.increment(v)
22
23  tallyfile = openFileWriteRobust('frequencies.txt')
24  sheet.writeTable(tallyfile)
25  tallyfile.close( )
26  print 'The tally has been written.'
```

FIGURE 8.10: Computing tallies from a file of integers.

Our second program reads a file of scores, presumed to have one integer per line. The complete program is shown in Figure 8.10, using a similar general approach to the first program. A complicating issue with this program is that we do not initially know the minimum and maximum scores we might encounter, and so we cannot initialize the TallySheet until after reading the file and locating the extreme values.

The input file is processed line by line, adding all valid integers to our own temporary list values. For robustness, we use a try statement when converting the line to an integer. If the line is not properly interpreted as an integer by the command **int**(line), a ValueError occurs. We do not want our program to crash, so we catch the potential error, yet there is nothing special we want to do with an offending line other than to ignore it. Syntactically, we cannot have an **except** statement without an associated clause. Therefore, we use a special command **pass** that serves as a body but does nothing when executed.

After reading the full file, we use the smallest and largest values that occurred as parameters when instantiating the TallySheet. At this point, we loop through the values, incrementing the tally for each. Then we write results to a file, just as in the first version.

TallySheet implementation

The top-level programs were written with the reliance upon the presumed behaviors of the TallySheet class. Before we can actually execute those programs, we must fully implement this class. Our complete class definition is given in Figure 8.11. We outline the highlights of that code in the following discussion.

We represent the sheet internally by storing the minimum and maximum values sent by the caller to delimit the legal range, together with a list of tallies, each initially zero. The most complicated aspect of our design is the need to map between the arbitrary value of the user and the associated range of indices into our list. We chose to define a private method _toIndex to encapsulate the details of that translation, thereby simplifying the rest of our code. We ensure that the minimum value results in index 0 and that all subsequent values are assigned consecutive indices. The overall length of our initial list depends upon the size of the gap between the maximum and minimum values, when translated to indices. The list itself is initialized at line 16 of our code, so that all counters are initially zero.

The implementations of increment and getCount are quite similar. In both cases we convert the caller's value to an underlying index for our list. We perform explicit error checking. If the resulting index is not in the proper range for our list, a ValueError is raised. Furthermore, a TypeError may be raised indirectly from within the _toIndex method if the given value is not compatible with the types of the original minimum and maximum values. Assuming the value is legitimate, the only difference between increment and getCount is that the former increments **self**._tallies[ind] while the latter returns the current count. The implementation of getTotalCount is trivial, relying upon the built-in function sum.

It is within the implementation of the private _toIndex method that we finally differentiate between tracking integers and characters. In either case, the general approach is to "subtract" off the minimum value as an offset (e.g., subtracting 1900 from a year, subtracting 'A' from a character). However, we cannot truly perform subtraction on strings. Instead, we rely on a combination of type checking and careful monitoring of exceptions. We use the official minimum value as a guide for the expected type. If that minimum is a string, then we expect it and the value to be single-character strings. In that case we rely upon the computation ord(val) − ord(**self**._minV) at line 50 to determine the index. That statement is still enclosed within a try clause just in case the user sends a nonstring or multicharacter string as a value; either of those scenarios results in a TypeError. If the representative minimum is not a string, then we expect it and the value in question to be integers. In this case the standard subtraction should work in calculating an index, although again we are ready to catch a TypeError in case anything goes wrong. It is worth noting that we intentionally caught the TypeError at line 53 only to re-raise a TypeError at line 54. Our reason for doing so is to provide our own custom error message.

The remaining functionality writes a table of results to a file. The primary job is handled by the writeTable method. After writing a table header to the file, this loops through each index of the underlying tally list, producing a single line of output for that entry. We use string formatting to properly align the columns of our table as desired. The biggest challenge here is in converting backward from the list index to the associated value for the caller's perspective. Intuitively, we just add back the offset that was subtracted within _toIndex, but we must again take care to properly handle the distinction between integers and characters. For simplicity, our writeTable method assumes that we will be printing a

```
1   class TallySheet:
2     """Manage tallies for a collection of values.
3
4     Values can either be from a consecutive range of integers, or a
5     consecutive sequence of characters from the alphabet.
6     """
7     def __init__(self, minVal, maxVal):
8       """Create an initially empty tally sheet.
9
10      minVal    the minimum acceptable value for later insertion
11      maxVal    the minimum acceptable value for later insertion
12      """
13      self._minV = minVal
14      self._maxV = maxVal
15      maxIndex = self._toIndex(maxVal)
16      self._tallies = [0] * (maxIndex + 1)        # a list of counters, each initially zero
17
18    def increment(self, val):
19      """Increment the tally for the respective value.
20
21      raise a TypeError if the given value is not of the proper type
22      raise a ValueError if the given value is not within proper range
23      """
24      ind = self._toIndex(val)
25      if not 0 <= ind < len(self._tallies):
26        raise ValueError('parameter '+str(val)+' out of range')
27      self._tallies[ind] += 1
28
29    def getCount(self, val):
30      """Return the total number of current tallies for the given value.
31
32      raise a TypeError if the given value is not of the proper type
33      raise a ValueError if the given value is not within proper range
34      """
35      ind = self._toIndex(val)
36      if not 0 <= ind < len(self._tallies):
37        raise ValueError('parameter '+str(val)+' out of range')
38      return self._tallies[ind]
39
40    def getTotalCount(self):
41      """Return the total number of current tallies."""
42      return sum(self._tallies)
```

FIGURE 8.11: Our TallySheet class (continued on next page).

```
43    def _toIndex(self, val):
44      """Convert from a native value to a legitimate index.
45
46      Return the resulting index (such that _minV is mapped to 0)
47      """
48      try:
49        if isinstance(self._minV, str):
50          i = ord(val) − ord(self._minV)
51        else:
52          i = int( val − self._minV )
53      except TypeError:
54        raise TypeError('parameter '+str(val)+' of incorrect type')
55      return i
56
57    def writeTable(self, outfile):
58      """Write a comprehensive table of results.
59
60      Report each value, the count for that value, and the percentage usage.
61
62      outfile    an already open file with write access.
63      """
64      outfile.write('Value  Count Percent \n----- ------ -------\n')
65      total = max(self.getTotalCount( ), 1)   # avoid division by zero
66      for ind in range(len(self._tallies)):
67        label = self._makeLabel(ind)
68        count = self._tallies[ind]
69        pct = 100.0 * count / total
70        outfile.write('%s %6d %6.2f%%\n' % (label, count, pct))
71
72    def _makeLabel(self, ind):
73      """Convert index to a string in native range."""
74      if isinstance(self._minV, int):
75        return '%5d' % (ind + self._minV)
76      else:
77        return '   %s   ' % chr(ind + ord(self._minV))
```

FIGURE 8.11 (continuation): Our TallySheet class.

string when reporting the value, and the creation of that string is encapsulated in another private function named _makeLabel. If the original value is an integer, we convert it to a right-justified string of length five (yes, this means we are in trouble if there are 100,000 or more occurrences of a single value). When the value is a character, we center it within a string of length five. That conversion, shown at line 77, makes careful use of a combination of the chr and ord functions.

8.6 Chapter Review

8.6.1 Key Points

- The **print** command can be followed by multiple arguments, separated by commas. Each argument will be automatically converted to a string, if not already so. Single spaces are printed between arguments.

- By default, **print** outputs a newline at the end. However, if a trailing comma is given after the last argument, then a single space is printed instead of the newline character.

- A newline character can be embedded in a string literal using the escape sequence '\n'.

- String formatting can be used to assemble new strings based upon a template string and a series of arguments to substitute, as in

    '%s: ranked %d of %d teams' % (team,rank,total)

- Python includes a built-in file class to support reading from and writing to files. A Python file object is constructed based upon an underlying file on the system using a syntax such as

    source = file(filename, 'r')

  where filename is a string. The second parameter specifies the access mode: 'r' is read-only (the default), 'w' (over)writes a file, and 'a' appends to the end of an existing file.

- If an unsuccessful attempt is made to open a file (either because it cannot be found or because it cannot be opened with the desired access mode), an IOError occurs.

- Three common ways to read data from textfile are the following, each of which returns the result in the form of a string:

  - textfile.read( ) — reads the entire remainder of the file.
  - textfile.read(numbytes) — reads the specified number of bytes next in the file.
  - textfile.readline( ) — reads the next line of the file, including the subsequent newline character.

- The **for** loop syntax can be used to iterate over lines of a file, as in

    for entry **in** scores:

  where scores is an open file object.

- A syntax result.write(text) is used to write a string text to a file. Unlike with the **print** command, arguments are not implicitly converted to strings and no spaces or newline characters are added (they must be explicitly part of the string parameter).

8.6.2 Glossary

access mode The type of use designated for a newly opened file. The most common modes are 'r' to read a file (the default), 'w' to (over)write a file, and 'a' to append information to the end of an existing file.

lexicon A collection of strings, for example all words or phrases in the English language.

string formatting A syntax of the form template % arguments for formatting a string with placeholders to be filled in by arguments.

8.6.3 Exercises

String Formatting

Practice 8.1: Assume that identifiers person, day, and month are set appropriately, with person and month being strings, and day an integer. Use string formatting to produce the form `"Susan's birthday is July 8."`

Exercise 8.2: Given an integer x show how to produce a string that corresponds to the algebraic expression $x + x = 2x$. For example, if x = 8, you should produce the string `'8 + 8 = 16'`.

Exercise 8.3: Assume that identifiers giver, present, event, and receiver are set appropriately. Use string formatting to produce a single string that appears as

```
    Dear George,

       Thank you so much for the toaster.
    What a thoughtful wedding gift!

    Warmly,
    Michael
```

where the italicized words are the values associated with the variables.

Exercise 8.4: For a baseball player, let H represent the number of hits and AB represent the number of at–bats. The batting average is computed as the ratio of hits to at–bats, printed in a form such as `.366` using three decimal places and no leading zero. Show how such a string can be created.

Exercise 8.5: In Exercise 4.39, the goal was to generate an $n \times n$ multiplication table with properly aligned columns. Revisit that task with the use of string formatting.

Files

Practice 8.6: Assume that the file `people.txt` contains one or more lines where each line is the name of a famous person followed by the year in which he or she was born. For example, the file might appear as

```
Athelstan 895
Edgar the Peaceable 942
Edward the Elder 877
Ethelred the Unready 968
Matilda 1102
St. Edward the Confessor 1003
```

You may assume that the file is formatted properly and that years are positive numbers. Give a complete program that reads the file and reports the name of the oldest person (you may assume this is unique). For example on the above input file, your program would output `Edward the Elder`.

Practice 8.7: Write a program that creates a new file named `message.txt`, having contents precisely matching the following:

```
This is a test.
How did I do?
```

Exercise 8.8: Write a program that reads a file named `famous.txt` and prints out the line with the longest length (in case of a tie, you may print out a single such line). For example, if the contents of the original file appears as

```
Alan Turing
John von Neumann
Donald Knuth
Charles Babbage
Grace Hopper
```

your program should output `John von Neumann`.

Exercise 8.9: Write a program that reads a file named `famous.txt` of the form shown below. Each line has the name of a person followed by the year in which he/she was born. Your program should print the name(s) of the youngest person(s) from the file. In the case of a tie, your program must print the names of *all* of the youngest people. For example, with input such as

```
Jimmy Carter 1924
Bill Clinton 1946
Gerald Ford 1913
George H. W. Bush 1924
George W. Bush 1946
```

your resulting output should be

```
Bill Clinton
George W. Bush
```

Exercise 8.10: Write a program that reads in a file `numbers.txt` consisting of an arbitrary number of floating-point values, each on a separate line, and outputs the average of those values. For example if `numbers.txt` has the following contents

```
4.0
3.4
5.2
```

the program should output

```
The average is 4.2
```

Exercise 8.11: There is a standard Unix tool named `grep`, that in simplest form performs the following task. For a given input file and a given search term, print out only those lines of the file that contain the given search term. Implement such a program yourself.

Exercise 8.12: Redo Exercise 2.37 regarding inverted pairs in DNA, but this time read the DNA strand from a file, input the marker from the user, and write the resulting DNA to a separate output file.

Exercise 8.13: Redo Exercise 8.5, writing the table to a file rather than printing it.

Case Studies

Exercise 8.14: In Section 8.5.2, we noted that our program for annotating a file always justifies line numbers using four spaces. While this is perfect for files that have from 1000 to 9999 lines, it is a waste of space for files that have fewer lines, and improper alignment for files that have more lines. Rewrite that program so that line numbers are justified using precisely the number of spaces that is necessary based upon the size of the file.

Exercise 8.15: Figure 8.10 contains a program for computing tallies from a file of integers. We tried to write a robust program that shields the user from experience any exceptions, but our program is flawed. Describe a scenario in which the end user is exposed to an uncaught exception.

Exercise 8.16: Add a drawGraph method to the TallySheet class that returns a graphical Canvas with a bar chart representing the current set of tallies.

Exercise 8.17: Add a method writeHistogram(entriesPerBucket) to the TallySheet class. Whereas the writeTable reports tallies for each individual value, a histogram should aggregate that report by pooling the tallies for a group of consecutive values. For example, if the original minimum and maximum values were originally 1900 and 2000, a call to writeHistogram(10) should produce a table of the form

```
 values      count  percent
 ---------   -----  -------
 1900-1909     88    7.33%
 1910-1919    143   11.91%
 . . .
```

The last bucket of the histogram might contain a smaller range of values.

Projects

Exercise 8.18: Write a program that reads a data set of two-dimensional points and calculates the "line of best fit" for that point set (namely, the line that minimizes the sum of the squares of the vertical distances between the points and the line).

You may assume that the file is formatted so that each line describes a single point, denoted by its x and y coordinate values separated by a space. Your output should report the equation for the line, in the form $y = mx + b$, where m is the slope of the line and b is the y-intercept. The best fit line for n points can be computed

using the formulae

$$m = \frac{n \cdot (\sum x_i \cdot y_i) - (\sum x_i) \cdot (\sum y_i)}{n \cdot (\sum x_i^2) - (\sum x_i)^2}, \qquad b = \frac{\sum y_i - m \cdot \sum x_i}{n}$$

Exercise 8.19: Redo Exercise 8.18, plotting the data and the resulting line graphically.

Exercise 8.20: Write a program that graphs a series of prices for a given stock. Assume that a file contains data for a stock with one line per day, reporting respectively the opening price, closing price, high price, and low price for that day. A common way to represent this data graphically is as follows.

Each rectangle represents one day, with the top of the rectangle being the daily high and the bottom being the daily low. The line to the left of a rectangle represents the opening price for that day and the line to the right the closing price.

Exercise 8.21: Implement a Lexicon class used to help manage a set of words belonging to a language. The constructor should accept a parameter that is an open file from which the words can be read. The underlying file will have one word per line. The constructor should read those lines and save each word into an internal list of words (akin to that on page 280).

Then implement the __contains__ method to test whether a given word is considered to be legal, based on the following rule. If a word in the lexicon is lower-case (e.g., python), then it may be legally spelled as either lowercase or uppercase; however, a word that is uppercase in the word list (e.g., Arthur) is only legal when uppercase. A sample test for this class follows:

```
language = Lexicon( file('words.txt'))
print 'Python' in language          # presumably True
print 'arthur' in language          # presumably False
```

Exercise 8.22: Use the Lexicon class of Exercise 8.21 to create a basic spell checker. The program should build a lexicon based on an underlying file of words for a language. Then it should read a document file indicated by the user. The goal is to produce a list of words from the document that do not appear in the lexicon. For the source document, you may presume that words are delimited with whitespace (and without any punctuation).

Exercise 8.23: Add additional functionality to your spell checker from Exercise 8.22. When reporting a misspelled word, give the line number at which it occurs in the source document. Furthermore, properly strip away leading and trailing punctuation from words in the source document before looking them up in the word list. For example, `'end.'` is a legitimate word despite the period.

Exercise 8.24: Redesign the spell checker from Exercise 8.23 to perform interactively. Display each apparent mistake and then prompt the user as to whether that mistake should be ignored or replaced. Then write the corrected version of the document to a new file.

Even better, augment the Lexicon class to support a getSuggestions behavior that takes a misspelled word as a parameter and produces a list of correct words that are in some way "close" to the misspelled word. Use this feature to offer your user a choice of suggested substitutions, in addition to the option to ignore or replace a misspelled word.

CHAPTER 9

Inheritance

A core principle of object-oriented programming is that instances of a given class support the same behaviors and are represented by a similar set of attributes. The design of software is based upon the identification of these underlying commonalities, allowing for greater reuse of code and minimizing the duplication of programming efforts. To take best advantage of object orientation, we must consider the relationships and commonalities between objects of different classes. In our opening chapter we introduced the concept of *inheritance*. This is a technique that allows us to define a new (child) class based upon an existing (parent) class. The child class inherits all of the members of its parent class, thereby reducing duplication of existing code.

We typically differentiate a child class from its parent in two ways. The child may introduce one or more behaviors beyond those that are inherited, thereby *augmenting* the parent class. A child class may also *specialize* one or more of the inherited behaviors from the parent. This specialization is accomplished by providing an alternative definition for the inherited method, thereby *overriding* the original definition. The techniques of augmentation and specialization are not necessarily used in isolation; a child class might specialize certain existing behaviors while introducing others. More generally, inheritance can be used to better organize relationships among many classes with the development of large class hierarchies. In such a context, a single class can serve as the parent for many different child classes. It is also possible to have a single child class inherit from multiple parent classes.

In this chapter we study inheritance, demonstrating technical aspects of its use as well as discussing its proper role in object-oriented design. We give several basic examples of augmentation and specialization. As a concrete example of a large class hierarchy, we explore the cs1graphics module and the use of inheritance in that design. We also take care to discuss some limitations of inheritance and alternative design strategies.

9.1 Augmentation

As our first example we consider the design of a deluxe version of our television, based upon our previous design of Section 6.3. We wish to add support for managing a set of so-called "favorite" channels. In particular, we have three new behaviors in mind:

- addToFavorites( ) — a method that adds the currently viewed channel to the set of favorites (if not already there).
- removeFromFavorites( ) — a method that removes the currently viewed channel from the set of favorites (if it is present).
- jumpToFavorite( ) — a method that jumps from the current channel setting to the next higher channel in the set of favorites. However, if no favorites are numbered higher than the current channel, it wraps around to the lowest favorite. If there are no favorites at all, the channel remains unchanged.

We develop a new class DeluxeTV that uses the previous Television class as its parent. We declare such a child class using a syntax as follows:

```
class DeluxeTV(Television):
```

The use of inheritance is indicated by giving the new class name (i.e., DeluxeTV) followed by parentheses surrounding the parent class (i.e., Television). With such a declaration, the new child inherits all existing methods of the parent class. Our responsibility is in specifying the details needed for the augmented functionality. In this case, we maintain a new instance variable **self.**_favorites that is a **list** of favorite channels.

Initially the favorites list should be empty, but we must establish this state for a newly constructed DeluxeTV. We do this by implementing the __init__ method as follows:

```
def __init__(self):
    Television.__init__(self)          # parent constructor
    self._favorites = [ ]
```

The final line establishes our list of favorites. We want to draw attention to the preceding line. The state of a deluxe television must not only include the list of favorites, but also tra-ditional attributes such as volume and channel. For the original Television class, those are established within the body of the constructor. Yet by implementing our own constructor for the DeluxeTV class, we have technically overridden the original __init__. Once we do this, it is our responsibility to ensure that all aspects of the state are properly initialized.

Although we could choose to set initial values for attributes like volume ourself, we still prefer to rely upon the original Television constructor. This is accomplished by the command Television.__init__(**self**). This is actually a function call, but syn-tactically it is quite different from other calls we have seen. Rather than the typical *object.method*(*params*) form, we use the pattern *class.method*(*params*). This allows us to draw a distinction between the __init__ method that was defined for the Television class versus the DeluxeTV.__init__ method that we are currently defining. A notable aspect of this syntax is that we must resend **self** as an *explicit* parameter to the parent constructor.

With the DeluxeTV constructor complete, we next provide implementations for our three new methods. The addToFavorites and removeFromFavorites methods are relatively straightforward. When addToFavorites is called, the goal is to add the current channel setting to the list of favorites. The only care we take is to check whether the power is on and to not reinsert the channel into the list if it is already present. We accomplish this as

```
def addToFavorites(self):
    if self._powerOn and self._channel not in self._favorites:
        self._favorites.append(self._channel)
```

Notice that we refer to the **self**._favorites attribute, established in our constructor, as well as the **self**._channel attribute, established by the parent constructor. The implementation of removeFromFavorites is quite similar and included in the complete source code given in Figure 9.1. The jumpToFavorite method is given at lines 30–51. The first major task is to determine the appropriate favorite channel based on the documented semantics. We use the following logic. We first determine the maximum of all favorites, at line 43. If the maximum favorite is not larger than the current channel, there are no strictly larger favorites. In this case, the proper behavior is to wrap around and jump to the minimum of all favorites, as determined at line 45. Otherwise, we know there exists one or more favorites that are larger than the current channel. In this case our goal is to determine which of those is truly closest to the current channel. We accomplish this with the for loop at lines 48–50, continually improving our guess until we have considered all options.

Having determined the desired channel, the second task is to enact the change. Although it is tempting to do something as simple as **self**._channel = closest, this would not suffice. We must properly maintain **self**._prevChan to support the jumpPrevChannel option (review Section 6.3 for a lengthy discussion of this lesson). Rather than risk a mistake in reprogramming that logic, we rely directly upon the inherited setChannel method, which already implements the proper semantics. This call is made at line 50 and then the final result is returned to the caller at line 51.

```
1   from Television import Television
2
3   class DeluxeTV(Television):
4     """A television that maintains a set of favorite channels."""
5
6     def __init__(self):
7       """Creates a new DeluxeTV instance.
8
9       The power is initially off, yet when turned on the TV is tuned to channel 2
10      with a volume level of 5. The set of favorite channels is initially empty.
11      """
12      Television.__init__(self)              # parent constructor
13      self._favorites = [ ]
```

FIGURE 9.1: The declaration of a DeluxeTV class (continued on next page).

```
14    def addToFavorites(self):
15       """Adds the current channel to the list of favorites, if not already there.
16
17       If power is off, there is no effect.
18       """
19       if self._powerOn and self._channel not in self._favorites:
20          self._favorites.append(self._channel)
21
22    def removeFromFavorites(self):
23       """Removes the current channel from the list of favorites, if present.
24
25       If power is off, there is no effect.
26       """
27       if self._powerOn and self._channel in self._favorites:
28          self._favorites.remove(self._channel)
29
30    def jumpToFavorite(self):
31       """Jumps to the "next" favorite channel as per the following rules.
32
33       In general, this method jumps from the current channel setting to the next higher
34       channel which is found in the set of favorites. However if no favorites are numbered
35       higher than the current channel, it wraps around to the lowest favorite. If there are
36       no favorites, the channel remains unchanged.
37
38       Returns the resulting channel setting.
39
40       If power is off, there is no effect.
41       """
42       if self._powerOn and len(self._favorites)>0:
43          closest = max(self._favorites)              # a guess
44          if closest <= self._channel:                # no bigger channel exist
45             closest = min(self._favorites)           # wrap around to min
46          else:                                       # let's try to get closer
47             for option in self._favorites:
48                if   self._channel < option < closest:
49                   closest = option                   # a better choice
50          self.setChannel(closest)                    # rely on inherited method
51          return closest
```

FIGURE 9.1 (continuation): The declaration of a DeluxeTV class.

9.2 Specialization

The jumpToFavorite method of the DeluxeTV class is somewhat complicated because the collection of favorite channels is *unsorted* within an internal **list**. Although we made do with that class, it was not truly the ideal tool for the job. Avoiding the insertion of a duplicate was rather easy, but locating the proper favorite when jumping was not. To facilitate the jump, we next consider maintaining the favorite channels in sorted order.

While we could embed the necessary logic within our DeluxeTV code, this is a great opportunity to develop a more appropriate storage mechanism as an independent class. In this section we develop a new SortedSet class that is well suited for the task. Defining this as a separate class, rather than as embedded logic in the DeluxeTV, allows us to better organize our efforts and also provides an opportunity for later reuse of the SortedSet abstraction, should the need arise in some other application.

Our SortedSet[1] will maintain a set of elements while ensuring that duplicates are removed and that the elements are ordered. Although we already noted that the **list** class is not ideal for this job, it still is quite useful. In our first approach for implementing the SortedSet class, we inherit from the existing **list** class and then specialize it. We begin the class declaration as

class SortedSet(**list**):

Unlike the DeluxeTV, which requires an additional attribute _favorites that is not part of the parent class, we are perfectly happy to rely on the underlying storage mechanism provided by the **list** class. We have no immediate reason to provide an alternative constructor since the default constructor provides an empty list, which by nature is sorted and without duplicates (we will come back to this issue when creating nonempty sets).

Looking at the menu of behaviors that are inherited from the **list** class, we find that many are perfectly appropriate for our context without modification. In fact all the accessor methods suffice (e.g., __contains__, __getitem__, __len__, __eq__, index). An accessor such as count may not be as significant since we do not allow duplicates, yet the answer it provides (either 0 or 1) is still meaningful. Even mutators such as pop and remove can be used without modification, as a sorted set remains a sorted set when entries are removed.

However, there are other methods that cannot be passively inherited in the context of a sorted set. For example, lists support a method insert(index, object) that allows a user to insert an arbitrary object at an arbitrary location within the list. For a SortedSet, the inherited behavior might introduce duplicates or violations to the sorted order, so we override this method to provide a specialized behavior. Our version of insert accepts a single parameter specifying the new value to insert; *we* determine where it is placed rather than the user and *we* ensure that it is not a duplicate.

We also introduce a new method indexAfter(value) as a convenient utility to determine a proper index for inserting a new element into a set. This method returns the index of the first element that is strictly larger than the given parameter. When there are no such values it returns the length of the entire set. For example, if a set has values [11, 206, 647]

---

1.   We should note that Python includes a built-in **set** class, although that class represents an *unordered* collection of elements. See Section 12.4 for details.

then a call to indexAfter(30) returns 1 (as 206 is the first larger value and located at index 1 of the set). Notice that if we were about to insert 30 into the set, this index would designate the proper placement for the new value. And if no elements of the set were larger than the parameter, the length of the set (e.g., 3 in this case) is the proper index for an insertion. We provide indexAfter as a public method because its use by others cannot harm the set, and it may be useful for other purposes. For example, in the DeluxeTV context the call indexAfter(30) can be used to determine the proper favorite channel when jumpToFavorite is invoked while the television is currently on channel 30.

Because we keep elements sorted, our implementation relies on a simple while loop to advance an index until surpassing the given value (for those wanting a more efficient algorithm for searching, look ahead to Section 11.4).

```
def indexAfter(self, value):
    walk = 0
    while walk < len(self) and value >= self[walk]:
        walk += 1
    return walk
```

Since our class is inherited from **list**, our instance is itself a **list**. So the syntaxes len(**self**) and **self**[index] are already defined based upon the inherited behaviors. With the indexAfter utility in hand, we can easily override the original insert method as follows:

```
def insert(self, value):
    if value not in self:              # avoid duplicates
        place = self.indexAfter(value)
        list.insert(self, place, value)    # the parent's method
```

The final line is explicitly invoking the *parent* form **list**.insert rather than our new form (i.e., SortedSet.insert). This syntax is reminiscent of our call to the parent constructor Television.__init__ in the preceding section. Using the parent form of insert allows us to precisely place the new value in the sequence.

To properly maintain the integrity of a sorted set, there are many other **list** mutators that must be overridden. For example, the natural version of append adds a new element to the end of a list. We override this method to make its behavior identical to our newly defined version of insert. In fact, we directly call our new version as follows:

```
def append(self, object):
    self.insert(object)
```

The syntax **self**.insert in this context causes an invocation of the SortedSet form of insert rather than the overridden **list** form. This is because our instance is most specifically a SortedSet. So when a method call is made it relies upon that class's behavior rather than the parent class version. The parent's methods are only applied in cases where there is no duly named method explicitly in the native context. This is an example of the principle of *polymorphism* and a key to the object-oriented paradigm. When the caller invokes a method on an object, the actual behavior depends upon the precise type of the given object.

```
1    from Television import Television
2    from SortedSet import SortedSet
3
4    class DeluxeTV(Television):
5      def __init__(self):
6        Television.__init__(self)          # parent constructor
7        self._favorites = SortedSet( )
8
9      def addToFavorites(self):
10       if self._powerOn:
11         self._favorites.append(self._channel)
12
13     def removeFromFavorites(self):
14       if self._powerOn and self._channel in self._favorites:
15         self._favorites.remove(self._channel)
16
17     def jumpToFavorite(self):
18       if self._powerOn and len(self._favorites)>0:
19         resultIndex = self._favorites.indexAfter(self._channel)
20         if resultIndex == len(self._favorites):
21           result = self._favorites[0]          # wrap around
22         else:
23           result = self._favorites[resultIndex]
24         self.setChannel(result)
25         return result
```

FIGURE 9.2: A DeluxeTV class that relies upon a SortedSet (documentation omitted).

Using our SortedSet to implement a DeluxeTV

Although we have not yet finished our complete implementation of a SortedSet, we know enough about its interface to show how it could be used. Figure 9.2 provides an alternative implementation of the DeluxeTV class that takes advantage of the SortedSet abstraction.

Further details

Although we already discussed the most important aspects of our SortedSet class, there is still a bit more work in creating a quality class. We have inherited many other behaviors from the **list** class and must ensure the integrity of our sorted set abstraction. For example, lists provide another mutator of the form extend(other), where the original list is modified by adding all elements of the other list to the end. For sorted sets, we do not want to blindly add those to the end, but instead to filter out duplicates and maintain the sorted order. We can again rely directly upon our revised version of insert.

```
def extend(self, other):
    for element in other:
        self.insert(element)
```

Earlier, we noted that the default constructor for the **list** class suffices, since an initially empty list qualifies as being a sorted set. However, the official **list** constructor accepts a sequence of existing objects as an optional parameter, for specifying initial contents of a nonempty list. For example the syntax **list**('hello') results in the list ['h', 'e', 'l', 'l', 'o']. This form is not naturally consistent with our convention of a sorted set, so we override __init__ as follows:

```
def __init__(self, initial=None):
    list.__init__(self)                    # calls the parent constructor
    if initial:
        self.extend(initial)
```

We make sure to call the parent constructor to configure the internal state of an empty list. Then, if the caller has specified a sequence of initial elements, we use our revised version of extend to insert each one (thereby filtering duplicates and ordering properly).

The __add__ method of the original **list** class is not a mutator, but instead creates and returns a new list that is a composition of two existing lists. For completeness we should override this method so that it produces a new SortedSet rather than a list. This is easily accomplished by relying upon the rest of our work.

```
def __add__(self, other):
    result = SortedSet(self)           # creates new copy of self
    result.extend(other)               # add other elements to this copy
    return result
```

As we continue looking through the catalog of inherited methods, there are a few unusual considerations. Lists support a sort method, which we inherit. Of course, our sets are already maintained in sorted order. Leaving this behavior alone does not violate the integrity of our sets. At the same time, the algorithm that is used to sort a list class takes time. It seems silly to spend any unnecessary time sorting a SortedSet, so we override the original behavior purely for the sake of efficiency.

```
def sort(self):
    pass
```

The command **pass** is a special one that does nothing at all when executed. However, syntactically it is a placeholder, serving as the body of a control structure.

There are two other inherited methods of concern, reverse and __setitem__. If we do not override these, their use may break our conventions for a sorted set. However, when overriding them, what behavior would be more appropriate? We really would prefer not to have the methods there at all, but removing inherited behaviors is not a standard object-oriented technique. Instead, we raise an exception whenever one of these methods is called. The __setitem__ override is done similarly. These functions are shown as part of a complete SortedSet implementation in Figure 9.3. Of course, we should provide full documentation for our class to describe its use for others.

```
 1  class SortedSet(list):
 2    def __init__(self, initial=None):
 3      list.__init__(self)              # calls the parent constructor
 4      if initial:
 5        self.extend(initial)
 6
 7    def indexAfter(self, value):
 8      walk = 0
 9      while walk < len(self) and value >= self[walk]:
10        walk += 1
11      return walk
12
13    def insert(self, value):
14      if value not in self:            # avoid duplicates
15        place = self.indexAfter(value)
16        list.insert(self, place, value)  # the parent's method
17
18    def append(self, object):
19      self.insert(object)
20
21    def extend(self, other):
22      for element in other:
23        self.insert(element)
24
25    def __add__(self, other):
26      result = SortedSet(self)         # creates new copy of self
27      result.extend(other)             # add other elements to this copy
28      return result
29
30    def sort(self):
31      pass
32
33    def reverse(self):
34      raise RuntimeError('SortedSet cannot be reversed')
35
36    def __setitem__(self, index, object):
37      raise RuntimeError('This syntax not supported by SortedSet')
```

FIGURE 9.3: A SortedSet class that inherits from **list** (excluding documentation).

9.3 When Should Inheritance (Not) Be Used

In the previous example, we implemented a SortedSet class by inheriting from **list** because it seemed that the **list** class was a good starting point. Many of the inherited behavior were perfectly suited. Some other behaviors, such as insert, needed to be specialized to capture the semantics of being a sorted set. The least pleasing aspect of that effort is the existence of several unnecessary methods. Our class has a sort method that does not do anything. While this is not a tragedy, we certainly would not include such a method if designing a SortedSet class from a clean start. Similarly we have two different methods insert and append that do exactly the same thing; we even have methods reverse and __setitem__ that are not supposed to be called.

There is an alternative way to take advantage of the existing **list** class without tech-nically using inheritance. We can design a SortedSet class from scratch, but using an instance of a **list** internally as an attribute, for storing our elements. A simple constructor might appear as

```
class SortedSet:
  def __init__(self):
    self._items = list( )
```

We establish the _items attribute as an initially empty list for our use. The relationship between a parent and child class when using inheritance is often termed an ***is-a relation-ship***, in that every DeluxeTV is a Television. When one class is implemented using an instance variable of another, this is termed a ***has-a relationship***. In our new implementa-tion, a SortedSet has a **list** (although the SortedSet is not itself a **list**).

Since we do not inherit from any parent class, we must explicitly provide support for any behaviors that we want to offer our users. For example, we might provide versions of indexAfter and insert in similar spirit to the version of SortedSet we gave in Section 9.2. Syntactically, we implement insert as follows:

```
def insert(self, value):
  if value not in self._items:
    place = self.indexAfter(value)
    self._items.insert(place, value)
```

If you compare this to the previous version of insert it is almost the same, but not precisely so. Most notably, there is no concept of calling the "parent" version of insert in this context. Instead, the final line of the body explicitly calls **self**._items.insert to invoke the insert method of the underlying **list** attribute.

The biggest advantage of avoiding inheritance is that we do not automatically inherit the unnecessary baggage of methods such as sort and reverse, or duplicate behaviors such as insert and append. In this version, we choose precisely what to offer. However, we do not inherit any of those useful **list** methods that were automatic in our previous version. We must explicitly provide methods such as remove, pop, index, __contains__, and so on. Each of those methods is easy to implement; we simply make the associated call on the _items attribute. For example, to remove an item from a set, we remove it from the list.

```
def remove(self, element):
    self._items.remove(element)
```

Such a function that makes an underlying call to a very similar function upon another object is known as a ***wrapper function***. Our complete implementation, shown in Figure 9.4, provides wrappers for several other desirable **list** methods.

In general, there is not always a clear-cut rule for when to use inheritance and when to use a has-a relationship. The decision comes down to the number of potentially inherited behaviors that are undesirable versus the number of desirable ones that would need to be explicitly regenerated if using a has-a relationship.

```
 1  class SortedSet:
 2    def __init__(self, initial=None):
 3      self._items = list( )
 4      if initial:
 5        self.extend(initial)          # extend the set (not the list)
 6
 7    def indexAfter(self, value):
 8      walk = 0
 9      while walk < len(self._items) and value >= self._items[walk]:
10        walk += 1
11      return walk
12
13    def insert(self, value):
14      if value not in self._items:
15        place = self.indexAfter(value)
16        self._items.insert(place, value)
17
18    def extend(self, other):
19      for element in other:
20        self.insert(element)
21
22    def __add__(self, other):
23      result = SortedSet(self)          # creates new copy of self
24      result.extend(other)              # add other elements to this copy
25      return result
26
27    def index(self, value):
28      return self._items.index(value)
```

FIGURE 9.4: A SortedSet class using a **list** as an attribute (continued on next page).

```
29      def remove(self, element):
30        self._items.remove(element)
31
32      def pop(self, index=None):
33        return self._items.pop(index)
34
35      def __contains__(self, element):
36        return element in self._items
37
38      def __getitem__(self, index):
39        return self._items[index]
40
41      def __len__(self):
42        return len(self._items)
43
44      def __eq__(self, other):
45        return self._items == other._items
46
47      def __lt__(self, other):        # lexicographic comparison
48        return self._items < other._items
49
50      def __str__(self):
51        return str(self._items)
```

FIGURE 9.4 (continuation): A SortedSet class using a **list** as an attribute.

9.4   Class Hierarchies and cs1graphics

Each of our examples of inheritance thus far captures the specific relationship between two classes, the parent and child. While this is typical, inheritance has even greater value as a framework for organizing a larger number of classes into a natural hierarchy.

As a tangible example of a rich hierarchy, we explore our own use of inheritance in developing the cs1graphics module of Chapter 3. That design leverages the commonality of various classes to minimize the duplication of effort and to provide greater uniformity in the programming interface. A large portion of that design was described in Figure 3.4, but there is even more to it behind the scene. In this section and the next, we explore the inner workings of this module demonstrating the use of inheritance in our own programming.

The role of inheritance in cs1graphics goes well beyond the convenience of its orig-inal development. The hierarchy of Drawable objects is intentionally designed to provide opportunity for other programmers to define new classes of objects. We will demonstrate several examples in which new classes leverage the original framework by augmenting or specializing existing classes.

FIGURE 9.5: Three instances of the Star class.

9.4.1 A Star Class

When designing the cs1graphics module, we tried to include support for many useful graphical objects. At the same time, we knew that other programmers would undoubtedly have their own creative ideas for objects that we did not envision. So we designed the hierarchy of Drawable objects in a way that could easily be extended by others to include new classes.

As our first example of such a class, suppose that you want to draw stars, such as those shown in Figure 9.5. Clearly, those shapes can be created by hand with the Polygon class, but specifying the geometry of each would be cumbersome. It would be much easier to imagine using a syntax such as

```
medal = Star(5)                          # a five-pointed star
paper.add(medal)
```

Although no such Star class is built into the official graphics module, you could design and implement the class yourself. Our goal in this section is to walk you through the process.

We use inheritance to avoid re-creating everything from scratch. Most notably, we recognize that a star is just a special case of a polygon. So we define a new Star class as a child of the existing Polygon class, starting with the syntax

```
class Star(Polygon):
```

By using Polygon as a parent class, we inherit many useful behaviors. These include the method for drawing a polygon, as well as behaviors from further up the hierarchy such as adjusting the border and fill color, and even moving, scaling, or rotating a star.

Our biggest challenge will be implementing a constructor that establishes the initial geometry of a star. As long as we are going to the trouble to design a separate class, we should do our best to support many different sizes and shapes of stars. This will make our class more useful. We want to allow stars with any number of rays and of varying sizes. Looking more carefully, a star with n rays is really a polygon with $2n$ points. The geometry of a star depends on both an outer radius, as measured from the center of the star to the tip of each ray, as well as an inner radius measured from the center to the place where two

```
1   class Star(Polygon):
2     def __init__(self, numRays=5, outerRadius=10, innerRatio=.5, center=Point(0,0)):
3       Polygon.__init__(self)              # call the parent constructor
4       top = Point(0, −outerRadius)         # top point is directly above the origin
5       angle = 180.0 / numRays
6
7       for i in range(numRays):
8         self.addPoint(top ^ (angle * (2 * i)))              # outer point
9         self.addPoint(innerRatio * top ^ (angle * (2 * i + 1)))    # inner point
10
11      self.adjustReference(0, outerRadius)   # move reference from top point to center
12      self.move(center.getX( ), center.getY( ))  # re-center entire star
13      self._innerRatio = innerRatio         # record as an attribute
14
15    def setInnerRatio(self, newRatio):
16      factor = newRatio / self._innerRatio
17      self._innerRatio = newRatio
18      for i in range(1, self.getNumberOfPoints( ), 2):        # inner points only
19        self.setPoint(factor * self.getPoint(i), i)
```

FIGURE 9.6: Our proposed Star class (excluding documentation and unit testing).

neighboring rays meet. Rather than have the inner radii be an independent parameter, we let the user specify the outer radius and then the ratio between the inner and outer radii. In this way, a larger outer radius automatically provides a proportionally larger inner radius.

We propose the implementation of a Star class in Figure 9.6. The constructor is responsible for configuring the initial state of the underlying polygon, based upon the user's parameters (or the default values of those parameters). To organize our effort, we design the geometry of a star as if centered around the origin, which also will serve as a natural reference point for our completed star (we will address centering our star elsewhere at the conclusion). The body of our constructor begins by explicitly invoking the parent constructor at line 3, as is usual with inheritance. By default, this initializes the internal state for an empty polygon. Our next challenge is adding the appropriate polygon points to represent our star. For a star with n rays, we need to add a total of $2n$ points, alternating between an outer and inner point, rotating around the center at equal intervals.

As a model for an outer point, we define the local variable top at line 4 to portray the topmost point of the star, located outerRadius units above the center. We will calculate all other locations by duly rotating and scaling this point (taking great advantage of the ^ and * operators of the Point class, as discussed on page 212 of Section 6.2). Since our $2n$ points must be spaced at equal intervals, the angle between each successive point is $\frac{360}{2n} = \frac{180}{n}$, as calculated at line 5. The actual points are added to the polygon during the loop of lines 7–9, with one outer and one inner point per pass.

This essentially completes the construction of a star-shaped polygon, but there are a few small details to address. First, as the designer of a new drawable object, we can choose an appropriate initial position for the reference point. For polygons, the default reference point is aligned with the first point to be added. For a star, the center location seems a good reference point. So at line 11, we adjust the reference point moving it down from the original top point to the center of our star's geometry. Next, we address the user's desire to place the center of the star elsewhere on a canvas or layer. By default, our star is centered at the origin, but the constructor accepts a final parameter center that can be used to place the star elsewhere. This is meant to parallel several of the existing graphics classes; for example, Circle(25) creates a new circle of radius 25 centered at the origin, yet Circle(25, Point(100,70)) creates a circle of radius 25 centered at the coordinates (100,70).

The purpose of line 13 is really in support of the coming method setInnerRatio, so we should first discuss the purpose of that behavior. We have given our users the ability to customize several aspects of a star upon instantiation. We might also want to provide convenient support for mutating a star after it has been created. Because a Star is a Polygon, which in turn is a Drawable, the user can already call move to change the location, or scale to effectively change the outer radius (and proportionally the inner radius). But the standard scale will not suffice for changing the relative ratio between the outer and inner radii. So we offer an additional behavior for stars to support just such a change. Calling setInnerRatio can be used to change the inner ratio to a new value. To implement this behavior, we leave the outer points alone and we scale all of the inner points by an appropriate factor to compensate for the difference between the existing ratio and the newly desired ratio. To facilitate the computation of this factor, we maintain an internal attribute _innerRatio that represents the current ratio. Notice that the initial setting for this ratio was treated as a parameter within the constructor. But parameters have local scope; those values are not directly accessible from within the body of other methods of the class. This is why we record that setting in line 13 of the constructor, so that we can later access it from line 16 of our method. With that information available, the rest of the process is straightforward, although requiring a bit of care. Looking back at our original construction, we inserted points starting with an outer point, then an inner, than an outer and so on. Therefore we know that all of the inner points are those with odd index in the underlying polygon. Since our Star is a Polygon, we can make use of methods getNumberOfPoints, getPoint, and setPoint that are supported by that class.

As a final comment, we will note that a user of our Star also has the ability to call methods that we inherit from Polygon. This means that a user could call deletePoint to remove an outer point (effectively lopping off a ray of our star), or even to remove an inner point (thereby directly connecting the two adjacent rays). The user could call addPoint to insert new points at any index of the underlying sequence. Not only would these mutations alter the appearance of a "star," they could potentially interfere with our implementation of setInnerRatio, which assumed that every other point was an inner point of the star. These issues really reflect back to the discussion of Section 9.3, as to the advantages and disadvantages of using inheritance. We will leave our implementation as is and let the user beware. If we really wanted, we could intentionally disable those mutators (much as we did for reverse in our first version of SortedSet). Alternatively, we could design a Star with a *has-a* relationship to Polygon rather than inheriting from it. This technique is demonstrated in Section 9.4.3 in the context of a Car. We leave it to Exercise 9.7 to develop such an alternative implementation for the Star class.

9.4.2 A Square Class

As our next example, we examine the actual code used in cs1graphics for defining the Square class as a child of the Rectangle class, as given in Figure 9.7. Just as a star is a special case of a polygon, we can view a square as a special case of a rectangle in which the width and height are equal. However, there are both advantages and disadvantages to this design. By representing a Square as a Rectangle, the primary advantage is the inheritance of an appropriate _draw method; after all, a square should be rendered just as a rectangle that happens to have equal width and height. The biggest disadvantage in this use of inheritance is the effort required to ensure that a square's width and height remain equal. This implementation relies upon a subtle combination of augmentation and specialization.

The size of a Square is specified as a single parameter to the constructor; we then use that value for both the width and height when calling the underlying Rectangle constructor at line 3. The Square supports three different mutators. The setWidth and setHeight methods were both included within the Rectangle class. Yet we must explicitly override those inherited versions or else risk allowing a user to alter one dimension of a square but not the other. So we redefine each to make a simple call to a new method setSize that will have the effect of changing both the width and height in tandem. The setSize method intentionally calls the *parent* versions of the setWidth and setHeight methods (lines 12 and 13) to change the two dimensions in the underlying state.

The Square inherits the getWidth and getHeight accessors from Rectangle; there is no need to override those since their use is consistent with a square. However, we introduce a new accessor named getSize to reinforce the preferred view of a square having a unified size. Internally, that method simply returns the width.

```
1   class Square(Rectangle):
2     def __init__(self, size=10, center=None):
3       Rectangle.__init__(self, size, size, center)
4
5     def setWidth(self, width):
6       self.setSize(width)
7
8     def setHeight(self, height):
9       self.setSize(height)
10
11    def setSize(self, size):
12      Rectangle.setWidth(self, size)       # parent version of this method
13      Rectangle.setHeight(self, size)      # parent version of this method
14
15    def getSize(self):
16      return self.getWidth( )
```

FIGURE 9.7: The actual implementation of the cs1graphics.Square class (documentation and error checking omitted).

9.4.3 A Car Class

In our initial exploration of cs1graphics, we introduced the Layer class for maintaining a collection of individual objects in a more unified way. As motivation at the time, Section 3.6 included an example of a very simple "car" which was composed of two tires and a body. By adding those components to a single layer, the car could subsequently be moved, scaled, or rotated as a single object. Still, that approach is not quite the same as having a true Car class. In particular, there was a burden upon the programmer to design the precise geometry of a car before embedding it in a scene. To provide more reusable code, we wish to encapsulate those details into a class that can be later used as simply as

```
myRide = Car( )
myRide.move(30,0)
```

Such a class would be convenient for creating many cars, and it would be something we could make available for others to import and use.

Ignoring artistic quality, a simple implementation of a Car class is given in Figure 9.8. If you compare this code to the original discussion of a car on page 110, you will find remarkable similarity. In the original version we created a Layer, and then created three shapes which were added to the layer. In this version, we define a Car to itself be a Layer. So after creating each component shape, we add it directly to the underlying layer calling the inherited method **self**.add (as in line 7).

```
 1   class Car(Layer):
 2     def __init__(self, bodyColor='blue'):
 3       Layer.__init__(self)                      # call the parent constructor
 4
 5       tire1 = Circle(10, Point(-20,-10))
 6       tire1.setFillColor('black')
 7       self.add(tire1)
 8
 9       tire2 = Circle(10, Point(20,-10))
10       tire2.setFillColor('black')
11       self.add(tire2)
12
13       self._body = Rectangle(70, 30, Point(0, -25))
14       self._body.setFillColor(bodyColor)
15       body.setDepth(60)                         # behind the tires
16       self.add(self._body)
17
18     def setBodyColor(self, bodyColor):
19       self._body.setFillColor(bodyColor)
```

FIGURE 9.8: A Car class implementation, inheriting from Layer.

The only other interesting aspect of our design is that we allow the user to specify the body color. The initial color is sent as a parameter to the constructor, and it can later be mutated with the setBodyColor. We explicitly track the rectangle that represents the body as attribute _body, so that we can access it from the other method (just as we did with the _innerRatio attribute in the previous Star example). In contrast, we do not bother to create attributes for the tires because once constructed and added to the underlying layer, we do not need to reference them.

Alternative design: inheriting directly from Drawable

Our implementation of the Car class is a reasonable design, but with Layer as a parent class, a car supports the add, remove, and clear methods. This could easily be documented as a "feature" rather than a "flaw." Car enthusiasts could make a custom car, perhaps adding a racing stripe or a diamond–studded grill. But those methods could be abused. Although a user cannot easily remove one of our own components (since he would not have a reference to the part), the clear method could be used to remove everything. We might prefer to develop a class that does not publicly support the Layer methods.

Staying with the theme of Section 9.3, we could use an alternative design in which a Car directly manages its individual components. Yet we will not forgo use of inheritance entirely. We still define our Car as a child class of Drawable. That class serves as the most generic class in our hierarchy and provides desirable behaviors such as the ability to move, scale, or rotate an object. In fact, any object that is to be drawn on a canvas must be directly or indirectly inherited from the Drawable class.

All descendants of the Drawable class are responsible for providing a private method named _draw that controls how that particular object is drawn. This is not a public method that users call directly, but it is invoked behind the scene when an object is first added to a canvas or when a canvas needs to be refreshed. However, there is no generic way to render a Drawable object; every child class must provide its own instructions on how its instances should be drawn. We have already provided the instructions for the various graphics primitives provided by the module (e.g., Circle, Polygon, Text). When we defined our own Star class we did not have to explicitly provide instructions for _draw because the instructions inherited from Polygon applied. Even when Car was inheriting from Layer, we did not have to explicitly provide those instructions because the process is handled by the Layer class (we will explain how that class works in Section 9.5).

By defining Car directly as a child of Drawable, the _draw method becomes our responsibility. This alternative implementation of a Car class is given in Figure 9.9. We inherit from Drawable at line 1 and call the parent constructor from line 3 of our constructor body. The rest of the constructor is used to create the components, laying out the geometry around the origin as in the first version. However, nothing else is done with those shapes within the constructor (in contrast, we explicitly added those components to the underlying layer in the previous version). The burden is shifted to the _draw method, explicitly imple–mented in lines 15–20. Informally, that code states that a car is drawn by drawing the body, then the first tire, then the second tire. Those three steps are implemented at lines 17–19 by directly calling the _draw methods for the individual components. Lines 16 and 20 are required for technical reasons for any implementation of a _draw method; simply con–sider this a protocol that must be followed. We are not relying upon the relative depths of

```
1   class Car(Drawable):
2     def __init__(self, bodyColor='blue'):
3       Drawable.__init__(self)                    # call the parent constructor
4
5       self._tire1 = Circle(10, Point(-20,-10))
6       self._tire1.setFillColor('black')
7       self._tire2 = Circle(10, Point(20,-10))
8       self._tire2.setFillColor('black')
9       self._body = Rectangle(70, 30, Point(0, -25))
10      self._body.setFillColor(bodyColor)
11
12    def setBodyColor(self, bodyColor):
13      self._body.setFillColor(bodyColor)
14
15    def _draw(self):
16      self._beginDraw()                          # required protocol
17      self._body._draw()
18      self._tire1._draw()
19      self._tire2._draw()
20      self._completeDraw()                       # required protocol
```

FIGURE 9.9: A Car class implementation, inheriting from Drawable.

our components in this version. The apparent depth is controlled literally by the order in which the individual components are drawn. This is commonly described as a "painter's algorithm" because the farther objects are painted first, and then closer objects painted on top of the earlier ones. In this example, we intentionally drew the body of the car before the tires so that the circles representing the tires are drawn on top of the body.

As a final comparison between the version of Figure 9.8 and Figure 9.9, we note that the tires and body are formal attributes in the second version. This is because we need to reference each component from within the _draw method.

 A WORD OF WARNING

When designing a new class that inherits directly from Drawable, you are respon- sible for providing an implementation of a method named _draw. By convention, the body of that method must begin with the command **self**._beginDraw( ) and end with the command **self**._completeDraw( ). Between those commands, you should draw individual components of your object, from farthest to nearest.

9.5 Multiple Inheritance

When inheritance is used to define a class, the new class typically inherits from a single parent, as with **class** Star(Polygon). We formally call this technique *single inheritance*, and it is the model we have used in all of our examples thus far. However, some languages, including Python, allow for the use of *multiple inheritance*. Although less common, this technique can be quite valuable in certain circumstances. In this section, we wish to demonstrate two such examples in the context of cs1graphics.

The Layer class

The Layer class is an extremely versatile tool, allowing programmers to logically organize a collection of underlying shapes into a single component. The nature of the Layer class itself is somewhat unusual. It shares a great deal in common with the Canvas class in that objects can be added and removed and that the rendering of objects within the same layer is affected by the relative depths of those components, just as is done when rendering objects directly to a canvas. At the same time a Layer is itself a Drawable object. It can be added directly to a Canvas, or for that matter, to yet another Layer. It can be moved, scaled, and rotated just as can any other drawable object. To leverage these underlying commonalities, multiple inheritance is used when defining the Layer class.

A Layer is defined as a child of Drawable so that it inherits the existing support for the various transformations such as scaling and rotating. Yet Layer is also defined as a child of a private class named _GraphicsContainer. We did not discuss the _GraphicsContainer class in earlier chapters because its existence does not effect the *public* interface for the graphics package. Its purpose is to serve as a parent class to both the Layer and Canvas classes, capturing their common aspects and thereby avoiding duplication of code that would otherwise be necessary if Layer and Canvas were defined independently. The graphics container keeps track of an internal list of drawable objects and supports methods add, remove, and clear. Since canvases and layers need to draw their contents in a back-to-front manner, the _GraphicsContainer class also provides a getContents method that returns the sequence of object sorted according to their respective depths, from largest to smallest.

An overview of the design is shown in Figure 9.10. Both the Layer and Canvas classes inherit the common support from _GraphicsContainer. The Canvas class defines further aspects, such as a title bar and background color, that are not supported by a Layer. The use of multiple inheritance lies in the declaration of the Layer class, which inherits from both Drawable and _GraphicsContainer. The actual definition of the Layer class from cs1graphics is shown in Figure 9.11. Syntactically, multiple inheritance is very similar to single inheritance. Rather than giving one parent class in the parentheses, we give a series of parent classes, separated by commas.

```
class Layer(Drawable, _GraphicsContainer):
```

The Layer class inherits the members from both of its parent classes. Its constructor makes sure to invoke *both* parent constructors (as each of those classes has an internal state that must be initialized). At this point, our work is almost done. We now have support for methods such as scale and rotate from Drawable as well as methods add and remove from _GraphicsContainer. However, there is one method we must provide: _draw.

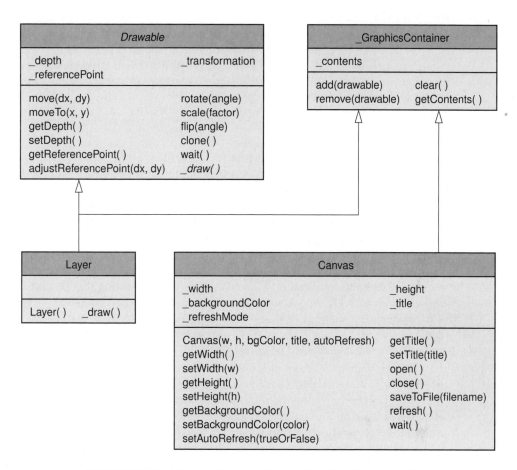

FIGURE 9.10: Using multiple inheritance to define the Layer class.

```
class Layer(Drawable, _GraphicsContainer):
  def __init__(self):
    Drawable.__init__(self)
    _GraphicsContainer.__init__(self)

  def _draw(self):
    self._beginDraw( )                  # required protocol
    for shape in self.getContents( ):
      shape._draw( )
    self._completeDraw( )               # required protocol
```

FIGURE 9.11: The actual implementation of the Layer class (excluding documentation).

Recall from our discussion in Section 9.4.3 that the Drawable class does not itself support a generic _draw method. That method should be implemented by any class that directly inherits from Drawable. In the case of a Layer, the process for drawing the layer is simply to draw each component of the layer, from back to front. We do this with a simple for loop, taking advantage of the fact that getContents guarantees to return the elements sorted in that fashion.

A LabeledRectangle class

As a second example of multiple inheritance, we develop a new class we choose to name LabeledRectangle. We have in mind a single composite shape composed of a rectangle with a centered text message displayed on top. This particular class is not officially part of the cs1graphics, but its implementation is quite similar to the Button class, which is included.

A LabeledRectangle could easily be designed as a Layer with a separate Rectangle instance and a Text instance, so long as the depths were set so that the text appears in front of the rectangle. However, we wish to show how this could be achieved through the use of multiple inheritance. A rather simple implementation that performs well is shown in Figure 9.12. An instance behaves both as displayed Text and as a Rectangle. This means that it supports methods such as setWidth, setFillColor, and setBorderWidth that are inherited from Rectangle, while also supporting methods like setMesssage and setFontColor that are inherited from Text.

We also indirectly inherit methods like move and scale from Drawable (as both Text and Rectangle were derived in some way from Drawable). But it is important to note that we cannot separately control the movement of the "rectangle" versus the "text." There are not two separate objects; an instance is simultaneously a rectangle and text. It has a single reference point, which by default is simultaneously aligned with the center of the displayed text and center of the rectangle. Our implementation of _draw intentionally over-rides the otherwise inherited versions so that we can make sure to display both underlying components, drawing first the rectangle's image and then the text on top.

```
1   class LabeledRectangle(Text, Rectangle):
2     def __init__(self, message, width, height):
3       Text.__init__(self, message)
4       Rectangle.__init__(self, width, height)
5       self.setFillColor('white')     # rectangle interior was transparent by default
6
7     def _draw(self):
8       self._beginDraw( )
9       Rectangle._draw(self)          # access the overridden Rectangle version of _draw
10      Text._draw(self)               # access the overridden Text version of _draw
11      self._completeDraw( )
```

FIGURE 9.12: Proposed implementation of a LabeledRectangle.

FOR THE GURU

The LabeledRectangle example was particularly subtle because both of the parents were themselves derived from a common class, namely Drawable. More generally, there is potential confusion anytime there is a ***name conflict*** between members from two different parent classes. In our first example, there were no such conflicts. The names of the members inherited from Drawable were entirely distinct from the members inherited from _GraphicsContainer.

In our LabeledRectangle class if we had not explicitly overridden _draw there would have been two conflicting versions of that method (one defined in the context of Text and one defined in the context of Rectangle). In case of such a conflict, the default resolution is that Python uses the member taken from the first of the parent classes, as ordered in the original declaration of multiple inheritance. So in our example, if we had not overridden _draw, users would only have seen the text portion actually displayed because our original declaration is LabeledRectangle(Text, Rectangle). Had we listed Rectangle as the first parent class, then that version of _draw would have been used. By providing our own implementation of _draw we effectively override both of the inherited versions. However, we can still access the overridden version by explicitly giving the underlying class name as a qualifier (as we did at lines 9 and 10).

When using multiple inheritance in Python, there is also a dangerous potential for name conflicts in underlying attributes. Here, the resolution is not based on the declaration order, but on the order in which the parent constructors are called. The latter constructor would effectively overwrite the initial value in such a scenario. In any event, we are likely in big trouble if there exists such a conflict. Correct use of multiple inheritance takes great care. Different object-oriented programming languages handle it in different ways. C++ offers a model for multiple inheritance that is different from Python's, while the designers of Java chose not to even support multiple inheritance.

9.6 Case Study: a Mailbox Class

As a final case study, we want to encourage creativity in designing your own graphical classes. Our earlier examples have generally shown ways to create additional shapes, such as stars, that are relatively static primitives. However, with inspiration these techniques can be used to create dogs that sit, wag their tails, and bark, birds that flap their wings and fly from point to point, or a horse that rears up on its hind legs.

As the designer of a class you have two responsibilities. First, you get to decide on the precise interface that your class supports. If creating a Dog class, perhaps you would want to support methods sit, wagTail and bark(message). Of course, you also need to decide on and document the semantics. For example, what would happen if someone calls sit when a dog is already sitting? Once you have decided upon the outward behavior, you

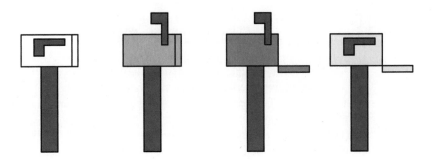

FIGURE 9.13: A Mailbox instance can have a variety of configurations.

must also consider how you will manage the underlying state of an object. What attributes will you maintain and how will those be initialized?

Our last example of this chapter is not quite so creative, but it is a step in the right direction. We develop a Mailbox class. Although a programmer could obviously design shapes that look like a mailbox using existing techniques, we want to make it easy. Besides handling the underlying geometry, our class will support additional semantics that make sense in the context of a mailbox, such as opening or closing the door, or raising or lowering the flag. We also allow the user to choose the primary color of the mailbox. This affects the box and door, but does not affect the flag, which must be red, nor the post, which is brown. Figure 9.13 demonstrates several configurations of the mailbox.

The complete code for our class, including documentation for the user, is given in Figure 9.14. Although we could inherit from Layer, we choose to use a design inheriting directly from Drawable, akin to the second version of the Car in Section 9.4.3. Our constructor initializes four components of our mailbox: the post, the box on top of the post, the door attached to the box, and the flag. Knowing that we may be rotating the flag and the door, we carefully choose natural reference points for those shapes. In particular, the reference of the door is its lower left corner, acting as a hinge when attached to the box; for the flag, we place the reference in the interior near the arm of the flag, as if attached to the box with a rivet. We also introduce two convenient boolean attributes _doorOpen and _flagUp to keep track of the current state of the door and flag.

The _draw routine is implemented to achieve the desired effect with the flag appearing closer than the rest of the box. The remaining methods provide support to the user for altering the color of the box or the configuration of the door and flag. We demonstrate two different styles for these manipulations. For the door, we offer two separate methods openDoor and closeDoor. Each of these carries out the intended task, assuming the door is not already positioned in such a way. For example, if openDoor is called when the door is already open, nothing is changed. For the flag, we offer a single method that toggles the position. If toggleFlag is called when the flag is down, it is rotated up; if up, it is rotated down. Finally, we have a little fun to achieve the effect of animation. These methods intentionally use loops to rotate the door or flag one degree at a time so that the user sees it in motion (although the exact speed will depend upon the system).

```
1   class Mailbox(Drawable):
2     """A graphical primitive representing a Mailbox.
3
4     The user can choose the color, open and close the door, and raise and lower the flag.
5     """
6     def __init__(self, flagUp=False, doorOpen=False, color='white'):
7       """Creates a new mailbox instance.
8
9       The reference point is initially at the bottom of the post.
10
11      flagUp        boolean determining whether flag is initially raise (default False)
12      doorOpen      boolean determining whether door is initially open (default False)
13      color         color of the box and door (default white)
14      """
15      Drawable.__init__(self)                     # call the parent constructor
16
17      # post sits on top of the origin
18      self._post = Rectangle(16, 80, Point(0,-40))
19      self._post.setFillColor('brown')
20
21      # box sits on top of post, slightly left to offset door
22      self._box = Rectangle(50, 30, Point(-3,-95))
23      self._box.setFillColor(color)
24
25      # door attaches to right-side of box
26      self._door = Rectangle(6, 30, Point(25,-95))
27      self._door.setFillColor(color)
28      self._door.adjustReference(-3, 15)          # act as hinge connected to box
29      self._doorOpen = doorOpen
30      if doorOpen:
31        self._door.rotate(90)
32
33      self._flag = Polygon(Point(15,-100), Point(15,-106), Point(-15,-106),
34                          Point(-15,-90), Point(-5,-90), Point(-5,-100))
35      self._flag.setFillColor('red')
36      self._flag.adjustReference(-3,-3)           # act as rivot holding flag
37      self._flagUp = flagUp
38      if flagUp:
39        self._flag.rotate(90)
```

FIGURE 9.14: The Mailbox class (continued on next page).

```
40    def _draw(self):
41      self._beginDraw( )                          # required protocol
42      self._post._draw( )
43      self._box._draw( )
44      self._door._draw( )
45      self._flag._draw( )
46      self._completeDraw( )                       # required protocol
47
48    def setColor(self, color):
49      """Change the color of the box and door to indicated color.
50
51      Note that the post and flag are unchanged.
52      """
53      self._box.setFillColor(color)
54      self._door.setFillColor(color)
55
56    def doorIsOpen(self):
57      """Returns True if door is currently open; False otherwise"""
58      return self._doorOpen
59
60    def openDoor(self):
61      """Opens the door.
62
63      If door is already open, has no effect.
64      """
65      if not self._doorOpen:
66        for i in range(90):                        # animate the motion
67          self._door.rotate(1)
68        self._doorOpen = True
69
70    def closeDoor(self):
71      """Closes the door.
72
73      If door is already closes, has no effect.
74      """
75      if self._doorOpen:
76        for i in range(90):                        # animate the motion
77          self._door.rotate(-1)
78        self._doorOpen = False
79
80    def flagIsUp(self):
81      """Returns True if the flag is currently raised; False otherwise"""
82      return self._flagUp
```

FIGURE 9.14 (continuation): The Mailbox class (continued on next page).

```
83    def toggleFlag(self):
84      """Switches the flag to the opposite setting.
85
86      That is, lowers the flag if currently raised; raises flag if currently lowered.
87      """
88      if self._flagUp:
89        increment = −1
90      else:
91        increment = 1
92      for i in range(90):                    # animate the motion
93        self._flag.rotate(increment)
94      self._flagUp = not self._flagUp
95
96  # unit test to demonstrate sample usage
97  if __name__ == "__main__":
98    paper = Canvas(300,300)
99    box = Mailbox( )
100   box.move(150,200)
101   paper.add(box)
102   raw_input('Press Return to Continue')
103
104   box.toggleFlag( )
105   raw_input('Press Return to Continue')
106
107   box.setColor('grey')
108   raw_input('Press Return to Continue')
109
110   box.toggleFlag( )
111   box.openDoor( )
112   raw_input('Press Return to Continue')
113
114   box.scale(1.5)
115   raw_input('Press Return to Continue')
116
117   box.closeDoor( )
118   raw_input("Press Return to End")
```

FIGURE 9.14 (continuation): The Mailbox class.

9.7 Chapter Review

9.7.1 Key Points

- Inheritance provides a way to avoid duplication of code by defining a new *child* class based upon existing *parent* classes.

- The use of inheritance is designated in a class definition by placing the name of the parent class within parentheses following the class name, as in **class** DeluxeTV(Television):.

- When the child class introduces a method that is not supported by the parent class we say that it *augments* the class.

- When the child class provides a method definition with the same name as one in the parent class, the new definition *overrides* the existing one, thereby specializing the behavior for instances of the new class. This is called *polymorphism* as the behavior of a particular object depends upon the precise type of that object.

- If a child class provides a specialized constructor, the first command within its body should almost always be to explicitly invoke the parent's version of the constructor. This can be done using a syntax such as Television.__init__(**self**).

- The advantage of inheritance is that a new class automatically inherits many useful methods of an existing class without providing additional code. However, this can create a problem if some of the inherited methods are not appropriate for the new class. One solution in this case is to override the unwanted methods providing new versions that do nothing or raise an error.

- Sometimes it is better to avoid inheritance altogether and instead have a new class that has an internal attribute of another useful class (a *has-a relationship*). No behaviors are inherited with this technique, but desired ones can be easily implemented by relying by wrapping the underlying functionality.

- Typically, a new class has a single parent class, but it is possible to designatee multiple inheritance using an initial syntax such as **class** LabeledRectangle(Text, Rectangle):.

- The hierarchy of Drawable objects for cs1graphics can be extended by designing new classes that inherit from existing ones. This can take several forms, depending upon the parent class that is used (most common choices are Polygon, Layer, and Drawable).

- When inheriting directly from the Drawable class, the new class must explicitly provide a _draw method and the body of that method must start with the command **self**._beginDraw( ) and end with the command **self**._completeDraw( ).

9.7.2 Glossary

augmentation A technique in which a child class defines one or more new behaviors beyond those that are inherited.

base class *See* parent class.

child class A class that is defined to inherit from another class, known as the parent class.

class hierarchy A taxonomy of related classes.

has-a relationship An instance of one class having an instance of another class as an attribute (e.g., a Course has a Teacher).

inheritance A technique by which one class is defined based upon another.

is-a relationship A description of the relation between child and parent classes (e.g., a Student is a Person).

multiple inheritance A form of inheritance in which a child class inherits from two or more parent classes.

override A technique by which a child class redefines the precise behavior associated with an inherited method.

parent class A class used as the basis for another (child) class through inheritance.

polymorphism A technique in which objects of different types support a common syntax or when a single function supports multiple behaviors depending upon the type of parameter it receives.

single inheritance The typical form of inheritance in which a child class inherits from a single parent class.

specialization A technique in which a child class overrides one or more inherited behaviors, providing an alternative implementation.

subclass *See* child class.

9.7.3 Exercises

Practice 9.1: Consider the following definitions:

```python
class Sneetch:
  def __init__(self):
    self._a = 3
    self._b = 4

  def x(self):
    print self._a

  def y(self):
    print self._b

class StarBellySneetch(Sneetch):
  def __init__(self):
    Sneetch.__init__(self)
    self._b = 7
    self._c = 8

  def y(self):
    print self._b, self._c

  def z(self):
    print self._a, self._c
```

Assume that we instantiate the following two objects:

```
alice = Sneetch( )
bob = StarBellySneetch( )
```

For each of the subsequent expressions, either describe the output that is generated or, in the case of an error, explain the cause of the error.

(a) alice.x( )

(b) alice.y( )

(c) alice.z( )

(d) bob.x( )

(e) bob.y( )

(f) bob.z( )

Exercise 9.2: Consider the following program:

```
 1  class MyClass:
 2    def __init__(self):
 3      self._x = 1
 4
 5    def increase(self):
 6      self._x += 1
 7
 8  class MyOtherClass(class MyClass):
 9    def __init__(self, z):
10      MyClass.__init__()
11      self._x = z
12
13    def decrease(self):
14      _x -= 1
15
16  a = MyClass( )
17  b = MyOtherClass( )
18  b.increase( )
19  a.decrease( )
```

This program has five distinct errors in its syntax and usage. Identify each of those errors.

Exercise 9.3: Consider the following class definitions:

```
class Person:
  def __init__(self, name, age):
    self.name = name
    self.age = age

  def printInfo(self):
    print 'Name: ', self.name
    print 'Age: ', self.age

class Student:
  def __init__(self, name, age, id):
    self.name = name
    self.age = age
    self.id = id

  def printInfo(self):
    print 'Name: ', self.name
    print 'Age: ', self.age
    print 'ID: ', self.id
```

The definitions above do not use inheritance. Rewrite the Student class as a child class of Person, reusing as much of the Person class functionality as possible. You may not, however, modify the Person class.

Exercise 9.4: Consider the version of SortedSet from Figure 9.4. Would the code still work if the constructor were implemented as follows?

```
2    def __init__(self, initial=None):
3      self._items = list( )
4      if initial:
5        self._items.extend(initial)        # changed from original code
```

If so, explain why and if not, explain what goes wrong.

Exercise 9.5: Consider the version of SortedSet from Figure 9.4. Would the code still work if indexAfter were implemented as follows?

```
7    def indexAfter(self, value):
8      walk = 0
9      while walk < len(self) and value >= self[walk]:  # changed from original code
10       walk += 1
11     return walk
```

If so, explain why and if not, explain what goes wrong.

Exercise 9.6: Consider the implementation of Star given in Figure 9.6. If we were to delete line 11 altogether would that have a noticeable impact on the semantics of the resulting star? Explain your answer.

Exercise 9.7: In Section 9.4.1 we used an "is-a" relationship to implement a Star as a child of the Polygon class. Show how to implement the class using a "has-a" relationship with Polygon (inheriting instead directly from the Drawable class, as demonstrated in the context of the second Car implementation of Section 9.4.3). Make sure that your new class still supports the useful methods setBorderWidth, setBorderColor, and setFillColor.

Exercise 9.8: Use inheritance to define a specialized RegularPolygon class, such that all side lengths and angles are consistent.

Exercise 9.9: As an experiment, create a variant of the Square class named FlawedSquare with lines 12 and 13 of Figure 9.7 replaced as follows:

```
12    setWidth(self,size)
13    setHeight(self,size)
```

Test your implementation, describe your observations, and in your own words explain the observed behaviors.

Exercise 9.10: Redesign the Mailbox class so that the user can specify a text message to be drawn upon the box.

Exercise 9.11: Rewrite the Mailbox class inheriting from Layer rather than Drawable (as demonstrated in the context of the first Car implementation of Section 9.4.3).

Exercise 9.12: Redesign the Mailbox class so that it displays an envelope coming out of the door at any point when the flag is up and the door is open.

Exercise 9.13: Rewrite the LayeredRectangle class using single inheritance from Layer (as demonstrated in the context of the first Car implementation of Section 9.4.3).

Exercise 9.14: Redesign the LayeredRectangle class to provide a method with signature crop(padding=5), that automatically resizes the rectangle to be the precise size of the text message plus the given padding on each side. See help(Text) for documentation on how to determine the width and height of the message.

Exercise 9.15: Exercise 7.14 assumed that you could modify the original Pattern class. In this problem, assume that you are not allowed to modify that class. Instead design a new RobustPattern class that has the additional feature.

Exercise 9.16: Exercise 8.16 assumed that you could modify the original TallySheet class. In this problem, assume that you are not allowed to modify that class. Instead design a new TallySheetWithGraph class that has the additional feature.

Exercise 9.17: Exercise 8.17 assumed that you could modify the original TallySheet class. In this problem, assume that you are not allowed to modify that class. Instead design a new TallySheetWithHist class that has the additional feature.

Exercise 9.18: In Chapter 8 we designed a FileUtilities module which provided two stand-alone functions for opening a file with error checking (see Figure 8.6). In this problem, we want you to build such functionality directly into the constructor of a new RobustFile class that is a child of the built-in file class. You should support the syntax RobustFile(name, mode), but if unable to successfully open the file, the program should reprompt the user for a new name rather than raising an IOError.

PART TWO

Advanced Topics

Deeper Understanding of the Management of Objects

The goal of the chapter is to provide a better explanation of what is happening behind the scene with Python, and more generally in a computer system. We explore the relation-ship between identifiers and the objects to which they refer. We examine the implications of a scenario in which two different identifiers are *aliases* for the same underlying object. We discuss the mechanism for passing information to and from a function. Finally, we look more closely at a configuration in which one object uses another object as an attribute. This has implications on storage, on making copies of such structures, and on testing the equivalence of two objects.

You may notice that this chapter begins the "Advanced Topics" portion the book. It is an unusual chapter in that we do not really introduce any new programming techniques nor do we use it to demonstrate new software applications. Instead, our goal is to set the groundwork as you progress to being a more advanced programmer. We will spend much of the chapter playing with "brain teasers" in the interpreter and drawing sketches of the behind the scene configurations that result.

In the first half of the book we made a genuine effort not to lie to you, but there were occasions when we intentionally avoided a discussion of the underlying subtleties. Ignoring those issues helped simplify life as a beginning programmer, but a solid under-standing is needed to become a good software developer. Many mistakes and inefficiencies are inadvertently introduced into software because of subtle misunderstandings of the way objects are managed. There is great value in having a broader knowledge of the larger sys-tem and the role of a programming language in controlling that system. While this chapter specifically focuses on the model Python uses for managing objects, we begin to touch on some themes that will carry over to a better understanding as you later learn additional programming languages.

10.1   Understanding Objects and References

Before we begin the lesson, we need a simple mutable class for the sake of example. To this end, Figure 10.1 gives a (very) simple implementation of an Account class. Given this definition, the command

```
>>> mySavings = Account()
```

accomplishes two things. It creates a brand new account and then it associates the identifier mySavings with that account. Although we often use the term mySavings as if it were the account itself, that identifier is really a separate entity serving as a ***reference*** to the account.

We wish to highlight the important distinction between an object and a reference to that object. In Chapter 2, we introduced the analogy of an identifier as a sticky label that is directly attached to an object. While that explanation sufficed for the time, we wish to subtly revise our analogy. Rather than viewing an identifier as a label stuck directly to the underlying object, we will view it as a ***pointer*** to the object, as shown in Figure 10.2(a). This helps clarify the distinction between the underlying object, which is the actual Account instance, and the identifier, which is the reference. Although we use the name mySavings as a way to identify the account when issuing Python commands, that name is not stored within the account's own state information, which is elsewhere in mem–

```
 1  class Account:
 2    def __init__(self, balance=0.0):
 3      self._balance = balance
 4
 5    def __eq__(self, other):
 6      return self._balance == other._balance
 7
 8    def __str__(self):
 9      return 'current balance is '+str(self._balance)
10
11    def getBalance(self):
12      return self._balance
13
14    def deposit(self, amount):
15      self._balance += amount
16
17    def withdraw(self, request):
18      if request > self._balance:
19        raise ValueError('Insufficient Funds')
20      self._balance -= value
21      return value
```

FIGURE 10.1: A very simple Account class.

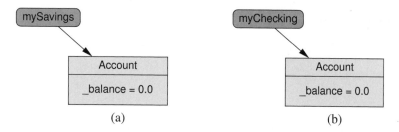

FIGURE 10.2: A change of style for drawing identifiers as distinct entities, rather than labels stuck directly onto an object.

ory. Each instance of a class has its own state information, so if we subsequently execute the command

```
>>> myChecking = Account()
```

this creates yet another account, shown in Figure 10.2(b). If you do not want to take our word for it, Python supports an id function that tracks the identities of underlying objects. We demonstrate its use as follows:

```
>>> id(mySavings)
402656
>>> id(myChecking)
403336
```

Your system may report values other than those shown here, but the two values will be distinct. Whenever a new object is created, Python designates an integer that serves behind the scene as its ID. On most computers, the ID will be related to the low-level memory address at which the object is stored; on other systems the ID may be somewhat arbitrary. What Python guarantees is that the ID of a particular object never changes and that each object has an ID that is unique from all other (current) objects.

10.1.1 Multiple References to the Same Object

A very different situation is indicated by the following assignment:

```
>>> myDebit = myChecking
```

This command does not establish any new account. Instead, it establishes a new iden-tifier myDebit, and assigns that identifier to the same underlying object that is currently referenced by myChecking. We can detect the underlying situation in several ways. An examination of the identities confirms that myChecking and myDebit are indeed referenc-ing the same object.

FIGURE 10.3: A scenario in which myChecking and myDebit are both referencing the same underlying object.

```
>>> id(mySavings)
402656
>>> id(myChecking)
403336
>>> id(myDebit)
403336
```

When two or more identifiers reference the same object, we call those **aliases**, just as we do when a person goes by more than one name. In this scenario, identifiers myChecking and myDebit are aliases for the same account, as shown in Figure 10.3. With this starting point in mind, carefully trace the following observed behavior:

```
>>> mySavings.deposit(100.0)
>>> myChecking.deposit(300.0)
>>> print mySavings
current balance is 100.0
>>> print myChecking
current balance is 300.0
>>> print myDebit
current balance is 300.0
>>> myDebit.withdraw(50.0)
50.0
>>> print mySavings
current balance is 100.0
>>> print myChecking
current balance is 250.0
>>> print myDebit
current balance is 250.0
```

Notice that an interaction with myChecking affects the same underlying object as referenced by myDebit, yet not the same as mySavings. So by the end of these interactions, mySavings has a balance of 100.0 because of the initial deposit. In contrast, the second account has an ending balance of 250.0 due to the deposit of 300.0 (nominally into myChecking) and the later withdrawal of 50.0 (nominally from myDebit).

10.1.2 Equivalence Testing

We have seen the expression a == b used to test the equivalence of the objects referenced by identifiers a and b. So when are they considered equivalent? Clearly, if those are aliases for the same underlying object, we would presumably consider them to be equivalent. But what if they reference two distinct objects? There may be natural contexts for defining the equivalence of different objects. For example, we might consider two bank accounts to be equivalent if they have equal balances.

There is no one–size–fits–all definition for what constitutes equivalency. For this reason, Python supports two different operators for testing equivalence. The operator **is** checks whether two identifiers are aliases to the same underlying object. The expression a **is** b evaluates to **True** precisely when id(a) is the same as id(b). It is also possible to use the syntax a **is not** b, which is a more readable form of **not**(a **is** b). Continuing with our ongoing example, we observe the following:

```
>>> mySavings is myChecking
False
>>> myDebit is myChecking
True
>>> myChecking is myChecking
True
>>> myChecking is not mySavings
True
```

In contrast, the semantics of the == operator is intended to capture the broader con–cept of equivalence. For each class, this notion is defined formally based upon the imple–mentation of the special method __eq__. Looking back at our Account definition in Figure 10.1, we define this method at line 5 so that two accounts are indeed considered *equivalent* if they have equal balances. Recalling that our two accounts most recently had balances of 100.0 and 250.0, we find the following:

```
>>> mySavings == myChecking
False
```

Yet if we were to deposit more money in the savings account, we can bring them to the same balance.

```
>>> mySavings.deposit(150)
>>> mySavings == myChecking
True
```

Although the accounts are still two distinct accounts, they each have a balance of 250.0, and so they meet the criteria for equivalence. For similar reasons, we find that

```
>>> myChecking == myDebit
True
```

We happen to know that these two identifiers are currently referencing the same underlying object, but all that is really being tested here is whether the balances of those "two" accounts are equal. A curious reader might wonder what happens if the == operator is used on objects from a user-defined class that does not provide an __eq__ method. Given the lack of an explicit test for equivalence, Python defaults to a safe interpretation where an underlying object is equivalent to itself but nothing else. That is, a == b evaluates as would a **is** b.

10.1.3 Garbage Collection

Continuing with our ongoing example, consider the effect of the following command:

```
>>> myChecking = Account()
```

We have described the semantics of such a command many times; a new account is created and the identifier myChecking is associated with that result. What is important to recognize is that this command has no effect whatsoever on the object that myChecking had previously referenced. In this particular case, that other object is still referenced by myDebit, as shown in Figure 10.4. Consider how the following command compares to the previous one:

```
>>> mySavings = Account()
```

As we know, this creates yet another new account and reassigns the identifier mySavings to that new account. What makes this situation slightly different from the last one is the treatment of the object that had previously been referenced by mySavings. We suggested that a reassignment of an identifier has no effect on that other object. However, in this

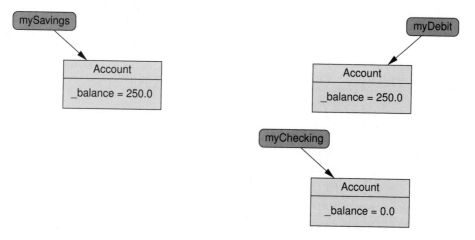

FIGURE 10.4: The scenario after reassigning myChecking to a newly created Account.

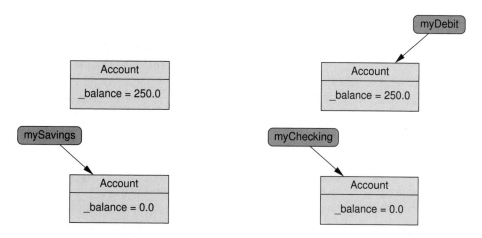

FIGURE 10.5: The scenario after reassigning mySavings to a newly created Account.

scenario as shown in Figure 10.5 we have an underlying object (the top left) stored in memory but with no apparent reference to it. Without a valid reference to an object, it can never be used. By analogy, if we lose all references to a real bank account, we have essentially lost our $250. Technically, the account may be there, but we cannot access it.

Continuing to store an inaccessible object is a waste of memory. Some languages (e.g., C++) rely upon the programmer to indicate when an object should be thrown away. Python (and Java) use a different approach known as *garbage collection*. If the Python interpreter detects an inaccessible object, it reserves the right to throw it away and reclaim the underlying memory for other purposes (such as for newly instantiated objects). The process for automatically detecting an inaccessible object is not always an easy task for a programming language, but there are some standard techniques that can help. For exam-ple, Python stores a *reference count* for each underlying object, noting how many current aliases exist for that object. Each time a new identifier is associated with the object the count is increased, and each time an associated identifier is reassigned to something else, the count is decremented. When that reference count reaches zero, the object can be thrown away (this is not the only way in which an object becomes inaccessible, but it is the most common). By taking on the burden of automatic garbage collection, Python allows the programmer to focus on higher-level decisions.

FOR THE GURU

If you want to further explore reference counts, import the sys module and read the documentation for the sys.getrefcount method.

10.1.4   Primitive Types

We know that calling a constructor for a class creates a new instance of that class. The same is often true when using literal forms to designate an instance of a primitive type in Python. Consider the following example:

```
>>> grades = ['A', 'B', 'C']
>>> alphabet = ['A', 'B', 'C']
>>> id(grades)
355312
>>> id(alphabet)
353776
```

We use the literal form ['A', 'B', 'C'] on the first line and the second line. Notice that each use of the literal results in a new underlying list. These two lists can be independently manipulated at this point (e.g., adding an 'F' to the alphabet does not directly add it to the list of grades). A similar observation can be made regarding the values returned by functions such as range. Each call produces a distinct list, as evidenced by the IDs.

```
>>> scores = range(90,100)
>>> temperatures = range(90,100)
>>> id(scores)
353808
>>> id(temperatures)
355344
```

Given the previous examples, you might be surprised to see the following:

```
>>> hello = 'aloha'
>>> goodbye = 'aloha'
>>> id(hello)
355328
>>> id(goodbye)
355328
```

Although the ID value on your system may not be 355328, you should see that the two IDs are the same as each other. This seems to contradict our previous discussion. The first use of the literal 'aloha' produces an underlying instance of the **str** class with the given characters. We might expect that the second use of the literal produces a second underlying object. But it does not.

The distinction is that strings are *immutable* while lists are *mutable*. The two lists must be represented separately in memory, because a change to one list must not have an effect on the other. With strings, there is no way to change the value once an instance has been created. So there is no apparent harm if Python allows several identifiers to alias the same underlying object. More so, there is an advantage in doing so. Using a single object rather than two in this situation saves memory.

Sometimes Python is clever in reusing an underlying immutable object, although there is no official guarantee as to when it does so. You may or may not find that id(4) is the same as id(2+2), or that id('aloha') equals id('Aloha'.lower( )). Therefore, it is very dangerous to rely upon a condition such as **raw_input( ) is** 'yes'. When dealing with immutable types, you should rely on equivalence such as **raw_input( ) ==** 'yes', which evaluates to **True** so long as the sequence of characters is the same.

10.2   Objects that Reference Other Objects

In the spirit of newfound honesty, we need to again revise our diagram style. Consider the simple scenario mySavings = Account( ), introduced at the beginning of this chapter. A picture in the style of Figure 10.6(a) was used to emphasize the identifier as a reference to an object. Yet the attributes that comprise the state of an object are also references to other objects. This is the essence of a classic ***has-a relationship***. So a more accurate portrayal of this scenario is given in Figure 10.6(b). We see that the _balance attribute of the Account is not technically the numeric value, but a *reference* to a **float** with value 0.0.

A **list** is another example of an object that references other objects. Our earlier diagrams (e.g., Figure 2.3 on page 46) seem to suggest that the contents of a list are stored as part of its state, but this is not so. In reality, the state of a list comprises a sequence of *references* to other objects, managed to reflect the desired order. So a more accurate portrayal of a list appears in Figure 10.7.

In more complex cases, objects reference objects that reference objects, and so on. For example, the DeluxeTV introduced in Section 9.1 includes an attribute _favorites that is a list of channel numbers. Therefore, a more technically accurate portrayal of a DeluxeTV is in Figure 10.8 (although for brevity, this picture omits some attributes from our original model).

So why do we bother making this distinction? There is little significance in a case where a reference is to an *immutable* object. The new diagram style is technically more

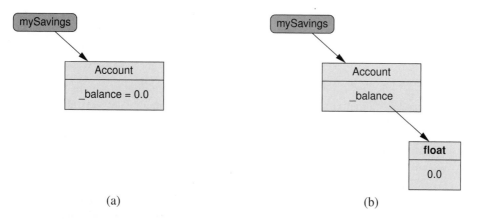

(a)   (b)

FIGURE 10.6: Yet another change of style. On the left is a recent style introduced in Figure 10.2(b). On the right is our newest style, highlighting that the _balance attribute itself references an object from the **float** class.

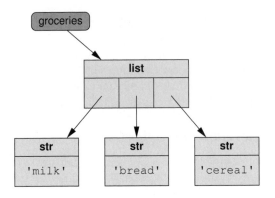

FIGURE 10.7: A portrayal of a list referencing its underlying contents.

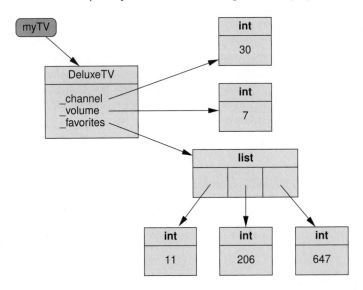

FIGURE 10.8: A more accurate portrayal of a DeluxeTV.

accurate, although we often continue to use the simpler style of Figure 10.6(a) to avoid unnecessary clutter. However, when a reference is to a mutable object, the distinction can be very significant. Consider the **tuple** of accounts portrayed in Figure 10.9 and declared as

```
frozenAssets = (mySavings, myChecking)      # not really frozen!
```

Despite the suggestive name, there is a paradox here. The accounts are not at all frozen. It is perfectly permissible to invoke mySavings.withdraw(100), or even to use the syntax frozenAssets[0].withdraw(100). A tuple is an immutable version of a list, and as such, it is represented as a sequence of references. But the immutability only constrains the sequence. That is, there is no way to insert, remove, or reorder the references within a tuple. But nothing stops us from mutating the underlying objects that the tuple references.

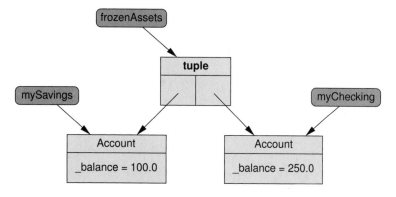

FIGURE 10.9: A tuple containing references to two accounts. The tuple is immutable but the accounts are not.

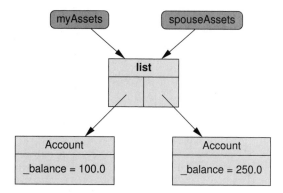

FIGURE 10.10: The result of the simple assignment spouseAssets = myAssets, modeling a couple that shares a single portfolio of accounts.

10.2.1   Deeper Forms of Aliasing

In Section 10.1, we showed a basic form of aliasing, whereby two identifiers reference the same underlying object. Aliasing is a powerful modeling technique when used appro-priately. When objects reference objects that reference objects and so on, many different forms of aliasing can occur with subtly different style yet dramatically different effect.

To frame the discussion, let's go back to the realm of a couple managing financial accounts. We begin with a basic list myAssets that references two underlying accounts (imagine a picture similar to Figure 10.9, but with a **list** rather than a **tuple**). Repeating a familiar lesson, the command spouseAssets = myAssets establishes an alias to the same list as shown in Figure 10.10. Such a configuration might accurately model a couple that maintains a single portfolio, consisting of accounts that are shared. Either identifier pro-vides access to the common list and indirectly to any of the shared accounts. Furthermore, any change to those accounts or even to the list itself will affect the apparent assets of

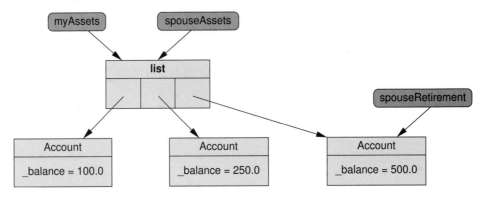

FIGURE 10.11: A subsequent configuration to Figure 10.10, having inserting a new account using the syntax spouseAssets.append(spouseRetirement).

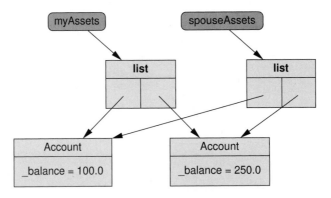

FIGURE 10.12: A model with two lists that happen to reference the same accounts.

each person. For example, the command spouseAssets.append(spouseRetirement) adds a third account to that common list, as portrayed in Figure 10.11.

Different portfolios with common accounts

A different configuration may be used to model a couple who maintain separate portfolios, but sharing the same underlying accounts. This scenario is shown in Figure 10.12. As before, any change to one of those accounts affects both people. However, the lists rep–resenting the two portfolios can be separately managed. For example, if the spouse adds a new account using the syntax spouseAssets.append(spouseRetirement), this adds that account to the spouse's portfolio but not to the original portfolio, as shown in Figure 10.13.

Complete independence

A third model for couples would portray complete financial independence. Each person could manage a separate list of accounts, where none of the accounts are shared. In this scenario, aliasing is entirely avoided (see solution to Practice 10.6 for a diagram).

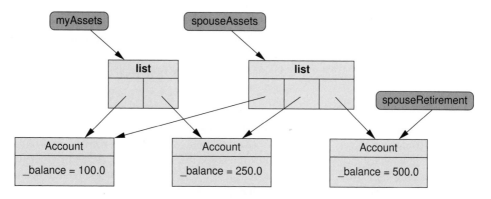

FIGURE 10.13: The subsequent configuration to Figure 10.12, having executed the command spouseAssets.append(spouseRetirement).

Advanced modeling

In the first chapter we used a typical student registration system as an example when discussing high-level modeling and objects that reference other objects. Proper use of aliasing is critical in the design of such a system. For example, if two different courses are being taught by the same instructor, the _instructor attribute of each Course should presumably reference a single underlying Professor, rather than having two distinct instances representing the same person. However, if a professor is teaching two sections of the "same" course, those two sections cannot really be represented as references to the same Course. Although components may be the same, such as the course number and name, other aspects of the state will differ, such as the meeting time and enrolled students.

There are many other cases where common notions of "same" and "different" must be carefully translated to form an accurate model. For example a Student may have a _curSchedule attribute that references a Schedule, which itself references one or more Course instances. Two friends may talk about having the "same" schedule for a given semester if they are taking all of the same courses. Yet we would want an internal model with two distinct Schedule instances that happen to reference the same set of courses. The reason is that if one student were to drop a course halfway through the term, we would not want that course implicitly dropped from the friend's schedule. This type of model is akin to the example of a couple with separate portfolios that include common accounts.

Revisiting equivalence testing

For most of the built-in classes, the definition of equivalence is natural. However, testing the equivalence of lists brings up a more interesting design issue. Each list models a sequence of *references* rather than a sequence of actual objects. So the question arises whether the lists are equivalent only when those references are the same, or more liberally, if the references are to equivalent (yet not identical) objects. In Python, the semantics of == is the latter interpretation, namely that two lists are equivalent if their respective underlying elements are pairwise equivalent. Thus expression a == b is evaluated as a[0] == b[0] **and** a[1] == b[1] **and** ... . By this definition, a given list is equivalent to itself, equivalent to another list that references the same elements, or to another list that refer-ences distinct elements so long as those elements are considered equivalent to the original list's elements. Notice that the subsequent equivalence tests between elements will be performed in a context that depends upon the type of objects involved.

10.2.2 Copying Objects

When objects reference other objects, we have to think very carefully about what it means to copy an object. There are two standard notions. A *shallow copy* of an original instance is a new instance whose attributes reference the same objects as the original. In contrast, a *deep copy* of an original instance is one whose attributes are assigned to be independent (deep) copies of the respective values referenced by the original. In certain contexts, there can also be intermediate notions of copying that fall somewhere between shallow and deep, depending on the desired semantics.

To explore the basic differences, we consider the following scenario. Assume that data is a list of points, each of which is represented by the Point class defined in Sec-tion 6.2. Our goal is to normalize each of those points, yet we also wish to retain a copy of the original data. A reasonable (yet flawed) attempt at achieving this goal is

```
backup = list(data)
for p in data:
  p.normalize( )
```

We introduced the syntax **list**(data) long ago as a way to copy a list (see Section 2.2.4). However, the new list is a *shallow* copy of the original, in that it references the same underlying points. After mutating the points in the for loop, we no longer have any record of the original point values.

What we need to do is to create a *deep* copy of the data. We can do this manually by creating a new list and placing a *copy* of each point on that list. We can even perform our normalization within that loop, so long as it is after we record the original value.

```
backup = [ ]
for p in data:
  newP = Point(p.getX( ), p.getY( ))   # a new Point instance
  backup.append(newP)
  p.normalize( )                        # normalize the original
```

FOR THE GURU

Taking a slice of an existing list produces a new list, but the new slice references the same objects as the original list (i.e., there is no deep copy of the contents).

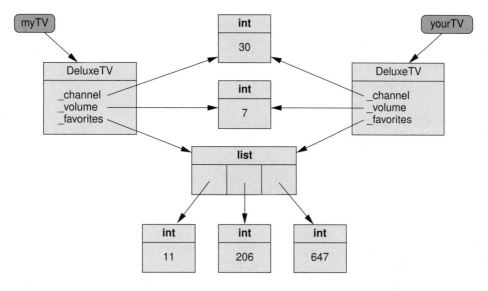

FIGURE 10.14: A shallow copy of a DeluxeTV.

The copy module

In the previous example, we made a deep copy of a list of points, but our technique relied upon our knowledge of the Point class. We used the syntax Point(p.getX( ), p.getY( )) to create a new Point instance that was in essence an independent copy of the existing point.

In other situations, we want to copy an object without having such specific knowl–edge. Python provides a general approach. There is a standard copy module that can be imported. That module includes two functions:

- copy(x) — produces a shallow copy of object x,
- deepcopy(x) — produces a deep copy of object x.

Each of these returns a newly created object that is appropriately copied from the given parameter. However, these functions are easily misused. Consider the DeluxeTV class. Executing the command yourTV = copy(myTV) produces a shallow copy. However, a shallow copy as shown in Figure 10.14 results in an inconsistent model. Notice that the attributes of the two televisions reference the same underlying objects. Interestingly, the aliasing of _channel and _volume is okay because the underlying objects are immutable. For example, if myTV.volumeUp( ) is invoked, this does not alter the **int** portrayed in the diagram. Instead, it creates a new **int** with value 8, and reassigns myTV._channel to that integer while leaving yourTV._channel unchanged. The problem here is the underlying alias of the (mutable) _favorites list. Calling myTV.addToFavorites( ) adds the current channel value 30 to that list. But this affects the apparent set of favorites from the perspec–tive of yourTV. In the case of a DeluxeTV, a deep copy is more appropriate.

Without understanding the internal representation of an object, it can be difficult to choose the proper copying model. For some classes, neither form of copying produces the correct semantics. For example, copying a Python file object is entirely disallowed since that object is just an interface to manage an underlying operating system file. If an open file object were copied, it would not be clear what is intended when subsequently reading or writing data using a combination of the objects, both of which presumably affect a single underlying file on the system.

10.3   Objects in the Context of a Function

With our deeper understanding of objects and references, we wish to take a closer look at several important issues in the context of a function. First, we consider how information is passed to and from a function in the form of parameters and return values. Then, we discuss how an optional parameter is assigned to a default value.

10.3.1   Information Passing

We discussed the correspondence between *formal parameters* and *actual parameters* when first introducing functions in Section 5.2. But for the sake of review, consider the follow-ing function implementation. This function verifies that an account holds assets of at least some given threshold, akin to a check that might be performed as part of a credit check.

```
def verifyBalance(account, threshold):
    """Check whether the balance of the given account meets a threshold."""
    meetsThreshold = account.getBalance( ) >= threshold
    return meetsThreshold
```

In this example the identifiers account and threshold serve as formal parameters. These are placeholders for the information that will later be sent by the caller. The caller invokes the function using a syntax such as

```
claimedAssets = 200.0
qualifies = verifyBalance(mySavings, claimedAssets)
```

In this context, the expressions mySavings and claimedAssets are actual parameters. That information must somehow be communicated so that it can be accessed from within the

FOR THE GURU

Deep copying provides a convenient way to make a complete and independent copy of an object. A related topic, known as *serialization*, is the process of saving the internal state of an object to a file and later re-creating the internal configura-tion by reading that file. For primitive data types, we could easily create a simple file format to save the data. However, for more complex, referential objects, this is a nontrivial task. Python provides a module pickle that supports such serialization.

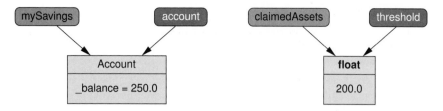

FIGURE 10.15: Assigning formal parameters to the actual parameters.

FIGURE 10.16: The result of the (re)assignment threshold = 2 * threshold.

function body. Different programming languages use different techniques for passing information. In Python, this is performed using the standard assignment semantics, ini‐tializing the formal parameters to reference the actual parameters. In our example, Python makes the following *implicit* assignments as soon as the function is invoked, resulting in the aliasing of Figure 10.15:

```
account = mySavings
threshold = claimedAssets
```

This parameter passing model is used for any type of object, but the consequences depend greatly on whether the actual parameters are mutable or immutable. When an *immutable* object is passed as a parameter, there is no way that the behavior of the func‐tion can affect the underlying object. For instance, although threshold references the same **float** as the caller's claimedAssets, a particular floating‐point instance cannot be mutated. A subsequent assignment from within the function body, such as

```
threshold = 2 * threshold
```

causes the function's identifier to be reassigned, but does not affect the value sent by the caller. The result of this hypothetical command is shown in Figure 10.16.

When the caller designates a *mutable* object as a parameter, the function has full access to the underlying object. This is important to keep in mind when designing func‐tions. For example, the following function can be used to transfer funds from one account to another.

```
def transfer(amount, here, there):
    """Transfer the given amount from here to there."""
    there.deposit( here.withdraw(amount) )
```

The second and third parameters are presumably accounts that are then mutated based on appropriate calls to withdraw and deposit. However, the passing of mutable objects can be abused as well. A deceptive implementation of the verifyBalance account could proceed as follows:

```
def verifyBalance(account, threshold):
    """Check whether the balance of the given account meets a threshold."""
    all = account.getBalance( )
    transfer(all, account, bermuda)
    return False                        # account is empty!
```

Based on the documentation, we would not expect this function to empty our account, but this is enforced in Python only as a matter of trust. The parameter passing is somewhat analogous to giving someone else a reference to your account (e.g., a bank account number) and trusting that he or she will use it appropriately.

Return values

The communication of a return value from a function back to the caller is managed precisely as the passing of parameters. In the case of verifyBalance (the original version), the function returns the object referenced within that context as meetsThreshold. The caller's assignment qualifies = verifyBalance(mySavings, claimedAssets) assigns the identifier qualifies to reference the very object returned by the function. When a function does not explicitly return anything, the special value **None** is returned.

Unnamed objects

In our first example of parameter passing, the caller specified the actual parameters using the identifiers mySavings and claimedAssets. However, actual parameters can be specified as a literal or expression. For example, the caller could have used the syntax

```
qualifies = verifyBalance(mySavings, 200.0)
```

We call that second parameter an ***unnamed object***. Although the caller does not have an explicit name for it, the system ensures that the value is represented with an underlying object that then serves as the actual parameter. A return value is often expressed as an unnamed object from within a function body. For example, rather than declaring and returning meetsThreshold, a more typical syntax is

```
return account.getBalance( ) >= threshold
```

This distinction in syntax is not apparent to the caller of the function. In either case, the caller sees a **bool** instance returned.

Information passing in other languages

Almost all modern programming languages include the concept of a function, with support for passing information from the caller to the function and returning a value from the function to the caller. However, not all languages use the same mechanism for passing the information. There are two basic ways in which information is generally communicated:

1. *by value* — a copy of the underlying data is passed,
2. *by reference* — a reference to the underlying data is passed.

As an analogy, imagine that you are in the library and find an interesting article that you would like a friend to see. Methodology 1 is akin to making a copy of the article to give to your friend. Methodology 2 is akin to telling your friend the call number for locating the article within the library. There are two primary issues to consider when choosing the model for passing information: convenience and data integrity.

Passing a reference is typically easier for the caller. Making a copy of the article would take you more time than simply telling your friend where to find it. The point is that the reference is inherently "smaller" than the complete information and thus easier to communicate. From the perspective of the friend, receiving a reference to the information is slightly less convenient than receiving an actual copy. It requires an additional step of using the reference to retrieve the full information (although on a computer system, this extra effort is relatively negligible). As for the data integrity, when you give your friend a copy it does not matter what she does with that copy. She may write on it, tear it up, or burn it; in any event, this has no effect on the original version sitting in the library. If you were to instead send your friend to the library to retrieve the original, there is a risk of losing data depending on your friend's actions.

The model for passing information in Python is akin to methodology 2; references to underlying objects are sent to and from a function. This provides the advantage of efficiency and allows a function to alter an underlying mutable object, if desired. The main disadvantage is that the caller cannot explicitly prevent a function from altering the object. If more secure protection is necessary, the caller must resort to first making an explicit copy of the original object (as discussed in Section 10.2.2), and then sending the function a reference to the copy. In this way, the function has the ability to mutate the copy, but this does not matter to the caller.

Other programming languages use a combination of approaches for passing information. In Java, the mechanism depends on whether the data being passed belongs to a primitive type. With a primitive type, the data is passed by value; typically, primitive types are small and so making a copy of the data is not such an undue burden. For all other types, information is passed by reference and so mutations made within the function affect the original underlying object. In C++, the programmer designates for each parameter whether it is to be sent by value or by reference. In fact, there is even a third style in which a reference to the underlying data is sent, yet with an explicit requirement that the function is not to mutate the object — a promise that is enforced by the language. This option provides the combination of efficiency and security when passing a large object quickly yet with "read only" semantics. With the choice of three models, an experienced programmer can choose the most advantageous for a given situation.

10.3.2 Optional Parameters

We introduced the use of an optional parameter in Section 5.2.2, with the following example:

```
def countdown(start=10):
  for count in range(start, 0, −1):
    print count
```

In the context of parameter passing, the designated value 10 serves as a default. The formal parameter will generally be assigned to reference the actual parameter indicated by the caller. But if the caller does not specify a value, the formal parameter is assigned to this default value. The use of optional parameters is quite natural—however, there is an important subtlety. In Python, the default object is instantiated when the function is being *defined* (as opposed to at the time the function is *called*). This fact has two important consequences.

Letting a default value depend upon other parameters

At times we may wish to have a default value that depends specifically on the values of other parameters. As a simple example, consider the presumed implementation of the pop method in the built-in **list** class. By default, this method removes the last item of a list; thus waitlist.pop( ) represents the person at the end of the waitlist growing impatient and leaving. However, the pop method accepts an optional parameter that is the index of the item to be removed. Thus waitlist.pop(0) removes the item at the front of the waitlist, per–haps because they are now being served and no longer waiting. Imagine looking behind the scene as if you were the original implementor of that class. How might you declare the signature of this method? At first glance, a reasonable approach might be

```
def pop(self, index = len(self)−1):
```

If the caller sends an explicit index, we will use that, but otherwise we intend to use the length minus one as this is the index of the final element of the current list. Unfortunately, this is not allowed. The formal parameter **self** is not yet associated with an actual object at the time the function is being declared. So the attempt to compute len(**self**) causes an immediate NameError as the function is first declared. When there is a need to base a default value upon the values of other parameters, this assignment must instead be done from within the function body. A typical solution starts with the following legitimate style:

```
def pop(self, index = None):
  if index is None:            # nothing sent by caller
    index = len(self) − 1      # so use this instead
  # ... now go ahead and perform the pop on self[index]
```

By waiting until we are within the body of the function, we can rely upon the fact that the other parameters, **self** in this case, have been properly established. To be fair, we should note there is a much easier approach in the case of pop. Since Python allows negative indices, a default value of index = −1 can be specified.

Beware of using a default value that is mutable

In most cases, we find ourselves wanting to use default values that are immutable (such as an **int** or **str**). Yet in some cases, we may be tempted to use a mutable object as the default value. While this is not outright illegal, it is very important to remember that the default is instantiated once, at the time the function is being declared. This can lead to serious aliasing problems. As an example of the risk, we go back to the DeluxeTV class originally introduced in Section 9.1. There we modeled a television that maintains a list of a viewer's favorite channels. Our original implementation used the following constructor:

```
def __init__(self):
    self._favorites = [ ]
```

and so every television starts with an empty list of favorites. Imagine that we wanted to support a feature allowing the user to specify an original list of favorite channels by using an optional parameter when constructing the television. It would be tempting to write that constructor as

```
def __init__(self, favorites = [ ] ):
    Television.__init__(self)
    self._favorites = favorites
```

Unfortunately, this implementation has a disastrous effect. If we create a television with the syntax myTV = DeluxeTV( ), everything may look okay at first. We get a new instance and because we did not specify an actual parameter, the underlying _favorites attribute is initialized to be a reference to the default value. If this were the only television, we would be okay. But if we were to create a second television yourTV = DeluxeTV( ), we soon have a problem. The problem is that the second television does not get its own empty list; its _favorites attribute is assigned to the same default instances as the first television. This is just another example of aliasing, leading to the same problem as with the shallow copy shown in Figure 10.14.

The proper way to implement the desired behavior is to rely upon **None** as the default parameter value, and then to wait until within the body of the constructor before instanti—ating a new empty list.

```
def __init__(self, favorites = None):
    Television.__init__(self)
    if favorites is None:
        favorites = [ ]              # truly a brand new list
    self._favorites = favorites
```

10.4 Case Study: Subtleties in the cs1graphics Module

We end this chapter by discussing some of the underlying issues in object management, as manifested in the design of cs1graphics. We begin by exploring the treatment of colors. Every instance of a FillableShape maintains an attribute _fillColor that is a reference to

```
1    scene = Canvas( )
2    trunkA = Rectangle(20, 50, Point(50,150) )
3    trunkA.setFillColor('brown')
4    trunkA.setDepth(60)
5    trunkB = Rectangle(20, 50, Point(150,150) )
6    trunkB.setFillColor('brown')
7    trunkB.setDepth(60)
8    scene.add(trunkA)
9    scene.add(trunkB)
10
11   leavesA = Circle(30, Point(50, 100))
12   leavesB = Circle(30, Point(150, 100))
13   seasonColor = Color('green')     # instance of Color class
14   leavesA.setFillColor(seasonColor)
15   leavesB.setFillColor(seasonColor)
16   scene.add(leavesA)
17   scene.add(leavesB)
18
19   raw_input('Press return to change seasons. ')
20   seasonColor.setByName('orange') # changes leaves of both trees
21
22   raw_input('Press return to change the right-hand tree. ')
23   leavesB.setFillColor('yellow')    # reassigns B to a new color instance
```

FIGURE 10.17: Demonstrating an intentional aliasing of colors.

an instance of the Color class representing the interior color. A shape's fill color can be changed by calling the setFillColor method. If the parameter sent to that method is an existing Color instance, the fill color will be reassigned to that instance. Alternatively, if a string or an RGB tuple is sent, the fill color is reassigned to a newly created Color instance matching those specifications.

Consider the code in Figure 10.17, which draws two simple trees (we do not display the image in this book, but invite you to execute the code on your own). Lines 1–9 of the program are straightforward, establishing rectangular trunks for each tree, with colors set according to a string name. The more interesting portion of this example involves the colors for the two circles that represent the leaves of the trees. At line 13 we create a Color instance that is initially green. We use this same instance when setting the fill colors of the two different trees at lines 14 and 15. This brings us to the underlying configuration portrayed in Figure 10.18. The identifiers leavesA and leavesB are pointing to two different circles. However, both circles are pointing to the same fill color. This sets the scenario for the command at line 20. That command mutates the Color instance itself, indirectly causing both circles to be redrawn with orange interior. In contrast, the command at line 23 reassigns the fill color for one of the circles. This results in the underlying configuration of Figure 10.19 and an outward change in the appearance of the second tree, but not the first.

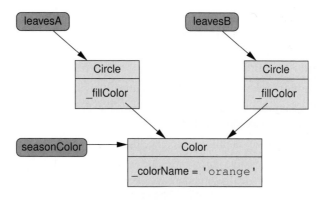

FIGURE 10.18: A brief view after line 20 of Figure 10.17 is executed.

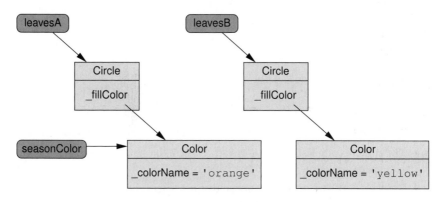

FIGURE 10.19: A brief view after line 23 of Figure 10.17 is executed.

The treatment of Point instances in cs1graphics is very different, by design. Many of the methods accept a point as a parameter, for example the Circle constructor. The fol–lowing code would appear to set up an intentional alias between the centers of two circles:

```
ourPoint = Point(100,100)
ballA = Circle(20, ourPoint)
ballB = Circle(30, ourPoint)
```

However, moving one of those circles does not have any effect on the other. Similarly, mutating the instance ourPoint has no effect on the circles.

Because of the way that the overall transformations of shapes are maintained inter–nally, the cs1graphics intentionally copies all points when they are passed as parameters or return values. This is a fact which is clearly documented within the module.

Fortunately, there is no need to have two objects alias the same underlying Point. Those shapes can be moved in unison by placing them together in a Layer. There was no corresponding way to achieve the effect of shared colors without the intentionally aliasing of a Color instance.

10.5 Chapter Review

10.5.1 Key Points

Objects and References

- An identifier serves as a *reference* to an underlying object.
- Given an identifier something, we can determine the identity of the object to which it points by using the syntax id(something). Distinct objects are guaranteed to have unique IDs.
- When two or more identifiers reference the same underlying object, we call them *aliases*.
- There are two possible forms of equivalence testing. The syntax a **is** b checks whether the two identifiers are referencing the same underlying object. The syntax a == b checks whether two identifiers reference objects that are considered equivalent (where the precise view of equivalence is defined by that class's __eq__ method).
- Python uses *garbage collection* to reclaim the memory used for an object that has become inaccessible to the program (for instance, because there are no longer any references to it).
- Each time a **list** literal is used in code, such as ['a', 'b', 'c'], this causes the instantiation of a new list. For immutable primitives, multiple uses of the same literal may be aliased to a single underlying object. The aliasing causes no harm since the object cannot be mutated.

Objects that Reference Other Objects

- The attributes stored in the state of an instance are actually references to other objects.
- The contents of a **list** are not stored directly in the state of that list. That state stores only a sequence of references to external objects.
- A form of aliasing occurs when two distinct objects both reference a third object. This can be a valuable modeling technique, yet when used improperly results can be disastrous.

Copying Objects

- The copy module can be imported. It supports two different functions, copy and deepcopy.
- The copy function creates a *shallow* copy of an object. The attributes of the new instance are references to the same underlying objects referenced by the original instance.
- When *deep* copying is used, each attribute of the new instance references its own (deep) copy of the corresponding attribute of the original instance.

Objects in the Context of a Function

- The formal parameter is simply an identifier assigned to reference the underlying object indicated by the caller as an actual parameter when the function is invoked.
- If the actual parameter is mutable, changes made within the function have a lasting effect.
- If the identifier serving as a formal parameter is itself reassigned within the body, this does not change the caller's object; instead, the function's identifier is just reassigned to the newly indicated value.
- The mechanism for communicating the return value works just as that for the parameters.
- When a default value is specified for an optional parameter within the declaration of a function, that value is instantiated at the time the function is first defined. If this default object is mutable, it will be shared by all instances that rely upon it.

10.5.2 Glossary

actual parameter The object that is sent by a caller when invoking a function; *compare to* formal parameter.

alias An identifier that refers to the same underlying object as another identifier.

deep copy A copy of an instance whose attributes are created as independent (deep) copies of the respective values referenced by the original.

formal parameter An identifier used in the signature of a function declaration that serves as a placeholder for the value of an actual parameter sent by the caller.

garbage collection A technique by which Python reclaims the memory used on objects for which there no longer exist any valid references.

reference A separate entity (often an underlying memory address) that is used to track the location of some information. For example, an ***identifier*** serves in Python as a reference to an underlying object.

shallow copy A copy of an original instance is one whose attributes are assigned to reference the same objects as the original.

10.5.3 Exercises

Understanding Objects and References

Practice 10.1: Using the new style, as in Figure 10.2(b), draw a diagram of the final con-figuration that results after executing the following program:

```
a = Account( )
a.deposit(200)
b = Account( )
b.deposit(100)
c = a
a = b
b = c
```

Practice 10.2: Consider the following program:

```
values = [1, 57, 34]
x = 47
values.append(x)
x = 13
numbers = values
numbers.append(x)

print values
print numbers
```

Show the output generated when this code is executed.

Exercise 10.3: Using the new style, as in Figure 10.2(b), draw a diagram of the final configuration that results after executing the following program:

```
v = Account( )
w = Account( )
x = v
v.deposit(100)
w.deposit(200)
x.deposit(400)
v.withdraw(25)
w.withdraw(25)
x.withdraw(25)
```

Exercise 10.4: The __contains__ method of the **list** class is used to determine whether a
given element is contained within a list. Given our knowledge of a list as a sequence
of references, we might re-examine the precise semantics of this built-in behavior.
There are two possible interpretations of containment: (A) that it checks whether a
given object is itself an element of the list; (B) that it checks whether the list contains
an element that is equivalent to the given parameter.

Your job is to perform experiments to conclusively determine which of these
interpretations is supported by Python's lists. In explaining your solution, give the
text of an interpreter session (including Python's responses) that constitutes your
"experiment." Then clearly state your conclusion and why the experiment supports
your conclusion.

Exercise 10.5: Implement a function hasAliasing(data) that takes a list data and returns
True if that list contains two or more elements that are actually references to the
same underlying object. As a test of your function, you should observe the following:

```
>>> a = range(5)
>>> b = range(4)
>>> c = range(5)
>>> hasAliasing( [a, b, c] )
False
>>> hasAliasing( [a, b, c, b] )
True
```

Objects that Reference Other Objects

Practice 10.6: On page 344 we describe a scenario with complete independence, in which
two people manage separate lists of accounts, where none of the accounts are shared.
Using the style of Figures 10.10–10.13, diagram such a configuration.

Practice 10.7: Using the style of Figure 10.7, draw a diagram of the final configuration
that results after executing the following program.

```
f = list('name')
g = f
g[0] = 's'
```

Practice 10.8: Using the style of Figure 10.7, draw a diagram of the final configuration that results after executing the following program:

```
j = list('name')
k = list(j)
k[0] = 's'
```

Exercise 10.9: Using the style of Figure 10.7, draw a diagram of the final configuration that results after executing the following program:

```
c = range(3)
d = c
c.append(7)
e = list(d)
e.append(8)
```

Exercise 10.10: Assume that someone uses the identifier myHouse as a reference to an object representing the actual house in which he or she lives. Using the real–world analogy of houses, explain the semantics that would be expressed by each of the following Python expressions.

    (a) myHouse **is** yourHouse

    (b) myHouse == yourHouse

    (c) myHouse = yourHouse

    (d) myHouse = copy(yourHouse)

    (e) myHouse = deepcopy(yourHouse)

    (f) In English, the familiar phrase "my house is your house" is used to welcome a guest into a host's home, suggesting that he share the house as if it were his own possession. None of the above Python expressions properly captures the spirit of this original phrase. Give a Python syntax that more accurately portrays this meaning.

Objects in the Context of a Function

Practice 10.11: The following method is designed to accept a **list** sent by the caller and change the state of that list so as to empty it (if not already empty):

```
def clear(data):
    """Empties the given list"""
    data = [ ]
```

Unfortunately, this implementation is flawed. Explain in your own words why the given code fails.

Exercise 10.12: Give a correct implementation of the clear(data) method, as was orig–inally discussed in Practice 10.11. The function should not return anything, but rather change the state of the list specified by the caller.

Exercise 10.13: On page 352, we gave the beginning of an implementation of the **list**.pop method that supports the syntax groceries.pop(5) as well as groceries.pop( ). Here is a very similar implementation, but unfortunately a flawed one.

```
def pop(self, index = None):
    if not index:                    # nothing sent by caller
        index = len(self) − 1        # so use this instead
    # ... now go ahead and perform the pop of self[index]
```

This attempt has a *very* subtle, yet critical bug. Suggest a specific setting in which the outward behavior of this implementation would differ from that of the standard implementation. Explain why the flawed syntax leads to that behavior.

C H A P T E R 11

Recursion

Computers get much of their power from repetition. For example, in Section 4.3 we used a loop to draw successive levels of the following pyramid:

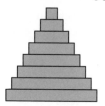

In this chapter, we introduce another form of repetition known as ***recursion*** that can be used to design classes and functions. We begin by demonstrating ***structural recursion*** as a natural way to define objects that have one or more (smaller) instances of the same class as attributes. For example the 8-level pyramid can be viewed as a single bottom level with a 7-level pyramid built on top. That 7-level pyramid is itself a bottom level with a 6-level pyramid on top of it, and so on. Eventually we reach a so-called ***base case*** in which recursion is no longer necessary; for this example, a 1-level pyramid is a single block. In this chapter we consider two detailed implementations using structural recursion. First we augment our graphics package to include a class that represents a bullseye pattern. Second, we we provide our very own (recursive) implementation of a list class.

A second form of recursion, known as ***functional recursion***, occurs when a behavior is expressed using a "smaller" version of that same behavior. For example a common childhood game involves one player guessing a number from 1 to 100 while the other gives hints as to whether the true answer is higher or lower than the guess. A wise strategy for a player is to guess the middle value, in this case 50. If that guess is not correct, the hint will narrow the remaining search to either the range 1 to 49 or the range 51 to 100. The strategy at this point can be described as a repetition of the original strategy, although adapted to consider the currently known lower and upper bounds. Much as a function can call another function, it is allowed to (recursively) call itself. We will explore several examples of functional recursion in the latter part of the chapter.

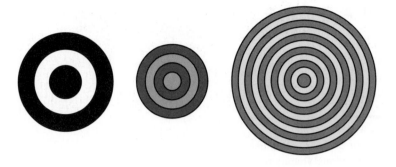

FIGURE 11.1: Bullseye instances with 3, 4, and 11 bands respectively.

11.1 A Bullseye Class

We begin by considering the development of a bullseye class within the framework of our graphics package. We envision a bullseye as a sequence of concentric circles with alternating colors, as shown in Figure 11.1. Although we could create this image using a loop, this is a natural opportunity to demonstrate recursion. A bullseye can be viewed as a single outer circle with a smaller bullseye drawn on top. Of course the smaller bullseye should be positioned so that its center is exactly the same as the outer circle.

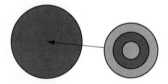

We use structural recursion to develop a Bullseye class. Internally, a bullseye instance maintains two attributes: _outer, which is the outermost circle, and _rest, which is a ref—erence to another bullseye providing the interior structure. For the public interface, we allow the user to specify the total number of bands, the overall radius of the bullseye, and the choice of two colors. Complete code for the class is given in Figure 11.2. Our class formally inherits from the Drawable class of the cs1graphics module so that it can be incor—porated as part of that graphics package (see Section 9.4 for similar use of inheritance).

The constructor accepts four parameters (numBands, radius, primary, secondary), where the bands alternate in color starting with primary as the outermost band. At line 10, we invoke the parent constructor to establish the relevant state of a Drawable object (as is standard when using inheritance). Lines 11 and 12 create a single circle to represent the outermost band of our bullseye. As such, its radius is set to the desired radius of the overall bullseye and its color is set to primary. Lines 14–18 are used to establish the rest of the bullseye. If the caller requests a bullseye with a single band, then the outer circle trivially suffices. In this case, we set **self.**_rest to **None** at line 15 to signify that there is no rest of the bullseye. This serves as our base case. More generally, we establish the rest of the bullseye as a smaller version of a bullseye. The inner bullseye is constructed at line 18 with different parameters than the original, having a smaller radius and inverted use of colors.

```
1    from cs1graphics import *
2
3    class Bullseye(Drawable):
4      def __init__(self, numBands, radius, primary='black', secondary='white'):
5        if numBands <= 0:
6          raise ValueError('Number of bands must be positive')
7        if radius <= 0:
8          raise ValueError('radius must be positive')
9
10       Drawable.__init__(self)                       # must call parent constructor
11       self._outer = Circle(radius)
12       self._outer.setFillColor(primary)
13
14       if numBands == 1:
15         self._rest = None
16       else:  # create new bullseye with one less band, reduced radius, and inverted colors
17         innerR = float(radius) * (numBands-1) / numBands
18         self._rest = Bullseye(numBands-1, innerR, secondary, primary)
19
20     def getNumBands(self):
21       bandcount = 1                                 # outer is always there
22       if self._rest:                                # still more
23         bandcount += self._rest.getNumBands( )
24       return bandcount
25
26     def getRadius(self):
27       return self._outer.getRadius( )              # ask the circle
28
29     def setColors(self, primary, secondary):
30       self._outer.setFillColor(primary)
31       if self._rest:
32         self._rest.setColors(secondary, primary)   # color inversion
33
34     def _draw(self):
35       self._beginDraw( )                            # required protocol for Drawable
36       self._outer._draw( )                          # draw the circle
37       if self._rest:
38         self._rest._draw( )                         # recursively draw the rest
39       self._completeDraw( )                         # required protocol for Drawable
```

FIGURE 11.2: Complete code for our Bullseye implementation (documentation excluded).

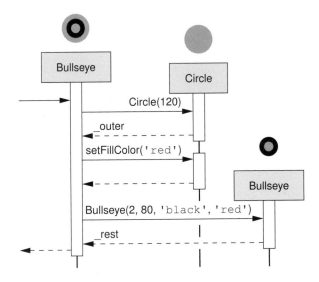

FIGURE 11.3: Top-level trace of Bullseye(3, 120, `'red'`, `'black'`)

Unfolding a recursion

There are two ways to envision the recursive process. When we discussed the flow of control in Section 5.2.1, we drew an analogy between calling a function and hiring a contractor to do some work. The original caller interacts with the contractor, yet does not follow the precise details of how that work is accomplished. As an example consider the construction of a three–banded bullseye, Bullseye(3, 120, `'red'`, `'black'`). Figure 11.3 portrays a top–level trace of the process. We first see the creation and configuration of the outer circle, and then the creation of an inner bullseye, instantiated as Bullseye(2, 80, `'black'`, `'red'`). In some sense, it is just that easy. But there is more happening behind the scene. Our code defining the creation of a bullseye relies upon the presumption that we have means for creating another bullseye (at line 18). How is that other bullseye created? Using the same algorithm!

To truly understand recursion, it helps to more carefully trace the complete execution through a process called ***unfolding a recursion***. Figure 11.4 provides such a diagram for our sample bullseye. If you take the perspective of the original bullseye, portrayed on the far left of the diagram, its interactions are identical to that shown in Figure 11.3. It initiates the construction of the outer circle, the coloring of that circle, and the construction of an inner bullseye. What is new in Figure 11.4 is the detailed portrayal of the subsequent construction Bullseye(2, 80, `'black'`, `'red'`). It progresses by creating a black outer circle with radius 80 and then its own inner bullseye, with parameters Bullseye(1, 40, `'red'`, `'black'`). The last case is traced as well, but the construction algorithm proceeds differently because the desired number of bands is one. An appropriate outer circle is constructed and colored, but the rest of this bullseye is set to **None**.

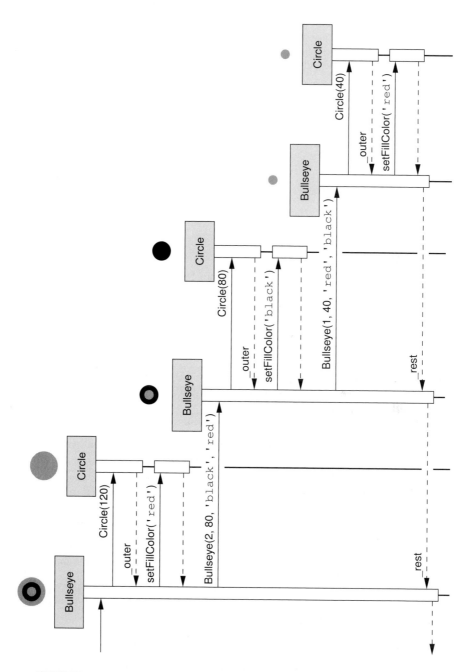

FIGURE 11.4: Unfolding the recursion Bullseye(3, 120, 'red', 'black')

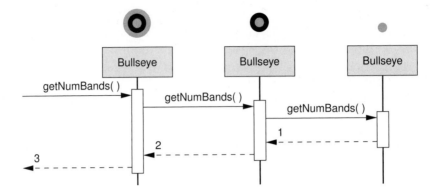

FIGURE 11.5: Sequence diagram for the call getNumBands( ).

Additional Bullseye methods

Our class supports several additional methods. The getNumBands method, at lines 20–24, returns the total number of bands to the caller. Although we did not explicitly record this value it is easily recalculated with the following recursion:

```
20   def getNumBands(self):
21     bandcount = 1                                # outer is always there
22     if self._rest:                               # still more
23       bandcount += self._rest.getNumBands( )
24     return bandcount
```

Each bullseye has an outer band, accounted for at line 21. If that were the only band then the answer is one. However, if we find that an inner bullseye exists, we must account for the bands that are contained within that inner portion. We use recursion at line 23 to ask the inner bullseye how many bands it contains, and then add that to our band count to get the final answer that we return to the original caller. We trace a sample execution of this method in Figure 11.5.

In contrast to the implementation of getNumBands, the getRadius method is natu-rally expressed without any use of recursion. To determine the radius of our bullseye, we simply need to know the radius of the outer circle.

```
26   def getRadius(self):
27     return self._outer.getRadius( )                # ask the circle
```

We note that the call to getRadius at line 27 is *not* recursive; rather this invokes the getRadius method of the Circle instance (not of another Bullseye instance). This is an example of polymorphism, as both classes support a getRadius method with different underlying implementations.

The mutator setColors(primary, secondary) recolors an existing bullseye. Thinking recursively, we simply change the outer circle to be the desired primary color and then tell the inner bullseye (if any) to recolor itself.

```
29    def setColors(self, primary, secondary):
30        self._outer.setFillColor(primary)
31        if self._rest:
32            self._rest.setColors(secondary, primary)    # color inversion
```

The only catch is that we need to instruct that inner bullseye to recolor itself so that it uses our secondary color as its primary, and vice versa. This inversion of the color parameters is quite similar to the technique we used in our original constructor.

Finally, having inherited from Drawable, our bullseye automatically supports interesting behaviors such as move, scale, rotate,[1] and clone. However, based on the protocol of cs1graphics, we are responsible for implementing the _draw method to display the bullseye. The core of our routine includes the following commands:

```
36        self._outer._draw( )              # draw the circle
37        if self._rest:
38            self._rest._draw( )           # recursively draw the rest
```

Notice that we always draw the outer circle, and in the case where there remains a rest of the bullseye, we draw that (recursively) on top of the outer circle. The order of these commands is significant to achieve the desired effect, as the depth attributes are not relevant when implementing the low-level _draw.

 A WORD OF WARNING

Every recursion must have a base case. Although recursion is a powerful technique, there must always exist at least one case that can be described without further use of recursion. Just as an improperly formed loop can repeat infinitely, so can an ill-formed recursion. Using our contractor analogy, we cannot have everyone passing off work to another person. For recursion to work, we must reach a scenario in which a person handles a request without assistance.

In our Bullseye class, the case of a single-banded bullseye serves as the base case. This is true not just of the initial construction, but of our implementation of the various behaviors. For example, a single-banded bullseye answers getNumBands without a recursive call because it recognizes its own lack of an inner bullseye.

---
1.   Admittedly, rotating a bullseye is not the most interesting behavior. But rotations are helpful for other recursive figures.

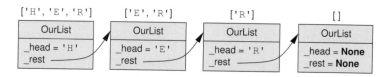

FIGURE 11.6: Underlying recursive structure for our list [' H ' , ' E ' , ' R '].

11.2   Our Own List Implementation

As our next example, we develop our own list implementation from scratch. Obviously, Python already includes the built-in **list** class,[2] so there is no need for us to do this. At the same time, it is empowering to realize that we can develop such an interesting class our-selves, had it not already been provided. The idea is to view a list as a recursive structure. Each list will be represented with two attributes: _head, which represents the first element of the list, and _rest, which is itself a list of all remaining items. So a list of three elements is represented as a first element and a remaining list of two items. That list of two items is represented as a single element followed by a list with one item. Even the list of length one is viewed as a single element followed by a list of zero remaining elements. We use an empty list as our base case and represent it by setting both _head and _rest to **None**. An example of our representation is shown in Figure 11.6, for the list [' H ' , ' E ' , ' R '].

Preliminaries

To begin our class definition, we provide a constructor that produces an initially empty list.

```
class OurList:
  def __init__(self):
    self._head = None
    self._rest = None
```

Many of our remaining methods use an empty list as the base case for the recursion, so to improve the legibility of these other methods, we introduce a private utility function _isEmpty that determines whether a given list matches the empty configuration.

```
def _isEmpty(self):
  return self._rest is None
```

append method

The append method is responsible for adding a given element to the end of the list. With our recursive view, this is rather straightforward. If we are adding a value to an empty list, we make the necessary modifications directly. That empty list should be turned into a list of one item, with the new value at its head and a new empty list to represent the rest. Alter-natively, if we receive a request to append a value to a nonempty list, we pass the buck.

---

2.   For the record, the actual implementation used for Python's version of **list** is not recursive; see Chap-ter 12 for discussion.

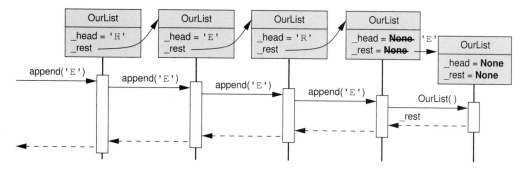

FIGURE 11.7: A call to append(`'E'`) upon list [`'H'`, `'E'`, `'R'`].

Appending the new item to the end of the *remaining* sublist serves the purpose of adding it to the end of the complete list. These intuitions lead to the following implementation:

```
def append(self, value):
    if self._isEmpty( ):
        self._head = value                  # we now have one element
        self._rest = OurList( )             # followed by new empty list
    else:
        self._rest.append(value)            # pass it on
```

A sample trace of this code is shown in Figure 11.7. As the recursion unfolds we eventually reach our base case, and therefore make the local modification to reflect the change.

count method

We next consider the count method. This accessor is responsible for counting the number of occurrences of a given value on the list. We implement it recursively as follows:

```
def count(self, value):
    if self._isEmpty( ):
        return 0
    else:
        subtotal = self._rest.count(value)   # recursion
        if self._head == value:              # additional match
            subtotal += 1
        return subtotal
```

An empty list serves as our base case, as it clearly has a count of zero. Otherwise, we use recursion to ask the rest of our list how many occurrences of the given value it has. Once we know that piece of information, we are almost ready to answer the question that was asked of us. But we must also consider the head of our list. If it matches the target value then the overall number of occurrences on our list is one more than that reported by our sublist.

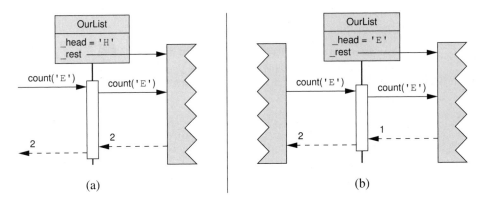

FIGURE 11.8: A local view of calls to count('E') upon list ['H', 'E', 'R', 'E'].
(a) Shows a view of the initial call; (b) shows a view of the next call.

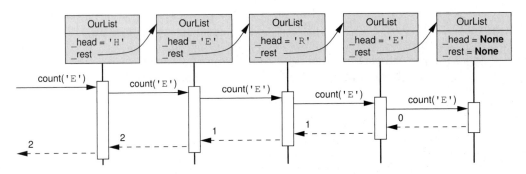

FIGURE 11.9: The complete trace of count('E') upon list ['H', 'E', 'R', 'E'].

The code for count is written from the perspective of a single level of the recursion. We can visualize the perspective of a single object as shown in Figure 11.8. Part (a) of that figure shows the top-level call. From the perspective of that instance, it learns (through recursion) that the remainder of the list has two occurrences of E. Given that its head is an H, it concludes that its entire list has only those two occurrences. Part (b) shows the perspective of the secondary recursion. That object is asked how many E's are on its list, and determines that there are two, one on its sublist and one at the head. If we were to stitch together all such local views, we get the fully unfolded recursion as shown in Figure 11.9.

The __contains__ method

The __contains__ method is used to provide support for a shorthand syntax of the form val **in** data. This method is responsible for returning **True** when the value is found within the list and **False** otherwise. What makes the style of this recursion different from count is the form of the base case. For count, the base case is an empty list. In any other scenario, there is no way to accurately report the count without examining the sublist. Our implementation of __contains__ relies upon two possible base cases, as shown in the following code.

```
def __contains__(self, value):
    if self._isEmpty( ):
        return False
    elif self._head == value:
        return True
    else:
        return value in self._rest        # recurse
```

If a list is empty, then clearly the element is not found. Alternatively, if the head of our list matches the target, then we may confidently return **True** without bothering to look at the remaining sublist. It is only in the third case that we apply recursion. If the value occurs on that sublist, then it occurs in the full list; if not on the sublist, it does not occur anywhere. We express this logic simply by returning the result of the expression value **in self._rest**, relying upon the implicit recursion that is used to evaluate the **in** operator.

The __getitem__ method

A different recursive pattern occurs in our implementation of the __getitem__ method, which is used to support a syntax such as data[i] for retrieving the element at a specified index of a list. There are several interesting aspects of the following implementation:

```
def __getitem__(self, i):
    if self._isEmpty( ):
        raise IndexError('list index out of range')
    elif i == 0:
        return self._head
    else:
        return self._rest[i−1]              # recurse
```

To begin, if someone attempts to access an element of an empty list, we immediately raise an IndexError, in accordance with the behavior of Python's built-in **list** class in this situation (see Section 5.5 for a discussion of raising exceptions). This serves as an important base case, guarding against use of an illegal index (see Exercise 11.14). Assuming our list is nonempty, the next task is to see whether the given index is 0. If so, the user is interested in the head of our list and we answer the question without examining the rest of the list. In the remaining case, we rely on the use of recursion, although with a changing parameterization. Retrieving the i-th element of a given list is equivalent to retrieving the (i-1)th element of the rest of the list. A sample trace of this behavior is shown in Figure 11.10.

Completing our class

With practice, we can go on to develop recursive implementations for almost all of the behaviors supported by Python's lists. A reasonably complete implementation of the class is given in Figure 11.11. Most of those methods are accomplished using similar techniques to the methods we have discussed. For example, count is quite similar to __len__, reaching an empty list as a base case. The three cases of __contains__ are very similar to those of index, and __getitem__ closely parallels __setitem__. We also provide an

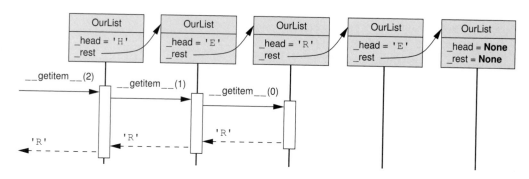

FIGURE 11.10: The underlying evaluation for the syntax data[2], using data
['H', 'E', 'R', 'E'].

implementation of __repr__ designed to mimic Python's list representation. The mutators insert and remove are similar to append in spirit, but their details are considerably
more subtle. Figure 11.11 includes a correct implementation of those routines, although
we suggest tracing through several sample executions to better understand the process (see
Exercise 11.12 and Exercise 11.13).

```
1   class OurList:
2     def __init__(self):
3       self._head = None
4       self._rest = None
5
6     def _isEmpty(self):
7       return self._rest is None
8
9     def __len__(self):
10      if self._isEmpty( ):
11        return 0
12      else:
13        return 1 + len(self._rest)              # recurse
14
15    def count(self, value):
16      if self._isEmpty( ):
17        return 0
18      else:
19        subtotal = self._rest.count(value)      # recursion
20        if self._head == value:                 # additional match
21          subtotal += 1
22        return subtotal
```

FIGURE 11.11: The implementation of OurList (continued on next page).

```
23    def __contains__(self, value):
24      if self._isEmpty( ):
25        return False
26      elif self._head == value:
27        return True
28      else:
29        return value in self._rest                    # recurse
30
31    def index(self, value):
32      if self._isEmpty( ):
33        raise ValueError('OurList.index(x): x not in list')
34      elif self._head == value:
35        return 0
36      else:                                            # look in remainder of the list
37        return 1 + self._rest.index(value)
38
39    def __getitem__(self, i):
40      if self._isEmpty( ):
41        raise IndexError('list index out of range')
42      elif i == 0:
43        return self._head
44      else:
45        return self._rest[i-1]                         # recurse
46
47    def __setitem__(self, i, value):
48      if self._isEmpty( ):
49        raise IndexError('list assignment index out of range')
50      elif i == 0:
51        self._head = value
52      else:
53        self._rest[i-1] = value                        # recurse
54
55    def __repr__(self):
56      if self._isEmpty( ):
57        return '[]'
58      elif self._rest._isEmpty( ):
59        return '[' + repr(self._head) + ']'
60      else:
61        return '[' + repr(self._head) + ',  ' + repr(self._rest)[1:]  # remove extra [
```

FIGURE 11.11 (continuation): The implementation of OurList (continued on next page).

```
62    def append(self, value):
63      if self._isEmpty( ):
64        self._head = value              # we now have one element
65        self._rest = OurList( )          # followed by new empty list
66      else:
67        self._rest.append(value)         # pass it on
68
69    def insert(self, index, value):
70      if self._isEmpty( ):              # inserting at end; similar to append
71        self._head = value
72        self._rest = OurList( )
73      elif index == 0:                   # new element goes here!
74        shift = OurList( )
75        shift._head = self._head
76        shift._rest = self._rest
77        self._head = value
78        self._rest = shift
79      else:                              # insert recursively
80        self._rest.insert(index−1, value)
81
82    def remove(self, value):
83      if self._isEmpty( ):
84        raise ValueError('OurList.remove(x): x not in list')
85      elif self._head == value:
86        self._head = self._rest._head
87        self._rest = self._rest._rest
88      else:
89        self._rest.remove(value)
```

FIGURE 11.11 (continuation): The implementation of OurList.

11.3 Functional Recursion

Our earlier examples of recursion are structural, as we have objects whose states include references to similar objects. Yet those examples also demonstrate the principle of functional recursion, as most of the behaviors depended upon recursive calls to the same algorithm. In the remainder of the chapter, we wish to demonstrate several classic examples of functional recursion (in the absence of any structural recursion).

We begin by discussing a simple mathematical example. The factorial of a number, commonly written as $n!$, is an important combinatorial concept. It represents the number of ways that n items can be ordered (so-called ***permutations***). It is defined as

$$n! = n \cdot (n-1) \cdot (n-2) \cdot (n-3) \cdots 3 \cdot 2 \cdot 1$$

since there are n possible choices for the first item, after which $n-1$ possible choices for the second item, $n-2$ choices for the third, and so on. Given this formula, it would

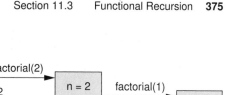

FIGURE 11.12: The trace of a call to factorial(4).

be quite easy to compute the factorial of a number using a loop. However, we wish to demonstrate a simple recursive approach. The key observation is the recognition that the formula corresponding to $(n-1)!$ factorial appears as a part of the $n!$ formula.

$$n! = n \cdot \underbrace{(n-1) \cdot (n-2) \cdot (n-3) \cdots 3 \cdot 2 \cdot 1}_{(n-1)!}$$

We see that $n! = n \cdot (n-1)!$ in general; as a base case we know that $1! = 1$. Going back to our definition of a factorial as the number of ways of arranging n items, we can view the recursion intuitively. We can select any of the n items to be first, and for each such choice we have $(n-1)!$ ways to subsequently order the remaining $n-1$ items. Turning this idea into code, we define the following recursive function:

```python
def factorial(n):
    """Compute the factorial of n.

    n is presumed to be a positive integer
    """
    if n <= 1:
        return 1
    else:
        return n * factorial(n-1)
```

In our earlier examples of structural recursion, we had a clear notion of distinct objects with their own states. We demonstrated the interactions between these distinct objects using sequence diagrams such as Figure 11.5. When dealing with a pure functional recursion, there are no such objects in play. Yet behind the scene, there is an underlying execution sequence and even a concept of state. This goes back to a lesson from *For the Guru* on page 171 of Section 5.2. Each time a function is called, the system creates an activation record to track the state of that particular invocation. In the context of recursion, each individual call to the function executes the same body of code yet with a separate activation record. We visualize this unfolding recursion as shown in Figure 11.12.

11.4 Binary Search

Assume that we have a list of values and we want to know whether a specific value occurs in that list. This is precisely the functionality provided by the __contains__ method of Python's **list** class. In fact for the remainder of the chapter, we presume that we are back to using the built-in **list** class supported by Python (as opposed to our own list implementation from earlier in this chapter). Behind the scene, the algorithm used by Python's **list** class is known as a ***sequential search***. It starts scanning from the beginning of the list until it either finds what it is looking for, or reaches the end of the list and thus reports a failure. In fact, we even considered a sequential search as an example of a **while** loop on page 162.

In this section, we focus our attention on a similar problem, but this time assuming that the list of values is known to be *sorted*. As a concrete example, we revisit the concept of a ***lexicon*** (a list of strings). We originally considered the task of reading a lexicon from a file as an example on page 280 of Chapter 8. Although we did not presume at the time that the strings were alphabetized in the file, we do so now (or we could explicitly call lexicon.sort( ) after reading the file). In real life, people commonly maintain lexicons in sorted order (e.g., phone books, encyclopedias, guest lists). The reason is that searching within a sorted list is *much* easier. In this section, we leverage our intuition to develop an efficient implementation for searching a sorted list.

11.4.1 Algorithmic Design

Imagine that you are handling security at a party and you have been provided a list of invited guests. As each person arrives you are responsible for checking whether that individual was invited. This is a very large party so there are many invitees and also a rather long line of people waiting to get into the party. It is important that you are as quick as possible in determining whether each name is on the list. If the names on the guest list were arbitrarily ordered, you would have no choice but to rely upon a sequential search. This can be very time consuming; each time someone arrives at the door, you may have to scan the entire list. It is much easier to look for an individual if the guest list is alphabetized. Why is this the case? How might you solve the problem?

The key intuition is the following. Rather than scanning the list from beginning to end, you can jump to a name near the middle of the list and compare that name to the one for which you are looking (let us call this the *target* name). If you are extremely lucky, that middle name may be the target. But the efficiency of our technique is not contingent on us being that lucky. The real key is that even if the middle name is not the same as our target, we get important information by considering whether the target should appear before or after that point in the alphabetized list. If our target should appear before the considered name, then we only have to continue our search on the first half of the original list; similarly, if the target should appear after the middle name, then we only have to search the second half of the original list. With this technique, we are guaranteed to make significant progress in paring down the effective size of the list. More importantly, after narrowing our search to half the list we do not revert to performing a sequential search; we apply recursion! That is, we again consider a name near the middle of the relevant portion of the list and we either find the target or further pare down the relevant portion to half its current size. Continuing in this fashion, we eventually find the target or reach a point when we have eliminated the entire list (and thus conclude that the person was uninvited).

This technique of searching a sorted list is commonly termed ***binary search***, because each step narrows the list into one of two halves. What is amazing is how much faster binary search can be versus a sequential search. Imagine that we start with a list of 1000 names. After one step of our process, we either find the target or reduce the range to 500 names. Even if we are not lucky, after a second step, we are down to at most 250 names, after three steps down to at most 125 names, after four steps, at most 62 names and so on. In fact after at most 10 such steps we will have either found the target or eliminated all possibilities. This is quite an improvement, comparing our target to a selection of only 10 names rather than sequentially comparing to all 1000 original names.

Of course, computers are very fast machines. Even a sequential search of 1000 names is evaluated quickly. But computers must often process significantly longer lists. A sequential search of millions or billions of items can become time consuming, even for fast machines. To analysis the cost of a binary search, we note that the overall number of steps is related to the number of times that we can repeatedly divide a list in half before running out of items. Mathematically, this is equivalent to the concept of a ***logarithm***, specifically a logarithm with base two. So if we start with n original entries, there will be at most $\log_2 n$ steps of a binary search. Putting this into perspective, we already noted that binary search over a list of 1000 entries requires at most 10 steps. For a list of one million items, it requires at most 20 steps; for a list of one billion items, at most 30 steps. Here we see the real victory. Rather than sifting through each of a billion entries, we can determine whether a value is on the list by examining only 30 well-chosen entries.

11.4.2   A Poor Implementation

Our goal is to convert this high-level idea into an actual implementation. Presumably, a reasonable interface for a user would be to provide a general function search(lexicon, target) that returns **True** if the target is found on a given list of strings and **False** otherwise.

In this section, we intentionally provide an awful implementation of the binary search algorithm. This implementation will seem natural and look innocent enough. In fact, it correctly determines the answer. The problem is that it is horribly inefficient — even worse than sequential search. Yet we choose to show this approach first because it is important to understand why it is so flawed. The code for this poor version is shown in Figure 11.13. The conditional at lines 7 and 8 provides an important base case.

```
7    if len(lexicon) == 0:                          # base case
8        return False
```

If we are asked about an empty list, clearly the target is not contained. In fact this is the only case where we definitively conclude that the target is absent.

In any other case, we consider comparing the target to the element at the middle of the list. The concept of the middle is well defined when the list has odd length. If the list has even length, we consider the element slightly right of center. Formally, our definition of the middle index is len(lexicon) // 2, as computed at line 10. As an example, if a list has length 7, the middle index is set to 3 (it truly is the middle of indices $\{0, 1, 2, \mathbf{3}, 4, 5, 6\}$). If a list has length 6, the division results in a choice of 3 for the "middle" (although there is slight asymmetry in $\{0, 1, 2, \mathbf{3}, 4, 5\}$).

```
1   def search(lexicon, target):
2       """Search for the target within lexicon.
3
4       lexicon     a list of words (presumed to be alphabetized)
5       target      the desired word
6       """
7       if len(lexicon) == 0:                            # base case
8           return False
9       else:
10          midIndex = len(lexicon) // 2
11          if target == lexicon[midIndex]:              # found it
12              return True
13          elif target < lexicon[midIndex]:             # check left side
14              return search(lexicon[ : midIndex], target)
15          else:                                        # check right side
16              return search(lexicon[midIndex+1 : ], target)
```

FIGURE 11.13: A bad implementation of the binary search algorithm.

Continuing our examination of the code, lines 11–16 contain the heart of the binary search algorithm. We compare the target to the middle element of the list. One of three things will happen. If we find an exact match, then we immediately report success. Otherwise, if the target is less than the middle item (in alphabetical order), we need only check the left side of the list. We accomplish this at line 14 by recursing upon the slice lexicon[:midIndex]. Recalling the definition of a slice, this is a list that contains the elements from the beginning of the original list, up to but not including the item at midIndex. We intentionally exclude that middle item because we have already determined that it was not a match. Lines 15 and 16 handle the symmetric case, where we wish to search the portion of the list strictly beyond the middle index.

This implementation is technically correct. As an illustrative example, Figure 11.14 gives a trace of the call search(['B','E','G','I','N','S'], 'F') upon this alphabetized list. For the initial call, the length of the lexicon is 6 and so the value of midIndex is set to 6 // 2 which is 3. Then the target 'F' is compared to the middle entry 'I'. This is not a match and since 'F' < 'I', line 14 of the code is executed. Therefore we recurse on the list lexicon[:3], which in this case is ['B','E','G']. The activation of that recursion is on a list with length 3, and so midIndex is set to 3 // 2 which is 1. Therefore the target is compared to 'E' and as 'F' > 'E', line 16 is executed with the slice lexicon[2:], which is simply ['G']. This list has length 1, and so we set midIndex to 1 // 2 which is 0 and so our target is compared to 'G'. We find that 'F' < 'G' and again line 14 is executed with lexicon[:0]. This slice is technically an empty list, as there are no elements at index strictly before 0. So we reach a base case as search([ ], 'F') is called. Having realized that 'F' is not contained in the empty list, we see that 'F' is not on the list ['G'], nor on the list ['B','E','G'] nor on the original list ['B','E','G','I','N','S'].

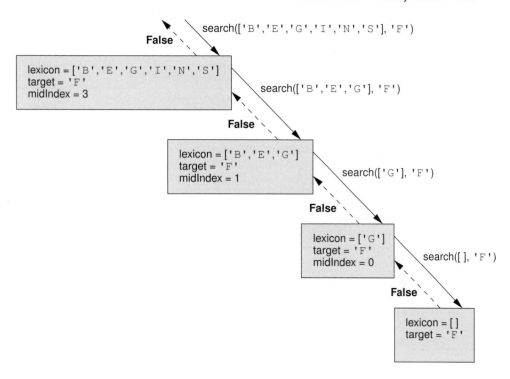

FIGURE 11.14: The trace of the call search(['B','E','G','I','N','S'], 'F') for the inferior implementation of binary search from Figure 11.13.

So what is wrong?

This version of the code correctly answers the question. However, it is very inefficient. Our implementation relies upon the use of Python's **list** class and in particular the following three operations upon those lists: determining the length of a list (lines 7 and 10), retrieving the middle element of a list (lines 11 and 13), and creating a slice of the list (lines 14 and 16). Python's lists are very efficient in reporting the length and in retrieving one particular element at a specified index (see Section 13.2 for more discussion). The culprit involves our use of slices when representing a sublist, as with the syntax lexicon[:midIndex] to designate the left half of the original list. Although a convenient Python syntax, slicing causes a new list to be created that is essentially a copy of the relevant portion of the original list. Creating this slice takes time proportional to the length of the slice, ruining the potential benefits of the binary search algorithm.

For intuition, consider again the analogy of checking a guest list at the door of a party. When processing a guest list with one thousand entries, we quickly compare the target to the middle entry. So far, so good. But if we determine that the first half of the list must be recursively searched, we do not want to be in a position of having to take time to copy those 500 names onto a new sheet of paper so that the sublist can be passed as a parameter to an assistant. We will have spent so much time creating the copy that we may as well have just looked for the target ourselves.

```
1   def search(lexicon, target, start=0, stop=None):
2     """Search for the target within lexicon[start:stop].
3
4     lexicon    a list of words (presumed to be alphabetized)
5     target     the desired word
6     start      the smallest index at which to look (default 0)
7     stop       the index before which to stop (default len(lexicon) )
8     """
9     if stop is None:
10      stop = len(lexicon)
11    if start >= stop:                              # nothing left
12      return False
13    else:
14      midIndex = (start + stop) // 2
15      if target == lexicon[midIndex]:              # found it
16        return True
17      elif target < lexicon[midIndex]:             # check left side
18        return search(lexicon, target, start, midIndex)
19      else:                                        # check right side
20        return search(lexicon, target, midIndex+1, stop)
```

FIGURE 11.15: Preferred implementation of the binary search algorithm.

11.4.3 A Good Implementation

Having recognized the problem with the preceding implementation, our goal in this section is to provide a truly efficient implementation of binary search. That approach is given in Figure 11.15. The key to our new approach is avoiding the use of explicit slicing when designating a sublist. Instead, we describe a sublist implicitly, passing a reference to the original list as well as the appropriate start and stop indices.

Passing a reference to the list is quite efficient, as it does not involve copying the object (see Section 10.3.1 for further discussion). We mimic slicing notation by using indices start and start, with the convention that the search proceeds beginning at index start of the lexicon, going up to but not including index stop. However, we want to support the original calling syntax, as in search(['B','E','G','I','N','S'], 'F'), so that our user need not be concerned with the extra parameters. We do this by making careful use of default parameter values. We set the value of start to zero by default, as this is the leftmost index of a full list. Setting a default for stop is more subtle. The problem is that we want to set it to len(lexicon), yet the list lexicon does not actually exist at the time we are declaring the function. Trying to use this expression in the signature would cause a syntax error if the default value were evaluated (see Section 10.3.2 for more on default parameter values). Instead, we initial set stop to the special value **None** in our signature. The desired value is computed, if necessary, at line 10 within the function body.

Other than the change to an implicit representation of the slice, our new version of the code is modeled upon the preceding bad version. The condition at line 11 is our way to

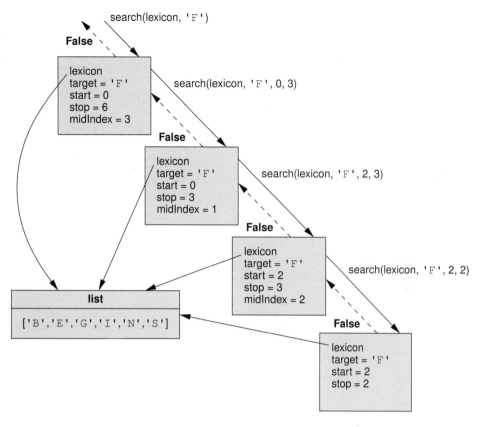

FIGURE 11.16: The trace of the call, search(['B','E','G','I','N','S'], 'F') for the improved implementation of binary search from Figure 11.15.

recognize a request to search an "empty" portion of the list. Line 14 computes the middle index of the current portion of the list and lines 18 and 20 recurse on the appropriate sublist. In Figure 11.16, we retrace search(['B','E','G','I','N','S'], 'F') using the revised implementation. Although very similar in style to the earlier version in Figure 11.14, the new style of parameter passing is more efficient.

 A WORD OF WARNING

If you take a slice of a list, this creates a new list that is a copy of the relevant portion of the original (see Section 10.2.2). This may be an unwanted expense in a recursive setting.

11.4.4 Searching for a Partial Match

We originally described binary search as an algorithm for finding an exact match of a value within a sorted list (for example, searching for 1492 within a sorted list of numbers). Yet the approach can be easily adapted for more general types of searches known as ***range searches***. For example, we can efficiently locate all numbers from a sorted list that are at least 1450 yet strictly less than 1500.

In the context of a lexicon of words, a common form of a range search is to check if any entry of the lexicon starts with a given *prefix*. For example, we might want to know if any word starts with the pattern `pyt`. Such a prefix-based search is quite easily accomplished, as shown in Figure 11.17. This implementation is almost identical to that given in Figure 11.15. Only one line of code has been changed. Originally, we looked for an exact match using the syntax

```
15    if target == lexicon[midIndex]:                          # found it
```

This time, we consider the search successful if the middle entry starts with the target string.

```
15    if lexicon[midIndex].startswith(target):                 # found prefix
```

```
1    def prefixSearch(lexicon, target, start=0, stop=None):
2        """Search to see if target occurs as a prefix of a word in lexicon[start:stop].
3
4        lexicon    a list of words (presumed to be alphabetized)
5        target     the desired word
6        start      the smallest index at which to look (default 0)
7        stop       the index before which to stop (default len(lexicon) )
8        """
9        if stop is None:
10           stop = len(lexicon)
11       if start >= stop:
12           return False
13       else:
14           midIndex = (start + stop)//2
15           if lexicon[midIndex].startswith(target):           # found prefix
16               return True
17           elif target < lexicon[midIndex]:                   # check left side
18               return prefixSearch(lexicon, target, start, midIndex)
19           else:                                              # check right side
20               return prefixSearch(lexicon, target, midIndex+1, stop)
```

FIGURE 11.17: Using binary search to check whether a prefix occurs within a list of words.

11.5   Case Study: Solving a Puzzle

Our next goal is to design a program that computes **anagrams** of a given word. An anagram is defined as a word that can be formed by rearranging the letters of another word. For example the word trace can be rearranged to form anagrams including caret, cater, crate, and react. We will develop a function that computes anagrams using a syntax such as anagrams(lexicon, 'trace'), where lexicon is again presumed to be an alphabetized list of words in a language. The return value of this call will be a list of lexicon entries that can be formed by rearranging the given string of characters.

We begin by noting a connection between this problem and the discussion of factorials from Section 11.3. Remember that a factorial, written as $n!$, is the number of ways there are to order n items. So if we start with an n-letter word, there are $n!$ possible ways to arrange the characters of that word when looking for anagrams (including the original ordering). Of course our program for computing factorials was only designed to calculate the *number* of orderings. For this case study, we must construct the various rearrangements.

The intuition introduced in the context of factorials can be used to develop a new recursion for computing anagrams. Rather than tackling the entire rearrangement problem at once, we begin by picking the first character. Of course we do not know which character to use as the first; instead we explore each possible choice, one at a time. For one such choice, we subsequently try all possible arrangements of the remaining characters. For example, if using the c from trace as the first character, we must subsequently decide how to arrange the remaining letters trae. We use recursion to handle this subtask. There is one catch in implementing this. The original goal of our function is to find solutions that are words in the lexicon. Yet when rearranging the rest of the letters, we need to recognize that aret, ater, and rate are meaningful, because when following the initial c, these form the words caret, cater, and crate. We therefore design a recursion that accepts a third parameter to designate an existing prefix. Our precise signature appears as

```
def anagrams(lexicon, charsToUse, prefix=' '):
```

The goal of the function is to return a list of words from the lexicon that start with the given prefix and are followed by an arrangement of charsToUse. We use a default parameter of an empty string for the prefix so that users may rely upon the two-parameter syntax, such as anagrams(lexicon, 'trace').

The heart of our implementation is based on trying each possible character as the next subsequent character. When facing an initial call of anagrams(lexicon, 'trace'), there are five choices for the first character, resulting in subsequent calls of the form:

```
anagrams(lexicon, 'race', 't')
anagrams(lexicon, 'tace', 'r')
anagrams(lexicon, 'trce', 'a')
anagrams(lexicon, 'trae', 'c')
anagrams(lexicon, 'trac', 'e')
```

Each one of these recursive calls will report a list of solutions (possibly empty). The overall list of solutions should be the union of these individual lists. We accomplish this with a simple loop shown at lines 12–16 of Figure 11.18. For each character of charsToUse we

```
 1  def anagrams(lexicon, charsToUse, prefix=' '):
 2      """
 3      Return a list of anagrams, formed with prefix followed by charsToUse.
 4
 5      lexicon         a list of words (presumed to be alphabetized)
 6      charsToUse      a string which represents the characters to be arranged
 7      prefix          a prefix which is presumed to come before the arrangement
 8                      of the charsToUse (default empty string)
 9      """
10      solutions = [ ]
11      if len(charsToUse) > 1:
12          for i in range(len(charsToUse)):        # pick charsToUse[i] next
13              newPrefix = prefix + charsToUse[i]
14              newCharsToUse = charsToUse[ : i] + charsToUse[i+1 : ]
15              solutions.extend(anagrams(lexicon, newCharsToUse, newPrefix))
16      else:       # check to see if we have a good solution
17          candidate = prefix + charsToUse
18          if search(lexicon, candidate):          # use binary search
19              solutions.append(candidate)
20      return solutions
```

FIGURE 11.18: Preliminary implementation of an anagram solver.

compute a new prefix which includes that character (line 13), we then compute a new string of remaining characters to use that does not include the selected one (line 14), and then we extend our list of solutions by the result of a recursion (line 15).

We must also define a base case for our recursion, namely a situation in which we can determine the answer without need for further recursive applications. Recall that our formal goal is to return a list of words that can be formed by taking the prefix followed by an arrangement of the remaining characters. If there is only one character remaining, we simply have to check whether the complete candidate word is in the lexicon. We rely upon the binary search function we implemented in Section 11.4.3 to perform this check. This base case is handled by lines 17–19 of Figure 11.18.

To fully understand how our anagram solver works, it may help to see a detailed trace as the recursion unfolds. For the sake of illustration, Figure 11.19 considers a very small example, computing anagrams of the word 'are'. The original activation relies upon three separate recursive calls, exploring the use of 'a', 'r', and then 'e' as the first character in a presumed anagram. Of course, the second call anagrams(lexicon, 'ae', 'r') does not actually begin until the first call anagrams(lexicon, 're', 'a') and all of its ancillary calls completes, returning control back to the original level.

The overall return value is the concatenation of the three lists returned by the secondary calls. We should note that the current version of our recursion does not make any explicit attempt to alphabetize the resulting list or to avoid duplicates. We explore these issues in Exercise 11.34 and Exercise 11.35 respectively.

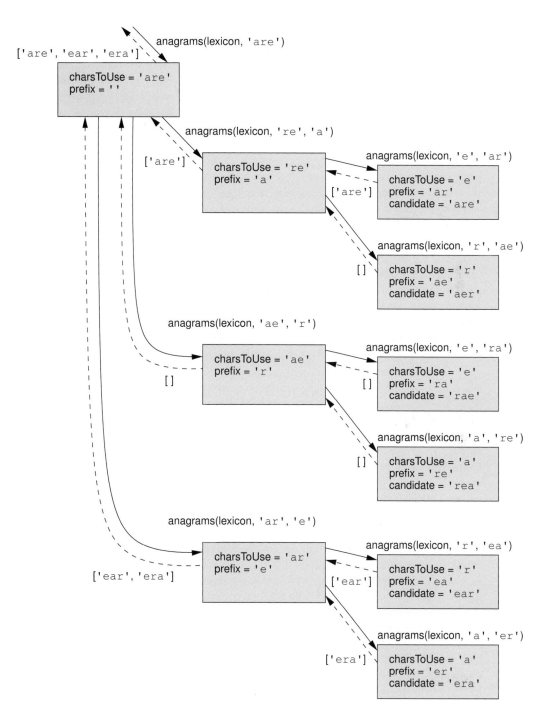

FIGURE 11.19: The trace of a call to anagrams(lexicon, `'are'`).

11.5.1 Improving Efficiency: Pruning a Recursion

As our final lesson of the chapter, we examine the efficiency of our preliminary anagram solver. The precise computation time depends upon the speed of the computer as well as the size of the lexicon being used. Of course, it also depends greatly on the number of characters in the anagram. For the sake of argument, we report running times observed on our own computer using a lexicon of over 100,000 words. We solve 7-letter anagrams in a fraction of a second, 8-letter anagrams in less than two seconds, even 9-letter anagrams in 15 seconds or so. But things soon get much worse. Finding anagrams of a 10-letter word (such as `coordinate` → `decoration`) takes 2.5 minutes. Analyzing an 11-letter word (e.g., `description` → `predictions`) takes about 28 minutes; we can solve a 12-letter puzzle (e.g., `impersonated` → `predominates`), yet only after 5.6 hours. Projecting this, we would have to wait over 3 days to find that `relationships` and `rhinoplasties` are anagrams and over 42 days to find that `disintegrations` and `disorientating` are anagrams.

The biggest impediment to efficiency is the growing number of ways to rearrange a set of characters, precisely what factorials describe. For example, there are $3! = 3 \cdot 2 \cdot 1 = 6$ ways to rearrange three letters. In fact, we saw those six candidate orderings as base cases in the example of Figure 11.19. There are similarly 24 orderings for a 4-letter anagram and 120 orderings for a 5-letter anagram. The number of arrangements soon grows out of control. There are over 3.6 million ways to arrange 10 letters, 40 million ways for 11 letters, 479 million for 12 letters, 6.2 billion for 13 letters, 87 billion for 14 letters.

Even the fastest computers will require significant time to evaluate this many pos-sibilities, especially given the many intermediate recursions used to generate those candi-dates and the subsequent search for each candidate within a large lexicon. Figure 11.20 summarizes the results of our own experiments. We measure the performance in two ways. We report the actual time it took to complete (using our computer). Although times may vary on your own computer, the comparison of the running times is telling. The other metric we display is an overall count of the number of intermediate recursive calls that are made along the way for each trial. The performance of the original version of our anagram solver is given in the middle of that figure.

Amazingly, with one simple change to our code, we can process all of these cases efficiently. For example, we can evaluate a 14-letter word in just under 16 seconds (rather than the projected 42 days that our original code would require). Although we might try to speed up the basic computations, the real improvement comes from simply avoiding as much of the work as possible. We use some intuition that would be very obvious to a person trying to solve anagrams by hand. Let's start by unfolding the recursion on the example anagrams(lexicon, `'trace'`). We begin with a loop that explores each possible first letter. The first such recursive call is to anagrams(lexicon, `'race'`, `'t'`). Each of the four remaining letters is next considered. Exploring some combinations, such as `'tr'`, lead to a real word (e.g., `trace`). Other prefixes, like `'ta'`, might seem reasonable even though they turn out not to uncover any solutions. Still other prefixes, such as `'tc'`, seem impossible to a person. If there are not any legitimate words in English starting with those letters, then it is a waste of time to consider all six arrangements of the final three let-ters (i.e., `tcrae`, `tcrea`, `tcare`, `tcaer`, `tcera`, `tcear`). Yet to avoid such waste, we have to know whether a prefix is impossible. Humans rely on intuition for this, but

word	len	Original		Improved	
		time (sec)	#recursions	time	#recursions
trace	5	0.006	206	0.010	108
parsed	6	0.031	1,237	0.040	256
editing	7	0.214	8,660	0.082	378
altering	8	1.72	69,281	0.193	1,097
diameters	9	15.3	623,530	0.521	2,625
coordinate	10	153	6,235,301	0.836	3,359
description	11	1668	68,588,312	1.60	5,842
impersonated	12	~5.6 hrs	823,059,745	3.90	12,371
relationships	13	~3 days	10,699,776,686	7.11	20,228
disintegration	14	~42 days	149,796,873,605	15.8	42,714

FIGURE 11.20: Efficiency of original and improved anagram implementations.

intuition might be flawed.[3] The computer has a way to accurately check whether a prefix occurs within a large lexicon; this is precisely what we accomplished in Section 11.4.4. Therefore, we rewrite the body of the for loop, changing it from the original version

```
13    newPrefix = prefix + charsToUse[i]
14    newCharsToUse = charsToUse[ : i] + charsToUse[i+1 : ]
15    solutions.extend(anagrams(lexicon, newCharsToUse, newPrefix))
```

to the following improved version:

```
13    newPrefix = prefix + charsToUse[i]
14    if prefixSearch(lexicon, newPrefix):    # worth exploring
15        newCharsToUse = charsToUse[ : i] + charsToUse[i+1 : ]
16        solutions.extend(anagrams(lexicon, newCharsToUse, newPrefix))
```

We only rearrange the remaining characters when we find that the new prefix exists in the lexicon. This general technique is called ***pruning a recursion***.

The code reflecting this change is given in Figure 11.21. Although this may appear to be a minor cosmetic change, its impact is enormous. On small examples, our "improve–ment" does not actually help; in fact for 5–and 6–letter words, our running times increase slightly. As shown in Figure 11.20, the overall number of recursions has been reduced somewhat in the new version, going from 206 down to 108 in the 5–letter example. How–ever, we spend a bit more time at each step due to the additional prefix search.

On bigger examples, the extra time checking prefixes is well spent. The overall num–ber of recursions still grows with the size of the word, but not nearly as fast. The savings occurs because as we process longer words, the majority of prefixes are not viable. At the extreme, we find that we can handle 14–letter words in a fraction of a minute because we use fewer than 43000 recursions rather than the 149 billion required by the naive approach.

---

3.   Did you remember the word `tchaviche`, which is on the Consolidated Word List for the Scripps National Spelling Bee? It is apparently a breed of salmon.

```
1    def anagrams(lexicon, charsToUse, prefix=' '):
2        """
3        Return a list of anagrams, formed with prefix followed by charsToUse.
4
5        lexicon        a list of words (presumed to be alphabetized)
6        charsToUse     a string which represents the characters to be arranged
7        prefix         a prefix which is presumed to come before the arrangement
8                       of the charsToUse (default empty string)
9        """
10       solutions = [ ]
11       if len(charsToUse) > 1:
12           for i in range(len(charsToUse)):           # pick charsToUse[i] next
13               newPrefix = prefix + charsToUse[i]
14               if prefixSearch(lexicon, newPrefix):   # worth exploring
15                   newCharsToUse = charsToUse[ : i] + charsToUse[i+1 : ]
16                   solutions.extend(anagrams(lexicon, newCharsToUse, newPrefix))
17       else:       # check to see if we have a good solution
18           candidate = prefix + charsToUse
19           if search(lexicon, candidate):             # use binary search
20               solutions.append(candidate)
21       return solutions
```

FIGURE 11.21: Improved implementation of our anagram solver. This prunes the recursion whenever an impossible prefix occurs.

11.6 Chapter Review

11.6.1 Key Points

General Issues

- Recursion provides another technique for expressing repetition.
- Structural recursion occurs when an instance of a class has an attribute that is itself another instance of the same class.
- Functional recursion occurs when the body of a function includes a command that calls the same function.
- A base case of a recursion is a scenario resolved without further use of recursion.
- One way to envision the recursive process is to maintain the local perspective for one particular recursive call. If the execution of that call causes another call to be made, we simply trust that the other call works and consider its impact on the original task.
- Another way to envision the recursive process is to *unfold* the entire recursion. Starting with the initial call, we can trace the precise execution of all subsequent calls.
- Each activation of a recursive function is managed separately, with the parameters and local variables for that call stored in a dedicated activation record.

OurList Implementation

- A list can be represented recursively by considering the element at the head of the list, and a subsequent list of all remaining items.

- We want to be able to represent an empty list, and so we use that as the base case for our recursion. A list of length one is represented by an element followed by a subsequent empty list.

- The empty list serves as a base case for all of our functions because when a command is issued to the empty list, there is no subsequent list for recursion.

- Several of the methods rely upon a second form of a base case, in scenarios when access to the head of the list suffices.

Binary Search

- A standard technique for finding a value in a list is known as *sequential search*. A loop is used to iterate through the elements one at a time, until either the desired value is found or the end of the list is reached (in which case the search was unsuccessful).

- When a list of values is known to be sorted, there is a more efficient approach known as *binary search*.

- The general idea of binary search is to compare a target value to an item near the middle of the list. If that is not the target value, we can rule out half of the original list based upon whether the target was less than or greater than the middle entry. The remaining sublist can be searched recursively.

- When using Python's slicing syntax, the slice is a newly constructed list and creating it takes time proportional to the length of that slice. For binary search, all of the potential gains in efficiency are lost if slices are created for recursion.

- Instead of creating slices, an efficient recursion can be designed by sending a reference to the original list, together with indices that delimit the "slice" of interest.

- Binary search can easily be adapted not just for finding an exact match, but also for finding matches that lie within a given range of values.

Solving a Puzzle

- Discrete puzzles can often be solved by recursively constructing and exploring partial solu-tions until finding a complete solution that suffices.

- The time for solving a puzzle depends greatly on the number of possible solutions that must be explored.

- Such a recursion can be made significantly faster by *pruning* the recursion, that is, by recursing only on those partial solutions that could lead to success.

11.6.2 Glossary

anagram A word that can be formed by rearranging the letters of another word.

base case A case in a recursive process that can be resolved without further recursion.

binary search A technique for searching a sorted list by comparing a target value to the value at the middle of the list and, if not the target, searching recursively on the appropriate half of the list.

functional recursion A technique in which a function calls itself.

lexicon A collection of strings, for example all words or phrases in the English language.

pruning a recursion A technique for speeding recursive searches by avoiding examination of branches that are clearly not useful.

range search A search for elements of a collection that have value in a given range (e.g., from 80 to 90), as opposed to a search for a single value.

recursion A technique in which a structure or behavior is defined based upon a "smaller" version of that same structure or behavior.

sequential search An algorithm used to find a value in a sequence by scanning from beginning to end, until either finding the value or exhausting the entire sequence.

structural recursion A technique in which a structure is defined using a "smaller" version of the same structure.

unfolding a recursion Tracing execution through all levels of a recursion.

11.6.3   Exercises

Bullseye

Practice 11.1: Using the style of Figure 11.4, give a sequence diagram showing a complete trace for the subsequent call sample.setColors('blue', 'white') upon that bullseye.

Exercise 11.2: Our original Bullseye class alternated between two colors. Write a new version supporting the constructor signature Bullseye(numBands, radius, colorlist), such that colorlist is a list of one or more colors. The bullseye should be drawn so that colorlist[0] is the primary color, colorlist[1] the secondary color, and so on, cycling when reaching the end of the list. Revise the setColors method accordingly.

Exercise 11.3: As a Drawable object, our bullseyes can be rotated. Of course, since the reference point is implicitly the center of many concentric circles, rotation is not very interesting. However, it can be used to produce an interesting optical illusion if we slightly alter our bullseye definition so that the circles are not perfectly concentric. We can bring the two-dimensional image to life, making it appear as a three-dimensional cone when rotated.

Modify the Bullseye class so that the rest of a bullseye is moved slightly to the right of center. Specifically, the default width of each band is radius/numBands; move the inner bullseye to the right by an amount equal to the band width times a coefficient. With a small coefficient, say 0.1, the perspective will appear to be above the tip of the cone; with larger coefficients, the view is from an angle (until eventually the illusion breaks down).

Exercise 11.4: At the beginning of the chapter, we discussed a pyramid as another natural example of a recursive structure. Implement a Pyramid class recursively, using an approach similar to that used for the Bullseye class. Allow the user to specify the number of levels and the overall width (which can be the same as the height).

The main difference in techniques involves the positioning of the components. For the bullseye, the outer circle and inner bullseye were concentric. For the pyramid, you will need to relocate the bottom rectangle and the upper pyramid to achieve the desired effect. Move the components so that the completed pyramid sits with its bottom edge centered on the origin (the default reference point).

Exercise 11.5: The following flower is based upon a recursive nesting of stars:

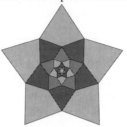

It is composed of an outer Star, as defined in Section 9.4.1, together with a inner flower. The outer radius of the inner flower is equal to the inner radius of the outer star and the inner flower is rotated so that its outer points coincide with the inner points of the star (try saying that ten times fast).

Exercise 11.6: Implement a Tree class for creating somewhat realistic looking trees with the use of recursion. Consider the following examples:

The general approach is to define a tree of order k that has a trunk and then two or more branches, which are actually trees of order $k - 1$. By defining a tree with the reference point at the bottom of the trunk, it is easy to rotate a subtree and attach it where desired. Variations can be achieved (as shown above), by altering the factor at which the trunk height and width decrease at each level, by altering the number of branches attached to the trunk or the angle between those branches. In our left two figures, all branches are attached to the top of the trunk. In the right two, the branch points are distributed vertically. The third and fourth figures are identical, except that leaves have been added as a base case, using a single small green circle at the end of each branch.

OurList

Practice 11.7: Several different recursive patterns are used by the methods of the OurList class. When one call results in a subsequent recursive call, we can examine whether the base case involves an empty list, the head of the list, or an index of zero. The parameterization may be the same at each level or vary between levels (or there may be no parameters whatsoever). Similarly, the return value might always be the same or might vary from level to level. For each method of Figure 11.11, fill in the following chart (we've gotten you started by doing __len__).

method	base case			parameters			return value		
	empty	head	index	same	vary	none	same	vary	none
__len__	✓					✓		✓	
__contains__									
__getitem__									
__setitem__									
__repr__									
count									
index									
append									
insert									
remove									

Practice 11.8: Give a recursive implementation of a method OurList.min that returns the smallest value on the list.

Exercise 11.9: The standard notion for comparing two Python lists is based on what is termed *lexicographical order*. The list with the smaller first element is considered the "smaller" list. However, in case the first elements are equivalent, the second elements are used as a tie–breaker, and so on. If all elements are pairwise equivalent yet one list has additional elements at the end, that list is considered "larger." If all elements are pairwise equivalent and they have the same length, the two lists are considered equivalent. Give an implementation of the method __le__(**self**, other) that returns **True** precisely when the original list is less than or equal to the other list, by lexicographical convention.

Exercise 11.10: In the chapter, we gave an implementation of the OurList.index method that took a single parameter value. That method returned the leftmost index at which the value occurs in the list. Python's lists support a more general signature, of the form

```
def index(self, value, start=0):
```

that returns the smallest index, at least as great as start, at which the value occurs. Use recursion to implement the more general form of OurList.index.

Exercise 11.11: Use recursion to implement the method OurList.pop(index). For simplic–ity, you do not need to support negative indices nor provide a default parameter.

Exercise 11.12: Assume that sample is an instance of OurList representing the corre–sponding list ['H', 'E', 'R', 'E']. Give an explicit trace showing the execution of sample.insert(2,'N').

Exercise 11.13: Assume that sample is an instance of OurList representing the corre–
sponding list `['H', 'E', 'R', 'E']`. Give an explicit trace showing the execution
of sample.remove(`'E'`).

Exercise 11.14: In the style of Figure 11.10, give a trace of the execution of syntax data[6]
on the list `['H', 'E', 'R', 'E']`.

Exercise 11.15: Our implementation of __getitem__ does not support Python's standard
notion of negative indices. Rewrite it so that it does. Hint: would it help if you knew
the overall length?

Exercise 11.16: In our implementation, a call to demo.index(`'T'`) on a list with contents
`['H', 'E', 'R', 'E']` raises a ValueError. This is a reasonable response since the
value was not found, yet our implementation exposes the underlying recursion to the
original caller, with the error appearing as

```
>>> demo.index('T')
Traceback (most recent call last):
  File "<stdin>", line 1, in ?
  File "OurList.py", line 61, in index
    return 1 + self._rest.index(value)
  File "OurList.py", line 61, in index
    return 1 + self._rest.index(value)
  File "OurList.py", line 61, in index
    return 1 + self._rest.index(value)
  File "OurList.py", line 61, in index
    return 1 + self._rest.index(value)
  File "OurList.py", line 57, in index
    raise ValueError('OurList.index(x): x not in list')
ValueError: OurList.index(x): x not in list
```

The problem is that the actual error is raised from deep within the recursion. From
the original caller's perspective, it would be better to see that error raised from the
context of the top–level call. Use a **try-except** clause to accomplish this.

Exercise 11.17: Provide an implementation of OurList.reverse. Think carefully about
your design. Hint: it's okay to rely upon calls to additional behaviors.

Exercise 11.18: Develop a strategy for implementing OurList.sort. One approach, known
as selection sort, involves finding the overall minimum item, rearranging so that it is
moved to the beginning of the list, and then sorting the rest accordingly.

Functional Recursion

Practice 11.19: Predict the output that results when TestA(1) is invoked on the following:

```
def TestA(count):
  if count != 4:
    print count
    TestA(count+1)
```

Practice 11.20: Predict the output that results when TestB(1) is invoked on the following:

```
def TestB(count):
  if count != 4:
    TestB(count+1)
    print count
```

Practice 11.21: Consider the following small program:

```
def fib(n):
  print 'n =', n
  if n <= 1:
    return n
  else:
    return fib(n−1) + fib(n−2)

print fib(4)
```

Predict the precise output of the program (not just the return value, all output).

Exercise 11.22: Consider the following program, where data is a Python **list**:

```
def getmax(data, start, stop):
  print 'What is max(data[%d:%d])?' % (start,stop)
  if stop == start + 1:
    answer = data[start]
  else:
    mid = (start + stop − 1) // 2
    sub1 = getmax(data, start, mid+1)
    sub2 = getmax(data, mid+1, stop)
    if sub1 > sub2:
     answer = sub1
    else:
     answer = sub2
  print answer, 'is max(data[%d:%d]).' % (start,stop)
  return answer
```

Predict the complete output that is printed when getmax([12, 35, 48, 19], 0, 4) is invoked.

Exercise 11.23: Give a natural recursive implementation of a gcd(u,v) function, based upon the intuition from *For the Guru* on page 10. Be careful to consider the base case.

Exercise 11.24: Write a function binary(n) that takes a nonnegative integer n, and returns a string of '0' and '1' characters that is the binary representation of the integer. Notice that the *rightmost* bit of the result is equal to **str**(n % 2), as even numbers end with 0 and odd numbers end with 1. The remaining prefix is exactly the binary representation of n // 2 (assuming that number is nonzero).

Exercise 11.25: A problem that is easily solved by recursion, but very difficult to solve by other means, is the classic Towers of Hanoi. The puzzle begins with three pegs and a tower of *n* disks on the first peg, stacked from largest at bottom to smallest at top. The goal is to move them all to the third peg, moving only one disk at a time. Moreover, you are not allowed to place a disk on top of a smaller disk.

Instructions for a correct solution can easily be generated by recognizing the following pattern. First, the top $n - 1$ disks can be moved from the original peg to the intermediate one (not as one step, but recursively). Then the bottom disk can be moved from the original to the end. Finally, the other $n - 1$ disks can be moved from the intermediate peg to the end. Write a program that generates a solution to the problem.

Exercise 11.26: Animate Exercise 11.25 with cs1graphics.

Binary Search

Practice 11.27: Using the style of Figure 11.14, diagram a full trace of the execution of call search(['A', 'L', 'M', 'O', 'S', 'T'], 'S') using the poor search implementation of Section 11.4.2.

Practice 11.28: Using the style of Figure 11.16, diagram a full trace of the execution of call search(['A', 'L', 'M', 'O', 'S', 'T'], 'S') using the good search implementation of Section 11.4.3.

Exercise 11.29: Had line 20 of Figure 11.15 read

```
return search(lexicon, target, midIndex, stop)
```

the code has the potential of entering an infinite recursion. Give a trace of a small example that demonstrates the flaw.

Exercise 11.30: The good implementation of binary search from Figure 11.15 produces the correct answer, even when executed on an instance of the OurList class (rather than the built-in **list** class). Unfortunately, the process is horribly inefficient. Explain why, noting which lines of the binary search code are bottlenecks.

Exercise 11.31: Use binary search to implement a more efficient version of the function SortedSet.insertAfter, as originally described in Section 9.2.

Exercise 11.32: Our version of prefixSearch simply returns **True** or **False**. Provide a new implementation that returns a list of all words from the lexicon with a prefix that matches the given target.

Anagrams

Practice 11.33: Using the style of Figure 11.19, trace the call anagrams(lexicon, 'tea').

Exercise 11.34: The list of solutions reported by our anagram solver are not necessarily alphabetized. Prove that if charsToUse is provided in alphabetical order, then the list of solutions will automatically be alphabetized.

Exercise 11.35: If the original word contains multiple occurrences of the same character, our anagram solver may report a solution multiple times in the results. Modify the code to avoid such duplicates. Hint: when looping over charsToUse, only start the recursion once for each distinct character.

Exercise 11.36: Since any given execution of our anagram program only depends upon words with the same length as the original, it would be more efficient to keep a separate lexicon for each word length. Modify the program to read the lexicon from a file, creating a list of sorted lists (one list for each length). Implement the anagrams function to take advantage of this new structure and see if you can measure any noticeable improvement in efficiency.

Exercise 11.37: A more interesting version of anagrams involve phrases with multiple words (e.g., `'use python'` is an anagram for `'pushy note'`). Write a function that locates such multiword anagrams. Hint: we suggest the parameterization anagrams(lexicon, charsToUse, precedingWords=' ', partialWord=' ').

Projects

Exercise 11.38: When computing anagrams, all of the original letters must be used as part of the solution. In the game of Scrabble™, a player has a collection of letters and must form a word by rearranging some (but not necessarily) all of those letters. Modify the anagram program to compute all possible words that can be formed from a given collection of letters.

Exercise 11.39: In the game of Boggle™, there is a four-by-four grid of letters and a player forms a word by spelling the word while tracing a path on that grid. The path can move horizontally, vertically, or diagonally, but the same spot cannot be used more than once for a given word. Write a program that computes all words from a lexicon that can be obtained from a given board configuration. One approach is to recursively trace paths through the board, pruning the search whenever a prefix is reached that does not occur in the lexion.

CHAPTER 12

More Python Containers

Certain classes are designed to provide storage and management of a larger collection of objects. A classic example of such a class is Python's **list**, which is used to represent an ordered sequence of elements. Yet there are several other classes that provide support for managing a collection. We call any such object a *container*.

In this chapter, we introduce four new container classes, drawing attention to the similarities and differences between these alternatives. By design, Python's containers all support certain common syntaxes. For example, each supports the syntax **for** element **in** data to iterate through its elements, the syntax element **in** data to determine whether a given element is contained, and len(data) to determine the overall number of elements.

Yet the various container classes are significantly different in their menu of behaviors and in the underlying efficiencies of their operations. Our goal is to compare and contrast these classes, enabling a more educated decision when choosing among the alternatives. We organize our discussion around the following aspects of a container:

order — The classes **list**, **tuple**, and (soon to be introduced) **array** are used to represent an *ordered sequence* of elements. Each of these uses the concept of an integer *index* for designating the location of an element within the sequence. While the relative order of data is significant in some applications, there are scenarios in which the ordering is irrelevant. Many operations can be implemented more efficiently using containers that are free of the responsibility of maintaining an explicit order among the elements.

mutability — The distinction between a **list** and a **tuple** is that the list is mutable whereas the tuple is immutable. So we can subsequently insert, replace, or remove elements of a list, even after it is created; we cannot do so with a tuple.

397

associativity — The contents of most containers are individual objects. For example, in Chapters 8 and 11 we used a list of strings to represent the collection of legal words for a language, known as a lexicon. However, there are many applications in which we want to separately store data associated with each element. For example, a language dictionary contains a definition associated with each term of the lexicon. We will introduce Python's **dict** class (a.k.a., "dictionary"), which is used to represent just such an association between what we will call a *key* and its underlying *value*.

heterogeneity — In Python, we can insert whatever type of data we want into a list. We do not just mean that we can have lists of strings and lists of integers; we can have a single list instance that contains elements of varying types. Such a collection is called *heterogeneous*. In contrast, a container that requires all objects to be of the same type is called *homogeneous*. Most of Python's containers support heterogeneity, although we will see one example that requires homogeneity.

storage — The final aspect that we consider is the model for storing the elements of a container. Most of Python's containers are referential, in that the value of the elements are not stored internal to the container, but indirectly as references to other objects (see Section 10.2). While this is convenient, and in fact is the reason that heterogeneity is easily supported, the indirect nature of the storage can be less efficient in terms of memory usage and access time. For high-performance applications, Python supports an **array** class, which provides compact storage for a collection of data drawn from a chosen primitive type.

The above discussion provides a framework for the chapter, but there are many more details to discuss and examples to demonstrate. The remainder of the chapter begins with a review of the **list** and **tuple** classes in this context. In subsequent sections, we introduce Python's **dict**, **set**, **frozenset**, and **array** classes. A brief comparison of the features of these classes is shown in Figure 12.1. At the conclusion of the chapter we provide an interesting exploration of the use of dictionaries as a tool by the creators of the Python language. We also provide a robust case study, using a combination of containers to implement an operable search engine.

	list	tuple	dict	set	frozenset	array
ordered	✓	✓				✓
mutable	✓		✓	✓		✓
associative			✓			
heterogeneous	✓	✓	✓	✓	✓	
compact storage						✓

FIGURE 12.1: A summary of the varying aspects of Python's containers.

12.1   Two Familiar Containers: list and tuple

Before introducing any new containers, we reflect upon Python's **list** and **tuple** classes. These containers are used to manage an *ordered sequence* of elements. The position of a particular element within that sequence is designated with an ***index***. For example, given groceries = ['bread', 'milk', 'cheese', 'bread'], the syntax groceries[2] accesses the particular value 'cheese'.

In general, we can consider the state of a **list** or **tuple** as an association between indices and values, as in

groceries[0]	⟶	'bread'
groceries[1]	⟶	'milk'
groceries[2]	⟶	'cheese'
groceries[3]	⟶	'bread'

It is important to remember that indices must be consecutive integers, from 0 to one less than the length of the sequence. The required numbering scheme for indices can be unnatural for certain applications. For example, the months of the calendar are typically numbered from 1 to 12. Yet in Section 2.10, we stored the month names in a tuple and relied upon the mapping,

monthNames[0]	⟶	'January'
monthNames[1]	⟶	'February'
...		...
monthNames[10]	⟶	'November'
monthNames[11]	⟶	'December'

Because of the zero-indexing in Python, we had to remember to subtract one from the standard number of the month when accessing the tuple.

We used a variant of this technique in Section 8.5.3 when computing frequency counts. We converted an arbitrary range of integers back to a zero-index range by subtracting an offset equal to the minimum value. For instance, when original values were in the range from 1900 to 2000, we used a list with the convention:

tallies[0]	⟶	number of occurrences of 1900
tallies[1]	⟶	number of occurrences of 1901
...		...
tallies[99]	⟶	number of occurrences of 1999
tallies[100]	⟶	number of occurrences of 2000

We even extended this technique with the appropriate mapping to allow us to track the frequencies of letters.

tallies[0]	⟶	number of occurrences of 'A'
tallies[1]	⟶	number of occurrences of 'B'
...		...
tallies[24]	⟶	number of occurrences of 'Y'
tallies[25]	⟶	number of occurrences of 'Z'

While we might be able to use such an approach for many scenarios, the fact of the matter is that lists and tuples are not perfectly suited for every situation. The use of an integer index in accessing an underlying element can be problematic.

12.1.1   Limitations to the Use of a list or tuple

Lack of permanency

Consider a relatively simple application in which a company wants to manage a collection of employee records. Let us assume that the company assigns each employee an "employee ID" that is an integer identifier. If the company assigns employees consecutive IDs, perhaps sequentially as they are hired, those IDs can be used as indices into a **list**. In this way, an expression such as employee[235] might be used to access a particular employee's record.

However, a problem may arise when an employee leaves the company. If employee[5] decides to retire and is removed from the list, this causes many other employees to be repositioned within the list. For example, the employee previously known as employee[235] becomes employee[234]. The issue is that the relationship between the integer index and the underlying element is *implicit*. Unfortunately, this means an index cannot serve as a meaningful and permanent identifier for an element (or alternatively, that the company cannot delete obsolete entries from the list).

The problem of large integers

The example of a company tracking its employees is further complicated if the identifiers for accessing employee records are not consecutively numbered by nature. For example, many companies use nine-digit social security numbers for identifying employees. To use those numbers directly as indices of a list would necessitate a list with a length of one billion. This is clearly an impractical solution, given that only a small fraction of those potential social security numbers actually belong to employees of a typical company.

The same problem occurs in many other common domains that use large integers as standardized identifiers. For example, published books each have a 13-digit ISBN, a credit card account is identified by a 16-digit number, the United States Postal Service uses 9-digit zip codes and, for certified mail, 20-digit tracking numbers.

In all of these cases, direct use of such large integers as indices is not practical. Yet there is no obvious way to convert the relevant values into a smaller range of integers more suitable as integers of a list.

Non-numeric identification

In other scenarios, there may not even be a natural numbering scheme. For example, we may wish to keep track of our favorite movies and the directors of those movies. However, movies do not have a widely used standard numbering system (such as ISBN for books). Although we could create such a numbering for our own purpose, we would still have to know how to tell which ID was used for which movie. It would be easier if we could simply use the title of the movie to look up a director, using a syntax such as director['Star Wars'].

In similar spirit, we might want to maintain a list of world capitals, but there is no natural numbering for the countries of the world. It would be more convenient to imagine a syntax such as capital['Bolivia'] for such a purpose. Unfortunately, we cannot do this with the **list** class. Yet this is precisely the syntax supported by Python's **dict** class, introduced as our next topic.

12.2   Dictionaries

In the chapter introduction, we briefly introduced the notion of a ***dictionary*** as an associa-tive container. A dictionary represents a mapping from objects known as ***keys*** to associated objects known as ***values***. The keys can be consecutive integers, as was the case with the implicit mapping represented by a list. But keys can be drawn from more general domains. For example, we can use a dictionary to represent the mapping from movies to directors, as follows:

director['Star Wars']	⟶	'George Lucas'
director['The Godfather']	⟶	'Francis Ford Coppola'
director['American Graffiti']	⟶	'George Lucas'
director['The Princess Bride']	⟶	'Rob Reiner'
...		...

In this example, the title of a movie serves as the *key* and the name of the associated director is the *value*. There is an important asymmetry between the role of a key and that of a value in such a mapping.

The keys

A key serves as an identifier when accessing a particular value in the dictionary. In this respect, a key's purpose is similar to that of an index of a list. However, unlike indices, a key does not represent a position within the collection. The keys do not need to be consecutive integers; in fact they do not even need to be integers, as we see here.

The keys within a dictionary are required to be *unique*. If we use the title of the movie as a key, yet there exist two different movies named 'Star Wars', there would be inherent ambiguity when using the expression director['Star Wars']. Python would have no way to tell which of the two movies we had intended. This is precisely why many industries rely upon a system for assigning unique keys. For example employers often rely upon a social security number or employee number, and the book industry uses the ISBN system for cataloging books. In the context of movies, there is no such standardized system, and there are cases where the same name is used for more than one movie. If we want to include such movies, we have to design a system to provide unique keys. For example, we might be more successful using a tuple of the form (title, year) as a key, distinguishing between director[('Shaft', 1971)] and director[('Shaft', 2000)]. Here, each tuple is a single object serving as a key, and the two tuples are indeed different. Of course, even this system breaks down if there are two movies with the same title in the same year (fortunately, an uncommon situation).

There is another important requirement when choosing keys of a dictionary. All keys must be drawn from an *immutable class*, such as **int**, **str**, or **tuple**. The reason for this is a technical one, related to the way that dictionaries are implemented behind the scene. The elements of a dictionary are not inherently ordered, as with a list. Python uses the key when deciding where to store an entry, and also uses that key when later trying to access that entry. If a key were allowed to change while an entry is stored in the dictionary, the original placement of the element may no longer match the expected placement based on the updated key (for those interested in more behind-the-scene details, we provide a complete implementation of a working dictionary class in Section 13.3).

A WORD OF WARNING

All keys within a given dictionary must be unique and immutable.

The values

In contrast to keys, there are no restrictions whatsoever on the allowable values in a dictio-nary. They can be drawn from any class we wish and they are not required to be unique. For example, we see that George Lucas was the director of both Star Wars and American Graf-fiti. This fact does not cause any ambiguity in our use of a dictionary, as the expressions director['Star Wars'] and director['American Graffiti'] are well defined.

In the above example the values happen to be strings, but we wish to emphasize that values can be anything we want. In many applications, a mutable value is used. For example an immutable student ID number might be used to access a mutable object that represents the student's record. Complete flexibility in choosing values is allowed because of the inherent asymmetry in access to a dictionary. The class is designed to efficiently look up the value associated with a given key (e.g., who directed Star Wars). However, a dictionary does not provide an efficient way to determine what keys are associated with a given value (e.g., what movies George Lucas has directed). The second question can be answered, but only by iterating over all entries of the dictionary (or by using what is known as a reverse dictionary, as introduced in Section 12.3.3).

12.2.1 Python's dict Class

Having introduced the concept of a dictionary, our next step is to demonstrate the use of Python's **dict** class. A dictionary can be instantiated in one of two ways. The first is by using the standard constructor syntax, as in

```
director = dict( )
```

This results in a new dictionary instance that initially contains zero entries. We can subse-quently add key-value pairs to our dictionary using an assignment syntax.

```
director['Star Wars'] = 'George Lucas'
director['The Godfather'] = 'Francis Ford Coppola'
director['American Graffiti'] = 'George Lucas'
director['Princess Bride'] = 'Rob Reiner'
```

Once established, the value associated with a key can be retrieved using a syntax such as director['Star Wars'] as part of a command.

Literal form

There is also a literal form for dictionaries delimited with the use of curly brackets { }. This is in contrast to square brackets [ ], used for list literals, or parentheses ( ), used for tuples. So the more common form for creating an empty dictionary is

```
director = { }
```

which is equivalent to director = **dict**( ). We can also use a literal form to initialize a nonempty dictionary. The desired mapping is described using pairs of the form key : value, with each such pair separated by a comma. As an example, we revisit the case study of Section 4.2 involving DNA transcription. Although we did not use dictionaries at the time, there was an implicit mapping between a DNA element and a corresponding RNA element, as follows:

DNA		RNA
'A'	⟶	'U'
'C'	⟶	'G'
'G'	⟶	'C'
'T'	⟶	'A'

We could encode this mapping directly using the following literal form:

```
dnaToRna = { 'A': 'U', 'C': 'G', 'G': 'C', 'T': 'A'}
```

For bigger dictionaries, it is also permissible to have a dictionary literal that spans multiple lines, so long as the initial { is on the first line. Therefore, we might write our initial director dictionary as,

```
director = {'Star Wars' : 'George Lucas',
  'The Godfather' : 'Francis Ford Coppola',
  'American Graffiti' : 'George Lucas',
  'The Princess Bride' : 'Rob Reiner'}
```

Supported behaviors

Figure 12.2 contains a table summarizing the syntax and semantics of the **dict** class. We discuss the most common of those behaviors in the remainder of this section. We can retrieve the value associated with a given key by using the standard "indexing" syntax, such as director['The Godfather']. If this syntax is used with a nonexistent key, a KeyError occurs, as shown in the following interpreter session:

```
>>> print director['The Meaning of Life']
Traceback (most recent call last):
  File "<stdin>", line 1, in -toplevel-
KeyError: 'The Meaning of Life'
```

Syntax	Semantics
d[k]	Returns the item associated with key k; results in KeyError if k not found.
d[k] = value	Associates the key k with the given value.
k **in** d	Returns **True** if dictionary contains the key k; **False** otherwise.
k **not in** d	Returns **True** if dictionary does not contain the key k; **False** otherwise.
len(d)	Returns the number of (key,value) pairs in the dictionary.
d.clear( )	Removes all entries from the dictionary.
d.pop(k)	Removes key k and its associated value from dictionary, returning that value to the caller; raises a KeyError if not found.
d.popitem( )	Removes and returns an arbitrary (key, value) pair as a tuple.
d.keys( )	Returns a **list** of all keys in the dictionary (in arbitrary order).
d.values( )	Returns a **list** of all associated values in the dictionary (in arbitrary order).
d.items( )	Returns a **list** of tuples representing the (key, value) pairs in the dictionary.
for k **in** d:	Iterates over all keys of the dictionary (in arbitrary order); this shorthand is equivalent to **for** k **in** d.keys( ):.

FIGURE 12.2: Selected behaviors of Python's **dict** class, for a prototypical instance d.

We have already seen a similar syntax used on the left–hand side of an assignment, as with our earlier director['The Godfather'] = 'Francis Ford Coppola', to establish an entry in the dictionary. If we make an assignment using a key that already exists, such as with the subsequent command

```
director['The Godfather'] = 'James Kirkwood'
```

this does *not* create a new entry in the dictionary. Instead, it changes the association, remapping the existing key to the newly declared value.

Entries can be removed from a dictionary by using the pop method, specifying the key as a parameter. The call director.pop('Star Wars') removes the key and its asso–ciated value from the dictionary, returning the removed value to the caller. If this method is invoked with a nonexistent key, a KeyError is raised. To avoid an unwanted KeyError, we can test whether a given key occurs in a dictionary using a boolean expression such as 'The Meaning of Life' **in** director.

Iterating through entries of a dictionary

A dictionary is highly optimized for retrieving individual elements based upon the use of a key as an index. However, a dictionary is a full–fledged container and can be used as such. The syntax len(director) tells us the number of (key, value) pairs currently stored in the dictionary. Two important issues arise when accessing the overall collection of elements. First, the dictionary gives no guarantee regarding the order in which entries are reported.

Behind the scene, this flexibility is critical to the efficient implementation of the dictionary class. Second, we have to draw a distinction between whether we wish to access all the keys of the dictionary, to access all the values of the dictionary, or all (key, value) pairs. For flexibility, dictionaries support three separate methods for accessing the underlying contents. The syntax director.keys( ) returns a list of all keys, the syntax director.values( ) a list of all values including duplicates, and director.items( ) a list of (key, value) tuples. These lists can be used in several ways.

They serve most naturally as a list upon which to iterate. Given the choices, iterating over the keys of a dictionary is most common. The reason for this is that once you have a key, it is easy to retrieve the associated value. In fact, in its most basic form the loop

```
for entry in director:
```

behaves identically to the more bulky syntax **for** entry **in** director.keys( ):. We can also manipulate these lists to control the order in which we process the entries of a dictionary. Although the default order is arbitrary, we can sort the list and then use that sorted list in the context of a for loop, as shown here.

```
titles = director.keys( )
titles.sort( )
for movie in titles:
    print movie, 'was directed by', director[movie]
```

To streamline the syntax in a situation like this, Python supports[1] a built-in function sorted, which returns a sorted copy of a container (while leaving the original unchanged). So it is legitimate to use the syntax

```
for movie in sorted(director):
    print movie, 'was directed by', director[movie]
```

which iterates over the dictionary keys in alphabetical order. If we wanted to iterate over all values of the dictionary in alphabetical order, we could use the syntax

```
for person in sorted(director.values( )):
    print person, ' is a director.'
```

However, notice that we have no immediate way to retrieve the key that was associated with a value. Furthermore, if a person has directed multiple movies, that value occurs multiple times in the iteration. Finally, we can iterate over the (key, value) pairs, using the syntax

```
for movie, person in director.items( ):
    print movie, 'was directed by', person
```

---

1.   This function was introduced in version 2.4 of Python.

12.3 Containers of Containers

The elements of a **list**, of a **tuple**, and the values of a **dict** can be whatever type of object we want. So it is perfectly acceptable to maintain a list of lists, a tuple of dictionaries, a dictionary of lists, and so on. Although nesting containers may seem unusual at first, it turns out to be a natural approach for many situations. We wish to demonstrate several examples, paying close attention to the proper syntax.

12.3.1 Modeling Multidimensional Tables

Often, data is viewed as a multidimensional table or matrix. As a simple example, consider the following Tic-tac-toe board"

X	X	O
O	O	X
X	O	X

One way to store this information is as a list of lists. We model the game board as a list of *rows*, with each row itself a list of entries from that row. Thus the configuration given above could be stored as follows:

```
game = [['X', 'X', 'O'], ['O', 'O', 'X'], ['X', 'O', 'X']]
```

Storing a two-dimensional data set in this way is called ***row-major*** order. A diagram of the underlying representation is given in Figure 12.3. If we want to access the bottom left square of the board, we could do so as follows.

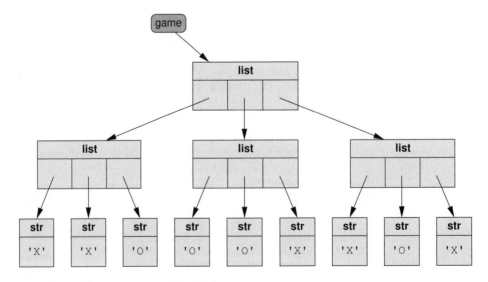

FIGURE 12.3: A diagram of the Tic-tac-toe representation as a list of rows, which themselves are lists of strings.

```
bottomLeft = game[2][0]
```

The double indexing may seem new, but this is just an artifact of the standard rules for evaluating an expression. The operators are evaluated from left to right, first evaluating game[2] and then taking that resulting object (which happens to be a list) and indexing it. More generally, the syntax game[i][j] gets the entry in the i-th row and j-th column, keeping in mind that everything is zero-indexed.

It would have been perfectly acceptable to have represented the original board in what is termed *column-major* order, as a list of columns. Of course in this case, the syntax game[i][j] refers to the i-th column and j-th row. It is also possible to generalize these techniques to data sets with three or more dimensions.

12.3.2 Modeling Many-to-Many Relationships

A dictionary represents a relationship between keys and values. In mathematical terms, we say this is a *many-to-one* relationship. Many different keys may map to a single underlying value, but a single key cannot simultaneously map to many values. For example, we considered the relationship between movies and directors as a typical example of a many-to-one relationship. There may be multiple movies directed by a typical individual, yet we do not expect a given movie to have multiple directors (although this is not inconceivable).

In contrast, the relationship between movies and actors is typically *many-to-many*. A typical movie will have many actors and a typical actor will appear in many movies. Modeling this relationship as a simple dictionary actor does not suffice. Consider the effect of the following sequence of assignments:

```
actor['The Princess Bride'] = 'Cary Elwes'
actor['The Princess Bride'] = 'Mandy Patinkin'
actor['The Princess Bride'] = 'Andre the Giant'
```

Each assignment overwrites the previous value. The key 'The Princess Bride' cannot simultaneously be mapped to multiple values. That key must map to a single value. Fortunately, that value can be whatever type of object we wish. So a natural way to store this many-to-many relationship is with a dictionary that maps each movie to a *tuple* of actors. To better reflect the purpose, we name our dictionary cast and add entries like the following:

```
cast['The Princess Bride'] = ('Cary Elwes', 'Robin Wright Penn',
    'Chris Sarandon', 'Mandy Patinkin', 'Wallace Shawn',
    'Andre the Giant', 'Christopher Guest', 'Fred Savage',
    'Peter Falk', 'Peter Cook', 'Billy Crystal', 'Mel Smith')
```

We could just as easily have used a list as the values, but we chose to model with a tuple because the cast of a movie is naturally immutable.

With such a container of containers, we must be careful in recognizing how expressions are evaluated. Consider, for example, the following containment queries.

```
>>> 'Andre the Giant' in cast
False
>>> 'Andre the Giant' in cast.values()
False
>>> 'Andre the Giant' in cast['The Princess Bride']
True
```

The first query fails because the syntax x **in** cast is used to check whether a given x is a key of the dictionary; `'Andre the Giant'` is not a key. The second query fails as well because the list of dictionary values is a list of tuples (not a list of strings that belong to those tuples). The third query is the more typical form and indeed succeeds in this case. The expression cast[`'The Princess Bride'`] references the value associated with that key in our dictionary. The value is itself a tuple, and so the operator **in** checks whether Andre is included in that tuple.

12.3.3 Reverse Dictionary

We have emphasized that a dictionary is designed to efficiently answer a question of the form "What value is associated with a given key?" Yet sometimes we want to know the converse, that is, what keys map to a given value. For example, suppose we want to know all movies that were directed by Francis Ford Coppola. Unfortunately, there is no direct way to answer such a question based upon the original director dictionary. We can construct a list of such movies as follows:

```
coppolaMovies = [ ]
for title in director:
   if director[title] == 'Francis Ford Coppola':
      coppolaMovies.append(title)
```

However, this approach is inefficient. We are iterating through all entries of a potentially large dictionary. If we want to efficiently answer many such queries, we can build what is called a ***reverse dictionary***. The reverse dictionary is a separate dictionary structure that maps each *value* of the original dictionary to a list of *keys* that are associated with the given value in the original dictionary. As a simple example, if we define an original dictionary as

original = { `'A'`: 1, `'B'`: 3, `'C'`: 3, `'D'`: 4, `'E'`: 1, `'F'`: 3 }

the reverse dictionary appears as follows:

{1: [`'A'`, `'E'`], 3: [`'C'`, `'B'`, `'F'`], 4: [`'D'`]}

Notice that in the original, the keys `'A'` and `'E'` both mapped to value 1; in the reverse dictionary, the key 1 is mapped to the **list** [`'A'`, `'E'`]. We use a list because there may be arbitrarily many keys from the original dictionary that map to the associated value. For consistency, we even use a list when there is only one value, as in the case of 4: [`'D'`]. Notice that we do not include any entries in the reverse dictionary for values that never appear in the original (e.g., 2).

   Building a reverse dictionary requires a complete iteration over all entries of the original dictionary, so it is not initially any more efficient than our earlier example with Francis

Ford Coppola. However, once the reverse dictionary has been constructed, all subsequent queries can be answered efficiently. We suggest the following function for computing a reverse dictionary:

```
1  def buildReverse(dictionary):
2      """Return a reverse dictionary based upon the original."""
3      reverse = { }
4      for key,value in dictionary.items( ):          # map value back to key
5          if value in reverse:
6              reverse[value].append(key)             # add to existing list
7          else:
8              reverse[value] = [ key ]               # establish new list
9      return reverse
```

At line 4, we iterate over the pairs in dictionary.items( ). We could have iterated over the keys and then looked up the associated value within the body of the loop, as we did in the earlier Coppola example. However, since we are interested in doing so for each key, there is some advantage to getting the values in advance (actually, the same could have been said for our earlier Coppola example). The condition at line 5 is important in differentiating between the first time a value is encountered and subsequent occurrences of that value. In general, we would like to append the current key to the list of associated keys for that value. However, if this is the first time we encounter the given value, no such list has been created. For this reason, the **else** body at line 8 instantiates of a new list to hold a single key; it is critical that the right-hand side of that assignment reads [key] as opposed to key.

12.4   Sets

The next container we introduce is used to represent the classic mathematical notion of a set, an *unordered* collection of *unique* elements. For example, we might want to keep the set of colors needed for drawing a picture or to keep track of the set of countries that have signed an international treaty. Before exploring the syntax of a new class, we wish to contrast the concept of a set to that of other containers.

The earliest versions of the language did not include a specific class for modeling the mathematical concept of a set. Individual programmers implemented their own versions based on use of a **dict** or **list**. The **dict** class is designed to efficiently test whether a given key exists. So we could use a dictionary to represent a set by relying on the keys of the dictionary as elements of the set. Syntactically, however, we must assign some associated value. For example, we might store a "set" of colors in a dictionary with entries such as colors['red'] = **True**. We would only place entries in the dictionary for those colors that exist in the set; there is no reason to explicitly insert **False** values for the many other colors that are not part of the set. There is still a slight inefficiency in this representation, as memory is being set aside to track those associated **True** values.

We could avoid the associated value by using a **list** or **tuple**, yet those classes are not specialized for efficient containment queries, relying instead on a sequential search. Also, unnecessary effort is spent to maintain the order of elements in such sequences.

As more programmers relied upon homespun adaptations to implement the concept of a set, the community decided to design more appropriate classes. Starting with Python 2.4, two new built-in classes were introduced into the language: **set** and **frozenset**. Both of these model the concept of a mathematical set, with the distinction that a **set** is mutable while a **frozenset** is immutable. Furthermore, with new dedicated classes, support was added for other common operations, such as computing unions and intersections of sets.

12.4.1 Python's set Class

We begin by introducing the use of Python's **set** class. Behind the scene, a set is implemented very much like a dictionary but without storing associated values. The implications of this design are as follows:

1. Containment queries, such as `'red'` **in** colors, are highly efficient.
2. The internal order of elements within a set is arbitrary.
3. Elements added to a **set** must be *immutable* (for similar reasons as with **dict** keys).

Constructor

A new set can be constructed with the syntax **set**( ), which by default produces an empty set. There is no literal form for a set, but if you know the elements you want, you can construct a set by passing some other container, such as a string, list tuple or dictionary, as a parameter. So the syntax **set**([1, 5, 8, 10]) is legal; in fact a similar form is used by Python when displaying a representation of a set. If the parameter to the constructor contains duplicates, those duplicates are automatically removed when building the set. For example, the expression **set**(`'this is a test'`) results in a set of the 7 unique characters **set**([`'a'`, `' '`, `'e'`, `'i'`, `'h'`, `'s'`, `'t'`]), albeit in an arbitrary order.

Accessors

A summary of the behaviors for examining aspects of a **set** is provided in Figure 12.4. These behaviors are similarly supported by a **frozenset** (see Section 12.4.2). To organize our overview, we group these behaviors into three major categories.

Standard container operations. These behaviors should look quite familiar, as they are supported by all containers. We can check for containment in a set (or the lack thereof) using the syntax `'red'` **in** colors (or alternatively `'red'` **not in** colors). The cardinality of the set is reported by len(colors) and we can iterate over the elements of a set using a for loop. Keep in mind that the order will be arbitrary.

Comparing the contents of two existing sets. It is possible to check whether two sets have the same contents using the notation s == t. This evaluates to **True**, so long as the sets are equivalent in the mathematical sense of sets. The order of the elements within the two sets is irrelevant for such a comparison. The syntax s < t has been overridden to check whether set s is a proper subset of set t. Consider the following examples.

Syntax (with alternate)	Semantics
len(s)	Returns the cardinality of set s.
v **in** s	Returns **True** if set s contains the value v, **False** otherwise.
v **not in** s	Returns **True** if set s does not contain the value v, **False** otherwise.
for v **in** s:	Iterates over all values in set s (in arbitrary order).
s == t	Returns **True** if set s and set t have identical contents, **False** otherwise (order is irrelevant).
s < t	Returns **True** if set s is a *proper* subset of t, **False** otherwise.
s <= t s.issubset(t)	Returns **True** if set s is a subset of t, **False** otherwise.
s > t	Returns **True** if set s is a *proper* superset of t, **False** otherwise.
s >= t s.issuperset(t)	Returns **True** if set s is a superset of t, **False** otherwise.
s | t s.union(t)	Returns a new set of all elements that are in either set s or set t (or both).
s & t s.intersection(t)	Returns a new set of all elements that are in both set s and set t.
s − t s.difference(t)	Returns a new set of all elements that are in set s but not in set t.
s ^ t s.symmetric_difference(t)	Returns a new set of all elements that are in either set s or set t but not both.

FIGURE 12.4: Accessor methods supported by the **set** and **frozenset**.

```
>>> set([3, 2]) < set([1, 2, 3])
True
>>> set([2, 3]) < set([2, 3])
False
>>> set([1]) < set([2, 3])
False
```

With the first expression, the set on the left is truly a proper subset of the set on the right. The second expression fails because the left-hand set is a subset, but not a *proper* subset (they are actually equivalent). The final expression fails as well, since element 1 is not in the right-hand set.

The expression s <= t operator is defined to check whether set s is a subset of set t (whether proper or not). Python also provides a named version of this behavior, that can be equivalently invoked as s.issubset(t). Which style to use depends somewhat on a programmer's comfort with the brevity of the operator form. It is also possible to use the operators >= and > to check whether a set is respectively a superset or proper superset of another.

Generating a third set based on two existing sets. Many common mathematical operations are supported by sets. For example, we can compute a union or intersection of two existing sets. Again, there are two different forms supported. A brief operator form[2] is supported using the symbol | for computing unions, and & for computing intersections, as follows:

```
>>> colors = set(['red', 'green', 'blue'])
>>> stoplight = set(['green', 'yellow', 'red'])
>>> print colors | stoplight
set(['blue', 'green', 'yellow', 'red'])
>>> print colors & stoplight
set(['green', 'red'])
```

Neither of the original sets is affected by these operations. It is simply that a new set is created with the desired contents. Those who wish to avoid use of symbols may instead rely upon duly named methods, as in color.union(stoplight) and color.intersection(stoplight). These forms have the same effect, generating a third set while leaving the original two unchanged.

There are two other mathematical operations supported, namely computing the difference between two sets and the symmetric difference between two sets. The summary of those operations is included in Figure 12.4; we leave it to the reader to review the various mathematical concepts when the need arises.

Mutators

Although the elements of a set are required to be *immutable*, the **set** itself is mutable. We can add or remove elements in a variety of ways. A single element can be added to a set by using a syntax such as colors.add('red'). If that element is already present, executing this command is legal, yet has no effect. A single element can be removed from a set in one of three ways. The syntax colors.remove('red') removes the designated element if it is in the set; however, a KeyError is immediately raised if the designated value does not belong to the set. A safer way to remove a potential element is the syntax colors.discard('red'). This removes the element when it exists, yet does nothing otherwise. Finally, an arbitrary element is removed and returned when calling colors.pop( ) and all elements are removed at once with the syntax colors.clear( ).

There also exist mutators that perform the standard mathematical set operations, yet by mutating the first of the existing sets rather than generating a third set. For instance, we saw that the syntax s & t computes a third set that is the intersection of the two. The

---

2.   The history of these symbols comes from their use in earlier programming languages. The | symbol is often associated with the "or" operator; thus elements in the union s | t must lie in set s or set t (or both). The & symbol is historically viewed as "and"; thus elements in the intersection s & t must lie in both set s and set t.

Syntax (with alternate)	Semantics
s.add(v)	Adds value v to the set s; has no effect if already present.
s.discard(v)	Removes value v from the set s if present; has no effect otherwise.
s.remove(v)	Removes value v from the set s if present; raises a KeyError otherwise.
s.pop( )	Removes and returns arbitrary value from set s.
s.clear( )	Removes all entries from the set s.
s |= t s.update(t)	Alters set s, *adding* all elements from set t; thus set s becomes the union of the original two.
s &= t s.intersection_update(t)	Alters set s, *removing* elements that are not in set t; set s becomes the intersection of the original two.
s −= t s.difference_update(t)	Alters set s, *removing* elements that are found in set t; set s becomes the difference of the original two.
s ^= t s.symmetric_difference_update(t)	Alters set s to include only elements originally in exactly one of the two sets, but not both.

FIGURE 12.5: Behaviors that mutate a **set**.

related syntax s &= t mutates the left-hand set, setting its contents equal to the intersection of the two. There is a named version of this behavior as well, s.intersection_update(t). Notice the use of the term "update" in the name, to differentiate it from the nonmutating s.intersection(t). The other set operations have similar mutating forms, both with operator syntax or a duly named method. Of particular note, the mutating form of union is named update (rather than the expected union_update). This stems from the similarity between this behavior and the already named update method supported by the **dict** class. The complete menu of mutating behaviors is given in Figure 12.5.

12.4.2   Python's frozenset Class

We have already noted that a **set** is mutable, while a **frozenset** is immutable. Therefore a **frozenset** supports all of the accessors listed in Figure 12.4, but none of the mutat–ing behaviors of Figure 12.5. The reason that Python includes a separate class for the immutable form is similar to the reason there is a **tuple** class alongside the **list** class. Remember that the elements of a **set** (or **frozenset**) must be immutable. Therefore we cannot have a set of sets; yet we could have a set of frozen sets. In similar fashion, we could use a **frozenset** as a key in a dictionary.

The only other issue worth noting is what happens when using operations that involve two (frozen or regular) sets. Quite naturally, the intersection of two **set** instances produces a **set** as a result; the intersection of two **frozenset** instances produces a **frozenset** as a result. If computing the intersection of one **set** and one **frozenset**, the result has the same type as the *first* of the two operands, as demonstrated below.

```
>>> colors = set(['red', 'green', 'blue'])
>>> stoplight = frozenset(['green', 'yellow', 'red'])
>>> print colors & stoplight
set(['green', 'red'])
>>> print stoplight & colors
frozenset(['green', 'red'])
```

12.5   Arrays

Beginning in Section 10.2, we made a point to describe a **list** as a collection of *references*. The actual values of the elements are not stored within the state of the list; only references to these objects are stored. As a concrete example, the list defined syntactically as

yearList = [1776, 1789, 1917, 1979]

can be portrayed as in Figure 12.6. This design makes lists remarkably versatile. The memory usage devoted to storing the state of the list depends upon the *number* of elements in the list, but it does not depend on the *type* of elements. In essence, a reference to an object is a memory address, which requires a fixed number of bits no matter whether it is a reference to the location of a "small" object or a "big" object. So it makes no difference whether storing a list of strings, a list of integers, or a list of canvases. In fact, it is perfectly acceptable to have a single list that contains different types of objects. Such a container is **heterogeneous**; in contrast, a container that can hold only objects of the same type is **homogeneous**.

Unfortunately, there is a slight inefficiency due to this design. The extra level of indirection increases the cost when accessing an element. Evaluating an expression such as yearList[3] becomes a two-step process. The computer has to map the identifier yearList to a memory address where the state of the list is stored. From there, the index 3 can be used to locate the appropriate *reference* to the desired element; that reference must

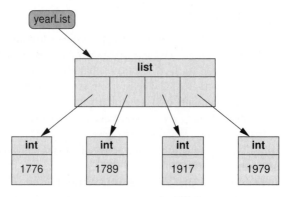

FIGURE 12.6: The underlying representation of a **list** of **int** objects.

then be followed to get to the place in memory where the actual value is stored. Another disadvantage is that the overall memory usage for this configuration may be twice as much as necessary; memory is being used to store an explicit memory reference as well as each corresponding value.

In most applications, these inefficiencies go unnoticed. However, for applications that are extremely data intensive, such as large–scale scientific computations, that additional memory usage and access time can be significant. Consider software designed to analyze a sequence of billions of numbers. A for loop over a **list** of those numbers would essentially proceed by finding the reference at index 0, then following that reference to the underlying number, then finding the reference at index 1, then following that reference to the underlying number, and so on. Notice that the numbers themselves are not necessarily near each other in memory, even though they are sequenced together in the list. Retrieving the data in this fashion can be unnecessarily time consuming.

For this reason, Python provides a more streamlined class named **array**, suitable for high–performance applications when running time is critical. Arrays provide a container for the efficient storage of a *homogeneous* collection of basic numeric or character data. Rather than storing references, the actual values of those primitives are stored within the state of the array. Arrays support most of the behaviors of the **list** class (see Figure 2.2 on page 42). However, the constructor requires a parameter that designates the specific type of data to be stored. For example, the syntax **array**(`'i'`) is used to create an initially empty array for storing integers, and **array**(`'f'`) to create an array for storing floating–point numbers. Once the array has been initialized, we can add elements to it or otherwise manipulate it as we wish. The constructor also accepts a second parameter that is a sequence of initial elements of the appropriate type.

The **array** class is *not* among the built–in types for Python so it must first be imported from a module, also named **array**. The following example produces an array, storing the same sequence of integers seen in our earlier list:

```
from array import array
yearArray = array('i', [1776, 1789, 1917, 1979])
```

The corresponding portrayal of the **array** storage is given in Figure 12.7. Because arrays are designed for large–scale use, they provide a few methods that are not supported by lists. For example, all the data in an array can be compactly stored into a file using a syntax such as measurements.tofile(f), where measurements is an array and f is an open file object. That data can subsequently be loaded from the file into an array using the fromfile method.

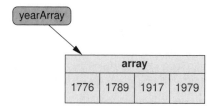

FIGURE 12.7: The compact representation of an **array** of integers.

12.6 Python's Internal Use of Dictionaries

Dictionaries are a very valuable tool for programmers. It turns out that they are equally valuable to the Python interpreter. In Chapter 10, we carefully distinguished between an identifier and the underlying object with which it is associated. If you reflect on the mapping from identifiers to values, you may start to recognize the familiar semantics of a dictionary. An identifier can only be assigned to one particular object at a time. Yet many different identifiers may be associated with the same underlying value. The fact is that the Python interpreter uses its own dictionary to track the relationship between identifiers and associated objects. The identifier (a string of characters) serves as a key in the dictionary; the underlying object is the value associated with that key.

In fact, Python does not just keep a single such dictionary of identifiers. It keeps a dictionary for each individual *namespace*. A namespace is a collection of unique identifiers that are declared within a particular *scope* of a program. Whenever an identifier is used in a command, the Python interpreter goes through a process called *name resolution*. Depending on the context, Python searches through several of these namespaces until it presumably finds the name, and retrieves the associated value from that underlying dictionary. If the name is not located, a NameError occurs (or an AttributeError in the case of an unsuccessful qualified name). In this section, we explore the various namespaces, the dictionaries used for managing them, and the process by which Python resolves a given name.

12.6.1 The Global Namespace

The global namespace consists of any declarations made at the top level of a program, module, or interpreter session. For example if you start a new program with the command processor = 8086, this establishes the string 'processor' as an identifier and associates it with the integer object 8086. Python maintains a global dictionary to keep track of these identifiers. We can examine that dictionary by using the built-in function globals( ). In our proposed example, this results in a dictionary with the following contents:

```
>>> print globals()
{'__builtins__': <module '__builtin__' (built-in)>,
 '__name__': '__main__', 'processor': 8086,
 '__doc__': None}
```

Recall that the order among entries in a dictionary is arbitrary, but you should see the string 'processor' as a key in the dictionary mapped to the integer value 8086. You will also notice several other entries in the global dictionary that were initialized by the system. For example we see that __name__ is set to '__main__' when we newly start a program (see Section 7.7). The global dictionary tracks all identifiers that are introduced in this top-level scope, including those used as names for functions and classes. Consider, for example, the following definitions.

```
def jam( ):
  print 'strawberry'

class room:
  def __init__(self):
    self._capacity = 30
```

After making these declarations, the global dictionary appears as

```
{'jam': <function jam at 0x37d270>,
 'room': <class __main__.room at 0x37c9f0>,
 '__builtins__': <module '__builtin__' (built-in)>,
 '__name__': '__main__', 'processor': 8086,
 '__doc__': None}
```

Notice that the names `'jam'` and `'room'` are included.

12.6.2 The Local Namespace

We have seen as early as Section 5.2 that identifiers introduced within the context of a function have *local scope*. Each time a function is invoked, a brand new dictionary is created to manage the local namespace for the duration of that call. Any identifiers that are established within the function, including the formal parameters, are stored within the local dictionary. When the function call completes, the local dictionary is destroyed. This is why the identifiers established locally during a function call are no longer accessible after the call completes. If the caller is to be informed, that information must be sent as a return value.

The transient nature of the local dictionary makes it difficult to observe, but we can do so by calling the built-in function locals( ) from within the actual function body. To demonstrate the principle, we consider the following function:

```
def demo(param = 'hello'):
  """An example of a function."""
  x = len(param)
  print 'local dictionary is', locals( )
  print 'global dictionary is', globals( )
```

Back at the global scope, we define a variable y and then invoke the demo function.

```
y = 'bon giorno'
demo(y)
```

The following shows the result.

```
local dictionary is {'x': 10, 'param': 'bon giorno'}
global dictionary is {
 '__builtins__': <module '__builtin__' (built-in)>,
 '__name__': '__main__', 'y': 'bon giorno', '__doc__': None,
 'demo': <function demo at 0x37d270>}
```

Notice that x and param are defined within the context of the local namespace. In the global namespace, we see the identifier y, and even the identifier demo (as that name has become associated with the function itself). But a NameError would occur if we try to access the identifier x after the function is complete.

However, it is legal for the body of the function to access a variable from the global namespace. For example, we could have legitimately included the statement **print** y within the body of the function. This is another lesson in Python's name resolution. When an command is executed within the body of a function, the system first checks the local dictionary looking for an identifier. If it cannot find it there, it then falls back to checking the global dictionary.

Still, we wish to emphasize that this coding style is very perilous because the function implementation relies upon the presumed knowledge about the identifiers used at the global scope. The direct access of a global identifier is rarely appropriate. We should also note that if the body of the function uses identifier y on the left-hand side of an assignment, as in y = 'arrivederci', this has no effect on the global dictionary. Instead, such an assignment adds the identifier to the local dictionary, which means subsequent uses of that identifier within the function call resolve to this local variable. This semantics is intentional; this is what allows us to choose local identifiers without having to worry about unintended conflicts outside of a function.

12.6.3 The Built-In Module

We have discussed the use of the global dictionary to resolve top-level identifiers. However, if we start a fresh interpreter session there are many identifiers that can be used even though they are not explicitly in the global dictionary. For example the identifier **int** refers to the class that represents integers, and identifier **abs** refers to a function for computing the absolute value of a number.

The careful observer may have noticed in earlier examples that the global dictionary includes a special module known as '__builtins__'. That module provides all of these built-in names and their associated values. All of the identifiers of that namespace are managed using another dictionary, which can be examined with the syntax vars(__builtins__). Due to the sheer volume of entries in this dictionary, we will not display its contents here, but you are welcome to take a look. The function vars is itself a built-in function that allows us to examine such underlying dictionaries used by Python.

When the interpreter encounters an identifier at the top level, it resolves its association in the following way. First, it looks for an explicit entry in the global dictionary. If it finds that, it will use it. However, if no such entry is found, it subsequently checks the dictionary for the __builtins__ module, seeking a match. If that fails as well, a NameError is generated. This resolution order explains an important subtlety. Although there are a handful of syntax terms that cannot be used as identifiers in Python, such as **for**, the names associated with built-in functions and classes are *not* reserved keywords. As an example, consider the following session:

```
>>> print abs(-5)
5
>>> abs = 'rock-hard'
>>> print abs
rock-hard
>>> print abs(-5)
Traceback (most recent call last):
  File "<stdin>", line 1, in -toplevel-
TypeError: 'str' object is not callable
```

In the first line, we are calling the built-in function for computing the absolute value of a number. The subsequent assignment places an entry in our global dictionary associating the identifier abs with a string value. From that point on, when the identifier abs is encountered, the name resolution finds the entry in the global dictionary and uses it. The reason for the last error is that abs, which now refers to a string instance, does not support a syntax of a function call. It is essentially trying to evaluate the expression `'rock-hard'`(5), which is not legitimate. It is not that the absolute value function has been destroyed. It is still defined in the __builtins__ module, but we can no longer refer to it by using the (unqualified) name abs. If we really wanted to, we can access that function by providing a *qualified name*.

```
>>> print __builtins__.abs(-5)
5
```

The __builtins__ prefix serves as an explicit guide to Python in the name resolution process. Still, we strongly advise that you not use the common built-in names as your own identifiers, unless you have a very good reason for doing so.

 A WORD OF WARNING

We strongly advise that you not use common built-in names as your own identifiers, because this has the effect of masking the original value. Although the syntax

```
str = 'Hello'
```

is allowed, we could not subsequently use the name **str** to reference Python's built-in string class, or to build new instances such as **str**(3.14).

12.6.4 Importing Modules

Python code is often organized into modules that can be imported into other programs to encourage code reuse. Our goal in this section is to better explain the relationship between modules and namespaces. Each module has its own distinct namespace with a dedicated dictionary to manage all of the identifiers declared as part of the module. To better demon-strate the principles, we revisit three different ways to import from a module, as originally introduced in Section 2.7. One approach is to use a syntax

from math **import** *

This command takes all of the identifiers defined in the math module (e.g., pi, sqrt) and introduces them into the current namespace, so we could subsequently use an expression like sqrt(2). While we use such a syntax at times in this book (mostly for convenience) it can be problematic. When there are a large number of definitions in a module, use of the wildcard syntax (i.e., **import** *) is said to "pollute" the namespace. The danger is that the identifiers being imported may conflict with identifiers that had previously been defined or imported into the current scope. For example, if we had our own identifier tan that represented a color and then we were to import the contents of the math module, that identifier would be reassigned to the function for computing tangents. It is generally risky to blindly import everything from a module unless you know for sure what is included.

A more preferable form is to explicitly name the particular items that you want imported into the current namespace. This can be done with a syntax, as

from math **import** sqrt, pi

In this case, those two items are imported into the current namespace, but no others.

A completely different way to import a module is to use a syntax such as

import math

This commands imports the module as a whole into the current scope, using the identifier math. If we were to start a program this way and then execute **print** globals( ), we would see something like the following:

```
{'__builtins__': <module '__builtin__' (built-in)>,
 '__name__': '__main__', '__doc__': None,
 'math': <module 'math' from '/usr/lib/python/math.py'>}
```

Notice that 'math' has been entered in the global dictionary but none of the entries from that module has been added to the global namespace. In this context, the syntax sqrt(5) results in a NameError. The contents of the math module remain in a separate dictionary for that module. We can examine the raw dictionary used for that namespace with the syntax vars(math). That dictionary will have the names of variables like pi and functions like sqrt. We can access those elements by providing a *qualified name*, as in math.sqrt(5). This causes Python to look for the name sqrt within the context of the math module.

12.6.5 Object-Oriented Name Resolution

There are many interesting lessons about object orientation that are more easily understood based upon knowledge of namespaces and dictionaries. With the exception of primitive types (e.g., **int**, **str**), the state of each individual object in Python is stored internally as a collection of member names and values, managed with a separate dictionary known as an ***instance-level*** dictionary. As a concrete example, suppose that we instantiate a Television instance based upon the class definition given in Section 6.3. We can examine its underlying dictionary with the expression vars(myTV) as follows:

```
>>> myTV = Television()
>>> print vars(myTV)
{'_prevChan': 2, '_volume': 5, '_channel': 2,
 '_powerOn': False, '_muted': False}
```

The dictionary contains identifying entries for values that are specific to this one instance. The syntax myTV._volume is just another example of a qualified name, accessing the _volume identifier from the context of myTV.

Notice that the dictionary for myTV does not contain an entry for the volumeUp method, yet the syntax myTV.volumeUp( ) is perfectly legal. The reason is that volumeUp was defined as part of the overall Television class, not as an individual attribute of this particular television. There is another dictionary used to manage names defined in the class-level namespace. We can observe that dictionary using the syntax vars(Television). Quite literally, the class-level dictionary includes all of the functions and data values that are defined within the original class definition. For example, in Section 6.5.1 we revised our Television class to include a shared Television._maxChannel. That association is stored in the class-level dictionary, but not in the instance-level dictionaries.

This approach works because of the name resolution mechanism. When a syntax such as myTV.*identifier* is applied, Python begins by looking for that name within the instance-level dictionary. If it is found there, that associated value will be used. Otherwise, the class-level dictionary is searched. In the context of inheritance, the search for a name continues to the context of the parent class, the grandparent class, and so on, using the first association that can be found (if never resolved, an AttributeError is raised). So given a Rectangle instance named brick, the syntax brick.scale(2) is evaluated as follows. The search for the identifier scale begins within the dictionary for the brick instance, then within the namespace of the Rectangle class, then the FillableShape namespace, the Shape namespace, and finally to the Drawable namespace, where it is found. If multiple inheritance is used, it (recursively) checks the namespaces based upon the order in which the parents are declared when defining the inheritance. For example in Section 9.5, we declared a Layer class beginning as

```
class Layer(Drawable, _GraphicsContainer):
```

When performing name resolution, it first searches in the Drawable namespace (and ancestors of that class, if any) before then proceeding to the _GraphicsContainer namespace.

This name resolution process is what allows a child class to override a behavior orig-inally defined in the parent class. For example, we defined a SortedSet class in Section 9.2 that inherited from **list**, yet provided its own definition for insert. That definition was placed in the dictionary for the SortedSet class. When the syntax s.insert(422) is invoked upon an instance, the name resolution algorithm finds the name insert in the SortedSet namespace, thereby masking the version that would otherwise have been inherited from the **list** class. When we want to force the use of a method from a specific level of the inheritance chain, we do so by using a qualified name. For example, line 16 of our original SortedSet implementation from Figure 9.3 uses the syntax **list**.insert(**self**, place, value) to designate the use of the insert method from the context of the **list** class rather than the similarly named method of the SortedSet class.

FOR THE GURU

With object-oriented name resolution, the expression myTV._maxChannel is permissible for retrieving a class-level value, even though we prefer to write Television._maxChannel to emphasize its class-level scope. The qualified scope is very important when making an assignment. Setting Television._maxChannel = 500 updates this value in the class-level dictionary, whereas myTV._maxChannel = 500 places a new entry in the dictionary for this instance, but leaves the class-level value unchanged.

12.7 Case Study: a Simple Search Engine

As a conclusion to the chapter, we combine use of several containers to develop the infra-structure for efficiently searching a ***corpus*** of one or more text documents. Our overall structure is an example of what is known as a ***search engine***. Given a particular word, our engine will efficiently determine the documents of the corpus that contain the word. We will support two different modes for reporting results. A brief summary can be gener-ated, listing only the names of the matching documents. Alternatively, a long report will provide context by displaying selected lines of those documents that demonstrate the use of the search term. Admittedly, professional search engines do a great deal more. They support querying for multiword phrases or for documents that contain all of a set of words. However, our initial version should demonstrate the basic principles used in practice.

The design of our search engine is very similar to the classic notion of an index of a book. If trying to locate a specific word in a book (e.g., `container`), someone could perform a sequential scan of the entire book. However, that approach is very time consuming, so a book (such as ours) typically has what is known as an ***index*** near the end of the book. The index is organized as a list of significant words, with each word followed by a sequence of page numbers on which the word occurs in the body of the book. A larger corpus, such as a set of encyclopedias or a collection of periodicals, may even provide a mega-index that catalogs the use of terms throughout the entire collection.

We rely on similar principles when implementing our search engine. We develop a container of containers, using one dictionary to map each word to a list of the associated documents in which it appears. Then for each individual document, a dedicated dictionary is maintained to track the line numbers at which each term appears. The overall concept is a variant of a reverse dictionary, as seen in Section 12.3.3.

What defines a word?

When analyzing a (text) document's contents, how should a "word" be defined? As a simple rule, we can split a long string of text into pieces using whitespace as a delimiter. This is what is done by the split( ) method of the string class. We might consider each resulting piece to be a word. However, this rule is imperfect. Consider the following sentence as an example:

```
When analyzing a (text) document's contents,
how should a "word" be defined?
```

The list of strings returned by split( ) is as follows:

```
['When','analyzing','a','(text)',"document's",'contents,',
    'how','should','a','"word"','be','defined?']
```

Although this is a valiant attempt, we would not want to directly use those strings as keys of a dictionary because of the mismatches that would result due to use of capitalization and punctuation. Someone looking for the word `defined` should be referred to this sentence even though the string we see from our view is `'defined?'`. Crafting a general rule for cleaning up these discrepancies is quite challenging. But we suggest a reasonable approach by defining a function ourStrip, as shown in Figure 12.8. The function accomplishes two goals. It strips off all nonalphabetic characters from the left and right ends of the param–eter while leaving internal punctuation (such as apostrophes and hyphens) undisturbed. Furthermore, the final result is intentionally lowercase to support case-insensitive queries.

```
 1  def ourStrip(w):
 2      first = 0                                      # locate first desirable character
 3      while first < len(w) and not w[first].isalpha( ):
 4          first += 1
 5
 6      last = len(w)−1                                # locate last desirable character
 7      while last > first and not w[last].isalpha( ):
 8          last −= 1
 9
10      return w[first:last+1].lower( )               # intentionally lowercase
```

FIGURE 12.8: A routine for stripping a word.

Building an index for a single document

Our next task is to build an index for a single text document. To encapsulate the concept, we define a TextIndex class as follows. We leave it to the user to gather the actual document into the form of a (perhaps lengthy) string. In this way, our code is shielded from the issue of how these documents are gathered (e.g., read from local files, downloaded over the network). For convenience, the user also provides a string that labels the source of the document (perhaps a filename or a URL).

The implementation of the constructor is shown in Figure 12.9. We begin processing the original contents by splitting the document string into a list of individual lines. We also create an initially empty dictionary named _wordAt, which we use as follows. The keys of that dictionary are the (stripped) words of the document, and the value associated with an individual word is an ordered list of line numbers at which that word appears. In the case where a word appears two or more times on the same line, we only record that line number once. The dictionary is populated as follows. We proceed line by line using the index-based for loop beginning at statement 16. This allows us to keep track of line numbers, which are zero-indexed internally. For a single line of text, we break it into a list of preliminary words by splitting on whitespace. Then we analyze each individual word

```
1   class TextIndex:
2     """Manage an index of words occurring in a work of text."""
3
4     def __init__(self, contents, sourceLabel):
5       """Construct a new index for the given document.
6
7       contents        a single string representing the complete contents
8       sourceLabel     a string which identifies the source of the contents
9       """
10      self._lines = contents.split('\n')
11      self._label= sourceLabel
12
13      # Now build a dictionary on the apparent words of the file.
14      # Each word is mapped to an ordered list of line numbers at which that word occurs
15      self._wordAt = { }
16      for linenum in range(len(self._lines)):
17        words = self._lines[linenum].split( )
18        for w in words:
19          w = ourStrip(w)
20          if w:                                    # not reduced to empty string
21            if w not in self._wordAt:              # this is first occurrence of the word
22              self._wordAt[w] = [ linenum ]
23            elif self._wordAt[w][-1] != linenum:   # occurring on a new line for this word
24              self._wordAt[w].append(linenum)
```

FIGURE 12.9: The TextIndex constructor.

with the nested for loop at statement 18. The first thing we do within that loop is to use ourStrip to get a clean version of the word. Assuming that the result is nonempty (i.e., there was at least one true alphabet character), we proceed to the body at statements 21–24.

Here, there are several cases. First we consider whether this word is one that we have previously encountered. The condition at statement 21 is designed to detect the first occurrence of a word. In this case, we add the word as a key to the dictionary together with a new *list* containing the current line number; note carefully the use of the square braces on the right-hand side of statement 22. Otherwise, when the word is already a key of the dictionary, we consider whether the current line number is already recorded. Since we process the file in order, the line numbers are added to the underlying lists in increasing order. If the current line were already on the list, it must be the last element. Therefore, we examine **self.**_wordAt[w][−1] at statement 23. If the current occurrence indeed occurs on a new line number, we append that line number to the appropriate list. After processing all words of all lines, our index is properly initialized.

Querying the index for a single document

In completing our implementation of the TextIndex class, we provide three additional behaviors, shown in Figure 12.10. The first simply echos the label that was provided to the constructor to identify the source of the document. The second method getWords retrieves the list of distinct words contained in this document. Behind the scene, those words serve as keys in our dictionary, so statement 31 simply returns a list of those keys.

The most intricate behavior is the getContext method, which provides a caller with appropriate context of the word occurring within the document. We typically provide context by giving three consecutive lines of the original document, showing the line before the word, the line with the word, and the line after the word. If the word occurs in multiple places within the document, we provide a three-line context for each occurrence. For a very frequent word, seeing the context for each occurrence may be an overwhelming amount of information. To provide flexibility, our signature for getContext accepts an optional parameter that is the maximum number of such contexts to display (10 by default).

A notable aspect of our design is that the method does not explicitly print out any context. Instead, it stores the entire result as a string that is returned to the caller. The caller can then determine the appropriate action (such as printing the string, formatting it differently, or filtering the results). To compose this potentially long result, we build an intermediate list of lines, denoted as output. This list is initialized at statement 39, augmented as we go, and finally joined at statement 47 to produce the return value. The rest of the method body is reasonably straightforward. We first check whether the given word occurs in the document (it is possible that the user queries for context of a nonexistent word). If it does, then the word is used as a key at statement 41, to retrieve the list of line numbers from the _wordAt dictionary. The for loop (statements 42–46) is used to produce each individual portion of the context, making sure to show at most the maximum number of desired results. A context is typically a three-line slice of the original list of lines, but statements 43 and 44 carefully handle some boundary cases. If we are showing context for the very first line of the file, there is no preceding line to show; similarly, the last line of the entire document does not have a following line.

```
25    def getLabel(self):
26        """Return the string which serves as a layer for this document."""
27        return self._label
28
29    def getWords(self):
30        """Return an unordered list of words appearing in this document."""
31        return self._wordAt.keys( )
32
33    def getContext(self, word, maxOccur=10):
34        """Return a string demonstrating occurrences of the word in context.
35
36        Will show up to maxOccur distinct occurrences (default 10)
37        """
38        word = ourStrip(word)                          # clean query term
39        output = [ ]                                   # build list of lines to output
40        if word in self._wordAt:
41            occurrences = self._wordAt[word]           # list of line numbers
42            for lineNum in occurrences[ : maxOccur]:   # limit the number of reported results
43                startContext = max(lineNum − 1, 0)     # typically the previous line
44                stopContext = min(lineNum + 2, len(self._lines))
45                output.append('-' * 40)
46                output.extend(self._lines[startContext : stopContext])
47        return '\n'.join(output)
```

FIGURE 12.10: The other methods of the TextIndex class.

This completes the definition of the TextIndex class, although this is only part of the larger search engine project. This is a perfect opportunity to perform unit testing on the TextIndex class before moving on to the larger project. For the sake of brevity we omit discussion here (but rest assured that we did perform our own tests).

Building the search engine for a corpus

A TextIndex instance serves as an index for a *single* document. We next define an Engine class that manages a larger collection of documents. Internally, the engine is represented using two different dictionaries. One of them, _hasWord, maps each word to the set of labels identifying the documents that contain the word. We use a set since each document is placed once, even when the word occurs multiple times, and since the order of the documents is arbitrary (see Exercise 12.9 for a discussion of ranking the documents). The second dictionary maintained by an engine, named _corpus, is a simple mapping from a document label to a TextIndex instance for that individual document.

The complete code for this class is contained in Figure 12.11. The constructor estab–lishes the two initially empty dictionaries. Documents to be cataloged are added to the corpus one at a time using the addDocument method. To enforce the uniqueness of labels, the document will only be processed if the name is different from all previous names. There are two distinct steps to successfully incorporate a document into the engine. First we must create a dedicated TextIndex for this document, as done at statement 19 of our code. That index is then added to the _corpus dictionary using the unique label as a key. Second, we must update the _hasWord dictionary to record this document label for all words occurring in the new document. The complete list of distinct words is conveniently retrieved from the TextIndex at statement 21. However, there are two possible cases for processing each word, depending upon whether that word has already occurred in some other document of the corpus. If this is the case, then statement 23 adds the new document label to the existing set of labels for that word. Alternatively, if a word is occurring for the first time in the entire corpus, we establish it as a key in the _hasWord dictionary at statement 25, associated with a newly created set containing this document label.

The remaining methods of the Engine class provide various forms of information about the corpus. We offer a lookup method that searches for a given term in the corpus and returns a set of labels for those documents that contain the term. The body of this method is relatively simple, since those documents can immediately be identified through the _hasWord dictionary. The most interesting part of this body is statement 30. Our goal

```
1   class Engine:
2     """Support word searches within a collection of text documents."""
3
4     def __init__(self):
5       """Create a new search engine.
6
7       By default, the initial corpus is empty.
8       """
9       self._corpus = { }          # maps each document label to the associated index
10      self._hasWord = { }         # maps each word to a set of labels
11
12    def addDocument(self, contents, sourceLabel):
13      """Add the given document to the corpus (if not already present).
14
15      contents        a single string representing the complete contents
16      sourceLabel     a string which identifies the source of the contents
17      """
18      if sourceLabel not in self._corpus:
19        newIndex = TextIndex(contents, sourceLabel)
20        self._corpus[sourceLabel] = newIndex
21        for word in newIndex.getWords( ):
22          if word in self._hasWord:
23            self._hasWord[word].add(sourceLabel)
24          else:
25            self._hasWord[word] = set([sourceLabel])      # new set with one entry
```

FIGURE 12.11: The Engine class definition (continued on next page).

is to return a set of document labels, and the value of **self**._hasWord[term] is precisely such a set. Yet since sets are mutable, we do not want the risk of sending the caller a reference to this very set. Instead, we intentionally return a copy of this set.

To further assist users of our Engine class, we provide a getContext method that returns a sample of the use of a given term within a given document. We had already implemented such a behavior as a public method of the TextIndex class. However, users of our Engine class were not given any direct access to the underlying TextIndex instances that we are using. Although we could provide such access, doing so would require our users to learn about this other class. Instead, we provide the convenient Engine.getContext method, which is really just a wrapper for a call to the underlying getContext method on the appropriate TextIndex for the designated document.

By combining calls to the lookup and getContext methods, our users can customize their own displays of search results. They could get the list of documents, and then select context samples for some or all of those documents. Yet for those who do not want to implement such efforts, we provide one additional accessor, named makeReport. This automates the process of performing the lookup and compiling sample contexts. This method returns one (possibly long) string as a result. Although the user cannot customize the format of the report, we do allow the designation of a maximum number of documents for the report and the maximum number of context samples per document.

Testing our engine

The conclusion of Figure 12.11 contains a relatively simple unit test to demonstrate use of the Engine class. In this case, we assume that documents are read from files and loaded into the engine. We will revisit this case study in Section 16.7, when we catalog documents downloaded from the web and provide a way to query our Engine through the network.

```
26    def lookup(self, term):
27        """Return a set of labels for those documents containing the search term."""
28        term = ourStrip(term)
29        if term in self._hasWord:
30            return set(self._hasWord[term])              # intentionally return a copy
31        else:
32            return set( )
33
34    def getContext(term, docLabel, maxOccur=10):
35        """Search a single document for a word, returning a string demonstrating context.
36
37        docLabel        the name of the underlying document to search
38        maxOccur        maximum number of distinct occurrences to display (default 10)
39        """
40        return self._corpus[docLabel].getContext(term, maxOccur)
```

FIGURE 12.11 (continuation): The Engine class definition (continued on next page).

```
41     def makeReport(self, term, maxDocuments=10, maxContext=3):
42         """Produce a formatted report about the occurrences of a term within the corpus.
43
44         Return a string summarizing the results.   This will include names of all documents
45         containing the term as well as a demonstration of the context.
46
47         term             the word of interest
48         maxDocuments  the maximum number of files to report (default 10)
49         maxContext       maximum number of occurrences to show per document (default 3)
50         """
51         output = [ ]                                      # lines of output
52         sources = self.lookup(term)
53         num = min(len(sources), maxDocuments)
54         labels = list(sources)[ :num]                     # choose first so many labels
55         for docLabel in labels:
56             output.append('Document:  ' + docLabel)
57             context = self._corpus[docLabel].getContext(term, maxContext)
58             output.append(context)
59             output.append('=' * 40)
60         return '\n'.join(output)
61
62  if __name__ == '__main__':
63      wizard = Engine( )
64
65      # Phase 1:  load original files
66      print 'Enter filenames to catalog, one per line.'
67      print '(enter a blank line when done)'
68      filename = raw_input('File: ')
69      while filename:
70          try:
71              source = file(filename)
72              wizard.addDocument(source.read( ), filename)
73          except IOError:
74              print 'Sorry. Unable to open file', filename
75          filename = raw_input('File: ')
76
77      # Phase 2:  let user enter queries
78      print
79      print 'Ready to search.  Enter search terms, one per line.'
80      print 'Enter a blank line to end.'
81      term = raw_input('Term: ')
```

FIGURE 12.11 (continuation): The Engine class definition (continued on next page).

```
82   while term:
83     documents = wizard.lookup(term)
84     if documents:  # found the term
85       print 'Containing files are:'
86       print '\n'.join(documents)
87
88       report = wizard.makeReport(term)
89       print
90       print 'Sample report:'
91       print report
92     else:
93       print 'Term not found'
94     term = raw_input('Term: ')
```

FIGURE 12.11 (continuation): The Engine class definition.

12.8   Chapter Review

12.8.1   Key Points

Dictionaries

- The built-in **dict** class is used to represent a mapping from *keys* to *values*.

- A dictionary's keys must be *unique* and *immutable*. A *value* can be any type of object.

- An empty dictionary can be constructed as **dict**( ), or more succinctly with the literal { }.

- A literal can be used to specify a dictionary's initial mapping, as in

    dnaToRna = { 'A': 'U', 'C': 'G', 'G': 'C', 'T': 'A'}

- A value can be entered into a dictionary using a syntax such as

    director['Star Wars'] = 'George Lucas'

  The expression director['Star Wars'] can later be used to retrieve the associated value.

Containers of Containers

- A typical two-dimensional table can naturally be stored as a list of lists, either in row-major or column-major order.

- A many-to-many relationship can be modeled by using a dictionary where each value is itself a container.

- A *reverse dictionary* is a separate mapping based on an original dictionary, identifying those keys that are mapped to each original value. In the reverse dictionary, elements are mapped to a list (as there may be more than one original key mapping to the same value).

Sets

- A **set** represents an unordered collection of unique elements.

- A **set** is a mutable object, but the elements of the set must themselves be immutable.

- The **frozenset** class represents an immutable form of a set.

Arrays

- The **array** class provides compact storage for a sequence of numeric or character types.

- Unlike a **list**, which is represented as a sequence of *references*, an **array** directly stores the data values as part of its state.

- In contrast to a list, the storage of data in an array uses less overall memory and supports more efficient access to the data.

Python's Internal Use of Dictionaries

- Each time an identifier is used as part of a Python command, the interpreter must determine what object is associated with that identifier. This process is called *name resolution*.

- Python uses dictionaries to handle the mapping from the identifier strings to the underlying values.

- A separate dictionary is used to manage the names declared in a given scope. We call such a collection of names a *namespace*.

- A global namespace consisting of identifiers declared at the top level is managed with a dictionary that can be accessed as globals( ).

- Each time a function is invoked, a local namespace is maintained to manage the identifiers established in the context of that call. When that call is completed, the underlying local dictionary is destroyed.

- The names of all Python's built-in functions and types are managed in a special module __builtins__. The dictionary for that namespace can be viewed as vars(__builtins__).

- There are several ways to import from a module.

    - **from** math **import** *
      This syntax takes all names defined in that module and enters those names directly into the current namespace. After this command, the contents of the module are accessed with an *unqualified* name, such as pi.

    - **from** math **import** sqrt, tan, pi
      This is most similar to the previous version, but rather than importing all of the names from the module into the current namespace, only those specifically identified names are imported.

    - **import** math
      This syntax imports the module name itself into the current namespace, but it does not directly import the contents of that module. The contents can be accessed by giving a qualified name, such as math.pi.

- Each instance of a class maintains its own dictionary to track members that are specific to that instance. The dictionary for an object can be viewed using a syntax such as vars(myTV).

- Members that are shared by all objects of a class, such as functions, are kept in a class-level namespace rather than with each individual instance. This dictionary can be viewed using a syntax such as vars(Television).

- When inheritance is used, name resolution proceeds from the instance namespace, to its class namespace, to a parent class namespace and so on.

- When we want to use something other than the default name resolution, we can use a qualified name to specify the namespace from which to look.

12.8.2 Glossary

column-major order A representation of a two-dimensional table as a list of columns, with each column represented as a list of entries in that column; *compare to* row–major order.

container An object whose purpose is to store and manage a collection of other objects.

corpus A collection of text documents.

dictionary A data structure used to manage a collection of keys and their associated values, such that an entry can be accessed quickly based upon a unique key. This structure is synonymously termed a *map* or an ***associative array***.

heterogeneous The property of a collection of objects that are *not* necessarily the same type. For example, a Python **list** can be heterogeneous; *compare to* homogeneous.

homogeneous The property of a collection of objects that are all of the same type. For example a Python **array** is homogeneous; *compare to* heterogeneous.

index An integer value used to identify a position in a sequential structure, such as a string or list. Indices are measured by the offset from the beginning, and thus the first position has index 0.

key An object used to access an associated value within a dictionary.

local scope The context of an identifier that is introduced within the body of a function and is only accessible for the duration of the function call.

name resolution The process by which Python determines which object is associated with an identifier in a given context.

namespace A collection of identifiers and associated values that are defined in a specific scope. A namespace is represented with a dictionary in Python.

qualified name A syntax using "dot" notation (e.g., math.pi) for accessing a name defined in another context (such as a module).

reverse dictionary A second dictionary, built relative to an original dictionary, where the roles of keys and values are interchanged. That is, for each value of the original dictionary, the reverse dictionary identifies the keys originally mapped to that value.

row-major order A representation of a two-dimensional table as a list of rows, with each row represented as a list of entries in that row; *compare to* column–major order.

scope The context of a program within which an identifier is defined.

search engine A data structure that supports efficient queries regarding the location of words within a document or set of documents.

value A piece of data within a dictionary associated with a key.

12.8.3 Exercises

Dictionaries

Practice 12.1: Assume that the method **dict**.values did not exist. Give a small code frag-ment that could be used to produce a list of values for a dictionary data.

Practice 12.2: On page 405, we demonstrated how to print information about movies and directors so that it would be sorted by movie titles (i.e., the keys). Why doesn't the following code fragment accomplish this goal?

```
for movie in director.keys( ).sort( ):
  print movie, 'was directed by', director[movie]
```

Exercise 12.3: Assume that the method **dict**.items did not exist. Give a small code frag-ment that could be used to produce such a result, namely a list of (key, value) pairs for a dictionary data.

Exercise 12.4: In Exercise 5.25, the goal was to implement a function pairSum(data, goal) that returns **True** if the data contains *two distinct* elements whose sum equals the goal, and **False** otherwise.

Reimplement such a function making use of dictionaries for efficiency. Hint: if you start with one number, what would the other have to be? If you find a pair with the correct sum, how could you ensure that the two elements are distinct?

Exercise 12.5: Consider the following program for tracking gifts that you give your friends and family:

```
presents = dict( )
name = 'unknown'
while name != ' ':
  name = raw_input('Who is the present for? ')
  if name != ' ':
    gift = raw_input('What did you give them? ')
    presents[name] = gift

for name in presents.keys( ):
  print 'You bought ', name, 'a(n)  ', presents[name]
```

This program works, so long as you give only one present to each person. Modify it so that you can give a person any number of presents.

Exercise 12.6: In Section 8.5.3, we developed a TallySheet class to compute frequencies for integer or character values. At the time, we worked hard to map general ranges to list indices. This task would have been much easier with the use of dictionaries. Reimplement the functionality of the TallySheet class making use of a dictionary. Use the same public interface, except that there is no need to provide a minimum or maximum value when constructing an instance.

Case Study: a Simple Search Engine

Practice 12.7: Look carefully at statement 25 of Figure 12.11. Why would the program be flawed had that line been written as follows?

> **self.**_hasWord[word] = **set**(sourceLabel)

Exercise 12.8: Consider statements 21–24 of the TextIndex constructor in Figure 12.9. The **if-elif** construct is used to handle two distinct cases. We intentionally ordered those two cases as given. Why would it be a mistake to reorder those cases, rewriting the code as follows?

> **if self.**_wordAt[w][−1] != linenum: # occurring on new line for this word
>   **self.**_wordAt[w].append(linenum)
> **elif** w **not in self.**_wordAt: # this is first occurrence of the word
>   **self.**_wordAt[w] = [linenum]

Exercise 12.9: The order in which Engine.query reports the matching documents is arbitrary. Redesign the software so that the TextIndex also track the number of occurrences of each term within a document. Then, modify Engine.query so that it orders the matching documents based upon the number of occurrences of the given term, ordered from greatest to least.

Exercise 12.10: Augment the Engine class with a method removeDocument(sourceLabel) that removes an existing document from the corpus. Hint: removing the entry from the _corpus dictionary is rather easy. The more difficult task is to remove all traces of that document from the entries of _hasWord.

Exercise 12.11: Our version of Engine.query only works when the search term is a single word. Redesign the software so that query accepts a list of words and identifies those documents that contain *all* of the given search terms.

Exercise 12.12: Our version of Engine.query only works when the search term is a single word. Redesign the software so that when the query string is a multiword phrase (e.g., 'hot dog'), the method identifies all documents that contain the desired phrase (e.g., the word 'hot' immediately preceding the word 'dog' in a document). Note: this is a difficult task.

Projects

Exercise 12.13: Write a main program that uses your solution to Exercise 12.6 to compute *word* frequencies rather than character frequencies. You may rely on the ourStrip function from Section 12.7. When writing a table of results, order it from most frequent to least frequent words (perhaps only showing the top ten words).

Exercise 12.14: As part of Exercise 8.24, we suggested a spell check that offers suggestions for misspelled words and an opportunity for the user to interatively correct a word. Take this one step further by keeping a dictionary of past corrections made by the user and adding those to the list of suggestions when re-encountering the same misspelling.

Implementing Data Structures

In this chapter, we examine the implementation of several classic data structures, focusing on how internal design choices affect the outward efficiency of the resulting structures. We focus on three particular examples. First we provide an overview of the representation of Python's built-in **list** class. You may recall that we implemented our own list class as part of Chapter 11. While that was an illustrative demonstration of the use of recursion, that is not how Python's **list** class is actually implemented; the built-in class uses a very different approach that is significantly more efficient.

The second example we discuss is that of a dictionary. We provide two different implementations for a dictionary class. The first is a rather simple implementation for handling the mapping from keys to values. The second approach is more intricate and very similar to the implementation used by Python's built-in **dict** class. Our final data structure is one known as a **_binary search tree_**. While it is not one of Python's built-in structures, it is an extremely powerful and versatile data structure, widely used in practice.

We have two broad goals for the chapter. The first is to introduce various approaches for organizing a data structure. A programmer may often need to develop a data structure that is not built into Python (such as a binary search tree). These examples should demonstrate techniques that are applicable in more general settings.

Yet we also spend effort in this chapter developing our own dictionary implementation, just as we spent time in Chapter 11 developing our own version of a list. We are not suggesting that anyone use our implementations in practice. Python's **list** and **dict** classes are extremely well designed and optimized for performance. Still, to make the best use of those classes, it is important to have a general understanding of their internal implementations. Our discussions are meant to give a peek at those internals. This goes somewhat against the principle of encapsulation, which is premised on the fact that we do not need to know about the internal design of a tool to be able to use that tool. While this is true in regard to the programming interface, the *efficiency* of our program depends intricately on the efficiency of those tools. When we invoke a function, our flow of control is passed to the function until it completes. It can make a great difference whether that function executes in a fraction of a second, a handful of seconds, minutes, hours, or days. Although the built-in classes are well defined, some behaviors are significantly less efficient than others.

13.1 Measuring Efficiency

The efficiency of a data structure has a direct impact on how large a data set software can process. Computers are definitely quick, yet we also ask a lot of them as data sets grow larger in society. Poor efficiency is often to blame for software that performs reasonably in initial testing yet fails miserably in large-scale deployment. This chapter provides a framework for measuring the efficiency of a piece of software and evaluating the impact of the size of a data set.

In some respects, the notion of efficiency is straightforward. Completing a task takes a certain amount of time and we would prefer that it use as little time as possible. The time can be measured in several ways. We could measure the elapsed time of a program manually by looking at a clock or using a stopwatch. For lengthy computations this may result in a reasonable approximation. Of course if the computer only takes a fraction of a second, our ability to accurately time it in a manual fashion is doomed. Fortunately, Python provides support for keeping track of elapsed time directly from within the program. The time module includes a function time( ) that returns the current time according to the computer's system clock. The return value is a **float** representing the number of seconds (or fractions thereof) that have passed since a canonical moment in time. The precise choice of that reference time depends upon the computer and operating system, but it is immaterial if we are only interested in elapsed time. A standard pattern for recording the elapsed time is shown as follows:

```
from time import time
start = time( )             # record the starting time
#   ... perform some task ...
stop = time( )              # record the finish time
elapsed = stop − start      # measured in seconds (or fraction thereof)
```

Even so, basing analysis on a precise measure of execution time poses significant challenges. The execution time for a task depends upon the amount of data being processed and the values being used. Furthermore, that execution time depends on other system factors and will vary from machine to machine, and even from trial to trial on the same machine.

Asymptotic analysis

In contrast to measuring elapsed time empirically, a common practice in computer science is to provide a mathematical analysis that estimates the order of growth of the running time in relation to the size of the data set. This approach is termed *asymptotic analysis*.

As our first example, we examine the time used by the count method of the **list** class (we will discuss lists more thoroughly in the next section). The process of counting is typically achieved by iterating over the entire list, comparing each element to the target value while keeping a count of the number of matches. Although we can measure the precise amount of time, this number does not have much meaning in isolation. We can gather more interesting empirical data by performing tests on different sized lists. In Figure 13.1, we suggest a test for measuring the performance of count on three different lists, with one hundred thousand, one million, and ten million elements respectively. Although we cannot

```
1  from time import time
2  testA = range(100000)
3  testB = range(1000000)
4  testC = range(10000000)
5  # small test
6  start = time( )
7  testA.count(12345)
8  stop = time( )
9  print 'testA time was', stop − start
10 # medium test
11 start = time( )
12 testB.count(12345)
13 stop = time( )
14 print 'testB time was', stop − start
15 # large test
16 start = time( )
17 testC.count(12345)
18 stop = time( )
19 print 'testC time was', stop − start
```

FIGURE 13.1: An empirical test of **list**.count.

accurately predict results on your system, you should see that the amount of time it takes for testB is approximately ten times greater than for testA, and that the time for testC is approximately ten times greater than for testB. In theory, if one list is ten times longer than another, it takes roughly ten times longer to iterate over its contents.

Formally, we describe this scenario by saying that the time used by count is *linear* with respect to the size of the list. To use a common notation in computer science, we write that the running time of count is $\Theta(n)$, where n represents the number of elements on the list. In short, this mathematical expression means that as n grows, the running time of the process increases proportionately. There are many other common asymptotic relationships. For example, in Section 11.4 we discussed why binary search has a running time that grows only logarithmically with the size of a list. Using this new notation, we more succinctly describe binary search as using $\Theta(\log n)$ time.

As another example, we explore the time used to compute the length of a list. At first thought, we might presume that this is similar to count, requiring code for iterating through the list to determine its length. However, if you modify the code of Figure 13.1 to compute len(testA) at line 7 and similarly at lines 12 and 17, you will find a very different result. The length is reported almost instantaneously for all three lists. This is because the internal state of a list includes direct knowledge of the current length. So querying the length of a long list takes no more time than the length of a shorter list. Using our formal notation, we say that the __len__ method runs in $\Theta(1)$ time, commonly described as *constant time*. In this case, the running time is completely independent of n.

13.2 Python's list Class

Python's **list** class is an extremely important tool, supporting many convenient methods. From a caller's perspective, those methods are all easy to use. Yet the relative efficiency of those methods varies greatly, as noted when examining count and __len__ in the previous section. While the precise implementation of the **list** class is subject to change in future versions of Python, some principles will remain at its core. A list is represented internally as a sequence of references, each of which points to an underlying object elsewhere in memory (see Section 10.2 for discussion). The references are stored in sequence, within a large block of memory known as an array.[1] By storing the references consecutively in memory, lists support extremely efficient access based upon the use of indices.

An index measures the offset from the beginning of that memory block to the desired item. The reference to data[0] will be found at offset zero from the beginning of that memory block. The reference to data[1] is found one step away from the beginning, and so on. Historically, this is the reason lists are zero-indexed. More importantly, there is no need to explicitly iterate over each of the preceding elements of the list. If someone is interested in examining the element with index 9876, that reference can be found by calculating the memory address that is at an offset of 9876 from the start of the array, measured according to the space used to store a single reference. Although references may point to objects of varying sizes, the references themselves each use the same amount of memory.

13.2.1 Accessors

With this representation in mind, let's begin to explore the efficiency of the behaviors of the **list** class. The accessors generally fall into one of three categories.

Constant time for any size list

The most important behavior in this category is the standard __getitem__ method. As we noted above, a syntax like data[9876] provides immediate access to that element of the list. The system does not need to iterate through the preceding elements to find the one in question. We have also already noted that the __len__ method returns its answer immediately, as that length is stored explicitly as part of the state information.

Require a complete iteration

The count method is a typical example of a behavior that requires iteration through the full list. Intuitively, the implementation must examine each value of the list in order to compute an accurate count of the number of matches. Therefore the execution time grows *linearly* with the size of the list. This same analysis is true of built-in functions min, max, and sum.

Require an iteration that may be partial

Although count requires a full examination of the sequence, many accessors fall into a middle category. Each of these requires some form of iteration through the list, but one that

---

1.   Although not to be confused with the **array** class introduced in Section 12.5, these follow the same concept. The **array** class is used to store a sequence of actual primitive values in a consecutive block of memory. Lists are correspondingly represented as an array of references; those references are stored consecutively in memory, yet the objects that they reference are stored elsewhere.

may or may not proceed through the entire list. As a typical example, consider the sequen-tial search used by __contains__. This iterates through the list, starting at the beginning, while looking for the desired value. As soon as it finds the value, it immediately stops the iteration and returns **True**, so the only way the iteration reaches the end is when the ele-ment is not found, or coincidentally is the last element. You can gather empirical evidence of these facts by timing the following individual steps (either formally or informally):

```
bigValue = 10000000
bigList = range(bigValue)
print 5 in bigList              # found near the beginning
print bigValue−5 in bigList     # found near the end
print −5 in bigList             # not found
```

When the value is found near the beginning, the method is quite efficient, but the overall running time is still linear when the value is found later in the list or never found.

Other behaviors fall into this category. The index method is responsible for find-ing the leftmost occurrence of a given value from some starting point and its efficiency depends upon how long it takes before finding such a value or else reaching the end of the list. The comparison between two lists, based on the __eq__ method, also falls into this category. A comparison is evaluated based upon what is known as *lexicographical order*. Corresponding elements of the two lists are compared until there is either a mismatch or the end of one or both of the lists is reached.

Taking a slice of a list requires partial iteration, although for a different reason. The slice is a shallow copy of the relevant portion of the original list. The time to construct the slice depends directly upon the desired length. Taking a slice such as data[30000:30005] is quite efficient. Python can easily access the desired portion of the sequence and build a new list composed of those same references. Yet computing the slice data[30000:40000] requires time to establish a new list containing the proper 10000 references.

13.2.2   Mutators

When altering a list, the efficiency depends greatly on the requirement that references be stored consecutively to support efficient indexing. We look at several variations.

Overwriting an element

Use of a syntax such as data[9876] = 54.3 is quite efficient. Just as an index provides effi-cient access when *retrieving* a reference to an underlying element, that reference can easily be reassigned to some other value. Changing that entry has no effect on the placement of the surrounding elements, so this action is performed in $\Theta(1)$ time.

Appending an element to the end of the list

The implementation of the append method is more interesting. A new element is tacked onto the end of the sequence. In spirit, since the list is aware of its own length, it knows precisely where this new reference should be stored in memory. So in most cases, this operation proceeds in $\Theta(1)$ time. However, there is a complicating factor.

The new reference must be integrated into the block of contiguous memory used to stored the list. The block has limited capacity, so there will eventually be a problem. Python handles this issue in a clever way. Rather than reserving only enough memory for the precise length of a list, it often requests a larger block of memory for such expansion. Presuming it has enough space, appending an item to the end of a list is efficient. However, after many insertions, that extra space will be exhausted. In this case Python has no choice but to relocate the underlying array into a larger block of memory. This step requires a linear pass to copy the references from the old memory block to a newer, larger memory block. Yet it intentionally moves to a *much* larger block, say one that is twice as large as the previous block. This provides a good reserve for further expansion so that an expensive relocation is not required often. The mathematical analysis of this approach is beyond the current discussion but, in short, append is guaranteed to run in constant time on average, with an occasional worst case that is linear in the current size of the list.

Popping from the end of the list

The default behavior for pop( ) is to remove the last item from the list. This is always efficient, running in $\Theta(1)$ time. Removing that entry never requires further reconfiguration.

Adding or removing general elements

Adjustments at the end of a list, via append( ) or pop( ), are quite efficient because one change does not affect the placement of any preceding elements. More time is needed when adding or removing elements from elsewhere in the sequence. Python must ensure that the altered sequence is stored sequentially in memory (for continued support of effi−cient indexing). So when a new value is inserted at a prescribed index, all subsequent elements must be shifted back one slot in the sequence to make room. For this reason, the running time of insert depends upon how far the new value is from the end of the list. When inserting near the end of the list, only a few elements need to be displaced, so the performance will be efficient. But in general, many elements may need to be shifted and the operation takes $\Theta(n)$ time.

The pop method has similar characteristics, as it requires all subsequent elements to be shifted forward one slot, to fill in the hole created by the removed item. When pop executes near the end of the list, such as with the default pop( ), the method runs in constant time. But popping from the heart of the list will require $\Theta(n)$ time. The remove method is closely related to the pop method, yet with an additional burden. With pop, the caller specifies the desired element according to index. When using remove, the parameter is a *value* and so this method has the extra burden of finding the leftmost occurrence of the value in addition to performing the underlying rearrangement once that location is found.

Reversing or sorting a list

Both reverse and sort affect the overall placement of elements within a sequence. When reversing a list, pairs of elements are swapped, starting at the opposite ends and proceeding until reaching the middle. This process requires $\Theta(n)$ time. Sorting is generally more expensive, requiring a more intricate rearrangement of the elements. In the worst case it requires $\Theta(n \log n)$ time; an explanation of why is the central theme of Chapter 14.

13.3 Our Own Dictionary Implementation

Python's **dict** class is a useful tool for representing general mappings from an unordered collection of *distinct* keys to their associated values. The concept of a dictionary was introduced in Section 12.2. In this section we look at several approaches that can be used to implement those behaviors, including the technique used by Python, and compare the efficiencies of these approaches. We will focus upon the representative subset of behaviors shown in Figure 12.2 on page 404.

13.3.1 Managing Coordinated Lists

As a simple first example, we revisit the mapping used in transcribing DNA to RNA.

DNA		**RNA**
'A'	⟶	'U'
'C'	⟶	'G'
'G'	⟶	'C'
'T'	⟶	'A'

A relatively easy way to manage this mapping is by using two coordinated sequences, one for the keys and one for the values. In fact this is precisely the strategy we used for the case study of Section 4.2. After determining the index of a key in the first sequence, we immediately locate its associated value in the second. That early example used two coordinate strings, since the mapping involved characters. We generalize the idea by designing a class DictWithLists. A dictionary instance maintains two lists, _keys and _values, that are carefully coordinated so that _keys[i] is associated with _values[i] for each index i. A diagram of this structure for our DNA mapping is shown in Figure 13.2.

A complete implementation based on this approach is given in Figure 13.3. Most of the work is devoted to a variety of methods that mimic Python's dictionary interface. Since there are so many situations in which we need the location of a given key, we provide a private _getIndex method at lines 6–10. This routine finds the location of the given key, if

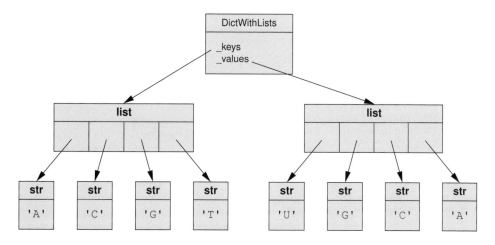

FIGURE 13.2: A simple example of a mapping, represented as a pair of coordinated lists.

it exists, and otherwise returns len(**self**._keys) as a special value to denote a key that was not found in the dictionary (notice that such an index could not be legitimate). We use that method as the first command for __getitem__, __setitem__, and pop. In the context of __getitem__, we raise a KeyError when detecting that the desired key was not found. Otherwise, we use the index to retrieve and return the associated value (line 22). There is never a KeyError in the context of __setitem__. However, the behavior depends on whether the given key exists. If so, then we overwrite its associated value at line 26; if it is a new key, we append it and the associated value to the end of the lists (lines 28 and 29). Within pop, we remove the indicated key and value from the respective lists, returning the value to the caller.

Efficiency

Although this approach suffices in simple cases such as the DNA mapping, the performance degrades as the size of a dictionary increases. In particular, the work to find the index at which a key occurs requires $\Theta(n)$ time in general. Since that method is used by most of the basic operations, we get linear performance for almost all operations. The only methods that are guaranteed to run in constant time are the constructor, __len__, clear, and popitem (since the underlying popping from the ends of the two lists is efficient).

```
1   class DictWithLists:
2     def __init__(self):
3       self._keys = [ ]
4       self._values = [ ]
5
6     def _getIndex(self, k):                      # Returns len(self) if key not found
7       i = 0
8       while i < len(self._keys) and self._keys[i] != k:
9         i += 1
10      return i
11
12    def __len__(self):
13      return len(self._keys)
14
15    def __contains__(self, k):
16      return k in self._keys
17
18    def __getitem__(self, k):
19      ind = self._getIndex(k)
20      if ind == len(self):
21        raise KeyError(repr(k))                  # k not found
22      return self._values[ind]
```

FIGURE 13.3: Representing a dictionary with coordinated lists (continued on next page).

```
23    def __setitem__(self, k, v):
24      ind = self._getIndex(k)
25      if ind < len(self):                    # reassign new value for existing key
26        self._values[ind] = v
27      else:                                  # new key/value pair
28        self._keys.append(k)
29        self._values.append(v)
30
31    def clear(self):
32      self._keys = [ ]
33      self._values = [ ]
34
35    def pop(self, k):
36      ind = self._getIndex(k)
37      if ind == len(self):
38        raise KeyError(repr(k))              # k not found
39      self._keys.pop(ind)
40      return self._values.pop(ind)
41
42    def popitem(self):
43      if len(self) == 0:
44        raise KeyError('popitem(): dictionary is empty')
45      return (self._keys.pop( ), self._values.pop( ))
46
47    def keys(self):
48      return list(self._keys)                # copy of internal list
49
50    def values(self):
51      return list(self._values)             # copy of internal list
52
53    def items(self):
54      result = [ ]
55      for i in range(len(self)):
56        result.append( (self._keys[i], self._values[i]) )
57      return result
58
59    def __repr__(self):
60      mapping = [ ]
61      for k,v in self.items( ):
62        mapping.append( repr(k) + ' :  ' + repr(v) )
63      return '{' + ',  '.join(mapping) + '}'
```

FIGURE 13.3 (continuation): Representing a dictionary with coordinated lists.

13.3.2 Hashing

We relied upon two coordinated lists, _keys and _values, in our previous implementation of a dictionary. To perform the mapping from a given key to its associated value, we used the first list in effect as a way to determine the index at which the associated value is stored in the second list. The time-consuming portion of the work is in searching for the key in the first list to determine the proper index; using the index to access the value in the second list is simple. Python's **dict** class uses a much more efficient approach for managing a dictionary, based on a general technique known as *hashing*.

If keys happened to be unique integers, say in the range from 0 to $T - 1$ for some T, we could completely bypass the need for the first of those two lists. We could use the key itself as an index into a list of size T. That is, we could use _values[key] as the place to store the value associated with the key. Inserting the value into the dictionary would be quite efficient, as would retrieving it at some later time. This is precisely the intuition we used when developing the TallySheet class back in Section 8.5.3. Of course, restricting keys to be integers is quite limiting as a general practice. This was the principal point we emphasized when originally discussing the use of dictionaries in Section 12.2. There are many scenarios in which the natural keys are not integers, or even if so, are so large that it is impractical to use them as indices. However, the underlying idea can be extended as follows.

To overcome the first hurdle, Python has a way to transform each immutable object into a somewhat arbitrary integer value, using the built-in function hash(key). Every piece of digital data is already represented at the core as a series of bits, so treating it as a large integer is not unimaginable. However, we will not try to explain the precise mathematics of how this value is computed. The second hurdle to overcome is the fact that such an integer may be too large to use as an index into a *reasonably* sized list. The solution here is to maintain a list with some size T that is more to our liking, and to fold those large integers into appropriate indices using modular arithmetic. By computing hash(key) % T, we get an index that is guaranteed[2] to be in the range from 0 to $T - 1$. Therefore, we can choose T to be the size of our preferred list and use hash(key) % T as an index into what is called a *hash table*.

Collisions and buckets

This use of hashing presents us with one additional hurdle. Although the original keys of a dictionary are required to be unique, there is a possibility that two or more distinct keys may get transformed into the same index by this process. This is so for two reasons. First there is a slight chance that two distinct keys have the same hash value and then a second chance that two different hash values get folded to the same index when using the modulus operator. When two different keys end up being mapped to the same index of our table, we call this a *collision*. Consider, for example, the following observations on our computer system[3] if converting string keys to indices within a list of length 7.

---

2. Other programming languages do not necessarily make such a guarantee. Some languages implement modular arithmetic in a way that can give a negative result when the original hash value is negative.

3. The actual hash values depends greatly upon the computer system and the version of Python, so it may be that you get different results for this example. However, there will certainly be cases in which two distinct keys lead to the same index.

key	hash(key)	hash(key) % 7
'A'	8320025024	3
'C'	8576025794	0
'G'	9088027334	1
'T'	10752032341	1

Notice that 'G' and 'T' both result in an index of 1 by this calculation. The problem with such a collision is that keys 'G' and 'T' presumably have independent values associated with them. We need to store both of those values, and know which goes with which key.

Since there is no way to avoid the possibility of collisions, we must prepare to cope with them. There are several strategies for collision management used in practice. The approach we take is to maintain a list of *containers* rather than a direct list of values. Using standard terminology, we will have one primary list known as a ***hash table***. At each location of that table, we will have a secondary structure which we call a ***bucket***. This is used to store all (key,value) pairs for keys that collide at a given index. Figure 13.4 shows a simple hash table for the above example.

Implementation

It is time to put these ideas together into a complete implementation of a class named DictWithHashing. The dictionary instance has two attributes: _table, which is a list of buckets, and _numItems, which is a count of the overall number of (key,value) pairs that are currently stored somewhere in the table.

The biggest remaining design issue is how to represent each bucket. Those buckets will have to store (key,value) pairs and allow us to later retrieve that information. In fact, the desired behaviors are precisely that of a *dictionary*. Although we could consider the use of recursion, we are going to use another common technique called ***bootstrapping***. We will use the much simpler DictWithLists implementation to represent each bucket. That earlier implementation is not as efficient for a large dictionary but, if things go well, we

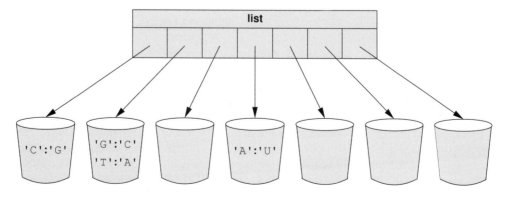

FIGURE 13.4: A simple example of a hash table.

expect relatively few elements in any particular bucket. For small sets, the DictWithLists is even more streamlined than the more complex hashing approach. The use of the simpler class also makes the code for our DictWithHashing quite legible. The constructor proceeds as follows:

```
def __init__(self):
    self._numItems = 0                    # no elements initially
    self._table = [None] * 7              # quick footprint;
    for h in range(len(self._table)):     # real buckets created by loop
        self._table[h] = DictWithLists()  # bootstrap with simpler version
```

For simplicity, we start with a table size of 7 and create each individual bucket as a new, empty DictWithLists instance. For most of the other routines, we proceed by finding the appropriate bucket for a given key and then manipulating that bucket. For this reason, we define a private utility _getBucket that handles the mathematics for performing a lookup in the table.

```
def _getBucket(self, k):
    return self._table[ hash(k) % len(self._table) ]
```

As we described in the introduction, the hash of the key is computed and then we use the modulus operator to get the appropriate index for our current table size. With these conventions, implementing most of the expected dictionary behaviors becomes easy. As an example, here is the implementation for __getitem__.

```
def __getitem__(self, k):
    bucket = self._getBucket(k)
    if k not in bucket:              # wasn't there
        raise KeyError(repr(k))
    return bucket[k]                 # retrieve associated value from bucket
```

Based upon the key we determine what bucket to examine. Of course, there is no guarantee that such a key had been inserted. So we use the test k **not in** bucket, which is supported by the underlying bucket. If the key is found, we retrieve the associated value with the syntax bucket[k].

The most complex aspect of our new implementation involves the management of the table size. Our bootstrapping was based upon the presumption that the individual buckets are not overwhelmed. The performance of our overall structure will seriously degrade if too many elements end up in individual buckets. The underlying mathematics of hashing is designed to distribute elements somewhat evenly, yet as more keys get inserted, the individual buckets will contain more and more elements. In our implementation, we arbitrarily started with a table size of 7. Clearly if millions of elements are inserted, even if uniformly distributed, there will be too many values in each bucket for an efficient dictionary.

One way to avoid the overload is to create a bigger initial table. But with what size? Unless we have specific knowledge as to the number of expected keys, we might still pick too small a table and be overwhelmed. Overestimating is also a potential problem, since too large a table is an unnecessary waste of space. The standard technique is to start with a small table but to expand the table if the overall load is getting too high. For example, let us assume that we are happy with the performance so long as the *average* number of elements per bucket is at most 2.0. Determining the average is easy, as it just depends on our overall count of elements relative to the current table size. Since new elements can only be added through the use of __setitem__, we look for an overloaded scenario from within that routine.

```python
def __setitem__(self, k, v):
    bucket = self._getBucket(k)
    if k not in bucket:
        self._numItems +=1                      # k is a new key
    bucket[k] = v                               # assign/reassign value
    if self._numItems > 2.0*len(self._table):   # load factor exceed
        self._expandTable( )
```

After inserting the new element, if we see that the resulting scenario has too high an average bucket size, we remedy the situation by expanding our table. The private _expandTable( ) routine proceeds as follows:

```python
def _expandTable(self):
    oldItems = self.items( )                    # save list of existing contents!!!

    # re-create bigger table of empty buckets
    newSize = 2 * len(self._table) + 1          # will be pow(2,j)−1 for some j
    self._numItems = 0
    self._table = [None] * newSize              # bigger footprint
    for h in range(len(self._table)):
        self._table[h] = DictWithLists( )       # empty bucket

    # reinsert contents from old to new
    for k,v in oldItems:
        self[k] = v
```

We essentially reconstruct a brand new table, in a style similar to the original constructor. However, we pick a bigger table size. The precise increase in table size can be customized based on performance. Our approach is a rather simple one that essentially doubles the current size (it actually adds an additional one because it turns out that hashing is better distributed when the table size is not a power of two). Because the table size is changing, and the mathematics for computing the location of a key depends upon dividing by the table size, we must redistribute all of the current items after re-creating the larger table. To do this we purposely get a list of those old items *before* disturbing the overall state. Then at the end, we redistribute those items back into the larger structure by relying upon **self**[k] = v (which triggers __setitem__). The rest of the behaviors are relatively straight-forward. Figure 13.5 provides the complete implementation.

```
1   class DictWithHashing:
2     def __init__(self):
3       self._numItems = 0                         # no elements initially
4       self._table = [None] * 7                   # quick footprint;
5       for h in range(len(self._table)):          # real buckets created by loop
6         self._table[h] = DictWithLists( )        # bootstrap with simpler version
7
8     def _getBucket(self, k):
9       return self._table[ hash(k) % len(self._table) ]
10
11    def __len__(self):
12      return self._numItems
13
14    def __contains__(self, k):
15      bucket = self._getBucket(k)
16      return k in bucket                          # is key actually in the bucket?
17
18    def __getitem__(self, k):
19      bucket = self._getBucket(k)
20      if k not in bucket:                         # wasn't there
21        raise KeyError(repr(k))
22      return bucket[k]                            # retrieve associated value from bucket
23
24    def __setitem__(self, k, v):
25      bucket = self._getBucket(k)
26      if k not in bucket:
27        self._numItems +=1                        # k is a new key
28      bucket[k] = v                               # assign/reassign value
29      if self._numItems > 2.0*len(self._table):   # load factor exceed
30        self._expandTable( )
31
32    def _expandTable(self):
33      oldItems = self.items( )                    # save list of existing contents!!!
34
35      # re-create bigger table of empty buckets
36      newSize = 2 * len(self._table) + 1          # will be pow(2,j)−1 for some j
37      self._numItems = 0
38      self._table = [None] * newSize              # bigger footprint
39      for h in range(len(self._table)):
40        self._table[h] = DictWithLists( )         # empty bucket
41
42      # reinsert contents from old to new
43      for k,v in oldItems:
44        self[k] = v
```

FIGURE 13.5: A dictionary based upon a hash table (continued on next page).

```
45      def clear(self):
46        for bucket in self._table:
47          bucket.clear( )
48        self._numItems = 0
49
50      def pop(self, k):
51        bucket = self._getBucket(k)
52        if k not in bucket:
53          raise KeyError(repr(k))                   # wasn't there
54        self._numItems -= 1
55        return bucket.pop(k)
56
57      def popitem(self):
58        if self._numItems == 0:
59          raise KeyError('popitem(): dictionary is empty')
60        h = 0                                        # must look for a nonempty bucket
61        while len(self._table[h]) == 0:
62          h += 1
63        self._numItems -= 1
64        return self._table[h].popitem( )
65
66      def keys(self):
67        allkeys = [ ]                                # must gather keys from all buckets
68        for bucket in self._table:
69          allkeys.extend(bucket.keys( ))
70        return allkeys
71
72      def values(self):
73        allvalues = [ ]                              # must gather values from all buckets
74        for bucket in self._table:
75          allvalues.extend(bucket.values( ))
76        return allvalues
77
78      def items(self):
79        allitems = [ ]                               # must gather items from all buckets
80        for bucket in self._table:
81          allitems.extend(bucket.items( ))
82        return allitems
83
84      def __repr__(self):
85        mapping = [ ]
86        for k,v in self.items( ):
87          mapping.append( repr(k) + ' : ' + repr(v) )
88        return '{ ' + ',  '.join(mapping) + ' }'
```

FIGURE 13.5 (continuation): A dictionary based upon a hash table.

Efficiency

If we are willing to trust that only a few items are stored in each individual bucket, then our DictWithHashing is quite efficient. With this assumption, adding or retrieving an item is processed in $\Theta(1)$ time on average. The most expensive process is the occasional expansion of the table, as this step requires $\Theta(n)$ time since each existing element must be reinserted. Yet by doubling the size of the table, this step does not need to be executed very often (the mathematics is quite similar to the discussion of Python's treatment of the **list** class, from Section 13.2.2). Because of their efficiency, hash tables are widely used in practice. In fact, this is the underlying technology used for Python's **dict** class (as well as the **set** class, introduced in Section 12.4).

13.3.3 Immutable Keys

When originally introducing the use of a dictionary, in Section 12.2, we emphasized the point that the keys of a dictionary must be drawn from an *immutable* class. At this point, we can explain why. The hash function used to convert a key to a representative integer depends upon that object's state. Imagine a hypothetical scenario in which a mutable object is inserted into a dictionary, perhaps placed into the bucket at index 3. After being inserted, some other action may cause the underlying state of this object to be mutated. The problem is that if we subsequently query the dictionary looking for that key, the recomputed hash function may lead us to a different bucket. This would cause us to report the absence of the key even though it was previously inserted. With an immutable key, all subsequent searches lead to the same bucket where an item was originally placed.

To enforce this restriction, immutable types support a special method __hash__ that is used to compute the expression hash(key) for a given key. That function has already been implemented for all of the built-in immutable types. If we try to use a *mutable* key (e.g., a **list**) with the **dict** class, we get the following TypeError reported:

```
>>> sample = dict()
>>> badKey = ['09', 'f9', '11', '02', '9d']  # mutable list
>>> sample[badKey] = 'oops'
Traceback (most recent call last):
  File "<stdin>", line 1, in -toplevel-
TypeError: list objects are unhashable
```

For user-defined classes, Python does not want to try to determine whether the object is semantically mutable or immutable. So instead it relies upon the existence of a __hash__ method to denote the presumed immutability of an object. In Section 6.4, we used the Fraction class as an example of a user-defined immutable class. It would be perfectly consistent, in spirit, to use fractions as keys of a dictionary. However, if you try to use a fraction, as defined in that earlier chapter, as a key into a dictionary the same TypeError is reported. As the designer of the class, it is our responsibility to implement __hash__ if we want the instances to be allowed as keys of a dictionary.

Designing a good hash function from scratch is a difficult task, as we need different values to be hashed to somewhat arbitrary integers to get good performance. Fortunately, there is a standard trick that can be used for typical cases of a user-defined class. We can rely upon the existing hash capabilities of built-in classes, most notably the **tuple** class. We compose a single tuple that includes all relevant attributes for the immutable state of our object. Then we consider our object's hash value to be the hash value of that tuple. For example, in the context of the Fraction class, that method could be implemented simply as

```
def __hash__(self):
    return hash( (self._numer, self._denom) )
```

13.4 Binary Search Trees

Hash tables, as introduced in the preceding section, are extremely efficient containers for supporting searches, as well as insertions and deletions. However, hash tables cannot be used to represent an *ordered* sequence. The efficiency of hashing relies upon the intentional scrambling of data via well-chosen hash functions. In this section we introduce another valuable data structure, called a ***binary search tree***, that is designed to efficiently manage an *ordered* sequence.

For the sake of comparison, we begin by reviewing the ***binary search*** algorithm of Section 11.4. That algorithm is used to search within a sorted **list**. The general idea is to compare a desired value to the middle value of the list. If that middle value does not match the target, we can narrow our search to either the left or right half of the list depending upon whether the target value is less than or greater than the middle value of the list. This recursive approach results in a search that is guaranteed to complete in at most $\Theta(\log n)$ rounds. That approach is excellent when managing a data set that never changes. Unfortunately, lists do not efficiently support arbitrary insertions and deletions. The problem stems from the fact that elements must be sorted for binary search to work and because underlying references must be stored sequentially in a list. As we noted in Section 13.2.2, a single insertion or deletion may require the shifting of linearly many existing elements.

The goal with a binary search tree is to provide support for an efficient search, akin to that of binary search, but to simultaneously support more efficient insertion and deletion operations. This is accomplished by maintaining the general order of elements, but not in a purely sequential fashion. We organize the data in a ***tree***, which is a hierarchical structure with a natural recursive definition. In general, a tree is composed of a single element (typically called the *root*) and two subtrees. The left subtree contains all additional elements that are *less* than that of the root; the right subtree contains all additional elements that are *greater* than that of the root. We implement a recursive version of a binary search tree modeled loosely in the style of the OurList class from Section 11.2. Much as we used an empty list as a base case for our lists, we represent an empty tree as one that does not store any elements, nor a left or right subtree. For simplicity, we will demonstrate the use of a binary search tree to manage a sorted set; the approach can easily be adapted to store duplicates or to track associated values, as with a dictionary. But before considering the code, let's take a few moments to explore the high-level concept.

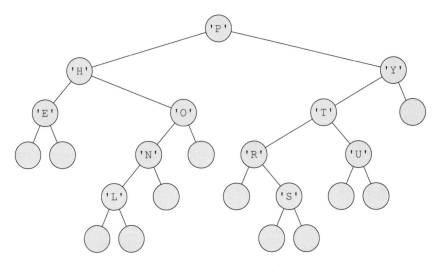

FIGURE 13.6: A basic example of a binary search tree. The characters are elements and the circles without characters represent empty subtrees.

As our first example, consider the binary search tree shown in Figure 13.6. In this example, the element located at the root of the tree is 'P'. All subsequent items are divided into those less than 'P' and therefore within the left subtree of the root, and those greater than 'P' and therefore in the right subtree of the root. This organizational structure continues at all levels of the tree. For example, if we look at the subtree rooted at 'H' we see that its left subtree has elements that are less than 'H' (namely 'E'). Its right subtree contains elements (namely 'L', 'N', and 'O') that are greater than 'H', although still less than 'P' since they belong to the left subtree of the original root.

The tree structure is precisely designed to support searching. In fact the strategy is quite similar in spirit to binary search on a list. We begin a search at the root and compare its element to the target value. One of four things will happen. If the root is empty, the search fails. If the element at the root matches the target, we have found it. Otherwise we decide which subtree to search based upon whether the target is less than or greater than the root's element. For example, when searching for 'R' we compare the target to the root. They do not match in this case and, since 'R' > 'P', we continue the search (recursively) in the *right* subtree of the root. Figure 13.7 shows the complete search path as the recursion unfolds. That right subtree has 'Y' at its root, and since 'R' < 'Y' we continue the search in the *left* subtree of that tree, and then continue to the left of 'T' until finally locating the desired element. As an example of an *unsuccessful* search, Figure 13.8 shows the search for 'M'. In this case, the recursion stops when the path reaches an empty subtree (namely the right subtree of 'L').

Efficiency

The efficiency of a binary search tree is closely related to our original analysis of binary search. By comparing the target to the root, we either find it or essentially eliminate half

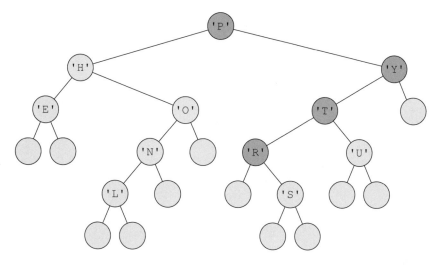

FIGURE 13.7: The path of a successful search for `'R'`.

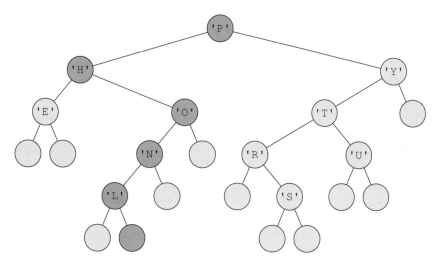

FIGURE 13.8: The path of an unsuccessful search for `'M'`, ending at an empty subtree.

the tree from contention. The main shortcoming in this analogy is that we specifically choose the precise midpoint when performing a binary search on a list. That allowed us to guarantee that the search would complete after at most $\Theta(\log n)$ steps. For a binary search tree, there might not be an equal number of elements on each side of the root. If they are approximately equal, the analysis holds. However, if one side is significantly bigger than the other and our search proceeds to the bigger half, the analysis fails. In an extreme case, the search path may be linear in the overall number of elements. Fortunately, a search tree is typically balanced enough to perform well if built with an arbitrary data set. There are more advanced techniques that can be used to reshape a tree to ensure sufficient balance.

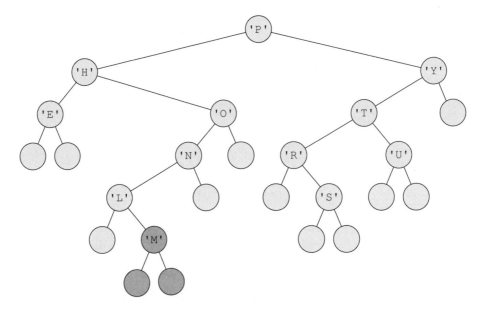

FIGURE 13.9: The tree, after inserting the new element 'M'.

Insertion

The greatest advantage of a binary search tree (versus a sorted list) is its support for adding new elements. The algorithm for inserting an element begins by following the same process as when searching. For instance, if we wish to insert the value 'M' into our sample tree, we consider where a subsequent search would expect to find it. It must be to the left of 'P' since it is smaller than 'P', yet must be to the right of 'H' by similar reasoning. In fact, a great place to store the new item is at the location of the empty subtree that we reached in Figure 13.8. Since we want to continue thinking of a nonempty tree as having two empty subtrees, we expand that subtree as shown in Figure 13.9.

Deletion

With a bit more care, an existing element can be efficiently deleted from a binary search tree. We give only a brief explanation of the strategy here. We begin with a search to locate the element. Then we must decide how to remove that value without disrupting the overall integrity of the tree structure. If the left subtree of the item to be removed is an empty tree (as is the case if deleting 'R' from our earlier example), we simply collapse that branch of the tree, essentially promoting the entire right subtree upward (the subtree rooted at 'S' in this case). By symmetry, if we delete an element with an empty right subtree (e.g., 'Y') we promote its left subtree upward (that rooted at 'T').

However, this strategy does not work when trying to remove an element that has two nonempty subtrees. For example, if deleting 'P' from the original tree, we cannot directly promote either subtree while maintaining the desired structure. Instead, we use the following approach. We find an element that can substitute for the one being removed.

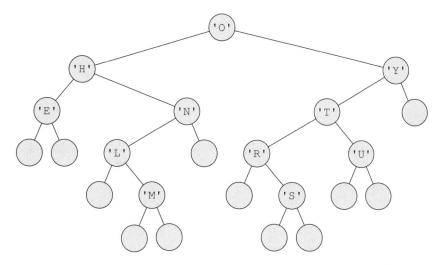

FIGURE 13.10: The previous tree, after deleting `'P'`. The element `'O'` was deleted from the original left subtree and used as a replacement for `'P'`.

Specifically, we remove the largest element from the left subtree and then use that element in place of the one being deleted. In our example, `'O'` is the maximum element in the left subtree of `'P'`. We are interested in the maximum of the left subtree because it is closest in value to the root itself. So everything that remains in the left subtree must be less than this value and everything that remains in the right subtree must be greater than this value. Deleting the maximum element from the left subtree turns out to be an easier process. That element must be at the end of the farthest rightward branch of the subtree (because it is bigger than all intermediate elements). Furthermore, its own right subtree must be empty, making this an easier deletion to enact. As a concrete example, Figure 13.10 shows the result of deleting `'P'` from the tree that was pictured in Figure 13.9.

13.4.1 Implementing a SortedSet with a Binary Search Tree

As an example of typical use, we use a binary search tree to implement a SortedSet class, mimicking the outward interface given in Section 9.3. Each instance of a tree maintains four attributes: _element is a reference to the element being stored at the root, _left, and _right are references to the respective subtrees, and _size is an integer tracking the overall number of elements currently stored in the given tree. Our class begins as follows:

```
class SortedSet:
    def __init__(self):
        self._element = None
        self._left = None
        self._right = None
        self._size = 0
```

A newly constructed tree is empty (represented with no elements or subtrees). Explicitly maintaining the _size attribute helps us when we later implement several of the index-based behaviors. It also provides us with a simple way to report the overall size of our container, without having to take time to explicitly count the elements. The __len__ method is simply implemented as

```
def __len__(self):
    return self._size
```

Since we trace a similar path through the tree when performing a search, an insertion or a deletion, we implement a private utility function _tracePath to avoid unnecessary duplication. By design, this recursive function is responsible for performing a search for a given value until either it is found or an empty subtree is reached at the bottom of the original tree. The utility returns a list of references marking the path, ordered from the root downward. We implement this as follows:

```
def _tracePath(self, value):
    if len(self) == 0 or value == self._element:
        return [ self ]
    elif value < self._element:
        return [ self ] + self._left._tracePath(value)
    else:
        return [ self ] + self._right._tracePath(value)
```

The first condition handles two forms of a base case. If searching an empty tree or if searching a tree that has an element at the root that matches the given value, the resulting search path consists solely of the current location. Otherwise we proceed recursively. If the target value is less than the root's element, then the overall search path will be the current location followed by the remaining path as traversed down the left subtree. Conversely, we combine the current location with the recursive path traced down the right subtree.

With this private method complete, we can go on to implement several public methods. As a simple example, the __contains__ method is used to determine whether a given value exists in our set. By tracing the search path, the only question is whether that search stops before reaching an empty node. If so, then the search is successful; otherwise, it was unsuccessful.

```
def __contains__(self, value):
    path = _tracePath(value)
    return path[-1]._size > 0      # check the end of the path
```

Implementing an insertion is only mildly more work. We begin in similar fashion, by computing the search path relative to the new value. If the value already exists in the set, we do not make any modification to our tree. Otherwise, our search path must have ended at an empty subtree. As originally shown in Figure 13.9, our goal is to expand that empty tree into a tree that has one element and two empty subtrees. Furthermore, we must remember to maintain the size accurately throughout the structure. By inserting a new element, not only is the empty subtree gaining one element, but all of the encompassing subtrees along the path are gaining one element. We implement this behavior as follows:

```
def insert(self, value):
    path = self._tracePath(value)
    endOfPath = path[-1]
    if endOfPath._size == 0:          # this is a new element
        for location in path:         # this subtree and all those above
            location._size += 1       # must have size increase by one element
        endOfPath._element = value
        endOfPath._left = SortedSet( )
        endOfPath._right = SortedSet( )
```

The for loop is used to increment all of the relevant sizes (including that at the end of the path). The final three lines are used to reconfigure the empty subtree to store the new element and to have two newly constructed (empty) subtrees.

Another interesting behavior is that of index. In the context of a SortedSet, this can be used to determine the relative index of a given element that is known to be in the set. Our implementation is as follows:

```
def index(self, value):
    if len(self) == 0:
        raise ValueError('SortedSet.index(x): x not in list')
    elif value == self._element:
        return len(self._left)
    elif value < self._element:
        return self._left.index(value)
    else:
        return 1 + len(self._left) + self._right.index(value)
```

To understand this code, keep in mind that the index of an element in a sequence can be viewed as the number of *other* elements that precede it. For example, the element with index 5 is actually the *sixth* element of the set; there are exactly 5 smaller elements. With that said, our implementation looks at four cases using a very similar recursion to that of tracing a path. However, we take advantage of the subtree sizes to compute the overall index of the specified value. As a base case, if someone asks for the index of a given value within an empty set, we raise a ValueError. This handles the obvious scenario, yet also serves as the eventual base case for an unsuccessful search on a larger tree. The other base case to our recursion is the special case when value == self._element. Having found the element at the root, we are responsible for returning the index, namely the number of other elements that are smaller than this one. Yet by the structure of our binary tree, all such elements must be located in the left subtree of the root. The number of elements, and thus the desired index, is precisely len(self._left).

The remaining cases are recursive, based upon whether the specified value is less than or greater than the element at the root. However, you may notice a slight asymmetry in the code. When the desired element is to the left of the root, then its overall index in the full tree is precisely the index as would be reported by the left subtree; if the index is viewed as a count of strictly smaller elements, all of those elements must also be in the left subtree. Yet when the specified value is in the right subtree, we already know that the root is smaller than it, as are all elements from the left subtree. There may also be some other elements in the right subtree that are smaller than the specified value. So the overall count of smaller elements is 1 + len(**self**._left) + **self**._right.index(value).

A closely related behavior is __getitem__. This is the inverse of index. The goal of index is to take a specified value and determine its index. The goal of __getitem__ is to take a given index and determine the element that has this index. Again we rely on the known sizes of the various subtrees and our knowledge of the binary search tree structure.

```
def __getitem__(self, index):
    index = self._cleanupIndex(index)   # handles negative indices properly
    if index == len(self._left):
        return self._element
    elif index < len(self._left):
        return self._left[index]
    else:   # look in right subtree, but discount the left elements and root when counting
        return self._right[index − (1 + len(self._left))]
```

The first call is to _cleanupIndex, a convenient utility that checks an index, converting a negative value to the corresponding positive index in accord with Python's standard conventions; we will show the implementation of that utility in our final presentation. The rest of the code uses similar logic to index, most notably our knowledge that the index of the root element is precisely len(**self**._left). So if this happens to be the index that the caller specified, we can return that element immediately. Otherwise, we resort to recursion, depending upon whether the desired index belongs left of the root or right of the root. If the user wants the element with an index (or equivalently, the number of smaller elements) that is strictly less than the size of the left subtree, then that element as well as all smaller ones must lie in the left subtree. So we simply look for **self**._left[index] as the desired element. However, when we determine that the desired element is to the right of the root, we must be more careful about the specification of the index. For example, if the user wants the element at index 13 and the size of the left subtree is 8, then the root itself has index 9. In this case, we want to return the element with index 4 (= 13 −9) in the right subtree. Such an element will be preceded by four items from the right subtree, together with the root and the eight elements in the left subtree, thus a total of 13 preceding elements.

The remainder of our code is given as part of the complete SortedSet implementation in Figure 13.11. The most intricate of the methods is remove. As before, we begin by tracing a search path for the specified value. If that value is never found, we do nothing, but otherwise it is our responsibility to make the necessary adjustments to the state of the tree. In similar fashion to our insert method, we begin with a for loop (lines 55 and 56) to account for the coming change in size for all subtrees on the search path. Then we consider the three possible cases for removing the value at the end of the path. As discussed in our high-level overview, if the left subtree of that location is empty, then we can simply promote the right child. For convenience, we encapsulate those low-level details in another

```
1    class SortedSet:
2      def __init__(self):
3        self._element = None
4        self._left = None
5        self._right = None
6        self._size = 0
7
8      def __len__(self):
9        return self._size
10
11     def _tracePath(self, value):
12       if len(self) == 0 or value == self._element:
13         return [ self ]
14       elif value < self._element:
15         return [ self ] + self._left._tracePath(value)
16       else:
17         return [ self ] + self._right._tracePath(value)
18
19     def __contains__(self, value):
20       path = _tracePath(value)
21       return  path[-1]._size > 0      # check the end of the path
22
23     def insert(self, value):
24       path = self._tracePath(value)
25       endOfPath = path[-1]
26       if endOfPath._size == 0:        # this is a new element
27         for location in path:         # this subtree and all those above
28           location._size += 1         # must have size increase by one element
29         endOfPath._element = value
30         endOfPath._left = SortedSet( )
31         endOfPath._right = SortedSet( )
32
33     def index(self, value):
34       if len(self) == 0:
35         raise ValueError('SortedSet.index(x): x not in list')
36       elif value == self._element:
37         return len(self._left)
38       elif value < self._element:
39         return self._left.index(value)
40       else:
41         return 1 + len(self._left) + self._right.index(value)
```

FIGURE 13.11: An implementation of SortedSet using a binary search tree (continued on next page).

```
42   def __getitem__(self, index):
43     index = self._cleanupIndex(index)   # handles negative indices properly
44     if index == len(self._left):
45       return self._element
46     elif index < len(self._left):
47       return self._left[index]
48     else:  # look in right subtree, but discount the left elements and root when counting
49       return self._right[index − (1 + len(self._left))]
50
51   def remove(self, value):
52     path = self._tracePath(value)
53     endOfPath = path[−1]
54     if endOfPath._size > 0:          # element was found
55       for location in path:
56         location._size −= 1          # these trees will each decrease by one element
57       # Now we must get rid of it
58       if len(endOfPath._left) == 0:
59         endOfPath._promoteChild(endOfPath._right)
60       elif len(endOfPath._right) == 0:
61         endOfpath._promoteChild(endOfPath._left)
62       else:                          # substitute maximum value removed from left subtree
63         endOfpath._element = endOfpath._left.pop( )
64
65   def pop(self, index=None):
66     if index == None:
67       index = len(self) − 1
68     value = self[index]
69     self.remove(value)              # reuse existing behavior, for convenience
70     return value
71
72   def _cleanupIndex(self, index):
73     if index < 0:
74       index += len(self)            # support Python's notion of negative index
75     if not 0 <= index < len(self):
76       raise IndexError('SortedSet index out of range')
77     return index
78
79   def _promoteChild(self, child):
80     self._element = child._element
81     self._left = child._left
82     self._right = child._right
```

FIGURE 13.11 (continuation): An implementation of SortedSet using a binary search tree.

utility _promoteChild, shown at lines 79–82. We also call that utility to promote the left subtree of the deleted element in the case that the right subtree is empty. The final case is when both subtrees are nonempty. In this case, our strategy was to explicitly delete the maximum element from the left subtree and to use that element as a replacement for the one being deleted. We handle this case at line 63 by relying on pop as a syntax for removing the largest value from a subtree.

Our implementation of pop is itself shown at lines 65–70. Although we could implement this behavior from scratch, we choose for convenience to rely on existing machinery. Note that the syntax **self**[index] used at line 68 invokes the underlying __getitem__ behavior, determining the value at the desired index. Once that value is known (and since all values are unique within a set), we rely on the call **self**.remove(value) at line 69 to enact the deletion of that value, making sure to return the deleted value to the caller.

13.4.2 Advantages of a Binary Search Tree

The general framework of binary search trees is enormously valuable. In addition to our basic SortedSet implementation, it is easy to use this as an alternative approach for a dictionary. As we have seen, the tree can easily be used to locate the minimum or maximum value from a collection without having to iterate over the entire set. A binary search tree can also be used to perform partial searches and range searches. For example, when an element is not in a collection, the tree can be used to identify an existing value closest to the target (it is guaranteed to be along the path traversed during an unsuccessful search for the target). A typical range search is to locate all entries that are between two given values. It is rather easy to produce a list of those results based upon a modified version of a recursive search.

In contrast, none of these additional behaviors can be efficiently supported by a hash table. The intentional scrambling of elements provides a good distribution for doing very efficient *exact* searches (even more efficient than with binary search trees). But it does not provide any means for these more general queries.

13.5 Chapter Review

13.5.1 Key Points

Measuring Efficiency

- The time.time( ) function returns a measure of the current time in seconds. Successive calls to this function can be used as an electronic stopwatch to measure the change in time from start to finish of a process.

- Asymptotic analysis is a mathematical approach for describing the relationship between the size of a data set and the processing time for a computation on that data.

- If a process requires time that is linearly proportional to the size n of data, we say it takes $\Theta(n)$ time.

- If a process requires time that is independent of the size of the data, we say it takes $\Theta(1)$ time.

Python's list class

- Behind the scene, a list is represented as an array of references stored consecutively in a single block of memory. A particular entry of the list can be located in constant time with use of an index.

- The efficiency of most list methods fall into one of three categories, those that do not use any iteration, those that may iterate only partially through the list, and those that are required to iterate through the complete list.

- Behaviors that do not require any iteration use $\Theta(1)$ time. This includes __getitem__, __setitem__, __len__, and typically append. The same is true of insert or pop when operating very near to the end of the list.

- Examples of tasks that require a complete iteration over a list are the methods count and reverse, as well as the built-in functions min, max, and sum.

- Examples of tasks that rely upon a partial iteration include __contains__, index, __eq__, as well as slicing. Also, the typical behaviors of insert and pop require iteration to move all subsequent elements respectively forward or backward to adjust for the change. The time for those depends upon how close the change is to the end of the list.

- The remove method is somewhat unusual, in that it requires an iteration from the beginning of the list to find the leftmost occurrence. Once found, a second iteration proceeds from that location to the end of the list to contract the subsequent elements.

Dictionaries

- A simple way to implement a dictionary mapping is to maintain two coordinated lists, one for keys and one for values, with a key and its associated value stored at the same index of the respective lists.

- The biggest drawback of coordinated lists is that most operations rely upon locating the index of the key within the list of keys. This requires linear time based upon a sequential search.

- A significantly faster implementation of a dictionary is based on a concept called *hashing*. The primary structure is a single list, known as a hash table. A mathematical function is applied to each key to determine an appropriate index into the hash table for placing the associated value.

- Although keys are distinct, it is possible that multiple keys end up leading to the same index in the hash table (a *collision*). One way to manage collisions is to use a secondary structure, informally termed a bucket, to hold all (key,value) pairs that fall at particular index of the table.

- With some reasonable assumptions about the hashing function, most of the common dictionary operations can be supported in $\Theta(1)$ time.

Binary Search Trees

- A binary search tree is a (typically recursive) structure used to manage an ordered sequence.

- A binary search tree can be viewed as a single root element together with two recursive subtrees. The left subtree is used to store all elements less than the root's value; the right subtree is used to store all elements greater than the root's value.

- This organization supports a very natural approach for searching. A target key is compared to the root. Assuming that the root is nonempty and the target was not found there, the search is made recursively on either the left or right subtree, depending respectively on whether the target was less than or greater than the key at the root.

- Insertions can be performed by mimicking a search and placing the new element at the end of the branch that is reached. Deletions can be performed efficiently as well, although with some manipulation to properly reconfigure the tree.

- Searches, insertions and deletions are typically processed in $\Theta(\log n)$ time, presuming the tree is sufficiently well balanced (or if additional techniques are used to guarantee such balance).

13.5.2 Glossary

asymptotic analysis A mathematical technique for estimating the efficiency of a process in relation to the amount of data. For example, a process that depends linearly on the size n of a data set is said to have $\Theta(n)$ running time.

binary search A technique for searching a sorted list by comparing a target value to the value at the middle of the list and, if not the target, searching recursively on the appropriate half of the list.

binary search tree A recursive branched structure used to manage an ordered collection. At each level of the structure, elements are organized so that smaller elements lie in the left subtree while larger elements lie in the right subtree.

bootstrap A technique by which a data structure is based on a more rudimentary implementation of that same structure.

bucket A secondary container used to manage collisions within a hash table.

collision The mapping of two different keys into the same index of a hash table.

dictionary A data structure used to manage a collection of keys and their associated values, such that an entry can be accessed quickly based upon a unique key. This structure is synonymously termed a *map* or an *associative array*.

hashing A technique for organizing elements based on a mathematical function that converts keys to indices of an appropriately sized table.

immutable The characteristic of an object whose state cannot be modified once constructed.

lexicographical order A convention for comparing two sequences to each other. The sequence with the smaller first element is considered the "smaller" sequence. If the first elements are equivalent, the second elements are used as a tie-breaker, and so on. If all elements are pairwise equivalent yet one sequence has additional elements at the end, that sequence is considered "larger." If they are the same length, the two sequences are considered equivalent.

recursion A technique in which a structure or behavior is defined based upon a "smaller" version of that same structure or behavior.

tree A hierarchical data structure often organized recursively as a root with two or more subtrees.

13.5.3 Exercises

Efficiency

Exercise 13.1: Run the experiment of Figure 13.1 on your own machine. Perform four separate trials for the entire experiment and make a chart of the observed times for each of the tests in each trial.

Exercise 13.2: Modify the experiment of Figure 13.1 to instead compute the time it takes for *constructing* each of the three original ranges. Report the observed times and your own conclusions.

Exercise 13.3: Repeat Exercise 13.2, but this time instantiate the ranges from largest to smallest. Rerun your experiments and discuss whether the change in order has any noticeable effect on the outcome.

Exercise 13.4: Modify the experiment of Figure 13.1 to perform a test of the **list.__len__** method. Report the observed times and your own conclusions.

Exercise 13.5: Modify the experiment of Figure 13.1 to perform a test of the **list**.index method with parameter 12345. Report the observed times and your own conclusions.

Exercise 13.6: Repeat Exercise 13.5, but this time reverse all three original ranges before beginning the timed tests. Report the observed times and your own conclusions.

Exercise 13.7: Perform the following experiment for a sufficiently chosen value N:

```
from time import time
big = range(N)
for pct in range(10, 100, 10):
    start = time( )                # record the starting time
    big.pop(int(N * pct // 100))
    stop = time( )                 # record the finish time
    print '%d percent:   %f seconds' % (pct, stop-start)
```

Report the observed times and your own conclusions.

Exercise 13.8: Perform the following experiment for a sufficiently chosen value N:

```
from time import time
big = range(N)
for pct in range(10, 100, 10):
    start = time( )                # record the starting time
    big.remove(int(N * pct // 100))
    stop = time( )                 # record the finish time
    print '%d percent:   %f seconds' % (pct, stop-start)
```

Report the observed times and your own conclusions.

Dictionaries

Practice 13.9: In our implementation of DictWithLists, line 48 returns **list(self**._keys) rather than returning **self**._keys. Why would the alternative be a potential problem? Why is the original implementation legitimate?

Practice 13.10: Our DictWithHashing implemention explicitly maintained a _numItems attribute to represent the current number of entries. Assuming that we did *not* have such an attribute, give an alternate implementation of the __len__ function.

Exercise 13.11: Our DictWithLists class uses two separate coordinated lists. Develop a similar dictionary implementation using a single internal list, whose elements are (key, value) tuples.

Exercise 13.12: Consider our implementation of DictWithHashing in Figure 13.5. Lines 4–6 are used to initialize the state of our table. If we had replaced all three of those lines with the single line

```
self._table = [ DictWithLists( ) ] * 7
```

there would be a problem. Explain the flaw.

Exercise 13.13: Consider our implementation of DictWithHashing in Figure 13.5. Assume that lines 26–28 of __setitem__ had been reordered to read as follows:

```
26    bucket[k] = v                      # assign/reassign value
27    if k not in bucket:
28        self._numItems +=1             # k is a new key
```

Unfortunately, there is a problem with this alternative. Clearly explain the flaw.

Exercise 13.14: Consider our implementation DictWithHashing._expandTable. Although that method changes the hash table size, the overall number of elements in the dictionary is unchanged by the expansion. So why do we set **self**._numItems = 0 at line 37 of Figure 13.5?

Binary Search Trees

Practice 13.15: For each of the following targets, describe what sequence of tree locations (including empty ones) are examined during a search of the tree shown in Figure 13.6:

(a) 'G'

(b) 'J'

(c) 'N'

Practice 13.16: Starting with an empty binary search tree, show the *final* tree that results after inserting the following entries in the following order: 'I', 'N', 'S', 'E', 'R', 'T', 'H', 'O', 'W'.

Exercise 13.17: For each of the following targets, describe what sequence of tree locations (including empty ones) are examined during a search of the tree shown in Figure 13.6:

(a) 'Q'

(b) 'T'

(c) 'W'

Exercise 13.18: Starting with an empty binary search tree, show the *final* tree that results after inserting the following entries in the following order: `'L'`, `'U'`, `'M'`, `'B'`, `'E'`, `'R'`, `'J'`, `'A'`, `'C'`, `'K'`.

Exercise 13.19: Starting with an empty binary search tree, show the *final* tree that results after inserting the following entries in the following order: `'C'`, `'O'`, `'M'`, `'P'`, `'U'`, `'T'`, `'E'`, `'R'`, `'S'`.

Exercise 13.20: Each SortedSet instance explicitly maintains a _size attribute to represent the current number of entries in that (sub)tree. Assuming that we did *not* have such an attribute, give an alternate implementation of the __len__ function.

Exercise 13.21: Add a method getRange(start, stop) to our SortedSet implementation that *efficiently* returns a sorted list of those entries that satisfy start <= value < stop.

Exercise 13.22: Add a method nextGreater(value) to our SortedSet implementation that returns the element of the set with value closest to but strictly greater than the specified value (or **None** if there are no greater elements). The parameter may or may not be an element of the set. Using our tree of Figure 13.6 as an example, a call to nextGreater(`'H'`) should return `'L'`, nextGreater(`'M'`) should return `'N'`, nextGreater(`'S'`) should return `'T'`, nextGreater(`'V'`) should return `'Y'`, and nextGreater(`'Y'`) should return **None**.

Hint: start by tracing the path to the parameter value. If that search is unsuccessful, the next greatest is the lowest entry on that path that qualifies as greater than the value. If the search is successful, the next greatest is the smallest element in the right subtree at the end of the path if that subtree is nonempty, or else it is the lowest element on the path that qualifies as greater.

Exercise 13.23: Adapt the concept of a binary search tree to give a full implementation of a dictionary class named DictWithTree.

CHAPTER 14

Sorting Algorithms

Sorting a list is an extremely important task, whether organizing numbers, strings, or some other data type. For this reason a great deal of effort has been spent on designing and implementing algorithms for sorting data. In fact, the developers of Python have already designed, implemented, and fine-tuned a sorting algorithm invoked as the sort method of the **list** class. With such a good implementation readily available, there is rarely need to implement a sorting algorithm ourselves. Even so, it is helpful to have knowledge of the underlying approaches that are used and to recognize the relative advantages and disadvantages that impact the efficiency of those algorithms. More generally, the task of sorting has served as a testbed for exploring algorithmic techniques that can be applied to other computational problems.

In this chapter, we discuss Python's built-in support for sorting and ways in which the process can be customized. Then we describe four classical sorting algorithms that rely upon starkly different techniques: *selection sort*, *insertion sort*, *merge sort*, and *quicksort*. At the conclusion, we will tell you which algorithm Python's developers chose. For consistency in our discussion, we let data represent a list of values to be sorted, and let n denote the length of that list.

14.1 Customizing Use of Python's Sort

Given a list named data, we can sort the list by using the syntax data.sort( ). This is one of the basic behaviors of the list class, introduced as early as page 45. It can be used to sort any type of data, relying on the natural definition of comparison between objects of that type. For example, when numbers are sorted, they are sorted from smallest to largest. When strings are sorted, they are sorted in a case-sensitive way according to standard alphabetical order. If our list were defined as,

```
data = ['bread', 'soda', 'cheese', 'milk', 'pretzels']
```

The standard use of sort results in

```
>>> data.sort()
>>> print data
['bread', 'cheese', 'milk', 'pretzels', 'soda']
```

However, there are often times when we want to sort data according to some notion other than the default view of comparison. As an example, consider the goal of sorting a list of strings relative to their lengths, from shortest to longest.

A comparison function

One approach for sorting items according to a nonstandard ordering is to explicitly provide a specialized *comparison function*. Such a function must take two elements of the expected data type as parameters, and then return an integer interpreted as follows:

> **-1** : the first element is smaller than the second
> **0** : the first element is equivalent to the second
> **1** : the first element is larger than the second

For the example of string length, we might write the following comparison function:

```
def lengthCmp(a, b):
  if len(a) < len(b):
    return −1
  elif len(a) == len(b):
    return 0
  else:
    return 1
```

In fact, we can write this function more concisely by taking advantage of a built-in function cmp, which provides this type of three-pronged comparison for two values. For example cmp(len('bread'), len('milk')) returns 1 since the first length is greater than the second length. By relying on cmp, we can define our own comparison function that is customized for string length, as

```
def lengthCmp(a, b):
  return cmp(len(a), len(b))
```

To use a comparison function with the sort method, we send the comparison function itself as a parameter, using a syntax such as

```
data.sort(lengthCmp)                    # use our function for comparing, not the default
```

In Python, a function definition is actually an object, identified by the chosen name of the function. So using the above syntax, we are sending the sorting method a parameter lengthCmp that literally identifies the function that we want it to use when comparing data elements to each other. This parameter is optional; the default value that we have been relying upon all along is that standard cmp function.

Note that when treating a function as an object, it is important that we do *not* include parentheses after the function name. For example, the following is invalid syntax:

```
data.sort(lengthCmp( ))                    # too many parentheses
```

Parentheses after a function name are used to invoke the function. This subtlety explains many earlier pitfalls, such as the difference between the expression groceries.sort( ) and groceries.sort, or flawed conditionals such as

```
if 'Hello'.islower:
  print 'Say what?'
```

Decorated tuples

Another approach for sorting by a nonstandard order exploits the standard *lexicographical order* that is used when comparing sequences. If two generic tuples (a0, a1, a2, a3) and (b0, b1, b2) are compared to each other, the first element of each is the most significant. That is, the values of items a0 and b0 are compared to each other. If those values are not the same, then the tuple containing the smaller of the two is considered the "smaller" tuple. However, in case of a tie, the decision turns to comparing the second elements, and so on. If all elements are pairwise equivalent yet one tuple has more entries at the end, that tuple is the "larger" one. The tuples are considered equivalent only when they have the same length and pairwise equivalent values. Notice that this lexicographical order is precisely the alphabetical order used when comparing two strings to each other, as sequences of characters.

Sorting data according to a nonstandard measure can thus be accomplished with what are known as *decorated tuples*. If we have in mind some notion of a key that should be used for comparing two pieces of data (e.g., a string's length), we can create a tuple with two entries, the first being the key, and the second being the original element. For example, the string 'bread' could be decorated as the tuple (5, 'bread'). If we create an auxiliary list of those strings, such as

```
[(5, 'bread'), (4, 'soda'), (6, 'cheese'), (4, 'milk'), (8, 'pretzels')]
```

and sort that list, we end up with the result

```
[(4, 'milk'), (4, 'soda'), (5, 'bread'), (6, 'cheese'), (8, 'pretzels')]
```

Notice that when the first components are equal, the lexicographical order breaks the tie based on a comparison between the next components, thus (4, 'milk') < (4, 'soda'). We can use this to accomplish our original goal of sorting strings according to length as follows. We create a decorated list, sort that list, and then strip away the decorations.

```
decorated = [ ]
for s in data:
    decorated.append( (len(s), s) )          # add a tuple starting with length
decorated.sort( )
for i in range(len(data)):
    data[i] = decorated[i][1]                # retrieve second piece of each tuple
```

Typically, the use of decorated tuples is more efficient than the use of a comparison func-tion. The reason is that the extra work of decorating and undecorating happens just once. In contrast, a specialized comparison function is called many times per element, each time the internal sorting algorithm needs to compare a pair of elements.

A decorator function

The technique of decorating, sorting, and undecorating a list is mechanical yet cumber-some. For this reason, starting with Python 2.4, the built-in sort function supports a more concise way to apply a decorator pattern. A special function can be designated to provide the decoration pattern. This function should accept a single data element as a parameter and produce the appropriate decorating key for that element. For example, in the case of string length, we could write our own function

```
def lengthDecorator(s):
    return len(s)
```

To use a function as a decorator, we invoke the sort method using the following syntax:

```
data.sort(key=lengthDecorator)          # use our decorator function
```

This syntax differs from our standard way to pass a parameter. It is known as ***keyword parameter passing***. In essence there exists an optional formal parameter key and we are assigning it to the function lengthDecorator.

Finally, we note that in the case of using string length as a decorator, there was no need to define our own decorator function. Look carefully; it is a function that takes a single parameter and returns the length. That is precisely the outward behavior of the __len__ method of the **str** class. If invoked with its qualified name, the calling syntax for that function is **str**.__len__('bread'); the explicit parameter in this form is the implicit **self** that is sent when using the method calling format. Therefore, we could accomplish our original goal with the single command,

```
data.sort(key=str.__len__)
```

The built-in function len would also suffice as the decorator, since it accepts a string as a parameter and returns an integer representing the length of that string. Thus we could have written data.sort(key=len).

14.2 Selection Sort

We begin our examination of sorting algorithms with a very simple approach known as *selection sort*. We make a pass through the entire data set, locating the smallest overall value. We then swap that value with the one in data[0], since that is where the smallest value belongs. Next, we make a pass through all remaining elements looking for the next smallest value. That value is switched into data[1]. The algorithm proceeds in rounds, selecting and relocating the next smallest element until all elements are properly placed (in fact, once we have properly placed the first $n - 1$ elements, the remaining element will naturally be the largest).

A complete implementation of this approach is shown in Figure 14.1. The variable hole is an index that represents the next "hole" to fill. Originally, it is set to 0 to reflect our interest in finding the correct value for data[0]. The **while** loop at line 3 continues so long as hole < len(data) -1, with its value incremented by one at the end of each pass (line 11). The body of that loop is responsible for finding the value that belongs in data[hole] and moving it there. Selecting each such value is accomplished using a relatively standard index-based loop. The variable walk is incremented through the range of indices from the hole to the end of the list, while the variable small is used to keep track of the *index* of the smallest value that we encounter along the way. We set small = hole as an initial default, in case no smaller element is found and we then begin with walk = hole + 1. Each time we find a smaller element, we record its position. By the time the inner loop completes, we will have found the smallest value of the remaining elements. Line 10 uses *simultaneous assignment* (see *For the Guru* on page 222) to swap that element into data[hole].

A demonstration of selection sort is given in Figure 14.2, displaying the state of the list immediately before and after line 10 is executed. For example, during the first pass the smallest overall value, namely 2, is located at data[4] and then swapped with the value originally at data[0] (in this case, value 18). During the next pass, the inner loop iterates over all entries from data[1] to the end of the list and determines that value 3, at data[7], is the smallest. So the elements at data[7] and data[1] are swapped as a result. Figure 14.2 continues in showing the first seven passes of the outer loop; we leave it as a simple exercise to complete the process.

```
1   def selectionSort(data):
2      hole = 0                              # next index to fill
3      while hole < len(data) −1:            # last item automatically ends in proper place
4         small = hole
5         walk = hole + 1
6         while walk < len(data):
7            if data[walk] < data[small]:
8               small = walk                 # new minimum found
9            walk += 1
10        data[hole], data[small] = data[small], data[hole]
11        hole += 1
```

FIGURE 14.1: Selection sort.

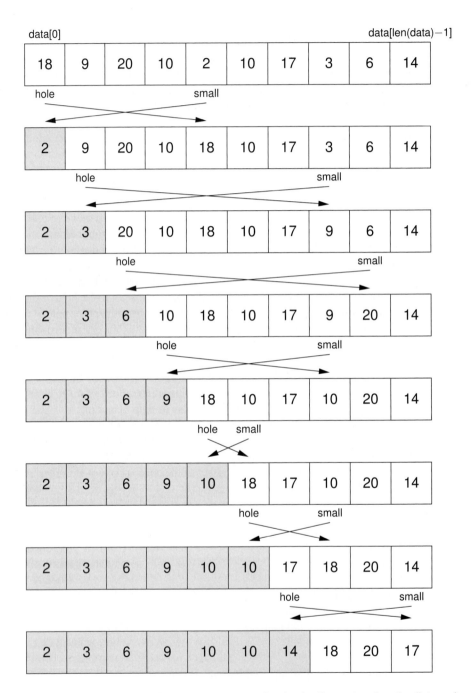

FIGURE 14.2: A trace of the first seven passes of selectionSort, showing the list each time line 10 is executed.

Efficiency

The running time of selection sort depends *quadratically* upon the length of the original list; that is, with *n* items in the original list, the algorithm requires $\Theta(n^2)$ time. To see this, we note that the outer loop executes $n-1$ times and that the inner loop executes an average of $\frac{n}{2}$ times for each pass of the outer loop. As a result, selection sort could be used for moderately sized lists. But there are certainly better approaches.

14.3   Insertion Sort

The next algorithm we describe is known as ***insertion sort***. The idea is similar to a technique often used by a person when physically sorting a pile of cards. Rather than going through the entire pile to look for the smallest overall value, insertion sort proceeds by considering values one at a time and ensuring that all values considered thus far are sorted relative to each other. To get started, we note that a single value is trivially sorted and that after considering all values, the entire list will be sorted. A complete implementation of this idea is given in Figure 14.3. The variable next represents the index of the next element to incorporate into the sorted portion of the list. Since data[0] is trivially a sorted sublist, the real work begins with next = 1 and continues so long as next < len(data).

The **while** loop starting at line 3 is responsible for relocating the value of data[next] relative to those previously considered values. This subtask is accomplished by creating an appropriate hole to place the newest value. The hole is created by an inner loop that slides *larger* intermediate values one at a time to the right. Before entering that loop, we keep a reference to the original value of data[next] (as we may soon be sliding some other element to that position of the list). The hole itself is initialized as hole = next because the new element might actually be larger than all previous values (in which case it can stay put). However, if the element immediately to the left of the hole is greater than the newest value, that element is moved into the hole, thereby moving the hole one more place to the left. This sliding is accomplished by the inner loop at lines 6–8. The loop condition at line 6 captures two necessary conditions for sliding the hole farther to the left. The hole should only be moved to the left if hole > 0 (thus the hole not already at the far left) and data[hole−1] > value (the element to the left of the hole is larger than the newest element).

```
 1  def insertionSort(data):
 2      next = 1                               # index of next element to insert (first is trivially okay)
 3      while next < len(data):
 4          value = data[next]                 # will insert this value in proper place
 5          hole = next
 6          while hole > 0 and data[hole−1] > value:
 7              data[hole] = data[hole−1]      # slide data[hole−1] forward
 8              hole −= 1                       # and the implicit hole one step backward
 9          data[hole] = value
10          next += 1
```

FIGURE 14.3: Insertion sort.

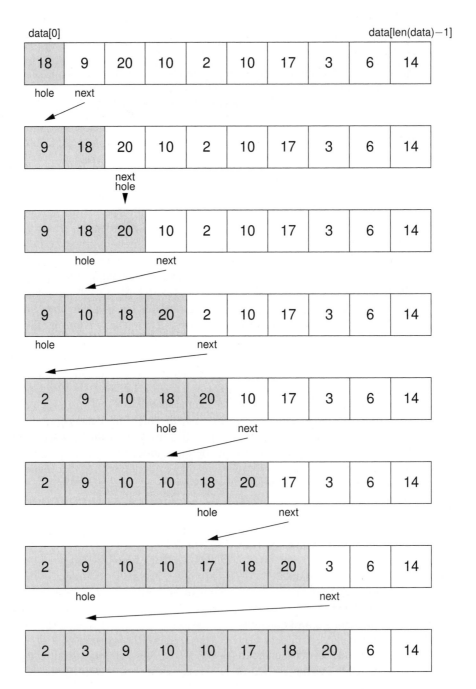

FIGURE 14.4: A trace of the first seven passes of insertionSort, showing the list each time line 9 is executed.

Figure 14.4 shows a trace of the algorithm. The first pass is devoted to correctly placing the value 9. In this case, since 18 is larger than 9, the 18 slides to the right and then the hole for 9 to the left. The inner while loop ends in this case because the hole reaches index 0. The second pass is used to correctly place the value 20. In this case, the condition for the inner while loop fails immediately and so no elements are moved. Instead, the new value is placed at the same position where it started. The third pass involves placing the value 10 relative to the previous items. This time the inner loop results in sliding value 20 to the right and then 18 to the right. The loop exits at that point because the value 9 is *not* larger than the new value. Therefore the new value is placed in the hole to the right of 9 but to the left of 18. Figure 14.4 continues in showing the first seven passes of the outer loop; we leave it as a simple exercise to complete the process.

Efficiency

The analysis of insertion sort is a bit more subtle than selection sort. It has the same basic structure, with an outer loop that executes $n - 1$ times, and an inner loop for each pass of the outer loop. The difference is that the inner loop of selection sort always considered all remaining elements and thus executed an average of $\frac{n}{2}$ times per pass. In the worst case, insertion sort uses the same number of iterations within the inner loop; if a new element is smaller than all previous elements, the hole slides all the way to the beginning. Even on random data, the hole is likely to slide halfway back to the beginning on average, still resulting in a $\Theta(n^2)$-time algorithm.

However, if we are extremely lucky, it may be that each newly considered element is already in or very near to its proper place. In fact, if the original list is already sorted, then insertion sort will only use $\Theta(n)$ time. Now it may not seem like such a feat to say that we can efficiently sort a list that was already sorted, but the same analysis can show that insertion sort is quite efficient for lists that are not perfectly sorted, but very nearly sorted. This is not such an unusual setting in real life, for example when only a handful of values have changed since the last time the data was sorted. For this reason, insertion sort is almost certainly better than selection sort and a reasonable approach in many settings.

14.4 Merge Sort

For larger data sets, it pays to use a more clever approach. The next algorithm we consider is based on a technique known as ***divide and conquer***, which is often expressed naturally through recursion. For analogy, consider the two approaches we considered for searching a list in Section 11.4, sequential search and binary search. Sequential search proceeds by iteratively comparing each element of the set to the target value. In contrast, binary search proceeds by comparing the target to the middle value of the data set, and by doing so divides the problem size in half. It then "conquers" the remaining half by recursively applying binary search.

For sorting, there are several divide-and-conquer algorithms. The first one we consider is known as ***merge sort***. We arbitrarily divide the list of values into two halves, and then independently sort each of those halves via recursion. Of course, getting two separately sorted halves is not the final goal; we want the full list to be entirely sorted. But it turns out that recombining the two halves into a single sorted list is relatively easy. The process, known as merging, is similar to what we might do by hand if combining two sorted piles. By looking at the next available item in each pile, the smaller of the two can be placed as the next item in the combined result. When one pile is empty, the next element is taken from the remaining pile. When both piles are empty, the merge is complete.

To implement the merging process, we define a _merge function as follows. In the big picture, we need this function not simply to merge the two halves of the original list, but to merge smaller sublists we encounter during intermediate levels of recursion. As was the case in Section 11.4, we prefer for efficiency to avoid taking unnecessary slices of lists. Instead, the extent of a sublist is delimited as follows. The caller sends a reference to the full original list data, as well as three indices start, mid, and stop. We interpret those indices as follows. The caller is expected to guarantee that the sublists data[start:mid] and data[mid:stop] are both sorted at the onset of a call. The responsibility of the _merge routine is to rearrange elements so that data[start:stop] is completely sorted by the conclusion.

There is one more wrinkle to our implementation. Although our physical analogy of merging two piles into one was straightforward, the simplicity relies upon our freedom to create a new third pile as a result. In the context of the list, it would be ideal if we could rearrange elements in place, that is, without using a significant amount of additional memory. For example, both selection sort and insertion sort are considered in-place sorting algorithms because most of the rearrangement is done by shifting or swapping values in the original list. Merging two sublists together is significantly easier if we allow ourselves to use a second list as a temporary buffer for holding elements. So in our implementation of the _merge function, we assume that we are sent a fourth parameter that is a reference to such an auxiliary list, with size equivalent to the original list.

Our complete implementation of the function is given in Figure 14.5. To make room for the merging process, lines 8–11 copy the relevant portion of the data into the temporary list. This way, when we begin to merge the two parts together, we can place the result back into the original list without fear of overwriting important information. The rest of the merging process proceeds by keeping three important indices as placeholders. mergedMark is maintained as an index into data[start:stop] that represents the next spot in which to place a merged item. Initially, that variable is set to start, as the smallest of the merged values should be placed in data[start]. We also maintain variables leftMark and rightMark to keep track of the "top" of the two respective piles from the temporary list, namely the first element from each half that has not yet been combined back into the merged data set. Therefore, we initialize leftMark to start and rightMark to mid.

The merging process itself is implemented by the while loop beginning at line 18. The general approach is quite simple. We move elements back into the original list one at a time until all have been moved back. The index mergedMark is incremented as each element is placed and the process continues while mergedMark < stop. Within the body of the loop, the goal is to determine whether the next smallest element is to be taken from the left half or the right half of the temporary buffer. The most subtle portion of that code is the boolean condition stated at line 19. Our goal is to express a condition that merits taking the next element from the left side. For this to be the proper action, there must remain elements on the left half that have not yet been merged. For this reason, we begin by requiring leftMark < mid, to ensure this condition. Of course, just because there remain elements on the left half does not ensure that the next element in the combined set comes from the left. We must also consider what is happening on the right side. There are two possibilities. It may be that we have exhausted the elements from the right side, that is rightMark == stop.

```
1   def _merge(data, start, mid, stop, temp):
2       """Merge data[start:mid] and data[mid:stop] into data[start:stop].
3
4       data[start:mid] and data[mid:stop] are presumed to be sorted.
5       temp is presumed to be a list with same length as data (serves as a buffer)
6       """
7       # copy data into temporary buffer
8       i = start
9       while i < stop:
10          temp[i] = data[i]
11          i += 1
12
13      mergedMark = start      # index into data[start:stop]
14      leftMark = start        # index into temp[start:mid]
15      rightMark = mid         # index into temp[mid:stop]
16
17      # merge values back into original data list
18      while mergedMark < stop:
19          if leftMark < mid and (rightMark == stop or temp[leftMark] < temp[rightMark]):
20              data[mergedMark] = temp[leftMark]
21              leftMark += 1
22          else:
23              data[mergedMark] = temp[rightMark]
24              rightMark += 1
25          mergedMark += 1
```

FIGURE 14.5: A routine for merging two (sorted) halves into one.

In this case, we should surely use the left-hand element next. Alternatively, both sides have remaining elements. In this case, the decision comes down to a comparison to find the smaller of the two leading elements. When temp[leftMark] < temp[rightMark] we should indeed take the next element from the left side. If our overall condition is true, lines 20 and 21 are executed to copy the relevant element from the left into the result and increment the mark accordingly. In the opposite case, lines 23 and 24 are used to copy the next value from the right side back into the original list.

To demonstrate the merging process, Figure 14.6 provides a trace of the process on some sample data. The diagram shows the contents of the *temporary* list, after the original data has been copied to that buffer. The task is then to determine how to properly order those elements back in the original list. The diagram provides a series of snapshots based upon each iteration of the while loop of line 18. The figure portrays the current setting for both the leftMark and rightMark indices. In general, those represent the two elements, one from each half, that are being considered as the next value in the combined result. We use a circle to highlight the element that is about to be chosen from those two (e.g., 2 in the first case). We do not actually show the original list in this diagram, but the circled elements

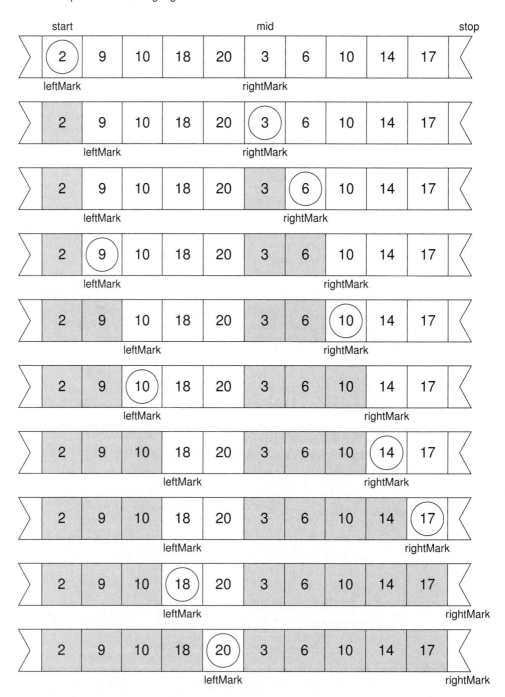

FIGURE 14.6: A trace of the _merge method. This shows the temp buffer each time the **while** condition at line 18 is evaluated. Each circle shows the next value to be copied back to the original list.

are being copied back into the original from left to right as we go (hence 2, then 3, then 6, then 9, and so on). The shaded squares represent elements that have already been copied back into the result; those elements are still in the temporary buffer, but no longer under consideration for being chosen.

For much of this process, unmerged elements remain in both halves of the buffer. Therefore the choice of next element typically depends upon the comparison between values temp[leftMark] and temp[rightMark]. However, by the second-to-last case in this diagram, the rightMark has advanced to stop, and so there are no more elements from that side. At this point, the conditional will always pick the next element from the left side until all of those are merged.

The recursion

Thus far, we have only implemented a function that merges two sorted portions of a list. We have not yet shown how an originally unsorted list can be sorted. Fortunately, this is quite easy to do using recursion. From a public point of view, we would like a caller to have a simple signature mergeSort(data) to begin the process. Behind the scene, we want to use recursion to our advantage. So we define a private function _recursiveMergeSort that has a better crafted signature for our recursion. The parameters for our private function include a reference to the original data and indices delimiting the implicit slice of interest, and a reference to a temporary buffer. The completed code appears as follows:

```
1   def mergeSort(data):
2       # create new temporary list for extra storage space
3       _recursiveMergeSort(data, 0, len(data), [None] * len(data))
4
5   def _recursiveMergeSort(data, start, stop, tempList):
6       if start < stop - 1:                          # more than one element to sort
7           mid = (start + stop) // 2
8           _recursiveMergeSort(data, start, mid, tempList)
9           _recursiveMergeSort(data, mid, stop, tempList)
10          _merge(data, start, mid, stop, tempList)
```

The user calls the mergeSort function and leaves the work to us. We in turn begin the recursion with start and stop values that delimit the whole list, and by creating a temporary list with the appropriate length, namely [**None**] * len(data). By creating this buffer once, at line 3, and reusing it throughout the recursion, we avoid unnecessarily taxing the memory management system (as would occur if instantiating a new buffer within each recursive call). The recursive function is itself quite simple. As a base case, a sublist with only one item is already sorted; this requires no action. It is only when there are two or more items, and thus start < stop - 1, that we need to do some work. In that case, we find the approximate midpoint of the current range, recursively sort the left half, recursively sort the right half, and merge the two halves back together. From this high-level perspective, the work proceeds as shown in Figure 14.7. Of course, if we want to dig deeper, we could trace the process used to sort the individual halves. For example, the left half of the original data was itself sorted by the recursive process diagrammed in Figure 14.8.

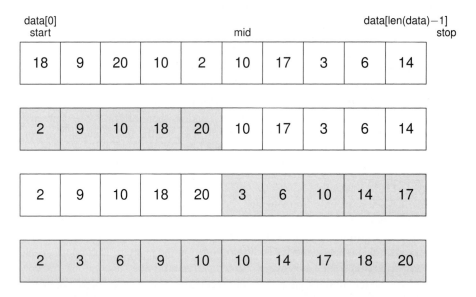

FIGURE 14.7: A high-level view of merge sort. The first row shows the original data, the second row after sorting the left half, the third row after sorting the right half, and the final row after performing the merge.

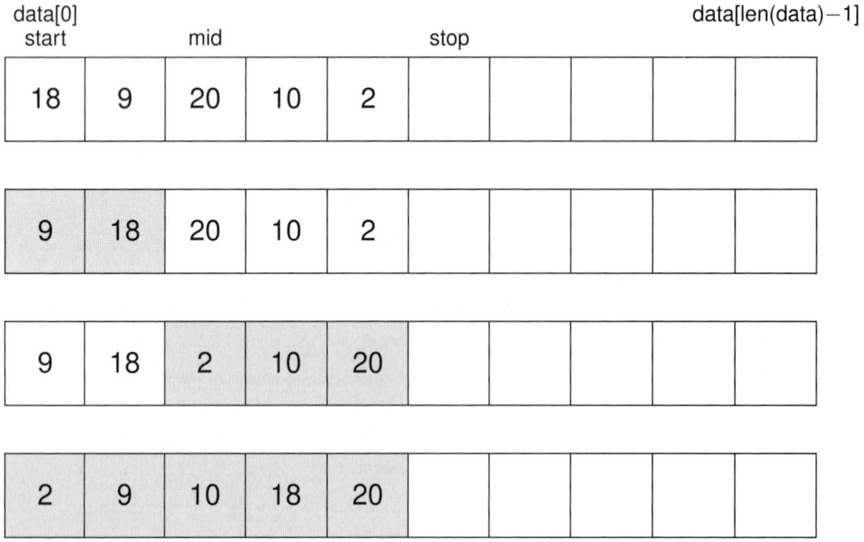

FIGURE 14.8: A view of an intermediate level of the merge sort recursion.

Efficiency

The analysis of merge sort is not quite as obvious as the earlier discussion of selection and insertion sort. However, the conclusion is important. For large data sets, merge sort can be significantly faster than either of those earlier sorts. In the worst case, the earlier sorts require $\Theta(n^2)$ time to sort a list of n elements. Merge sort completes in $\Theta(n\log n)$ time, no matter how the original values are arranged. *This is a significant improvement.* The advantage relates to the difference between a logarithmic term and a linear term, just as with binary search versus sequential search.

In practice, selection or insertion sort might be reasonable to sort tens of thousands of elements, but after that the time requirement may become impractical. In contrast, sorting a million elements with merge sort requires roughly 20 million operations (as $\log_2 1000000$ is approximately 20). This number of operations is quite reasonable for a computer to perform in a practical amount of time. In contrast, sorting one million items with selection sort requires approximately 500 *billion* operations — about 25000 times longer than merge sort!

The biggest drawback in using merge sort is our requirement for a temporary buffer that is equal in size to the original list. When sorting very large data sets, the use of extra memory can become a more significant drawback than the required computation time. Still, merge sort is a very practical approach, even when sorting billions of items.

FOR THE GURU

Analysis of merge sort

There are several ways to explain the $\Theta(n\log n)$ time requirement of merge sort. We draw a comparison to our earlier analysis of binary search. The logarithmic factor stems from the fact that a data set of size n can only be cut in half $\log_2 n$ times before reaching a base case of one element. The same is true for the depth of the merge sort recursion. The difference between binary search and merge sort is the time spent at each step of the recursion. With binary search, we had to only look at a single value in order to start the appropriate recursion and analyze the result of that call.

With merge sort, we have to start two recursions rather than just one, and we also have to spend linear time to perform the _merge to put those two pieces together again. So unfolding the recursion, we need to call merge for the final set of n elements, but also perform two intermediate merges when analyzing the sets of $\frac{n}{2}$ elements, as well as four merges of $\frac{n}{4}$ elements, and so on. In this way, each "level" of the recursive computation accounts for an additive term of n and there are $\log_2 n$ levels before finally reaching the n sublists of size 1.

14.5 Quicksort

In this section, we look at one more approach, known as *quicksort*. This is also a divide–and–conquer approach that we implement recursively, but the idea is really quite different from merge sort. Merge sort spent very little time on the "divide" step; it simply calculates a midpoint and starts the recursion on the two halves of the original set. The most significant work of merge sort is *after* the recursive calls are completed; this is when time must be spent to merge the two separate halves into one coherent order.

Quicksort takes a very different approach. Rather than blindly dividing the original group into two arbitrary halves, the goal is to partition the set into a group of "small" elements and a group of "large" elements. If we can accomplish that step, then when we sort the small group and separately sort the large group, our work will be done; the overall sorted list is simply the (sorted) small values followed by the (sorted) large values.

The catch is how to perform the partitioning step. In fact, it is not even clear how to define "small" versus "large" without spending some time to analyze the particular set of values that we are given. The approach most often used is the following. We pick an arbitrary element from the set and use this element as a *pivot*. All elements that are less than or equal to the pivot are considered "small" and all elements strictly greater than the pivot are considered "large." As a simple rule, we will use the *rightmost* element of the group as a pivot.

It would be quite easy to create two new lists that contain the small and large elements. However, what makes quicksort most useful in practice is that it can be performed in place, that is, without need for large auxiliary lists. Remember that this was the most significant disadvantage of merge sort. We perform the partition step by scanning through the list from left to right maintaining indices that divide the list into three portions. First will be those elements that we have determined to be less than or equal to the pivot, then elements greater than the pivot, and finally "unknown" elements (those we have not yet classified). Figure 14.9 provides a general schematic view of this division. From such a scenario, we can easily incorporate one additional unknown element as follows. If the leftmost unknown value is greater than the pivot, we simply shift the dividing line so as to include that element within the "large" section. No elements need be displaced. If, however, the next unknown value is less than or equal to the pivot, we must rearrange. Our approach here is to swap that unknown element into the *leftmost* location of the current "large" section. After doing this we advance both delimiters. Notice that the newly swapped element becomes part of the "small" group as a result, and the value for which it had been swapped is still considered part of the "large" group (though now at the right–most end rather than the leftmost end). Each time we repeat this process, we classify one additional unknown element, so eventually all elements are partitioned.

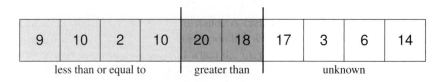

FIGURE 14.9: An intermediate stage of our partitioning algorithm with a pivot value of 14.

```
1   def _quickPartition(data, start, stop):
2       """Rearrange data[start:stop] so that values are partitioned around a pivot value.
3
4       Return index at which pivot element is eventually placed. At the conclusion,
5           data[start:pivot] will have values less than or equal to pivot's
6           data[pivot] is the pivot itself
7           data[pivot+1:stop] will have values strictly greater than pivot's
8       """
9       # Algorithm proceeds with the following invariant,
10      #    data[start:big] entries must be less than or equal to pivot value
11      #    data[big:unknown] entries must be greater than pivot value
12      #    data[unknown:stop] entries can be anything
13
14      pivotVal = data[stop−1]              # rightmost element of range
15      big = unknown = start                # initially, everything is unknown
16      while unknown < stop:
17          if data[unknown] <= pivotVal:
18              data[big], data[unknown] = data[unknown], data[big]
19              big += 1
20          unknown += 1                     # in either case, one less unknown element
21      return big − 1                       # index where pivot has just been placed
```

FIGURE 14.10: The implementation of quicksort's partitioning step.

With this high-level approach in mind, the actual code for the partitioning is quite simple. Figure 14.10 gives an implementation of a function _quickPartition that accomplishes this goal. The caller sends the list data, as well as the two outermost delimiters start and stop. Our goal is to partition only the portion of the list denoted as data[start:stop]. At the conclusion of the partitioning, we guarantee that there is an index pivot such that data[start:pivot] are values that are known to be less than or equal to the pivot value, that data[pivot] is the actual pivot value, and that data[pivot+1:stop] contains values known to be greater than the pivot. We return the index pivot to the caller upon competition.

Internally, we maintain two additional delimiters big and unknown, so that at all times data[start:big] are the "small" values, data[big:unknown] are the "large" values, and data[unknown:stop] are the unknown values. Since everything is initially viewed as unknown, we first set big = unknown = start (so that data[start:big] and data[big:unknown] are trivially empty). The only other subtlety in our code is the placement of the pivot element itself. We do not want it to be at an arbitrary place in the left group; we want to ensure that it lies at the boundary of the two groups. Our code relies upon the fact that the pivot element was chosen as the rightmost original element. This means that it will be the last unknown element processed. By definition it will be less than or equal to itself, so it will be swapped into the rightmost entry of the "small" group. Therefore, we return the index big − 1 with confidence that this is the final resting place of the pivot value.

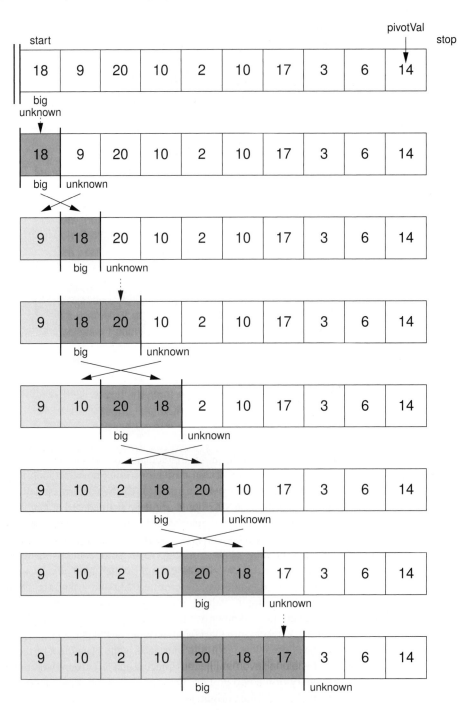

FIGURE 14.11: A trace of the _quicksortPartition method, showing the state each time the **while** condition at line 16 is evaluated (continued on next page).

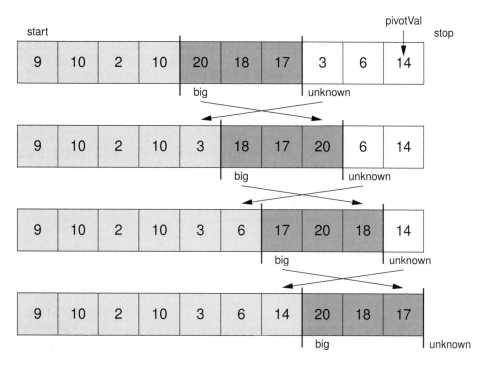

FIGURE 14.11 (continuation): The remaining trace of the _quicksortPartition method, continuing from the bottom configuration on the preceding page.

A demonstration of _quickPartition is shown in Figure 14.11. In this case, the right–most element with value 14 is used as the pivot. We demonstrate the two basic maneuvers. During the transition from the sixth line to the seventh, the value 10 is the element being classified from the unknown group. Because that value is less than the pivot value, we swap it for the leftmost "big" element (18 in this case) and then we advance both marks. In the next case, the unknown element has value 17, which is greater than the pivot value. In this case, we leave that element where it is, but advance the unknown marker to reflect that value 17 is now considered part of the "big" group. We draw attention to the final case, when the pivot element is itself swapped into position at the boundary of the two regions.

The recursion and analysis

Implementing the rest of the quicksort algorithm is quite easy. The partition does most of the work in separating the original list into two groups. Those groups can each be recursively sorted at which point the contents of the entire list will be sorted. The recursive version of the sort can be implemented as shown in Figure 14.12. Since the pivot element is already in its proper place, it is not included in either of the recursive calls. This means that the size of a recursive problem is at least one less than the preceding group and again we use a sublist of size one as a base case. Given the initial partition from Figure 14.11, the recursive process proceeds as shown in Figure 14.13.

```
def _recursiveQuicksort(data, start, stop):
   if start < stop−1:                              # more than one element to sort
      pivot = _quickPartition(data, start, stop)
      _recursiveQuicksort(data, start, pivot)
      _recursiveQuicksort(data, pivot+1, stop)
```

FIGURE 14.12: The implementation of quicksort's recursion.

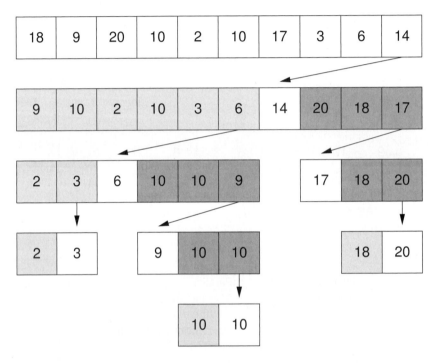

FIGURE 14.13: A complete trace of quicksort's recursion. Each arrow represents the movement of a pivot element during a subsequent recursive call.

The most interesting facet when analyzing quicksort's divide-and-conquer approach is that the two groups that result from _quickPartition are not necessarily equal in size. With merge sort, the division into two equal parts led to the guarantee that the base case of the recursion was reached after at most $\log_2 n$ splits, and therefore in an overall $\Theta(n \log n)$ running time. With quicksort, the analysis can again be bounded by n times the maximum recursive depth. It is quite likely that the two sides of a partition are not equal. In the most extreme case, the partition places all other elements on one side. If each pivot turns out to be extreme, quicksort degenerates to a $\Theta(n^2)$-time algorithm. Worse yet, this extreme behavior occurs when the original list was already sorted. This is quite ironic, that sorting a sorted list brings out the *worst* efficiency of an algorithm.

If, however, we assume that the order of the data is initially random, quicksort uses $\Theta(n\log n)$ time. To avoid the poor behavior that results from special cases (like data that is sorted), the standard approach is to intentionally *randomize* the process. This can be done by picking each pivot element at random from the given subset, but we use an even easier approach. We shuffle the original data once, at the beginning of the process, and then leave the rest of the code as is. We take advantage of a function for shuffling a list, imported from Python's random module. Our public quicksort function is then written as follows:

```python
from random import shuffle
def quicksort(data):
    shuffle(data)                               # in hope of getting good partitioning
    _recursiveQuicksort(data, 0, len(data))
```

After shuffling the data once and then starting the standard recursive process, it can be proven that quicksort runs in $\Theta(n\log n)$ time for any initial configuration with very high probability. For this reason, quicksort is a common algorithm choice in practice. Its major advantage over the variant of merge sort that we presented is that quicksort does not require an auxiliary list for temporary space. Also, the partitioning code is very streamlined and tends to perform well with little overhead.

14.6   Which Algorithm Does Python Use?

Now that we have examined several sorting algorithms, we should reiterate the fact that Python's lists already support a very efficient sort method. In fact, none of our own imple-mentations outperform that built-in method. The built-in method has two advantages. First, it is allowed to directly manipulate the internal representation of a list while our algorithms rely only upon the public access to that state. Second, the creators of Python worked quite hard on optimizing their sorting algorithm.

So which algorithm do they use? Giving an accurate answer to this question takes care. First, the principle of encapsulation dictates that the internal approach is officially none of our business. There is no guarantee that the algorithm remains the same from ver-sion to version or system to system. If the designers of Python wish to change their minds, that approach may change. In fact, the internal sorting algorithm has been redesigned in past versions of Python to improve its performance.

That said, the Python interpreter is open-source software, which means that its source code is available to the public for examination. So the current sorting algorithm is not a secret. Yet the approach is a hybrid of several algorithms. It is based on a divide-and-conquer approach for large lists, yet it switches over to insertion sort once the recursion reaches a sufficiently small sublist. Early versions of Python relied upon quicksort for the primary sorting. Although its worst-case performance is slower than merge sort, quicksort performs quite well on average, and uses minimal excess memory as an in-place algo-rithm. With Python 2.3, **list**.sort was reimplemented using an optimized variant of merge sort. The common version of merge sort, as described in Section 14.4, is impeded by the requirement for a secondary list with capacity roughly matching that of the original list. With greater care, merge sort can be implemented with lesser need for auxiliary memory.

The switch to insertion sort on small sublists may seem counterintuitive since our analysis suggests that merge sort is theoretically more efficient than insertion sort. Yet managing the divide–and–conquer approach requires extra manipulations that are worth–while for big data sets but overkill for small lists. In practice, experiments show that inser–tion sort can outperform the more complex algorithm when the size of a sublist is below a certain threshold. Insertion sort can also be helpful in cases where the original data is mostly ordered (in that case, the inner loop does not iterate as often, on average).

 A WORD OF WARNING

To be clear, we strongly suggest making use of the built–in sort method whenever possible. It is very difficult to implement a sorting routine that will outperform the built–in version, unless the data set is drawn from a known distribution that favors a specialized algorithm.

14.7   Chapter Review

14.7.1   Key Points

Using Python's Sort

- Sorting a list using a syntax data.sort( ) orders those elements based upon the default com–parison operator that is defined for the data type. However, there are ways to sort a list according to other notions of order.

- One approach for sorting with a nonstandard order is to provide an optional parameter that is a *comparison function*, as in data.sort(lengthCmp). The comparison function must compare two parameters and return –1 if the first is strictly smaller, 0 if they are equivalent, or 1 if the first is strictly greater.

- Another approach for sorting data according to a nonstandard order is to use *decorated tuples*. An auxiliary list is created with tuples of the form (key(element), element) as entries, for an appropriate function key that captures the desired notion of order. When the auxiliary list is sorted, it will be sorted primarily according to those keys. The sorted version of the original list can then be reconstructed by retrieving the original elements from the tuples.

- Starting with Python 2.4, the built–in sort supports a more concise way to apply a dec–orator pattern. If the caller provides a function to compute a decorator key for a given element, the sort function will take care of the actual decorating and undecorating process. The decorator function is specified using a special syntax known as *keyword parameter passing*. As an example, we could use the built–in len function as a decorator with syntax data.sort(key=len).

Selection and Insertion Sorts

- The selection sort algorithm proceeds by locating and placing the smallest element at the first location of the list, then the second smallest element at the second location, and so forth, until all elements have been placed. It runs in $\Theta(n^2)$ time.

- The insertion sort algorithm proceeds by maintaining the sorted order of a growing sublist. During each pass, one more element is incorporated in that sublist by sliding the larger elements rightward to open up a hole for the newest element. In the worst case, it runs in $\Theta(n^2)$ time, although in special cases it may run as quickly as $\Theta(n)$ time.

Merge Sort

- Merge sort is an example of a *divide-and-conquer* algorithm. It independently sorts (via recursion) the first half and second half of the original list. Then it merges the two halves together for the final result.

- The merging process is handled by selecting an element at a time, choosing the smallest remaining item from the two halves as the next element of the merged result.

Quicksort

- Quicksort is another divide-and-conquer approach, but quite different from merge sort. Rather than dividing the data based upon the original order, a *pivot* value is chosen and time is spent dividing the original values into those that are less than or equal to the pivot and those that are greater than the pivot.

- One of the most convenient aspects of quicksort is that partitioning, and thus the full sorting algorithm, can be performed in place (that is, without significant auxiliary memory).

14.7.2 Glossary

comparison function A function designed to compare two elements, often with a semantic that is different from the standard comparison. Such a function can be used to customize the order when sorting.

decorated tuple A tuple of the form (key(element), element), which can be used to sort elements based upon a nonstandard key.

divide and conquer An algorithmic technique in which a large data set is processed by dividing it into smaller portions, processing those portions, and then combining the results as needed.

insertion sort A sorting algorithm that proceeds by maintaining a sorted subset of elements, incrementally adding one new element at a time.

keyword parameter passing An alternative style for specifying an optional parameter to a function, such as sort(key=len). The syntax relies on an explicit assignment to initialize the formal parameter, rather than the more customary parameter passing that assigns formal parameters to actual parameters based on a designated order.

lexicographical order A convention for comparing two sequences to each other. The sequence with the smaller first element is considered the "smaller" sequence. If the first elements are equivalent, the second elements are used as a tie-breaker, and so on. If all elements are pairwise equivalent yet one sequence has additional elements at the end, that sequence is considered "larger." If they are the same length, the two sequences are considered equivalent.

merge sort   A sorting algorithm that proceeds by dividing a set into two, sorting the halves independently, and then recombining those halves.

pivot   A value used in quicksort to partition the data, specifically into those elements less than the pivot and those greater than the pivot.

quicksort   A sorting algorithm that proceeds recursively by dividing a data set according to those values that are less than a chosen pivot and those that are greater.

selection sort   A sorting algorithm that proceeds by finding and relocating the smallest value, then the second smallest value, and so on.

14.7.3 Exercises

Using Python's Sort

Practice 14.1: Given a list of strings identified as words, the behavior for words.sort( ) is case sensitive by default. All uppercase words are placed before any of the lower-case words. Show how to perform a *case-insensitive* version of sorting by using a comparison function.

Practice 14.2: Repeat Practice 14.1, but this time using a decorator function.

Practice 14.3: Suppose that data is a list of numbers and our goal is to sort those numbers based upon their distance from 100, ordered from closest to farthest. For example, the list [90, 93, 98, 101, 107, 111] would be sorted as [101, 98, 93, 107, 90, 111] by this rule (although you may break ties arbitrarily). Show how this can be accomplished using a comparison function.

Exercise 14.4: Repeat Practice 14.3, but this time using a decorator function.

Exercise 14.5: Assume that words is a list of lowercase strings. Our goal is to order those strings from those having the most e's to those having the least. Thus the list ['bee', 'beetle', 'clam', 'eel', 'elephant', 'reindeer'] might be sorted as ['beetle', 'reindeer', 'bee', 'eel', 'elephant', 'clam']. Show how this can be accomplished using a comparison function.

Exercise 14.6: Repeat Exercise 14.5, but this time using a decorator function.

Selection Sort

Practice 14.7: Figure 14.2 shows only the first seven passes of the outer loop. Diagram the completion of the process, continuing in the same style.

Practice 14.8: Using the style of Figure 14.2, give a complete trace of selection sort executing on the original list [15, 8, 12, 3, 7, 19, 14]

Practice 14.9: Give an example of an initial list of eight elements such that when selection sort is executed, one particular *data element* is repositioned seven times.

Exercise 14.10: Using the style of Figure 14.2, give a complete trace of selection sort executing on the original list [11, 5, 14, 13, 6, 9, 10]

Exercise 14.11: Give an example of an initial list of eight elements such that when selection sort is executed, one particular *index* is involved in all seven swaps.

Exercise 14.12: Our implementation of selection sort was given in Figure 14.1. There is a potential problem if we replace line 4 of the original code with the following:

```
4    small = hole + 1
```

Demonstrate the flaw by providing a specific data set and explaining what goes wrong with that execution.

Insertion Sort

Practice 14.13: Using the style of Figure 14.4, give a complete trace of insertion sort executing on the original list [15, 8, 12, 3, 7, 19, 14].

Exercise 14.14: Using the style of Figure 14.4, give a complete trace of insertion sort executing on the original list [11, 5, 14, 13, 6, 9, 10].

Exercise 14.15: Give an initial configuration of five elements that presents the worst possible performance of insertion sort in terms of efficiency.

Exercise 14.16: Our implementation of insertion sort was given in Figure 14.3. There is a potential problem if we replace line 6 of the original code with the following:

```
6    while data[hole−1] > value:
```

Demonstrate the flaw by providing a specific data set and explaining what goes wrong with that execution.

Merge Sort

Practice 14.17: Using the style of Figure 14.6, give a complete trace of the execution of a call _merge(data, 0, 3, 6, temp) with data = [2, 10, 11, 5, 8, 14].

Exercise 14.18: Using the style of Figure 14.6, give a complete trace of the execution of a call _merge(data, 0, 3, 6, temp) with data = [3, 6, 15, 7, 10, 12].

Exercise 14.19: Our implementation of _merge given in Figure 14.5 is based on a careful choice of a boolean condition given at line 19. There is a potential problem had we replaced that condition with the following:

```
19    if rightMark == stop or temp[leftMark] < temp[rightMark]:
```

Demonstrate the flaw in the following way. Give specific numeric values for a list data = [a, b, c, d] with a < b and c < d, such that _merge(data, 0, 2, 4, temp) fails to produce a properly sorted result. As part of your answer, show the final (erroneous) result that occurs after executing the flawed code on your data.

Exercise 14.20: Our implementation of _merge given in Figure 14.5 is based on a careful choice of a boolean condition given at line 19. There is a potential problem had we replaced that condition with the following:

```
19    if leftMark < mid and temp[leftMark] < temp[rightMark]:
```

Demonstrate the flaw in the following way. Give specific numeric values for a list data = [a, b, c, d] with a < b and c < d, such that _merge(data, 0, 2, 4, temp) fails to produce a properly sorted result. As part of your answer, explain the problem that occurs when executing the flawed code on your data.

Quicksort

Practice 14.21: Using the style of Figure 14.11, trace a call to _quickPartition(data, 0, 7) with data = [15, 8, 12, 3, 7, 19, 14]. Note: you do not need to do the complete sort, just the partitioning.

Practice 14.22: Using the style of Figure 14.13, show the complete trace of quicksort's recursion with data = [15, 8, 12, 3, 7, 19, 14] (but without any random shuffle). Note: you do not need to show the details of each partition (see Practice 14.21 for that).

Practice 14.23: In the original implementation of _quickPartition of Figure 14.10, we establish the pivot at line 14 as the rightmost original element. There is a potential problem with the correctness of the process if we had changed line 14 to use the leftmost element, as follows.

```
14    pivotVal = data[start]                        # leftmost element of range
```

Demonstrate the flaw by providing a specific data set and explaining what goes wrong with that execution.

Exercise 14.24: Using the style of Figure 14.11, trace a call to _quickPartition(data, 0, 7), with data = [11, 5, 14, 13, 6, 9, 10]. Note: you do not need to do the complete sort, just the partitioning.

Exercise 14.25: Using the style of Figure 14.13, show the complete trace of quicksort's recursion for data = [11, 5, 14, 13, 6, 9, 10] (but without any random shuffle). Note: you do not need to show the details of each partition (see Exercise 14.24 for that).

Exercise 14.26: Our implementation of _quickPartition is given in Figure 14.10. There is a potential problem (albeit, a subtle one), if we had changed line 17 to read as follows.

```
17    if data[unknown] < pivotVal:                  # strict inequality
```

Demonstrate the flaw by providing a specific data set and explaining what goes wrong with that execution.

Exercise 14.27: Our original version of quicksort performs inefficiently when sorting a list with a large number of equivalent values, for example quicksort([6] * 100000). The problem stems from our implementation of _quickPartition, which places all elements that are equal to the pivot in the left group. When there are many such elements, we get a very unbalanced partition.

This can be fixed as follows. Each time an element that equals the pivot value is encountered, toggle a boolean flag. If that flag is **True**, go ahead and swap that element to the small group; if it is **False**, leave the element as part of the big group. The only extra rule is that the rightmost such element, the pivot, must be swapped so that the return value is assured to be the index of a pivot value. Implement and test such a version of _quickPartition.

CHAPTER 15

Event-Driven Programming

Up to this point, we would describe the style of our programs as flow driven. They proceed sequentially, executing one command after another until the end of the program is reached. Control structures might be used to more creatively express the desired sequence of operations, yet still the execution follows one continuous flow, finishing one command and immediately executing another.

In this chapter, we examine another very important style known as *event-driven programming*. In this paradigm, an executing program waits passively for external *events* to occur, and then responds appropriately to those events. Consider for example, a modern word processor. Even when the software is running, it typically sits quietly unless the user of the program does something. When an event occurs, such as the selection of a menu item, the typing of characters, or the pressing of a button, the software reacts appropriately. Each event may be handled with a different response.

In coding how various events should be handled, we will use familiar Python programming techniques (e.g., control structures, functions, and objects). The major shift in thinking will involve the high-level design of a program and our view of how an executing program should proceed.

We focus primarily on *graphical user interfaces (GUIs)*, which are classic examples of event-driven programming. The user's actions are viewed as events that trigger reactions from the software. When a particular type of event occurs, a method is executed to deal with this event. If multiple events occur then a method is initiated for each event. A web server is another classic example of event-driven software. The server simply waits until a request is received for information, only then working to properly handle the request. That request is considered an external event to the server, because it was triggered by some other entity. We will explore some examples of network programming in Chapter 16.

493

15.1   Basics of Event-Driven Programming

We have already seen a basic form of event–driven programming in our earlier endeavors. We use the **raw_input** function in order to get user input. Consider the following simple program:

```
print 'What is your name?',
name = raw_input( )                          # wait indefinitely for user response
print 'Hello %s. Nice to meet you.' % name
```

When the **raw_input** function is called, our flow of control comes to a halt, waiting indef–initely until the user enters a response. Once that user event occurs, we continue on our way. A similar example, introduced on page 115 of Chapter 3, uses the wait( ) method of the graphics library.

```
paper = Canvas( )
cue = paper.wait( )                          # wait indefinitely for user event
ball = Circle(10, cue.getMouseLocation( ))
ball.setFillColor('red')
paper.add(ball)
```

The paper.wait( ) call causes the execution of our program to be delayed until the user triggers an appropriate event on the canvas, such as a mouse click.

However, both of these examples are still sequential. The flow of control is expressed just as all of our other programs. One statement is executed after the next; we can simply view **raw_input**( ) as any other function call, although one that may take a while before returning. Unfortunately, waiting for events in this way is not very flexible. When writing a program, we have to forecast the precise opportunities for user interaction, and the user must follow this script.

In most software, the user has more freedom to control the actions of a program. At any point, a user has the option of selecting menu items, entering keyboard input, using a scroll bar, selecting text, and much more. For example, a simple drawing program might allow the user to click on one button to add a shape, on another button to delete a shape, to drag a shape with the mouse from one position to another, or to save an image through an appropriate menu selection or the correct keyboard shortcut. When implementing this type of software, a sequential train of thought is not as meaningful. Instead, the program is described through *event handling*. The program declares various events that should be available to the user, and then provides explicit code that should be followed to handle each individual type of event when triggered. This piece of code is known as an ***event handler***.

Event handlers

Often, a separate event handler is declared for each kind of event that can be triggered by a user interaction. An event handler is typically implemented either as a stand–alone function or as an instance of a specially defined class. When programmed as a stand–alone function, event handlers are known as ***callback functions***. The appropriate callback function is reg–istered in advance as a handler for a particular kind of event. This is sometimes described as registering to *listen* for an event, and thus handlers are sometimes called *listeners*. Each time such an event subsequently occurs, this function will be called.

With object-oriented programming, event handling is typically implemented through an event-handling class. An instance of such a class supports one or more member functions that will be called when an appropriate event occurs. The advantage of this technique over use of pure callback functions is that a handler can maintain state information to coordinate the responses for a series of events.

The event loop

The design of event-driven software is quite different from our traditional flow-driven programming, although there is still a concept of the main flow of control. When the software first executes, initialization is performed in traditional fashion, perhaps to create and decorate one or more windows and set up appropriate menus. It is during this initialization that event handlers are declared and registered. Yet once initialization is complete, the execution may reach a point where the next task is simply to wait for the user to do something.

We want our software to be ready to handle any number of predefined events triggered in arbitrary order. This is typically accomplished by having the main flow of control enter what is known as an *event loop*. This is essentially an infinite loop that does nothing. Yet when an event occurs, the loop stops to look for an appropriately registered handler, and if found that handler is called (otherwise the event is ignored). When a handler is called, the flow of control is temporarily ceded to the handler, which responds appropriately. Once the handler completes its task, the default continuation is to re-enter the event loop (although there are techniques to "quit" the event loop, if that is the appropriate consequence of a user action). Figure 15.1 provides a simple view of such an event-driven flow of control.

Threading

There are several forms of event-driven programming. The first question at hand is what happens to the program's flow of control once an event loop begins. In one model, the primary program cedes the flow of control to the event loop. Another model uses what is known as *multithreaded* programming, allowing the main program to continue executing, even while the event loop is monitoring and responding to events. The main routine and this event loop run simultaneously as separate *threads* of the program. Threading can be supported by the programming language and the underlying operating system. In reality, the threads are sharing the CPU, each given small alternating time slices in which to execute.

Just as we distinguish between the case of the event loop running in the primary thread (thus blocking the main program), or in an independent thread, we can ask how the event loop invokes a handler. In some models, the handler executes using the same thread as the event loop, thus blocking the loop's monitoring of other events in the interim. However, it is possible to make further use of threads by having the event loop invoke each handler with an independent thread. In this way, the handler can continue to run even while the event loop continues listening for other events.

Main Program

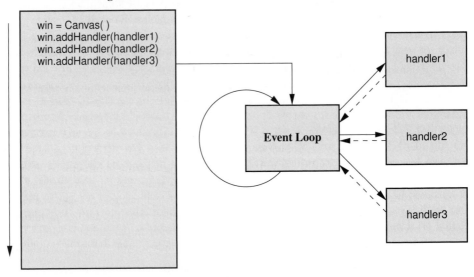

FIGURE 15.1: The flow of control in an event-driven program.

15.2   Event Handling in Our Graphics Module

The precise model for event-driven programming depends not only on the programming language, but on the underlying package that is being used for the graphical user interface. The graphics package receives the low-level user events, such as mouse clicks, and must decide how to process them. For the remainder of this chapter, we describe event handling with the cs1graphics module. As described in Chapter 3, that package supports a simple wait( ) model for basic support. However, it also supports more robust event handling.

15.2.1   The Event Loop

Without knowing it, every time you have used the cs1graphics package, an event loop has been running concurrently with the rest of your program. Every time you have clicked on the canvas's window or typed on the keyboard the event loop was informed. In most cases nothing occurred, as no handlers had been associated with the events. One exception is when you clicked on the icon to close the window; the event loop triggered a built-in handler that closed the window. When all canvas windows were closed, the event loop terminated. This starting and stopping of the event loop happens automatically.

15.2.2   The EventHandler Class

The module includes a generic EventHandler class that should be used as a parent class when defining your own handlers. Figure 15.2 outlines the two methods of that class, namely the constructor and a handle method. The handle method of the EventHandler class does not itself do anything. This method is overridden by a child class to describe the proper action in case of an event. The parameter to the handle method is an instance

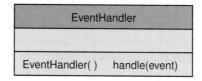

FIGURE 15.2: The EventHandler class.

of an Event class, used to describe the particular event that occurred. We will explore use of that parameter in Section 15.3. For now, we demonstrate a very simple handler which prints `Event Triggered` each time an event is detected:

```
class BasicHandler(EventHandler):
  def handle(self, event):
    print 'Event Triggered'
```

Registering a handler with a graphics object

For an event handler to be active, it must be registered with one or more graphical objects. Both the Canvas and Drawable classes support two additional methods named addHandler and removeHandler to register and unregister a handler. For example, an instance of our BasicHandler class can be registered with a canvas as follows:

```
simple = BasicHandler( )
paper = Canvas( )
paper.addHandler(simple)
```

Each time the user clicks on the canvas window or presses a key while the canvas is active, an event is created triggering our handler which displays `Event Triggered`.

Using a similar technique, we can register an event handler directly with a particular drawable object. For example in the following scenario,

```
sun = Circle(30, Point(50,50))
sun.setFillColor('yellow')
paper = Canvas( )
paper.add(sun)
simple = BasicHandler( )
sun.addHandler(simple)          # register directly with the sun
```

the handler is only triggered when an event is received by the circle. Clicking on any other part of the canvas will not suffice. In our model, it is possible to register a single handler with multiple shapes or canvases, and to have multiple handlers registered with the same shape or canvas. If there are multiple handlers registered with an object and a relevant event is triggered, then *each* of those handlers is called in the order that they were registered. A single mouse click could initiate several reactions, one for each handler.

15.2.3   A Handler with State Information

In our first example, the handler did not have any state information. As our next example, we create a handler that counts the number of times that it has been triggered.

```python
class CountingHandler(EventHandler):
    def __init__(self):
        EventHandler.__init__(self)  # call the parent constructor!
        self._count = 0

    def handle(self, event):
        self._count += 1
        print 'Event Triggered. Count: ', self._count
```

In this example, we define our own constructor to establish the initial state of the _count attribute, which is later used from within the handle routine. Note that when overriding the constructor, we call the parent constructor so that the underlying state for the handler is properly established. In contrast, there is no need to call the parent version of the handle method, because that method is clearly documented as one that does not do anything.

As a further example, Figure 15.3 provides a program that updates a *graphical* count, in the form of a Text object, each time the user clicks on the canvas. In this case, the handler must be given a reference to the existing Text object in order to manipulate it. Therefore, we send this text object as a parameter when instantiating the actual handler at line 15. The reference to this object is then stored as an instance variable within the handler, at line 5, so that it can be used from within handle at line 10.

```python
 1  class TallyHandler(EventHandler):
 2      def __init__(self, textObj):
 3          EventHandler.__init__(self)
 4          self._count = 0
 5          self._text = textObj
 6          self._text.setText(str(self._count))      # reset to 0
 7
 8      def handle(self, event):
 9          self._count += 1
10          self._text.setText(str(self._count))
11
12  paper = Canvas(100, 100)
13  score = Text(' ', 12, Point(40,40))
14  paper.add(score)
15  referee = TallyHandler(score)          # create the handler
16  paper.addHandler(referee)              # activate the handler
```

FIGURE 15.3: A handler that increments a graphical counter.

```
class HandleOnce(EventHandler):
  def __init__(self, eventTrigger):
    EventHandler.__init__(self)
    self._trigger = eventTrigger

  def handle(self, event):
    print "That's all folks!!!"
    self._trigger.removeHandler(self)

paper = Canvas( )
oneTime = HandleOnce(paper)
paper.addHandler(oneTime)
```

FIGURE 15.4: An event handler that can only be triggered once.

By default, handlers continue responding to events as long as the program runs. In contrast, we may want to have a handler that intentionally unregisters itself the first time it is triggered. This provides a one-time handling mechanism that is more naturally accomplished from within the context of the handler class. Figure 15.4 shows an example of this. When the handler is triggered, the call to removeHandler deactivates itself. So the first click on the canvas will trigger the print statement, but subsequent clicks will not.

15.3 The Event Class

Sometimes, an event handler may need information about the triggering event, such as the mouse location or the type of event that was received. To support this, the handle method of our EventHandler class is always passed an additional parameter that is an instance of an Event class, as originally introduced in Section 3.8.

Thus far in this chapter, you will see that all of our handlers have a signature

```
def handle(self, event):
```

although they do not use the event parameter within the body. To use that parameter, we need to know more about the Event class. One method that it supports is getTrigger( ), which returns a reference to the underlying object upon which the event was originally triggered (a canvas or drawable object). This knowledge can often be used to simplify the design of a handler. For example, the HandleOnce class defined originally in Figure 15.4 needed to call the removeHandler method upon that trigger object. In that implementation we passed the identity of that trigger as a parameter to the constructor so that the handler could access it from within the handle method. However, we could have written the code more succinctly using getTrigger, as shown in Figure 15.5.

The Event class also supports a getDescription( ) accessor that returns a string indi-cating the kind of event that occurred. In the remainder of this section, we discuss several kinds of events, most notably those involving mouse or keyboard activity.

```
class HandleOnce(EventHandler):
  def handle(self, event):
    print "That's all folks!!!"
    event.getTrigger( ).removeHandler(self)


paper = Canvas( )
oneTime = HandleOnce( )
paper.addHandler(oneTime)
```

FIGURE 15.5: Another implementation of an event handler that can only be triggered once.

15.3.1 Mouse Events

There are several distinct kinds of mouse events: the mouse might be single clicked, released, or dragged while the button is being held down. The particular kind of event can be determined by calling getDescription( ), which returns a string, 'mouse click', 'mouse release', or 'mouse drag' respectively. If the user clicks the button and then releases it two events will be triggered, the first identified as mouse click and the second as mouse release. When the mouse is dragged across the screen the sequence of events sent to the handler is a mouse click, followed by one or more mouse drags, and finally a mouse release event.

For some applications, we might be interested in the precise position of the mouse at the time the event occurred. The getMouseLocation( ) method of the Event class returns a Point instance, identifying the location of the mouse with respect to the coordinate system of the object that triggered the event.

As a first example using these techniques, Figure 15.6 gives a program that places circles on a canvas centered where the mouse is clicked. The handle function checks, at line 3, whether the event corresponded to a mouse click. If so, then line 4 create a new circle centered at the mouse location, and line 5 adds this circle to the underlying canvas. Notice that this handler intentionally ignores other kinds of events, such as when the mouse

```
1  class CircleDrawHandler(EventHandler):
2    def handle(self, event):
3      if event.getDescription( ) == 'mouse click':
4        c = Circle(5, event.getMouseLocation( ))
5        event.getTrigger( ).add(c)
6
7  paper = Canvas(100, 100)
8  handler = CircleDrawHandler( )
9  paper.addHandler(handler)
```

FIGURE 15.6: A program for drawing circles on a canvas.

is released or a key is pressed. Observe that the circle is created when the mouse button is pressed down and if the mouse is dragged it creates a circle when the button is first depressed. Try changing the code so that it draws the circle on a `mouse release` and observe the difference.

In the case of a `mouse drag` event, the getOldMouseLocation( ) method indicates where the mouse was before the dragging occurred. The combination of this knowledge and that of the current location can be used to figure out how far the mouse was moved. We will demonstrate use of this on a later example, in Section 15.4, showing how to drag objects across the screen.

Dragging the mouse across the screen triggers a `mouse click` event, followed by one or more `mouse drag` events, and finally a `mouse release` event. In some cases, we want a program to respond differently to a mouse drag than to a stationary click and release. This requires a handler that keeps track of the state as shown in Figure 15.7.

The attribute _mouseDragged is used to keep track of whether we are in the middle of a sequence of events corresponding to a mouse drag. The handle method in lines 6–15 responds to each mouse event. Note that the actual response is triggered when the mouse is released and other events are used to update the object's state. When the mouse is first clicked on _mouseDragged is set to **False**. This ensures that if the next event is a `mouse release` then the handler will indicate that the mouse was clicked without dragging. However, if a `mouse drag` event occurs before the mouse button is released then as soon as the mouse button is released we are informed that the mouse was dragged.

```
 1  class ClickAndReleaseHandler(EventHandler):
 2    def __init__(self):
 3      EventHandler.__init__(self)
 4      self._mouseDragged = False
 5
 6    def handle(self, event):
 7      if event.getDescription( ) == 'mouse click':
 8        self._mouseDragged = False
 9      elif event.getDescription( ) == 'mouse drag':
10        self._mouseDragged = True
11      elif event.getDescription( ) == 'mouse release':
12        if self._mouseDragged:
13          print 'Mouse was dragged'
14        else:
15          print 'Mouse was clicked without dragging'
16
17  paper = Canvas( )
18  dragDetector = ClickAndReleaseHandler( )
19  paper.addHandler(dragDetector)
```

FIGURE 15.7: Differentiating between a mouse click and release and mouse dragging.

```
1   class KeyHandler(EventHandler):
2     def __init__(self, textObj):
3       EventHandler.__init__(self)
4       self._textObj = textObj
5
6     def handle(self, event):
7       if event.getDescription() == 'keyboard':
8         self._textObj.setText(self._textObj.getText() + event.getKey())
9       elif event.getDescription() == 'mouse click':
10        self._textObj.setText('')    # clear the text
11
12  paper = Canvas()
13  textDisplay = Text(' ', 12, Point(10,10))     # empty string initially
14  paper.add(textDisplay)
15  echo = KeyHandler(textDisplay)
16  paper.addHandler(echo)
```

FIGURE 15.8: A program for echoing characters upon a canvas.

15.3.2 Keyboard Events

When the user presses a key on the keyboard, this triggers a keyboard event upon whatever object currently has the "focus." Depending upon the operating system, the focus is deter–mined either by where the mouse is currently located or perhaps which object was most recently clicked. From within a handler, this type of event is reported as 'keyboard' by getDescription(). If needed, the getMouseLocation() is supported for a keyboard event. But keyboard events also support a behavior getKey() that returns the single character that was typed on the keyboard to trigger the event. Note that if the user types a series of characters, each one of those triggers a separate event.

Figure 15.8 gives a simple program showing how to display characters graphically as they are typed within a canvas. The main flow begins by creating a canvas and adding a new Text instance, although one that displays the empty string. When the handler is instantiated at line 15, we must explicitly send it a reference to this underlying Text object.

Within the class definition, we record the identity of the text object as an attribute at line 4 and then use it within the handle body at lines 8 and 10. When a user types a character, that character is added to the displayed string. If the user clicks on the canvas, the text is reset to the empty string.

15.3.3 Timers

Mouse and keyboard events are originally triggered as a direct result of the user's activi–ties. When using event-driven programming, there are other scenarios in which we want our program to respond to an event that we generate internally. The cs1graphics module includes a definition of a Timer class for this purpose. A timer is not itself a graphical object, nor is it an event or an event handler. A timer instance is a self-standing object that is used to *generate* new events (almost like a ghost who generates events as if a user).

A Timer has an interval, measured in seconds, that can be specified as a parameter to the constructor. Thus the syntax Timer(10) creates a timer that generates an event after ten seconds has elapsed. However, the timer does not start counting upon instantiation; the start( ) method must be called to begin the timer's clock. After the specified time interval passes, it generates a timer event. The constructor for the Timer class takes an optional second parameter that can be used to specify if the timer should be automatically restarted after it triggers an event. By default, the timer does not restart itself. However, a timer constructed with the call Timer(5, **True**) will repeatedly trigger an event every five seconds, once it is started. Its internal timer can be explicitly interrupted with the stop( ) method.

For a timer to be useful, there must be a corresponding handler that is registered to listen for those events. For example, we could register one of our CountingHandler instances from page 498 to listen to a timer, creating the following event-driven stopwatch:

```
alarm = Timer(1, True)
stopwatch = CountingHandler( )
alarm.addHandler(stopwatch)
print 'Ready...'
alarm.start( )                    # yet never stops...
```

Once per second, an event is generated, triggering the handler. The user will see the count displayed each second. Notice that the earlier CounterHandler method handles all events in the same way, and therefore we do not need to do anything special for it to recognize the `timer` event. We could similarly use such a timer to trigger some action on the canvas. For example, animating a rotating shape.

```
class RotatingHandler:
  def __init__(self, shape):
    self._shape = shape

  def handle(self, event):
    self._shape.rotate(1)

paper = Canvas(100,100)
sampleCircle = Circle(20, Point(50,20))
sampleCircle.adjustReference(0,30)
paper.add(sampleCircle)

alarm = Timer(0.1, True)
rotator = RotationHandler(sampleCircle)
alarm.addHandler(rotator)
alarm.start( )
```

This creates a circle and draws it on the canvas and every tenth of a second rotates around the reference point (the center of the canvas). The circle will continue on its path around the screen until the canvas is closed.

15.3.4 Monitors

In some cases, we want to blend event–driven programming with the more sequential flow–driven approach. For example, we have already seen how a command like **raw_input** causes the current flow of control to wait indefinitely until the user responds. Sometimes we want a similar way to wait indefinitely, until triggered by some combination of events.

For simple cases, we provided the wait( ) behavior as introduced in Chapter 3 and reviewed on page 494 of this chapter. However, that behavior cannot be customized. It blocks the flow of control until any kind of event is triggered upon the one particular canvas or drawable object. There are times where we may want to wait until one particular kind of event occurs, or to wait until an event happens on any one of a larger set of objects.

To this end, we introduce a Monitor class. The class is so named because it can be thought of as "monitoring" some condition and alerting us once that condition is met. The class supports two methods, wait( ) and release( ). When wait( ) is called, control of that flow will not be returned until the monitor is somehow released, presumably by some event handler. Yet we can use many different handlers to potentially release a given monitor.

Figure 15.9 gives an example of the use of a monitor. We create a Monitor instance at line 11, and then a dedicated handler at line 12, which will later be used to release the

```
1   class ShapeHandler(EventHandler):
2     def __init__(self, monitor):
3       EventHandler.__init__(self)
4       self._monitor = monitor
5
6     def handle(event):
7       if event.getDescription( ) == 'mouse drag':
8         self._monitor.release( )
9
10  paper = Canvas( )
11  checkpoint = Monitor( )
12  handler = ShapeHandler(checkpoint)
13
14  cir = Circle(10, Point(50,50))
15  cir.setFillColor('blue')
16  cir.addHandler(handler)
17  paper.add(cir)
18  square = Square(20, Point(25,75))
19  square.setFillColor('red')
20  square.addHandler(handler)
21  paper.add(square)
22
23  checkpoint.wait( )
24  paper.setBackgroundColor('green')
```

FIGURE 15.9: The use of a monitor.

monitor. Notice that the handler is registered with both the circle and the square, and that it is programmed to only respond to mouse drag events. At line 23, the wait( ) method of the monitor is invoked, essentially blocking the main flow of control. Line 24 is not immediately executed. In fact, it will not be executed until the monitor is released. This will only occur when the user drags the mouse on either the circle or square; at that point the original flow of control continues to line 24 and the background color is changed. Technically, the handler continues listening for mouse drags, rereleasing the monitor each time. However a rerelease has no subsequent effect. Notice that the use of a monitor has a similar style to invoking wait( ) directly upon a drawable object, except that it allows us to wait for only specific kinds of events, or to simultaneously wait upon multiple objects.

15.4 Programming Using Events

Our preliminary examples have been rather simple, demonstrating each new concept individually. In this section, we combine the basic techniques to produce three programs with more interesting results.

15.4.1 Adding and Moving Shapes on a Canvas

As our next example, we design a program to create and modify shapes. Each time the mouse is clicked on the background, a new shape is created and added to the canvas. Dragging the mouse on an existing shape can be used to move it, while clicking on it enlarges the shape. Typing on the keyboard when a shape has the focus changes its color.

We use two different handlers for this task, one that listens for events on the background of the canvas, and a second that listens for events on any of the existing shapes. The complete program is given in Figure 15.10. Let's examine how that program works. At lines 1–19, we define a ShapeHandler class. This will eventually be used to manage the shapes that have already been added to our canvas. The handler has three distinct behaviors, depending upon whether the user is dragging the mouse, clicking on the shape, or typing on the keyboard. The handler needs to respond differently to mouse drags than to clicking and releasing the mouse. This will be dealt with using the same style as the program in Figure 15.7. When dragging, notice that we use the difference between the new mouse location and the old mouse location to determine how far to move the shape. When the user triggers a keyboard event, our current implementation switches to a random color, although we could easily modify this code to pick a specific color depending upon what letter was typed (see Exercise 15.4).

In lines 21–42, we define a NewShapeHandler that will listen for events on the canvas background. Each time the user single clicks, a new shape is added to the canvas at that location. This implementation automatically cycles through four different shapes. Within the constructor, a _shapeCode attribute is initialized to control which type of shape is next created (that integer code is later "advanced" at line 37). The other attribute created in the constructor, at line 25, is an instance of the ShapeHandler class. We will use a single handler to manage all of the shapes that are created. This handler is registered to each new shape at line 42.

With these class definitions, the main part of the program creates a canvas, and then instantiates a NewShapeHandler while immediately registering it with the canvas. Once this is done, the user may begin playing.

```
1   class ShapeHandler(EventHandler):
2     def __init__(self):
3       EventHandler.__init__(self)
4       self._mouseDragged = False
5
6     def handle(self, event):
7       shape = self.getTrigger()
8       if event.getDescription() == 'mouse drag':
9         old = event.getOldMouseLocation()
10        new = event.getMouseLocation()
11        shape.move(new.getX()-old.getX(), new.getY()-old.getY())
12        self._mouseDragged = True
13      elif event.getDescription() == 'mouse click':
14        self._mouseDragged = False
15      elif event.getDescription() == 'mouse release':
16        if not self._mouseDragged:
17          shape.scale(1.5)
18      elif event.getDescription() == 'keyboard':
19        shape.setFillColor(Color.randomColor())
20
21  class NewShapeHandler(EventHandler):
22    def __init__(self):
23      EventHandler.__init__(self)
24      self._shapeCode = 0
25      self._handler = ShapeHandler()   # single instance handles all shapes
26
27    def handle(self, event):
28      if event.getDescription() == 'mouse click':
29        if self._shapeCode == 0:
30          s = Circle(10)
31        elif self._shapeCode == 1:
32          s = Square(10)
33        elif self._shapeCode == 2:
34          s = Rectangle(15,5)
35        elif self._shapeCode == 3:
36          s = Polygon(Point(5,5), Point(0,-5), Point(-5,5))
37        self._shapeCode = (self._shapeCode + 1) % 4   # advance cyclically
38
39        s.move(event.getMouseLocation())
40        s.setFillColor('white')
41        event.getTrigger().add(s)          # add shape to the underlying canvas
42        s.addHandler(self._handler)        # register the ShapeHandler with the new shape
43
44  paper = Canvas(400, 300, 'Click me!')
45  paper.addHandler(NewShapeHandler())   # instantiate handler and register all at once
```

FIGURE 15.10: Creating and modifying shapes using events.

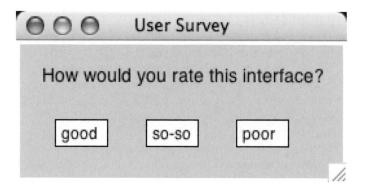

FIGURE 15.11: A screenshot of a sample dialog box.

15.4.2 A Dialog Box Class

Our second advanced example is to create what is known as a dialog box. This is a common technique for blending the event-driven and flow-driven styles. Often graphics-based programs need to ask a specific question of the user and to await that response before proceeding. For example when closing an open file, a pop-up window might appear warning the user that all data will be lost and asking if they want to continue. Buttons may offer alternatives such as "OK" or "Cancel" that the user can click on to respond. Other dialogs may offer choices like "Yes" and "No", or more than two choices such as "Save", "Exit without saving", and "Cancel". A typical sample of a dialog box is shown in Figure 15.11.

To support such dialogs, we will design a utility class Dialog. Before looking at the implementation, we focus on the programming interface for those wanting to use our dialogs. The constructor is called with the signature

```
Dialog(prompt, options, title, width, height)
```

although our implementation will offer default values for these parameters. The prompt is a string that will be displayed as part of the dialog box, options is a sequence of strings to be offered as choices, and the parameters title, width, and height affect the window settings.

Instantiating a Dialog instance configures it, but does not display it. The user interaction is accomplished by calling the display( ) method, which waits for a user response and then returns the string corresponding to the chosen option. The dialog can be redisplayed whenever the same interaction is needed. An example of its use might appear as follows:

```
survey = Dialog('How would you rate this interface?',
            ('good','so-so','poor'),'User Survey')
answer = survey.display( )     # waits for user response
if answer != 'good':
  print "Let's see you do better (see exercises)"
```

When displayed, the user would see the window shown in Figure 15.11. Once the user clicks on a button, the answer is returned and our program continues.

```
1   class Dialog(EventHandler):                        # Note: handles itself!
2       """Provides a pop-up dialog box offering a set of choices."""
3
4     def __init__(self, prompt='Continue?', options=('Yes', 'No'),
5                   title = 'User response needed', width=250, height=100):
6        """Create a new Dialog instance but does not yet display it.
7
8        prompt     the displayed string (default 'Continue?')
9        options    a sequence of strings, offered as options (default ('Yes', 'No') )
10       title      string used for window title bar (default 'User response needed')
11       width      width of the pop-up window (default 250)
12       height     height of the pop-up window (default 100)
13       """
14       EventHandler.__init__(self)
15       popup = Canvas(width, height, 'lightgray', title)
16       popup.close()                                 # hide, for now
17       popup.add(Text(prompt, 14, Point(20,20)))
18
19       xCoord = (width − 70*len(options)/2           # Center buttons
20       for opt in options:
21          b = Button(opt, 40, 20, Point(xCoord, height−30))
22          b.addHandler(self)                         # we will handle this button ourselves
23          popup.add(b)
24          xCoord += 70
25
26       self._monitor = Monitor()
27       self._response = None
28
29     def display(self):
30        """Display the dialog, wait for a response and return the answer."""
31        self._response = None                        # clear old responses
32        popup.open()                                 # make dialog visible
33        self._monitor.wait()                         # wait until some button is pressed
34        popup.close()                                # then close the popup window
35        return self._response                        # and return the user's response
36
37     def handle(self, event):
38        """Check if the event was a mouse click and have the dialog return."""
39        if event.getDescription().startswith('mouse'):
40           self._response = event.getTrigger().getText()   # label of chosen option
41           self._monitor.release()                          # ready to end dialog
```

FIGURE 15.12: A dialog box class.

The complete implementation of the Dialog class is given in Figure 15.12. The con-structor initializing a pop–up window, but immediately hides the window at line 16 for the time being. This allows us to work behind the scene in configuring our dialog box based upon the given parameters. We add a text prompt and, below that, a row of buttons labeled with the indicated options. Our initial implementation does a rough job of guessing at the geometry (designing a more robust layout is left as Exercise 15.5).

Since the constructor is responsible for preparing this dialog for future use, it also creates a Monitor instance at line 26 and initializes a response to **None** at line 27. The monitor will be used to intentionally delay the progression of code until the user has chosen one of the buttons. That user interaction is started by calling the display method. This method resets the response to empty, makes the pop–up window visible, and then waits on the monitor at line 33. We are not yet prepared to give an answer to the caller of this method. However, once a button has been pressed, the monitor will be released and we go on to lines 34 and 35, to close the dialog window and to return the chosen response.

The actual code for handling the buttons is given in lines 37–41. There is a great deal of subtlety tying all of this code together. Most significantly, we use inheritance at line 1 of our class definition to declare the Dialog instance itself as an EventHandler. We could have used two different classes, one for the dialog window and the other for a handler class, but the sharing of information is much more convenient as a single object. Notice that the event handling code needs to access two objects, as it must store the chosen response in a way that can later be accessed by the dialog code, and it must release the dialog's monitor so that the original call can proceed. If we were to create a separate handler, we would have to construct that handler while passing it references to those underlying objects (as was done with ShapeHandler in Figure 15.9). By having our class serve as its own handler, it already has the needed access! When a button is pressed, the chosen option string is retrieved at line 40 from the specific button that triggered the current event, and then the monitor is released at line 41 to allow the primary flow of control within the display method to continue beyond the wait initiated at line 33.

15.4.3 A Stopwatch Widget

As our third example, we design a basic stopwatch. Unlike the Dialog class, which brings up its own pop–up window, our stopwatch is designed to be a component that can itself be used on a canvas. Such graphical components are often called *widgets*. A picture of our stopwatch is shown in Figure 15.13. It displays a time, measured in minutes and seconds, and has three buttons. The left button is used to start (or restart) the stopwatch. The middle button is used to stop the watch, and the third button is used to reset the time to zero.

Again, we begin by considering the *use* of our presumed class. We offer the follow–ing simple demonstration.

```
paper = Canvas(400,400)
clock = Stopwatch( )
paper.add(clock)
clock.move(200,200)
```

Notice that the Stopwatch instance is added to the canvas as with any Drawable object.

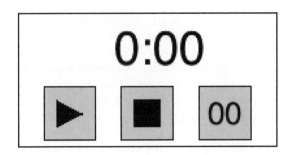

FIGURE 15.13: A screenshot of the Stopwatch widget.

Our Stopwatch design is based upon the use of multiple inheritance. We want a stopwatch to be treated as a single graphical component, and so we inherit from the Layer class (as done in Section 9.4.3). At the same time, we find it convenient to have our objects handle their own events, as we did with the preceding Dialog example, so our class inherits from EventHandler as well. Therefore, we use multiple inheritance and begin the class definition with the syntax **class** Stopwatch(Layer, EventHandler). We will ensure that our constructor calls the parent form of the constructor for both the Layer and EventHandler classes.

The complete implementation is given in Figure 15.14. Much of the constructor is dedicated to laying out the graphical components of the stopwatch, namely a border, a text display, three buttons, and appropriate icons. The border and icons are identified with local variables because we will not need to access them when handling an event. However, the display and the three buttons are designated as data members so that we can reference them from the event handling routine. The loop at lines 28 and 29 is used to explicitly add all of our intended components to ourself (as a Layer).

Perhaps the most interesting part of the constructor is given in lines 31–34. Here we initialize our internal clock to zero and create a periodic Timer object (although one that is not yet started). In lines 33 and 34 we formally register our Stopwatch instance as the handler for the four event-triggering components, namely the timer and the three buttons.

The getTime method at lines 36–42 is a simple utility that converts the current internal clock to an appropriately formatted string for displaying the time in minutes and sec-onds (we do not use hours as a unit of time, although this could easily be accomplished). We see this utility used from lines 51 and 59 of the subsequent handle routine.

The complete handle routine is given in lines 46–63. It is written to handle potential events from four different components. If an event is triggered by the timer, we update our internal clock and refresh the displayed time (lines 49–51). If the event is a mouse click, it must have occurred on one of the three buttons; our response depends upon which button. When the start button is pressed, we start the internal timer (even if it was already running), and similarly we stop the timer when the user clicks on the stop button. Otherwise, the reset button was pressed, so we reset the internal clock to zero and update the displayed time. Notice that our reset behavior does not change the Timer instance. Pressing reset when the clock is running causes it to go back to zero but it continues to run. Pressing the reset button on a stopped clock, resets it to zero while leaving the clock stopped.

```
1   class Stopwatch(Layer, EventHandler):
2     """Display a stopwatch with start, stop, and reset buttons."""
3
4     def __init__(self):
5       """Create a new Stopwatch instance."""
6       Layer.__init__(self)
7       EventHandler.__init__(self)
8
9       border = Rectangle(200,100)
10      border.setFillColor('white')
11      border.setDepth(52)
12      self._display = Text('0:00', 36, Point(-25,-40))
13
14      self._start = Square(40, Point(-60,25))
15      self._stop  = Square(40, Point(0,25))
16      self._reset = Square(40, Point(60,25))
17      buttons = [self._start, self._stop, self._reset]
18      for b in buttons:
19        b.setFillColor('lightgray')
20        b.setDepth(51)   # in front of border, but behind icons
21
22      startIcon = Polygon( Point(-70,15), Point(-70,35), Point(-50,25) )
23      startIcon.setFillColor('black')
24      stopIcon = Square(20, Point(0,25))
25      stopIcon.setFillColor('black')
26      resetIcon = Text('00', 24, Point(47,15))
27
28      for obj in buttons + [self._display, border, startIcon, stopIcon, resetIcon]:
29        self.add(obj)    # add to the layer
30
31      self._clock = 0                  # measured in seconds
32      self._timer = Timer(1, True)
33      for active in (self._timer, self._start, self._stop, self._reset):
34        active.addHandler(self)  # we will handle all such events
35
36    def getTime(self):
37      """Convert the clock's time to a string with minutes and seconds."""
38      min = str(self._clock // 60)
39      sec = str(self._clock % 60)
40      if len(sec) == 1:
41        sec = '0'+sec  # pad with leading zero
42      return min + ':' + sec
```

FIGURE 15.14: Implementation of a Stopwatch class (continued on next page).

```
43    def handle(self, event):
44        """Deal with each of the possible events.
45
46        The possibilities are timer events for advancing the clock,
47        and mouse clicks on one of the buttons.
48        """
49        if event.getDescription( ) == 'timer':
50            self._clock += 1
51            self._display.setText(self.getTime( ))
52        elif event.getDescription( ) == 'mouse click':
53            if event.getTrigger( ) == self._start:
54                self._timer.start( )
55            elif event.getTrigger( ) == self._stop:
56                self._timer.stop( )
57            else:   # must have been self._reset
58                self._clock = 0
59                self._display.setText(self.getTime( ))
60
61    if __name__ == '__main__':
62        paper = Canvas(400,400)
63        clock = Stopwatch( )
64        paper.add(clock)
65        clock.move(200,200)
```

FIGURE 15.14 (continuation): Implementation of a Stopwatch class.

15.5   Case Study: a Full GUI for Mastermind

If we combine all of these techniques for dealing with events we can write a full graphical interface for the Mastermind game developed in Chapter 7. Our goal is to have the user control the entire game, from start to finish, with the mouse. Figure 15.15 shows a screen-shot of the game in action; to select a peg color, the user clicks on the peg and our interface displays a box of choices. Once all of the peg colors have been selected the button labeled "Guess" is activated; pressing this button finalizes the guess. This provides a fairly natural user interface with minimal changes made to the original code.

For flexibility, the design of the Mastermind program had separate classes for dealing with user input and output. For input we used the TextInput class and for output we used either the TextOutput or GraphicsOutput classes. A full GUI for the game involves both input and output involving the same graphical objects, so a single class MastermindGUI will be written to take the place of both the input and output classes. See Figure 15.16 for the methods it must support.

Since all of the display functions are the same as in GraphicsOutput, we will inherit the GUI class from it. However, all of the input routines need to be completely rewritten since they were originally text based. Below are the changes to the main routine for starting the Mastermind game. First an instance of the MastermindGUI is created. Since the new class handles both input and output there is no need for two separate class instances being

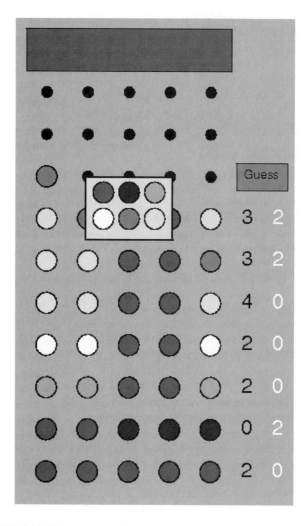

FIGURE 15.15: A screenshot for the new interface to Mastermind.

sent to the constructor for Mastermind. These are the only changes to necessary when starting the game.

```
if __name__ == '__main__':
  palette = ('Red', 'Blue', 'Green', 'White', 'Yellow', 'Orange',
             'Purple', 'Turquoise')
  interface = MastermindGUI(palette)
  game = Mastermind(interface, interface)
```

The full implementation of MastermindGUI is in Figure 15.17. The first group of methods are used to query the user for game parameters in lines 9–28. Comparing the code to the TextInput class on pages 258–258 of Chapter 7, we see that each call to the

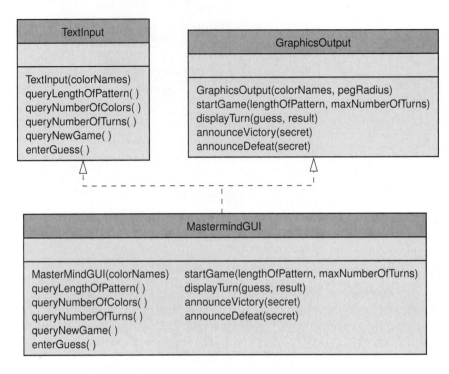

FIGURE 15.16: The MastermindGUI must perform all of the tasks of both the input and output classes.

_readInt function has been replaced by the creation of a dialog box. This utilizes the Dialog class written in Section 15.4 to display the possible options for each query. This provides a straightforward way to use existing code to enter these game parameters. (In Exercise 15.9 you will have an opportunity to improve upon this user interface.)

The GraphicsOutput class has a method _setupBackground that is used to render the game board. This method is overridden in lines 35–50. When it comes time for the user to enter the pattern we will need to add handlers for the pegs so that the user can click on them to select a color. To do this we need to keep track of each pegs, so we store the location of the Circle instances for each peg location in the member variable _holes.

The enterGuess method in lines 52–77 allows the user to enter a pattern using the mouse. When the user clicks on a peg, a small window appears with the color options. When the user selects a color, a peg of that color peg is placed in the hole. The user can change the color by selecting that peg location again. When the user is done, he presses the button labeled "Guess." For this to operate properly, we need two handler classes: PegHandler for clicking on the peg, and ButtonHandler for clicking the button. When enterGuess is called, a PegHandler instance is created for each hole in the current row of the board and associated to the corresponding circle in lines 59–61. In lines 64–67 a ButtonHandler is created to respond when the user clicks on the button to complete the guess. Much of the complexity of the two handler implementations is present to ensure that a color must be selected for each peg before the "Guess" button is pressed. The attribute _pegEntered keeps track of which pegs have had their colors selected.

The PegHandler class is implemented in lines 78–116. The constructor initializes two attributes to keep track of the MastermindGUI instance and which peg is currently having its color selected. When the peg is clicked on, the handle method renders a rectangle containing a circle for each color option. Each circle has an instance of ChoiceHandler that is triggered when that color is selected. The monitor created in line 115 will be released when the handle method of ChoiceHandler is called. This handler also sets the color choice for that peg and indicates that the peg color has been selected.

```
1   from cs1graphics import *
2   from Mastermind import Mastermind
3   from GraphicsOutput import GraphicsOutput
4   from Dialog import Dialog
5
6   class MastermindGUI(GraphicsOutput):
7     """Class to provide full graphical interface to Mastermind"""
8
9     def queryLengthOfPattern(self):
10      """Ask the user how many pegs in the secret pattern."""
11      dialog = Dialog('How many pegs are in the secret?',
12        'Length of pattern',['4','6','8','10'])
13      return int(dialog.display())
14
15    def queryNumberOfColors(self):
16      """Ask the user how many colors to use for secret pattern."""
17      inputOptions = []
18      for i in range(2,len(self._palette)+1):
19        inputOptions(str(i))
20      dialog = Dialog('How many colors are available?',
21        'Number of color', inputOptions)
22      return int(dialog.display())
23
24    def queryNumberOfTurns(self):
25      """Ask the user maximum number of guesses to be allowed."""
26      dialog = Dialog('How many turns are allowed?',
27        'Number of turns',['5','10','15','20'])
28      return int(dialog.display())
29
30    def queryNewGame(self):
31      """Offer the user a new game. Return True if accepted, False otherwise."""
32      dialog = Dialog('Would you like to play again?',
33        'Again?',['Yes','No'])
34      return dialog.display() == 'Yes'
```

FIGURE 15.17: The GUI for Mastermind (continued on next page).

```
35    def _setupBackground(self):
36       """Draws the backgound to the graphics canvas."""
37       block = Rectangle(4*self._lengthOfPattern*self._pegRadius, 4*self._pegRadius,
38          Point((1 + 2*self._lengthOfPattern)*self._pegRadius, 3*self._pegRadius) )
39       block.setFillColor('brown')
40       block.setDepth(10)
41       self._canvas.add(block)
42
43       self._holes = [ [None] * self._lengthOfPattern ] * self._numberOfGuesses
44       for row in range(self._numberOfGuesses):
45          for col in range(self._lengthOfPattern):
46             self._holes[row][col] = Circle(self._pegRadius/2, self._getCenterPoint(row,col))
47             self._holes[row][col].setFillColor('black')
48             self._holes[row][col].setDepth(10)
49             self._canvas.add(self._holes[row][col])
50       self._canvas.refresh()
51
52    def enterGuess(self):
53       """Have user enter guess and return response."""
54       self._guess = Pattern(self._lengthOfPattern)
55
56       # Turn on handlers for each of the pegs
57       handlers = [ ]
58       self._pegEntered = [False] * self._lengthOfPattern
59       for i in range(self._lengthOfPattern):
60          handlers.append(PegHandler(self, i))
61          self._holes[self._currentGuess][i].addHandler(handlers[i])
62
63       # Create the button and add a handler for it
64       self._button = Button('Guess', 4*self._pegRadius, 3*self._pegRadius)
65       self._button.move((4*self._lengthOfPattern+5)*self._pegRadius,
66          (4*(self._numberOfGuesses-self._currentGuess-1)+9)*self._pegRadius)
67       handler = ButtonHandler(self)
68
69       # Wait for the button to be pressed
70       self._wait = Monitor()
71       self._wait.wait()
72
73       # Disable the handlers
74       for i in range(self._lengthOfPattern):
75          self._holes[self._currentGuess][i].removeHandler(handlers[i])
76
77       return self._guess
```

FIGURE 15.17 (continuation): The GUI for Mastermind (continued on next page).

```
78   class PegHandler(EventHandler):
79       """Dealing with the user setting the color of a peg.
80
81       When the peg is clicked on options are presented to the user to select.
82       """
83
84       def __init__(self, gui, peg, location):
85           """Create a new PegHandler instance.
86
87           gui  reference to the user interface
88           peg  integer indicating which peg is being set
89           """
90           EventHandler.__init__(self)
91           self._gui = gui
92           self._peg = peg
93
94       def handle(event):
95           """Display options when the user mouse clicks on a peg."""
96           if event.getType == 'mouse click':
97               # Create a box of options and display
98               box = Layer()
99               box.move(self._gui._holes[self._peg].getCenter)
100
101              size = 11*self._gui._pegRadius
102              background = Rectangle(size, size, Point(−size/2, −size/2))
103              background.setBackgroundColor('light gray')
104              box.add(background)
105
106              for i in range(3):
107                  for j in range(3):
108                      if 3*i + j <= len(self._gui._pegColors):
109                          peg = Circle(self._gui._pegRadius,
110                              Point((−4+3*j)*self._gui._pegRadius, (−4+3*i)*self._gui._pegRadius))
111                          handler = ChoiceHandler(self, 3*i+j)
112                          peg.addHandler(handler)
113                          box.add(handler)
114
115              self._monitor = Monitor()
116              self._monitor.wait()
```

FIGURE 15.17 (continuation): The GUI for Mastermind (continued on next page).

```
117   class ButtonHandler(EventHandler):
118       """Handler for user submitting a guess."""
119
120       def __init__(self, gui):
121           """Create a new ButtonHandler."""
122
123           EventHandler.__init__(self)
124           self._gui = gui
125
126       def handle(event):
127           """Release the monitor waiting for a guess."""
128           release = True
129           for peg in self._gui._pegEntered:
130               release = release and peg
131           if release:
132               self._gui._wait.release()
133
134   class ChoiceHandler(EventHandler):
135       """Handler class for the selection of a colored peg."""
136       def __init__(self, pegHandler, colorChoice):
137           """Create a new instance."""
138           EventHandler.__init__(self)
139           self._pegHandler = pegHandler
140           self._color = colorChoice
141
142       def handle(event):
143           """Set the choice of color and close the popup."""
144           self._pegHandler._gui._guess.setPegColor(self._pegHandler._peg, self._color)
145           self._pegHandler._gui._pegEntered[self._pegHandler._peg] = True
146           self._pegHandler._monitor.release()
147
148   if __name__ == '__main__':
149       palette = ('Red', 'Blue', 'Green', 'White', 'Yellow', 'Orange',
150                  'Purple', 'Turquoise')
151       interface = MastermindGUI(palette)
152       game = Mastermind(interface, interface)
```

FIGURE 15.17 (continuation): The GUI for Mastermind.

The ButtonHandler class in lines 117–132 responds each time the "Guess" button in pressed. However, the handler only responds if every peg has been entered. This is checked by examining the values held in the _pegEntered list stored in the MastermindGUI instance. When all of these values are **True** the monitor in the MastermindGUI class is released. In line 71, the enterGuess method is waiting on a monitor. Once this monitor is released by the ButtonHandler, all of the handlers for the pegs are removed and the guess is returned.

The code for entering the guess is rather complicated. But by carefully examining the classes and their interactions, it is possible to see how it works. Notice that it relies on several helper classes that need access to each others' states in order to work together. With time and experience you will be able to write similar programs yourself.

15.6   Chapter Review

15.6.1   Key Points

- The flow of an event-driven program responds to user interaction. Each time an event occurs, code is run to respond appropriately.

- A routine to respond to events is called a handler. Every object that needs to respond to an event derives a class from EventHandler to process events for that object.

- An event loop waits for user interaction or other events to occur and call the appropriate handler. This loop will continue to run until the program is terminated.

- When an event occurs, the handle method of the handler class is called with an instance of Event as its only parameter. This instance stores the type of event that has occurred, the location of the mouse when the event was triggered and any other pertinent information.

15.6.2   Glossary

callback function *See* event handler.

event An external stimulus on a program, such as a user's mouse click.

event-driven programming A style in which a program passively waits for external events to occur, responding appropriately to those events as needed.

event handler A piece of code, typically a function or class, used to define the action that should take place in response to a triggered event.

event loop A potentially infinite loop that does nothing other than wait for events. When an event is triggered, an event handler is called to respond appropriately. Once that event handler completes, the event loop is typically continued.

listener *See* event handler.

thread An abstraction representing one of possibly many active flows of control within an executing program.

widget An object that serves a particular purpose in a graphical user interface.

15.6.3   Exercises

Practice 15.1: Write a handler that will display the type of event and the mouse location whenever a mouse event has occurred.

Practice 15.2: Write a program that draws a circle in the center of a graphics window whenever the mouse button is clicked down, and erases it when the button is released.

Exercise 15.3: Write a program to draw circles on a canvas. When the canvas is first clicked a circle should appear. As the user drags the mouse the radius should change so that the mouse is on the boundary of the circle. Once the mouse button is released the circle's geometry should remain fixed.

Exercise 15.4: Our program for creating and modifying shapes, in Figure 15.10, picks an arbitrary color when it receives a keyboard event. Modify this program so that the user can select from a palette of colors based on the key that was typed (e.g., 'r' for red, 'b' for blue).

Exercise 15.5: The Dialog class from Figure 15.12 could be made more robust by having the geometry adjust properly to the number of options and the length of those strings. As originally implemented, the overall height and width of the pop-up window, and the spacing of the buttons is hardcoded. Rewrite that program to do a better job of laying out the geometry based upon the option list.

Exercise 15.6: Modify the Stopwatch of Section 15.4.3, so that it measures time in hundredths of a second, displayed as 0:00.00.

Exercise 15.7: Using techniques similar to the Stopwatch of Section 15.4.3, redesign the Mailbox from Section 9.6 so that the flag automatically toggles when it is clicked upon and so that the door opens and closes when it is clicked upon.

Exercise 15.8: Write a program to animate an analog clock face with hour, minute, and second hands. The program should take a time as input, and the clock should display this time and move the hands the appropriate amount each second.

Exercise 15.9: The Mastermind interface in the case study has separate dialog boxes to enter each game parameter. Modify the implementation so there is a single dialog box to enter all of the game parameters.

Projects

Exercise 15.10: Write a sliding tile game. There are tiles numbered 1 to 15 randomly placed on a four by four grid with one empty space. If a tile adjacent to the empty position is clicked on, then it should move to that spot. When any other tile is clicked on nothing should happen.

Exercise 15.11: Write a checkers game that draws the board and the initial placement of the checker pieces. The user should be able to drag a piece from one square to another if it is a legal move. When the piece is released it should always be placed in the center of a square.

Exercise 15.12: Write an alarm program. When started the program should ask the user what time they want the alarm to go off and the message to display. At the specified time a window should open that displays the message in flashing colors.

Exercise 15.13: Exercise 6.22 involved the use of graphics to animate our earlier Television class, but even that exercise assumed that the standard method calls were used to manipulate a television instance. For this exercise, create a graphical user interface which resembles a remote control, with buttons for triggering behaviors such as channelUp and channelDown.

CHAPTER 16

Network Programming

Computer networks play a critical role in society. They allow for information to be transmitted from one computing device to another, forming the basis for email, web browsing, chat rooms, instant messaging, and many other networked applications.

At its heart, a network connection is another means of input and output. Just as our programs use **print** and **raw_input** to interact with a local user, or use write and read to get information into and out of a file, network connections allow us to send information to another computer, or to receive information sent by that computer.

In this chapter, we introduce several tools to support network programming in Python. We demonstrate working implementations for simple forms of several applications includ– ing a web browser, a web server, a chat room, and even our own networked search engine.

16.1 A Network Primer

To begin, we need to describe how network connections are established and how pro– grams communicate. When you type `http://www.prenhall.com/goldwasser` into your web browser, communication takes place behind the scene to bring you the desired information. This string of characters is known as a *uniform resource loca– tor (URL)* and serves as a general identifier for a networked resource.

The `www.prenhall.com` portion of that URL is termed a *host name* and sym– bolizes a machine somewhere on the network. Host names are chosen to be memorized by humans but have little to do with the true locations of underlying machines. Behind the scene, network connections are established using a number known as an *IP address* (e.g., 165.193.123.253). To translate a host name to its underlying IP address, your com– puter will query a special computer on the Internet known as a *domain name server (DNS)*.

The `http` portion of the URL denotes a particular *network protocol* that will be used for the transmission of information (in this case the *Hypertext Transfer Protocol*). The protocol specifies a convention for the transmission of data. Since networks are used to transmit many different kinds of information, the sender and receiver must have an agreement as to the particular format that will be used. The protocol used for requesting a web page is different from that used to send email or to stream live video. If the two machines are not using the same protocol they cannot effectively communicate, much like two people speaking different languages. Because so many different protocols exist, a machine will often execute different software depending upon which data format is being used. To help quickly segment incoming network traffic according to the protocol, each network connection to a remote machine must be designated at a specific ***port***. A port is really just a number ranging from 0 to 65535, but there are established conventions for using certain port numbers for certain types of activity. For example, queries to a web server are typically sent through port 80, and so a machine might automatically handle network traffic from that port with software designated for `http` activity.

Finally, the `/goldwasser` portion of our sample URL is a path to some particular information on Prentice Hall's web server.

A network socket

To manage the use of a specific network connection, programmers rely upon an abstraction known as a ***socket***. For a connection between two machines, a separate socket is maintained at each end, used to track the incoming and outgoing data for that machine. As a programmer, the socket serves as the interface for sending or receiving data from the opposite machine. In Python, this is modeled using a socket class, which itself is imported from the socket module. We can instantiate such an object as

```
>>> from socket import socket
>>> s = socket()
```

This socket is not yet connected to any remote machine. This class supports a variety of behaviors, although we will only use the most basic ones summarized in Figure 16.1. For example, to open a network connection to a remote host, we must specify both the host address and the network port number. This is done by calling the connect method with a single parameter that happens to be a (host, port) tuple. The host can be specified using either an IP address or a host name. For example, we might use our socket s as follows:

```
>>> s.connect( ('www.prenhall.com', 80) )
```

If the network connection cannot be made successfully, an exception is raised.

Once a connection has been successfully established, the socket can be used to send and receive data, in the form of strings. The send method is used to transmit data to the remote host. This takes a single parameter that is a string to be transmitted. This works in much the same fashion as the write method for writing to a file.

If we expect to receive data from the remote host, we call the recv method, which returns a string of characters. Although somewhat analogous to reading from a file, the precise use differs due to the nature of networks. First, a parameter must be specified when calling recv to designate the maximum number of characters that we are willing to accept at the moment. It is not possible to accept an unbounded amount of data at one time.

Syntax	Semantics
s.connect((host,port))	Connects socket s to the remote host at the specified port, raising an error if the connection fails.
s.send(data)	Sends the given string to the remote host.
s.recv(maxNumChars)	Returns a string of character that have been received from the remote host, up to the specified maximum number. If fewer characters are returned, this means that no further characters are currently available. If an empty string is returned, this signifies that the connection is no longer open. If the connection is open yet no new data has been received, this call waits indefinitely before returning.
s.close( )	Disconnects socket s from the remote host (this instance cannot be reconnected).

FIGURE 16.1: Selected behaviors of Python's socket class, on prototypical instance s.

When a call to recv is made, there are four possible responses. The most natural is when the call returns a string of the indicated length. In this case, there may exist additional data sent through the network, yet not returned by this call due to the specified limit. Such further data is buffered by the socket instance and returned by a subsequent call to recv. A second scenario is when recv returns *less* data than the specified maximum, presumably because no further data has thus been sent by the remote host.

A third scenario occurs when we call recv, yet no additional data is currently available. Rather than return empty handed, this call waits indefinitely for more data to be received through the network. This saves us the trouble of making multiple calls while waiting for an expected transmission to arrive. Yet it can cause trouble when the remote host has no intention of sending data. Consider the following session:

```
>>> from socket import socket
>>> s = socket()
>>> s.connect( ('www.prenhall.com', 80) )
>>> print s.recv(1024)           # there's no reply at all
```

That final call to recv never returns. Although we established an initial connection with Prentice Hall's web server, that server does not bother to send further information unless we send it a specific query. This is precisely why network protocols are so important. Both participants must have a clear understanding of when each is to send data, and the format used for transmitting the information. If the software on the two ends do not cooperate properly, the communication will not succeed.

There is a final scenario, in which a call to recv returns an empty string. This indicates that the connection has been closed (either by the remote host or a network disruption), so there is no reason to continue waiting. We can terminate a network connection from our end by invoking the close method upon the socket. Once we have closed a connection, any subsequent call to send or recv will result in an error.

A WORD OF WARNING

Throughout this chapter, we introduce network programming with source code that demonstrates the basic principles. You should be able to run those programs on your own machine, but there are potential complications. Your ability to open up network connections at various ports will be dependent upon the combination of your operating system, your network settings, your Internet service provider, and any firewalls that are designed to protect your system.

Also, when trying to use our sample clients with remote servers, the coherency of the software will depend upon whether the remote host supports the same protocol versions assumed by our client.

16.2   Writing a Basic Client

There are several models for network communication. The two most common are the *client-server* model and the *peer-to-peer (P2P)* model. In a client–server model the two connected machines have a very *asymmetric* role. A machine acting as a *server* typically sits passively, waiting for a *client* who initiates contact. For example, a web server does not do any work unless someone makes an explicit request to receive content from that website. The protocols used for the client–server model typically involve the client sending a request and the server sending a response to that request. For this reason, the software for controlling a client is usually different from the software for controlling a server.

In a peer-to-peer network, two connected machines have more symmetric capabilities and thus each run the same software. Peer-to-peer software is often implemented by combining the separate capabilities seen in client software and server software.

Whether using a client–server or peer-to-peer model, it is critical that a clear protocol be used for any network connection. In this section, we begin our examination by demonstrating several simple examples of *client* software for existing protocols, specifically accessing a time server and accessing a web server. In Section 16.3 we will give several examples of software written to support a server. In later sections, we will combine these techniques to produce more robust applications.

16.2.1   Fetching the Time and Date

For our first client program, we use the Internet to figure out what time it is. The National Institute of Science and Technology (NIST) runs servers that, when queried, report the current time. These servers are connected to atomic clocks so their time is precise (although the time when it is received may not be precise, due to network delay).

Our reason for using this as the first example is that the time servers support a very simple protocol on port 13 known as *daytime*. Whenever a client opens a connection to one of these time servers, the server immediately returns a string that contains the time and date information. The client need not even send an explicit request; the mere act of opening a connection implies the client's desire to know the time.

Here is an example of the actual format returned by the daytime protocol.

```
'\n54169 07-03-10 02:43:18 52 0 0 594.5 UTC(NIST) *\n'
```

The full specifications of this protocol are documented by NIST, but the key information that we need is present. The second field of the string is the date in YY–MM–DD format and the third is the time in HH:MM:SS format. The timezone for this date and time is universal time (UTC), which is the timezone of Greenwich, England.

To warm up, let's try to find out what time it is by opening a connection to one of NIST's servers manually in the interpreter.

```
>>> from socket import socket
>>> connection = socket()
>>> connection.connect( ('time.nist.gov', 13) )
>>> print connection.recv(1024)

54169 07-03-10 02:43:18 52 0 0 594.5 UTC(NIST) *

>>>
```

First we import the socket class and then instantiate an instance of that class. In the third step, we establish a connection to one of NIST's servers. In accordance with the protocol, the server immediately sends the formatted string once the connection is made. We retrieve that string by calling recv. The value of 1024 is the maximum number of bytes of data we are prepared to receive (in the case of the daytime protocol, fewer characters are sent).

This same idea can be incorporated into a self-standing client for retrieving the current time, as shown in Figure 16.2. Notice that we use split to break apart the server's response upon the white space, and then retrieve the relevant portions of that string. Of course, if we preferred to display the data with a different format or to change the time to the local timezone, we could use tools from the time and datetime modules.

```
 1   from socket import socket
 2
 3   connection = socket( )
 4   server = 'time.nist.gov'
 5   connection.connect( (server, 13) )
 6
 7   fields = connection.recv(1024).split( )
 8   date = fields[1]
 9   time = fields[2]
10
11   print 'Date (YY-MM-DD) is %s, time is %s (UTC)' % (date,time)
```

FIGURE 16.2: Software for a client that retrieves the current time.

16.2.2 Downloading a Web Page

In our second example, we develop a client that downloads and saves a web page. This process is similar to the time client, but the protocol for retrieving a web page is more involved. After the connection is made, the client must explicitly send a request to the server for the desired web page. We will base our code on version 1.0 of the HTTP protocol. This is not the most current version of the HTTP protocol, but it is a simple one and still supported for backward compatibility by many (but not all) web servers.

To request a page, the client sends a `GET` message to the server. For example, the request `'GET /index.html HTTP/1.0'` asks a server to send the `index.html` page using version 1.0 of the HTTP protocol. If the indicated file is available, the server sends the contents of that file back to the client over the connection. If the file is unavailable, the server sends an appropriate error page. According to the HTTP protocol, the precise data sent back by the server contains not only the contents of the web page, but additional header information, such as the file type, last modification time, and length of the file. The contents of a header differ somewhat from server to server, but a typical response is shown in Figure 16.3. The header begins with a response that indicates the protocol being used and a success code for the indicated page. The header may include various other information and eventually is guaranteed to be followed by a blank line.

What makes fetching a web page more complicated than fetching the time is that the length of a response varies. For our purpose, the most relevant piece of information within the header is the content length (94 in this case). Remember that when we call the `recv` method, we are required to provide a limit on the maximum amount of data that is to be returned. Knowing the overall length, we might be tempted to try to receive the remainder

```
HTTP/1.0 200 OK
Date: Thu, 21 Dec 2006 00:38:32 GMT
Server: Apache
Content-Length: 94
Content-Type: text/html

<HTML>
<TITLE>
My Web page
</TITLE>

<BODY>

<H1>Welcome to my web page</H1>

</BODY>

</HTML>
```

FIGURE 16.3: A typical raw response from a web server.

at once, but we have no control over how quickly that data is received through the network. Instead, we read a little bit of the response at a time, keeping track of how many characters of content we have read. We continue doing this until receiving the full content length.

Figure 16.4 provides a complete program to download a single web page and save the contents (but not the header) to a file. After prompting the user for the URL of the web page at line 6, we carefully break that apart at lines 7 and 8 to properly identify the host name and the page that is to be retrieved. The name of the server appears between the second and third slashes and everything following that is considered the name of the page.

```
1   from socket import socket
2
3   print 'Enter the web page you want to download.'
4   print 'Use the format http://domain.name/page/to/download'
5
6   url = raw_input( )
7   server = url.split('/')[2]                    # e.g., domain.name
8   page = '/' + '/'.join(url.split('/')[3:])     # e.g., /page/to/download
9   connection = socket( )
10  connection.connect( (server, 80) )
11  connection.send('GET %s HTTP/1.0\r\n\r\n' % page)
12
13  raw = connection.recv(1024)                   # read first block (header + some content)
14  sep = raw.index('\r\n\r\n')
15  header = raw[ :sep]
16  content = raw[sep+4: ]
17
18  length = 0                                    # just in case header doesn't say
19  for line in header.split('\n'):
20      if line[:15] == 'Content-Length: ':
21          length = int(line[15:])
22
23  outputFile = file('download.html', 'w')
24  outputFile.write(content)                     # write out content we have seen thus far
25
26  contentRead = len(content)
27  while contentRead < length:                   # still more...
28      content = connection.recv(1024)
29      contentRead += len(content)
30      outputFile.write(content)
31
32  outputFile.close( )
33  connection.close( )
```

FIGURE 16.4: A program to download and save a web page.

Once the connection is open, we make a request for the web page by sending the message at line 11. Then we wait at line 13 to receive the first chunk of data from the network
socket. We specify a large enough limit to ensure that a typical header is included. Each
line of the header is terminated with '\r\n' and the entire header will not have any blank
lines but will be followed by one. Therefore, we can recognize the string '\r\n\r\n'
as a separator between the header and the beginning of the true content.

In lines 18–21, we sift through each line of the header looking for one that begins
'Content-Length:'. Assuming that we find it, we record the value of that length for
reference. The rest of the original block received is the beginning of the actual web page.
We open an output file and write that remaining content (but not the header) to the file. Of
course, we may not be done, so we keep track of how many characters of the web page we
have already read. If the server has promised more, we continue retrieving data from the
socket during the loop of lines 26–30, until we reach the proper length. The precision is
necessary. If we stop early, then some of the web page would be missing, yet if we call
recv one time too many, we might end up waiting forever (as the web server is no longer
sending us information).

An easier way

Our program for downloading a web page is meant to be instructive, showing the low-level
steps that take place when retrieving a web page from a server using the HTTP protocol.
Of course this high-level task is so common in practice, Python already includes a similar implementation within its libraries. Specifically, there is a urllib module that contains
several tools for web processing. In particular there is a function urlopen, which takes a
string parameter specifying a URL, and returns a file-like object from which we can read
the downloaded contents. All the low-level steps for the download are encapsulated within
this function (using a more modern version of HTTP than 1.0).

Figure 16.5 provides a more succinct client for downloading a web page that makes
proper use of this module. Line 7 does the primary work, opening the specified URL and
then reading the downloaded contents.

```
1   from urllib import urlopen
2
3   print 'Enter the web page you want to download.'
4   print 'Use the format http://domain.name/page/to/download'
5   url = raw_input( )
6
7   content = urlopen(url).read( )
8
9   outputFile = file('download.html','w')
10  outputFile.write(content)
11  outputFile.close( )
```

FIGURE 16.5: Downloading a web page making use of the urllib module.

16.3   Basic Network Servers

Writing a server is quite different from writing a client. The flow of control for a client was rather straightforward. A client typically establishes a connection, makes a request, and processes the response. When a server begins running there may be some initialization, but soon there is nothing to do except wait until one or more clients connect to the server and make requests.

Implementing a server at a low level consists of listening on a particular port for incoming connections, creating a socket to manage each such connection, and then following the chosen network protocol for communication with the client. Because these low–level steps are common to all servers, Python provides a SocketServer module with some convenient tools that ease the burden of writing a server.

The TCPServer class handles all the details of listening on a specified port for incoming connections and creating a dedicated socket for each such connection (the term TCP is an acronym for the ***Transmission Control Protocol***, which is used for establishing connections on the Internet). What needs to be customized are the precise interactions that should take place once a client has connected to the server. This response depends upon the type of server we are creating and the protocol that is being followed. The technique used to customize a TCPServer is to provide a second class that will be used to handle each connection. This style is called event–driven programming (and was discussed more fully in Chapter 15).

In this context, our task is to define a special–purpose class that inherits from the BaseRequestHandler class (also imported from Python's SocketServer module). Our specially defined class must minimally support a handle method that will be called each time a new connection is established by a client. By the time the body of that method is executed, the TCPServer will have already initialized a socket, identified as **self**.request, that can be used for communicating with the client. It is important to keep in mind that this is the server's socket. So the send method is used to send data *from the server to the client*. The recv method is used to retrieve data sent from the client to our server.

In the remainder of this section, we give two explicit examples of complete software for implementing a server. Our first example, known as an echo server, provides a very simple demonstration of the techniques used. Our second example is a functional web server that can be used to allow others access to content stored on the server's machine.

The commonality of these two examples is as follows. After defining a custom handler class, we must initialize our TCPServer and activate it. To construct an instance of that class, we use a general syntax such as TCPServer((host, port), HandlerClass). With this syntax, host must be either the host name or IP address for the machine that will function as the server. The port can be whatever number we choose, but there must be an agreement so that the client software uses the same port when connecting.[1] The HandlerClass is the *name* of the customized handler class (as opposed to an instance of that class).

Instantiating a TCPServer is the first step, but the server is not automatically activated. We do so by calling the method serve_forever( ), essentially telling the server to continue running so long as the Python program is executing (we can terminate the server by intentionally interrupting the Python interpreter).

---

1.   As we warned earlier, your local network configuration may disallow use of certain ports.

```
1   from SocketServer import TCPServer, BaseRequestHandler
2
3   class EchoHandler(BaseRequestHandler):
4     def handle(self):
5       message = self.request.recv(1024)
6       self.request.send(message)
7
8   # may need to customize localhost and port for your machine
9   echoServer = TCPServer( ('localhost', 9000), EchoHandler)
10  echoServer.serve_forever( )
```

FIGURE 16.6: The echo server.

16.3.1 Echo Server

As a first example, we implement what is known as an echo server, as shown in Figure 16.6. This has one of the simplest protocols. As soon as the client sends us a message, we simply send back the precise same string and let the connection close.

Line 1 imports the relevant tools from the SocketServer module. Lines 3–6 provides the customized handler class, which we chose to name EchoHandler to indicate its purpose. Notice that it inherits from the imported base class and then overrides the handle method to provide our desired protocol. Each time a connection is established to our server, this method gets called with **self**.request referencing the controlling socket. For our echo server, we simply get the message received from the client and send that same string right back. As soon as the handle method ends, the server automatically closes the connection, and so this echo server can only be used to echo a single message.

After defining the appropriate handler class, line 9 creates a server instance. Note that the first parameter to the constructor is a tuple ('localhost', 9000). You may very well have to customize those values to be able to run the server on your own machine. Also note that the second parameter to the constructor is the class EchoHandler itself as opposed to an instance of that class, which would be EchoHandler( ).

Line 10 is necessary to activate the server. If all goes well, you can execute the script and have a running server. To test it, start up a second Python interpreter session on the same machine or even some other machine, and try the following (again, using your chosen host name and port):

```
>>> from socket import socket
>>> echo = socket()
>>> echo.connect( ('localhost', 9000) )
>>> echo.send('This is a test.')
15
>>> print echo.recv(1024)
This is a test.
```

The return value displayed after the **send** command is the number of characters that were successfully sent. This was provided by the socket (not the echo server). The final line shows the response sent by the echo server. If you were to try to echo a second message on this existing socket, you will find that the connection has been closed. However, you could create a new socket and echo as long as the echo server software is executing.

You may also be able to use existing network tools to connect to your echo server. If `telnet` is installed on your machine, you might use it to connect to your server as follows:

```
command prompt> telnet localhost 9000
Trying 127.0.0.1...
Connected to localhost.
Escape character is '^]'.
Is anybody listening?
Is anybody listening?
Connection closed by foreign host.
```

16.3.2 Basic Web Server

Writing an echo server was easy, but what if we wanted to do something useful, like write a web server? It turns out that a (basic) web server is almost as easy. Complete code for a web server is given in Figure 16.7. We know that the client sends us a request of a basic form such as `'GET /index.html'`. So assuming that the incoming request matches this form, we start to process the request.

```
 1  from SocketServer import TCPServer, BaseRequestHandler
 2
 3  class WebHandler(BaseRequestHandler):
 4    def handle(self):
 5      command = self.request.recv(1024)
 6      if command[:3] == 'GET':
 7        pagename = command.split( )[1][1:]        # remove leading '/' for filename
 8        try:
 9          requestedFile = file(pagename, 'r')
10          content = requestedFile.read( )
11          requestedFile.close( )
12          header = 'HTTP/1.0 200 OK\r\n'
13          header += 'Content-Length: %d\r\n\r\n' % len(content)
14          self.request.send(header)
15          self.request.send(content)
16        except IOError:                           # could not open the file
17          self.request.send('HTTP/1.0 404 Not Found\r\n\r\n')
18
19  webServer = TCPServer( ('localhost', 8080), WebHandler)
20  webServer.serve_forever( )
```

FIGURE 16.7: The basic web server.

For this web server, our intent is to only give access to files or directories located in the same place that we run our script. So line 7 is used to identify the presumed name of the underlying file, but without the leading '/'. In this way, when we attempt to open the file at line 9 it will be relative to the current directory. If we are unable to open the file, we report this error at line 17 using a standard HTTP protocol. Otherwise we are ready to prepare our response. We get the content by reading our local file, and produce a (simple) header that matches the expectations of our web client in Section 16.2.2. This includes an acknowledgment of success, the designated content length, and a blank line. After that we send the content itself.

That is all there is to it. Lines 19 and 20 use this new class to start up a web server, in this case on port 8080 (rather than using the standard, port 80). To see this in action, create a few files in your directory with simple content, such as `index.html`, and then execute the web server software.

You should be able to retrieve the sample files using a web client, such as either of the ones we gave in Section 16.2.2. Note that the standard version from urllib presumed that a web server would be running on port 80. You can specify a nonstandard port as part of a URL using a form such as `http://localhost:8080/index.html` (again substituting your own host name in place of `localhost`). Of course, if you want to really be impressed, use your favorite web browser as a client! Type the URL into your browser and if all goes well, it will display the contents of that file.

 A WORD OF WARNING

Running our web server implementation on your own computer for any extended length of time is a huge security risk. This is a simple example that does not provide much error checking. If someone happened to find the proper host name and port for your server, they may have the ability to view essentially any file on your computer. We will address a few improvements in Exercises at the end of the chapter, but even then, our server remains insecure.

16.4   Case Study: Network Chat Room

Our next goal is to build software that supports a network chat room. We will use a client–server model, providing full code for both pieces. This project will require more effort than the previous examples for several reasons. First, our previous examples were based on existing protocols. We do not have such a standard for chat rooms, so we develop our own protocol and then write a server and client based on it.

The chat room is also quite different from our previous examples because the connection between a client and server has more permanence. In the case of the echo server the flow of control for each individual connection followed a pattern of: client connects, client sends request, server sends response, connection is closed. Although the server keeps running, each such interaction is handled sequentially.

In the case of a chat room application, a client will connect to the server and stay connected for quite a while. This is called a ***persistent connection***. The server cannot be solely devoted to handling that connection until it is closed, or else it would become unresponsive to other connection attempts (making this a very lonely chat room). The client also needs to do two things at once, monitoring the keyboard in case the user enters any commands, but also monitoring the socket to listen for transmissions from the server. So our solution will be to use a concept known as ***multithreading***, that allows several different pieces of software to execute at the same time. We will explain more about this as we go.

16.4.1   Communication Protocol

To begin, we consider the design of our own network protocol. This design will not be seen by the user of our software, but becomes the basis for all network communication between the server and the clients. We have to be particularly careful in implementing a chat room to differentiate between messages that users send to each other and messages that the client and server software send to each other.

There are many possible actions that occur for an interesting chat room. Users may come and go while others remain. A particular user may type a message that is supposed to be shown to everyone currently in the room. Also, we may wish to support a way for one user to send a private message to another user. Notice that all of these events are initiated by a user interacting with the *client* software. Behind the scene, the local client will have to inform the server of the news, and then the server may have to relay relevant information to one or more other clients. So our protocol will have one set of transmissions that are sent from a client to the server and another set of transmissions that are sent from the server back to a client.

Figure 16.8 shows the format we have chosen for the protocol used from a client to the server. These options are needed to announce activity that happen at the client side for a particular user. We only allow four such events: the user may join the room, the user may quit the room, the user may send a message to the entire room, or the user may send a message to a specified individual. Each of the network transmissions begins with an uppercase keyword that identifies the type of activity and is followed by the subsequent data, if any. For example, the transmission `'ADD coolcat\n'` would be used to inform the server of a person entering the chat room with `'coolcat'` as a screen name. When forwarding a private message, the protocol requires two subsequent arguments: the screen name of the recipient and the message text. Notice that the screen name of the *sender* is not retransmitted here. The server will know who is sending the message based on the identity designated by this same client with the earlier `ADD` command.

The remainder of the network protocol, shown in Figure 16.9, is used by the server to pass information to an individual client.   The server will inform a client whenever another individual joins or leaves the room, and whenever messages have been entered that are supposed to be seen by this client's particular user. We differentiate between messages that are viewable because they were broadcast to the whole room and messages that are viewable because they were privately sent to this user (you want to recognize when someone is telling you a secret). Finally, the server will explicitly acknowledge when it receives word that a particular user is quitting the chat room.

Message Type	Format
Join the room using given identity	`'ADD %s\n'` % screenName
Broadcast the message to everyone	`'MESSAGE %s\n'` % content
Send a private message	`'PRIVATE %s\n%s\n'` % (recipient,content)
Quit the chat room	`'QUIT\n'`

FIGURE 16.8: The protocol for messages from the client to the server.

Message Type	Format
New user has joined	`'NEW %s\n'` % screenName
Message was broadcast to everyone	`'MESSAGE %s\n%s\n'` % (sender, content)
Private message was sent to user	`'PRIVATE %s\n%s\n'` % (sender, content)
Someone has left the room	`'LEFT %s\n'` % screenName
Acknowledges request to quit	`'GOODBYE\n'`

FIGURE 16.9: The protocol for messages from the server to the client.

16.4.2 The Server

The complete source for the server is shown in Figure 16.10. Most of the work involves the definition of a ChatHandler class that specializes BaseRequestHandler. This general technique is similar to the one used in our echo server and basic web server. The primary difference is that for the chat and web server, each connection represented a single query, which is processed and dismissed. In the case of a chat server, the handle routine is called whenever someone connects to the server and the routine continues for the full duration of that user's participation. So the handle routine consists primarily of one big while loop at lines 13–34 that begins as soon as a client connects. It remains active until finally receiving the QUIT command from the client (line 30) or until the connection fails, as signaled when recv returns an empty transmission (thus reaching the **else** at line 33).

To better explain the code, we should discuss the _socketLookup dictionary and _broadcast function, which are defined at lines 3–7 outside of the formal class definition. There will be a separate ChatHandler instance to manage each user's connection to our server. At the same time, activity from one client may need to be announced to other clients and, in the case of a private message, based upon the user's screen name. So the _socketLookup dictionary is maintained to map a screen name to the actual socket that is being used to manage the connection to that user's client. We see a new entry added to that dictionary at line 21 when a user initially joins the room, and the user's socket removed at line 37 after the connection is closed. The _broadcast function is a utility for transmitting network activity to each current client.

Looking again at the while loop of lines 13–34, we see that the server begins each pass at line 14 by listening for further communication from this client. By our protocol, the first word characterizes the type of activity and the rest of the line contains supplemental

```
1   from SocketServer import ThreadingTCPServer, BaseRequestHandler
2
3   _socketLookup = dict( )                              # intentionally shared as global
4
5   def _broadcast(announcement):
6     for connection in _socketLookup.values( ):        # uses the global dictionary
7       connection.send(announcement)
8
9   class ChatHandler(BaseRequestHandler):
10    def handle(self):
11      username = 'Unknown'
12      active = True
13      while active:
14        transmission = self.request.recv(1024)        # wait for something to happen
15        if transmission:
16          command = transmission.split( )[0]
17          data = transmission[1+len(command): ]       # the rest
18
19          if command == 'ADD':
20            username = data.strip( )
21            _socketLookup[username] = self.request
22            _broadcast('NEW %s\n' % username)
23          elif command == 'MESSAGE':
24            _broadcast('MESSAGE %s\n%s\n' % (username,data) )
25          elif command == 'PRIVATE':
26            rcpt = data.split('\n')[0]
27            if rcpt in _socketLookup:
28              content = data.split('\n')[1]
29              _socketLookup[rcpt].send('PRIVATE %s\n%s\n'%(username,content) )
30          elif command == 'QUIT':
31            active = False
32            self.request.send('GOODBYE\n')             # acknowledge
33          else:
34            active = False                             # socket failed
35
36      self.request.close( )
37      _socketLookup.pop(username)
38      _broadcast('LEFT %s\n' % username)               # inform others
39
40  myServer = ThreadingTCPServer( ('localhost', 9000), ChatHandler)
41  myServer.serve_forever( )
```

FIGURE 16.10: The complete implementation of our chat server.

arguments. Each case implements the appropriate reaction from the server. For example, at line 19 when a user formally joins the room, we add the socket to the dictionary and then broadcast news of the arrival to the room. When a public message reaches the server at line 23, that message is immediately broadcast to the entire room. In contrast, when a private message is received by the server at line 25, that message will only be sent to the socket for the indicated user (assuming that the recipient is indeed found in the room). When the loop finally completes, several things happen. The socket is formally closed at line 36, and then removed from the lookup dictionary at line 37. Finally, all other users are informed of the departure.

An important distinction between this implementation and our earlier servers is that we use the ThreadingTCPServer class, not the TCPServer class used in Section 16.3. The issue is that connections to our chat room are persistent. The handle method will be running for a long time as one particular user remains in the chat room. We cannot allow our server to be fully devoted to that one person, at the expense of ignoring all other network activity. The "threaded" version of the TCP server uses a technique known as multithreading (described in the next section). This distinction is relatively minor in terms of our source code, but is critical for a properly functioning chat room server.

16.4.3 The Client

The client turns out to be more complicated than the server. It too needs to be multi–threaded, but in a way that requires a deeper understanding of the principle. The issue is that we want the user to interact with software that does two things simultaneously. It should allow the user to type commands yet should also display messages received from the other users. The problem is that if we call **raw_input** to wait for the user to type some–thing, this will block our flow of control. If we are not careful, this means that nothing new will be displayed to the user's screen while waiting. At the same time, we need to listen for activity on the network socket to be able to learn of new activity in the room, but this requires a call to the recv method on that socket. Again, that call will block our flow of control if there is silence in the room, meaning that we would be unable to process commands typed by the user while our program listens to the socket. Before getting to our actual client implementation, we need a bit of background about multithreading in Python.

Multithreading

Modern software appears to simultaneously execute multiple flows of control. For exam–ple, a modern web browser can download and display data, managing multiple windows at once. This is accomplished with a technique known as multithreading in which one or more *threads* take turns using the processor, perhaps a fraction of a second at a time.

For the chat client to do two things "at once" we will have each task run in a separate thread. To create a new thread within a Python program, we use inheritance to specialize the Thread class imported from the threading module. Our child class overrides the run method to provide the desired sequence of commands. To use such a thread, we construct an instance of our new class and then call the start( ) method, which indirectly initiates the call to run. The key is that the start function returns immediately, rather than waiting until the underlying run method completes. This allows us to continue executing the primary flow of control in parallel.

Figure 16.11 gives a simple example of a program that starts a second thread. In lines 4–7 the class for the thread is defined. When run, it announces itself, waits 5 sec−onds, and then announces its completion. We create the second thread based on this new class at line 10, and then invoke the start method at line 11. The start( ) functions returns immediately, and so our primary program continues immediately to line 12 and announces its completion. Yet at the same time, the second thread has started. Figure 16.12 provides a schematic for the program flow. As an end user, we might see the following output:

```
Second thread begins.
The program is done.
Second thread is done.
```

In this case, the second thread is still executing while the primary thread completes. On some systems, the first two of these three output statements might be reversed as the threads compete with each other for time on the processor.

```python
1  from threading import Thread
2  from time import sleep
3
4  class MyThread(Thread):
5    def run(self):
6      print 'Second thread begins.'
7      sleep(5)
8      print 'Second thread is done.'
9
10 secondThread = MyThread( )
11 secondThread.start( )
12 print 'The program is done.'
```

FIGURE 16.11: A multithreaded program.

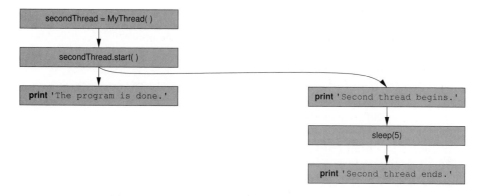

FIGURE 16.12: The flow of a multithreaded program.

The client source

We use multithreading to implement the chat room client, as shown in Figure 16.13. Two threads share a single network socket identified as server. The IncomingThread class defined at lines 4–26 is devoted to monitoring *incoming* messages from that socket. It executes a while loop that repeatedly waits for more information from the server (line 8). When receiving network traffic, it uses knowledge of our protocol to interpret the meaning.

Each line of an incoming transmission is broken into two components, the keyword designating the command and any subsequent data from that line. Based upon our proto-col, MESSAGE and PRIVATE are followed by an additional line with the content of the message to be delivered. If we receive the GOODBYE designator from the server (confirm-ing our intent to QUIT), the overall while loop is exited. All output displayed to the user is prefaced with the ==> symbol, to help demarcate the session.

The primary thread executes lines 27–46. It begins by establishing the shared socket connection (line 28) and registering the user in the chat room using the ADD protocol

```
1  from socket import socket
2  from threading import Thread
3
4  class IncomingThread(Thread):
5    def run(self):
6      stillChatting = True
7      while stillChatting:                          # wait for more incoming data
8        transmission = server.recv(1024)            # 'server' will be defined globally at line 27
9        lines = transmission.split('\n')[:-1]
10       i = 0
11       while i < len(lines):
12         command = lines[i].split( )[0]             # first keyword
13         param = lines[i][len(command)+1: ]         # remaining information
14         if command == 'GOODBYE':
15           stillChatting = False
16         elif command == 'NEW':
17           print '==>', param, 'has joined the chat room'
18         elif command == 'LEFT':
19           print '==>', param, 'has left the chat room'
20         elif command == 'MESSAGE':
21           i += 1                                   # need next line for content
22           print '==>', param + ': ' + lines[i]
23         elif command == 'PRIVATE':
24           i += 1                                   # need next line for content
25           print '==>', param + ' [private]: ' + lines[i]
26         i += 1
```

FIGURE 16.13: The chat client (continued on next page).

```
27   server = socket( )                                # shared by both threads
28   server.connect( ('localhost', 9000) )             # could be a remote host
29   username = raw_input('What is your name: ').strip( )
30   server.send('ADD %s\n' % username )
31   incoming = IncomingThread( )
32   incoming.start( )
33
34   active = True                                     # main thread for user input
35   while active:
36     message = raw_input( )                          # wait for more user input
37     if message.strip( ):
38       if message.rstrip( ).lower( ) == 'quit':
39         server.send('QUIT\n')
40         active = False
41       elif message.split( )[0].lower( ) == 'private':
42         colon = message.index(':')
43         friend = message[7:colon].strip( )
44         server.send('PRIVATE %s\n%s\n' % (friend,message[1+colon:]) )
45       else:
46         server.send('MESSAGE ' + message)
```

FIGURE 16.13 (continuation): The chat client.

(line 30). Then the primary thread spawns the secondary thread for monitoring incoming network activity (lines 31 and 32). The remaining responsibility of the primary thread is to monitor input entered by the local user via the keyboard. This proceeds with the while loop of line 35. Each pass of the loop begins with a call to **raw_input**( ) at line 36. The primary thread waits until something is entered by the user (yet the secondary thread continues to run independently). Once the user enters something (other than whitespace), our code determines what to do based upon what the user types, and then forwards an appropriate message to the server using our network protocol.

Note that the user is not expected to follow the *network protocol*; we have a simpler interface for the user. The single word quit is used to leave the room and close the software. A command of the form,

```
private hotdog:  Are you hungry?
```

is used to send a private message to one other user (in this case hotdog). Anything else that the user types is presumed to be a public message, to be broadcast to the entire room.

A sample session as viewed by the user of this software appears in Figure 16.14. Lines 5, 10, 12, 14, and 16 are commands typed by this user. The rest is a trace of the relevant chat room activity. Notice that the message issued at line 5 is reflected back at line 6 as it is broadcast to the entire room. The commands issued at lines 12 and 14 are private messages to hotdog and thus not broadcast to the room. The incoming message at line 13 was received privately from user hotdog.

```
 1  What is your name: coolcat
 2  ==> coolcat has joined the chat room
 3  ==> coldturkey has joined the chat room
 4  ==> coldturkey: Hi everyone!
 5  Hi turkey
 6  ==> coolcat: Hi turkey
 7  ==> hotdog has joined the chat room
 8  ==> hotdog: How's everyone doing?
 9  ==> coldturkey: pretty good
10  I'm okay
11  ==> coolcat: I'm okay
12  private hotdog: Are you hungry?
13  ==> hotdog [private]:  Sure. Wanna get some food?
14  private hotdog: Yep
15  ==> hotdog has left the chat room
16  quit
```

FIGURE 16.14: The perspective of `coolcat` using our chat client.

16.5   Peer-to-Peer: Instant Messenger

Our implementation of the chat room software is a classic example of a client–server approach. There were asymmetric roles, with a single client in charge only of the communication involving one user and the server in charge of coordinating the transfer of information between those clients. Not only did we use different software for the two roles, but also two different protocols.

In this section, we demonstrate a peer–to–peer network approach, developing software that allows two people to communicate without a centralized server. Both people will execute the identical software for this application and, once a connection is established, we use a completely symmetric network protocol. This protocol is much simpler than the one we designed for the chat room. There are only three commands. When a socket connection is first established, both parties are responsible for sending a CONNECT message to inform the peer of the user's identity. All of the users' messages will be transmitted directly as a string. Finally, if either party is planning on terminating the connection, a formal QUIT command is passed to the peer.

The complete source code for the program is shown in Figure 16.15. Although the same software is used by both ends of the connection, we frame our discussion as seen from one side of the connection. We use the global identifier peer to represent the open network socket; we delay, for the moment, our discussion of the process used for establishing this connection. Once open, we use two different threads to manage the interaction, as was the case with our chat client. The primary thread gets input from the user and transmits it to the peer, while the secondary thread handles all incoming transmissions from the peer.

We begin our examination of the code with the manageConversation function in lines 5–24. This is called from within the primary thread just after the connection is established. We immediately start the secondary thread at line 6 (we will describe this thread next). The rest of this function consists of repeatedly waiting for user input from **raw_input**, so long as the connection remains active. For the user of the software, the single word `quit` is used to exit the conversation; anything else is presumed to be a message to be sent to the peer. In the case when `quit` is indicated, the peer is informed and then the loop is exited. Otherwise, the entered line is transmitted to the peer, demarcated with a trailing newline. The **try-except** construct is used to detect an error during either of the calls to peer.send, indicating a failed socket (either because the peer closed the socket or the network connection was lost).

Next, we examine the inner working of the secondary thread, defined in lines 25–46. This thread repeatedly polls the socket for incoming data. Each time a transmission is received, it is broken apart into lines; although only a single line is sent at one time by our protocol, it may be that several lines are delivered at once due to network delays. There are three possible scenarios. If a QUIT command is received, we announce that the peer is leaving and prepare to exit the loop. The CONNECT message is used as part of our process when establishing the connection. We will discuss that process more in a moment; the relevant part here is that it provides us an identifying name for the peer. In any other scenario, the transmission is presumed to be a string exactly as typed by the opposite user.

```
1   from socket import socket, gethostname
2   from threading import Thread
3   from SocketServer import TCPServer, BaseRequestHandler
4
5   def manageConversation( ):
6     IncomingThread( ).start( )        # start secondary thread for monitoring incoming traffic
7
8     print
9     print 'Enter a message and hit return to send it.'
10    print 'Type quit to stop the program.'
11    print
12    active = True                      # primary thread handles user's direct input
13    while active:
14      message = raw_input( )                         # wait for more user input
15      try:
16        if message.rstrip( ).lower( ) == 'quit':
17          peer.send('QUIT\n')
18          active = False
19        else:
20          peer.send(message+'\n')
21      except:
22        print 'connection to peer was lost'
23        active = False
24    peer.close( )
```

FIGURE 16.15: The peer-to-peer instant messenger (continued on next page).

```
25   class IncomingThread(Thread):
26     def run(self):
27       connected = True
28       while connected:
29         transmission = peer.recv(1024)
30         if transmission:                              # successful transmission
31           lines = transmission.rstrip('\n').split('\n')
32           i = 0
33           while i < len(lines):
34             if lines[i] == 'QUIT':                    # peer is leaving
35               print name, 'has quit'
36               connected = False
37             elif lines[i].startswith('CONNECT '):
38               name = lines[i][8:]
39               print name, 'is connected'
40             else:
41               print name+': ', lines[i]               # an actual message
42             i += 1
43         else:
44           print 'connection to peer was lost'
45           connected = False                           # socket failed
46       peer.close()
47
48   class RegistrationHandler(BaseRequestHandler):
49     def handle(self):
50       global peer
51       peer = self.request                             # socket to peer
52       peer.send('CONNECT %s\n' % username)            # announce our identity
53       manageConversation()
54
55   username = raw_input('What is your name: ').strip()
56   print 'Enter the Internet address (e.g., computer.domain.com)'
57   print 'of the computer to which you want to connect,'
58   print 'or hit return to wait for an incoming connection.'
59   address = raw_input()
60   if address:
61     peer = socket()
62     peer.connect((address, 9000))
63     peer.send('CONNECT %s\n' % username)              # announce our presence
64     manageConversation()
65   else:     # Start server to await incoming connection
66     localHost = gethostname()  # or you may hardwire your computer's hostname
67     incomingServer = TCPServer( (localHost, 9000), RegistrationHandler)
68     print 'Waiting for connection at', localHost
69     incomingServer.handle_request()
```

FIGURE 16.15 (continuation): The peer-to-peer instant messenger.

The remainder of the code involves the initialization of the connection. This is the one aspect in which the peer-to-peer protocol is not perfectly symmetric. To establish the connection from a technical perspective, one of the two ends must set itself up as a network server and await a connection from the other. The software is written so that the primary thread begins at line 55, asking for the name of the user and then asking the user to either provide an address (presumably of a previously started peer), or else to hit return to be the host and await a connection.

When the user provides an address of a peer, the code takes the traditional role of a client. Lines 61–64 create the peer socket and connect it to the given address. Once a connection is established, we send a formal CONNECT message to our peer as per our protocol, and then we call the manageConversation routine as discussed earlier.

Alternatively if no known address is given, we establish ourself as a server. To this end, we create a TCPServer at line 67 using a simple RegistrationHandler class as defined at lines 48–53. The call to handle_request at line 69 starts up the server in a similar fashion to calls to serve_forever that we saw in earlier examples this chapter, but only for the duration of a single inbound session. When that connection is presumably initiated by a peer, the body of the handle routine at line 49 is triggered.

As a technical note, we comment on the command at line 50. Recall that in several places in our code we have assumed that identifier peer has been established as a socket to the peer. For the case of a server, the connecting socket is automatically identified as **self**.request from within the context of the handler. However we want to keep a reference to that socket for the global context. If we were to make an assignment, peer = **self**.request within a typical function body, this establishes peer as a *local* variable to that body, and thus would be useless for the larger context. The command **global** peer at line 50 informs Python that we wish to have any subsequent assignments to the identifier peer made within the global scope rather than the local scope.

As a final step, once a connection has been established from the perspective of a server, line 52 sends the official CONNECT protocol to the peer and then we revert to a call to manageConversation to manage the remaining interactions.

16.6 Server-Side Scripting and CGI

Another way that Python is commonly used on the Internet is to perform what is known as *server-side scripting*. A classic web server, such as the one we developed in Section 16.3.2, is used to transmit the contents of *pre-existing files* that serve as web pages. We typically call such files *static* content. Another technique that is commonly employed by websites is to generate content *dynamically* in response to a particular request. For example, when entering a term into a search engine, that search engine sends back the relevant information formatted using the *Hypertext Markup Language (HTML)*, which is then displayed by your browser. But that search engine did not previously have that precise page formatted and sitting in a file. Instead, it runs software to interpret the query and to generate an appropriate response to be sent back.

Rather than building that dynamic behavior directly into the web server software, there is a specification known as the *Common Gateway Interface (CGI)* that provides an industry standard for performing such tasks. This allows users to more easily implement their own server–side processing in a way that is compatible with various web server tech–

nologies. CGI programming can be done in a variety of languages, including Python. In this section, we wish to provide a few simple examples to show how this is done in Python, using tools from the cgi module. These examples rely upon a bit of knowledge of HTML, but they should be easy to follow.

16.6.1 Getting Started

Our first example is rather elementary, but allows us to introduce the tools for generating web content dynamically. Performing server-side scripting begins by having a true static web page that appears something like the one shown in Figure 16.16. The important part of that file for this lesson is line 6. This makes the phrase Run CGI script a live link on the user's browser. When the user clicks on it, rather than taking them to a static page, the server will run our simple.cgi script and return the output generated by that script as the web page.

The file simple.cgi should presumably be accessible to the web server and might appear as the one given in Figure 16.17. Although the suffix for that file is .cgi it is actually Python source code. The first line begins with the # character, and so it is ignored as a comment by the Python interpreter. However, it serves a particular purpose for the web server. Since CGI scripting can be performed in many languages, this lets the web server know that this particular script should be executed with the Python interpreter (which is typically installed on systems at /usr/bin/python). Because the output of this program is to be sent back and interpreted by a web browser, we send relevant header information, followed by a blank line, and then our content. In this case, our content is just plain text (as opposed to HTML), and so line 2 denotes this content type as part of the header. Line 3 is the blank line that ends the header and line 4 is the remaining content. The user will see the result of this "dynamic" web page as a text file with the words

```
1  <html>
2    <head>
3      <title>Say Hello!</title>
4    </head>
5    <body>
6      <a href="simple.cgi">Run CGI script</a>
7    </body>
8  </html>
```

FIGURE 16.16: A simple web page that relies upon CGI scripting.

```
1  #!/usr/bin/python
2  print 'Content-type: text/plain'
3  print
4  print 'Hello World Wide Web'
```

FIGURE 16.17: The simple.cgi script to support the web page of Figure 16.16.

Hello World Wide Web. Of course, since this program always generates the same response in this simple case, we really had no need for server-side scripting.

16.6.2 HTML Forms

As a more interesting example, we look at a case where dynamic content is generated based upon specifications sent by the viewer. One way this is done is by appending extra parameters as part of a URL. You may have noticed when browsing that sometimes you get taken to a page with a URL of the form,

`http://www.sample.edu/page.html?name=Foo&date=today`

The strings after the question mark set values for variables. In Python these get stored in a dictionary that can be accessed using the cgi library. Once this library is imported, a call to FieldStorage returns a dictionary-like object that maps the existing variable names to their associated values. For example, if a page were accessed via the URL

`http://www.mysite.com/hello.cgi?name=Beth`

then we would find that FieldStorage['name'].value is 'Beth'.

Another way that information is gathered from the user is through something called an ***HTML form***. Figure 16.18 provides a simple example of the static HTML code that is used to display a form. The viewer of this page will originally see labels, First name: and Last name:, and next to each an empty text box in which he can type. There will also be a button below them that is used to submit the form. When he clicks that button, the form is submitted and evaluated by a script processForm.cgi, as is designated at line 6. When that program is executed, the corresponding Python dictionary will have two entries based upon the keys 'firstName' and 'lastName'.

An actual script we might use to dynamically generate a response is shown in Figure 16.19. It imports the FieldStorage function from the cgi module, and then calls it at line 4 to retrieve the dictionary of user parameters. In this case, rather than generate plain

```
1   <html>
2     <head>
3       <title>Python CGI Demo</title>
4     </head>
5     <body>
6       <form method="post" action="processForm.cgi">
7         First name: <input type="text" name="firstName"><br>
8         Last name: <input type="text" name="lastName"><br>
9         <input type="submit" value="Enter">
10      </form>
11    </body>
12  </html>
```

FIGURE 16.18: A web page using an HTML Form and CGI scripting.

```
1   #!/usr/bin/python
2   from cgi import FieldStorage
3
4   form = FieldStorage( )
5
6   print 'Content-type: text/html\n'   # includes extra blank line
7   print '<html><head>'
8   print '<title>', form['firstName'].value + "'s Page</title></head>"
9   print '<body><h1>'
10  print 'Hello', form['firstName'].value, form['lastName'].value
11  print '</h1></body></html>'
```

FIGURE 16.19: The `processForm.cgi` script used to support the web page of Figure 16.18.

text, we chose to dynamically generate HTML code that will be sent back to the user's browser. Line 6 generates the appropriate header entry to denote the coming content type (as well as the blank line to end the header). Everything from lines 7–11 is the actual content of our dynamic web page, including the appropriate HTML tags to make our result pretty. Note that the resulting page is intentionally customized to include the user's first name and last name, as retrieved from the form in lines 8 and 10.

This may not be the most impressive example, but it demonstrates all that is necessary to get the data into and out of our Python program. The rest of the chapter relies upon our existing knowledge of Python programming and shows some more inspiring web page design.

16.7 Case Study: Searching the Web

In the case study of Section 12.7, we developed a basic search engine with a text-based interface. In this section, we expand upon the original tool, using the techniques of this chapter to develop a more robust client-server model for web searching.

Our original engine was a single piece of software that indexes a corpus of documents loaded from a local file system, subsequently allowing the user to make queries on the corpus. Our new version has several improvements. First, rather than cataloging locally stored files, our server build an indexing engine based upon web pages that are downloaded when crawling the web from a given starting page.

Secondly, rather than have a single executable that builds the index and interacts with a user, we break this into two distinct components. The first piece acts as a server, initially gathering and analyzing the corpus and then opening up a TCPServer that supports incoming queries. Paired with this, we develop two different versions of a client to interact with our search engine. The first is a simple text-based client that performs the query over the network, displaying the results on the console. The final version is a web-based client that relies upon an HTML form for gathering the user's search term, and a CGI script for querying the server and dynamically displaying the results as a web page.

16.7.1 Web Crawler and Server

Our first piece of software, shown in Figure 16.20, is designed to gather a corpus of documents directly from the web, to load them into an Engine instance as was defined in Section 12.7, and then to start a TCPServer with a simple protocol used to query the underlying search engine.

To gather the corpus, we use a technique known as ***web crawling***. A crawler automates the exploration of the web by taking an initial web page, and recursively looking for embedded links to other pages. We accomplish this with the recursiveCrawl function at lines 6–19 of our code. Our high-level approach is to take a starting URL, to fetch the contents of that page from the web, to add the document to our search engine, and to look for links that it contains referencing additional web pages for exploration.

We highlight two technical issues used to manage this process. First, we need to somehow limit the scope of our crawling (unless we have resources available for downloading the entire web). So when configuring the server, the software asks for a maximum recursive depth for the crawling. A depth of zero includes only the initial page. A depth of one includes the initial page as well as any pages to which it links. A depth of two includes the initial, its linked pages, and pages linked from those. To manage this recursion, the maxDepth is given as a parameter on line 6, checked at line 13 before further recursing, and reduced to maxDepth-1 at line 17 when starting the recursive crawl.

The second issue is that we want to avoid having the same page indexed more than once by our engine (for example, when several pages link to a common page). To avoid duplication, we maintain a set of knownPages as a parameter to our recursion; it is an empty set by default. As we crawl a particular page, we add its URL to this set at line 8. Then at line 16, prior to starting a recursive exploration of a "new" page, we check if the URL is already included among the set of known pages.

Because our search engine is presumed to catalog plain text documents, we must strip away all HTML constructs before adding the content to our engine. So at line 12, we make a call to removeHTMLTags before inserting the document contents into our engine. The implementation of this routine is at lines 21–31, relying on knowledge that all ***HTML tags*** are bracketed between the symbols < >. These symbols and all characters between them are removed.

Similar text processing is used to find the HTML links embedded within the current (unstripped) web page. This is managed by the getLinks method, which is called from line 14 and implemented at lines 32–52. Usually a link in an HTML file is formatted as

```
href="http://some.domain/directory/webpage.html"
```

The getLinks function loops through all occurrences of such a pattern to identify the URLs of interest (we only consider pages with the suffix `.html` or `.htm` or those in nested directories). We take care in lines 42–45 to adjust for embedded links that are relative to the containing page or server.

The next portion of the program is the definition of a SearchHandler class that will be used to manage incoming connections to our search engine server. This uses an extremely simple protocol and relies heavily on the existing machinery of the Engine class from

Section 12.7. The search term is transmitted directly through the socket. We pass that term to the makeReport method of the underlying search engine. That returns the report as one (possibly long) string. We prepare to send the report back to the client, but since reports vary in length, we preface the transmission with a single line forecasting the number of characters to be sent (we will later see how the client uses this length when receiving the report).

Finally, lines 63–74 control the main flow of control of our program. The first step is to initialize the wizard based upon our recursive crawl of the web. Then we create and activate a server, which awaits incoming connections from the clients.

```python
1  from Engine import Engine
2  from urllib import urlopen
3  from socket import gethostname
4  from SocketServer import TCPServer, BaseRequestHandler
5
6  def recursiveCrawl(pageURL, wizard, maxDepth, knownPages = set( )):
7    print 'Crawling', pageURL
8    knownPages.add(pageURL)
9
10   try:
11     contents = urlopen(pageURL).read( )
12     wizard.addDocument(removeHTMLTags(contents), pageURL)
13     if maxDepth > 0:      # look for pages linked from this one
14       links = getLinks(contents, pageURL)
15       for newURL in links:
16         if newURL not in knownPages:
17           recursiveCrawl(newURL, wizard, maxDepth−1, knownPages)
18   except:
19     pass       # if anything goes wrong, ignore the current page but do not crash
20
21 def removeHTMLTags(html):
22   text = ' '
23   insideTag = False
24   for c in html:
25     if not insideTag and c != '<':
26       text += c
27     elif not insideTag:
28       insideTag = True
29     elif c == '>':
30       insideTag = False
31   return text
```

FIGURE 16.20: Crawling the web to build an index (continued on next page).

```
32   def getLinks(contents, page):
33     links = [ ]
34     indexStart = 0
35     length = len(contents)
36     while indexStart < length:
37       indexStart = contents.find('href="', indexStart)
38       if indexStart > -1:
39         indexEnd = contents.find('"', indexStart + 6)
40         link = contents[indexStart+6:indexEnd]
41         if link[:7].lower( ) != 'http://':   # look for relative URLs
42           if link[0] == '/':                 # this link is relative to the current domain
43             link = 'http://' + page.split('/')[2] + link
44           else:                              # this link is relative to the current URL
45             link = '/'.join(page.split('/')[:-1]) + '/' + link
46         if link[-5:].lower( )=='.html' or link[-4:].lower( )=='.htm' or link[-1]=='/':
47           links.append(link)
48         indexStart = indexEnd + 1
49       else:
50         indexStart = length
51
52     return links
53
54   # Server for searching
55   class SearchHandler(BaseRequestHandler):
56     def handle(self):
57       searchTerm = self.request.recv(1024)
58       searchResult = wizard.makeReport(searchTerm)
59
60       self.request.send('Length:  ' + str(len(searchResult)) + '\n')
61       self.request.send(searchResult + '\n')
62
63   startingPage = raw_input('Enter the URL of the initial web page: ')
64   searchDepth = int(raw_input('Enter the maximum crawling depth: '))
65
66   # First crawl the web to build the index
67   wizard = Engine( )
68   recursiveCrawl(startingPage, wizard, searchDepth)
69
70   localHost = gethostname( )  # or you may hardwire your computer's host name
71   searchServer = TCPServer( (localHost, 9000), SearchHandler)
72   print
73   print 'Starting the server on', localHost
74   searchServer.serve_forever( )
```

FIGURE 16.20 (continuation): Crawling the web to build an index.

```
1   from socket import socket
2
3   address = raw_input('Enter hostname for the search engine: ')
4   connection = socket( )
5   connection.connect( (address, 9000) )
6
7   searchTerm = raw_input('Enter a term to search for: ')
8   connection.send(searchTerm)
9   response = connection.recv(1024)
10
11  totalLength = int(response.split('\n')[0][8:])
12  if totalLength > 0:
13    result = '\n'.join(response.split('\n')[1:])
14    while len(result) < totalLength:
15      transmission = connection.recv(1024)
16      result += transmission
17    print result
18  else:
19    print 'No matches found.'
```

FIGURE 16.21: Text-based client for querying the search engine.

16.7.2   Text-Based Client

To demonstrate the use of our networked search engine, we begin with a simple text-based client, shown in Figure 16.21. The user must provide the host name of an active server and then a query term. A connection to the server is made, the search term is transmitted, and then we await the response.

Recalling our server's protocol, the first line of the response is presumed to be of a form `'Length: 123'`, designating the actual length of the search result. If the report length is zero, this means that the search term was not contained in the corpus. Otherwise, we reconstruct the result from the remainder of the first transmission, and from subsequent transmissions as necessary until reaching the total length.

16.7.3   Web-Based Client

For a more user-friendly interface to our search engine, we create an HTML form for entering a search term, and then use CGI scripting to process the query and to dynamically reformat the result as a web page.

The entry form is quite simple and shown in Figure 16.22 (feel free to create a prettier design). From a technical perspective, the only significant issues are that the user enters the search term into a text box that is named `term` within the form, and that the submitted form will be processed by a script named `WebSearch.cgi`.

The underlying CGI script is shown in Figure 16.23. Its basic flow generally parallels the text-based client. The difference include how we gather input and how we display the

```
1   <html>
2     <head>
3       <title>Seach the web</title>
4     </head>
5
6     <body>
7
8       <h2>Enter a search term</h2>
9       <form method="post" action="WebSearch.cgi">
10        <input type="text" name="term">
11        <input type="submit" value="Enter">
12      </form>
13
14    </body>
15  </html>
```

FIGURE 16.22: Web page for querying the search engine.

output. In the text–based example, we use **raw_input** to ask the user for the location of the search engine server and the desired search term. In this case, we hardwire the identity of our networked search engine at line 16 of the script, and we gather the search term from the designated field of the submitted form.

The report that we receive from the search engine is plain text. It is gathered at lines 15–25 in much the same way as with our text–based client, which subsequently echos the report to the console. Since the output for the web–based client will be displayed to a user in a web browser, we choose to format it as an HTML page. The initial header is produced by lines 6–9, and the closing of the page is produced at line 39.

When the report is nonempty, we convert it at lines 27–32 to a more well formed web page. There are two distinct types of changes that we make, relying upon our knowledge of the format of the Engine.makeReport result. We know that the URL of each matching document is presented, followed by examples of the search term used in context. We look specifically for the line containing the URL so that we can convert that URL to a live link in the HTML. This is accomplished by lines 29–31. Our original text format uses a line of equal signs to demarcate the sections of the report. We detect this at line 32 and instead place a horizontal rule into the HTML. For all other lines of our report, we make sure to insert a <br> tag to keep displayed line breaks similar to that of the original document.

In the case when we receive an empty report (detected as the **else** at line 36 matching the **if** at line 22), we choose to explicitly inform the user of the lack of matches. We have intentionally wrapped the non–trivial portion of this script within a **try** clause starting at line 12, followed by the **except** statement at line 38. Our reason for doing this is to ensure that our CGI script succeeds even if the attempted connection with the underlying search engine fails. In this case, we inform the user with an appropriate error message.

With extra work, there are many ways to improve our search engine. However, we will stop our case study here, having demonstrated the basic techniques.

```
1   #!/usr/bin/python
2   from socket import socket
3   from cgi import FieldStorage
4
5   # Display HTML header info
6   print 'Content-type: text/html\n\n'
7   print '<html>'
8   print '<head><title>Search results</title></head>'
9   print '<body>'
10  print '<h2>Search results</h2><hr>'
11
12  try:
13    form = FieldStorage( )
14    searchTerm = form['term'].value
15
16    connection = socket( )
17    connection.connect( ('localhost', 9000) )  # will need to adjust server name
18    connection.send(searchTerm)
19    response = connection.recv(1024)
20
21    totalLength = int(response.split('\n')[0][8:])
22    if totalLength > 0:
23      result = '\n'.join(response.split('\n')[1:])
24      while len(result) < totalLength:
25        transmission = connection.recv(1024)
26        result += transmission
27
28      for line in result.split('\n'):
29        if line.startswith('Document: '):
30          filename = line[10:]
31          print 'Document: <a href="%s">%s</a><br>' % (filename,filename)
32        elif line == 40 * '=':
33          print '<hr>'                  # horizontal rule
34        else:
35          print line + '<br>'
36    else:
37      print 'No matches found.'
38  except:
39    print 'Sorry.  Our server is not responding.'
40
41  # Display HTML footer info
42  print '</body></html>'
```

FIGURE 16.23: Script `WebSearch.cgi` supporting the web-based query.

16.8   Chapter Review

16.8.1   Key Points

Network Basics

- A networked resource is identified using a *uniform resource locator (URL)*, as in `http://www.prenhall.com/goldwasser`.

- In the above URL, `www.prenhall.com` represents the *host name*, and symbolizes a machine somewhere on the network. The actual server for that website has an alternative numeric *IP address* which is used by the Internet protocol. The translation from host name to IP address is performed by a special machine known as a *domain name server (DNS)*.

- In the above URL, `http` specifies the *network protocol* that is to be used for the transmission of information. This particular acronym denotes the *Hypertext Transfer Protocol*.

- Because there are so many protocols, incoming network traffic to a machine is often segmented according to the notion of a *port*, perhaps with a different protocol used for each port. For example, the default port used for HTTP is port 80.

- In the above URL, `/goldwasser` is a path to some particular information on Prentice Hall's web server.

Python's socket Class

- To manage the use of a specific network connection, programmers rely upon an abstraction known as a *socket*. In Python this is modeled using a socket class, which itself is imported from the socket module.

- When a socket is initially constructed, it is not connected to any network resource. The connection is established by calling the method connect((host, port)), using an appropriate tuple as a parameter. The host can be identified either by IP address or as a domain name.

- Once open, information can be transmitted from the local machine to the remote machine by calling the send method, with a string instance as the parameter.

- Once open, information can be retrieved from the remote machine by calling the recv method. This method requires a parameter designating the maximum number of characters that we are willing to accept, and it returns a string of up to that maximum length. After receiving that maximum-length string, it may still be that more information is ready to be transmitted through another call to recv. The call to recv may return fewer characters that the specified limit, if that is all that is available for transmission at the time.

- In the case when a call to recv is made yet *no* information is available from the remote machine, the call waits indefinitely, perhaps returning information at a later time. If, however, the connection associated with the socket has been closed or otherwise fails, a call to recv returns an empty string (further waiting would be pointless).

Client-Server Network Model

- In a client-server network model, the client and server have asymmetric roles. The client is responsible for initiating the connection, while the server passively listens for incoming connections on a particular port.

- Once a connection is established, both parties must follow a prescribed protocol regarding their communication. A typical protocol has the client sending a request to the server, and the server replying with an appropriate response.

- Servers are implemented by creating a handler class inherited from BaseRequestHandler. The handle function must be overridden to describe the behavior of the server once an incoming connection has been established. The socket for that connection is automatically designated as **self**.request with the handler.

- The handler class is designated as a parameter when constructing a server, for example as server = TCPServer(('my.ip.address', 9000), MyHandler). The server is activated by calling handle_request( ) to process a single connection, or serve_forever( ) to continue handling incoming connections until terminated.

- If a server needs to process multiple connections simultaneously, it should be created as an instance of the ThreadingTCPServer class.

Peer-to-Peer Network Model

- In a peer-to-peer network, the two parties have more symmetric roles, but the initial connection must still be established with one "client" party initiating a connection to the other "server" party.

The Web: HTTP and HTML

- Documents on the World Wide Web are typically transmitted using the *Hypertext Transfer Protocol (HTTP)*.

- By this protocol, a client makes an explicit GET request for a specific path on the server's system. The server responds by first sending a header that includes information such as the length and format of the requested document. Following that header, the document itself is transmitted.

- Web pages are often written in the *Hypertext Markup Language (HTML)*. This allows for structural and formatting information to be embedded with the use of *tags* denoted between the symbols < >.

- Python's urllib module contains convenient tools for retrieving data from the web.

Server-Side Scripting and CGI

- A *static* web page is one whose content is based upon a pre-existing file saved on the server. However, it is possible to generate a *dynamic* web page with content generated at the time of the request, depending upon given parameters.

- Dynamic web pages are often generated by executing a script on the server, typically with the *Common Gateway Interface (CGI)*. Python provides a cgi module with tools to aid in the development of server-side scripts.

- One approach to gathering parameters from a viewer of a web page is to use an *HTML Form*. The values entered with that form can be retrieved from within a script using the FieldStorage class of the cgi module. This serves as a dictionary-like structure mapping form parameters to actual values.

16.8.2 Glossary

client The designated role for any machine that is making a request of a networked server; *see also* client–server network.

client-server network A centralized configuration in which some machines act as clients, making requests for information from another machine known as a server; *compare to* peer–to–peer (P2P) network.

Common Gateway Interface (CGI) A protocol for sending data from a web server to a web client.

domain name server (DNS) A server that converts the host name of a computer on the Internet to an IP address.

dynamic web page A web page whose contents are generated by the server at the time of a request, often by executing a server–side script using the Common Gateway Interface (CGI).

host name An alphanumeric string that typically identifies a single device on a network (e.g., `www.prenhall.com`).

HTML Form A component of an HTML document used to gather information from a viewer. The form is typically submitted with a button click, at which time its contents are transmitted to the web server and processed with a server–side script.

Hypertext Markup Language (HTML) A language used to embed structural and formatting information in the form of *tags* within a text document. HTML is commonly used for transmitting a web page.

Hypertext Transfer Protocol (HTTP) The standard protocol used for communication of information on the World Wide Web, often in the form of the Hypertext Markup Language (HTML).

IP address An Internet protocol address, which is a number usually expressed in bytes, such as 165.193.123.253

multithreading A technique allowing a computer program to execute (or appear to execute) multiple flows of control at the same time.

network protocol A particular convention used by two connected computers when transmitting information.

peer-to-peer (P2P) network A configuration in which all machines behave symmetrically and communicate directly with each other; *compare to* client–server network.

persistent connection A network connection that remains open throughout multiple rounds of communication.

port A special number used to segment incoming network traffic, often according to the desired communication protocol.

server A machine that awaits incoming network connections from other client machines; *see also* client–server network.

server-side script A program that runs on a web server to generate a dynamic response to a query.

socket An entity managing one end of a connection between two machines in a network.

static web page A web page whose contents are predefined within a file on the server.

thread An abstraction representing one of possibly many active flows of control within an executing program.

Transmission Control Protocol (TCP) An Internet protocol used for establishing network connections.

uniform resource locator (URL) A string of characters that identifies the source of a networked resource and often the particular protocol that should be used to get the resource (e.g., `http://www.prenhall.com/goldwasser`).

web crawler A piece of software that explores the web automatically by recursively looking for links in known documents.

16.8.3 Exercises

Implementing a Server

Practice 16.1: Change the echo server implementation so that it prefaces the echo with the string `'ECHO: '`.

Practice 16.2: Our echo server from Section 16.3.1 was not persistent. After a connection is established it can echo the first message sent by the client, but then the connection is closed. Reimplement a persistent echo server that can repeatedly echo messages for the duration of a connection.

Exercise 16.3: Implement your own time server, using a protocol consistent with that of Section 16.2.1. You do not need to worry about the precise meaning of the other fields in the response string, but fake them so that things line up for use with our client. You may use a call to time.localtime( ) to get a tuple that contains the relevant data for the current time and date on your machine. You do not need to convert to UTC (unless you want to try).

Exercise 16.4: Implement a KnockKnockServer supporting the following protocol. A single connection includes three rounds of communication. The client initiates with the message `'Knock. Knock.'` to which the server responds `"Who's there?"`. In the second round, the client sends an arbitrary message (e.g., `'blah'`), to which the server responds `'blah who?'`. In the third round, the client sends the punch line of a joke, to which the server responds `'Ha ha.'`.

Our Web Client and Server

Exercise 16.5: On page 532, we described how `http` in a URL assumes port 80 by default, but that a nonstandard port can be specified using a syntax such as
`http://talk.google.com:5222/about.html`.
The web client in Figure 16.4 does not support such a syntax. Rewrite that software so that it uses a nonstandard port, when so indicated.

Exercise 16.6: A major problem with the web server of Figure 16.7 is that it potentially provides access to all files on the server machine. A more robust web server may be configured to restrict access to a designated subdirectory of the computer. This

is accomplished by automatically remapping URLs relative to the desired subdirectory. For example, a request for `http://www.typical.edu/sample.txt`
might actually retrieve the file `public/sample.txt` on the server's file, for a
designated subdirectory `public`. Modify our web server software to support such
a configuration.

Exercise 16.7: Even with the proposed modification of Exercise 16.6, there is another
security flaw. Even if a path is interpreted relative to a particular subdirectory, many
operating systems consider the expression `. .` to indicate a parent directory. This
might provide a backdoor for someone accessing a file that was not in the intended
subdirectory, perhaps with a request `GET ../hidden.txt`. Modify the web
server software to disallow use of `. .` within a request path.

Our Chat Room

Exercise 16.8: The chat room server of Figure 16.10 takes care to terminate a client's
handler thread if it detects that the connection to that client has failed. However, the
implementation of the chat room client of Figure 16.13 does not gracefully handle
the case of a dropped connection to the server. If the server fails, the client continues
to run but without ever receiving any activity from the server. Although there is no
way to recover the connection, rewrite the client software so that it explicitly informs
the user that the connection has been lost.

Exercise 16.9: Consider the following behavior of our chat room software. When a user
broadcasts a message to the group (such as that on line 5 of Figure 16.14), that
message is then echoed on that user's client as it is received from the server (as with
line 6 of that figure). Rewrite the *client* software so that it does not display an echo
of a message sent by this uers. Accomplishing this task does not require any change
to the server's code nor to the underlying protocol being used.

Exercise 16.10: If a person sends a private message to an unrecognized screen name, our
server ignores the request. However, the user who sent the message is not informed
of this failure. A better protocol is to have the server transmit an `UNKNOWNUSER`
message back to the client in this scenario. Rewrite both the server and client software based on such a protocol, ensuring that the user is appropriately informed.

Exercise 16.11: Our chat room software has the following flaw. If a new person connects
to the server using the same screen name as an existing person, the new person's
connection wipes out the first person's connection in the _socketLookup dictionary.

A better approach is to adapt the protocol as follows. When a new person sends
an `ADD` request to the server, the server should reject the request by transmitting
an `UNAVAILABLE` message back to the client. Rewrite both the server and client
software based on such a protocol, ensuring that the user is given an appropriate
explanation and an opportunity to select a new screen name.

Exercise 16.12: When a new person comes into the chat room, they have no initial idea
who else is in the room. Redesign the network protocol and reimplement the client
and server, so that a person is informed about the existing members when joining.
Your design should not effect the view of the existing members, who are simply
informed of the one new uesr.

Exercise 16.13: Extend the chat room software so that private messages can be sent simul–taneously to more than one person.

Exercise 16.14: The software we have written for the chat room server and client work well together. However a third party could crash our server by writing client–like software that abuses our protocol. Consider the following interactive session with an active server s:

```
>>> s.connect( ('localhost', 9000) )
>>> s.send('ADD hacker')
10
>>> s.send('\n')
1
>>>
```

The final transmission causes our server to crash. First, explain the underlying cause of the crash, and then rewrite the server software to avoid such a scenario.

Projects

Exercise 16.15: Adapt the Mastermind program of Chapter 7 (or the event–driven version of Section 15.5), producing a networked version of the game. Remember, all of the user interactions were encapsulated by special inputManager and outputManager instances.

APPENDICES

APPENDIX A

Using IDLE

A.1 Using the Python Interpreter within IDLE
A.2 Working with Files

IDLE is an integrated development environment (IDE) for Python. It incorporates in a single package the Python interpreter, a text editor, and tools for managing and debugging source code. Here, we discuss the basics for using IDLE.

A.1 Using the Python Interpreter within IDLE

IDLE can be started from the command-line with the idle command, or started from the application menu. At first glance there is very little difference when using the interpreter with or without IDLE. See Figure A.1 for a screenshot of an IDLE window. However, IDLE does provide more support than the standard interpreter. For example, Python syntax is highlighted in color, see Figure A.2. Comments are in red, strings in green, definitions in blue, keywords in orange, and output in green.

IDLE leverages existing documentation to provide automatic help for the proper use of methods and functions. When a programmer types a method or function name followed by an opening parenthesis, IDLE's interpreter displays a pop-up hint as shown in Figure A.2. The hint displays the formal parameters and the first line of the documentation. These tips show up for both built-in and user-defined types.

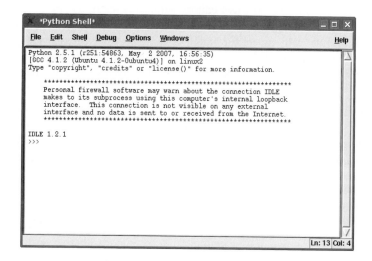

FIGURE A.1: An IDLE session.

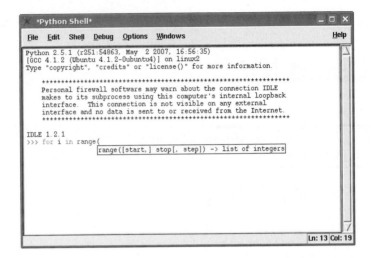

FIGURE A.2: Entering a command into IDLE.

IDLE's interpreter window also has some basic text editing features. For example, you can copy and paste within the shell, allowing you to easily reenter statements that you had previously typed. You can also use this feature to save your entire Python session.

A.2 Working with Files

IDLE also includes a fully functional text editor. Selecting the "New File" item in the "File Menu" will open an empty window in which you enter a program (see Figure A.3). You can also open existing files by selecting "Open File" in the "File" menu. The editor works the same as most text editors with a few extra features. When you work with a program it will highlight the syntax giving more readable code. As you enter the code, it will automatically indent for you. For example, after entering **for** i **in** range(10,−1,−1)**:** and hitting enter, IDLE will automatically indent the next line for you. Also, the same hints that were given in the interpreter are displayed when using IDLE's text editor.

Once you have entered your program in the editor window, you may select "Run Module" in the "Run" menu (if you have not yet saved your file, you will be prompted to do so before it is run). Running the modules causes the file to be executed using the Python interpreter. At this point, one window displays the original source code and a second displays the interpreter session, as shown in Figure A.4. Notice that the interpreter session first displays a line "==== RESTART ====" before running the program. The output of the program is displayed in blue, and after it completes a Python prompt is displayed. You may continue from this prompt to enter more Python commands or to access any of the top-level variables (just as when starting an interpreter from the command line as `python -i`.

If your program uses multiple files, or imports libraries such as cs1graphics, all of the source code for those modules must be located either in the same directory as the primary file, or located in Python's system-wide library directory.

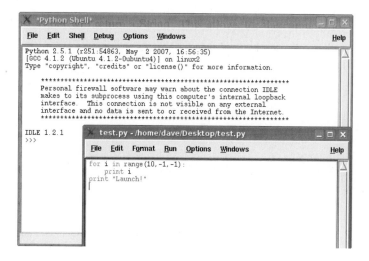

FIGURE A.3: Opening an editor

If your program has an error when you run it, the error message will indicate the line of your file at which it has occurred. You can then return to the editor to make the appropriate fixes, and save and run the program again. Another way you can find bugs in your program is to use the "Check Module" item of the "Run" menu. This cannot find all possible errors, but it will find syntax errors, for example, if you do not have matching parentheses or have forgotten a colon at the end of a **for** statement.

There are more advanced features of IDLE that we do not discuss here, such as debugging tools for tracing an executing program (see the "Debug" menu option).

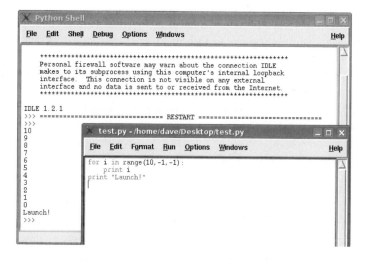

FIGURE A.4: Running the program in the editor.

APPENDIX B

Python, Java, and C++:
a Transition Guide

B.1 The Purpose of This Guide

Python is a wonderful programming language and we expect that readers of this book will find many opportunities to use it. That said, there are many different programming languages used by software developers. Each language has its own strengths and weaknesses, and professionals must become accustomed to programming in different languages. Fortunately, once you have a solid foundation in one language it becomes easier to transition to another language. This appendix is designed for readers choosing Java or C++ as a second language. Those are among the most widely used languages in industry. As object-oriented languages, they have a great deal in common with Python. Yet there exist significant differences between the three languages.

This transition guide is not meant to serve as a complete self-contained reference for either of the languages. Our goal is to provide an initial bridge, built upon the knowledge and terminology that we have gained in Python. We begin in Section B.2 by providing a high-level discussion about programming languages and the more significant differences between Python, Java, and C++. Section B.3 provides our first direct comparison between Python source code and Java/C++ code. Then we diverge into a more detailed comparison of Python and Java, given in Section B.4, and a separate comparison of Python and C++ in Section B.5. We expect those interested in transitioning to Java to read the former, and those transition to C++ the later; we intentionally avoid a detailed three-way comparison, as we do not suggest learning two additional languages at once.

As much as possible, we rely upon earlier examples in Python and then translate these to Java and C++ respectively. In this appendix, we provide basic examples of the major language constructs. For those interested in more details, we provide a longer transition guide from Python to Java and from Python to C++ through our publisher's website.

With that said, let the tour begin...

B.2 High-Level Programming Languages

To begin, we recommend that you reread Section 1.3, where we first describe the distinction between *low-level* and *high-level* programming languages. At its core, a computing architecture supports an extremely limited set of data types and operations. For this reason, we describe a CPU's machine language as a *low-level* programming language. It is possible to develop software directly for that machine language. In fact, this is often done for specialized applications where execution speed is of utmost concern. However, it is extremely inconvenient to develop complex software systems in a low-level language. High-level programming languages were conceived to better support a programmer's expressiveness, thereby reducing the development time of software systems, providing greater opportunity for code reuse, and improving the overall reliability and maintainability of software.

B.2.1 Convenience versus Efficiency

In effect, high-level languages offer convenience. They support a greater range of data types and a richer syntax for expressing a series of operations. Yet this additional support is somewhat artificial. In the end, the software must be translated back to the CPU's machine language in order to be executed on a computer. For high-level languages, this translation has been automated in the form of a compiler or interpreter. As a result, software written in a high-level language is no more powerful than equivalent software that could have been written directly in the low-level language (given enough time and expertise). The convenience afforded by a high-level language often comes at the expense of some slight inefficiencies in the performance of the resulting software. The automated translation from high level to low level has been carefully optimized, but still the generated low-level code is not always as streamlined as code crafted directly by an expert in the field.

Yet as a society, we simply cannot afford to have each and every piece of software hand-crafted in a low-level language. While there are slight discrepancies in efficiency, those are quickly negated by improvements in hardware, networks, and other aspects of a computing environment. A more significant concern is the software development time, that is, the time it takes to carry an idea from the initial inspiration to the final software for a consumer. The design and development of quality software applications is extremely labor-intensive, and can take months or years depending on the project. The single biggest factor in the cost of a software project is employing the developers. So there is great benefit in use of a high-level language that can better support abstractions and thereby reduce the overall development cycle.

More than a thousand high-level languages have been developed over time, with perhaps a hundred that are still actively used for program development. What makes each language unique is the way in which concepts are abstracted and expressed. No single language is perfect, and each strikes its own balance in trying to support the development of efficient, maintainable, and reusable software. This guide is limited to the examination of three specific *object-oriented* languages, yet the object-oriented paradigm is just one example of an abstraction for program development. Even within the object-oriented framework, there are differences between languages. In the remainder of this section, we discuss the most significant ways in which Python, Java, and C++ differ.

B.2.2   Interpreter versus Compiler

An important aspect of any high-level language is the process by which it is translated back to the low-level machine code to be executed. Python is an example of an *interpreted* language. We "run" a typical Python program by feeding its source code as input to another piece of software known as the Python interpreter. The Python interpreter is the software that is actually executing on the CPU. It adapts its outward behavior to match the semantics indicated by the given source code. In effect, the translation from the high-level code to low-level operations is performed on-the-fly, each time the program is run.

In contrast, C++ is an example of a *compiled* language. Progressing from the original source code to a running program is a two-step process. During the first phase ("compile-time"), the source code is fed as input to a special piece of software known as a *compiler*. That compiler analyzes the source code based on the syntax of the language. If there are syntax errors, they are reported and the compilation fails. Otherwise, the compiler translates the high-level code into machine code for the computing system, generating another file known as an executable. During the second phase (the "run-time"), the executable is independently started by the user; the compiler is no longer needed unless a new executable must be generated, for example when a change is made to the original source code.

Java uses somewhat of a hybrid approach in the progression from high-level source code to a running program, relying upon a compiler and an interpreter. The original source code is first fed to a compiler, using a process akin to that of C++. For this reason, we tend to discuss Java as more of a compiled language from the point of view of a programmer. However, the compiler does not directly generate machine code, but an intermediate platform-independent form known as Java bytecode. When it comes time to run the software, that bytecode is fed to an interpreter typically known as a Java Virtual Machine (or JVM, for short). The hybrid approach is designed to balance the relative advantages and disadvantages between compiled and interpreted languages.[1]

The greatest advantage of the compilation model is execution speed. In essence, the more that can be handled at compile-time, the less work there is to be done at run-time. By performing the full translation to machine code in advance, the execution of the software is streamlined so as to perform only those computations that are a direct part of the software application. A second advantage is that the executable can be distributed to customers as free-standing software. So long as it was designed for the particular machine code of their system, it can be executed by those users without any further requirement of software installations (e.g., an interpreter). A consequence of this model is that the machine code can be distributed by a company without exposing the original source code that was used to generate it (although some companies choose to "open source" their software).

In contrast, there is no distinction between compile-time and run-time for a purely interpreted program. The interpreter bears the burden of translating the original source code as part of the run-time process. Furthermore, distributing the source code is only useful to a customer who has a compatible interpreter installed on his or her system. The primary advantage of an interpreted language is greater platform-independence. The same source code can be distributed for use on different computing platforms, so long as each platform has a valid interpreter. In contrast, a compiled executable is catered to one partic-

---

1.   Python also balances these considerations by automatically pre-compiling an imported module into an intermediate form, saved as a file with the `.pyc` suffix.

ular machine language; different versions of the executable must be distributed for use on different computing platforms.

For software developers, the debugging cycle varies a great deal when working with an interpreter language versus a compiled language. For example, we have readily used Python's interpreter not just as a means for running a final version of a program, but to provide useful feedback and interaction when problems arise. The compiler can be helpful in detecting purely syntactical errors at compile–time, but it is no longer of use when run–time errors occur.

B.2.3 Dynamic versus Static Typing

For compiled languages, there is an advantage in doing as much work as possible at compile–time, so as to streamline the run–time process. It is this fact that motivates the single greatest distinction between Python and either of Java or C++. Python is known as a *dynamically typed* language. Within a given scope an identifier can be assigned to an underlying value using an assignment statement, as in

```
age = 38
```

We happen to know that age is being assigned to an integer value in this case, yet we did not make any syntactic declaration regarding the data type. In fact, we could later reassign that same identifier to the string 'Stone'. Types are not formally associated with the identifiers, but rather with the underlying objects (thus the value 38 knows that it is an integer). When identifiers are used in expressions, the legitimacy depends upon the type of the underlying object. The expression age + 1 will be valid when age is an integer yet illegal if age is a string. The method call age.lower( ) will be legitimate when age is a string yet illegal when age is an integer.

In Python, these expressions are evaluated at run–time. When encountering an expres–sion such as age.lower( ), the interpreter determines[2] whether the object currently associ–ated with the name age supports the syntax lower( ). If so, the expression is evaluated successfully; if not, a runtime error occurs. The same principle of dynamic typing applies to the declaration of functions. The formal parameters in the signature serve as place–holders for the required number of actual parameters, yet there is no explicit statement of type. The identifiers are assigned to the objects sent by the caller. The dynamic typing also applies to the attributes within a class definition, which are generally initialized in the constructor, but never explicitly declared.

In general, code works so long as the objects support the expected members; other–wise an exception is raised. This flexibility allows for various forms of polymorphism. For example, the sum function accepts a parameter that is assumed to be a sequence of num–bers. It works whether that sequence is in the form of a **list**, a **tuple**, or a **set**, so long as the parameter is iterable. Another form of polymorphism is a function that displays markedly different behaviors depending upon the parameter type. For example in Section 6.2 we provided a Point.__mul__ implementation that used explicit type checking at run–time to determine the appropriate semantics for the use of multiplication.

---

2.   See Section 12.6 for a much more detailed explanation of the name resolution process in Python.

Java and C++ are statically typed languages. An explicit type declaration is required for every identifier before it can be used. The following demonstrates a type declaration followed by an assignment, as it might appear in Java or C++:

```
int age;
age = 38;
```

The first line is a declaration that establishes the identifier age as an integer value in the current scope. Type declarations apply in many contexts. For example, a function signature must include explicit type declarations for all formal parameters, as well as for the resulting return type. All data members must be explicitly typed as part of a class definition. The reason for requiring programmers to make such declarations is that it allows for significantly more work to be done at compile–time rather than run–time. For example the legality of the subsequent assignment age = 38 is apparent at compile–time based upon knowledge of the data type. In similar spirit, if a programmer attempts to send a string to a function that expected a floating–point number as in sqrt("Hello"), this error can be detected at compile–time. In some scenarios, type declarations can help the system in better managing the use of memory.

The choice between dynamically–versus statically–typed languages is often (though not always) paired with the choice between interpreted and compiled languages. The primary advantage of static typing is the earlier detection of errors, yet this early detection is more significant for a compiled language, for which there is a distinction between compile–time errors and run–time errors. Even if static typing is used in a purely interpreted language, those errors will not arise until the program is executed. The primary advantages of dynamic typing is the reduced syntactical burden associated with explicit declarations, together with the simpler support for polymorphism.

B.3   A First Glance at Java and C++

To warm up, we begin with a side–by–side example of a Python code fragment and the corresponding code in Java and C++. In particular, Figure B.1 demonstrates the code for a function that computes the greatest common denominator of two integers using Euclid's algorithm. The Python version is similar to the solution for Practice 5.19, given on page 631. Notice that the Java and C++ versions for this example are identical.

The similarity between Java and C++ in our first example is more than a coincidence. Though there are many differences between Java and C++, the low–level syntax of the languages are similar because both are patterned after an earlier programming language named C. The C programming language was introduced in 1973 and widely used for software development for decades (in fact, its use is still prevalent). Its greatest strength is its run–time efficiency, however it is non object–oriented.

C++ is a direct extension of C, initially developed in the early 1980s at Bell Labs. It adds support for object orientation while preserving aspects of the original syntax of C. Java is a programming language that was originally developed by Sun Microsystems in 1995. Java is *not* a true extension of C, rather an independent language. However, the creators of Java intentionally borrowed aspects of C's syntax to provide greater familiarity for programmers transitioning from C to Java.

Python

```
1   def gcd(u, v):
2     # we will use Euclid's algorithm
3     # for computing the GCD
4     while v != 0:
5       r = u % v        # compute remainder
6       u = v
7       v = r
8     return u
```

Java/C++

```
1    int gcd(int u, int v) {
2      /* We will use Euclid's algorithm
3         for computing the GCD */
4      int r;
5      while (v != 0) {
6        r = u % v;     // compute remainder
7        u = v;
8        v = r;
9      }
10     return u;
11   }
```

FIGURE B.1: A function for computing the greatest common denominator, as seen in Python, Java, and C++.

Looking more carefully at Figure B.1, we see that the Java/C++ version is a bit more bulky than the Python code. It should hopefully seem legible, yet there are definitely syntactical differences. First we draw attention to Python's use of whitespace versus Java and C++'s use of punctuation for delimiting the basic syntactic structure of the code. An individual command in Python (e.g., u = v) is followed by a newline character, officially designating the end of that command. In Java and C++, each individual command must be explicitly terminated with a semicolon. For example, we see the semicolon after the command u = v on line 7.

There is also a difference in designating a "block" of code. In Python, each block is preceded by a colon, and then indentation is used to clearly designate the extent of the block. We see the body of a while loop consisting of lines 5–7 of the Python code, and that loop nested within the larger body of the gcd function, comprised of lines 2–8. In Java and C++, these blocks of code are explicitly enclosed in curly braces { }. The body of the while loop in the Java/C++ version consists of everything from the opening brace at the end of line 5 until the matching right brace on line 9. That loop is itself nested within the function body that begins with the left brace on line 1 and concludes with the right brace on line 11.

There is a difference in punctuation, as Java and C++ require that the boolean con—dition for the while loop on line 5 be expressed within parentheses; we did not do so in Python, although parentheses could be used optionally. We also see a difference in the punctuation usage when providing inlined comments.[3] In Python, the # character is used to designate the remainder of the line as a comment, as seen at lines 2, 3 and 5. Two dif—ferent comment styles are allowed in Java and C++. A single-line comment is supported, though using the // pattern, as seen at line 6. Another style is demonstrated on lines 2 and 3, starting with the /* pattern, and ending with the */ pattern. This style is particularly convenient as it can span multiple lines of source code.

---

3.   We wait until later to visit the corresponding issue of embedding official documentation.

For the most part, the use of whitespace is irrelevant in Java and C++. Although our sample code is spaced with one command per line, and with indentation to highlight the block structure, that is not formally part of the language syntax. The identical function could technically be defined in a single line as follows:

```
int gcd(int u, int v) { int r; while (v != 0) { r = u % v; u = v; v = r; } return u; }
```

To the compiler, this is the same definition as our original. Of course, to a human reader, this version is nearly incomprehensible. So as you transition from Python, we ask that you continue using whitespace to make your source code legible.

The more significant differences between the Python and Java/C++ versions of our example involve the difference between *dynamic* and *static* typing, as we originally discussed in Section B.2.3. Even in this simple example, there are three distinct manifestations of static typing. The formal parameters (i.e., identifiers u and v) are declared in the Python signature at line 1 without any explicit type designation. In the corresponding declaration of parameters in the Java/C++ signature, we find explicit type declaration for each parameter with the syntax gcd(**int** u, **int** v). This information serves two purposes for the compiler. First, it allows the compiler to check the legality of our use of u and v within the function body. Second, it allows the compiler to enforce that integers be sent by the caller of our function.

The second manifestation of static typing is the explicit designation of the *return type* as part of a formal signature in Java and C++. In line 1 of our Java/C++ example, the declaration **int** at the beginning of the line labels this as a function that returns an integer. Again, the compiler uses this designation to check the validity of our own code (namely that we are indeed returning the correct type of information at line 10), as well as to check the caller's use of our return value. For example, if the caller invokes the function as part of an assignment g = gcd(54,42), this would be legal if variable g has been declared as an integer, yet illegal if g has been declared as a string.

Finally, we note the declaration of variable r at line 4 of our Java/C++ code. This designates r as a local variable representing an integer, allowing its use at lines 6 and 7. Had we omitted the original declaration, the compiler would report an error "cannot find symbol" regarding the later use of r (the analog of a NameError in Python). Formally, a declared variable has scope based upon the most specific set of enclosing braces at the point of its declaration. In our original example, the variable has scope as a local variable for the duration of the function body (as is also the case with our Python version). Technically, since this variable's only purpose is for temporary storage during a single invocation of the while loop body, we could have declared it within the more narrow scope of the loop body (Python does not support this form of a restricted scope).

You may have noticed that this first example is not at all object oriented. In fact, the Java/C++ code fragment that we give is essentially a C code fragment (the only aspect of the fragment which is not in accordance with the C language is the // style of comment at line 6). Where Java and C++ vary more significantly from each other (and from Python), is in their type system and their support of object–orientation. The remainder of our transition guide is organized into Section B.4, which is devoted to a further exploration of Java, and Section B.5, which is similarly focused on C++.

B.4   Java Guide

Java is a programming language that was originally developed by Sun Microsystems. The first public release of the language came in 1995. A second major revision was released in 1998, and several more revisions have come since. For consistency, the Java source code in this guide adheres to what is formally known as Java 2 Standard Edition 5 (or informally as Java 5.0). Some aspects of Java's syntax are superficially different than Python yet conceptually the same. We will do our best to show corresponding examples of code in both languages. Other aspects of Java are remarkably different in design than Python, warranting greater discussion within this guide.

B.4.1   Data Types and Operators

Figure B.2 provides a summary of Java's primitive data types, noting the correspondence to Python's types. Ironically, none of the type names are the same. The boolean type in Java is formally named **boolean**, versus Python's **bool**. Furthermore the literals **true** and **false** are uncapitalized in Java while capitalized in Python.

Java gives the programmer more fine-grained control in selecting the underlying precision of integers, supporting four fixed-precision integer types (**byte**, **short**, **int**, and **long**). The precision of Python's **int** class is system-dependent, although often akin to Java's **long**. Python's **long** type serves a completely different purpose, representing integers with unlimited magnitude. In Java, this functionality is supported by the BigInteger class, which is available from the standard libraries. Java supports two different floating-point types (**float** and **double**) with a choice of underlying precisions. The **double** type in Java is the more commonly used, and more akin to what is named **float** in Python.

Java Type	Description	Literals	Python analog
boolean	logical value	**true** **false**	**bool**
byte	8-bit integer		
short	16-bit integer		
int	32-bit integer	38	
long	64-bit integer	38L	**int**
BigInteger[a]	arbitrary-precision integer		**long**
float	32-bit floating-point value	3.14f	
double	64-bit floating-point value	3.14	**float**
char	single character	`'a'`	
String[a]	character sequence	`"Hello"`	**str**

FIGURE B.2: Java's primitive data types.

[a]Not technically a built-in type; defined within standard libraries.

Java supports two different types for representing text. The **char** type provides a streamlined representation of a single character of text. Java's String class serves the same purpose as Python's **str** class, representing an *immutable* sequence of characters (which may happen to be an empty string or a single-character string). To distinguish between a **char** and a one-character string, a String literal must be designated using double quote marks (as in `"a"`). The use of single quotes is reserved for a a **char** literal (as in `'a'`). An attempt to misuse the single-quote syntax, as in `'impossible'`, results in a compile–time error. The String class supports a different set of behaviors than Python's **str** class, although many are quite similar. A summary of the most commonly used operations is in Figure B.3.

Type declarations

The basic form of a type declaration was demonstrated in our first glance of Section B.3:

4
```
int r;
```

A variable declaration can be combined with an initial assignment statement, using a syn–tax such as

```
int age = 38;
```

Furthermore, we can declare multiple variables of the same type in a single statement (with or without initial values), as in

```
int age = 38, zipcode = 63103;    // two new variables
```

Operators

With a few notable discrepancies, the two languages support a similar set of operators for the primitive types. The same basic logical operators are supported, yet Java uses the following symbols (borrowed from the syntax of C):

&& for logical **and**
|| for logical **or**
! for logical **not**

For numeric values, Python differentiates between *true division* (i.e., /), *integer division* (i.e., //), and *modular arithmetic* (i.e., %), as originally discussed in Section 2.4. Java supports operators / and %, but not // (in fact we already saw this pattern used to desig–nate inline comments in Java). The semantics of the / operator depends upon the type of operands. When both operands are integral types, the result is the integer quotient; if one or both of the operands are floating–point types, true division is performed. To get true divi–sion with integral types, one of the operands must be explicitly cast to a float (as described starting on page 575).

Syntax	Semantics
s.length( )	Returns the number of characters in string s.
s.charAt(index)	Returns the character of string s at the given index.
s.concat(t)	Returns a concatenation of strings s and t.
s + obj	Returns a concatenation of string s and arbitrary object obj (automatically converts other object to a string, if not already so).
s.equals(t)	Returns **true** if strings s and t have same contents, **false** otherwise.
s.equalsIgnoreCase(t)	Similar to equals but case insensitive.
s.contentEquals(seq)	Returns **true** if seq is any form of a character sequence with contents equal to string s, **false** otherwise.
s == t	Returns **true** if s and t are the identical instance, **false** otherwise.
s.compareTo(t)	Returns a negative value if string s is lexicographical less than string t, zero if equal, and a positive value if s is greater than t.
s.compareToIgnoreCase(t)	Similar to compareTo but case insensitive.
s.contains(pattern)	Returns **true** if the given pattern occurs as substring of string s, **false** otherwise.
s.startsWith(pattern)	Returns **true** if string s starts with the pattern, **false** otherwise.
s.endsWith(pattern)	Returns **true** if string s ends with the pattern, **false** otherwise.
s.indexOf(pattern)	Returns the least index at which the pattern begins within string s. When the pattern is not found, returns −1.
s.indexOf(pattern, start)	Returns the least index, greater than or equal to start, at which the pattern begins within string s. When the pattern is not found, returns −1.
s.trim( )	Returns a copy of s with leading and trailing whitespace removed.
s.toLowerCase( )	Returns an entirely lowercase copy of string s.
s.toUpperCase( )	Returns an entirely uppercase copy of string s.
s.substring(start, stop)	Returns a new string that is a slice of string s, including characters of the original from index start, up to but not including index stop (if not specified, stop defaults to the end of the string).
s.replace(old, new)	Returns a copy of string s, with every occurrence of the old substring replaced with the **new** string.
s.split(pattern)	Splits string s according to pattern and returns array of substrings.
s.split("\\s+")	Splits strings according to whitespace and returns array of substrings.

FIGURE B.3: Selected behaviors supported by Java's String class.

As is the case for Python, Java supports an operator–with–assignment shorthand for most binary operators, as with x += 5 as a shorthand for x = x + 5. Furthermore, since incrementing a number by one is so common, Java supports a ++ operator for this purpose. In fact there are two distinct usages known as ***pre-increment*** (e.g., ++x) and ***post-increment*** (e.g., x++). Both of these add one to the value of x, but they can be used differently in the context of a larger expression. For example, if indexing a sequence, the expression groceries[i++] retrieves the entry based upon the original index i, yet subsequently increments that index. In contrast, the syntax groceries[++i] causes the value of the index to be incremented *before* accessing the associated entry of the sequence. A −− operator is simi– larly supported in pre–decrement and post–decrement form. This combination of operators can be valuable for an experienced programmer, but their use also leads to very subtle code and sometimes mistakes. We recommend that they be used sparingly until mastered.

Strings in Java are manipulated primarily with the named methods of Figure B.3 rather than by operators. For example, you should use methods like equals and compareTo to check the equivalence or natural ordering of two strings.[4] Strings support the same zero–indexed concept as Python, but accessing an individual character is performed using a syntax such as s.charAt(3), as opposed to s[3] in Python.

An important operator supported by a Java String is the + symbol, used to generate the concatenation of strings as in "over"+ "load". More so, if one of the operands is a string and the other is not, the nonstring is automatically converted to a string to perform the concatenation. For example, if variables rank and total are declared as integers, it is perfectly acceptable to use the following expression:

```
String standing = rank + "  of  " + total;
```

The integers are automatically converted to their string representation before the concate– nation. Recall that in Python, arbitrary objects were implicitly converted to strings when printed, but not when using concatenation. The above command would require explicit conversions in Python, as

```
standing = str(rank) + "  of  " + str(total);
```

Converting between types

In Python, we saw several examples in which implicit type conversion is performed. For example, when performing the addition 1.5 + 8, the second operand is coerced into a floating–point representation before the addition is performed. As noted above, the Python command **print** 8 implicitly converts the integer argument to a string before it is printed.

There are similar settings in which Java implicitly casts a value to another type, as we saw above when concatenating a string and a nonstring. Because of the static typing, additional implicit casting may take place when assigning a value of one type to a variable of another. Consider the following example:

---

4.   Java supports operators ==, <, and so on, but these have a very misleading interpretation in the context
      of strings. We will discuss this issue further in Section B.4.7.

```
int a;
double b;
a = 5;
b = a;           // sets b to 5.0
```

The final command causes b to get an internal floating-point representation of the value 5.0 rather than the integer representation. This is because variable b was explicitly designated as having type **double**. Java allows this type of implicit conversion because we are switch-ing from a "narrower" range (integral values) to a "wider" range (floating-point values); that is, integers have a natural floating-point representations. However, Java does not allow casting from a wider range to a narrow range. For example the following code generates a compile-time error:

```
int a;
double b;
b = 2.67;
a = b;           // compile-time error
```

In such cases, we can force a conversion by using an *explicit cast*. In Python, we performed explicit conversions using a syntax such as **int**(b) that truncates the fractional part. The truncation is similar in Java, but the syntax differs. The name of the desired type is itself placed within parentheses (rather than the value to be converted). Here is the legitimate conversion in Java.

```
int a;
double b;
b = 2.67;
a = (int) b;     // explicit type-cast
```

Even so, explicit casts are only allowed between what Java considers convertible types. For example, it will not allow you to convert a **boolean** to a **double**, or vice versa. It also will not allow you to convert the other primitive types to a string in this form. The syntax to convert a val of some other primitive type to a string is String.valueOf(val). Converting from a string to some other primitive type is done with another special syntax, for example, **int** age = Integer.parseInt(response).

B.4.2 Input and Output

The syntax for gathering input or display output is very different between the two lan-guages, although the same underlying abilities exist.

Console output

In Python, typical console output is generated with the **print** command. This command can be followed by any number of arguments, separated by commas. Each will be converted to a string and spaces are automatically inserted between arguments. A newline character is automatically generated, unless a trailing comma is present.

In Java, console output is generated using a special object named System.out. This object supports a println method to display a string followed automatically by a newline character, a print method to display a string (but without a trailing newline), and a printf method to display formatted strings. We begin by discussing print and println, which are identical other than the trailing newline character. Each of these functions accepts a *single* parameter. If that parameter is a string, it is printed. If it is any other data type, it is automatically converted to a string and printed. If you wish to display multiple values, those values must be concatenated into a single string, which serves as the parameter to println. To demonstrate several typical usage patterns, we provide the following side-by-side examples in Python and Java. In both cases, we assume that variables first and last have previously been defined as strings, and that count is an integer.

Python	**Java**

```
1  print "Hello"
2  print
3  print "Hello, ", first
4  print first, last       # automatic space
5  print count
6  print str(count) + "."    # no space
7  print "Wait...",  # space; no newline
8  print "Done"
```

```
1  System.out.println("Hello");
2  System.out.println( );
3  System.out.println("Hello,  " + first);
4  System.out.println(first + "  " + last);
5  System.out.println(count);
6  System.out.println(count + " . ");
7  System.out.print("Wait...  ");
8  System.out.println("done");
```

Formatted output

To conveniently generate formatted strings in Python, a string literal serves as a template with embedded placeholders (e.g., `%7.3f`) that designate the data type and format to be substituted. The actual values are provided within a trailing tuple. Our first example in Section 8.2 was the following:

```
print '%s: ranked %d of %d teams' % (team, rank, total)
```

In Java, similar template strings are used, but the arguments are provided as separate parameters to the printf function. This same example appears in Java as

```
System.out.printf("%s: ranked %d of %d teams\n", team, rank, total);
```

In the Java version, notice that we explicitly include a newline at the end of the string; otherwise, no newline would be printed (in our Python example, the newline is not technically part of the formatted string, but the **print** command inserts one for us). As a side note, we were able to use string formatting in Python not just for generating output, but also for creating other string instances. The same can be done in Java by using a format method of the String class, as follows:

```
String msg = String.format("%s: ranked %d of %d teams", team, rank, total);
```

File output

File output is handled very similarly to console output in Java, using a special PrintWriter object rather than System.out. You can open a new output file as,

```
PrintWriter result = new PrintWriter('sample.txt');
```

and then issue commands such as result.println("Hello"). The underlying file is saved when the PrintWriter object is closed using a syntax such as result.close( ).

Input

The most convenient way for reading input in Java is through use of the Scanner class. This class is not built into the core language, but can be imported with the command

```
import java.util.Scanner;
```

An instance of this class can be used to gather input from the standard console or an exist–ing file by using one of the following two styles:

```
Scanner console = new Scanner(System.in);          // read from standard console
Scanner datafile = new Scanner(new File("data.txt")); // read from given file
```

This class supports many useful behaviors for text processing, although we only demonstrate the most basic ones. The analog of Python's **raw_input** command is the nextLine method of the Scanner class. As an example, the Python command

```
name = raw_input('What is your name?)
```

might be equivalently expressed by the following pair of Java commands (assuming console is the scanner we previously opened):

```
System.out.print("What is your name? ");     // display the prompt
String name = console.nextLine( );
```

The returned string includes characters up to but not including the next newline character.

Java's Scanner offers additional functionality not directly supported by Python. It is able to process incoming data one "token" at a time; by default, tokens are delimited by whitespace. The most basic command is next( ), which returns a string representing the next token read from the source. For example, if we assume that a name has precisely two components, we could read those using the commands

```
String firstname = console.next( );
String lastname = console.next( );
```

This works even when the user enters both components on a single line, as in

```
What is your name? John Doe
```

In Python, we would have to read the entire line as a string `'John Doe'`, and then split it into the components after reading it.

The Java version is also different from Python as it continues waiting until finding a legitimate token (i.e., a nonwhitespace block). If the user were to enter a blank line, the Java code would continue waiting for a first name and subsequently a second name.

When trying to read nonstring data in Python, we had to read the string and then explicitly convert it, using a syntax such as age = **int**(**raw_input**(`'How old? '`)). In Java, nonstring primitive types can be read from the source using dedicated methods, such as console.nextInt( ) which interprets the next token as an integer value. As is the case with Python, an exception may be thrown if the characters entered do not match a legitimate literal for the indicated type. The ability to read several tokens from the same line makes certain tasks much easier in Java than in Python. For example, here is a code fragment that asks the user to enter two numbers on the same line and computes their sum.

```
Scanner console = new Scanner(System.in);
System.out.print("Enter two integers: ");
System.out.printf("Their sum is %d.\n", console.nextInt( ) + console.nextInt( ));
```

For the sake of comparison, a Python version is given as the solution to Practice 2.31.

We have noted that the delimiter used to separate tokens is any form of whitespace. That delimiter can be changed to any pattern that we want, somewhat akin to the difference between str.split( ) and str.split(delim) in Python. For example, if we want to process the input one line at a time, we can change the delimiter to a newline character, as console.useDelimiter(`"\\n"`); for the sake of brevity, we wish to ignore the reason for the double slash in this literal at this time.

B.4.3 Control Structures

We already saw an example of a **while** loop as part of our first example in Section B.3. The basic structure is similar, with only superficial differences in syntax. Most notably, parentheses are required around the boolean condition in Java. In that first example, curly braces were used to delimit the commands that comprise the body of the loop. Technically those braces are only needed when the body uses two or more distinct statements. In the absence of braces, the next single command is assumed to be the body.

Java also supports a **do-while** syntax that can be a convenient remedy to the "loop-and-a-half" problem, as see with while loops on page 165. Here is a similar Java code fragment for requesting a number between 1 and 10 until receiving such a number:

```
int number;
do {
  System.out.print("Enter a number from 1 to 10: ");
  number = console.nextInt( );    // assuming we already initialized console Scanner
} while (number < 1 || number > 10);
```

We should note that we have not properly caught the exception if a noninteger is entered.

Conditionals

A basic **if** statement is quite similar in style, again requiring parentheses around the boolean condition and curly braces around a compound body. As a simple example, here is a construct to change a negative number to its absolute value.

```
if (x < 0)
    x = −x;
```

Notice that we do not need braces for a body with one command.

Java does not use the keyword elif for nesting conditionals, but it is possible to nest a new **if** statement within the body of an **else** clause. Furthermore, a conditional construct is treated syntactically as a single command, so a typical pattern does not require excessive braces. Our first example of a nested conditional in Python was given on page 144 of Section 4.4.2. That code could be written in Java to mimic Python's indentation as follows (assuming groceries is an adequate container[5]):

```
if (groceries.length( ) > 15)
    System.out.println("Go to the grocery store");
else if (groceries.contains("milk"))
    System.out.println("Go to the convenience store");
```

For loops

Java supports two styles of a **for** loop. The first is borrowed from the syntax of C. Its original use was to provide a more legible form of the *index-based* loop pattern described in Section 4.1.1. An example of a loop used to count downward from 10 to 1 is as follows:

```
for (int count = 10; count > 0; count−−)
    System.out.println(count);
System.out.println("Blastoff!");
```

Within the parentheses of the for loop are three distinct components, each separated by a semicolon. The first is an *initialization* step that is performed once, before the loop begins. The second portion is a *loop condition* that is treated just as a loop condition for a while loop; the condition is tested before each iteration, with the loop continuing while true. Finally we give an *update* statement that is performed automatically at the very end of each completed iteration. In fact, the for loop syntax is just a convenient alternative to a while loop that better highlights the logic in some cases. The above example is essentially identical in behavior to the following version.

---

5.   We will discuss Java's containers in Section B.4.8.

```
int count = 10;                        // initialization step
while (count > 0) {                     // loop condition
  System.out.println(count);
  count--;                              // update statement
}
System.out.println("Blastoff!");
```

The for loop syntax is far more general. For example, it is possible to express *multiple* initialization or update steps in a for loop. This is done by using *commas* to separate the individual statements (as opposed to the semicolon that delimits the three different components of the syntax). For example, the sum of the values from 1 to 10 could be computed by maintaining two different variables as follows:

```
int count, total;
for (count = 1, total = 0; count <= 10; count++)
  total += count;
```

Foreach loops

The first style of **for** loop was the only one that Java supported for many years. As part of the Java 5 release in 2004, the language added support for use of a for loop to iterate through a container, akin to Python's standard for loop. Although we will not formally discuss Java's container types until Section B.4.8, we wish to demonstrate this basic syntax on a presumed container. Our first example of such a loop in Python was the following:

```
for person in guests:
  print person
```

In Java, the general syntax for such an iteration is **for** (*type identifier* : *container*) with a body that follows. Assuming that groceries is a container of strings (as it was in our original Python version), this loop would be written in Java as

```
for (String person : guests)
  System.out.println(person);
```

Note that the explicit type designation is required when establishing the loop variable. In Java, this loop variable is limited to having scope for the duration of the loop. Its final value cannot be accessed beyond the loop (as opposed to Python, where the loop variable has a wider scope).

B.4.4   Defining a Function

We already provided an example of a Java function in our initial demonstration from Section B.3. In this section we give a few other examples.

With that first example, we emphasized the need to explicitly designate the type of each individual parameter as well as the returned type. If the function does not provide a return value, there is a special keyword **void** that designates the lack of a type. Here is such a function that prints a countdown from 10 to 1.

```
void countdown( ) {
  for (int count = 10; count > 0; count−−)
    System.out.println(count);
}
```

To demonstrate the use of optional parameters in Python, Section 5.2.2 provided an alternate implementation of this function, appearing as follows:

```
def countdown(start=10, end=1):
  for count in range(start, end − 1, −1):
    print count
```

This allows the caller to invoke the function with one of three distinct forms: countdown( ), countdown(5), or countdown(4,2). Java does not technically support the declaration of default parameter values, but the same effect is accomplished in a different manner. Multi−ple definitions of a function can be declared, so long as their parameterizations vary either in the number of parameters or the respective types of those parameters. Because of static typing, the compiler can discern which form to use based upon the actual parameters des−ignated by the caller. This general technique is called *overloading* the signature.

Therefore, we can translate the above Python example to Java by providing three different declarations of a countdown function, respectively accepting two, one, or zero parameters. Of course, it would be silly to duplicate the internal code for the three, so we allow the second and third forms to rely upon a call to the first.

```
void countdown(int start, int end) {
  for (int count = start; count >= end; count−−)
    System.out.println(count);
}

void countdown(int start) {
  countdown(start, 1);  // invoke original with given default for end
}

void countdown( ) {
  countdown(10, 1);    // invoke original with both defaults
}
```

When the caller explicitly invokes countdown(4,2), the compiler matches that with the first of our three forms. When the caller invokes countdown(5), this matches the second of our functions and as a result, an internal call is made to countdown(5,1). An original call to countdown( ) invokes the third of our forms, but again falling back to an internal call to the first form based on our desired defaults.

B.4.5 Defining a Class

Classes are even more important in Java than in Python because every command and function must formally be defined as part of a class. There is no such notion of "top-level" code
as there is in Python. To demonstrate the syntax for a Java class, we rely upon several of
the examples that we first used in Chapter 6, beginning with the simple version of the Point
class as given in Figure 6.3 on page 206. The corresponding Java version of that class is
given in Figure B.4. There are several important aspects to discuss in comparing Java's
syntax to Python's. Please bear with us as we highlight the key differences.

Access control

The first notable distinction shows up with the first word **public**, on the first line. In fact
we see many other occurrences of the terms **public** and **private**. These designate what is
known as *access control* and are used to support the concept of *encapsulation*.

   With Python, we addressed this issue in Section 7.6, differentiating at the time
between what we considered "public" versus "private" aspects of a class design. Public

```
 1   public class Point {
 2     private double x;
 3     private double y;
 4
 5     public Point( ) {
 6       x = 0;
 7       y = 0;
 8     }
 9
10     public double getX( ) {
11       return x;
12     }
13
14     public void setX(double val) {
15       x = val;
16     }
17
18     public double getY( ) {
19       return y;
20     }
21
22     public void setY(double val) {
23       y = val;
24     }
25   } // end of Point class
```

FIGURE B.4: Implementation of a simple Point class.

aspects are those that we expect other programmers to rely upon, while private ones are considered to be internal implementation details that are subject to change. Yet Python does not strictly enforce this designation. Instead, we rely upon a naming conventions, using identifiers that start with an underscore (e.g., _x) to infer privacy.

In Java, we explicitly declare the desired access level for each individual member of a class (both data members and functions). In fact, we can even designate the access level for the class as a whole (sometimes we define utility classes that are not to be used by others). In this particular example, we define the Point class as a whole to be **public** at line 1, the two data members to be private at lines 2 and 3, and each of the subsequent functions to be **public**.

Explicit declaration of data members

The issue of static typing arises prominently in a class definition, as all data members must be explicitly declared. Recall that in Python, attributes of a class were simply introduced by assignment statements within the body of the constructor. In our Java example, we declare the data members at lines 2 and 3 and then initialize them at lines 6 and 7 within our constructor.

Alternatively, since each attribute is a **double**, we could have combined lines 2 and 3 into a single declaration of the form **private double** x, y. In fact, since the initial values are known in advance, we could have initialized them to 0 with the initial declaration, as **private double** x=0, y=0. In this case there would be no need to assign values from the constructor (in fact, for this particular example, no need for the constructor).

Constructor

In the previous discussion, we have already noted that the constructor is the function shown at lines 5–8. We wish to highlight two particular aspects of this syntax. First, the name of the constructor must be precisely the name of the class (i.e., Point). Secondly, you will notice that there is no designated return value in the signature (not even **void**). This too is a requirement for a valid constructor. If we mistakenly declare a return type in the signature at line 5, this defines a standard member function rather than a constructor, invoked on an existing instance as p.Point( ).

Implicit self-reference

A careful reader will have already noticed another major distinction between the class definition in Java and the same class in Python. The **self** reference does not appear as a formal parameter nor is it used when accessing members of the instance. Remember that we have explicitly declared x and y to be attributes of a point. Because of this, we can freely use those identifiers from within the body of our methods; the compiler will know what we mean.

For those who miss the **self** reference, it exists in Java as well, although it is named **this**. So we could use the syntax **this**.x rather than x, but there is no good motivation in this case. In other scenarios, there may be need for the self-reference, for example to pass our object as a parameter to an outside function.

A robust Point class

To present some additional lessons about a class definition, we provide a more robust implementation of a Point class, modeled upon the Python version from Figure 6.4 on page 213. Our Java version is shown in Figure B.5.

Our first lesson involves the constructor. In Python, we declared a constructor with signature **def** __init__(**self**, initialX=0, initialY=0). The use of optional parameters allows a caller to set initial coordinates for the point if desired, but to use <0,0> as a default. Since we cannot formally support default parameters values in Java, we use the technique demonstrated in Section B.4.4. We offer two distinct signatures, the first accepting two parameters (lines 5–8) and the other accepting zero (lines 10–12); for brevity, we omit the one-parameter version supported by our Python version.

Notice our use of reference **this** at line 11 when invoking the first form of the constructor from within the body of the second. We definitely do not want to reconstruct a second instance of a point; we simply want to invoke the other routine. Java uses **this** as a function in such a context, to apply an alternate constructor to the same instance.

As a minor issue, we note the use of the sqrt function at line 37. We qualify it as Math.sqrt because this function is technically supported by the Math class. That class is part of the core Java library so we do not need to explicitly import it, but we do need to use the qualified name in this case (in contrast, the Scanner class, which we imported in Section B.4.2, was from a portion of the Java library that is not automatically included).

```
1   public class Point {
2       private double x;
3       private double y;
4
5       public Point(double initialX, double initialY) {
6           x = initialX;
7           y = initialY;
8       }
9
10      public Point( ) {
11          this(0,0);      // invoke alternate version of constructor
12      }
13
14      public double getX( ) {
15          return x;
16      }
17
18      public void setX(double val) {
19          x = val;
20      }
```

FIGURE B.5: Implementation of a robust Point class (continued on next page).

```
21    public double getY( ) {
22       return y;
23    }
24
25    public void setY(double val) {
26       y = val;
27    }
28
29    public void scale(double factor) {
30       x *= factor;
31       y *= factor;
32    }
33
34    public double distance(Point other) {
35       double dx = x − other.x;
36       double dy = y − other.y;
37       return Math.sqrt(dx * dx + dy * dy);
38    }
39
40    public void normalize( ) {
41       double mag = distance(new Point( ));
42       if (mag > 0)
43          scale(1/mag);
44    }
45
46    public String toString( ) {
47       return "<" + x + ", " + y + ">";
48    }
49
50    public Point add(Point other) {
51       return new Point(x + other.x, y + other.y);
52    }
53
54    public Point multiply(double factor) {
55       return new Point(x * factor, y * factor);
56    }
57
58    public double multiply(Point other) {
59       return x * other.x + y * other.y;
60    }
61
62  } // end of Point class
```

FIGURE B.5 (continuation): Implementation of a robust Point class.

Our next lesson is to re-emphasize that we can access members of the class without explicitly using a self-reference. This was already made clear in our use of names like x rather than **this**.x. The same is true in calling member functions. So at line 43, we see a call to the scale method. This is implicitly invoked on the current instance, akin to **this**.scale(1/mag). Line 41 has a similar invocation of the distance method.

Line 41 brings up another discrepancy between Java and Python. The parameter sent to the distance function is a newly instantiated point (equivalent to <0,0> by default). What is significant here is that we must use the syntax **new** Point( ) to instantiate an object (as opposed to simply Point( ), which is the syntax used in Python). Similar instantiations take place at lines 51 and 55 when generating a new point as a return value. This syntax is used, not just within our own class definition, but whenever we instantiate an object from a class. If you look back at our use of Scanner in Section B.4.2, you will find similar treatment.

The toString method of lines 46–48 is the analog of __str__ in Python. The name has significance in Java as a method that produces a string representation for an instance. This method is relied upon for implicit conversion between an object and a string, for example when printing output. By default, all objects inherit a default version that produces a generic representation (akin to Python's default __str__). Providing toString is used to customize the display.

Java is somewhat different from Python in that is does not allow a programmer to overload operators. Although we may wish to support a syntax, such as p+q, for adding points, we cannot. Instead, user-defined classes typically offer a named method to provide such functionality. The choice of name is flexible, but there are some strong conventions for common usage. In our case, we provide an add method, allowing for a syntax p.add(q). Note that our behavior does *not* mutate the point p, but instead generates a new point that represents the sum of the original two.

Finally, our implementations of multiply demonstrate another use for overloading a method signature. We wish to support two distinct notions for multiplication: multiplying a given point by a numeric constant, and computing the dot product of two points. Our original Python implementation accomplished this with a single function definition that accepted one parameter. Internally it performed dynamic type checking of that parameter and determined the appropriate behavior depending on whether the second operand was a point or a number. In Java, we provide two different implementations. The first accepts a **double** and returns a new Point; the second accepts a Point and (coincidentally) returns a **double**. Since all data is explicitly typed, Java can determine which of the two forms to invoke at compile-time, based upon the actual parameters.

Class-level members (a.k.a., static members)

Moving on to another example, we reflect on the issue of *class-level* scope. We introduced this concept in Section 6.5.1, using an advanced version of our Television class as an example. We later discussed Python's maintenance of this scope in Section 12.6.5. As a brief review, there are times when we wish to support certain members that should be shared by all instances of a class, rather than replicated for each. Our first example was the introduction of a _minChannel attribute of the Television class. Syntactically, we qualified its class-level nature using the syntax Television._minChannel.

Java allows for class-level members (both data members and function) to be defined. Syntactically, this is done by inserting an additional keyword **static** in front of its declaration. If we were defining such a Television class in Java, it might begin as follows.

```
public class Television {
    private static int minChannel;   // class-level scope
    private static int maxChannel;   // class-level scope
    private int channel;             // instance-level scope
    ...
```

The same technique can be used to define static methods. These methods are not invoked directly upon a particular instance of the class, but rather using the class name to qualify it. We have already snuck in a few examples of this earlier in our guide. For example, the syntax String.valueOf(val) was introduced on page 576 as a way to generate a new string based upon some value of another type. This valueOf method is not being invoked on an existing string and it is not formally using the constructor syntax. It is being invoked with the class name qualifier. As another example, Math.sqrt is technically a static method supported by the Math class.

Unit testing and the main routine

A very good practice in software development is to embed a unit test along with each class definition (see Section 7.7). In Python, this was accomplished by placing the source code for a class in a dedicated module (i.e., file) and then using the construct

```
if __name__ == '__main__':
    # unit test here
```

When the Python interpreter is executed directly upon this file, this condition is satisfied and the unit test is performed. However, if the module were indirectly imported by some other program, the condition fails and so the unit test is bypassed.

In Java, a unit test can be embedded in a class by providing a *static* method named main. Formally, such a function should have the form

```
public static void main(String[ ] args) {
    // unit test here
}
```

This method behaves somewhat like the __main__ conditional in Python; it is executed when the user invokes the Java interpreter upon this particular class, but not when this class is used as part of a larger program. As a side note, the parameter in this signature is used to transfer what are known as ***command-line arguments*** specified to the interpreter. We will ignore this issue for simplicity (we similarly ignored it in Python, although command-line arguments can be accessed through the list sys.argv).

Embedding documentation

Another very good software practice is to provide formal documentation on the use of your classes and functions. In Python, these could be embedded directly in the source code as **docstrings**, which are then displayed through the help command within the interpreter or through web pages generated by the `pydoc` utility (see Section 7.5). Although the syntax differs, the same general principle is supported in Java through the use of **doc comments** within the source code. That documentation can then be parsed using the `javadoc` utility, which generates web pages having a standard look and feel.

As a brief example, the Pattern.compareTo method was documented in Python as part of the Mastermind project on page 247. The corresponding Java documentation for that method might appear as

```
/**
 * Compare the current pattern to otherPattern and calculate the score.
 *
 * @param  otherPattern   the pattern to be compared to the current one
 * @return               a {@link Score} instance representing the result
 */
public Score compareTo(Pattern otherPattern) {
```

The doc comment immediately precedes the declaration of a method or class. From the compiler's point of view, it is a standard comment, delimited by /* and */. However, because it begins with an extra asterisk, as /**, this is treated as official documentation by the `javadoc` tool. Within the documentation comment, the @ character denotes components that will be formatted differently or hyperlinked to other parts of the documentation.

B.4.6　Managing a Complete Program

We have thus far discussed many aspects of the Java language, but we have not actually shown a complete self-contained program that can be compiled and run. In this section, our interest is in providing an overview of the process of managing such software. Our supplemental website provides complete translations of the text-based Mastermind program from Chapter 7 as well as the frequency-counting case study from Section 8.5.3 based on the design of the TallySheet class.

Java rigidly requires that all code be written in the context of a class. The top-level flow of control of a program must be expressed as a static method main of a chosen class. Although we described the main routine as a means for providing a unit test, in the larger project one particular class can be elevated so that its main routine serves as the final product. For example if we look back at our Python implementation of the Mastermind project, many classes (e.g., Score, Pattern) used a "main" construct to provide a unit test. Yet the main code of the Mastermind class served as the driver for the complete software.

We use a similar model for the Java version of our game. Each public class in Java must be defined in a separate file and the name of that file must be precisely the class name (including capitalization) followed by the `.java` suffix. For example, we define our Score class in the file `Score.java`, our Pattern class in the file `Pattern.java` and our Mastermind class in the file `Mastermind.java`.

As described in Section B.2.2, Java is both a compiled and interpreted language. The original source code is compiled into an intermediate form known as ***bytecode***. That bytecode is then executed by feeding it to a separate piece of software known as the Java interpreter. If using the standard Java Development Kit,[6] the source code from an individual file can be compiled using a command such as

```
javac Pattern.java
```

This compiles the code producing a file `Pattern.class` that is the intermediate byte-code for that class. When the compiler is invoked on the project's primary class, for example as `javac Mastermind.java`, this not only compiles the indicated class but also all classes on which it depends. Once the code has been successfully compiled, the main function for a class is executed using the Java interpreter, with a command such as

```
java Mastermind
```

Notice that the interpreter command is `java` rather than `javac`, and that the indicated class name is given, yet without any suffix. This same syntax is used to execute a unit test for one particular class, as in `java Pattern`.

Finally, we wish to note that it is permissible to write a program as a main routine for a "class" that has no real methods or attributes. As an example, if we look at our Python development of the programs for computing frequency counts, we developed a TallySheet class but we did not provide the front-end program as part of that class. In fact we developed two separate applications `CountLetters.py` and `CountScores.py` that were meant for the end user. Those files do not use the typical **if __name__ == '__main__'** construct because we do not intend for those files to be imported as part of other projects. They use top-level code controlling the overall software. In translating that project to Java, we design the TallySheet class in its own `TallySheet.java` file and we provide two additional files `CountLetters.java` and `CountScores.java`. Formally, the `CountLetters.java` file defines a public class CountLetters that has a static main routine and nothing else. We do not expect anyone to instantiate a CountLetters object, we simply must use the class definition to be consistent with Java's requirements.

B.4.7   Assignments and the Object Model

Python presents a consistent model in which all identifiers are inherently references to underlying objects. Use of the assignment operator as in a = b causes identifier a to be reassigned to the same underlying object referenced by identifier b. These semantics are consistently applied to all types of objects.

This situation in Java is a bit more complex as it relies upon two distinct models for the semantics of a variable. For the majority of types, including all user-defined classes, Java relies upon what are known as ***reference variables***. They serve an identical purpose

---

6.   The Java Development Kit (JDK) is a set of standard tools distributed by Sun Microsystems, for compiling and running Java programs. However, many developers use Integrated Development Environments (IDEs) for Java to provide a graphical interface to the creation and management of source code, much as IDLE is used for Python. When using an IDE, compilation and execution is usually triggered through the use of buttons or menu selections.

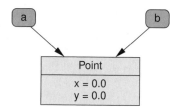

FIGURE B.6: Two reference variables a and b, pointing to the same underlying point.

to Python's identifiers. They are entities that can be mapped to an underlying value, with that association determined at *run-time*. A declaration of such a variable in Java establishes the name as a reference, but it does not cause the creation of a new underlying object. Thus,

```
Point a;
```

creates a new reference variable a, but does *not* instantiate any underlying Point. By default, such a reference variable is set to the special value **null** designating the lack of a referenced object (the analog of Python's **None** value). The instantiation of a point is indicated by invoking the constructor with the syntax **new** Point( ). A reference variable can be assigned to that newly created point with an assignment statement, as in

```
a = new Point( );
```

However, a reference variable can also be assigned to an existing instance, perhaps one returned by some other function or one that is currently identified with another variable. Aliasing, as shown in Figure B.6, occurs with the following continuation:

```
Point b;
b = a;        // two variables referencing the same underlying point
```

Other than the use of the keyword **new** for instantiation, use of Java's reference variables should seem very familiar to Python programmers.

What makes Java quite different is its treatment of the primitive data types, namely **boolean, byte, short, int, long, float, double**, and **char**.[7] These types are managed using what are known as *value variables*. A declaration such as

```
int count;
```

causes the compiler to reserve memory for storing an actual integer value (0 by default), rather than a reference to an integer. It is a subtle distinction, but an important one. The name count is associated to an underlying memory location at *compile-time* (in contrast to the run-time mapping of a reference variable). For this reason, we prefer to diagram a value variable as shown in Figure B.7, without any independent concept of a reference.

---

7.   We note that String is not a true primitive in Java. Strings are objects managed with reference vari-
       ables; they are simply objects from a class that is part of the standard library.

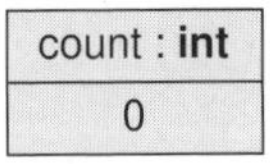

FIGURE B.7: The representation of a value variable.

Java implements primitive types using the value model, rather than the reference model, for the sake of efficiency. The memory allocation is possible because each primitive type uses a fixed number of bits in its representation; with more general objects, the number of bits of the internal representation may change over time as the state is manipulated. The reference model has the disadvantage that it requires more effort at run-time to trace the reference to the underlying object. Also, the reference model requires the use of memory for both the reference and the underlying value.

If all of these issues were simply internal implementation details for the creators of Java, we would not spend so much effort highlighting the distinction. However, the difference between value variables and reference variables impacts our life as a Java pro–grammer. Most significantly, the semantics of an assignment is different when using value variables rather than reference variables. As an example, let's add one additional variable to our earlier setting, declaring and initializing a second integer variable as follows:

```
int age = 38;
```

This leads us to the scenario diagrammed in Figure B.8. count is a name associated with the integer value shown on the left, while age is a name associated with the integer value shown on the right. Consider the following assignment statement:

```
count = age;
```

This is a *value* assignment. As a result, the value of the integer count is mutated to match the value of the integer age. An updated representation is given in Figure B.9. At this point, both integers have the value 38, yet these are still two separate integers. The identifiers count and age are not aliases for the same value, and a subsequent change to the value of age has no effect on the value of count.

FIGURE B.8: The declaration of a second variable, initialized to 38.

FIGURE B.9: The effect of assignment count = age on our representation.

The distinction between the assignment semantics for value variables versus refer–ence variables carries over to the way information is passed to and from a function. For Python, we described parameter passing in Section 10.3.1. Identifiers serving as formal parameters within the function signature are automatically assigned to the actual param–eters indicated by the caller. We gave an example of a Python function with signature verifyBalance(account, threshold), for which the first parameter was assumed to be an Account instance and the second a floating–point value. Figure 10.15 on page 349 showed the scenario that results when making the call verifyBalance(mySavings, claimedAssets), effectively based upon the implicit assignments:

```
account = mySavings
threshold = claimedAssets
```

In Java, that same function would be implemented as follows:

```
boolean verifyBalance(Account account, float threshold) {
   boolean meetsThreshold = account.getBalance( ) >= threshold;
   return meetsThreshold;
}
```

Parameter passing is again based on the implicit assignment of formal parameters to actual parameters, as in

```
Account account = mySavings;
float threshold = claimedAssets;
```

However, this leads to a very different internal representation in Java. The assignment of account to mySavings creates an alias, just as in Python. This style is commonly termed *passing by reference*. The declaration and assignment of the formal parameter threshold establishes a new value variable that is assigned the same value as the actual parameter. This style is commonly termed *passing by value*. Figure B.10 portrays this situation. A significant consequence of the parameter passing style is the following. The function has the ability to mutate the caller's object when passed by reference. The function does not have any way to change the caller's object when passed by value. In this example, changes made to threshold from within the function affect the copied value, not the caller's original.

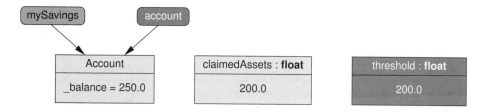

FIGURE B.10: Parameter passing in Java, where account is a reference parameter and threshold is a value parameter.

B.4.8 Container Classes

Python provides several valuable built-in classes for managing collections of objects. Most notable are the **list** class for managing an ordered sequence, the **dict** class for managing an associative mapping, and the **set** class for managing an unordered collection of unique values. Java offers support for similar concepts through a series of definition known as the Java Collections Framework. These definitions are not built into the core language but can be imported from the java.util library. Figure B.11 provides a summary of the most commonly used classes from this framework.

We start by discussing the ArrayList class, which is the closest analog to Python's **list** class. The most important distinction regarding their usage relates to the issue of static versus dynamic typing. Python's lists are naturally homogeneous in that we can insert whatever type of objects that we wish, even inserting a mix of different types into the same list. As we describe in Section 10.2, a list's internal state is maintained as a sequence of references to other objects. It makes no difference what kind of objects those are.

Java's ArrayList uses the same internal mechanism, storing a sequence of references to other objects. However, because of static typing, the method signatures for that class must be explicit. That is, a method to add a new element into the list must have a well-defined parameter type. Similarly, methods that return an underlying object to the caller must have a declared return type. For example, if we wanted to maintain a grocery list as a sequence of strings, we could imagine a class that provides a method with signature **void** add(String element), or a method with signature String get(**int** index). But if we had a Photo class and wanted to maintain a list of photographs, we would want a class with signatures such as **void** add(Photo element) and Photo get(**int** index). Rather than having many different list classes to support various element types, recent versions of Java rely upon a technique termed *generic programming*.

The declaration or instantiation of an ArrayList requires the explicit specification of a class of objects that can be inserted into the list. This means that a particular list is homogeneous, yet the class can support a list for any chosen type. For example, if we wished to maintain a grocery list as a list of strings, we might write code as follows:

```
ArrayList<String> groceries = new ArrayList<String>( );
```

Because of the designation of the String class, the signature for add will accept a String

Java Type	Description	Python analog
ArrayList	ordered sequence	**list**
HashMap	associative mapping	**dict**
HashSet	set of unique elements	**set**
TreeMap	*sorted* associative mapping	
TreeSet	*sorted* set of unique elements	

FIGURE B.11: Commonly used classes from Java's collection framework.

parameter, just as get will return a String. This allows for the compiler to perform static checking of our code. We might continue as

```
groceries.add("bread");
groceries.add("milk");
groceries.add("cheese");
String mostRecent = groceries.get(2);      // will be "cheese"
```

There is one additional complexity when trying to use an ArrayList to maintain a collection of primitive types. The designation of the element type must be a reference type; you can‑not declare an ArrayList<**int**>. Instead, Java supports what is known as a *wrapper* class for each primitive type. For example, there is a built‑in class Integer that serves to reference an underlying integer value. These wrapper classes allow for the use of primitive types in a manner more consistent with the reference types (as is done by Python). So if we want to maintain a list of integers, our code might look like

```
ArrayList<Integer> lottoPicks = new ArrayList<Integer>( );
lottoPicks.add(15);
lottoPicks.add(16);
lottoPicks.add(17);
lottoPicks.add(43);
int mistake = lottoPicks.remove(1);
System.out.println(lottoPicks);            // prints [15, 17, 43]
```

For the sake of brevity, we refer the reader to formal documentation for a com‑plete menu of an ArrayList's behaviors, as well as those for other common collections; rest assured that most of Python's behaviors are supported in one form or another. The HashMap provides the equivalent concept of a dictionary using an internal implementa‑tion akin to the hash table we presented in Section 13.3.2. The key type and value type must be designated for such a mapping, using a syntax like HashMap<Movie,Director>, presuming that we have Movie and Director classes. As with Python, the key type must be hashable. Java's HashSet is implemented essentially the same as Python's set class. Java offers two additional classes, TreeMap and TreeSet, that provide similar functionality to the hash‑based classes, but instead use a binary search tree for internal organization, thereby preserving elements in their natural order (as we did with our SortedSet class of Section 13.4).

B.4.9   Inheritance

In Chapter 9, we provided several examples of the use of inheritance in Python. We will show two of those examples, translated to Java. First we define a DeluxeTV class modeled closely after the version in Figure 9.2 that used a SortedSet. Although we omit the pre‑sumed definition for a basic Television class, our complete code for the DeluxeTV class is given in Figure B.12. The use of inheritance is originally indicated at line 3 by use of the keyword **extends** followed by the name of a parent class, in this case Television. With that designation, our new DeluxeTV class immediately inherits all attributes (e.g., powerOn,

```
1   import java.util.*;
2
3   public class DeluxeTV extends Television {
4     protected TreeSet<Integer> favorites;
5
6     public DeluxeTV( ) {
7       super( );                              // calls parent constructor
8       favorites = new TreeSet<Integer>( );
9     }
10
11    public void addToFavorites( ) { if (powerOn) favorites.add(channel); }
12
13    public void removeFromFavorites( ) { if (powerOn) favorites.remove(channel); }
14
15    public int jumpToFavorite( ) {
16      if (powerOn && favorites.size( ) > 0) {
17        int result;
18        // compute the subset of strictly greater channels
19        SortedSet<Integer> greaterChoices = favorites.tailSet(channel+1);
20        if (greaterChoices.size( ) > 0)
21          result = greaterChoices.first( );
22        else
23          result = favorites.first( );       // wrap around to smallest channel
24        setChannel(result);
25      }
26      return channel;
27    }
28  } // end of DeluxeTV
```

FIGURE B.12: Implementing a DeluxeTV class through inheritance.

channel) and all methods (e.g., setChannel) from the parent. What remains is for us to define additional attributes or to provide new or updated implementations for methods that we want supported.

At line 4, we declare a new attribute to manage the set of favorite channel numbers. Although we used our custom SortedSet class in our Python version, this is an excellent opportunity to make use of Java's TreeSet container introduced in the previous section. We wish to draw particular attention to the use of the word **protected** in the declaration of that attribute. Until now, we have used two forms of access control: **public** and **private**. Members that are public can be accessed by code outside of the class definition, while members that are private can only be accessed from within the original class definition. The purpose of privacy is to encapsulate internal implementation details that should not be relied upon by others. Yet with the use of inheritance, there is need for a third level of access. When designing a class that inherits from another, the question arises as to whether code for that new class should be able to directly access members inherited from the parent. This is determined by the original access control designated for those members. A child class cannot access any members from the parent that are declared as **private**. However, the child is granted access to members designated as **protected** by the parent.

In this particular setting, the important point is not actually our use of **protected** at line 4. What matters to us is how the original attributes of the Television class were defined. For our DeluxeTV code to work, the television attributes must be declared originally as

```
protected boolean powerOn;
protected int channel;
...
```

If those had been declared as **private**, we would not have the necessary access to implement our DeluxeTV. Of course, the original designer of the television may not have known that we would come along and want to inherit from it. However, an experienced Java program will consider this possibility when designing a class. In our DeluxeTV definition, the declaration of attribute favorites as **protected** at line 4 is not for our own benefit, but to leave open the possibility that someone else may one day want to design a SuperDeluxeTV that improves upon our model.

The second aspect of our example we wish to discuss is the definition of our constructor, at lines 6–9. In our Python version, the new constructor begins with an explicit call to the parent constructor, using the syntax, Television.__init__(**self**). That was used to establish the default settings for all of the inherited attributes; then we take care of initializing the new favorites attribute. In Java, the syntax for invoking a parent constructor is through use of the syntax **super**( ) at line 7. This calls the parent constructor without sending any explicit parameters. To be honest, in this particular example, line 7 is superfluous. If the first line of our constructor body does not explicitly call the parent constructor, Java will do it implicitly. However, explicit use of **super** is necessary when parameters are to be sent to the parent constructor (as in our second example).

The rest of our DeluxeTV code is used to provide three new behaviors. With use of the TreeSet, the technique is rather simple. The most complicated portion is achieving the wrap-around behavior in jumpToFavorite. Even that could be greatly simplified if we allowed ourselves to use a new method named higher, introduced in the release of Java 6. What we wish to highlight is our ability to access the underlying attributes powerOn and channel, which were inherited from the parent class.

A Square class

As a second example of inheritance, Figure B.13 provides a Java rendition of our original Square class from Section 9.4.2. The Square inherits from a presumed Rectangle class. At line 3 we use the **super** syntax to call the parent constructor with the appropriate dimensions and center. Had we not done this explicitly, an implicit call would have been made to the *default* version of the rectangle constructor, leading to incorrect semantics for our square. As a side note, we admit that our Square implementation does not itself provide a default version of the constructor, although this could easily be accomplished as we did for our robust point class in Figure B.5.

```
1   public class Square extends Rectangle {
2     public Square(double size, Point center) {
3       super(size, size, center);                    // The Rectangle constructor
4     }
5
6     public void setWidth(double w) { setSize(w); }   // override inherited setWidth
7     public void setHeight(double h) { setSize(h); }  // override inherited setHeight
8
9     public void setSize(double size) {
10      super.setWidth(size);                          // make sure to invoke PARENT version
11      super.setHeight(size);                         // make sure to invoke PARENT version
12    }
13
14    public double getSize( ) { return getWidth( ); }  // inherited getWidth suffices
```

FIGURE B.13: Implementing a Square class based upon a Rectangle.

The remainder of the definition is meant to provide new getSize and setSize meth−ods, while also overriding the existing setWidth and setHeight methods so that a change to either dimension affects both. We use the same approach as our Python version. We override the existing methods at lines 6 and 7, changing their behaviors to call our new setSize method. Our setSize method then relies upon the *parent* versions of the over−ridden setWidth and setHeight methods to enact the individual changes to those values. Notice at lines 10 and 11 that we again rely on use of the keyword **super** to invoke a call using the parent version of a behavior rather than the new version.

Polymorphism and Java's interfaces

Java does not allow for multiple inheritance, but it does provide language support for a somewhat related topic known as an **interface**, used to support a form of polymorphism. We again base our explanation on the issue of dynamic versus static typing. In Python, there are many examples of classes that are not technically dependent upon each other but that intentionally support similar method signatures. For example, many containers define an underlying __contains__ method to support a syntax, item **in** data, that checks whether a particular item exists in the container. If we have a reference to an object that we believe to be such a container, we can simply use this syntax and all goes well. The check for the necessary method is performed at run−time.

In Java, the legitimacy of all such calls is verified at compile−time. To allow for a more generic view of multiple classes that support a common set of behaviors, Java uses a notion of an **interface**. The definition of an interface is somewhat like that of a class, except that an interface does not provide any data members nor implementations for any methods. It only formalizes the *method signatures* that are to be supported by classes that respect the interface. For example, the official Container interface in Java includes a definition for methods add, remove, size, and contains, among others. There is also a SortedSet interface that designates additional methods such as first( ) and last( ). In some respects, an interface serves as a contract that is to be respected. A true class can then designate that it **implements** one or more interfaces.

We relied subtly on this mechanism as part of our implementation of DeluxeTV in Figure B.12. At line 19 of that code we made a call to a method tailSet upon our TreeSet instance named favorites. That method returns in a sense an ordered subset of elements that have values at least as great as the designated value. That method provides a secondary container as a return value, although not necessarily a TreeSet. However, it guarantees that whatever gets returned will satisfy the requirements of the SortedSet interface. So our declared variable greaterChoices is designated to be a reference to some form of a SortedSet. This serves as a guarantee that the first method will be supported, thereby satisfying the compile–time checking at line 21.

B.4.10   Conclusions

There is certainly much more to learn about Java (and much more to learn about Python, for that matter). All of our advanced techniques from Python carry over in some form to programming in Java (e.g., exception handling, recursion, graphics, event–driven program–ming, network programming). But our goal for this transition guide was to provide you with the initial bridge to transfer your knowledge and experience in Python to learning a new language. So it is time that we say goodbye.

We offer a more complete transition guide from Python to Java on the supplemental website, for this book. That version expands upon this appendix, offering further examples of Python concepts and source code translated to Java. If that is not enough, hundreds of books, tutorials, websites, and other references are available offering further lessons about programming in Java.

B.5   C++ Guide

In comparison to other object–oriented languages, the greatest strength of C++ is its poten–tial for creating fast executables. This efficiency stems from a variety of factors. C and C++ provide great flexibility in controlling many of the underlying mechanism used by an executing program. A programmer can control low–level aspects of how data is stored, how information is passed and how memory is managed. When used wisely, this control can lead to a more streamlined result. Furthermore, because of the long history of C and C++ and their widespread use, the compiler technology has been highly optimized.

The greatest weakness of C++ is its complexity. Ironically, this weakness goes hand–in–hand with the very issues that we described as strengths of the language. As a language with decades of prominence, its evolution has been somewhat restricted by the desire to remain backward compatible in support of the large body of existing software. Some addi–tional features have been retrofitted in a more awkward way than if the language had been developed with a clean slate. As a result, parts of the syntax have grown cryptic. More significantly, the flexibility given to a programmer for controlling low–level aspects comes with responsibility. Rather than one way to express something, there may be five alter–natives. An experienced and knowledgeable developer can use this flexibility to pick the best alternative and improve the result. Yet both novice and experienced programmers can easily choose the wrong alternative, leading to less–efficient, and possibly flawed, software.

B.5.1   Data Types and Operators

Figure B.14 provides a summary of primitive data types in C++, noting the correspondence to Python's types. The **bool** type is supported by both languages, although the literals **true** and **false** are uncapitalized in C++ while capitalized in Python. C++ gives the program-mer more fine-grained control in suggesting the underlying precision of integers, support-ing three different fixed-precision integer types (**short**, **int**, and **long**). The precision of Python's **int** class is akin to C++'s **long**. Python's **long** type serves a completely different purpose, representing integers with unlimited magnitude. There is no such standard type in C++ (although some similar packages are independently available). C++ supports two different floating-point types (**float** and **double**) with a choice of underlying precisions. The **double** type in C++ is the more commonly used, and akin to what is named **float** in Python.

C++ also supports two different types for representing text. A **char** type provides a streamlined representation of a single character of text, while the **string** class serves a purpose similar to Python's **str** class, representing a sequence of characters (which may happen to be an empty string or a single-character string). To distinguish between a **char** and a one-character string, a **string** literal, must be designated using double quote marks (as in `"a"`). The use of single quotes is reserved for a **char** literal (as in `'a'`). An attempt to misuse the single-quote syntax, as in `'impossible'`, results in a compile-time error.

In contrast with Python's immutable **str** class, A C++ **string** is *mutable*. A summary of the most commonly used string operations is given in Figure B.15. Notice that the expression s[index] can be used to access a particular character, as well as to change that character to something else, when used on the left-hand side of an assignment. Also, the syntax s+t is used to generate a third string that is a concatenation of the others, while syntax s.append(t) mutates instance s.

C++ Type	Description	Literals	Python analog
bool	logical value	**true** **false**	**bool**
short	integer (often 16 bits)		
int	integer (often 32 bits)	38	
long	integer (often 32 or 64 bits)	38L	**int**
			long
float	floating-point (often 32 bits)	3.14f	
double	floating-point (often 64 bits)	3.14	**float**
char	single character	'a'	
string[a]	character sequence	"Hello"	**str**

FIGURE B.14: Most common primitive data types in C++.

[a]Not technically a built-in type; included from within standard libraries.

Non-mutating Behaviors	
s.size( ) or s.length( )	Either form returns the number of characters in string s.
s.empty( )	Returns **true** if s is an empty string, **false** otherwise.
s[index]	Returns the character of string s at the given index (unpredictable when index is out of range).
s.at(index)	Returns the character of string s at the given index (throws exception when index is out of range).
s == t	Returns **true** if strings s and t have same contents, **false** otherwise.
s < t	Returns **true** if s is lexicographical less than t, **false** otherwise.
s.compare(t)	Returns a negative value if string s is lexicographical less than string t, zero if equal, and a positive value if s is greater than t.
s.find(pattern, start)	Returns the least index, greater than or equal to start, at which pattern begins; returns **string**::npos when not found.
s.rfind(pattern, start)	Returns the greatest index, less than or equal to indicated start, at which pattern begins; returns **string**::npos when not found.
s.find_first_of(charset, start)	Returns the least index, greater than or equal to indicated start, at which a character of the indicated string charset is found; returns **string**::npos when not found.
s.find_last_of(charset, start)	Returns the greatest index, less than or equal to indicated start, at which a character of the indicated string charset is found; returns **string**::npos when not found.
s + t	Returns a concatenation of strings s and t.
s.substr(start)	Returns the substring from index start through the end.
s.substr(start, num)	Returns the substring from index start, continuing num characters.

Mutating Behaviors	
s[index] = newChar	Mutates string s by changing the character at the given index to the new character (unpredictable when index is out of range).
s.append(t)	Mutates string s by appending the characters of string t.
s.insert(index, t)	Inserts copy of string t into string s at the given index.
s.insert(index, t, num)	Inserts num copies of t into string at the given index.
s.erase(start)	Removes all characters from start index to the end.
s.erase(start, num)	Removes num characters, starting at given index.
s.replace(index, num, t)	Replace num characters of current string, starting at given index, with the first num characters of t.

FIGURE B.15: Selected behaviors supported by the **string** class in C++.

Type declarations

The basic form of a type declaration was demonstrated in our first glance of Section B.3:

4
```
int r;
```

It is also possible to combine a variable declaration with an initial assignment statement, as in **int** age=38. However, the preferred syntax for initialization in C++ is the following:

```
int age(38);
```

Furthermore, we can declare multiple variables of the same type in a single statement (with or without initial values), as in

```
int age(38), zipcode(63103);     // two new variables
```

Immutability

Python often makes a distinction between mutable and immutable types (e.g., **list** vs. **tuple**). C++ takes a different approach. Types are generally mutable, yet a program—mer can designate an individual instance as immutable. This is done by use of the **const** keyword as part of the declaration, as in

```
const int age(38);   // immortality
```

This immutability is strictly enforced by the compiler, so any subsequent attempt to change that value, as with age++, results in a compile–time error.

Operators

With a few notable discrepancies, the two languages support a very similar set of operators for the primitive types. The same basic logical operators are supported, yet C++ uses the following symbols (borrowed from the syntax of C):

&& for logical **and**
|| for logical **or**
! for logical **not**

For numeric values, Python differentiates between *true division* (i.e., /), *integer division* (i.e., //), and *modular arithmetic* (i.e., %), as originally discussed in Section 2.4. C++ supports operators / and %, but not // (in fact we already saw this pattern used to desig–nate inline comments in C++). The semantics of the / operator depends upon the type of operands. When both operands are integral types, the result is the integer quotient; if one or both of the operands are floating–point types, true division is performed. To get true division with integral types, one of the operands must be explicitly cast to a float (a discussion of type conversion begins on the following page).

As is the case for Python, C++ supports an operator–with–assignment shorthand for most binary operators, as with x += 5 as a shorthand for x = x + 5. Furthermore, C++

supports a ++ operator for the common task of incrementing a number by one. In fact, there are two distinct usages known as ***pre-increment*** (e.g., ++x) and ***post-increment*** (e.g., x++). Both of these add one to the value of x, but they can be used differently in the context of a larger expression. For example, if indexing a sequence, the expression groceries[i++] retrieves the entry based upon the original index i, yet subsequently increments that index. In contrast, the syntax groceries[++i] causes the value of the index to be incremented *before* accessing the associated entry of the sequence. A −− operator is similarly supported in pre-decrement and post-decrement form. This combination of operators can be valuable for an experience programmer, but their use also leads to very subtle code and sometimes mistakes. We recommend that they be used sparingly until mastered.

Converting between types

In Python, we saw several examples in which implicit type conversion is performed. For example, when performing the addition 1.5 + 8, the second operand is coerced into a floating-point representation before the addition is performed.

There are similar settings in which C++ implicitly casts a value to another type. Because of the static typing, additional implicit casting may take place when assigning a value of one type to a variable of another. Consider the following example:

```
int a(5);
double b;
b = a;          // sets b to 5.0
```

The final command causes b to get an internal floating-point representation of the value 5.0 rather than the integer representation. This is because variable b was explicitly designated as having type **double**. We can also assign a **double** value to an **int** variable, but such an implicit cast may cause the lost of information. For example, saving a floating-point value into an integer variable causes any fractional portion to be truncated.

```
int a;
double b(2.67);
a = b;          // sets a to 2
```

There are many scenarios in which C++ implicitly converts between types that would not normally be considered compatible. Some compilers will issue a warning to draw attention to such cases, but there is no guarantee.

On a related note, there are times when we want to force a type conversion that would not otherwise be performed, we can indicate an ***explicit cast***. This is done using a syntax similar to Python, where the name of the target type is used as if a function.

```
int a(4), b(3);
double c;
c = a/b;            // sets c to 1.0
c = double(a)/b;    // sets c to 1.33
```

The first assignment to b results in 1.0 because the coercion to a **double** is not performed until after the integer division a/b is performed. In the second example, the explicit conversion of a's value to a **double** causes a true division to be performed (with b implicitly coerced). However, we cannot use such casting to perform all such conversions. For example, we *cannot* safely mimic Python's approach for converting a number to a string, as with **str**(17), or to convert a string to the corresponding number, as with **int**('17'). Unfortunately conversions back and forth between strings require more advanced techniques, related to the handling of input and output, which we next discuss.

B.5.2   Input and Output

Input and output can be associated with a variety of sources within a computer program. For example, input can come from the user's keyboard, can be read from a file, or transmitted through a network. In similar regard, output can be displayed on the user's screen, or written to a file, or transmitted through a network. To unify the treatment of input and output, C++ relies on a framework of classes to support an abstraction known as a "stream." We can insert data into a stream to send it elsewhere, or extract data from an existing stream. A stream that provides us with input is represented using the istream class, and a stream which we use to send output elsewhere is represented using the ostream class. Some streams (iostream) can serve as both input and output. Then there are more specific classes devoted to certain purposes (e.g., a file is managed with an fstream).

Necessary libraries

Technically, the definitions that we need are not automatically available in C++. Most are defined in a standard library named iostream (short for "input/output streams"). A C++ library serves a similar purpose to a Python module. We must formally include the definitions from the library before using them.

```
#include <iostream>
using namespace std;
```

Technically, the first of these statements imports the library, while the second brings those definitions into our default namespace. In addition to the basic class definitions, that library defines two special instances for handling input to and from the standard console. **cout** (short for "console output") is an object used to print messages to the user, and **cin** (short for "console input") is used to get input typed by the user.

Console output

In C++ we generate console output through the **cout** stream from the iostream library. Streams support the operator << to insert data into the stream, as in **cout** << "Hello". The << symbol was chosen to subliminally suggest the flow of data, as we send the characters of "Hello" into the stream. As is the case with print in Python, C++ will attempt to create a text representation for any nonstring data inserted into the output stream. Multiple items can be inserted into the stream in a single command by repeated use of the operator, as in **cout** << "Hello"<< " and "<< "Goodbye". Notice that we explicitly insert

spaces when desired, in contrast to use of Python's print command. We must also explicitly output a newline character when desired. Although we can directly embed the escape
character, \n, within a string, C++ offers the more portable definition of a special object
endl that represents a newline character.

To demonstrate several typical usage patterns, we provide the following side-by-side
examples in Python and C++. In both cases, we assume that variables first and last have
previously been defined as strings, and that count is an integer.

	Python		**C++**
1	**print** "Hello"	1	**cout** << "Hello" << **endl**;
2	**print**	2	**cout** << **endl**;
3	**print** "Hello, ", first	3	**cout** << "Hello, " << first << **endl**;
4	**print** first, last # automatic space	4	**cout** << first << " " << last << **endl**;
5	**print** count	5	**cout** << count << **endl**;
6	**print str**(count) + " . " # no space	6	**cout** << count << " . " << **endl**;
7	**print** "Wait...", # space; no newline	7	**cout** << "Wait... "; // no newline
8	**print** "Done"	8	**cout** << "Done" << **endl**;

Formatted output

In Python, we use string formatting to more conveniently generate certain output, as in the
following example:

print '%s: ranked %d of %d teams' % (team, rank, total)

The use of the % sign for this purpose is designed to mimic a long-standing routine named
printf, which has been part of the C programming language. Since C++ is a direct descen-
dant of C, that function is available through a library, but it is not usually the recommended
approach for C++ (printf does not work consistently with the C++ **string** class). Instead,
formatted output is generated directly through the output stream. Since data types are automatically converted to strings, the above example can be mimicked in C++ as

cout << team << ": ranked " << rank << " of " << total << " teams" << **endl**;

This approach is not quite as pleasing as the previous, but in this case, it does the job. More
effort is needed to control other aspects of the formatting, such as the precision for floating-
point values. In Python, the expression 'pi is %.3f' % 3.14159265 produces the
result 'pi is 3.142'. In C++, output streams support additional methods for setting
or resetting the default formatting options. For example, the command **cout**.precision(3)
changes the default floating-point precision to 3 digits after the decimal point. This call
affects the formatting of all floating-point numbers (unless a subsequent call to precision
is made). The command **cout**.width(7) changes the minimum width for the next *individual*
item to be printed (akin to the %7 placeholder for most types). Although we will not give
a complete overview here, there are many more ways to control the precise output format
and even further support available in the <iomanip> library.

Console input

Just as **cout** is an output stream for the console, **cin** is an input stream used to read from the console. Here is a simple example of its use.

```
int number;
cout << "Enter a number from 1 to 10: ";  // prompt without newline
cin >> number;
```

The >> operator *extracts* data out from the stream and stores it in the given variable. The static typing of C++ actually helps us here, in comparison to Python. Since number was already clearly designated as an integer, C++ automatically converts the input as a number. Recall that in Python, we had to get the raw input string and explicitly convert it as in,

```
number = int(raw_input('Enter a number from 1 to 10: '))
```

There are other differences regarding the treatment of input. In Python, the **raw_input** command reads one line at a time. In C++, extracting data from a stream uses up only as many characters as are necessary. For example, here is a code fragment that asks the user to enter two numbers on the same line and computes their sum.

```
int a, b;
cout << "Enter two integers: ";
cin >> a >> b;
cout << "Their sum is " << a+b << "." << endl;
```

For the sake of comparison, a Python version is given as the solution to Practice 2.31. To be fair, both of our versions crash if a user enters characters that cannot be interpreted as integers.

When a string is requested, the stream advances to the first nonwhitespace character and goes from there up until the next whitespace character. This is quite different than with Python. Assume that we execute name = **raw_input**('What is your name?'), and the user responds as follows:

```
What is your name? John Doe
```

In Python, that entire line would be saved as a string 'John Doe'. If the same user interaction were given to the following C++ code,

```
string name;
cout << "What is your name? ";
cin >> name;
```

the result would be that name is assigned "John". The other characters remain on the stream until a subsequent extraction. If we want to read a full line at a time in C++, we can do so by using the syntax getline(**cin**, name).

File streams

File streams are defined in a library named <fstream>. Everything we have discussed about input and output apply to file streams as well. If the name of a file is known in advance, an associated file stream can be declared as

```
fstream datastream("data.txt");
```

If the filename is not known in advance, the stream can first be declared and then later opened, as

```
fstream datastream;
datastream.open("data.txt");
```

This syntax is typically used for opening an input file. The syntax which would correspond to Python's `'w'` access mode is

```
fstream datastream("data.txt", ios::out);
```

Append mode can be specified by using ios::app in place of ios::out above.

String streams

A stringstream class, included from a <sstream> library, allows us to use our formatting tools to produce an internal string rather than external output. In essence, such a stream serves as a buffer, allowing us to use the stream operators to force data into the buffer, or extract data from the buffer. At the end of Section B.5.1, we avoided the issue of how to convert an **int** to a string. This can be accomplished using a stringstream as follows:

```
stringstream temp;
temp << i;          // insert the integer representation into the stream
temp >> s;          // extract the resulting string out from the stream
```

B.5.3 Control Structures

We already saw an example of a **while** loop as part of our first example in Section B.3. The basic structure is similar, with only superficial differences in syntax. Most notably, parentheses are required around the boolean condition in C++. In that first example, curly braces were used to delimit the commands that comprise the body of the loop. Technically those braces are only needed when the body uses two or more distinct statements. In the absence of braces, the next single command is assumed to be the body.

C++ also supports a **do-while** syntax that can be a convenient remedy to the "loop-and-a-half" problem, as seen with while loops on page 165. Here is a similar C++ code fragment for requesting a number between 1 and 10 until receiving such a number:

```
int number;
do {
    cout << "Enter a number from 1 to 10: ";
    cin >> number;
} while (number < 1 || number > 10);
```

We should note that we have not properly handled the case when a noninteger is entered.

Conditionals

A basic **if** statement is quite similar in style, again requiring parentheses around the boolean condition and curly braces around a compound body. As a simple example, here is a construct to change a negative number to its absolute value.

```
if (x < 0)
    x = −x;
```

Notice that we did not need braces for a body with one command. C++ does not use the keyword elif for nesting conditionals, but it is possible to nest a new **if** statement within the body of an **else** clause. Furthermore, a conditional construct is treated syntactically as a single command, so a typical pattern does not require excessive braces. Our first example of a nested conditional in Python was given on page 144 of Section 4.4.2. That code could be written in C++ to mimic Python's indentation as follows (assuming groceries is an adequate container[8]):

```
if (groceries.length( ) > 15)
    cout << "Go to the grocery store";
else if (groceries.contains("milk"))
    cout << "Go to the convenience store";
```

For loops

C++ supports a **for** loop, but with very different semantics that Python's. The style dates back to its existence in C. The original use was to provide a more legible form of the typical *index-based* loop pattern described in Section 4.1.1. An example of a loop used to count downward from 10 to 1 is as follows:

```
for (int count = 10; count > 0; count−−)
    cout << count << endl;
cout << "Blastoff!";
```

Within the parentheses of the for loop are three distinct components, each separated by a semicolon. The first is an *initialization* step that is performed once, before the loop begins. The second portion is a *loop condition* that is treated just as a loop condition for a while loop; the condition is tested before each iteration, with the loop continuing while true.

---

8.   We will discuss C++ containers in Section B.5.8.

Finally we give an *update* statement that is performed automatically at the end of each completed iteration. In fact, the for loop syntax is just a convenient alternative to a while loop that better highlights the logic in some cases. The previous example is essentially identical in behavior to the following version:

```
int count = 10;                    // initialization step
while (count > 0) {                // loop condition
    cout << count << endl;
    count--;                       // update statement
}
cout << "Blastoff!";
```

The for loop is far more general. For example, it is possible to express *multiple* initialization or update steps in a for loop. This is done by using *commas* to separate the individual statements (as opposed to the semicolon that delimits the three different components of the syntax). For example, the sum of the values from 1 to 10 could be computed by maintaining two different variables as follows:

```
int count, total;
for (count = 1, total = 0; count <= 10; count++)
    total += count;
```

B.5.4 Defining a Function

We already provided an example of a C++ function in our initial demonstration from Section B.3. In this section we give a few other examples.

With that first example, we emphasized the need to explicitly designate the type of each individual parameter as well as the returned type. If the function does not provide a return value, there is a special keyword **void** that designates the lack of a type. Here is such a function that prints a countdown from 10 to 1.

```
void countdown( ) {
    for (int count = 10; count > 0; count--)
        cout << count;
}
```

We used an alternative version of this function in Section 5.2.2, to demonstrate the use of optional parameters in Python. The same technique can be used in C++, with the syntax

```
void countdown(int start=10, int end=1) {
    for (int count = start; count >= end; count--)
        cout << count;
}
```

B.5.5 Managing a Complete Program

We need to discuss one last detail before developing a complete C++ program. What should happen when the program is executed? Where does the flow of control begin? With Python, the flow of control begins at the beginning of the source code. The commands are interpreted one after another, and so a trivial Python program might appear simply as:

```
print 'Hello World.'
```

In C++, statements cannot generally be executed without any context. When an executable is started by the operating system, the flow of control begins with a call to a special function named main. The above Python code is most directly translated into C++ as the following program:

```
1  #include <iostream>
2  using namespace std;
3  int main( ) {
4      cout << "Hello World." << endl;
5      return 0;
6  }
```

The return value for main is a bit of a technicality. The signature must designate an **int** return type. The actual value returned is reported back to the operating system at the conclusion of the program. It is up to the operating system as to how to interpret that value, although zero historically indicates a successful execution while other values are used as error codes.

To demonstrate how to compile and execute a C++ program, we introduce a second example in Figure B.16. This is a rather simple program that pulls together several earlier techniques to compute and display the greatest common denominators of numbers entered by the user. Let's assume that the source code is saved in a file gcd.cpp. The most widely used compiler is from an organization known as GNU, and the compiler is most typically installed on a system as a program named g++. The compiler can be directly invoked from the operating system command line with the syntax,

```
g++ -o gcd gcd.cpp
```

The compiler will report any syntax errors that it finds, but if all goes well it produces a new file named gcd that is a true executable. It can be started on the computer just as you would start any other executable (with the Windows operating system, that executable might need to be named gcd.exe). There also exist integrated development environments for C++ (such as Python's IDLE). Those typically rely upon the same underlying compiler, but provide a more interactive control for the process.

The process is more involved when the software combines source code from multiple files (as is typical for larger applications). Our supplemental website demonstrates two such large projects, the text–based Mastermind program from Chapter 7, and the frequency–counting case study from Section 8.5.3 based on the design of the TallySheet class.

```
1   #include <iostream>
2   using namespace std;
3
4   int gcd(int u, int v) {
5      int r;
6      while (v != 0) {
7         r = u % v;    // compute remainder
8         u = v;
9         v = r;
10     }
11     return u;
12  }
13
14  int main( ) {
15     int a, b;
16     cout << "Enter first number: ";
17     cin >> a;
18     cout << "Enter second number: ";
19     cin >> b;
20     cout << "The gcd is " << gcd(a,b) << endl;
21     return 0;
22  }
```

FIGURE B.16: A complete C++ program that computes the gcd of two numbers.

B.5.6   Defining a Class

To demonstrate the syntax for a C++ class, we rely upon several of the examples that we first used in Chapter 6, beginning with the simple version of the Point class as given in Fig–ure 6.3 on page 206. The corresponding C++ version of that class is given in Figure B.17. There are several important aspects to discuss in comparing C++'s syntax to Python's. Please bear with us as we highlight the key differences.

Explicit declaration of data members

The issue of static typing arises prominently in a class definition, as all data members must be explicitly declared. Recall that in Python, attributes of a class were simply introduced by assignment statements within the body of the constructor. In our C++ example, we explicitly declare the type of the two data members at lines 3 and 4.

Constructor

Line 7 of our code is the constructor, although the syntax requires some explanation. The line begins with the name of the class itself (i.e., Point) followed by parentheses. The constructor is a function, with this particular example accepting zero parameters. However, unlike other functions, there is no designated return value in the signature (not even **void**).

```
1   class Point {
2   private:
3     double _x;
4     double _y;
5
6   public:
7     Point( ) : _x(0), _y(0) { }
8
9     double getX( ) const { return _x; }
10
11    void setX(double val) { _x = val; }
12
13    double getY( ) const { return _y; }
14
15    void setY(double val) { _y = val; }
16
17  };    // end of Point class (semicolon is required)
```

FIGURE B.17: Implementation of a simple Point class.

The next piece of syntax is the colon followed by _x(0), _y(0). This is what is known as an *initializer list* in C++. It is the preferred way to establish initial values for the attributes (we are not allowed to express initial values on lines 3 and 4). Finally, we see the syntax { }. This is technically the body of the constructor. Some classes use the constructor body to perform more intricate initializations. In this particular case, having already initialized the two variables, there is nothing else for us to do. But the { } serves as a placeholder syntactically (somewhat like **pass** in Python).

Implicit self-reference

A careful reader will have already noticed another major distinction between the class definition in C++ and the same class in Python. The **self** reference does not appear as a formal parameter nor is it used when accessing members of the instance. Remember that we have explicitly declared _x and _y to be attributes of a point. Because of this, the compiler recognizes those identifiers when used within the body of our methods (for example at line 9). For those who miss the self-reference, it is implicitly available in C++, although it is named **this**. This can be useful, for example, when passing our object as a parameter to an outside function.

Access control

Another distinction is the use of the terms **public** and **private** within the class definition. These relate to the issue of *encapsulation*. With Python, we addressed this issue in Section 7.6, differentiating at the time between what we considered "public" versus "private" aspects of a class design. Public aspects are those that we expect other programmers to rely upon, while private ones are considered to be internal implementation details that are subject to change. Yet Python does not strictly enforce this designation. Instead, we rely upon a naming conventions, using identifiers that start with an underscore (e.g., _x) to infer privacy.

In C++, these designators serve to declare the desired *access control* for the various members (both data members and functions). The use of the term **private** at line 2 affects the subsequent declarations at lines 3 and 4, while the term **public** at line 6 effects the subsequent declarations. The compiler enforces these designations within the rest of the project, ensuring that the private members are not directly accessed by any code other than our class definition.

Designating accessors versus mutators

In Python, we used the notion of an *accessor* as a method that cannot alter the state of an object, and a *mutator* as a method that might alter the state. This distinction is formalized in C++ by explicitly placing the keyword **const** for accessors at the end of the function signature but before the body. In our example, we see this term used in the signature of getX at line 9 and again for getY at line 13. We intentionally omit such a declaration for the mutators setX and setY.

As with access control, these **const** declarations are subsequently enforced by the compiler. If we declare a method as **const** yet then try to take an action that risks altering any of the attributes, this causes a compile-time error. Furthermore, if a caller has an object that had been declared as immutable, the only methods that can be invoked upon that object are ones that come with the **const** guarantee.

A robust Point class

To present some additional lessons about a class definition, we provide a more robust implementation of a Point class, modeled upon the Python version from Figure 6.4 on page 213. Our C++ version is shown in Figure B.18.

Our first lesson involves the constructor. In Python, we declared a constructor with the signature **def** __init__(**self**, initialX=0, initialY=0). This provided flexibility, allowing a caller to set initial coordinates for the point if desired, but to use the origin as a default. The C++ version of this constructor is given at lines 7 and 8.

Our next lesson is to re-emphasize that we can access members of the class without explicitly using a self-reference. This was already made clear in our use of names like _x rather than Python's **self**._x. The same convention is used when the body of one member function invokes another. At line 29, we see a call to the scale method. This is implicitly invoked on the current instance. Line 27 has a similar invocation of the distance method. Notice the use of Point( ) at line 27 to instantiate a new (default) point as a parameter to the distance function; this style is the same as we used in Python.

Lines 32–34 are used to support the + operator, allowing for the addition of two points. This behavior is akin to the __add__ method in Python, although in C++ the semantics are defined using **operator**+ as the "name" of a method. In the case of the syntax p + q, the point p technically serves as the implicit instance upon which this method is invoked, while q appears as a parameter in the signature. Technically, the **const** declaration that we make at line 32 designates that the state of p is unaffected by the behavior.

```cpp
1   class Point {
2   private:
3     double _x;
4     double _y;
5
6   public:
7     Point(double initialX=0.0, double initialY=0.0)
8       : _x(initialX), _y(initialY)        { }
9
10    double getX( ) const { return _x; }
11    void setX(double val) { _x = val; }
12    double getY( ) const { return _y; }
13    void setY(double val) { _y = val; }
14
15    void scale(double factor) {
16      _x *= factor;
17      _y *= factor;
18    }
19
20    double distance(Point other) const {
21      double dx = _x - other._x;
22      double dy = _y - other._y;
23      return sqrt(dx * dx + dy * dy);      /* sqrt imported from cmath library */
24    }
25
26    void normalize( ) {
27      double mag = distance( Point( ) );
28      if (mag > 0)
29        scale(1/mag);
30    }
31
32    Point operator+(Point other) const {
33      return Point(_x + other._x, _y + other._y);
34    }
35
36    Point operator*(double factor) const {
37      return Point(_x * factor, _y * factor);
38    }
39
40    double operator*(Point other) const {
41      return _x * other._x + _y * other._y;
42    }
43  };    // end of Point class (semicolon is required)
```

FIGURE B.18: Implementation of a robust Point class.

```
44   Point operator*(double factor, Point p) {
45     return p * factor;
46   }
47
48   ostream& operator<<(ostream& out, Point p) {
49     out << "<" << p.getX( ) << ", " << p.getY( ) << ">";
50     return out;
51   }
```

FIGURE B.19: Supplemental operator definitions involving Point instances.

Lines 36–42 support two different notions of multiplication: multiplying a given point by a numeric constant, and computing the dot product of two points. Our original Python implementation accomplished this with a single function definition that accepted one parameter. Internally it performed dynamic type checking of that parameter and determined the appropriate behavior depending on whether the second operand was a point or a number. In C++, we provide two different implementations. The first accepts a **double** and returns a new Point; the second accepts a Point and (coincidentally) returns a **double**. Providing two separate declarations of a method is termed *overloading* the signature. Since all data is explicitly typed, C++ can determine which of the two forms to invoke at compile–time, based on the actual parameters.

Technically, line 43 of Figure B.18 ends our Point class declaration. However, we provide two supporting definitions shown in Figure B.19. The first of those supports use of a syntax such as 3 * p. The earlier definition of **operator*** from lines 36–38 technically supports the * operator when a Point instance is the *left-hand* operator (e.g., p * 3). C++ does not allow the formal class definition to affect the operator behavior in the case where the only instance of that class is the right-hand operator. Instead, we define such a behavior independent of the official class definition. So at lines 44–46, we provide a definition for how * should behave when the first operator is a **double** and the second is a Point. Notice that both operands appear as formal parameters in this signature since we are no longer within the context of the class definition. The body of our method uses the same simple trick as in our Python implementation, commuting the order so that the point becomes the left-hand operand (thereby, invoking our previously defined version).

Finally, lines 48–51 are used to produce a text representation of a point when inserted onto an output stream. A typical syntax for such a behavior is **cout** << p. Again we define this behavior outside of the context of the class because the point serves as the right-hand operator. Line 49 inserts our desired output representation onto the given output stream. We use the formal parameter out rather than **cout** so that a user can apply this behavior to any type of output stream. The declared return type on line 48 and the return statement at line 50 are technically required to allow for multiple << operations to be applied on a single line; the syntax **cout** << p << " is good" is evaluated as (**cout** << p) << " is good", with the result of the first evaluation being an output stream used in the second operation. The use of the & symbol twice on line 48 is another technicality, leading to our next topic of discussion.

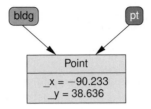

FIGURE B.20: An example of parameter passing in Python.

B.5.7 Assignments and the Object Model

Python presents a consistent model in which all identifiers are inherently references to underlying objects. Use of the assignment operator as in a = b causes identifier a to be reassigned to the same underlying object referenced by identifier b. These semantics are consistently applied to all types of objects. The assignment semantics also affect the passing of information to and from a function, as described in Section 10.3.1. Upon invocation, the formal parameters are assigned respectively to the actual parameters indicated by a caller. The return value is communicated in a similar fashion.

As a simple example, assume that we define the following Python function for determining whether a given point is equivalent to the origin:

```python
def isOrigin(pt):
    return pt.getX( ) == 0 and pt.getY( ) == 0
```

Now assume that the caller invokes this function as isOrigin(bldg), where bldg is an identifier that references a point instance. Figure B.20 diagrams the underlying configuration. This scenario is the precise result of the system performing an implicit assignment of formal parameter to actual parameter pt = bldg.

In this section, we consider the same issues in C++, namely the correspondence between an identifier and an underlying value, the semantics of an assignment statement, and the subsequent affect on passing information to and from a function. C++ provides more fine-tuned control than Python, allowing the programmer a choice between three different semantic models.

Value variables

The most commonly used model in C++ is that of a *value variable*. A declaration such as

```cpp
Point a;
```

causes the compiler to reserve memory for storing the state of a point. The translation from the name a to this particular instance is handled purely at *compile-time*, providing greater run-time efficiency than if that mapping were evaluated at run-time (as with Python). In the above case, the default constructor is applied, initializing both coordinates to zero. We could otherwise use an initialize statement to parameterize the construction of a value variable, with a syntax such as the following.

a : Point
x = 0.0
y = 0.0

b : Point
x = 5.0
y = 7.0

FIGURE B.21: The declaration of two separate value variables.

a : Point
x = 5.0
y = 7.0

b : Point
x = 5.0
y = 7.0

FIGURE B.22: The effect of an assignment a = b upon value variables.

```
Point b(5,7);
```

Note that the parameters are enclosed in parentheses that follow the variable name (as opposed to the type name). Furthermore, note that we did not use any parentheses in the earlier case, when relying on the default constructor.

To portray the semantics of a value variable, we prefer a diagram in the style of Figure B.21, without any independent concept of a reference. The assignment semantics for a value variable is very different from Python's. The assignment a = b causes the Point a to take on the *value* of Point b, as diagrammed in Figure B.22. Notice that a and b are still names of two distinct points.

The difference between C++ and Python assignments has a notable effect on the semantics of a function. Going back to our earlier Python example, we might implement that function in C++ as follows:

```
bool isOrigin(Point pt) {
    return pt.getX( ) == 0 && pt.getY( ) == 0;
}
```

The parameter passing model in this case is based on the implicit initialization of a formal parameter to the value of an actual parameter.

```
Point pt(bldg);
```

This initialization has very different consequences for a value variable. In this case, the formal parameter does not become an alias for the actual parameter. It is a newly allocated Point instance with state initialized to match that of the actual parameter. Figure B.23 portrays this scenario. As a result, changes made to the parameter from within the function body have no lasting effect on the caller's object. This style of parameter passing is generally termed *by value*, as originally discussed on page 351.

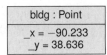
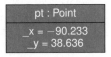

FIGURE B.23: An example of passing by value in C++.

Reference variables

The second model for a C++ variable is commonly termed a ***reference variable***. It is declared as

```
Point& c = a;   // reference variable
```

Syntactically, the distinguishing feature is the use of the ampersand. This designates c as a new name, but it is not a new point. Instead, it becomes an alias for the existing point, a. We choose to diagram such a situation as in Figure B.24.

This is closer to the spirit of Python's model, but still not quite the same. A C++ reference variable must be bound to an existing instance upon declaration. It cannot be a reference to nothing (as is possible in Python with the None value). Furthermore, the reference variable's binding is static in C++; once declared, that name can no longer be reassociated with some other object. The name c becomes a true alias for the name a. The assignment c = b does not rebind the name c; this changes the *value* of c (also known as a).

Reference variables are rarely used as demonstrated above, because there is little need in a local context for a second name for the same object. Yet the reference variable semantics becomes extremely important in the context of functions. We can use a *pass-by-reference* semantics by using the ampersand in the declaration of a formal parameter, as in the following revision of the isOrigin function:

```
bool isOrigin(Point& pt) {
    return pt.getX( ) == 0 && pt.getY( ) == 0;
}
```

This leads to a model similar to Python in that the formal parameter becomes an *alias* for the actual parameter. There are several potential advantages of this style. For larger objects, creating a copy is typically more expensive than creating an alias (which simply requires the communication of an underlying memory address). In fact, some classes do not even support the notion of creating a copy. For example, creating and manipulating a "copy" of an output stream is not allowed by the ostream class. For this reason, we see

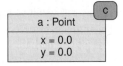

FIGURE B.24: The name c is an example of a reference variable in C++.

the use of references in the signature of **operator<<**, looking back at Figure B.19; both the parameter stream and return value are communicated in such a way.

A second potential benefit of passing by reference is that it allows a function to intentionally manipulate the caller's object (in contrast to when a parameter is passed by value). In cases where a programmer wishes to get the efficiency of passing by reference, but without the risk of allowing the object to be mutated, the **const** modifier can be used in declaring a parameter, as in

```
bool isOrigin(const Point& pt) {
  return pt.getX( ) == 0 && pt.getY( ) == 0;
}
```

With this signature, the point will be passed by referenced, but the function promises that it will in no way modify that point (a promise which is enforced by the compiler).

Pointer variables

C++ supports a third form of variable known as a ***pointer***. This provides a semantics which is closest to Python's model, although the syntax is quite different. A C++ pointer variable is declared as follows:

```
Point *d;     // d is a pointer variable
```

The asterisk in this context declares d not to be a Point itself, but to be a variable that can store the memory address of a Point. This is related to a reference, but pointers are more general in that a pointer is allowed to point to nothing (using the keyword NULL in C++). Also, the pointer can be reassigned to different instances over time. A typical assignment statement is as follows:

```
d = &b;
```

This leads to a configuration diagrammed in Figure B.25. We intentionally portray d as a separate entity because it is itself a variable stored in memory and manipulated, whose value just happens to be a memory address of some other object. In order to manipulate

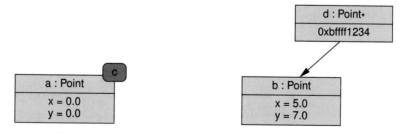

FIGURE B.25: The variable d is an example of a pointer whose value is assigned to the address of instance b.

the underlying point with this variable, we must explicitly dereference it. The expression *d is synonymous with b in this configuration. For example, we could call the method (*d).getY( ), which returns the value 7.0 in this case. However, since this syntax is bulky, C++ introduced a new operator in the context of pointers, allowing the syntax d−>getY( ).

Passing a pointer provides a third alternative in the context of a function.

```
bool isOrigin(Point *pt) {
   return pt−>getX( ) == 0 && pt−>getY( ) == 0;
}
```

However, the only advantage to using a pointer variable rather than a reference variable is to allow for the possibility of sending a null pointer (recall that reference variables cannot have such a value).

Dynamic memory management

With value variables, C++ handles all issues of memory management. When a declaration, as Point a, is made, the system reserves memory for storing the state of this point. Furthermore, when that variable declaration goes out of scope (for example, if a local variable within a function body), the system automatically destroys the point and reclaims the memory for other purposes. Generally, this automatic memory management eases the burden upon the computer.

However, there are some circumstances when a program wants to take a more active role in controlling the underlying memory management. Pointer variables serve a valuable role in this regard. In our first example of a pointer variable, we assigned its value to the address of an *existing* object. We can also use an existing pointer to keep track of a brand new object, instantiated as follows:

```
d = new Point( );
```

This instantiation syntax is different from that of a value variable. The use of the keyword **new** designates this as what is termed a ***dynamic*** allocation. Memory will be set aside for storing and initializing this new Point, but the object is never automatically destroyed. It is up to the programmer to explicitly throw it away when it is no longer necessary, using a syntax **delete** d (just one more way that C++ allows a programmer to fine-tune software).

B.5.8   Container Classes

Python provides several valuable built-in classes for managing collections of objects. Most notable are the **list** class for managing an ordered sequence, the **dict** class for managing an associative mapping, and the **set** class for managing an unordered collection of unique values. C++ offers support for similar concepts through a series of definition known as the Standard Template Library (STL). These definitions are not built into the core language but can be imported from the standard libraries. Figure B.26 provides a summary of the most commonly used classes from this framework. Although we already discussed the **string** class earlier, we include it here as it is mutable and technically a container in STL (specifically a container of characters).

C++ Type	Description	Python analog
string	character sequence	**str**
vector	homogeneous sequence	**array**
map	associative mapping (homogeneous)	**dict**
set	set of unique elements (homogeneous)	**set**

FIGURE B.26: Commonly used classes from C++'s Standard Template Library (STL).

We begin by examining the **vector** class, which can be included from the **<vector>** library. This is probably the closest analog to Python's list class, but we more accurately compare it to Python's **array** class because a vector is homogeneous and stored as a collection of *values* (rather than as a collection of references to values, as with Python's **list**). To support static typing, the precise type of objects that can be inserted must be specified as part of a **vector** declaration. For example, if we wish to maintain a grocery list as a vector of strings, we might write code as follows:

```
vector<string> groceries;
groceries.push_back("bread");
groceries.push_back("milk");
groceries.push_back("cheese");
cout << groceries[2] << endl;          // will be "cheese"
```

By declaring groceries as **vector<string>**, it becomes clear that objects inserted into the container must be a string, and that objects retrieved from the container will be strings. The push_back method is the C++ analog of Python's **append**, adding the new value to the end of the sequence. We see that elements of a vector can be accessed by index, using a syntax similar to Python's **list**. However, for the sake of efficiency, C++ does not check the validity of an index at run-time, it simply trust the programmer (with potential disaster if the programmer is wrong). A safer (yet slower) way to access an element is using the syntax groceries.at(2), which calls a method that performs a run-time check of the given index. For the sake of brevity, we refer the reader to formal documentation for a complete menu of the **vector** behaviors, as well as those for other common collections; rest assured that most of Python's behaviors are supported in one form or another.

B.5.9 Inheritance

In Chapter 9, we provided several examples of the use of inheritance in Python. We will show two of those examples, translated to C++. First we define a DeluxeTV class modeled closely after the version in Figure 9.2 that used a SortedSet. Although we omit the presumed definition for a basic Television class, our complete code for the DeluxeTV class is given in Figure B.27. The use of inheritance is originally indicated at line 1 by following the declaration of the new class with a colon and then the expression **public** Television.

```
1    class DeluxeTV : public Television {
2    protected:
3      set<int> _favorites;
4
5    public:
6      DeluxeTV( ) :
7        Television( ),     // parent constructor
8        _favorites( )      // empty set by default
9        { }
10
11     void addToFavorites( ) { if (_powerOn) _favorites.insert(_channel); }
12
13     void removeFromFavorites( ) { if (_powerOn) _favorites.erase(_channel); }
14
15     int jumpToFavorite( ) {
16       if (_powerOn && _favorites.size( ) > 0) {
17         set<int>::iterator result = _favorites.upper_bound(_channel);
18         if (result == _favorites.end( ))
19           result = _favorites.begin( );     // wrap around to smallest channel
20         setChannel(*result);
21       }
22       return _channel;
23     }
24   };   // end of DeluxeTV
```

FIGURE B.27: Implementing a DeluxeTV class through inheritance.

With that designation,[9] our DeluxeTV class immediate inherits all attributes (e.g., powerOn, channel) and all methods (e.g., setChannel) from the parent. What remains is for us to define additional attributes or to provide new or updated implementations for methods that we want supported.

At line 3, we declare a new attribute to manage the set of favorite channel numbers. Although we used our custom SortedSet class in our Python version, this is an excellent opportunity to make use of the C++ **set** container. We wish to draw particular attention to the use of the word **protected** at line 2. Until now, we have used two forms of access control: **public** and **private**. Members that are public can be accessed by code outside of the class definition, while members that are private can only be accessed from within the original class definition. The purpose of privacy is to encapsulate internal implementation details that should not be relied upon by others. Yet with the use of inheritance, there is need for a third level of access.

When designing a class that inherits from another, the question arises as to whether code for that new class should be able to directly access members inherited from the parent. This is determined by the original access control designated for those members. A

9.   For the sake of simplicity, we will not discuss the precise significance of the term **public** on line 1.

child class cannot access any members from the parent that are declared as **private**. How-ever, the child is granted access to members designated as **protected** by the parent. In this particular setting, the important point is not actually our use of **protected** at line 2. What matters to us is how the original attributes of the Television class were defined. For our DeluxeTV code to work, it must be that television attributes were originally declared as

```
protected:
  bool _powerOn;
  int _channel;
  ...
```

If those had been declared as **private** we would not have the necessary access to implement our DeluxeTV. Of course, the original designer of the television may not have known that we would come along and want to inherit from it. However, an experienced C++ program will consider this possibility when designing a class. In our DeluxeTV definition, the declaration of attribute favorites as **protected** is not for our own benefit, but to leave open the possibility that someone else may one day want to design a SuperDeluxeTV that improves upon our model.

The second aspect of our example we wish to discuss is the definition of our con-structor, at lines 6–9. In our Python version, the new constructor begins with an explicit call to the parent constructor, using the syntax, Television.__init__(**self**). That was used to establish the default settings for all of the inherited attributes; then we take care of initial-izing the new favorites attribute. In C++, we can invoke the parent constructor as part of the initializer list using the syntax Television( ) at line 7. This calls the parent constructor without sending any explicit parameters. To be honest, in this particular example, line 7 is superfluous. If we do not explicitly call the parent constructor, C++ will do so implicitly. However, an explicit call is necessary when parameters are to be sent to the parent con-structor (as in our second example). In a similar spirit, we choose to explicitly initialize the favorites attribute at line 8, although this too is superfluous, since we rely upon the default form of the constructor.

The rest of our DeluxeTV code is used to provide three new behaviors. The precise details of those methods depends greatly on our knowledge of the **set** class (which we admit we have not tried to explain). Our purpose for this example is to demonstrate the use of inheritance. We draw attention to the fact that we are able to access the inherited attributes, _powerOn and _channel, as well as our new attribute _favorites when imple-menting the methods. We also make a call to the inherited method setChannel at line 20 of our code.

A Square class

As a second example of inheritance, Figure B.28 provides a C++ rendition of our original Square class from Section 9.4.2. The Square inherits from a presumed Rectangle class. We do not introduce any new attributes for this class, so our only responsibility for the constructor is to ensure that the inherited attributes are properly initialized. To do this we call to the parent constructor at line 4. In this case, we needed to do an explicit call to pass the appropriate dimensions and center. Had we not done this explicitly, an implicit

```
1   class Square : public Rectangle {
2    public:
3     Square(double size=10, Point center=Point( )) :
4       Rectangle(size, size, center)    // parent constructor
5       { }
6
7     void setHeight(double h) { setSize(h); }
8     void setWidth(double w) { setSize(w); }
9
10    void setSize(double size) {
11      Rectangle::setWidth(size);    // make sure to invoke PARENT version
12      Rectangle::setHeight(size);   // make sure to invoke PARENT version
13    }
14
15    double getSize( ) const { return getWidth( ); }
16  };   // end of Square
```

FIGURE B.28: Implementing a Square class based upon a Rectangle.

call would have been made to the *default* version of the rectangle constructor, leading to incorrect semantics for our square.

The remainder of the definition is meant to provide new getSize and setSize methods, while also overriding the existing setHeight and setWidth methods so that a change to either dimension affects both. We use the same approach as our Python version. We override the existing methods at lines 7 and 8, changing their behaviors to call our new setSize method. Our setSize method then relies upon the *parent* versions of the overridden setWidth and setHeight methods to enact the individual changes to those values. The use of the expression Rectangle:: before the method names at lines 11 and 12 designates our desire to use the parent version of those behaviors, rather than the default Square versions.

B.5.10   Conclusions

There is certainly much more to learn about C++ (and much more to learn about Python, for that matter). All of our advanced techniques from Python carry over in some form to programming in C++. But our goal for this transition guide was to provide you with the initial bridge to transfer your knowledge and experience in Python to learning a new language. So it is time that we say goodbye.

We offer a more complete transition guide from Python to C++ on the supplemental website for this book. That version expands upon this appendix, offering further examples of Python concepts and source code translated to C++. In particular, we offer complete translations of the text–based Mastermind program from Chapter 7 as well as the frequency–counting case study from Section 8.5.3 based on the design of the TallySheet class. If that is not enough, hundreds of books, tutorials, websites, and other references are available offering further lessons about programming in C++.

APPENDIX C

Solutions to Practice Exercises

Chapter 1: Cornerstones of Computing

Practice 1.1: ASCII is an acronym for American Standard Code for Information Interchange. It was introduced in 1963 as a standard numbering for 128 common characters (mostly the Roman alphabet, together with numerals and punctuation). Unicode is a more recent industry effort, started in 1991, to standardize the representation of more characters in support of the internationalization of computing applications.

Practice 1.5:

1. Write down the two numbers, one above the other, so as to align columns starting with the rightmost (the "ones digit").

2. Repeat the following steps for each column, starting with the rightmost:

   (a) Add the numerals in the current column to produce a subtotal.

   (b) If that subtotal is strictly less than 10, write that value at the bottom of the column as a result.

   (c) Otherwise, write a 1 above the column to the left (a "carry"), and then subtract 10 from the subtotal, writing the result at the bottom of the column.

3. The sum of the two numbers is indicated at the bottom.

Practice 1.11: When the volume reaches the lowest setting, the volumeDown behavior has no effect; the volume remains as is. When the channel reaches its lowest setting and channelDown is applied, the channel typically wraps around to the largest channel number.

Practice 1.15:

Attributes:

title	—	The name of the course.
dept	—	The department offering the course.
code	—	The code number (e.g., 101, as in CS-101).
hours	—	The number of credit hours for this course.
seats	—	The maximum number of students that can be enrolled.
students	—	A list of students currently enrolled.
instructor	—	The instructor for the course.

Behaviors:

getTitle( )	—	Returns the course title.
getDept( )	—	Returns the department offering the course.
getCode( )	—	Returns the number serving as the course code.
getInstructor( )	—	Returns the name of the instructor.
getNumHours( )	—	Returns the number of credit hours associated with the course.
getNumOpenSeats( )	—	Returns the number of currently available seats in the course.
getCapacity( )	—	Returns the overall number of seats in the course.
requestSeat(student)	—	Used to request a seat in the course for the given student. Returns **True** if the request is approved (and hence the student added to the role), returns **False** otherwise.
setInstructor(person)	—	Used by the department to assign a faculty member as the instructor of the course.

Practice 1.20:

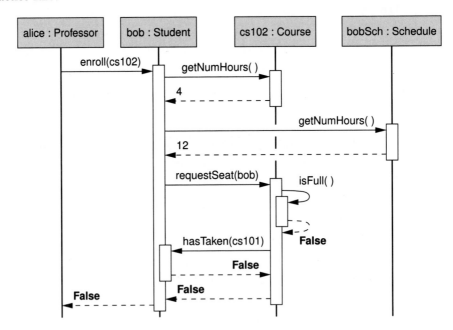

Practice 1.25:

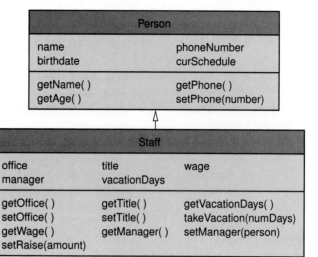

Practice 1.28:

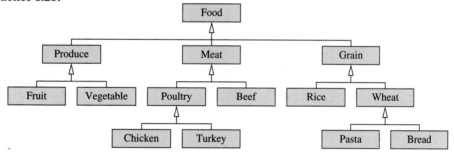

Chapter 2: Getting Started in Python

Practice 2.1: astronauts.insert(1, 'Alan Shepard')

Practice 2.2:

people.sort( )
people.reverse( )

Practice 2.3: someHouses = houses[1: :2]

Practice 2.4: range(2, 9, 2)

Practice 2.14:

(a) **str** with value 's'

(b) **str** with value 's a te'

(c) **int** with value 4

(d) **int** with value 8

(e) **int** with value 18

(f) **list** with value ['This is ',' test. This is only ',' test']

Practice 2.15: stringA.lower( ) == stringB.lower( )

Practice 2.16: There are two natural approaches. The first is to separately count the two cases, as song.count('b') + song.count('B'). Another approach is to create an entirely lowercase version and then to count, as in song.lower( ).count('b').

Practice 2.17: We describe two different ways of doing this. The first is to make use of the string operators to find the location of the space, to use slices to pull aside the individual first and last name, and then to use the + operator to concatenate the resulting strings.

```
space = person.index(' ')
name = person[space+1:] + ',  ' + person[ :space]
```

A second approach is to split the string at the space, resulting in a list of the two pieces of the name, to reverse that list, and then to rejoin the list using ', ' as the separator.

```
pieces = person.split(' ')
pieces.reverse( )
name = ',  '.join(pieces)
```

Practice 2.18: `Hello, my name is Ann.`

Practice 2.26:

(a) Type: **int**, value: 31	(j) Type: **bool**, value: **False**
(b) Type: **float**, value: 2.4	(k) Type: **list**, value: ['h', 'cusp', 'cus']
(c) Type: **float**, value: 6.2	(l) Type: **bool**, value: **False**
(d) Type: **float**, value: 3.4	(m) Type: **int**, value: 13
(e) Type: **int**, value: 3	(n) Type: **int**, value: 10
(f) Type: **float**, value: 5.2	(o) Type: **str**, value: 'press'
(g) Type: **bool**, value: **False**	(p) Type: **int**, value: 3
(h) Type: **str**, value: '121212'	(q) Type: **bool**, value: **True**
(i) Type: **str**, value: 'abbb'	(r) Type: **bool**, value: **True**

Practice 2.27: 3.14159 * r * r or alternatively math.pi * pow(r,2)

Practice 2.28:

(a) A TypeError occurs. You can multiply a string by an integer, to get repetitions of the string. But you cannot multiply a string by another string.

(b) A TypeError occurs. The parameter to the join method must be a list of strings. In this case the parameter range(10) is a list of integers.

(c) An AttributeError occurs. The result of range(10) is a list. The list class does not support a split method.

(d) A TypeError occurs. First, range(10) is evaluated, resulting in a list. Then the reverse method is applied to that list. However, that method does not have any return value. Therefore the subexpression range(10).reverse( ) evaluates to the special value **None**. This object cannot be indexed with [3].

(e) A TypeError occurs. The expression range(10).pop( ) evaluates to the integer 9. Integers do not support the len syntax.

Practice 2.32:
```
name = raw_input('What is your name? ')
print 'Hello ' + name + '!'
```

Practice 2.33:
```
numberString = raw_input('Enter two integers: ')
numbers = numberString.split( )
sum = int(numbers[0]) + int(numbers[1])        # convert to integers
print 'Their sum is ' + str(sum) + '.'
```

Chapter 3: Getting Started with Graphics

Practice 3.1: Line 5 should read screen.add(disk), as the disk should be added to the canvas, not the canvas added to the disk.

Practice 3.2:
```
paper = Canvas( )
triangle = Polygon(Point(100,80), Point(120,110), Point(80,110))
triangle.setFillColor('yellow')
paper.add(triangle)
```

Chapter 4: Elementary Control Structures

Practice 4.1:
```
g
r
e
a
t
```

Practice 4.2:
```
dramatic = ''
for char in original:
   dramatic += char + char
```

Practice 4.3:
```
strList = [ ]
for val in intList:
   strList.append(str(val))
```

Practice 4.4: This is very similar to the pyramid. However, instead of each center having the same x-coordinate, the horizontal placement of the center depends upon the level number.
```
from cs1graphics import *
numLevels = 4
unitSize = 12                                # the height of one level
screenSize = unitSize*(numLevels+1)
paper = Canvas(screenSize, screenSize)
# create levels from top to bottom
```

```
for level in range(numLevels):
    width = (1+level)*unitSize              # width varies by level
    block = Rectangle(width, unitSize)      # height is always unitSize
    centerX = (numLevels−level/2.0)*unitSize
    centerY = (1+level)*unitSize
    block.move(centerX, centerY)
    block.setFillColor('gray')
    paper.add(block)
```

Practice 4.19:

```
count = 0
for obj in collection:
    if obj == value:
        count += 1
```

Practice 4.20:

```
shortWords = [ ]
for w in words:
    if len(w) <= 3:
        shortWords.append(w)
```

Practice 4.21:

```
0 is divisible by 9
3 is divisible by 3
6 is divisible by 3
9 is divisible by 9
12 is divisible by 3
15 is divisible by 3
18 is divisible by 9
```

Practice 4.22:

(a) answer is D

(b) answer is B

(c) answer is C

(d) answer is B

Practice 4.32: dramatic = ' '.join([2 * char **for** char **in** original])

Practice 4.33: strList = [**str**(val) **for** val **in** intList]

Practice 4.34: shortWords = [w **for** w **in** words **if** len(w) <= 3]

Chapter 5: Additional Control Structures

Practice 5.1:

```
6
7
8
9
10
```

Practice 5.2:

```
2  1
2  7
4  7
6  7
8  7
8  13
10  13
```

Practice 5.3:

```
count = 0
total = 0.0
number = 999    # just used to force our way into the loop
while number != 0:
    number = float(raw_input('Enter a number: '))
    total += number
    count += 1
print 'The average is', total/count
```

Practice 5.18:

```
start silly
5
start funny
10
start goofy
11
end goofy
end funny
start goofy
4
end goofy
end silly
```

Practice 5.19:

```
def gcd(u, v):
    while v != 0:
        r = u % v     # compute remainder
        u = v
        v = r
    return u
```

Practice 5.20:

```
def dramatic(original):
    result = ' '
    for char in original:
        result += char + char
    return result
```

Practice 5.21:
```
def sumOfSquares(n):
    total = 0
    for k in range(1, n+1):          # range includes n itself
        total += k * k
    return total
```

Practice 5.31:
```
def yesOrNo(prompt):
    response = raw_input(prompt)
    while response not in ('yes','no'):
        print 'You must respond with "yes" or "no"'
        response = raw_input(prompt)
    return response == 'yes'
```

Practice 5.32:
```
def gcd(u, v):
    if not isinstance(u,int) and isinstance(v,int):
        raise TypeError('args must be integers')
    if u < 0 or v < 0:
        raise ValueError('args must be nonnegative')
    while v != 0:
        r = u % v
        u = v
        v = r
    return u
```

Chapter 6: Defining Our Own Classes

Practice 6.1:

line 1   —   **def** Widget: should be **class** Widget: .

line 3   —   **def** Widget(**self**): should be **def** __init__(**self**): .

line 6   —   Must have colon after **def** replace(**self**).

line 7   —   **self**.index('w') should be **self**._msg.index('w').

line 8   —   Two errors: identifier g undefined; perhaps meant literal 'g'. Also strings are immutable; you cannot use the syntax **self**._msg[index] on the left–hand side of an assignment. If need be, a new string could be constructed as
self._msg = **self**._msg[:index−1] + 'g' + **self**._msg[index+1:].

line 11   —   the **print** should be replaced with **return** as this is the expected result of __str__ method.

Practice 6.3: Yes, in general there is an effect, namely the call will leave the television instance with a value of 9 for both the channel and prevChan attributes (whereas the television in general may have had some other prevChan value at the onset).

Practice 6.5:

(a)

```
def getDay(self):
    return self._day
```

(b)

```
def setYear(self, yr):
    self._year = yr
```

(c)

```
def __str__(self):
    return Date.monthNames[self._month−1] + '  ' \
        + str(self._day) + ',  ' + str(self._year)
```

Practice 6.6:

```
def count(self, value):
    count = 0
    for object in self:
        if object == value:
            count += 1
    return count
```

Practice 6.7:

```
def __contains__(self, value):
    i = 0                               # index-based search
    found = False                       # pessimism
    while i < len(self) and not found:
        if self[i] == val:
            found = True                # we found it
        else:
            i += 1                      # keep looking...
    return found
```

Chapter 7: Good Software Practices

Practice 7.1:

(a) foo is a function.

(b) Widget is likely a class (or perhaps a module).

(c) bar is an object.

(d) data is an object; _analyze is a private method of that object.

(e) myFoo is an object; fooBar is a method of that object.

(f) my is an object; _stuff is an attribute of it.

(g) helpMe( ) is a function.

(h) Table is a class.

Practice 7.2:

```
def volumeUp(self):
    """Increment the volume of the Television by one increment.

    If power is currently off, there is no effect.

    Otherwise, update the volume setting appropriately, and
    return the new setting value to the caller.
    If television is currently muted, it will be unmuted as a result.
    If volume was at maximum level, it remains at maximum level.
    """
```

```
def jumpPrevChannel(self):
    """Change the channel to most recent other channel to have been viewed.

    Return the resulting channel setting.
    If power is off, there is no effect.
    """
```

Practice 7.6:

```
if Fraction(13,6) + Fraction(-7,15) != Fraction(51,30)
    print 'Error in addition of fractions.'
if Fraction(0,1) + Fraction(41,17) != Fraction(41,17)
    print 'Error in addition of fractions when adding zero.'
```

Practice 7.13: To describe the scoring, we refer to the lowest guess in the figure as guess 1, and the pegs of each guess as pegs 1 through 5, from left to right.

Guess 1:   the one black is because of the match at peg 4.

Guess 2:   the one white is because peg 1 of the guess matches peg 4 of the secret.

Guess 3:   the one black is at peg 5; the additional white is because peg 2 of the guess matches peg 4 of the secret.

Guess 4:   the one black is at peg 2; the additional two whites are because peg 1 of the guess matches peg 5 of the secret, and peg 3 of the guess matches peg 4 of the secret.

Guess 5:   the one black is at peg 4; the additional four white are because pegs 1, 2, 3, and 5 of the guess match respectively pegs 5, 1, 2, and 3 of the secret.

Guess 6:   the one black is at peg 5; the additional four white are because pegs 1, 2, 3, and 4 of the guess match respectively pegs 2, 1, 4, and 3 of the secret.

Guess 7:   everything is correct.

Chapter 8: Input, Output, and Files

Practice 8.1: `"%s's birthday is %s %d."` % (person, month, day)

Practice 8.6:

```
namefile = file('people.txt')
name = ' '
for line in namefile:
    rightSpace = line.rindex(' ')        # delimiter before year
    year = int( line[rightSpace+1: ] )
    if name == ' ' or year < earlyYear:
        earlyYear = year
        name = line[ : rightSpace]       # everything prior to the year
print name
```

Practice 8.7:

```
result = file('message.txt', 'w')
result.write('This is a test.\nHow did I do?')
result.close( )
```

Chapter 9: Inheritance

Practice 9.1:

(a) 3

(b) 4

(c) This generates an error, as a Sneetch does not support any method z.

(d) 3

(e) 7 8

(f) 3 8

Chapter 10: Deeper Understanding of the Management of Objects

Practice 10.1:

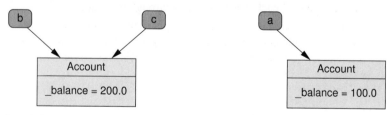

Practice 10.2:

```
[1, 57, 34, 47, 13]
[1, 57, 34, 47, 13]
```

Practice 10.6:

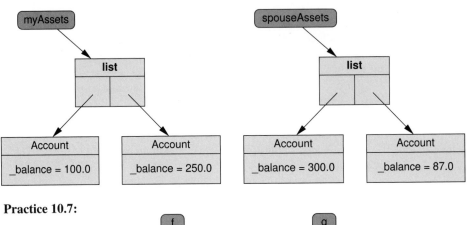

Practice 10.7:

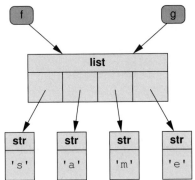

Practice 10.8:

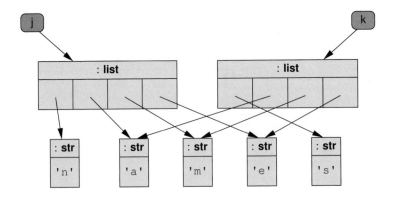

Practice 10.11: The assignment statement data = [ ] reassociates the identifier data to a newly created empty list. However, this does not have any effect on the original list sent by the caller as an actual parameter. This issue is similar to the discussion of the threshold parameter on page 349.

Chapter 11: Recursion

Practice 11.1:

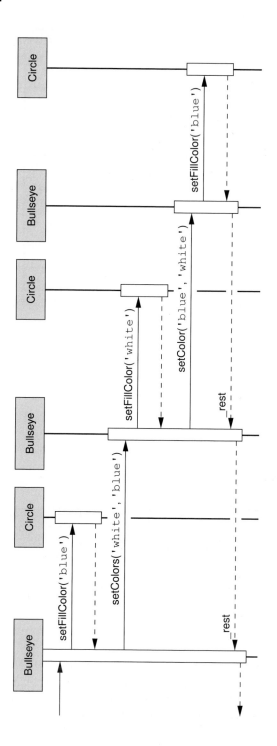

Practice 11.7:

method	base case			parameters			return value		
	empty	head	index	same	vary	none	same	vary	none
__len__	✓					✓		✓	
__contains__	✓	✓		✓			✓		
__getitem__	✓		✓		✓		✓		
__setitem__	✓		✓		✓				✓
__repr__	✓					✓		✓	
count	✓			✓				✓	
index	✓	✓		✓				✓	
append	✓			✓					✓
insert	✓		✓		✓				✓
remove	✓	✓		✓					✓

Practice 11.8:

```
def min(self):
  if self._isEmpty( ):
    raise ValueError('min() of empty sequence')
  else:
    if self._rest._isEmpty( ):
      return self._head
    else:
      candidate = self._rest.min( )
      if self._head < candidate:
        candidate = self._head
      return candidate
```

Practice 11.19:

```
1
2
3
```

Practice 11.20:

```
3
2
1
```

Practice 11.21:

```
n = 4
n = 3
n = 2
n = 1
```

```
n = 0
n = 1
n = 2
n = 1
n = 0
3
```

Practice 11.27:

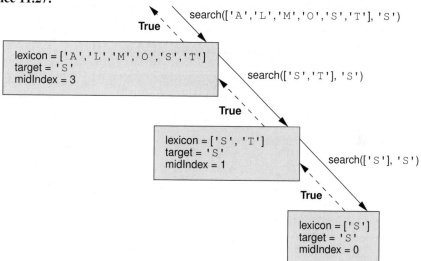

Practice 11.28:

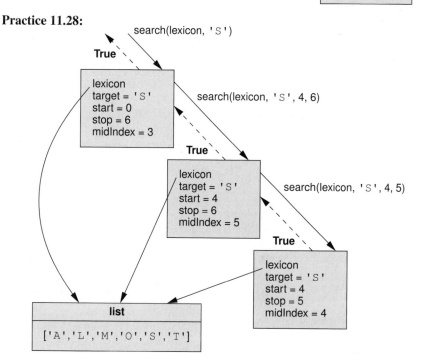

Practice 11.33:

['tea', 'era', 'eat', 'ate']

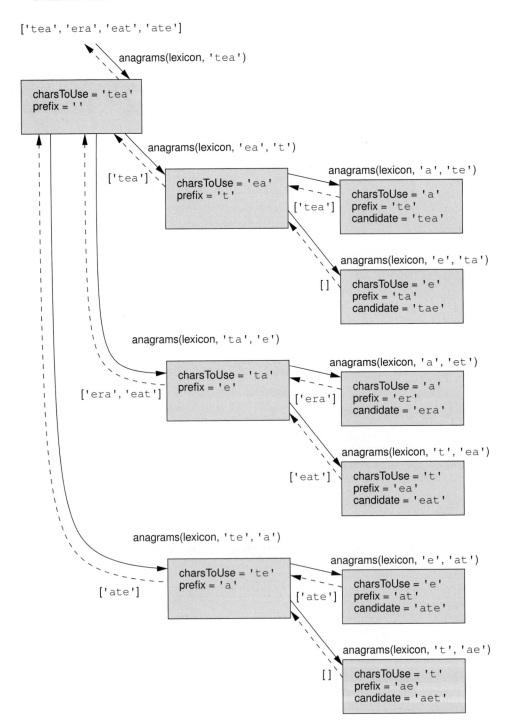

Chapter 12: More Python Containers

Practice 12.1:
```
values = [ ]
for key in data:
    values.append(data[key])
```

Practice 12.2: The problem is that the sort method does not actually return anything; the expression director.keys( ).sort( ) evaluates to **None** (this is a variant of the problem originally shown on page 45).

Practice 12.7: Keep in mind that sourceLabel is a string, and thus a sequence of characters. The **set** constructor, when given a string, forms the set of unique characters from that string, as demonstrated in the chapter with **set**('this is a test').

The purpose of the original line is to create a set that contained a single element, that element being the designated string. This is accomplished by sending the parameter [sourceLabel], which is a list of one item, to the **set** constructor.

Chapter 13: Implementing Data Structures

Practice 13.9: The problem with this alternative is that the caller receives a reference to our internal list. Once he has that access, he might alter the structure of the list, breaking the necessary coordination. By handing back a shallow copy, the caller does not have a way to mutate our internal list. He has access to the elements themselves, but since keys are presumed to be immutable they cannot be altered.

As a side note, the shallow copy returned by values at line 51, may have elements that are mutable, but changing those values has no effect on the integrity of our dictionary.

Practice 13.10:
```
def __len__(self):
    num = 0
    for bucket in self._table:
        num += len(bucket)
    return num
```

Practice 13.15:

(a) 'O', then 'H', then 'E', and finally the right child of 'E'.

(b) 'O', then 'H', then 'N', then 'L' and finally the left child of 'L'.

(c) 'O', then 'H', then 'N'.

Practice 13.16:

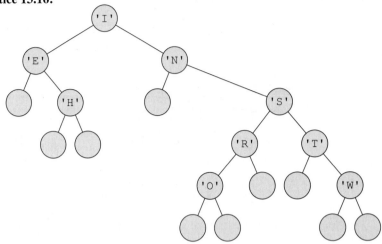

Chapter 14: Sorting Algorithms

Practice 14.1:
```
def insensitive(a,b):
  return cmp(a.lower( ), b.lower( ))
words.sort(insensitive)
```

Practice 14.2: words.sort(key=**str**.lower)

Practice 14.3:
```
def nearHundred(a,b):
  return cmp(abs(a−100), abs(b−100))
data.sort(nearHundred)
```

Practice 14.7:

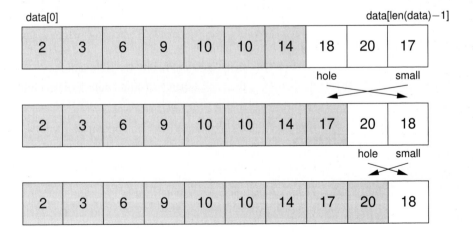

Practice 14.8:

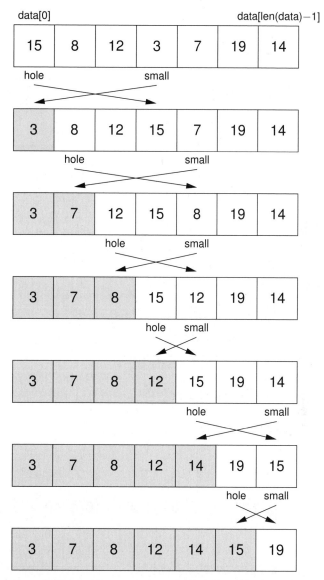

Practice 14.9: For data = [80, 10, 20, 30, 40, 50, 60, 70], the value 80 will be involved in each swap.

Practice 14.13:

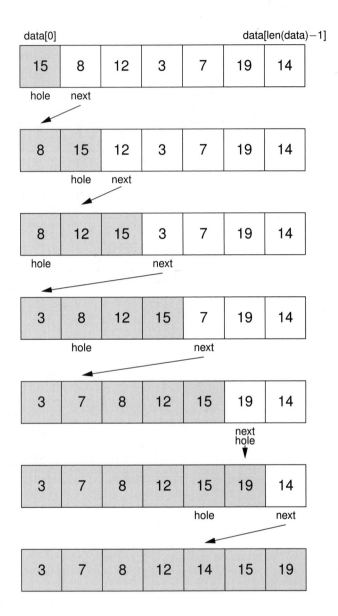

Practice 14.17:

Practice 14.21:

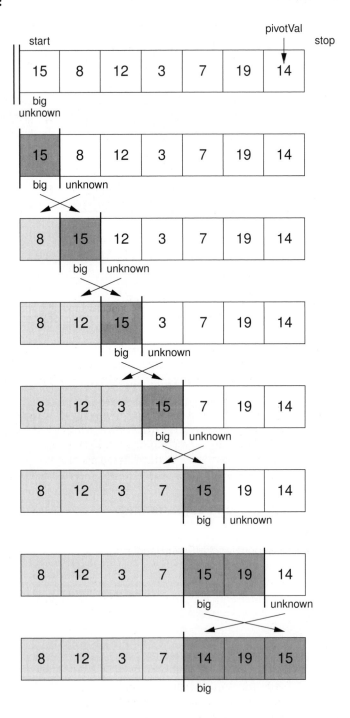

Practice 14.22:

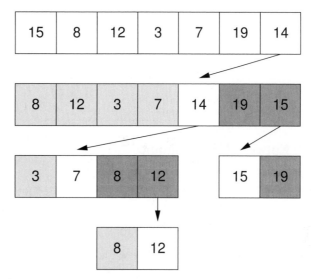

Practice 14.23: Using the leftmost element as a pivot is not a problem in general, but we must be careful. It is important that the pivot element itself is at the boundary of the two resulting sides, as its index is returned and used for the subsequent recursions. In the original code, this was assured because the rightmost element was considered as the very last pass of the while loop, and since data[unknown] <= pivotVal at that point, the exchange takes place moving the pivot to what becomes the rightmost side of the "small" subset.

As is, look at what happens when partitioning data = [20, 30, 10]. It so happens that 20 is swapped with itself, then 30 is initially left alone, then 10 is swapped with 30. By the end of partitioning, the list appears as [20, 10, 30] with big = 2 and thus the index 1 returned to the caller. This causes trouble at the upper-level of the recursion, as no more work is completed and the final result is improperly sorted.

Chapter 15: Event-Driven Programming

Practice 15.1:

```
class ReportHandler(EventHandler):
    def handle(self, event):
        if event.getDescription[:5] == 'mouse':
            print event.getDescription( ), event.getMouseLocation( )
```

Practice 15.2:

```
class CircleHandler(EventHandler):
    def __init__(self, canvas):
        EventHandler.__init__(self)
        self._canvas = canvas
        self._circle = Circle(20, Point(100,100))
        self._circle.setFillColor('red')
```

```
  def handle(self, event):
    if event.getDescription( ) == 'mouse click':
      self._canvas.add(self._circle)
    elif event.getDescription( ) == 'mouse release':
      self._canvas.remove(self._circle)


paper = Canvas( )
handler = CircleHandler(paper)
paper.addHandler(handler)
```

Chapter 16: Network Programming

Practice 16.1:

```
from SocketServer import TCPServer, BaseRequestHandler

class EchoHandler(BaseRequestHandler):
  def handle(self):
    message = self.request.recv(1024)
    self.request.send('ECHO: ' + message)  # notice the change

# may need to customize localhost and port for your machine
echoServer = TCPServer( ('localhost', 9000), EchoHandler)
echoServer.serve_forever( )
```

Practice 16.2:

```
from SocketServer import ThreadingTCPServer, BaseRequestHandler

class EchoHandler(BaseRequestHandler):
  def handle(self):
    active = True
    while active:
      message = self.request.recv(1024)
      if message:
        self.request.send(message)
      else:
        active = False     # connection has failed


# may need to customize localhost and port for your machine
echoServer = ThreadingTCPServer( ('localhost', 9000), EchoHandler)
echoServer.serve_forever( )
```

APPENDIX D

Glossary

abstraction A high-level model for a piece of information or an algorithmic process, independent of low-level implementation details.

access mode The type of use designated for a newly opened file. The most common modes are `'r'` to read a file (the default), `'w'` to (over)write a file, and `'a'` to append information to the end of an existing file.

accessor A method whose invocation cannot affect the state of the callee.

activation record An internal record kept by the system to track each invocation of a function. It maintains the state of all parameters and local identifiers as the execution proceeds.

actual parameter The object that is sent by a caller when invoking a function; *compare to* formal parameter.

algorithm A step-by-step procedure for accomplishing a task.

alias An identifier that refers to the same underlying object as another identifier.

anagram A word that can be formed by rearranging the letters of another word.

ASCII A standard ordering for an alphabet of 128 common characters, used for representing text digitally.

assignment A statement that associates an identifier on the left-hand side of the = operator with the object expressed on the right-hand side.

asymptotic analysis A mathematical technique for estimating the efficiency of a process in relation to the amount of data. For example, a process that depends linearly on the size n of a data set is said to have $\Theta(n)$ running time.

attribute One of the pieces of data used in representing the state of an object. Equivalently termed a data member, field, or instance variable.

augmentation A technique in which a child class defines one or more new behaviors beyond those that are inherited.

base case A case in a recursive process that can be resolved without further recursion.

base class *See* parent class.

behavior *See* method.

binary search A technique for searching a sorted list by comparing a target value to the value at the middle of the list and, if not the target, searching recursively on the appropriate half of the list.

binary search tree A recursive branched structure used to manage an ordered collection. At each level of the structure, elements are organized so that smaller elements lie in the left subtree while larger elements lie in the right subtree.

bit A binary digit; the smallest unit of memory. It can be set to one of two distinct states.

body A block of (indented) code used within the context of a control structure.

bootstrap A technique by which a data structure is based on a more rudimentary implementation of that same structure.

bottom-up implementation Writing and testing low-level classes first and then using them in the implementation of higher-level code.

bucket A secondary container used to manage collisions within a hash table.

callback function *See* event handler.

callee The object whose method is being executed.

caller The object that initiates the execution of a method.

canvas A graphics window on which objects can be drawn.

casting A conversion of data from one type to another.

central processing unit (CPU) The hardware component that controls the computer.

child class A class that is defined to inherit from another class, known as the parent class.

class A group of objects that share commonality in their underlying encoding and supported behaviors.

class diagram A figure used to model the design of a class by identifying its name, its attributes, and its methods.

class hierarchy A taxonomy of related classes.

class-level attribute An attribute introduced within the context of a class, as opposed to one introduced within the context of an *instance* of the class.

client The designated role for any machine that is making a request of a networked server; *see also* client-server network.

client-server network A centralized configuration in which some machines act as clients, making requests for information from another machine known as a server; *compare to* peer-to-peer (P2P) network.

clone A copy of an object.

code reuse Writing portions of a program so that components can be applied in several places of the same program or as part of other projects.

collision The mapping of two different keys into the same index of a hash table.

column-major order A representation of a two-dimensional table as a list of columns, with each column represented as a list of entries in that column; *compare to* row-major order.

comment An explanatory note in the source code that is ignored by the Python interpreter yet visible to a programmer.

Common Gateway Interface (CGI) A protocol for sending data from a web server to a web client.

comparison function A function designed to compare two elements, often with a semantic that is different from the standard comparison. Such a function can be used to customize the order when sorting.

conditional statement A control structure that specifies one or more blocks of code to be executed only if certain conditions are true.

constructor A special method that is implicitly called whenever an object is instantiated. It is responsible for establishing the initial state of the object.

container An object whose purpose is to store and manage a collection of other objects.

control structure A command that describes the order in which some other instructions are executed.

corpus A collection of text documents.

CPU *See* central processing unit.

data The low-level representation of information, as stored and manipulated by a computer.

data member *See* attribute.

data type A definition that associates a particular form of high-level information with an underlying representation scheme.

decorated tuple A tuple of the form (key(element), element), which can be used to sort elements based upon a nonstandard key.

deep copy A copy of an instance whose attributes are created as independent (deep) copies of the respective values referenced by the original.

default parameter value *See* optional parameter.

dictionary A data structure used to manage a collection of keys and their associated values, such that an entry can be accessed quickly based upon a unique key. This structure is synonymously termed a *map* or an *associative array*.

divide and conquer An algorithmic technique in which a large data set is processed by dividing it into smaller portions, processing those portions, and then combining the results as needed.

docstring A Python string embedded within source code to provide formal documentation. Technically, a docstring is a string literal that is placed as the very first element within the body of a module, class, or function.

domain name server (DNS) A server that converts the host name of a computer on the Internet to an IP address.

double buffering A technique for avoiding flicker in animation by computing incremental changes internally before displaying a new image to the viewer.

dynamic web page A web page whose contents are generated by the server at the time of a request, often by executing a server-side script using the Common Gateway Interface (CGI).

encapsulation A principle by which internal implementation details of a software component are treated as private (as opposed to the public interface to that component, which must be well documented for others).

encoding *See* representation.

error checking The general practice of ensuring that data (for example, that sent by a caller or entered by a user) has the appropriate type and value.

event An external stimulus on a program, such as a user's mouse click.

event-driven programming A style in which a program passively waits for external events to occur, responding appropriately to those events as needed.

event handler A piece of code, typically a function or class, used to define the action that should take place in response to a triggered event.

event loop A potentially infinite loop that does nothing other than wait for events. When an event is triggered, an event handler is called to respond appropriately. Once that event handler completes, the event loop is typically continued.

exception A general class used to report unexpected errors during the execution of a program.

exclusive or Meeting one of two conditions but not both.

executable A low-level program that can be run directly by a computer's hardware.

expression A single statement consisting of one or more operations.

field *See* attribute.

flow of control The order in which a series of statements is executed.

flowchart A diagram demonstrating the sequence of steps associated with a particular algorithm.

for loop A control structure used to iterate a block of code for each item of a sequence.

formal parameter An identifier used in the signature of a function declaration that serves as a placeholder for the value of an actual parameter sent by the caller.

function A programming construct for encapsulating a (user-defined) behavior.

functional recursion A technique in which a function calls itself.

garbage collection A technique by which Python reclaims the memory used on objects for which there no longer exist any valid references.

global scope The context of an identifier that is introduced at the top level of a program.

graphical user interface (GUI) A design allowing a user to interact with software through a combination of mouse movements, clicks, and keyboard commands.

has-a relationship An instance of one class having an instance of another class as an attribute (e.g., a Course has a Teacher).

hashing A technique for organizing elements based on a mathematical function that converts keys to indices of an appropriately sized table.

heterogeneous The property of a collection of objects that are *not* necessarily the same type. For example, a Python **list** can be heterogeneous; *compare to* homogeneous.

high-level programming language A language designed to ease the task of specifying a complex set of instructions to be followed by a computer. High-level languages support more general abstractions than low-level programming languages.

homogeneous The property of a collection of objects that are all of the same type. For example a Python **array** is homogeneous; *compare to* heterogeneous.

host name An alphanumeric string that typically identifies a single device on a network (e.g., `www.prenhall.com`).

HTML Form A component of an HTML document used to gather information from a viewer. The form is typically submitted with a button click, at which time its contents are transmitted to the web server and processed with a server-side script.

Hypertext Markup Language (HTML) A language used to embed structural and formatting information in the form of *tags* within a text document. HTML is commonly used for transmitting a web page.

Hypertext Transfer Protocol (HTTP) The standard protocol used for communication of information on the World Wide Web, often in the form of the Hypertext Markup Language (HTML).

identifier A name associated with some underlying object.

if statement *See* conditional statement.

immutable The characteristic of an object whose state cannot be modified once constructed.

inclusive or Meeting at least one of two conditions.

index An integer value used to identify a position in a sequential structure, such as a string or list. Indices are measured by the offset from the beginning, and thus the first position has index 0.

index-based loop A loop that iterates over a range of integers representing indices of a list, rather than iterating directly over the elements of that list.

infinite loop A while loop that executes indefinitely because the loop condition remains satisfied.

inheritance A technique by which one class is defined based upon another.

insertion sort A sorting algorithm that proceeds by maintaining a sorted subset of elements, incrementally adding one new element at a time.

inspector *See* accessor.

instance A single object drawn from a given class.

instance variable *See* attribute.

instantiation The construction of a new object in a given class.

IP address An Internet protocol address, which is a number usually expressed in bytes, such as 165.193.123.253

is-a relationship A description of the relation between child and parent classes (e.g., a Student is a Person).

iteration The process of repeating a step for each item in a sequence.

key An object used to access an associated value within a dictionary.

keyword parameter passing An alternative style for specifying an optional parameter to a function, such as sort(key=len). The syntax relies on an explicit assignment to initialize the formal parameter, rather than the more customary parameter passing that assigns formal parameters to actual parameters based on a designated order.

left-associative Operators that are evaluated from left to right as part of an expression, as in 18 − 5 + 2 which is equivalent to (18 − 5) + 2.

lexicographical order A convention for comparing two sequences to each other. The sequence with the smaller first element is considered the "smaller" sequence. If the first elements are equivalent, the second elements are used as a tie-breaker, and so on. If all elements are pairwise equivalent yet one sequence has additional elements at the end, that sequence is considered "larger." If they are the same length, the two sequences are considered equivalent.

lexicon A collection of strings, for example all words or phrases in the English language.

list A built-in class used to manage a mutable sequence of elements.

list comprehension A syntax for creating a new list that is populated based upon the contents of an existing list, as in deposits = [entry **for** entry **in** transactions **if** entry > 0].

listener *See* event handler.

literal An explicit value of an object drawn from one of the built-in classes.

local scope The context of an identifier that is introduced within the body of a function and is only accessible for the duration of the function call.

loop variable An identifier that is assigned to each element of the sequence during the execution of a for loop.

low-level programming language A programming language with very basic support for primitive data types and operations, for example, a CPU's machine language.

machine language The particular low-level programming language supported by a CPU.

main memory The portion of the computer system's storage in which the program and its data are stored while the program is executing.

member Any of the attributes or methods associated with a class or an instance of that class.

member function *See* method.

merge sort A sorting algorithm that proceeds by dividing a set into two, sorting the halves independently, and then recombining those halves.

method A formal operation supported by all objects of a given class.

modularity The design of a program as a series of smaller independent pieces.

module A library defining a combination of identifiers, functions and classes. Modules must be imported when needed.

multiple inheritance A form of inheritance in which a child class inherits from two or more parent classes.

multithreading A technique allowing a computer program to execute (or appear to execute) multiple flows of control at the same time.

mutable The characteristic of an object whose state can be changed by one or more of its methods.

mutator A method whose invocation may affect the state of the callee.

name resolution The process by which Python determines which object is associated with an identifier in a given context.

namespace A collection of identifiers and associated values that are defined in a specific scope. A namespace is represented with a dictionary in Python.

nesting A technique in which one control structure is placed within the body of another.

network protocol A particular convention used by two connected computers when transmitting information.

object An entity of an executing program, which typically represents some real-world item or concept.

object-oriented programming A paradigm in which data and operations are modeled as intimately paired, rather than as separate elements.

operation A basic instruction that may be performed by a computer.

operator A symbol (e.g., +) that triggers a special behavior in Python.

optional parameter A parameter that can be sent to a function, yet which is assigned a default value if not sent.

override A technique by which a child class redefines the precise behavior associated with an inherited method.

paradigm A general approach to conceptualizing and expressing computer software (e.g., the object-oriented paradigm).

parameter A piece of information sent from the caller to the callee upon invocation of a function.

parent class A class used as the basis for another (child) class through inheritance.

peer-to-peer (P2P) network A configuration in which all machines behave symmetrically and communicate directly with each other; *compare to* client-server network.

persistent connection A network connection that remains open throughout multiple rounds of communication.

pivot A value used in quicksort to partition the data, specifically into those elements less than the pivot and those greater than the pivot.

pixel The smallest displayable element in a digital picture.

polymorphism A technique in which objects of different types support a common syntax or when a single function supports multiple behaviors depending upon the type of parameter it receives.

port A special number used to segment incoming network traffic, often according to the desired communication protocol.

precedence When one operation is performed before another in evaluating an expression. Python defines strict rules for how precedence is determined.

primitive data type A data type that is so commonly used it is already defined as part of a programming language.

private The designation of a class, or member of a class, as one that is not meant for public use from outside the component. Private aspects are typically named with a leading underscore in Python (e.g., _channel).

pruning a recursion A technique for speeding recursive searches by avoiding examination of branches that are clearly not useful.

public The designation for a class, or member of a class, that is designed to provide an external means of interaction.

pure function A function that is defined outside the context of any class.

Python interpreter The software that accepts and executes Python commands.

qualified name A syntax using "dot" notation (e.g., math.pi) for accessing a name defined in another context (such as a module).

quicksort A sorting algorithm that proceeds recursively by dividing a data set according to those values that are less than a chosen pivot and those that are greater.

range search A search for elements of a collection that have value in a given range (e.g., from 80 to 90), as opposed to a search for a single value.

recursion A technique in which a structure or behavior is defined based upon a "smaller" version of that same structure or behavior.

reference A separate entity (often an underlying memory address) that is used to track the location of some information. For example, an *identifier* serves in Python as a reference to an underlying object.

reference point A particular location for a cs1graphics.Drawable instance that is used when determining the placement of the object upon a canvas's coordinate system. The reference point remains fixed when the object is scaled, rotated, or flipped.

representation A low-level way of storing some high-level information.

return value A piece of information sent back from the callee to the caller at the conclusion of a function call.

reverse dictionary A second dictionary, built relative to an original dictionary, where the roles of keys and values are interchanged. That is, for each value of the original dictionary, the reverse dictionary identifies the keys originally mapped to that value.

RGB value A form for specifying a color as a triple of integers representing the intensity of the red, green, and blue components of the color. Typically, each color is measured on a scale from 0 to 255.

row-major order A representation of a two-dimensional table as a list of rows, with each row represented as a list of entries in that row; *compare to* column-major order.

scope The context of a program within which an identifier is defined.

search engine A data structure that supports efficient queries regarding the location of words within a document or set of documents.

selection sort A sorting algorithm that proceeds by finding and relocating the smallest value, then the second smallest value, and so on.

semantics The underlying meaning associated with a particular syntax.

sequence diagram A figure used to model the chronological flow of control between interacting objects.

sequential search An algorithm used to find a value in a sequence by scanning from beginning to end, until either finding the value or exhausting the entire sequence.

server A machine that awaits incoming network connections from other client machines; *see also* client–server network.

server-side script A program that runs on a web server to generate a dynamic response to a query.

shallow copy A copy of an original instance is one whose attributes are assigned to reference the same objects as the original.

short circuiting A technique used by the computer in evaluating compound boolean expressions, whereby a partial evaluation suffices as soon as the outcome can be properly determined.

signature The interface of a function; specifically its name, parameters, and return value.

single inheritance The typical form of inheritance in which a child class inherits from a single parent class.

slice A selected portion of a sequence, such as a **list**, **str**, or **tuple**, using a syntax such as data[start:stop].

socket An entity managing one end of a connection between two machines in a network.

source code The characters that comprise commands for a program in a high-level language. Source code is typically stored in one or more text files and translated with an interpreter or compiler.

special method A method that provides implicit support for an alternative syntax in Python. For example, the __add__ method supports the + operator.

specialization A technique in which a child class overrides one or more inherited behaviors, providing an alternative implementation.

state The current condition of an object, as represented by its set of attribute values.

static web page A web page whose contents are predefined within a file on the server.

string formatting A syntax of the form template % arguments for formatting a string with placeholders to be filled in by arguments.

structural recursion A technique in which a structure is defined using a "smaller" version of the same structure.

subclass *See* child class.

syntax The precise rules for the use of characters, words, and punctuation when writing in a particular programming language.

thread An abstraction representing one of possibly many active flows of control within an executing program.

top-down design An approach for software development in which functionality is first described at a very high level and subsequently organized into smaller and smaller components suitable for coding.

Transmission Control Protocol (TCP) An Internet protocol used for establishing network connections.

tree A hierarchical data structure often organized recursively as a root with two or more subtrees.

try statement A control structure used to encase a block of code that might generate an exception.

type checking A technique by which data is explicitly examined to ensure that it belongs to the expected class.

unfolding a recursion Tracing execution through all levels of a recursion.

uniform resource locator (URL) A string of characters that identifies the source of a networked resource and often the particular protocol that should be used to get the resource (e.g., `http://www.prenhall.com/goldwasser`).

unit testing Testing to ensure that a class or function works properly in isolation.

user-defined type A custom data type that is defined by a programmer (as opposed to a primitive type of the language).

value A piece of data within a dictionary associated with a key.

web crawler A piece of software that explores the web automatically by recursively looking for links in known documents.

while loop A control structure used to repeat a block of code so long as a given condition remains true.

widget An object that serves a particular purpose in a graphical user interface.

Index